Career Directions

Career Directions

Third Edition

Donna J. Yena
Johnson & Wales University

GLENCOE
McGraw-Hill

New York, New York   Columbus, Ohio   Woodland Hills, California   Peoria, Illinois

Copyright for the first edition was held by PAR, Incorporated.

Copyright © 1997 by Glencoe/McGraw-Hill. All rights
reserved. Copyright © 1993, 1989. No part of this publication may be reproduced, stored in a retrieval system, or
transmitted, in any form or by any means, electronic,
mechanical, photocopying, recording, or otherwise,
without the prior written permission of the publisher.

Library Of Congress Cataloging-in-Publication Data

Yena, Donna J.
    Career directions/Donna J. Yena. 3rd ed.
        p. cm.
    Includes bibliographical references and index.
    ISBN 0-256-19085-2
    1. Vocational guidance.   I. Title
HF5381. Y46   1997   96-11237
 650.1   dc20

Send all inquiries to:
Glencoe/McGraw-Hill
21600 Oxnard St., Suite 500
Woodland Hills, CA 91367-4906

Printed in the United States of America

    9 10   079   02 01

Preface

The goal of your education is to prepare you for a career in your field of study. *Career Directions,* Third Edition, is your guide to managing your own career into the 21st century and throughout your lifetime. Although you may receive assistance from your school in securing your first job, you need to master job search skills so that you can make successful career moves on your own. Technical skills are only one component of a successful career. You also need to develop self-confidence, career focus, communication skills, and job search skills. Finally, it is important to understand the world in which you work. As we move toward the 21st century, the workplace is becoming more global and more culturally diverse. Technology has created new techniques for you to use to conduct your job search and function in your everyday work environment. Mastery of these areas will enable you to stand out in today's competitive and changing workplace. *Career Directions* puts you in control of your future!

Students in career schools, colleges, community colleges, and universities can all benefit from this book in professional development courses and career workshops. *Career Directions* can be used independently for those who want to direct their own career planning and job search efforts.

Career Directions provides instruction and resource materials that will help you find your first job, enter a new profession, or move to a new job within an existing career. Regardless of what stage you are in, *Career Directions* can help you assess yourself and take the right next step in your career.

How to Use This Book

The material in this book can be studied in a variety of ways. You may complete all of the material at once in your professional development course or study certain topics through a series of professional development workshops offered at your school. It is also possible to study *Career Directions* independently. It is best first to complete all the material thoroughly so that you master the process of managing your career. At various stages of your career, you may find it helpful to go back to certain chapters that can help you with a particular decision.

There is a deliberate sequence to the material presented in *Career Directions.* Part One focuses you first on preparing for your career through self-assessment, personal development, and an overview of the career paths open to you. It directs you toward

building workplace skills that have been identified as important by employers through SCANS, the Secretary's Commission on the Achievement of Necessary Skills. Finally, it guides you through the process of building and presenting a career portfolio. Part Two provides job search techniques, including résumés and job applications, letters to write during your job search, interviewing techniques, and advice on both accepting a job and handling rejection when you don't get the job. Information on how to use current recruitment technology such as the Internet, CD-ROM, disk and video résumés, and electronic résumés and cover letters is also included. Part Three helps you manage your career from your first months on the job and gives advice on growing with your job. You are introduced to contemporary issues in the workplace that may affect you in your work environment and are provided with techniques for building professional relationships in a culturally diverse work environment.

Selected chapters contain tips on how to apply the information in the chapter to an international job search. These tips are easily identified in sections called International Career Directions (ICD).

The last section of the book is your personal Career Handbook, which contains tools you can use to successfully direct your career. "Career Paths" provides an opportunity to review the many career options available to you. It also shows you the jobs you may hold as you move through your career in a particular field. These career paths should be explored along with the information in Chapter Four, "Career Paths Overview," and can be referred to again when considering future career moves.

The "Glossary of Terms Used in Job Descriptions" is designed to help you understand the job descriptions in the "Index of Job Descriptions." This glossary can be used in conjunction with Chapter Seven to help you express your qualifications more effectively in your résumé. The "Index of Job Descriptions" provides a brief description of what each job listed in "Career Paths" entails. This gives you an idea of what the actual day-to-day responsibilities are in the jobs that might interest you.

Finally, "Career Resources" contains a list of resource materials that you can use to supplement much of the information presented in Career Directions. Should you want to explore one or more topics in depth, you can start by using some of these additional resources.

Skills You Will Develop

The most important benefit you will gain from studying Career Directions is mastery of the essential skills necessary to managing a successful career. You will learn how to:

- Assess your personal and professional strengths and weaknesses, and relate your values, interests, personality, and skills to your career choice.
- Compare your professional qualifications with those employers identified as critical through SCANS.
- Set goals for self-improvement.
- Improve your communications skills.
- Convince an employer you are the best candidate for the job.
- Present your best professional image.
- Evaluate the many career paths available to you.
- Conduct an independent job search.
- Conduct an international job search.
- Apply new recruitment technology to your job search.
- Prepare a career portfolio.
- Write effective résumés.

- Complete job applications.
- Write job search letters.
- Secure a job interview.
- Conduct a successful job interview.
- Compete in a global job market.
- Complete proper follow-up after an interview.
- Accept the best job.
- Be successful on the job.
- Deal with workplace issues.

Special Features of Career Directions

New special features of *Career Directions* include information about SCANS, new recruitment technology, career portfolios, an international job search, and building relationships in a culturally diverse workplace. By applying this information you can gain a competitive edge in the job market as we approach the 21st century. In addition, "Contemporary Issues in the Workplace," the "Career Handbook," and the "Interview Hall of Fame" remain as special features from the previous edition with enhanced and updated information.

A summary of growing career fields gives you an idea of some of the industry trends influencing job growth over the next five years. Tips on how to recession-proof your career teach you how to stay marketable during tough economic times.

These special features provide you with specific information so that you can make better career choices, market yourself more competitively to prospective employers, and successfully manage your career in a changing environment.

Acknowledgments

The content of this text incorporates my own work experience with the valuable input I have received from students, employers, and career development professionals throughout the country.

During my 18 years of involvement with students, they have willingly shared their most common concerns about their careers during individual career counseling sessions and in personal and professional development courses I have taught. The hundreds of employers I have worked with over the years have applauded our students' clear focus, realistic attitudes, and professional experience, and have offered candid assessments of students' strengths and weaknesses as they prepare to enter the workplace.

My thanks to the many career development professionals I have met throughout the country at placement workshops I have conducted and to my own Career Development staff at Johnson & Wales University, who have openly discussed their challenge and success with assisting students in job placement.

Specifically, I would like to thank the reviewers and survey respondents whose input has allowed me to refine this third edition:

Lori Abrams	*DeVry Institute of Technology (Phoenix)*
Kim M. Benson	*Bay State College, Boston, MA*
Helen Blair	*Santa Barbara Business College (Santa Maria)*
Celeste Brantolino	*Johnson & Wales University*
MK Brennan	*Bryant & Stratton*
Sandy Christianson	*National College*
Darrell Costa	*DeVry Institute of Technology (Pomona)*

Patrick DeBold	*Concorde Career Colleges Inc.*
Kimberley Dumouchel	*Central Connecticut State University*
DiAnna Eason	*Chaparral College*
Barbara Friedrich	*American Business & Fashion Institute*
Carol Gauer	*National College Corporation*
Ann Golubeff	*Stratton College*
Fred Hawk	*Chaparral Career College*
Jay S. Hollowell	*Commonwealth College*
Larry Johnson	*Lamar Community College*
Robert Laheta	*ETI Technical College*
Lynn Le Blanc	*Louisiana Technical College—Lafayette Campus*
Sandy Martin	*Eastern Maine Technical College*
Melinda E. Miller	*Massey College of Business and Technology*
Karen W. Nichols	*University of Mississippi*
Casey Shannon	*Cabrillo College*
Lynne Shapiro	*Academy of Computer Careers*
Rita Shourds	*Sullivan College*
Diane Verdolotti	*Johnson & Wales University*

Finally, I would like to thank the Career Education Division of Richard D. Irwin for the professional guidance and support they have given me throughout this project. I am particularly grateful to the marketing professionals and sales representatives for their input from the market.

I owe personal thanks to Jean Roberts, Senior Developmental Editor, for the partnership we developed as we worked to produce this manuscript. My thanks also to Karen Anderson for her hard work in producing the final manuscript.

The success of *Career Directions* is shared by everyone who contributed to making it a practical and complete guide to helping students launch their careers.

Thank you!

Contents

Part Three • Career Management   221

Career Handbook   254

Photo Credits for
Chapter Opener
Photos

Chapter 1:   © Robert Frerck/Tony Stone Worldwide
Chapter 2:   © Margot Granitsas/Photo Researchers, Inc.
Chapter 3:   © Joseph Pobereskin/Tony Stone Worldwide
Chapter 4:   © Johnson & Wales University
Chapter 5:   © Gabe Palmer/The Stock Market
Chapter 6:   © Johnson & Wales University
Chapter 7:   © Chuck Savage/The Stock Market
Chapter 8:   © Andrew Sacks/Tony Stone Worldwide
Chapter 9:   © Jon Riley/Tony Stone Worldwide
Chapter 10:   © David Grossman/Photo Researchers, Inc.
Chapter 11:   © Jeff Greenberg/Photo Researchers, Inc.
Chapter 12:   © Blair Seitz/Photo Researchers, Inc.
Chapter 13:   © Bruce Ayres/Tony Stone Worldwide
Chapter 14:   © Steven Peters/Tony Stone Worldwide

Part One

Career
Planning

Chapter One

The World of Work in the 21st Century

Chapter Objectives

After completing this chapter, you will:

Understand how world trends are affecting the workplace.

Understand how American businesses and workers are responding to workplace challenges.

Know that your success in tomorrow's workplace depends on skills-based and lifelong learning.

I t is important to have an awareness of the world around you as you prepare for tomorrow's workplace. Now more than ever, societal and economic trends will affect your job and your work environment on a regular basis. This chapter discusses how world trends are reshaping your world of work by focusing on the major challenges today's workers face, how American businesses and people are responding to these challenges, and the skills you will need for success in the 21st century. A major part of your own professional development will depend on your ability to respond and adapt to some of these changes.

World Trends and Tomorrow's Workplace

As you prepare to enter the workplace, you should be aware of how that environment is changing. A major part of your professional development will depend on your ability to anticipate and adapt to changes in the economy, technology, globalization, and cultural diversity.

The Economy

Careers, jobs, and the workplace are affected by ongoing fluctuations in the world economy. In general, growth in the economy means growth in jobs. The level of job growth and the types of jobs available change as new industries emerge and others decline. For example, while the age of technology has created many new jobs in technical fields, it has automated many jobs in other fields. This has resulted in a decrease in the number of certain manufacturing jobs and other jobs previously dependent on human expenditure of effort instead of technology.

An increase in foreign trade and deregulation are two of the many factors creating more business competition. As businesses compete with one another, hiring trends fluctuate with changing demands for a company's product. As market demand goes up, hiring goes up. As market demand declines, fewer workers are needed in a given firm. For many companies, survival means doing more with fewer people. However, jobs are there for workers who bring job-specific skills that help create new products or markets or help keep current products competitive.

Today's fluctuations in staffing due to changing markets create mobility among workers, who move to and from firms where their skills are in most demand. Whereas the worker of the past often only had one or two jobs in an entire lifetime, today the typical American worker stays on a job for an average of four to six years, and thus may have 10 or more jobs in his or her lifetime.

Increased competition has also spurred the growth of small business, causing new jobs today to emerge at a faster rate in small companies than in large corporations.

Finally, education levels and earnings are closely related. In general, tomorrow's jobs will require education beyond high school and sometimes beyond college. However, not all college education provides the same level of opportunity for launching a successful career. The key for those who go to college is to select programs where there is a high demand for graduates. As the number of college graduates increases, competition for jobs will remain high. Tomorrow's jobs will be many in number, but increased competition for those jobs from candidates making career changes plus additional entry-level candidates may make high-quality career opportunities more rare.

Altogether, this means that you must have strong qualifications and know how to market them in order to stand out as the right candidate for the job. You must develop competitive skills, a clear goal, and a careful plan for achievement in your chosen field.

New Technology

New technology is re-creating the way we do business throughout the world. Everything from fax machines, video conferencing, and the Internet to robotics, distance learning, and cybernetics is changing the way we communicate with one another on a daily basis. Technology increases our productivity, allowing us to spend less time on tasks that involve generating data and more time on jobs requiring us to interpret data, problem-solve, and make decisions within our organizations. In most cases, technology is not replacing workers, but is redefining what we do and how we do it. Familiarization and competency with current technology in your field are now critical qualifiers for a successful career.

New technology has allowed us more leisure time, increasing the amount of time we spend dining out, traveling, and generally enjoying various sources of entertainment. Our lifestyles are changing and the way we communicate with each other is changing. Get ready—technology is changing the world of work!

Globalization

The world's workforce is becoming more mobile, and employers are reaching across borders to find highly skilled people. A global workforce will result from:

- Extensive relocations of people, including temporary workers, retirees, and visiting workers. The greatest relocation will involve young, well-educated workers flocking to the world's major cities.
- A reevaluation of immigration policies in many parts of the world, as all countries begin to rely on and compete for foreign-born workers.
- Gradual standardization of labor practices among industrialized countries. For example, it is possible that by the year 2000, European standards for vacation time (five weeks) will be common in the United States or the 40-hour workweek will be accepted in Japan.
- A hunger for talent in industrialized nations, while the developing world educates more workers than it can productively employ. This will increase the opportunities for professionals in all fields to fill jobs available in many different parts of the world.

Cultural Diversity

The workplace is becoming increasingly more diversified as more people with culturally different backgrounds enter it. "By the year 2000, minorities and immigrants will hold 26 percent of all jobs, 60 percent of all women will be working, and the average age of the workforce will be 39 years old."[1] The composition of the workforce is changing dramatically as the number of minorities and immigrants working in the United States grows. This blending of culturally diverse people into the workplace brings new skills and different perspectives to businesses.

The increase in culturally diverse work settings will mean that you must learn to appreciate and recognize others' different educational experiences and cultural values. For example, as the number of Spanish speaking workers continues to grow in the United States, you may need to study Spanish to better communicate with your co-workers or those you supervise. Some Asian workers may be less likely to be as assertive as some American workers about asking questions or asking for help on the job. This is due to the Asian culture, where it is sometimes considered insulting to ask too many questions of a speaker or supervisor because it may indicate the person was not a clear communicator. These are just a few examples of divergent thinking and backgrounds that require you to bring an open mind and a broader understanding of culturally diverse people to the workplace.

American Responses to Workplace Challenges

"Although technical skills are important, they must be balanced with interpersonal skills."
PATRICIA ABURDENE, CO-AUTHOR WITH JOHN NAISBITT OF *RE-INVENTING THE CORPORATION*

Qualifications for Tomorrow's Careers

Technical skills   +   High energy level
Positive attitude
Flexibility
Interpersonal skills
Work experience
Willingness to learn

[1]"Riding the Tide of Change," *The Wyatt Communicator,* Winter 1991, pp. 4–11.

Business leaders report that graduates with solid technical and interpersonal skills, a positive attitude, and some work experience are hired more frequently than those with technical skills alone.

As you train to enter your profession, you must be sure to become involved in experiences, in and out of the classroom, that will help you sharpen your competence in these areas. This will ensure that your education is truly a preparation for the changing workplace.

American businesses and people are responding to today's challenges through new ways of interacting with one another and with their customers.

Customer Service and Quality

W. Edwards Deming, a leading expert on quality in business, has said, "Quality is defined by the customer. Improvements in products and processes must be aimed at anticipating customers' future needs."

Today's businesses compete primarily on the basis of customer service and quality because customers consider these to be important when deciding which products or services they want to use. We hear a lot about the service economy that exists today. This simply means that the business of most companies is focused on delivering to customers some type of product, such as computer equipment, or providing a service, such as delivering clothes by mail. In the past, companies focused more on actually making the goods than on showing how they could be used. The focus on service means that the jobs available to you will probably require good product knowledge and an ability to communicate well to customers about how the product can benefit them.

By treating the customer right the first time and providing a high-quality service or product, a company can attract and retain good customers. *You* will be the link between the customer and the company that will cause the customer either to come back again or to go elsewhere to fill his or her needs. Your ability to relate to others is critical to success in your career.

The New Management Team

The new management team involves close working relationships between management and support staff. There are no longer sharp differences in the importance of different jobs but rather recognition that each person performs a critical function for the organization. Such support positions as data entry operator and secretary have grown in responsibility and taken on a new significance in the management of information and services within companies. Managers work more directly with support staff than ever before in setting and achieving company goals. Managers and support staff work together to create the new management team.

With an increasing number of professionals seeking top-management jobs, there is a decline in the number of qualified support personnel in organizations throughout the country. That's where many jobs will be. Businesses are recognizing the importance of support personnel who are committed to quality, customer service, and teamwork. To be successful, it is no longer necessary to climb to the top, but rather to become the best at whatever you do to keep the day-to-day operations of the business thriving. Your ability to work with a team will be important throughout your entire career.

The New Management Team

Management   +   Support staff
(Accountants, computer specialists, reservationists, sales representatives, distributors, cooks, night auditors, front desk clerks, secretaries)

Entrepreneurship

Around the world, as mentioned earlier, small businesses and multinational corporations are creating more new career opportunities than domestic corporations. Many graduates are now being hired by small and medium-sized enterprises. While such companies might recruit only one or two people, the number of companies recruiting at this level and being given the opportunity to attract top-quality graduates is increasing steadily. An increasing number of recent graduates and experienced professionals are abandoning traditional employment where they work for someone else and are becoming their own bosses by starting their own businesses. Many start-up businesses are being developed by young entrepreneurs before they even graduate from high school. Some examples include lawn care businesses; pest control businesses; gift basket services, and desserts-to-go businesses. One young woman with a flair for creative writing supplies card messages for publication by a national greeting card company.

Success in the 21st Century: Skills-Based and Lifelong Learning

Each individual who hopes for success in the world of work in the 21st century must be committed to learning job-specific skills and continuing the learning process for a lifetime.

Skills-Based Learning

In the United States, workforce training is being driven by changing workplace requirements. As part of the U.S. Department of Labor's role in helping American workers prepare for their future, the Secretary's Commission on Achieving Necessary Skills (SCANS) defines a common core of skills and competencies that constitute work readiness for the jobs of today and tomorrow. SCANS identifies three major foundation skills for the workplace:

1. Basic skills: reading, writing, arithmetic and mathematics, speaking, and listening.
2. Thinking skills: thinking creatively, making decisions, solving problems, seeing things in the mind's eye, knowing how to learn, and reasoning.
3. Personal qualities: individual responsibility, self-esteem, sociability, self-management, and integrity.

SCANS further identifies five competencies for the workplace:

1. Resources: Identifies, organizes, plans, and allocates resources.
2. Interpersonal: Works well with others.
3. Information: Acquires and uses information.
4. Systems: Understands complex social, organizational, and technological systems and interrelationships.
5. Technology: Works with a variety of technologies.

These competencies and foundation skills have been identified as critical to success in the workplace. They have become the basis for curriculum development in schools and colleges and universities as well as employer training programs. The more you can develop these skills before you go to work, the less training you may need on the job and the greater the value you can bring right away to the company you work with. SCANS is an excellent example of a concerted effort to bridge the gap between education and employers' needs.

INTERNATIONAL CAREER DIRECTIONS

A Global Need for Basic Skills

The basic skills that SCANS emphasizes are important not only to U.S. employers but also to employers outside the United States. In a recent edition of *The European*, an international newspaper, international employers reported that they are increasingly looking at job applications for evidence that prospective employees have the skills that will be required to do a job successfully. These skills might include technical know-how, leadership, teamwork, communication, motivation, and management. Rather than being developed through just academic study, these skills might also be displayed through extracurricular activities.

Chapter Summary

The information presented in this chapter on the world of work in the 21st century will help you adapt to a new work environment and develop a broader perspective on what is happening around you. This foundation is critical because adaptability and versatility need to become your way of responding to the constant change that will be an integral part of your professional career.

Self-Assessment

Chapter Objectives

After completing this chapter, you will:

Identify your own values, interests, personality, and skills.

Define success.

Recognize how well you meet employer expectations.

Identify areas for self-improvement and set goals for self-improvement.

Clarify the value you add to an employer.

This chapter is focused on helping you better understand yourself and what employers expect of you. Knowing yourself is an important first step toward a successful career because what you do needs to be compatible with who you are. Self-assessment is the process of identifying your values, interests, personality traits, and skills; relating them to your definition of success; and comparing how well you meet employer expectations. Once you do this, you can set your own goals for self-improvement to bring you closer to reaching your individual personal and professional goals. By completing a detailed self-assessment, you will have a clear picture of your current strengths and weaknesses as they relate to your qualifications for employment. You will take the next vital step of creating an action plan for your self-improvement. The goal of your self-improvement program is to successfully bridge the gap between your qualifications and employers' needs.

Understanding Yourself

Having a clear understanding of yourself helps you choose a career that meets your individual needs. Your unique talents and needs influence your choice of career and your overall lifestyle.

Values

Your values are the standards you choose to live by. Your values affect most of the choices you make every day. The sum total of your own personal values or standards makes up your value system. Values by themselves are not right or wrong. What is an acceptable choice for one person may be unacceptable for you because of your value system. For example, one person may feel little or no obligation to spend time helping others through some sort of community work. For you, this may be very important because one of the standards you have set for yourself is helping others. The following are some examples of values:

- Time with family.
- Financial reward.
- Community service.
- Professional position.
- Personal relationships.
- Social status.
- Where you live.

One way to clarify what values are most important to you is to ask yourself: What are the top priorities in my life? These priorities may tell you a lot about the values you have. The examples listed above may reflect some of your values. There are probably some you would add to or subtract from this list. Knowing what's important to you makes you aware of your own value system.

ACTIVITY 2-1 • *Values Checklist*

Values affect most of the choices we make every day. The career you choose should be compatible with your values. Rank the following major sets of values, with 1 being the most important to you and 5 being the least important to you.

⬚ Family values	⬚ Professional values
⬚ Social values	⬚ Ethical values
⬚ Personal values	

Within each of the following major sets of values, rank individual values, with 1 being the most important to you and 5 being the least important to you.

Family Values

⬚ Free time—enjoy free time with family	⬚ Role model—set example for other family members
⬚ Financial provider—provide financial support for family members	⬚ Love
	⬚ Responsibility

Social Values

2 Altruism   5 Membership

4 Volunteerism   1 Leadership

3 Community service

Personal Values

5 Health   2 Financial reward

6 Free time for yourself   3 Where you live

4 Position/title   1 Education

Professional Values

1 Reliability   4 Job security

3 Loyalty   2 Quality work

5 Recognition

Ethical Values

2 Honesty   5 Morality

1 Justice   3 Fairness

4 Integrity

How do you think your values affect your career choice? _My mentality doesn't allow_
me to use values if I had any because my first priority
is to be financially succesful.

Values and Your Career Choice.   Your values affect your career choice in many ways. For example, if you value nights and weekends with your family, you'll probably require a career with a workweek that does not include much overtime or weekend work. Frequent travel is also something you may prefer to avoid. If your career choice is to be a secretary, you will generally find that spending time with your family will be possible because most secretarial jobs have standard workweeks, with work hours of 8:30–4:30 or 9:00–5:00 Monday through Friday.

When your career choice seems to conflict with your values, take a second look. For example, if you are considering a career in sales, you may need to travel and work some nights and weekends. Perhaps if you rethink what is important to you, you may realize that time with your family, rather than a standard schedule, is what really counts and that good planning gives you the free time you want while you pursue a sales career.

Interests

Interests are the activities you choose to do because you enjoy them. Your interests may lean toward individual or group activities. Most people enjoy some combination of both. Having a variety of interests helps you develop and grow and is a good source of fun and relaxation.

ACTIVITY 2-2 • *Interests Checklist*

Interests affect most of the choices we make every day. The career you choose should be compatible with your interests. Rank the following major sets of interests, with 1 being the most important to you and 5 being the least important to you.

3   Arts
5   Travel
2   Clubs/organizations

4   Sports
☐   Professional

Fill in a list of your own interests under each major heading and then rank each interest you listed in order of importance to you, with 1 being the most important to you and 5 being the least important to you.

Arts (Example)

1   Music
2   Literature
4   Theater
5   Paintings
3   Poetry

Clubs/Organizations

2 / 1   Friends
1   Family
3   Church
4   Baseball
5   ~~None~~ Gym

Sports

☐ *Football*
☑ *Baseball*
☑ *Basketball*
☑ *Boxing*
☑ *Running*

Travel

☐ _____
☐ _____
☐ _____
☐ _____
☐ _____

Professional

☐ _____
☐ _____
☐ _____
☐ _____
☐ _____

How do you think your interests affect your career goal? _____
_____
_____

Interests and Your Career Choice. How you spend your free time says a lot about you—your likes, dislikes, and motivation. This information can provide you with leads to the career that's best for you. For example, if you spend some of your free time as an officer in a club or organization, you may have an interest in a job that puts your leadership skills to work. If you enjoy fixing cars or repairing computers or household items during your free time, you may be suited for a career as a technician. An interest in writing may mean you are suited for a career as a claims analyst or administrative assistant. Pay attention to what you enjoy doing, and you may discover interests that apply to a variety of careers.

Personality

Personality can be your biggest asset as you prepare for a career in the service industries. Your personality is the sum total of the way you act and react to everyday events. A personality trait is a distinguishing quality or characteristic that belongs to you.

Personality and Your Career Choice. Certain types of personalities may be better suited for certain careers than for others. For example, if you are pursuing a career in retailing, you will need a high energy level and an outgoing personality. In contrast, if you are pursuing a career in court reporting, you may be quiet by nature and able to work at a set pace for a long period of time. Both careers offer excellent opportunities but are better suited to different personalities.

The more you develop your positive personality traits, the more you'll be viewed as someone other people like to be with. A pleasing personality is a plus when looking for any job because many employers see this as one indicator of your own confidence in yourself and your ability to get along with others. Of course, while there is much more to career success than having a pleasing personality, it is a big advantage to bring to any professional setting.

ACTIVITY 2-3 • *Personality Checklist*

Developing an effective personality is critical to your success. The career you choose should be compatible with your personality. Rank the following major personality traits, with 1 being the most important to you and 5 being the least important to you.

1 Attitude

3 Motivation

4 Commitment

5 Aesthetic appreciation

2 Global understanding

Attitude

4 Positive

2 Realistic

3 Flexible

5 Enthusiastic

1 Confident

Aesthetic Appreciation

2 Appreciation for music/art

4 Creativity

5 Imagination

3 Environmental awareness

1 Social responsibility

Motivation

5 Self-motivated

4 Energetic

1 Competitive

2 Persistent

3 Extroverted

Commitment

5 Focused

1 Self-disciplined

3 Determined

4 Responsive

2 Hardworking

Global Understanding

2 Well-read

4 Culturally sensitive

5 Adaptable

1 Independent

5 Multilingual

How does your personality affect your career choice? _____

_____

_____

List five of the above personality traits you wish to develop and write a plan for each trait you desire:

Example	Plan
Confidence	I will offer my opinions more often in class even when they are different from those of others.

1._____   _____

_____

_____

2._____   _____

_____

_____

3._____   _____

_____

_____

4._____   _____

_____

_____

5._____   _____

_____

_____

Skills

A skill is an ability you have developed or an area in which you have expertise. As you assess your skills, you will find they generally fall into one of the following three categories: personal, interpersonal, or technical (see the table). Personal skills are your own way of dealing directly with situations. For example, organizing your time or work well, being able to solve problems on your own, and seeing a project through from start to finish are personal skills that can help you succeed in your job. Interpersonal skills are your methods of dealing with others. For example, being a good listener or a great public speaker helps you communicate well with others. Technical skills are the abilities you can demonstrate through work with your mind or your hands. With a little effort, most of us can learn new skills that may help us in our personal and professional lives.

Types of Skills

Personal	Interpersonal	Technical
Memorizing	Listening	Word processing
Organizing	Teamwork	Shorthand
Problem solving	Understanding	Filing
Initiating	Sales	Reception work
Completing	Public speaking	Computer operation
Planning	Negotiation	Letter writing
Prioritizing	Teaching	Drafting
Budgeting	Training	Cooking
	Coaching	

ACTIVITY 2-4 • Skills Checklist

Rank the following starting with 1 being your strongest skills/competencies and the highest number being the skills/competencies you need to develop further.

Skills/Competencies Checklist

- ☐ Basic skills
- ☐ Thinking skills
- ☐ Personal qualities
- ☐ Resources

- ☐ Interpersonal
- ☐ Information
- ☐ Systems
- ☐ Technology

Basic Skills

- ☐ Reading
- ☐ Writing
- ☐ Arithmetic/mathematics

- ☐ Listening
- ☐ Speaking

Thinking Skills

☐ Creative thinking   ☐ Knowing how to learn

☐ Decision making   ☐ Reasoning

☐ Problem solving

Personal Qualities

☐ Responsibility   ☐ Self-management

☐ Self-esteem   ☐ Integrity/honesty

☐ Sociability

Resources

☐ Time management   ☐ Management of material and facilities

☐ Money management   ☐ Management of human resources

Interpersonal

☐ Participate as team member   ☐ Exercise leadership

☐ Teach others new skills   ☐ Negotiate decisions

☐ Serve clients/customers   ☐ Work with cultural diversity

Information

☐ Acquire/evaluate information   ☐ Use computers to process information

☐ Organize/maintain information

☐ Interpret/communicate information

Systems

☐ Understand systems   ☐ Improve/design systems

☐ Monitor/correct performance

Technology

☐ Select technology   ☐ Maintain/troubleshoot technology

☐ Apply technology to task

How do you think your mastery of the above basic skills and competencies affects your career goals? ____

_____

_____

Skills/Competencies and Your Career Choice.   You may find that you are interested in a career that uses the skills you already have, or you may wish to develop new skills that will set you in a different career direction. For example, if you are understanding and a good listener, you may have what it takes to be a customer service representative for an airline. You may need to learn computer skills as well. By combining the skills you already have and the ones you want to develop, you can begin to make yourself a stronger candidate for the job you want. If you are unsure about whether you will fit into the career field that interests you, remember there is a wide range of jobs that may suit you within each field.

If you tend to have many hands-on mechanical skills, such as machine repair or computer operation, you may enjoy a job as a technician. If you have good interpersonal skills, such as working well as a team member or teaching, and prefer using them on a daily basis, you may enjoy a job that focuses more on dealing with people. Within every career field, jobs range from high people orientation to high task orientation. The travel/tourism field is a good example. If you are in a travel/tourism program in school and you find that many of your good skills are interpersonal ones, you will probably enjoy a job such as a tour escort, where you would deal with people a lot. If you find your personal and technical skills to be stronger than your interpersonal skills, you may enjoy a job as a data analyst in the travel industry. The

---

ACTIVITY 2-5 • *Skills Assessment*

Skills are something we all can develop. Skills can be either technical or personal.

Technical Skills	Personal Skills
Typing 55 words per minute	Ability to plan
Shorthand 120 words per minute	Ability to organize
Computer skills	Ability to develop

Write down the skills that you have right now, both technical and personal.

Technical Skills	Personal Skills
_____	_____
_____	_____
_____	_____
_____	_____
_____	_____

Next, list which of these skills you would like to develop, or new ones you would like to have.

_____	_____
_____	_____
_____	_____
_____	_____
_____	_____
_____	_____
_____	_____

Write a plan for developing each skill from your list above. Follow this example:

Skill: <u>Increase the speed at which I take shorthand.</u>

Plan: <u>Practice on my own; ask my employer if I can use shorthand more on the job.</u>

Skill: _____

Plan: _____

Skill: _____

Plan: _____

Skill: _____

Plan: _____

Skill: _____

Plan: _____

Skill: _____

Plan: _____

tour escort spends most of his or her time working with the public individually and in groups, while the data analyst may independently review population trends in a city and write a recommendation on whether or not to build a new hotel or restaurant there. Both jobs are in the travel/tourism industry, but each requires a different type of person.

Defining Success

Everyone has his or her own definition of success. You won't get to where you want to go with someone else's dream—you must create your own. For many people, success is defined as carving out their own niche—finding something they want to do and doing it well. Your idea of success may be to reach a feeling of personal fulfillment, or it may be to reach a certain financial status. As you attempt to define your own success, think about what's important to you, not to those around you. Don't limit yourself to traditional ideas of success, such as a top position in a large corporation, but broaden your idea to something you can really feel in your gut! When you feel the drive for something that strongly, you must want it badly enough to really go after it.

Changing Perspectives

Over the years, there have been changing perspectives on success. Talk to some successful people and ask what their definition of success was when they first started their careers. They might say something like:

"I'd like to be earning $100,000 a year by the time I am 30 years old."
"I'd prefer to be my own boss."
"I want to own a vacation home on one of the islands."
"I want to own a new sports car."
"I'd like to get my book published."

Then ask if that definition of success has changed over the years. In almost all cases, the answer will be yes. People who are well established in their careers will probably give some very different answers, like:

"I'd like to balance my time between job, family, and friends."
"I'd like to be challenged in my work."
"I'd enjoy helping someone else reach one of his or her goals."
"I want to be the best secretary in my department."
"I'd like to be debt-free."

Your changing values affect your attitudes about success. Both your age and the society in which you live affect your values. At an early age, your symbols of success may be focused on approval from others and independence demonstrated by owning material things. As you grow older and gain more experience, your symbols of success may change as your value system changes. You may experience a shift away from needing outside sources of approval toward wanting inner satisfaction. For example, some of the new symbols of success are having more control over one's time, viewing work as fun, receiving affection and understanding from others, involvement with community work, and teaching or helping others.

As you progress through your career, changes in your personal life and in the world around you will have an impact on your goals. An emphasis on human resources will cause employers to develop new approaches to rewarding performance in the workplace. The traditional meaning of the words *reward, recognition,* and *compensation* will change to meet the new values of the worker in the 21st century. The values of tomorrow's workers—including you—are changing the workforce as we've known it in the past. For these reasons, successful lifelong career planning involves periodic review of your definition of success and your strategies for achieving it.

As you plan your career today, decide what your definition of success is right now and base your immediate decisions on that. If success to you right now is being hired by one of the leading employers in your field, focus on achieving that. Just under-

ACTIVITY 2-6 • *Success Checklist*

It is time to really think about what success means to you. Rank the following indicators of success according to which you would like to achieve. Start by placing a 1 next to the term that most represents your personal definition of success and end by placing a 10 next to the term that least represents your personal definition of success.

- ☐ Financial status
- ☐ Position/title
- ☐ Reputation/fame
- ☐ Respect from others
- ☐ Family unity
- ☐ Recognition as a leader in community service

- ☐ Top recognition in profession, sports, or church
- ☐ Independence
- ☐ Creating something new
- ☐ Balance in life

How do you think your perspective on success may affect your career choice?

_____

_____

stand that by looking ahead and at least thinking about the lifestyle you may want in the future, your present decisions may take a different focus.

Quality of Success

Some qualities of success include clear goals, a positive attitude, risk taking, enthusiasm, and motivation. Successful people share many common characteristics. By having goals, they take each one of their small successes and use them to build bigger successes in the future. Successful people make the most of their intelligence. They have and use common sense. They are willing to explore new avenues of information. Some of the most interesting individuals are those who read extensively, listen well, and absorb all the facts they can from the world around them. Successful people are usually positive, a trait which attracts people to them. They have ways of preventing disappointments and setbacks from becoming obstacles. Along with a positive attitude comes the ability to trust and believe in oneself and others. Successful people are good risk takers and are willing to accept failure as part of the course. They think you fail only when you are not able to cash in on the experience you have.

Successful attitudes are built on *enthusiasm*. Enthusiasm is the demonstration of a strong interest in something. It comes from within and has a strong effect on other people. Enthusiasm lends credibility to what you do and results in your own satisfaction. It builds spirit around an idea and is a great basis for creativity. A fantastic idea that is presented with little enthusiasm can be rejected in favor of another idea that is delivered more enthusiastically.

Successful people are usually highly motivated. *Motivation* is an inner drive that makes you do something. Motivation makes you productive and allows you to work well independently. If you are motivated, you have a healthy interest in yourself. Motivation goes hand in hand with a love for what you do. All these qualities of success must come from within. They are not something anyone else can give you. Above all else, *success is really an attitude*. It is a choice you make to respond to problems as opportunities, to see alternate routes to your goals when others see only a path with a dead end.

Success and Your Career Choice

As you decide on the career you will pursue, think about how well it will allow you to meet your individual definition of success. For example, will it provide you the level of financial stability you are looking for? Will promotion eventually require a higher level of education than you are currently pursuing? Will it enable you to satisfactorily maintain your family relationships? Ultimately, you must ask yourself if your career choice will allow you to have the overall lifestyle you want. A successful career helps you lead a successful life.

Employer Expectations

Generally speaking, employers prefer candidates who possess some combination of the positive personality traits, skills, and qualities of success just discussed. Some employers may have additional expectations when considering you as a job candidate. The following sections will give you some information about these expectations and how important they are to employers.

Goals. When you have goals, an employer may recognize your commitment to your career, believe you will stay in a job for a reasonable length of time, and realize where your self-motivation will come from.

Positive Personality. A person with a positive personality has certain characteristics, including a good attitude, poise, self-confidence, decisiveness, and a tendency to

be extroverted. Having one or more of these attributes may convince an employer that you can do the job well.

Appropriate Technical Skills.   Employers must first be concerned with filling their job openings with candidates who possess the basic aptitude to do the job. Whether or not it is important that your skills be fully developed depends on the job, but in most cases you must demonstrate at least the basic skills to start in the job. An employer will evaluate how much more training you need and decide whether it is possible to provide you with this additional training. You must be sure to convince an employer that you can perform the tasks the job requires. Remember that the attitude you present with those skills may convince an employer to hire you even when more technical training is needed on the job.

Application Skills.   Human resource professionals often agree on what various industries are looking for from students with a postsecondary education. Many repeat all the qualities discussed so far but unanimously agree that these three attributes are most important: the ability to *analyze* information, *apply* how it can be used, and then take appropriate *action* were the most necessary skills for success in their corporations. These "think and do" skills are the most basic to any business situation because they are a source of ideas that develop new products, and they ensure that workers learn how to act independently on the job, providing growth for themselves and for the company.

Leadership.   Successfully influencing and inspiring other individuals and groups toward a common goal is one proof of leadership ability. Leaders usually emerge from within a group because of their ability to draw followers. Companies seek individuals with proven leadership ability to become change agents in their organization.

Work Ethic.   Proving you have a strong work ethic may include giving examples that show you are willing to work hard and perform to the best of your ability on a regular basis. Even if you haven't had a lot of work experience, the hard work you put into your studies or into a project or hobby are good examples of your strong work ethic.

Realistic Expectations.   Realistic expectations of job candidates about starting salaries and job responsibilities are important to employers because they may improve job satisfaction. When a job candidate fully understands what is expected of him or her on a day-to-day basis, there is less chance of disagreement or disappointment about the job.

Maturity.   Employers evaluate maturity in a variety of ways. Your ability to remain poised in different situations, tolerate differences of opinion, and assume responsibility with little supervision are some examples of how an employer may evaluate your maturity level. Immaturity in the workplace can lead to personality conflicts, poor performance, or inappropriate social behavior. Employers try to avoid hiring immature workers because they may be disruptive or unproductive in the workplace, show less likelihood of success, or require more supervision and training than an employer is willing to provide.

Enthusiasm.   Enthusiasm is one indicator of how excited you really are about your career and about life. Employers prefer candidates who seem genuinely excited about their job, because usually people perform best when they are doing what they like to do. Lack of enthusiasm may be interpreted as a lack of interest or confidence on your part.

Focus.   Your ability to be focused on your career goals tells the employer you have already thought through many options and have decided to make a commitment to a specific career. This means there is a greater chance that you are choosing a job you really want, and that you will concentrate on doing what is necessary to be successful.

Scholastic Record.   Your scholastic record is one way an employer may judge whether you have developed skills appropriate to the job. Reviewing your record will indicate

if the courses you studied provided the skills you will need, and good grades in these courses will indicate an understanding of the subject. Good grades may also be concrete evidence that you have the motivation, enthusiasm, and focus needed to succeed.

Community Service.   A personal commitment to the community (communities) you serve is helpful to you in your job search and in your career. Employers view your community involvement as an expression of your concern for others. An attempt to make the community in which the company does business a better place for its residents and a more attractive place for other new businesses is evidence of your ability to balance your time, energy, and talents effectively. It is also a great effort toward your own professional development.

Company Knowledge.   Your ability to convince an employer that you understand and like the business field you are about to enter is important. When you have thoroughly investigated both the industry and the company you may be dealing with, you demonstrate sincerity about wanting to work for that company and give the impression that you're not just shopping around for any job that comes along.

Follow-Through.   An ability to independently follow directions on projects is important. Employers want to know you can complete your work on your own without constant supervision. When you need to be supervised constantly, you take away from the time the supervisor has to do his or her own job and you cost the company money.

Handling Conflict.   Think of some times you successfully handled conflict. Such incidents may have occurred within your family, with friends, or between co-workers. Conflicts between people happen frequently in the workplace, and an employer needs to know that you are able to handle them on your own. This is both a sign of maturity on your part and a time-saver for the employer, who would prefer not to waste valuable time settling differences between people instead of getting the job done.

Self-Discipline.   Self-discipline is helpful on the job because it helps keep you focused on your job until it is completed. The ability to avoid distraction and be self-driven helps you perform your job well.

Outside Interests.   Employers look at how involved you are in activities outside the classroom in order to understand your likes and dislikes, your level of initiative, your leadership potential, and your ability to manage your time well. Employers understand if you simply have not been able to explore many outside interests because you've been working or have family responsibilities, but they often prefer some evidence of involvement beyond the classroom. It is important to realize that very often an employer will accept a candidate with weaker skills over another because the candidate seems to be the *right type* for the job. Usually, the right type is someone who demonstrates positive personality traits and qualities of success, and meets the employer's overall expectations.

Loyalty.   You should be able to give a prospective employer examples of situations that demonstrate your ability to be loyal to your employer. An example might be a time when you defended the reputation of your company, which had just gotten negative publicity in the newspaper. Another example might be a time when you knew a co-worker was recording more hours on his or her time card than he or she had actually worked, and you told your supervisor about it.

Professionalism.   Reliability, an excellent appearance, and proper business manners are all part of professionalism. Good attendance in class and at work can be one indicator of your reliability. Meeting your industry's standards on grooming and dress is also an important part of professionalism. In fact, your appearance creates an employer's first impression of you. If that first impression is not positive, you will probably not be considered further in the hiring process.

2/26/02

Good Speaking Skills.   Being able to express yourself verbally to an employer can give the impression that you will interact well with others on the job and that you can promote your skills and your ideas confidently. A good appearance may leave the employer thinking you really care about the impression you make on others and that you would present a positive image of the company.

Reviewing this list of qualities is one way to understand what employers look for in job candidates. Another way to understand employer expectations is to read the classified ads. Employers may indicate certain personality traits they are looking for or give other clues as to their expectations by the way they have described the job

ACTIVITY 2-7 • *Reading Classified Ads*

Carefully read each of the classified ads listed below.

MARKETING ASSISTANT

Responsible for handling clerical functions for Director of Marketing. Membership Manager and Database Manager including:

- correspondence
- travel arrangements
- preparation of reports
- coordination and transmission of communications during the Director of Marketing's or Department Manager's absence
- assist in other duties as assigned to ensure the smooth operation of the Marketing Division

Good communication and organizational skills necessary. Computer experience important. Strong keyboarding ability necessary. Accuracy and promptness a must.

The Society is an equal opportunity employer and provides excellent benefits. The building is wheel-chair accessible. Interested applicants should send resumé and salary requirements to:

Personnel Manager
American Mathematical Society
PO Box 6248
Providence, RI 02940

Equal Opportunity Employer

INVESTOR RELATIONS

We have an excellent opportunity for an aggressive, high energy self-starter with strong knowledge of finance and equity securities. Responsibilities include client and investment community contact, arranging and handling analyst meeting and report writing. Travel is required. Three to five years experience as a securities analyst, stockbroker or IR professional. Experience with marketing equities, knowledge of financial statements, strong written and verbal communication skills. New York based agency.

Send letter and resumé to:
Box NY193, Wall Street Journal
420 Lexington Ave., NY, NY 10170

Make a list of the skills and personality traits sought by each employer:

_____	_____
_____	_____
_____	_____
_____	_____
_____	

Compare the skills and personality traits that employers expect for each position.
   Repeat this exercise with classified ads in your local newspaper for positions you are interested in, and think about the skills and personality traits you will need to qualify for these positions.

and the person they are seeking to fill it. Read the qualifications sought for a wide variety of careers in and out of your chosen field. List all of the common attributes that appear in the ads. Do you see many similarities or much repetition? This is a good indication to you that, regardless of differing technical skill requirements, employers expect candidates to demonstrate certain qualities. These qualities are important to the employer because they are, to a large measure, predictors of success.

Setting Goals for Self-Improvement

Throughout this self-assessment process, you have identified your own values, interests, personality traits, skills, and ideas of success. You have also reviewed those that many employers prefer in the professionals they hire. Preparing for your career involves evaluating how well you compare to what employers expect and then setting goals for self-improvement so that you will better meet employers' expectations.

Characteristics of a Goal

A goal is the difference between where you are and where you want to be. Careers move in a positive direction when you set goals. Before setting your goals for self-improvement, you should be aware of the basic characteristics of successful goals. A goal should be all of the following:

Conceivable: Can you picture the goal in your mind?

Believable: Do you really believe it can happen?

Desirable: Do you really want it?

Achievable: Is your goal realistic?

Measurable: When will your goal be accomplished?

   Goals provide you with the *motivation* or drive to produce top performance on a daily basis. This drive can come from having a clear idea of the direction in which you want to go. It is much easier to get excited about what you are doing if you can see the end results. In the case of personal goals, the end result can be both gaining personal satisfaction and becoming more qualified for the job you want.

Setting Goals into Action

In developing your personal goals, you will develop an *action plan* and identify *action steps* for each area you want to improve. For example, if one of the personality traits you want to develop is confidence, your action plan may be to offer your opinions more often, even when they are different from others'. Your first action step may be to do this more in class, while your second action step may be to speak up more in social conversations as well. With each action plan, you should decide how you want to monitor your progress and determine how you will really know you've achieved your goal. The act of speaking up more in class may be a way to develop your confidence, but the final measure of whether or not you've developed confidence may be the level of comfort and ease

you feel with your new actions. The measure of success as well as the strategies for achieving that success will vary with everyone. What is important is that you think through how you are going to work on your goals and how you will know when you've achieved them.

The process of setting goals for self-improvement really involves turning a weakness into a strength. In the process, remember that acknowledging your weaknesses in a positive way can be important to you and to a prospective employer. Being comfortable with your weaknesses is the result of having a plan for improving them. With this plan, you gain control of the areas you need to improve, rather than letting those areas control you. Your ability to express your weaknesses in a positive way to an employer can mean the difference between the job you really want and the job you may settle for. If an employer asks what your major strengths and weaknesses are and your thoughts are "I am an excellent typist, but my shorthand is only 60 wpm," your response should be "I am an excellent typist. I am working at bringing my shorthand speed up by practicing on my own (or by taking an extra class, or by asking my boss to let me use it more on the job I have now). I like shorthand and realize it is an important skill. I am confident that my speed will improve with practice."

Through this process of setting goals for self-improvement, you can honestly turn something that may sound negative into a positive response. This is easier to do if you already have your action plans and success measures in place.

Proof by Example: How You Add Value to an Employer

Now that you have assessed what skills you have and compared them to what employers look for, you need to focus on how to *convince* an employer that you have excellent qualifications for the job. An employer must be able to *visualize* your value to his or her organization. It is essential that you *create* a *word picture* of your skills, abilities, and past accomplishments and that you link these to the employer's needs.

ACTIVITY 2-8 • *Proof by Example*

Help the employer visualize what you can do for them. Here's how:*

Proof by Example	Sample Exercise
	Job candidate: Richard Carlson
	Job available: Marketing Assistant
1. Present three concrete examples of a skill you wish to offer to a potential employer (*one at a time, most extraordinary*).	1. Leadership skills, sales skills, writing skills.
2. Qualify examples by describing circumstances (*who, what, when, where, why, how*).	2. I recruited 20 of my classmates in three days to sell ad space by phone to employers for a special edition of the school newspaper so that the career development office could do a special promotion for our Career Day.
3. Quantify examples with measurable data (*numbers, percentages, frequency, volume, years, months, weeks, etc.*).	3. The 20 volunteers sold 15 ads which covered 100 percent of the printing cost of the special edition. I wrote the articles for the insert.
4. Specify results . . . What happened? (*data, specific outcomes*)	4. As a result of this special promotion, student attendance at Career Day increased by 5 percent and the career development office reduced its overall

5. Link and think. How will each statement help the employer visualize *increased profits, decreased turnover, improved productivity, improved worker morale, less personal frustration, solution to problems*?

5. This means that at your company I can properly select and motivate an effective sales team, increase sales, and suggest new ways of doing things to increase effectiveness.

Help the employer visualize what you can do for the company.

1. *Present* three concrete examples of a skill you wish to offer to a potential employer (one at a time, focusing on the most extraordinary skills you have to offer):

   Customer service
   Reliable
   Responsible ; punctual, courteous

2. *Qualify* examples by describing circumstances (who, what, when, where, why, how):

   _____
   _____
   _____

3. *Quantify* examples with measurable data (numbers, percentages, frequency, volume, years, months, weeks, etc.):

   _____
   _____
   _____

4. Specify results . . . What happened? (data, specific outcomes):

   _____
   _____
   _____

5. Link and think: How will each statement help the employer visualize the following?

   Increased profits: _____
   Decreased turnover: _____
   Improved productivity: _____
   Improved worker morale: _____
   Less personal frustration: _____
   Solution to problems: _____
   Other benefits to the employer: _____

*Source: Excerpted from Career Development Seminars, Robert Morris College.

INTERNATIONAL CAREER DIRECTIONS

Self-Assessment for International Careers

Values, interests, personality, and skills take on new meanings in different parts of the world. The interests individuals pursue and the personality and skills they develop are very much affected by the culture in each country. For example, some societies emphasize family, hard work, or study as core values which may limit the pursuit of extensive outside interests because little time is left for additional involvement. Other societies are more social and encourage a balance between work and social activity. While individual privacy is the norm in one culture, strong interrelationships and socialization are key in another.

The important things to think about in your self-assessment for an international career is to be aware that people in other cultures may have different values, interests, personality and skills than we do in the United States. This awareness does not mean you should change to become like your international colleagues, but you do need to understand cultural differences in thinking and self-image in order to more effectively live and work in a different country. The following list provides you with some things to think about.

Tips for Self-Assessment for International Careers

1. Realize that what is considered a personal strength in one country may be perceived as a weakness in another country.

2. These are important personal qualities to develop: flexibility, patience, resourcefulness, follow-through, risk taking, versatility.

3. You must be comfortable with the unknown or unexpected.

4. You must not be easily offended by abruptness or aloofness.

5. Identify what transferable skills you can develop for the workplace in most countries.

6. You should know or be able to learn a new language.

7. Keep in perspective other cultures' symbols of success or status.

8. You must deal with the fact that personal lofe and work are completely separate in most other countries.

9. In many countries, the family is valued as a top priority and the job does not interfere with this.

10. In most other countries, an American education is valued even more than work experience.

Example

Aggressive behavior can be viewed as a strength *or* a weakness depending on your cultural perspective. The following comparison of how aggressive behavior is viewed in the United States, the Pacific Rim, and the Middle East and Europe shows why it is important to understand different cultural perspectives on behavior when pursuing an international career.

• *U.S. culture:* Candidates are encouraged to be aggressive in a job search so that the employer will see the candidate as someone with initiative and a real motivation for the job. In general, aggressiveness is valued as a positive trait in the United States.

- *Some Pacific Rim cultures:* When I recently asked a student from Malaysia why her classmates from other Pacific Rim countries did not ask many questions in class, she responded that these students don't want to risk embarrassing a speaker or teacher who may not know the answer or feel as though the presentation was not well prepared. In this case, these students thought questioning the instructor is offensive.

- *Some Middle Eastern and European cultures:* In certain Middle Eastern and European countries, students are taught to be assertive to get ahead. During the interviewing process in the United States, several European students were identified as arrogant and very aggressive by employers.

You need to be aware of the fine balance between aggressiveness and arrogance. Knowing some of the background of the company you will be applying to, as well as of the person who will interview you, would help you prepare your presentation style before your interview.

Chapter Summary

In order to compete effectively in the job market, you need to know what specific value you bring to an employer. While self-assessment is useful to your career planning, it is important to use the results to develop a strategy for self-improvement that will convince an employer to hire you because you bring unique talent to the company. Now that you have mastered the proof-by-example exercise, you can refer back to it as an exercise to help you prepare for each future job interview.

Personal Development

Technical skills alone are not enough to ensure a successful career. Focusing on your personal development, which will help you project a positive self-image and communicate well with others, is important because the majority of jobs available throughout the next century will be in the service industries requiring direct customer contact. This chapter will help you improve your self-image by focusing on communication skills, personal care and personal appearance, time and stress management, business manners, role models, and awareness of the world around you.

Communication Skills

You may spend more than 85 percent of your day communicating with others.[1] Communication takes many forms: speaking, writing, listening, and body language. Each interaction we have with others results in either a positive or a negative impression. First impressions consist of things people notice about you when they first meet you. *It takes only two to four minutes to make a first impression.* First impressions are important because they can lead others either to pay further attention to you or to disregard you before they get to know you. Communication skills are necessary to enhance your technical skills. Excellent communication skills may even make up for weaknesses in technical skills with some employers. For example, if a secretary must spend a lot of time dealing with clients, strong communication skills may compensate for a slow typing speed; it may be easier for a good communicator to improve typing skills through practice than for a poor communicator to become an effective communicator.

Speaking

Speaking is a form of communication. The spoken word can be powerful, depending on the content of the message and the style in which it is delivered. Being aware of what you sound like can help you know how you may be coming across during a job interview, an oral presentation, or a one-on-one discussion. Factors that influence how your voice is received include how fast you speak (rate), how high or low your voice is (pitch), how positive you sound (tone), and how clear your speech is (articulation).

The quality of your message should ultimately make the difference in whether or not your message is credible to others. However, *what* you say is not always as important as *how* you say it. The relationship between how you say something (your voice) and what you say (your message) is critical. Learning how to match your voice with the content of your message is key to being an effective communicator. Let's look at some examples of the relationship between the two.

Say the following sentences two times, putting verbal emphasis on the italicized word in each: "Did you know he *succeeded* on the third try?" "Did you know he succeeded on the *third* try?" Most people would interpret this sentence in two distinct ways, given the different verbal emphasis in each case. The first statement emphasizes the word *succeeded*. The thought that the person was successful, regardless of how many times he tried, is foremost in the listener's mind. The second statement emphasizes the word *third*. The thought that it took three attempts before this person was successful is emphasized. The tone of each sentence implies different meaning.

As you move forward in your career, you will have many opportunities to create a positive impression by how you speak. When you use the telephone to respond to a want ad or ask people for career advice, your voice is your only tool for making a good impression. Let someone hear a smile in your voice by being enthusiastic. Speak slowly and clearly pronounce all your words. Project your voice so you can be heard. If you have an accent, you should be conscious of how well you are understood by others. If the clarity of what you say is not diminished by your accent, there is no need to work on eliminating it. If your accent sometimes interferes with your ability to deliver a clear message, you should work on changing it.

In today's global workplace, you should evaluate whether or not learning to speak one or two other languages may be helpful to you. Studying other languages not only helps you communicate better with your international colleagues in written or verbal form but also helps put into context the mind-set of the person you are speaking with from another country. This happens because when you study another language, you cannot help but also study much of the overall culture in which that language is spoken. Knowing more than one language will be a big plus for you when you interview with prospective employers.

[1]Janet G. Elsea, "The First Four Minutes," *First Impression, Best Impression* (New York: Simon & Schuster, 1984), p. 18.

Listening

Listening is the communication skill that is most often overlooked. Listening is paying attention to what someone is saying. A good listener hears the message being conveyed and evaluates its meaning. Good listening is a form of learning because it reveals knowledge of others. Hearing what is being said but not concentrating on what it means is called *passive listening*. In contrast, *active listening* means hearing what is being said and interpreting its meaning as well. Active listening makes you a more effective communicator because you react to what you have heard.

As you are planning your career, you will find active listening to be helpful in many ways. Listening to business and personal acquaintances may lead you to a new contact. Listening to how someone talks about a company can tell you a lot about how the company is run and the morale of the employees.

Good listening skills include being able to distinguish important from unimportant information, to detect inconsistencies in information, and to understand the main points of a message. When parts of a message are unclear, the best thing to do is to take notes, jot down your questions, and wait until the entire presentation or discussion is finished. It may also be appropriate to provide comments about what was presented or to provide feedback on what was said and how it was said. Remember that many times we have difficulty listening to what is being said because we are distracted by things that are bothering us or by the environment around us. Another distraction can be our own emotions about what is being presented or about the speaker. The key to overcoming these distractions is concentration. By developing basic communication skills, you will become more confident in yourself and more effective in your interaction with others.

ACTIVITY 3-1 • *Active Listening*

Some characteristics of an active listener are being attentive, maintaining eye contact, not interrupting, and being tuned in to the other person's facial expression, gestures, body language, and tone of voice. To understand the importance of effective active listening, sit across from a partner and, facing each other, prepare to engage in a brief conversation. Decide who will be Person A, the listener, and Person B, the storyteller. The storyteller should tell a three- to four-minute story about personal interests, family background, and career plans. The listener will repeat the storyteller's story, including as much detail as possible.

To determine how accurate Person A's listening skills are, you will both assess how effectively Person A listened. Place a check (✔) in the boxes that describe the listener's behavior while hearing the story.

Listening Skills Checklist

The Listener's Self-Evaluation	The Storyteller's Evaluation of the Listener
If you were the listener, check the appropriate boxes below.	If you were the storyteller, check the appropriate boxes below.
I think I:	**I think Person A:**
☐ Maintained eye contact	☐ Maintained eye contact
☐ Was attentive	☐ Was attentive
☐ Did not interrupt	☐ Did not interrupt
☐ Nodded to show agreement	☐ Showed positive acknowledgment
☐ Took appropriate notes	☐ Took appropriate notes

When communicating with others, it is important that they perceive you to be a good listener. Very often you may think you have appeared to listen well, only to find the speaker has a different perception of how well you listened.

Different Perceptions of Active Listening

After each of you has completed the listening skills checklist, discuss how similar or different your responses were. Discuss with each other the behaviors you agreed on and those you did not agree on. By discussing those you did not agree on, Person A can gain a better understanding of how well he or she is perceived to be an active listener.

Assessing Active Listening

Even though it is important to appear to be an active listener, the true measure of creative listening is how well you can recall and interpret what you heard. Discuss how accurate the listener was in relaying back the storyteller's story. Were any key points missing? How much detail was repeated? Did the listener provide any interpretation of observations of body language, facial expressions, gestures, or tone of voice?

Body Language

Body language is a form of nonverbal communication conveyed by certain body movements. Body language includes your facial expression, poise, posture, and mannerisms. When someone looks at you, certain clues can be detected through your body language as to how you feel or what you may be thinking. Facial expressions can reveal your inner thoughts and feelings or present a controlled reaction by choice. Facial expression can show a variety of emotions. The following are just a few simple illustrations of how you communicate with your face, before any words are spoken:

Facial Expression	Message to Others
Smile	Acceptance or approval
Frown	Anger, confusion, or disappointment
Wide-open eyes	Interest and confidence
Raised brows	Surprise
Wandering eyes	Boredom or distraction

Poise is your ability to act with ease and dignity. When you are poised, you appear self-assured and composed in almost every situation. A poised person appears to be in control of most actions and reactions. Posture is one indicator of poise. Standing or sitting straight and still, without appearing tense or uncomfortable, creates an impression that you are confident about the situation you are in. Think about people you know who are noticeable when entering a room just by the way they hold their body. The way a person carries himself or herself indicates total confidence. Poised people can create energy just by walking into a room.

Each of us has certain mannerisms that either add to or detract from our image. Mannerisms are part of our body language and are formed by habits we have developed. Mannerisms include using your hands a lot to emphasize a point when you speak, tapping your foot while waiting or in a hurry, or rocking back and forth or pacing when standing in front of an audience to make a presentation. While certain mannerisms may have a positive effect, mannerisms like the ones just mentioned may not. Some positive mannerisms that can help you communicate well in most business settings include maintaining direct eye contact, using a firm handshake, nodding your head to show support or approval, extending your right arm with open hand to let someone go ahead of you or tell them to start first, scanning the entire audience or

group with your eyes when making a presentation, or nodding once to acknowledge someone's presence or give that person the signal to go ahead with something.

Facial expressions, poise, posture, and mannerisms are all important parts of body language because they influence someone's impression of you before you even speak. By developing appropriate nonverbal responses to situations, you are in better control of the image you portray and have a better chance of making a good long-lasting impression on others.

The Art of Conversation

There is a difference between talking with someone and engaging in interesting conversation. A good conversationalist keeps interested and interesting and shows concern for the listener(s). Stay well informed on a wide variety of subjects. Know when to talk business and when not to. Avoid talking about topics that may be too personal, boring, or controversial, such as your health, other people's health, how much things cost, family problems, or harmful gossip. Show interest in what the other person likes to do. Avoid correcting the other person in public. Be excited about others' good news. Don't interrupt. Know how to ask questions that show your interest, but don't pry. Give and accept compliments gracefully. Address everyone within a group, not just one or two people.

Having varied cultural interests and awareness of world events is important to being a good conversationalist. This is especially true when you are hosting visitors from another country or when you travel abroad on business or for pleasure.

When you show through your conversation that you care about other people as well as yourself, you will be received in a more positive way. Balancing your conversations between a focus on yourself and the other person will allow you to express yourself and at the same time make the other person feel good.

Telephone Skills

Telephone skills are an important part of business communication because much of your time in your job search, and even in your current part-time job, will be spent on the telephone. Although you are not seen while speaking on the telephone, you are heard and judged by how you handle the call.

Here are some guidelines for making telephone calls:

- Before placing a telephone call, know the name of the person you are calling, his or her title, and the department he or she works in.
- First identify yourself by giving your name and the reason for your call, then ask to be connected to the party you are calling.
- Always refer to the person you are calling by Mr., Ms., or Mrs. and the last name. If you know they have a specific title, such as Dr. or Professor, use it.
- Learn the proper pronunciation of the person's name before calling.
- If you reach your party, greet him or her by the proper name and title, introduce yourself, and state the purpose of your call.
- If you cannot reach your party because he or she is unavailable, leave a message that you called and indicate that you will return the call.
- Ask when would be a good time to do so, and then call back when you said you would.
- *Always* remain pleasant and professional, even when your frustration level is high. You don't want the message to read that you were rude.

Here are some rules for receiving telephone calls:

- The telephone should always be answered within three rings. Answering on the first ring is best.
- No one should ever be left on hold for more than one minute. The first call always has priority.

- Transferring a call within a company requires thorough knowledge of the organization, of the different divisions' duties and responsibilities, and of the names of key people who will handle the call properly.
- If you are not sure where to transfer the call, put the caller on hold briefly, explaining that you are trying to find the proper source to serve the caller's needs, then find out where the call should go. When you are sure you can make the proper transfer, do so.
- If it's your job to screen calls, remember to do so in a professional manner.
- If you are a secretary, you may help an executive return calls by keeping a neat list of calls at your desk and asking the executive if you can place the return call.
- If you must take a message, politely explain that the party being called is unavailable and that you will be sure that the person gets the message.

It is important to remember that the way you handle yourself on the telephone says a lot about you and reflects an image of the company you represent.

Finally, be aware that taking a good message is an art. The following are elements of a good message:

- Name of the caller (correctly spelled).
- Telephone number, including area code if needed, and extension.
- Name of caller's company.
- Date and hour of the call.
- Your name or initials.

IMPORTANT MESSAGE

FOR __*Dr. Smith*__

DATE __*10/5/95*__   TIME __*2:15*__   AM/PM

WHILE YOU WERE OUT

M __*r. Allen Jones*__

OF __*Cartwright Industries*__

PHONE NO. __*(401) 885-6666*__

TELEPHONED	✔	PLEASE CALL	✔
CALLED TO SEE YOU		WILL CALL AGAIN	
WANTS TO SEE YOU		RUSH	
	RETURNED YOUR CALL		

MESSAGE __*The contract has been received and he has some questions. Please try to call back on Thursday, 10/8 between 2-4 pm.*__

SIGNED __*Cheryl Anderson*__

- A request to call back immediately, if the call is urgent.
- The message.

Voice Mail and E-Mail

Today's technology changes the art of message taking to one of message processing through the use of voice mail and E-mail (electronic mail). There are pros and cons to the use of these automated systems for leaving messages. The advantages are that the message sender can be sure the message is delivered exactly the way he or she wants. In both voice mail and E-mail, the recipient gets the sender's actual message rather than an abbreviated version that may come when a secretary or receptionist takes the message over the phone. Also, with voice mail and E-mail, messages can be sent any time of day, without the need to reach someone physically in the office.

The disadvantages are that not everyone is as fervent about reading E-mail as most people are about checking their message slips, especially those who work in an environment that is not technologically advanced. Also, taking down messages on slips usually brings both parties together verbally at some point. With voice mail and E-mail, the two parties may never communicate with each other verbally. This could lead to a feeling of depersonalization in the communication process. Finally, more people may hear or see the message left on voice mail or E-mail, causing the need for the sender to be conscious of the language in and the content of the messages sent.

In all, the benefits of voice mail and E-mail are tremendous. But as we move toward using these forms of communicating with one another, we should adhere to quick response times and professionalism in the way we communicate.

Benchmark: Interoffice E-mail

Most of the users that make up the Internet's impressive growth statistics aren't using the Web or downloading files. They're simply sending and receiving electronic mail along the Net's phone lines. But our sampling of small businesses indicates that those companies' E-mail isn't wired to the world quite yet. The majority limit E-mail to internal or telecommuting employees. Very few businesses use the Net to contact clients, prospects, or advisers. "Our industry just hasn't accepted E-mail yet as a regular form of communication," says Harvey Friedman of Hatfield Electric, an electrical contractor based in Scottsdale, Ariz. Hatfield has Windows-driven PCs with desktop modems for most of the office employees, who use Lotus cc:Mail. "We do a lot of faxing via modem but no E-mail. Our vendors and other contractors just aren't using E-mail technology at this point," says Friedman.

The results of the survey

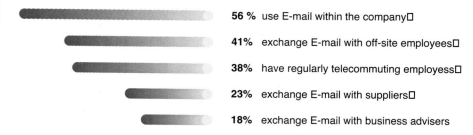

56 % use E-mail within the company

41% exchange E-mail with off-site employees

38% have regularly telecommuting employess

23% exchange E-mail with suppliers

18% exchange E-mail with business advisers

Source: A survey of 273 small to midsized businesses, conducted by the Executive Committee, San Diego, April 1995.

Although electronic modes of communication are becoming popular, they will not replace the human factor completely, nor do they diminish the need for or power of effective telephone skills in the workplace.

Writing

Writing effectively can also help you gain a competitive edge in your job search when writing letters or résumés or completing a job application. Throughout your career, almost any job will require you to produce written documents. You may also want to show a prospective employer a report you did for one of your classes. People form an impression about you through your writing. Well-organized thoughts and good grammar, spelling, and punctuation show the reader that you care about the quality of your work. The neatness of any document you produce is important. This means having no white-outs, erasures, or bent or soiled papers.

You can take several steps to become a good writer. These include deciding on the content, sequence, and style of your writing. *Content* is the first thing you need to think about. Focus on what you want your message to be. Ask yourself what you are really trying to tell someone. To get started, jot down some of the key words or phrases that begin to define your message.

Sequencing the information you want to convey means listing your key points in the order you want to present them. Look to see if there is a flow in the thought process you are using, and be sure there are no gaps.

Choose a *style* of writing to reflect your personality or to fit the degree of formality required in different situations. When writing is required as part of your job search, you should be sure to let your individuality come through. Very often, how you express yourself in the written word can differentiate you from others saying the same thing in writing:

Factual: "I have all the necessary qualifications to work at your company."

Professional: "My education, coupled with my work experience, makes me a well-qualified candidate for the job you offer."

Distinctive: "The secretarial award I won for my typing accuracy and speed and the A I received in my communications class make me an excellent choice for your administrative assistant position."

Notice that in the last statement, the human resource manager may learn about the unique qualifications you personally bring to the job. Being specific about the skills you offer when presenting yourself to an employer may help you stand out among other applicants.

In general, the writing style for almost all job-search situations should be professional. To develop an effective professional writing style, you should know your reader, know your message, and be concise. Having this type of focus helps you get to the point so that what you say is clearly understood. Sound confident. Your confidence helps the reader feel that you can support what you say. Use proper form (grammar, spelling, punctuation) so that the quality of your work will not be questioned. Keep the language simple. When you do this, the reader can understand what you say better, and there is less chance of confusing the reader. Proofread your own work so that there are no mistakes. Have someone else proofread your work. You will want the opportunity to correct errors and make improvements on your work before it is in final form. It is not proper form to use slang or abbreviations in your professional writing. Avoid copying form letters. Form letters should serve as a guide for you to get started with your work, but what you say and how you say it should be original. Sound enthusiastic!

The Sales Process

Any employer will hire any applicant as long as he or she is *convinced* that the applicant will bring in more value than it costs to hire that person. It has already been

well established that knowing yourself and being able to communicate effectively are important to your success. Once you have your own sense of direction and have determined what you want, you need to know how to get it. To successfully compete in tomorrow's workplace, you need to be *convincing*. Knowing yourself and your goals is the first step, but communicating them effectively to the people that count is the key to successfully managing your career.

The person with the hardest job of convincing another person of something is the salesperson. The sales process is really the process you will go through on a job interview. Before learning the many specific interviewing techniques that exist, you will want to consider the sales process as an approach to obtaining the jobs you want. In the employment process, think of the *employer as the customer* and *you as the product*. You have a certain set of skills and attributes to bring to the employer, and the employer offers an opportunity for you to use them.

Why are some people with similar skills and attributes hired and others not if their qualifications meet those needed for the job? The difference lies in the candidates' ability to sell themselves. There is a difference between marketing and sales. Both are important in the employment process. *Marketing* involves surveying the market, both employers and potential employers, and assessing their needs and wants. *Sales* is the formal process of exchanging what you have for what someone else has.

Selling also involves being convinced. In the employment process, your skills are exchanged for a job. Both you and the employer benefit if the match is right. If it is not, neither one of you benefits. So beyond having effective sales ability, you need to be sure you want the job you are going after and that the employer really needs you. Identifying customer needs is one of the keys to effective salesmanship. Let's take a look at why people buy and compare it to why an employer might hire you.

Why People Buy	Employer Interests
To satisfy a need	To fill a job opening
Cost effectiveness	To increase profitability
Comfort and convenience	Employees' professional preparation and ability to fit in

It costs a company money to hire you. The company loses money if you don't work out in the job. High company recruiting costs result in competitive candidate selection. The Bank of Boston recently estimated that it costs $80,000 before new managers get through their training program. The bank spends $10,000 on recruiting, $50,000 on training, and $20,000 on relocating and travel expenses. The costly hiring process makes companies highly selective. In a typical year, the Bank of Boston interviewed 1,800 students. They then cut down to 1,200 interviews to hire 50 people. The average recruiting cost per new recruit is $1,600. Whether a company visits your school to interview you or runs ads in the newspaper, it costs money to hire someone new.

You stand a good chance of competing for a job if you have the skills to do the job, if you are sure that you want the job before taking it so that replacement costs will not skyrocket for the company, and if you can reinforce the employer's feelings that you've been professionally trained.

An important part of "selling" your professional training is knowing how your coursework and other accomplishments have provided you with specific workplace competencies. As you prepare to convince an employer that your education has provided you with unique qualifications, review the following:

- What your specialized course work consists of.
  Example: If you are pursuing a program in fashion and retailing management, specialized courses may include Merchandising Mathematics and Merchandise Buying.

- Training you have received on specialized equipment.
  Example: Desktop publishing, computers, court reporting machines, hotel reservations systems.
- Work experience that is not part of your formal program of study or work programs that you have earned credit for.
  Example: Internships, cooperative education, and externships.
- Skills developed through work experience.
  Example: If you pursued a work experience in the fashion and retailing management field, some skills acquired may include sales forecasting, decision making, profit generation, stock and sales, and quantitative skills.

By identifying how the training and work experience you receive as part of your education develops skills sought by employers, you translate the relevance of your

---

ACTIVITY 3-2 • *Summary of Training, Experience, and Skills*

By completing this exercise, you will be better able to articulate what you bring to an employer. Remember, an important part of successful selling is product knowledge. In this case, the product is you!

Training: Write a list of some of the specialized courses you completed in your program of study and special equipment you can operate:

Courses: _____

_____

_____

Equipment: _____

_____

_____

Work experience: Write a list of work experience programs you have participated in:

_____

_____

_____

Skills:*   Write a list of skills you will have developed upon completion of your program of study:

_____

_____

_____

The second part of presenting your unique features to an employer is tying in individual experiences that have had relevance to your career. To complement the unique features of your career training you need to summarize the related activities that you have pursued in preparation for your career. Such activities may include the following:

Part-time employment	Trade shows visited
Summer employment	Extracurricular activities
Industry guest speakers' programs	Volunteer work
Field trips	Special interests
Special accomplishments	

Briefly describe the value of your:

Part-time employment: _____

Summer employment: _____

Industry guest speakers' programs: _____

Field trips: _____

Trade show visits: _____

Extracurricular activities: _____

Volunteer work: _____

Special interests: _____

Special accomplishments: _____

*Many schools have defined lists of employment skills for each course or program offered as part of their outcomes assessment program. Check with your instructor to see if your school can provide you with a list of your program outcomes to help you better explain your employment skills to a prospective employer.

education to preparation for a job. When you can do this with your program of study, it will become easy to convince an employer you have mastered skills important to your profession, as opposed to simply completing a degree or diploma.

Business Manners

Having business manners means knowing how to move through sometimes awkward situations with ease and grace. Business manners are an essential ingredient to success in today's service industries. With today's emphasis on people in organizations, the art of successful interaction depends on your ability to handle yourself professionally in many different situations. Your ability to do the right thing at the right time or to say the right thing at the right time is not only important in the job interview but especially important once you are on the job. Business manners span the whole company from the secretary to the president. Secretaries now have broader responsibilities that require an awareness of proper protocol.

Many meetings between executives occur at luncheons, breakfasts, and dinners, as well as in the boardroom. Salespeople are constantly creating an image for their company with clients. There is no doubt that no matter what your role will be in the organization in which you choose to work, you will play a major role in portraying the company's image. In fact, people really are the company image. In every daily business contact you have, you will be in the powerful position of creating a positive or a negative response in others. Those others will be your superiors, subordinates, associates, and, most important, your customers. How all of these people see you is critical to your own career success. Remember, you have the power to elicit the response you want from them by exercising basic business manners.

The following section on dining etiquette offers a number details, but the basic principles of courtesy and manners may be applied to almost any business situation.

Dining Etiquette As you prepare for and develop your career, you will have many opportunities to share a meal, attend a reception, or be at a party with businesspeople. Perhaps you will dine with a corporate executive at one of your school's industry recognition dinners or network with businesspeople at a party. You may be invited to attend a

reception as part of a company's open house where you can learn about working for that company. Certainly there is a chance one of your job interviews will be conducted over lunch. In these business settings, practicing proper dining techniques is very important to portraying a professional image.

Restaurants.   As the person seeking employment or career advice, you will probably be receiving invitations to dine at a restaurant. If someone has extended you an invitation, it is generally up to that person to decide where you will go. The person extending the invitation generally offers to pay the full bill.

Since you are the guest in this situation, the waitperson will probably ask for your order first. Order a meal in the medium price range. Select foods that are easy to eat. Avoid finger foods such as chicken wings or shellfish. You want to be able to focus on your conversation, not on keeping your fingers clean. Generally avoid ordering alcohol with your meal, especially if this is your first meeting. Always try not to smoke. If you are in a smoking area, you should still ask those you are with whether or not your smoking will bother them. In most cases, you should avoid smoking at all.

Wait for all the meals to be served before you begin eating. If you are not sure which utensils to use, remember to start with those on the outside and work in toward your plate. During your meal, remain active in conversation. Be sure to thank your host for the hospitality extended. If you have occasion to dine with that person again, offer to pay the bill.

Receptions.   Occasionally a prospective employer may invite you to the firm for a company open house or reception intended to familiarize you with the company. Or you may find yourself at a social reception where there are many good contacts that may be helpful to you in your job search. Keep in mind that, although these settings may seem more social in nature, if you want to make a professional impression, treat them as business settings. This means not overindulging in the alcoholic beverages or food that are available. It will also be helpful to dress professionally and not come dressed in the fancy attire you may wear at a strictly social party. Be sure you move around and speak to a lot of people, making a special effort to speak to the hosts of the reception. An invitation usually gives a specific time frame for the reception, for example, 5:00–8:00 PM. You should not arrive before nor remain after the designated time.

These occasions are great opportunities for expressing the enthusiasm, good communication skills, and technical skills you have developed. Remember, your positive attitude is key to making a great impression.

Awareness of the World around You

A final step in your personal development is keeping current on what is happening in the world. Develop the habit of either reading the newspaper or watching the news on television every day. It may be helpful to read magazines like *Time* or *Business Week,* or magazines or trade journals specific to your career interest. The point is that being aware of happenings outside your personal world is important to your ability to hold interesting conversations and relate well to others.

What to Be Aware Of	Possible Sources of Information
Current corporate mergers or acquisitions	CNN
Cost of living trends in different U.S. states and in different countries	*The Wall Street Journal*
The current 10 most successful businesses in your career field	*U.S.A. Today*

What to Be Aware Of	Possible Sources of Information
Health-related issues	*Time* magazine
International business trends	*Business Week*
National and international political events	*Fortune* magazine
Bills being voted on that may affect you	Your local and national political representatives
Employment trends in different regions of the country and in different countries	The Internet

Personal Care and Personal Appearance

Personal care and personal appearance are both an important part of your personal development because they help you create a positive impression with prospective employers. Proper grooming, personal hygiene, wellness, and professional dress all help you to portray your best professional image.

Grooming

A professional appearance is a statement of confidence. People are more apt to listen to you if you look like you take your job seriously. In fact, many employers follow grooming standards set for their industry. The food service industry is a good example of one industry where adherence to grooming codes is mandatory. These codes do not only exist for you to portray a professional image with the public, but also to meet sanitation and health codes set for professionals who handle food and related products that will be served to the public. Another example of where strict grooming standards exist is the health care industry. Once you begin the interviewing

process, you have stepped into the world of work and you need to present yourself as a professional, even if you are still a student. Your professional appearance begins with good grooming from head to toe.

- Hair should be short for men, short enough not to hit your shirt collar. Long hair, multi-length hair, and brightly colored hair must be changed prior to your first interview.
- Clothing should fit properly. Do not try to use your suit from high school since, for most of you, the sleeves will be too short or worn or just will not help you present a crisp image. If you borrow clothes for your job interviews, be sure they fit and are attractive on you. Wear an ironed shirt or blouse. A crumpled look is unprofessional.
- Shoes are an important part of your clothing. Buy new shoes for your interviews.

These efforts to create a well-groomed look are all critical to your credibility with a prospective employer. Too many times, job applicants fail to build a well-groomed image by addressing only one area rather than concentrating on the total look. For example, time after time, students have arrived for interviews with a new, well-fitted suit and old or casual shoes or long hair that is not properly maintained. Unless you commit to your whole look, employers may not view you seriously as a professional.

Personal Hygiene   Cleanliness is important to how you look and to your health. Personal hygiene involves the following practices:

- Bathe or shower daily.
- Use underarm deodorant after you bathe or shower to avoid possible body odor.

- Be clean shaven. Women should shave their legs and underarms. Men should shave their beards. In some professions a beard may be acceptable, but most often you will find it necessary to have no beard.
- Brush your teeth at least twice a day. It doesn't hurt to carry a travel-size tube of toothpaste and a toothbrush so that you can brush after lunch or dinner if you are away from home.
- Keep nails clean and nicely cut.
- Keep hair clean and well-shaped by having it cut on a regular basis. Avoid extreme styles or striped colors (green or orange), and be sure hair color or highlights are subtle.
- If you wear makeup, be sure to apply it lightly so that it accentuates your features instead of changing your looks.

Wellness

Proper exercise and diet can help you look and feel brighter, more alert, and more energetic. Diet and exercise are often neglected because of constantly changing work or school schedules. Here are some guidelines for building healthy habits:

- Control total fat and salt intake. It is recommended that total fat intake not exceed 30 percent of total caloric intake. Reading food labels can help you be aware of how much fat and salt are in the foods you eat.
- Avoid substance abuse that can result in overuse or misuse of alcoholic beverages, drugs, or tobacco. Overindulgence of any of these substances can seriously impair your health.
- Drink plenty of water. Drinking eight glasses of water per day helps keep the body in balance. If you find eight glasses excessive for you, be sure to incorporate a good amount of water in your diet every day.
- When restaurant dining, you can follow these same healthy guidelines if you choose the right items on the menu. Most restaurants offer a variety of leaner foods (pasta, chicken, fish, and salads) and a choice of how food is prepared (baked, broiled, poached, steamed, or grilled).
- If you can, exercise moderately every day. You may join a fitness center or a health spa, or you may develop your own routine, such as walking briskly for 20 minutes per day.

Professional Dress

Developing your own personal style by how you dress can be a lot of fun. The styles, colors, and degree of formality of the clothes you wear can express a lot about your personality. What is important to know as you prepare for your career is the type of dress that will create your best professional image.

Some of the factors that influence your choice of career wardrobe include the type of work situation you will be in every day, the professional look you are trying to achieve, regional differences, and enhancing your own personality and body type. You can enhance your professional image by knowing which colors and fabrics work best for you. Before you begin to plan your business wardrobe, you should know how all of these factors can influence the selections you make.

Work Situations. Different work situations require different styles of dress. The type of work you do and the work setting define your work situation. For example, some jobs require uniforms. Most jobs require a professional look appropriate to the job setting—for example, an office, a store, a bank, or a restaurant. Projecting a good image in "off-the-job" situations is also important.

Uniforms. Jobs in many fields of work require uniforms. This is especially true in the health care, technical, food service, and hospitality industries. If your profession

requires you to wear a uniform, don't assume that you can be lazy about your professional attire. When uniforms are required for work or the classroom, treat them as you would any other good clothing you would buy. Keep them clean, pressed, and new looking at all times. Uniforms should not be an excuse "not to have to worry about dressing for work every day." Buy a good number of uniforms to be sure you always have a clean one available. Only wear uniforms that look crisp and clean. Replace a uniform when the fabric or color begins to wear. Wear shoes that are appropriate for the uniform. Do not overaccessorize a uniform with scarves, jewelry, and so on.

Professional Look.   You should always strive for a professional look when dressing for the workplace. Carefully choosing the right clothes for work makes you feel better about yourself on the job and tells an employer you care about the image you are projecting for yourself and the company. To help you understand what a professional look is, here are basic dress rules to follow that seem to be universal for both men and women:

- Choose well-coordinated outfits. This means mixing and matching colors and styles tastefully. For example, if you wear a blazer, wear tailored trousers or a skirt to go with it. You wouldn't wear a casual flared skirt or balloon pants with a blazer.

- Suits and dresses are usually worn to conduct business. Don't assume you can dress casually. Even if you are working at your own desk most of the time, your look should always be professional enough to go to an unexpected meeting, greet guests into your area, or represent the company unexpectedly at a social or professional event in the evening. If you are not required to wear a suit, it is always better for women to wear a skirt or dress rather than slacks and for men to wear a sport coat rather than just shirtsleeves.

- Wear long- or short-sleeved blouses or shirts. Avoid sleeveless tops, unless you intend to keep a jacket over them. Do not wear tank tops to work.

- Accessorize tastefully with ties, scarves, or jewelry that is not too gaudy or trendy. For example, even though it is a trend for some men to wear earrings, this is not appropriate in the workplace. A studded belt that might look great with your denim jeans is not fitting for the workplace.
- Wear closed-toe shoes that are new looking and well polished.

Sound simple? It is easy to begin a business wardrobe with these basic guidelines. Although you may think this sounds boring, having a few outfits that will give you a well-put-together, conservative look is essential for everyone. Activity 3-3 lists basic wardrobe items that are important to building your professional look. Determine which items you have or need, and develop an approximate budget to make any purchases.

There may be some jobs, such as a recreation coordinator, in which very casual attire is common because of comfort, safety, or convenience. However, most research shows that the professional look described is accepted and most often expected. When considering your work situation and how you will dress, keep in mind that you should also use good judgment when dressing for company social events—formal or casual. If you are invited to attend a sporting event or a picnic, choose nice, casual clothing. Try to avoid jeans; wear casual slacks instead. Don't wear T-shirts that have writing or pictures on them; wear polo shirts or short-sleeved shirts or blouses instead. You want to portray a neat yet stylish image and avoid any clothing that might make you look cheap or sloppy. When attending more formal social events, such as a Christmas party or awards dinner, avoid wearing low-cut or sheer outfits, or any type of dress that may be better suited for a school dance.

All of these different work situations require your good judgment when it comes to dress. If you are not sure what is appropriate, observe what other people are wearing or ask ahead of time if there is a preferred dress style for the situation.

Business Casual. Many businesses now have a "casual day" each week or month enabling employees to dress casually. While the purpose of a casual day is to create a more

ACTIVITY 3-3 • *Wardrobe Inventory*

Complete the following wardrobe inventory to determine what pieces of business attire you have and what pieces you need, indicating the approximate cost for each. This will help you plan to buy only what you need and budget properly for each purchase.

Basic Wardrobe Chart

	Women		
	Have	**Need**	**Approximate Cost**
Suits			
Blazers			
Blouses			
Sweaters			
Skirts			
Dresses			

Basic Wardrobe Chart, *concluded*

Women

	Have	Need	Approximate Cost
Slacks			
Coats			
Shoes			
Boots			
Handbags			
Belts			
Scarves			
Gloves			
Total			

Men

	Have	Need	Approximate Cost
Suits			
Blazers			
Shirts			
Sweaters			
Vests			
Slacks			
Pants			
Coats			
Shoes			
Boots			
Hats			
Belts			
Ties			
Scarves			
Gloves			
Total			

relaxed working environment throughout the company, you should still follow some basic guidelines for business casual dress. These guidelines include no jeans, shorts, sneakers, old T-shirts, or athletic wear. You should avoid tight-fitting or extremely short clothing. It is best to wear nice casual slacks or skirts, and tops or shirts that are casual but crisp and neat looking. Casual dress in the workplace is an invitation to be yourself yet still maintain a certain level of professionalism. Remember that you are still

likely to attend meetings and perhaps greet visitors or customers coming into your work area, and it is important to maintain a positive image of yourself and the company in these situations. In any situation, the way you dress makes a statement about you.

Regional Differences. In different parts of the country, professional dress may vary according to a region's culture or climate. The North and Northeast are generally the most conservative in business dress, reflecting the overall conservative attitude in these areas. The colder climate also influences the selection of colors and fabrics. Colors tend to be darker and fabrics heavier (wool, gabardine, polyester blends). The South is not as conservative but is somewhat more formal in its attitude toward dress. In this warmer climate, colors and fabrics tend to be lighter (cotton, linen, silks).

The hotter climates of the West and Southwest tend to dictate less formal attire and certainly lighter fabrics and colors. However, it is important to note some things about this region. Even though the hot climate may be suitable for lighter-weight clothes, it does not give you license to wear low-cut, sheer, or see-through (voile, lace) clothing. These are simply not appropriate at any time in any business setting.

Accessories. You can enhance your look by dressing according to your personality and body type. Choose clothes because they complement your figure and not just because they are the latest style. Remember that dark (black, brown, gray) and cool (blue, green) colors minimize size, while light (white, pink, peach) and warm (red, purple, yellow) colors maximize size. Vertical lines in clothes can help you look taller, while horizontal lines can make you look fuller.

Colors and styles can also reflect your personality. Bold colors (red) or combinations of colors (black and white) often depict an outgoing personality. Cooler colors (beige, light blue) might reflect a calmer or quieter personality or mood. Finally, business accessories can enhance your professional style.

Luggage: Discard your outdated and worn bags and invest in some good luggage.

Briefcase: Regardless of the position you hold, using a briefcase is the best way to transport your paperwork to and from the office. Briefcases are not limited to use by executives; they are a useful and efficient way to keep important information organized.

Leather-bound notebook: These are for holding or for attending meetings, keeping daily "to do" lists, or attending conferences and workshops. They look better than a note pad or loose-leaf paper and provide a convenient way to keep papers together.

Calendars: Keep one on your desk, one at home, and one in your pocket or handbag. There will be many times you will not be in your work area when you are asked if you are available, and it is very frustrating not to be able to check your schedule immediately. Keeping a calendar at home that records your business schedule is extremely helpful when starting a new week or day.

Watch: Wear a watch so you can be on time. Punctuality is an important habit to develop.

Personalized stationery: Two types of personalized stationery can suit your needs—one that you use for personal correspondence and a different one for business. When you use either kind, your correspondence is more professional.

Subscriptions to trade journals: Useful information about current trends in your career field is found regularly in trade journals. Make a habit of reading at least one regularly.

These are just a few examples of items that indirectly add to your professional image. These items also make up a terrific gift list for graduation, holiday giving, birthdays, or the start of your first job.

Dress can help you present a positive image of yourself if you choose clothing that is appropriate to your job, the area you live in, and your own body type. Dress is a great form of self-expression which can reflect your individuality. How you dress for work can tell a lot about you and help you project confidence and pride in yourself.

ACTIVITY 3-4 • *Self-Image Checklist*

Whatever you decide needs to be done to make you look or sound better, do it now! Check off what you need to do:

- ☐ Exercise
- ☐ Lose weight
- ☐ Buy a new wardrobe
- ☐ Sit up straight
- ☐ Practice facial expressions in the mirror
- ☐ Smile
- ☐ Walk with more confidence
- ☐ Make more direct eye contact
- ☐ Hear yourself as others do
- ☐ Listen to your voice samples
- ☐ Practice out loud and listen to your progress
- ☐ Change your language (choice of words, organization, and support of your ideas)

Strategies

- Do it yourself.
- Hire an expert.
- Work with a group.

Which strategy will you choose? _____

Your Action Plan

Goal: _____

Start date: _____

Completion date: _____

When your action plan is complete, you will have improved your: _____

_____

_____

How will this be an advantage to you in your career? _____

_____

_____

Time and Stress Management

Time Management A well-known author once wrote, "Nothing is easier than being busy, and nothing more difficult than being effective." Do you know someone who is constantly busy,

has a lot of different activities going on at once, and never seems to get any of them done? Sometimes you are never really sure what that person has done, but he or she displays a sense of urgency about everything. You may eventually view that person as being extremely competent, but not until you have had a chance to see exactly what he or she has accomplished.

Time management is the ability to see a task through from start to finish. To be able to see an *important* task through on time, and with *quality* results, is good time management. The amount of time spent doing something says nothing about the quality of the results or the person's ability. Time management is also defined informally as becoming more efficient at doing things that are important. In this case, *efficient* refers to quality and productivity, while *important* refers to what really needs to be done.

Here are some ways to develop time management skills:

- First, and most important, believe that you are in control!
- Learn to say no graciously.
- Delegate appropriately. Don't give the very important work to someone else, yet don't be afraid to ask for help.
- Handle interruptions; don't let them handle you.
- Prioritize. You prioritize by evaluating and asking:

    "How critical is the work?"

    "How long will it take from start to finish?"

    "What do you need to do to get it done?"

    "Who do you need to deal with?"
- Set a timetable to measure how you are doing.
- If the job seems overwhelming, break it down into more easily manageable steps. Finish one at a time.
- Have alternatives for how you will spend your time if you have to wait for someone or something.
- Build in some free time. During very busy times, it is important to take care of your physical and mental health. The quality of your work is easily affected by burnout. Have fun, and don't take yourself too seriously. Instead of becoming consumed with getting things done, enjoy each accomplishment along the way. Take time to pat yourself on the back for a job well done. Look at the challenge in whatever you are doing. When you do, the reward will bring you more satisfaction.

Stress Management

Stress is a physical, psychological, or performance-related reaction to internal or external events.

Many such events cause stress in our daily lives. Challenges that seem overwhelming to us are a cause of stress. These challenges can include everything from schoolwork to overcoming a handicap, or the sickness or death of a loved one. Financial concerns create stress for us. Determining ways to help you afford your education is often first on the minds of students beginning a college career. Poor health habits can create stress. Lack of proper exercise or diet does not give proper physical energy or mental alertness needed to resist stress. Overinvolvement in activities that you cannot handle all at once can leave you frustrated at your inability to do any of them well. Like everyone, you need to feel you belong. When you leave friends and family to pursue your education or career, you leave a tremendous support system. Not connecting with new friends or not being bonded to your family can leave you feeling isolated and anxious. The wrong friend can create peer pressure for you to be like everyone else, leaving you the feeling that you won't belong unless you give in to that pressure. When you feel pressured to be

ACTIVITY 3-5 • *Managing Your Time*

Look over the following list of activities for the month of May:

At School	On the Job
Term paper	Your performance review
Final exams	Proposal deadline
Counseling session	Monthly statements
Graduation	Train a temporary worker
Oral report	Attend a company function

Either of these scenarios may be familiar to you. If both of them are, chances are you have already had a lot of experience with time management. Read each list carefully. Think about how you would accomplish these activities successfully. List a few of the decisions you need to make.

For School

Example: Give up one night out a week to work on assignments

_____

_____

_____

_____

For the Job

Example: Work Saturday morning to get caught up

_____

_____

_____

_____

If it were April 1, what actions would you take, knowing your schedule in May?

For School

Example: Start research now for term paper

_____

_____

_____

_____

For the Job

Example: Start list of things you wish to discuss on your performance review.

_____

_____

_____

_____

Did these decisions come easily to you? For many people, there isn't even a decision process, but rather a "do whatever comes next" approach. That approach may even have worked for you up to now, but what will happen when you receive another important school assignment that *must* get done by April 15? When you get sick the second week of May? When your car breaks down on Saturday morning? *Will you still meet your deadlines efficiently?*

someone you are not, you feel stressed. A lack of goals can leave you unsure of where you are headed and anxious about your future. A lack of confidence or personal problems can cause you to withdraw or internalize feelings that create anxiety and tension.

There are many causes of stress in your daily life. These are just a few of the many situations that you may find yourself in and that can create some level of stress in your life.

Symptoms of stress include procrastinating, rushing or skipping meals, difficulty with listening or sleeping, misplacing things, forgetfulness, lack of energy, lack of social time, frequent lateness, or stifled creativity.

The results of prolonged stress may include a lack of productivity, depression, sickness, burnout, chronic tiredness, obesity, headaches, and a general lack of enjoyment or enthusiasm.

Being aware of some of the symptoms of stress will help you recognize your own stress level. In order to manage stress in your life, it is best to try to determine the cause of your stress by talking with friends, family members, teachers, counselors, and other professionals trained to help you work through stress in your life. Once you've determined the source of your stress you can take positive steps to help yourself. Try a few of the following techniques to ward off stress and increase your productivity:

1. Develop a daily schedule.
2. Get a part-time job.
3. Maintain a positive attitude.
4. Eat and sleep right; get plenty of exercise.
5. Limit involvement in outside activities to what you can manage.
6. Complete one thing at a time.
7. Familiarize yourself with the resources available to you.
8. Talk to family, friends, teachers.
9. Set goals for yourself.
10. Join a club, attend social functions, get involved.
11. Seek advice from counselors.
12. Don't quit!

ACTIVITY 3-6 • *Stress Checklist*

Check your major sources of stress:

☐ Schoolwork   ☐ Personal problems

☐ Finances   ☐ No goals

☐ Lack of confidence   ☐ Peer pressure

☐ Poor health habits   Others:

☐ Involvement in too many activities   ☐ _____

☐ Lack of friends   ☐ _____

☐ Family   ☐ _____

List the strategies you will take to reduce each of the stressors you identified:

_____

_____

_____

_____

Your Action Plan

Goal: _____

Start date: _____

Completion date: _____

When your action plan is complete you will be able to manage stress previously caused by: _____

_____

_____

How will this be an advantage to you in your career? _____

_____

ACTIVITY 3-7 • *Selecting a Role Model*

Think about some people who are possible role models for you. Write their names down and the reason(s) they would make a good role model.

Names   **Reasons Why**

_____   _____

_____   _____

_____   _____

_____   _____

   Now review the names and the reasons you selected them. Think about your own career goals and what skills and style you need to develop to achieve your goal. Which of the people you named comes closest to helping you achieve your goal? _____ Why? _____

This person will probably be your most effective role model. If this person is living, write him or her a letter expressing your feelings about the thought process you just went through and why you chose him or her. Having this role model is important because you can always have a concrete image of success in mind, even when you are finding it difficult to achieve your goals. Knowing that someone else experienced some obstacles on the path to success and overcame them can be a source of encouragement for overcoming your own obstacles.

Role Models

A role model is someone you choose to be your frame of reference as you strive for success. Your role model usually has qualities you admire and has gone about achieving success in a way you think is admirable.

Role models may be living or dead, employed by the same company you work for or known to you from another source. It is important to select a role model as part of your career planning process because we all need a source of inner strength and an image of success that serves as our constant drive to achieve our own goals. Role models are important because most times their success did not just happen. Like most successful people, the role models you choose probably had to overcome adversity and defeat a few times before experiencing success. Knowing what those obstacles were and studying how that person overcame those obstacles shows that it is possible to take charge of your own life and offers you some strategies for how to do it.

Chapter Summary

By developing techniques to improve communication skills, grooming and dress, business manners, and time and stress management skills, you improve your chances for launching and maintaining a successful career. To promote your technical skills as an asset is only half of what you need to do to build your career. The effective interpersonal skills you have begun to develop will help launch your first job and also help you perform well enough to advance successfully in your job and in your profession. Perhaps out of all of the critical skills that the SCANS report highlights, effective communication skills may have the greatest impact on your career. Using those skills to explain your unique qualifications to a prospective employer to convince that employer to hire you is your proof that your personal development is moving in the right direction!

Career Paths Overview

One of the best ways to ensure career success is to establish a clear focus on the career path you wish to pursue. When you choose your career path, you understand how you will put your education to work and what jobs and other experiences will help you reach your career goal. Establishing your career path allows you to see your career as a progression of many different experiences. A career path is a way of identifying both your ultimate career goal and the set of jobs you may need to succeed in before reaching that goal. Too often, graduates want to be hired into jobs at levels higher than what is realistic. This is because they have established a long-range career goal without a plan for getting there. In this chapter you will learn how to plan the steps in your career by looking at how a job differs from a career, the phases of a career, where the jobs are, types of universal careers, and what the growing career fields are.

Job versus Career

What does work mean to you? By definition, work is labor—an expenditure of physical energy. In your past experience, *work* may have been nothing more than something done to earn money. Work has also been defined as a place. To work has traditionally meant to be at a specific place for specific time periods on specific days because the job required it. The job, not the person holding it, was important.

This perspective has changed dramatically. Personnel officers have become human resource managers as corporations have begun to focus on people as key contributors in a struggle for quality, excellence, and innovation. The workplace is now identified as people-centered. With 80 percent of the workforce in service jobs, corporations have become extremely dependent on their human resources for competitive advantage and growth. The difference between a successful company and one that loses its competitive edge lies in the quality of its people. Corporations are only as successful as the people who work in them.

The phrase *job versus career* is used over and over again while people struggle to define the real differences. Rather than looking at the differences, consider how the terms complement each other. Since there will probably be many phases of your career, you may hold many jobs throughout your lifetime. At some point, you will probably stop changing jobs and will remain in a key position for a long period of time. It may even be the final job you hold. But the growth you experience in that same job for an extended period of time is also a significant phase in your career.

The difference between a job and a career is not how many jobs you have but rather the meaning that your jobs have for you. To remain in one job for 10 years can be just as successful a career direction as holding a number of successive jobs. The real determining factors concerning careers are these:

- Your attitude and commitment to what you do go beyond the tasks you perform every day.
- You have the ability to determine what you want and how to get it, as opposed to taking what comes your way.
- Rewards include, but go beyond, financial rewards.
- Rewards are characterized both by growth and change in you and in the challenges they provide for you.
- What you do provides a certain degree of psychological and emotional satisfaction.
- Rewards are the result of a planned sequence of related jobs.

Richard Bolles in *What Color Is Your Parachute?* defines a job as "a flexible combination of tasks—which can be arranged in a number of different tantalizing ways."[1] Bolles defines careers as "a flexible combination of skills that can be applied to a wide variety of situations." Flexibility will create job security for you and the confidence that you really are in control of your career.

A major difference between a job and a career is one's attitude. It is possible for two people who perform the same task, have the same title, and have similar educational backgrounds to have very different outlooks on their work. If your job is only what you do to pay the bills, it can quickly become routine drudgery. You may develop the attitude that life begins when the workday ends. You will probably be less willing to look beyond the tasks you need to perform, and you may have little enthusiasm for performing them. In a job that is not part of a career direction, you may not strive for promotion or plan for the future.

If you see your job in the context of larger career goals, your motivation is different. You see it as a challenge, as an opportunity to gain new skills that will help you in the

---

[1]Richard N. Bolles, *What Color Is Your Parachute?* (Berkeley, Calif.: Ten Speed Press).

future. You see a next step. You have goals to achieve. You will probably see the job as part of a lifelong learning process. In Section A of the Career Handbook, "Career Paths," you will see the many jobs that comprise the career you choose. You will notice that the jobs are all somewhat related; they just vary in degree of responsibility. You may stop at any point along the path to become a member of senior management. *Remember, a career is not determined by where you stop or how far you continue, but rather by the attitude with which you perform the job you have at any point in time.*

Career Phases

As you follow along your particular career path, you will notice changes in the nature of the jobs you hold. Throughout any career, different types of jobs are characterized by three phases: the entry-level phase, the second phase, and the third phase.

In the entry-level phase of your career, you will probably be more of a generalist, being trained in and exposed to a wide variety of company procedures. The purpose of the broad scope of entry-level jobs is to acquaint you with an overall picture of your job and how it fits into the company. This first phase may last anywhere from six months to several years.

The second phase of your career will be characterized by jobs that are more specialized. You can expect to spend many years in middle-management and/or specialist jobs. It is during the second phase of your career that you may change jobs most often as you move through a variety of specializations. In each career path, you will notice that the widest variety of jobs exists in the second phase.

It is important to note that many successful careers revolve around staying in middle-management and specialist jobs. These jobs play a significant role in the company because senior management relies so heavily on the expertise and specific knowledge of people in those jobs. A rewarding career can result in maintaining jobs within this area due to the tremendous impact they have on the company and the challenge and variety they can offer individuals.

The third phase of your career is management, which moves you back to more of a generalist position. If you choose to pursue your career into management at some point, you will find yourself relying on the specialists because your focus will be on many broad areas on a day-to-day basis.

Thus, there are many ways of looking at jobs and careers. The most important point to remember is that you manage your career by the jobs you choose and the attitude with which you perform them. *You* determine those jobs and what you want, and *you* take responsibility for getting there.

Career Trends

The most noticeable trend in the kinds of jobs that will be available through the year 2005 is the shift toward service professions.

In the United States, by the year 2005:

- The number of manufacturing jobs will decrease by 300,000.
- Service jobs will account for 23 million of the 24.6 million new jobs created.
- The number of technical jobs will increase by 37 percent, from 4.2 to 5.8 million.
- The number of operators and laborers will decrease by 700,000.
- Retail jobs will grow by more than 7 million.
- More managers, professionals, and marketing and sales personnel will be needed to develop and sell new competitive products.
- Demand for electronic engineers will increase by more than 40 percent.

- The number of installers and repairers of technology will increase by 16 percent overall, with a 63 percent increase in computer equipment repairers.
- Demand for all computer-related occupations will grow by almost 5 percent a year through the remaining 1990s.

Growing Career Fields

Many new career opportunities are available as a result of social and economic trends in the United States and abroad.

Accounting.   Career opportunities in accounting usually remain high regardless of the state of the economy. When businesses are booming, accountants are needed to manage firms' finances. When business is poor, accountants advise firms on how to maintain their financial stability. The advice that accountants provide is often the most important information for the decision-making process in a business. The fastest-growing jobs within the accounting field include consultants and credit specialists. Consulting services are aimed at assisting companies in applying the factual information they have about their finances to an effective business decision. The need for credit specialists is growing because of the problems plaguing the credit and loan industry. Public accountants, management accountants, government accountants, and internal auditors are always in demand.

Administrative Service.   Office careers have traditionally encompassed a wide variety of support and management positions from entry-level clerical work to office management. The responsibility of administrative service managers surpasses these traditional roles. They are charged with overseeing the day-to-day operations of a business. In a large company, the scope of responsibility might be for one or more departments. In a small company, duties may include overseeing all of the business's operations. Administrative service managers have the prime responsibility for ensuring cost savings and efficiency, while not jeopardizing the quality of work performed.

By 2005, employment in administrative services will grow by 13 percent.

Computer-Aided Drafting and Design (CADD). The use of computer-aided drafting and design (CADD) and computer-aided manufacturing (CAM) is widespread in U.S. corporations. The efficiency such innovative computer applications can generate for drafting technicians is revolutionizing the drafting profession. Basically, drafters use computers to draft layouts, line drawings, and designs. Drafters are able to sketch and modify shapes instantly on their computer screens, allowing time for more creativity, accuracy, and flexibility in the design process. CADD technicians work in such fields as architecture and electronics, and they frequently find employment with auto and aerospace factories.

By 2005, 1.2 million new jobs will be created in this field.

Computer Security. Computer security experts work in major corporations and industries to prevent illegal use of computer resources. This may include preventing an unauthorized user of a system from having access to the equipment. It may also include ensuring against unauthorized release of certain data and/or safeguarding the system from computer viruses. Computer security experts sometimes create guidelines for using the system. Jobs are available in industries where computer usage is high, including the federal government. With computer crime on the rise, this position is extremely valuable to companies that store confidential data on their computer systems.

Computer Systems. Computer systems analysts evaluate how computer applications can be used to make business procedures easier. The job includes interviewing the person in need of information from the system to determine how to program the computer to produce that information.

Customer Service. This position applies to almost any business whose prime focus is customer satisfaction. The customer service representative's job can take on different meanings. In the past, the term was used more to describe a person who took requests from customers and then tried to find the appropriate person to respond to the request. Today, the customer service representative generates new business through sales calls, and interviews customers with complaints, so as to get to the root of the problem and make recommendations for solving it. Because customer service representatives are the frontline people dealing directly with the customers, they can provide feedback on how well customers' needs are being met. Today, companies value the input of customer service representatives and sometimes alter their course of business based on that input. It is a much more proactive and critical role today than in the past.

Entrepreneurship. As many large corporations continue to downsize and restructure, and more small to medium-sized firms emerge, the opportunities for entrepreneurs are multiplying. Most entrepreneurs own businesses involved in delivering services or in creating and manufacturing products. Entrepreneurs must be resourceful enough to bring together the right combination of talent to make their business work. They must be comfortable with risk taking, be flexible and versatile, and have a high level of confidence in order to succeed.

By 2005, the number of new U.S. business incorporations will near 1 million, compared to 300,000 in 1990.

Financial Services. Financial planners help individuals and corporations make decisions on how to manage their financial resources. They provide input on changing tax laws and on the many investment options available to their clients. Other financial planners sell financial products such as insurance, stocks, and securities. The trend in this field is for careers to move from larger corporations to smaller firms that specialize in a particular service. Specialization may enable financial planners to provide more personalized service to their clients. Other career opportunities include consulting work with financial firms that are reorganizing. As existing firms continue

to consolidate and new firms emerge, expert advice is often sought to structure the new firm and effectively market its services.

Experts predict that employment in financial, insurance, and real estate services will grow 21 percent overall, adding 1.4 million jobs to the U.S. economy by 2005.

Food Service.   By the year 2000, at least 500,000 managerial and administrative positions will exist in the food service industry. Annually, $300 billion is spent in the United States on food sales, and over 9 million employees work in the industry. One of the fastest-growing segments of the business is off-premise food service sales. Off-premises catering involves restaurateurs and others providing food service away from their own sites. This may involve catering at homes, institutions, or other commercial properties, or even selling prepared food items through gourmet sections in large supermarket chains.

Health Service.   By 2005, the number of employees in the health service industries will grow from 8.9 to 12.8 million. Part of the growth in jobs is due to an increasing number of outpatient facilities and a higher demand for nursing and personal care facilities. Some of the jobs available include nursing and medical technologist positions. Nurses and technologists are most needed in hospitals, nursing homes, and home health agencies. Jobs in hospital sales involve working to recruit patients from the community and from major corporations. Lab technician positions are growing in number because technicians are needed by corporations now testing job candidates and employees for drug use. As the population of elders increases in the United States, there will be expanded career opportunities for geriatric health care workers, which include nurses, rehabilitation specialists, nursing assistants, and home health care workers. Finally, as senior fitness programs become more popular, the need for fitness trainers and advisers with medical backgrounds is growing.

Hospitality.   Recent acquisitions and mergers of some independent hotels by larger chains has produced many new company structures in the hospitality field. Careers are plentiful in this fast-paced industry; however, the jobs of today are not the same as they were even two years ago. Many major hotel chains have eliminated their formal management training programs and have opted for direct placement instead. This means that instead of being hired into a central training program at corporate headquarters you will be hired to fill available positions and train directly at individual properties in and out of the country. Jobs will continue to be available for hotel managers, assistant managers, and support staff. Tremendous growth in international travel has kept this industry thriving, even during recent times when it seemed to be overbuilt. Trends in the industry include hotels individualizing their marketing strategies to serve the needs of different customers, and a movement toward developing properties as "life care" facilities to address the housing and health care needs of the elderly.

Marketing.   Due to increased competition between businesses in this country and abroad, marketing careers are growing. Businesses must rely on creative marketing strategies to differentiate themselves to customers. One aspect of marketing careers is sales. Sales positions have been the most frequently available opportunities for entering the marketing field. These opportunities still remain strong, especially in advertising and computer sales.

There is a renewed emphasis on market research careers because of new interest on the part of service businesses in measuring quality and customer satisfaction on a regular basis. There is a need for qualified people to develop customer surveys and interpret the results. Professionals with good sales backgrounds will fit best into market research positions because they are already familiar with the needs of the customers. Once the customers' needs are identified, a marketing strategy can be devel-

oped to specify which sales, advertising, sales promotion, and public relations efforts will address those needs.

By 2005, the number of employees in the marketing field will increase by 24 percent, from 14.1 to 17.5 million.

Retail. The retail industry has undergone a lot of change in recent years, shifting emphasis from large department stores to specialty, discount, and off-price stores. Career opportunities exist in all of these segments despite the trend from one type of operation to another. However, the quality of the career opportunity varies.

There are some things you can look for to determine whether or not the company you are considering for employment offers a strong career track. First, look at companies that have developed almost a total focus on the customer. These firms develop ways to find out what types of products and services their customers want and then think of creative marketing techniques to attract and retain those customers. The retail industry, as a whole, is extremely competitive right now. The companies that are thriving are those that provide a quality product at a competitive price and have reinforced the importance of excellent customer service.

Spurred by higher personal income and the growing participation of women in the workforce, the fastest projected job growth in retail trade is in apparel and accessory stores.

Technical Services. Technical services usually involve repairing, servicing, installing, or inspecting certain types of equipment. For example, CADD technicians, computer service technicians, and electronics technicians are all involved with servicing a variety of computers and other electronic equipment. These opportunities have emerged in recent years in response to the tremendous surge in new technology.

As technical careers continue to grow, new opportunities exist in telecommunications, broadcasting, data communications, and with local area networks. Telecommunications technicians work with voice line-switching equipment. Broadcast

technicians are hired by stations needing to maintain or improve the quality of their broadcast equipment. Data communications technicians deal with transmitting computer data over telephone lines. Finally, local area network technicians are responsible for working with communication systems that are within limited geographic areas.

Overall employment in technical services will grow by 16 percent, from 4.9 to 5.7 million jobs, by 2005.

Travel/Tourism.   The greatest need for professionals is for well-trained travel agents and corporate travel managers. Although there are many other types of career opportunities in the travel/tourism field, these two jobs are experiencing the fastest growth due to a more global business and social climate; business and personal travel are on the rise. As with the hotel industry, the travel/tourism industry has been positively affected by increased international travel. This creates a need for agents who give advice on destinations and make arrangements for transportation, hotel accommodations, car rentals, tours, and recreation. For international travel, agents provide information on customs regulations, required papers (passports, visas, and certificates of vaccination), and currency exchange rates. The corporate travel manager is usually employed in-house by a large business firm to work with outside travel agencies on making all travel plans for that company.

Travel and tourism will create 144 million jobs worldwide between now and the year 2005.

Home-Based Careers   Technology has made people more mobile by providing them access to professional resources to do their job from almost anyplace in the world. This, coupled with a growing number of families interested in at least one spouse having more involvement in child rearing at home, has led to the growth of home-based careers. These entrepreneurial career paths include jobs in the following areas:

- Career services.
- Bed-and-breakfasts or inns.
- Word processing services.
- Desktop publishing.
- Gift basket services.
- Image consulting.
- Child care.
- Publicity consulting.
- Home instruction.
- Cleaning services.
- Event planning services.
- Bookkeeping and accounting.
- Adult day care.
- Information broker services.

Career Opportunities for Women   Many fields provide wide-open career opportunities for women. Recently, women have found employment readily available to them in the fields of communications, sales, marketing, and finance. This is in addition to the careers more traditionally pursued by women, such as those in the areas of health, education, office technology, and human resources. Women are beginning to assume more positions as computer specialists, paralegals, electronic technicians, financial consultants, and business managers. Finally, many women enjoy successful entrepreneurial careers in a variety of fields, including travel, child care, financial consulting, employment agencies, and food service.

Working Women: Findings from a Sweeping New Study

Working women may sense real obstacles to professional advancement today, but lack of education or training isn't viewed as a big barrier. That's one of the findings in a sweeping new survey by the Families and Work Institute, the Whirlpool Foundation, and Louis Harris and Associates. Additional results from the study follow.

• **What's your current work status?**

Self-employed	8%
Work full time	45%
Work part time	15%
Retired	1%
Unemployed	4%
Student	7%
Homemaker	17%

• **If you had enough money to live comfortably, would you prefer to:**

	Women	Men
Work full time	15%	33%
Work part time	33%	28%
Do volunteer work	20%	17%
Work at home caring for the family	31%	21%

• **Share of family income earned by working women:**

	Total	White	Black
All	18%	17%	32%
More than half	11%	11%	9%
About half	26%	27%	26%
Less than half	44%	46%	33%

• **Given a choice, would you prefer to have more time or more money?**

	Total	White	Black
More time	44%	46%	31%
More money	50%	47%	63%

• **How much do you think others value you for fulfilling your responsibilities:**

	At home	At work
Very valued	59%	59%
Somewhat valued	35%	37%
Not too valued	4%	3%
Not at all valued	1%	1%

• **Which of these workplace issues is your greatest worry?**

Employers providing fewer benefits	19%
Balancing work and family life	13%
Pressure from work affecting family	13%
Not being valued by employer	10%
Lack of opportunities for women to advance	10%
Possibility of job loss for men	9%
Lack of opportunities to grow and learn	5%
Sexual harassment	5%
Possibility of job loss for women	5%

• **Of the 80 percent of women who expect the next generation of women to have *more* opportunities, the top reasons:**

More opportunities in the workplace	51%
More education	37%
Less discrimination against women	22%

• **Of the 15 percent of women who expect the next generation of women to have *fewer* opportunities, the top reasons:**

Scarce market, slower economy	33%
Younger generation lazy, fun-loving	17%
Education not as good or accessible	12%

Women were only 40 percent of the workforce in 1995; by 2005, they will constitute 47 percent.

Career Opportunities for Minorities

Overall, career opportunities for minorities are growing in most fields. As the number of minorities enrolled in career education programs increases, minorities provide the right qualifications for many jobs. Some fields tend to hire more minorities than others. These include the hospitality industry and health services. Minority candidates are also actively sought, along with other qualified candidates, in the technical fields. There has been substantial improvement in the recruitment of minority candidates, but work still needs to be done in this area.

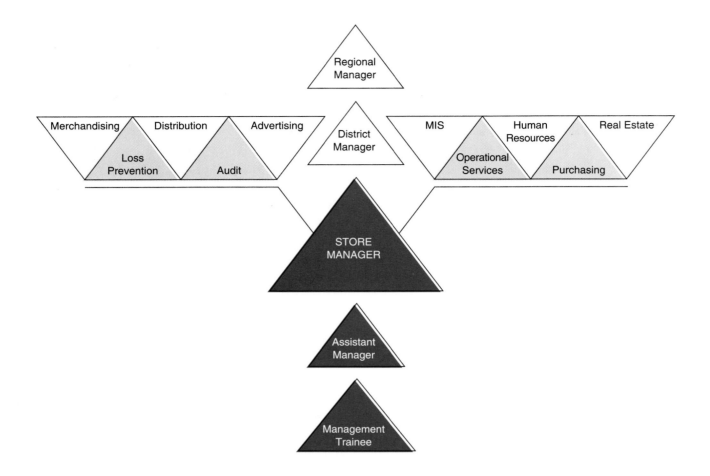

The best ways for minority candidates to sustain a competitive edge in the hiring process are to complete the educational training necessary to do the job, to sharpen communication skills, and to gain work experience while in school.

Your Career Path

Understanding the career phases you will go through, where the jobs are, and career trends is the beginning of establishing your own career path. Your career path is the sequence of jobs you plan to take to build your professional experience. These jobs can lead you to the job in your career field that you think matches your interests and abilities. For example, if your career goal is to be a retail store manager, you may first work as a sales associate, department manager, and assistant store manager (see the Sample Career Path figure). This series of jobs is your career path.

To build your career path, you should start by choosing the job you would like to have in the future, for example, store manager. Then you should strive to obtain the jobs that will give you the experience you need to get there.

As you begin thinking about your own career path, it is important to remember that you must gain entry-level technical experience in your first jobs in order to qualify for the long-range jobs you are thinking about. All entry-level jobs are part of paying your dues so that you can qualify for more responsible positions.

Activity 4-1 serves as a place for you to gather information about a potential career path.

ACTIVITY 4-1 • *Career Path Inventory*

This inventory has been designed as a guide to help you identify the career path you wish to pursue. As you gather facts about one career, be on the lookout for related areas that could provide career alternatives.

Introduction

Write down the nature of the career you think you might like to pursue:

_____

Describe the career you chose and how you feel about it. State clearly what a person in this occupation does (e.g., a placement counselor helps students consider career alternatives, arranges for on-campus interviews, and maintains a library of career information).

_____

_____

_____

How would you describe the working environment?

_____

What do you especially like about this occupation?

_____

What don't you like about this occupation?

_____

(Examples: work inside or outside, vacations, salary, helping others, working with people, data, or things, etc.)

Values and Interests

How might your values and interests be satisfied by this occupation?

_____

_____

Training or Qualifications Required

Check the amount of education the career requires:

☐ Vocational training beyond high school   ☐ Master's or doctoral degree

☐ Associate or two-year degree   ☐ Other: _____

☐ Bachelor's degree

What particular skills are involved in this occupation?

_____

_____

What academic majors lead to this occupation?

_____

Is your major one of these? _____

Entrance and Advancement

Entrance: Where might you get your first position? Name the kinds of employers who would be likely to hire you.

_____

_____

Advancement: As you look beyond the entry-level position in this occupation, consider the following questions.

• To what positions in this occupation may you advance?

_____

• Into what related occupations may this occupation lead?

_____

Employment Outlook

List the national projections for employment in this field that you find in *The Occupational Outlook Handbook*.

_____

_____

Do you have a preference for a particular geographic region? If so, what is the employment outlook in that region?

_____

Salaries

	National	Geographic Area of Interest
Beginning wage	_____	_____
Average wage	_____	_____
Top wage	_____	_____

Sources of Additional Information

List names and addresses of major professional associations from which you may get helpful information.

_____

_____

Summary

Review the notes you made in response to these sections. If you had to decide today whether or not to pursue this career path, what would you decide and why?

_____

_____

Where the Jobs Are

Employment opportunities exist in many different areas. Understanding the options available will help you make more educated decisions about your career path.

The three main avenues for employment are the private sector, the public sector, and the foreign sector. Within the private sector, career opportunities exist with individuals, corporations, and institutions. The public sector deals with government employment, and the foreign sector with business or government agencies conducting transactions overseas. The private and public sectors make up our national economy and, with the foreign sector, make up our economy outside of the United States.

Private Sector

Small businesses, large corporations, franchises, entrepreneurial enterprises, and nonprofit corporations are examples of where jobs are in the private sector. Currently, 5 of 6 American employees work in institutions with fewer than 1,000 employees. The share of new jobs created by firms with fewer than 100 employees has increased to 40 percent. Although there are increased employment opportunities with smaller firms, large corporations still employ the majority of American workers.

Franchise opportunities are expanding. A franchise is developed when one company assigns to another the right to supply its product. Kentucky Fried Chicken and McDonald's are examples of successful franchise operations. Individual franchisees are required to put up the capital, with the franchisor providing training, technical assistance, specialized equipment, and advertising and promotion.

Entrepreneurs are people who bring together their product knowledge and business expertise to start their own business and make a profit. The individual takes on the risk associated with the new venture and the responsibility for successfully organizing the company.

Nonprofit corporations are developed to provide a service, usually aimed at helping the human services, supporting environmental projects, or doing other work related to improving the world we live in. Although nonprofit corporations are not established to make a profit, they are usually run like successful businesses and may generate a profit. When they do, the money goes back into the operation rather than to the individuals who own it.

Public Sector

Most opportunities in the public sector are careers with the government. Some federal agencies where employment opportunities exist include the following:

- U.S. Air Force.
- U.S. Army.
- Department of Health and Human Services.
- Housing and Urban Development.
- Department of the Interior.
- Justice Department.
- U.S. Navy.
- Department of Transportation.
- Treasury Department.
- Legislative and judicial agencies.

All of these offer opportunities with a wide variety of options for professionals.

There are some distinct advantages and disadvantages of working for the government. Some advantages are challenging work, job location throughout the country, considerable responsibility, diversity of career paths, and flexible hours. Some disadvantages may be the extensive paperwork and procedures associated with most

public-sector jobs, uncompetitive pay, lack of personalization because of vast size, and poor working environments.

Many career opportunities also exist in state and local governments; your state department of personnel can provide you a list of job openings and the qualifications needed to fill them.

International Sector

International jobs are becoming more popular as the communication and ease of travel among countries throughout the world have increased. When considering an international career, you should determine the reason you want this experience. Experience with other countries and their cultures can be professionally and personally rewarding because it broadens your perspective of the world. You may think about an international career in or outside of the United States. Many foreign-based companies operate within the United States. Abroad, you will find opportunities with American-based companies and companies based within each individual country.

You may find the same variety of private-sector opportunities as available in the United States, as well as many opportunities in the public sector. For example, the Peace Corps is an independent agency of the federal government with paid as well as volunteer career opportunities both in and outside of the United States.

Portable Careers

In addition to deciding which sector your career path will be in, you may want to think about some career options that exist in almost any field. These *portable careers* can be developed as a result of having expertise in a particular discipline. For example, consulting, teaching, writing, or owning and operating your own business are possible in almost any field. Usually these career paths can be pursued after you have attained a high level of professional experience in your particular field.

If you are considering work abroad, the portable career areas listed on pages 73 and 74 can move with you wherever you go. For professionals who relocate frequently because of their own initiative or because a spouse has been transferred to a new job in a new country, it is wise to develop a portable career.

INTERNATIONAL CAREER DIRECTIONS

International Career Paths

You should be aware of some ways in which international career paths differ from those in the United States. As Americans use different job titles, along with descriptions that correspond to certain levels of responsibilities, so do employers in other countries. But the job titles in other countries do not always correspond to the job descriptions and responsibilities you might expect. When speaking to the French about different levels of jobs, for example, you will frequently hear them describe each level as a *stage*.

Job titles are an important factor to research carefully if you are planning an international career path because you may be surprised to find yourself involved in a job abroad that requires more qualifications than that same job in the United States or vice versa. There is also sometimes different prestige given to certain jobs in different countries. Although a service (front-of-the-house) position is not considered the ultimate goal for most U.S. food service professionals, a service position in Europe usually carries with it a good amount of prestige.

The United States is one of the few countries in the world in which professionals frequently move from job to job and company to company. In most other countries, professionals stay with the same employer for a relatively long period, and someone's career is not considered to be stagnant if he or she is in the same position for many years. This means that you cannot necessarily compare a career path in another country with a similar-sounding one in the United States.

Some Tips for Planning an International Career Path

1. Find out what categories of work exist in different companies.
2. Find out where the jobs are. Focus on researching current economic trends in the technological sector, importing and exporting divisions, and international sections of service industries.
3. Know the different approaches used to compensate people in each country.
4. Find out how long it takes to move from one position to another.
5. Keep in mind that starting a business may require a very different set of requirements than in the United States.
6. Determine how long you plan to stay; your length of stay may affect the job you are eligible to receive.

Protable Career Areas

- *Office administration:* Multilingual secretaries with knowledge of the latest electronic office systems have a good chance of finding work almost anywhere in the world.
- *Computer systems:* Businesses worldwide use automated systems and need specialists who can write computer programs and teach employees how to use the latest equipment.
- *Training seminars:* If you have a specialty area in which you are very knowledgeable or have considerable experience, training in business and industry can be applied in many different settings.
- *Teaching English:* For those with the proper certification, many jobs are usually available in language schools or corporations to teach English throughout the world.

- *Sales representative:* Selling products or services for an American company operating abroad or a firm based in another country can be an excellent career in any country, if you have an inclination toward sales and learning about new products and customers.
- *Entrepreneur:* Create your own product or business and try your hand at being an independent businessperson in whatever country you find yourself in.
- *Interpreter:* If you are fluent in more than one language and have a great capacity for listening and for articulating concepts clearly, you may be a successful interpreter in social, business, or educational settings.
- *Chef:* If food service is your profession, you can take your culinary expertise with you anywhere in the world and find a restaurant, hotel, resort, or other place in which to flaunt your talent.
- *Hotel manager:* Major hotels operate in large cities around the world, and thus opportunities for experienced managers exist worldwide.

Keep in mind that the greater your professional versatility, the greater chance you have of moving through different workplace environments successfully.

Chapter Summary

Deciding on a specific focus within your career field is important. Having a targeted career goal will help you remain motivated with your studies now and will allow you to make effective decisions about what experiences you need to obtain the position you want.

Chapter Five

Your Career Portfolio

Chapter Objectives

After completing this chapter, you will:

Know the employment skills you need to demonstrate to employers.

Identify "career passport" opportunities that build employment skills.

Collect evidence of your employment skills.

Develop a career portfolio.

Plan a portfolio presentation.

Your career portfolio is a tool you can use to present your unique employment skills to a potential employer on a job interview. Your career portfolio should contain samples of work and other documentation of your skills and credentials that employers in your career field are interested in. This will be an enhancement to using only a résumé to present yourself professionally. While certain fields, such as advertising and public relations, have traditionally required job candidates to have portfolios, the use of portfolios is becoming more widespread as employers focus more on finding job candidates with specific workplace competencies.

Because usually you do not assemble your actual portfolio until just before a job interview, you might make the common mistake of not starting early enough to focus on developing and collecting evidence of your skills for a portfolio presentation. If so, your portfolio will be incomplete and therefore less effective for self-promotion.

At the very beginning of your career education you should develop your plan to build the skills employers value and collect evidence of those skills on an ongoing basis. Together, your plan and your collection of accomplishments and skills will be your career passport to success. Just as your travel passport helps you gain entry to different countries, your career passport will help you gain entry to jobs throughout your career.

Build Skills Employers Value

On your road to career success you should know the paths you will follow to reach your goals. Employers provide you the map they think will be your best guide by identifying the skills you need for a successful career. Your school provides you the opportunities to build and collect evidence of your skills, thus helping you gain entry to the world of work. With the information you have from employers and your school, you can develop your plan to build and demonstrate the skills that will become your unique career passport to success.

Passport (noun)

a. Permission or authorization to go somewhere.

b. Something that secures admission or acceptance.

    For example: Education is a passport to career success.

To ensure that your plan to build skills is headed in the right direction, review the skills employers say they value most. In Chapter 2 we discussed the findings of the Labor Secretary's Commission on the Achievement of Necessary Skills (SCANS), which highlighted basic skills, thinking skills, and personal qualities as necessary workplace competencies. Within each of these areas are specific skills that are important because of their direct application on the job. The following table lists some examples to help you visualize how these skills may be applied on the job.

Examples of How Some Skills Are Used on the Job

Necessary Skills	Possible Applications on the Job
Basic Skills	
Math	Reconciling differences between inventory and financial records
	Estimating discounts on the spot while negotiating sales
	Projecting resource needs over next planning period
	Calculating food and beverage costs
	Projecting revenue for your business
Writing	Writing proposals to justify resources or explain plans
	Preparing instructions for operating simple machines
	Developing a narrative to explain graphs or tables
	Drafting changes to company procedures
	Writing company handbooks
Reading	Interpreting blueprints and materials catalogs
	Reading patients' medical records and medication instructions
	Reading the text of technical manuals from equipment vendors
	Dealing with letters and written policies or complaints
Speaking	Explaining product features to customers on a sales call
	Making a presentation at a staff meeting
	Interviewing for a new job in your company
	Addressing an audience as a guest speaker
	Calling clients for a telemarketing campaign
Thinking Skills	
Creative thinking	Developing a new advertising campaign for your restaurant
	Devising new ways to do more with less cost

Necessary Skills	Possible Applications on the Job
Decision-making	Identifying the most qualified staff members for promotion Choosing to expand your business or not Selecting investment options
Problem-solving	Devising a new system to reduce customer complaints Adjusting production schedules to reduce machine stoppage due to overloading Recommending solutions to an employee dispute Recommending corrective actions to an employee to improve performance
Visualization (seeing things in the mind's eye)	Picturing the layout of a new facility Seeing your company win recognition Anticipating someone's response to your proposal
Knowing how to learn	Asking someone to teach you to work on the new computer Observing how your boss handles conflicts Volunteering for a new job
Reasoning	Drawing conclusions based on past events Understanding the meaning of events and behaviors
Personal Qualities	
Responsibility	Taking ownership to see an important project through Being accountable for the results of a team you are leading Being trusted with confidential information Finding solutions to customer complaints
Self-esteem	Volunteering to do a different job Continuing to work toward your career goal after experiencing some setbacks Promoting yourself as the best candidate on a job interview Taking criticism well
Sociability	Working successfully with a team Representing your company at industry trade shows or conventions Making sales calls
Self-management	Successfully handling multiple projects Working with little or no supervision Working the hours necessary to get the job done Building in time to further your education while you work fulltime
Integrity	Refusing to take short cuts that could compromise work quality Refusing to talk negatively about a former employer Refusing to make a popular decision, if you believe it is the wrong decision
Honesty	Not accepting credit for something someone else did Identifying areas of your own performance that need improvement Offering constructive criticism to an employee who works for you

17 Pathways to Success

A 1995 study of employers by Johnson & Wales University revealed that employers identify 17 pathways to success. This study supports the findings of SCANS and points to other skills required of entry-level job candidates: career planning, job

search, career management, work experience, and financial responsibility, to name a few. Employers said what they wanted most was for job candidates ultimately to demonstrate the added value they could bring to the firm, that is, what they could contribute to the growth and development of the business. Examples of how you can bring added value to a firm include your ability to increase profits, reduce employee turnover, or develop a new product line. The accompanying box summarizes the results of the Johnson & Wales survey.

Employers' 17 Pathways to Success

1.	Career planning	A clear career goal and strategy for achieving it
2.	Academic achievement	Ability to acquire the basic skills needed for employment
3.	Technical skills	Ability to perform the technical tasks for your job
4.	Work experience skills	"Real-world" experience and realistic expectations
5.	Leadership	Ability to lead, coordinate, and contribute
6.	Community service	Commitment to contribute to society
7.	Financial responsibility	Commitment demonstrated through financing your education; ability to manage your finances
8.	Professionalism	Attendance, grooming, and dress; work ethic
9.	Global perspective	International work, study, or living experience
10.	Effective communication skills	Writing, speaking, listening
11.	References	Proven success recognized by others
12.	Job search skills	Ability to secure employment independently
13.	Personal qualities	Ability to manage yourself and deal effectively with others
14.	Role models and mentors	Learning from others
15.	Special distinctions	Personal achievement, standing out from the competition
16.	Career management	Making successful career moves
17.	Added value	What value do you bring to the employer?

As you move through each experience of your career passport, you will acquire new workplace skills and obtain documentation that provides evidence of your skills. This documentation will help you create a personal portfolio that can be used on your job interviews to prove your qualifications to a potential employer.

Reprinted from the Johnson & Wales University Career Passport System with permission from Johnson & Wales University.

Identify Opportunities to Build Skills

The more employment skills you build in school, the more career opportunities you will have and the higher your earnings can be over your lifetime. The results of a 1993 current population survey taken by the U.S. Census Bureau prove that the median earnings for those who complete a college degree are higher than for those without one. You should take advantage of every opportunity your education affords you to build employment skills. The following sections show you how to develop a plan to do just that.

Opportunities in the Classroom

Each course you complete as part of your program of study is designed to help you develop employment skills. While some courses teach you technical skills like cost accounting, ice carving, or desktop publishing, others teach you life skills like lead-

ership, time management, or critical thinking. At the beginning of each course you take, you should identify, with your instructor, the employment skills you can develop throughout the course. When you complete the course, review and record the skills you have developed.

ACTIVITY 5-1 • *Skills Developed through Coursework*

For each course you complete, begin to record the employment skills you have developed, as follows:

Course Name	Skills Developed
1. English Composition	1. Write a research paper
2. Communications	2. Deliver a presentation at a meeting

Course Name	Skills Developed

You will use this list to help you organize your résumé, prepare for a job interview, and work with your career counselor to assemble your portfolio. (You may need to develop your own or additional lists to record all the courses in your program of study.)

Opportunities Outside the Classroom

Opportunities to develop employment skills outside the classroom include, but are not limited to, part-time and summer jobs and internship, externship, and cooperative education experiences. Beyond work experience, opportunities outside the classroom include volunteer work, involvement in clubs or professional associations, and sports activities. In order to take full advantage of the opportunities available outside the classroom, you need to know what they are. Complete Activity 5–2 to help you identify these opportunities and Activity 5–3 to help you choose those you wish to take advantage of.

Refining Your Plan

Your Job Target

Your self-assessment process and development of a targeted career path have helped you identify your career destination. Knowing about the segment of your *industry* you want to work in, the type of *job* you want, and eventually the *employer* with whom you want to work will help you build an effective career passport. Employers' needs drive what credentials you should build and what competencies you must develop. However, for most of you, your initial decisions about your career goal will not be permanent but will evolve over time. New information about jobs in your field will come via input from employers, your own work experiences, and new job trends and employment rates in your industry.

ACTIVITY 5-2 • *Opportunities to Develop Skills Outside the Classroom*

Working with your instructor or a student service professional at your school, list all of the opportunities available outside the classroom to help you build employment skills.

Opportunities Outside the Classroom	Possible Skill Development
Example: National student organizations	Leadership

Opportunities Outside the Classroom	Possible Skill Development

(You may need to develop your own or additional lists to record all of the opportunities available to you.)

ACTIVITY 5-3 • *Choose Your Opportunities*

Review the list of opportunities available to you outside the classroom and the skills they can help you develop (Activity 5-2). Based on your knowledge of the job you want and the skills you need to qualify for the job, prepare a list of the opportunities outside the classroom you will choose to become involved with. For each opportunity you choose, indicate the skills you plan on developing.

Opportunities Outside the Classroom	Skills to Develop
Example: Varsity sports	Teamwork

Opportunities Outside the Classroom	Skills to Develop

You will use this to help you organize your résumé, prepare for a job interview, and work with your career counselor to assemble your portfolio. (You may need to develop your own or additional lists to record all the opportunities you choose.)

Employment skills can be developed through your accomplishments in any of these areas. For example, if you are an accounting major, you may learn how to complete an income tax return in your tax accounting class, prepare computerized monthly budget reports on your part-time job, and teach high school students how to balance a checkbook through your volunteer work in the community. Developing a plan to select experiences that will build your career skills is the first step to developing a career portfolio. The more experiences you have, the more entries you can make in your portfolio.

While it is natural to refine your job target from time to time, it is important also to refine your plan for building proper credentials for that job if necessary.

Example

Original job target: Financial analyst for a firm in the United States
Defined job target: Financial analyst for a U.S. firm overseas.

The basic job target is the same in both situations, but to work in that same job overseas may require the addition of proficiency in a foreign language or a work or study experience abroad. Your job target is a constant reminder of why you are pursuing your education!

Your Graduation Date

No matter how sophisticated your plan to reach your job target is, you cannot complete your plan unless you graduate. Although many experiences outside the classroom will be key to your career development, your classroom experiences will provide you with the strongest foundation to develop the critical skills you need for the workplace.

If you are less interested in or have more difficulty with some courses than others, don't get discouraged. Seek the help you need to keep you on track academically. You may not always see how your coursework is preparing you for your job. When you can see this connection, you will probably become more motivated to succeed academically.

Forms of Evidence

There are many forms of evidence that can document your skills. Even though you may not use all of the documentation you collect for every job search, you should still be sure to collect as much evidence as you can to demonstrate and verify your skills. The following are some examples of evidence you can collect and explanations of how each one can help you.

Résumé. A well-prepared résumé is evidence of good career planning and job search skills. In particular it demonstrates your ability to set and communicate your career goal. A good résumé can convince an employer you have the best background for the job.

Photographs. Photographs may include those of your work, of you receiving an award or recognition, of you in a professional publication, or of an event you planned. Try to collect photographs that are processed well and that portray your message professionally. As you collect your photographs, keep them stored in a plastic sleeve, album, or photo box to avoid damage.

Computer Disks. Many employers prefer to receive résumés on disk so that candidates' qualifications can be sorted and stored for easy access in a databank. You may also use a computer disk to illustrate a facilities plan you designed, to provide evidence of the computer program you designed to create a new system or procedure at your job, or to show a computerized accounting procedure you can work with. These are only a few of the many skills you can demonstrate on a computer disk.

Writing Samples. Writing samples may include a term paper, an article for the school newspaper, an ad campaign written for your advertising class, business letters, or any other of your original writings. Only use writing samples that demonstrate the following: good grammar, proper spelling and punctuation, and clearly organized thoughts. Seek the advice of a faculty member when deciding what your best writing sample may be.

Audiotapes. Audiotapes can be used as evidence of your verbal communication skills. For example, a tape of a speech that you delivered particularly well is a strong indicator of your public speaking skills. Audiotapes can also be used as a means of

walking the employer through the contents of your résumé or portfolio, or to demonstrate foreign language or translation skills.

Letters of Reference.   Your current and past employers are your best resource of reference letters. Most employers will be willing to write a reference letter for you if your employment with them has been a positive experience for the company as well as for you. Letters from past or current employers to prospective employers should prove your ability to perform in the workplace. Other sources of reference letters are professional associations, teachers, and in some cases personal contacts.

Letters of Commendation.   Any congratulatory letters you receive for winning an award or competition, receiving academic honors, or performing well on the job should be saved as evidence of your outstanding accomplishment. If you have customer contact, you should focus on receiving letters from customers that praise the level of service you provided them. These can be used to demonstrate that you have good customer service skills, one of the most widely sought-after skills by employers.

Employer Evaluations.   When you successfully complete an internship, externship, or cooperative education assignment, you will probably have at least one written employer evaluation of your work performance. Employer evaluations from part-time, full-time, summer, or volunteer work are also worth keeping if they are good.

Performance Reviews.   Like employer evaluations of your work, your performance reviews are worth keeping. Most often, employers share with an employee written copies of his or her review both as documentation of what occurred during the review and as a guide to help the employee target the areas of performance that need improvement.

News Article.   If a newspaper has published an article about one of your jobs, awards, honors, or other accomplishments, be sure to save a copy.

Blueprints.   A sample set of blueprints you have designed is a great example of your computer-aided drafting and design (CADD) skills.

Menus.   If you are in the food service profession and have designed some menus of your own or helped someone else design menus, copies of those menus should be kept to show a prospective food service employer. Menus that illustrate meals you have actually prepared, even if someone else created the menu, are also great samples of the types of cuisine you can prepare.

Facilities Designs.   If you have learned how to lay out the design for new office space, a new restaurant or hotel, or a new retail store, you have a skill a prospective employer should know about. If you have designed more than one space, keep copies of your work to show the variety of designs you have worked with.

Business Plans.   Writing a business plan utilizes many different skills employers will be interested in. In addition to demonstrating your business writing techniques, your business plan communicates your ability to conceptualize, plan, promote, and potentially operate a business.

Certificates of Completion.   Certificates of completion are often given to you when you attend a professional workshop, conference, or seminar. Keeping these types of certificates is important because they confirm your participation in a program that

has contributed to your professional growth and shows your commitment to continued education and lifelong learning.

Grades/Transcripts.   It may be worthwhile to show employers that you have done well in the courses aimed at developing the particular skills they are looking for. If all of your grades are good, then it can be a help to show your transcripts to an employer. If some of your grades are below average but you have done well in the courses that specifically trained you to do the job you are applying for, then it isn't a problem to show an employer your transcripts. If your academic performance is consistently below average, then you may want to focus more on skills gained from your volunteer work, work experience, or involvement in sports or clubs and organizations.

Attendance Record.   Many college students do not think of attendance in school as a factor that can affect their employment prospects, but employers say good attendance in school is a potential indicator of good attendance on the job. Good attendance is evidence to an employer of your reliability, dependability, and work ethic—all of which are important to success on the job. Keep your record of attendance to demonstrate both your commitment to your education and your professionalism.

Manuals/Procedures Developed.   A procedural manual you helped develop through one of your jobs, for a club or organization, or through your volunteer work is a great sample of the work you are capable of doing.

Honors/Certificates.   The reason you are working toward developing a career portfolio is to show employers your special distinctions. Any honor or award you receive usually recognizes some type of accomplishment that gives you special distinction. Keep copies of letters or certificates you receive for doing something special. For example, a certificate of achievement for completing a leadership course or a certificate verifying you were the employee of the month at your part-time job would be good evidence of your special achievements.

Licenses.   Certain professions require job candidates to have a license for work in the field. Whether it is required or not, if you have a special license that attests that you can perform certain skills, keep it ready to show to an employer.

Now that you know the types of documentation that can be presented in your portfolio, you can set goals toward accomplishments that will help you collect evidence of your employment skills. In this process, it is very important to remember that the items listed above are only a few of the many possible items you can accumulate. You do not need all of them to prepare an effective portfolio. Also keep in mind that you should mainly collect evidence of your best work. If you have any of the items listed above that do represent some of your best work, then be sure to save them. On the other hand, you may have improved significantly in a skill area and want to show an employer the progress you made because of your persistence and hard work. In this case, it may be helpful to keep both a sample of your average work and a sample of your excellent work to show how much improvement you have made over time.

In any case, do not feel compelled to keep work that is not your best. Everyone is better at some things than at others. You should end up with a portfolio that focuses on your strengths, not your weaknesses. Remember, the purpose of creating a portfolio is to promote your unique talents and skills.

ACTIVITY 5-4 • *Your Documentation Record*

As you collect evidence of some of your skills, keep a list of the documentation you have and the skill(s) you think it helps you demonstrate to a prospective employer. By maintaining this record you will readily know the possible portfolio items available to you when you prepare for your job interviews.

Record of Evidence/Documentation	What It Proves
1. Example: Attendance record	Reliability; work ethic
2.	
3.	
4.	
5.	
6.	
7.	
8.	
9.	
10.	
11.	
12.	
13.	
14.	
15.	
16.	
17.	
18.	
19.	
20.	

Develop Your Career Portfolio

At this point, you have already collected much of the evidence to show you have industry credentials. When you are about to interview with potential employers, it is important to select the evidence that is most valued by each employer and to plan to present that evidence effectively.

Types of Portfolios   There are many different types of portfolio products. The product you choose will largely depend on the career field you are in and the types of samples (photos, written material, etc.) you are likely to present.

Three-ring binders ($8\frac{1}{2}'' \times 11''$) that hold acetate-covered pages or plastic sleeves are commonly used as portfolios. These are practical because the pages or sleeves can hold all types of written evidence as well as photographs. Special vinyl slide sheets, three-hole punched, can be added to hold slide samples if appropriate.

Larger portfolio cases ($17'' \times 22''$) are available in most art supply stores and are usually needed by writers, journalists, and advertising professionals who need

enough space to display full-page ads and printed articles from all sizes of newspapers and magazines.

Both types of portfolios are excellent vehicles for saving and displaying your work samples and other credentials. Be sure to make copies of whatever you put into your portfolio in case an employer asks you to leave your portfolio behind. You should try not to leave any original pieces of your work. To respond to an employer's request to keep the contents of your portfolio a little longer for others in the company to see, have copies of as many things as you can.

Art supply stores and bookstores at colleges that offer a degree in art are two great places to purchase some of the materials necessary to assemble your portfolio.

Portable Portfolios   The prime limitation of using a three-ring binder or portfolio case is that, for the most part, you must present it in person. It is difficult to forward such portfolios to employers by mail before or after an interview. Computer disks and videotapes are two means by which to make your portfolio portable. A videotape may be used to show you presenting the pages of your portfolio to an employer as you would in person. With this technique, an employer whom you cannot meet face to face can get an impression of both how you present yourself verbally and what you actually present in your portfolio. Of course, you can also videotape yourself demonstrating a skill such as speaking to a large group, teaching a class, or carving ice.

Today, you can assemble, store, and transmit your entire portfolio electronically. In fact, by displaying your portfolio on the Internet you can readily reach employers all over the world. Even long or numerous writing samples can be stored on a single floppy disk.

While portable portfolios give you instant access to employers worldwide during your job search and make it easy for you to retain all the original copies of your work, they do not substitute for the chance to enter into conversation about the contents of your portfolio in person.

This challenge is being met with access to video conferencing. Soon it will be more common for job candidates to interview with employers worldwide without ever leaving a single room; that room, of course, will be equipped with cameras that transmit a video image of you and the employer to each other.

Thinking of ways to make your portfolio portable—whether it is through computer disk, videotape, or video conferencing—can help you obtain interviews with employers not within your immediate geographic area.

Planning Your Portfolio Presentation

Deciding what you will put into your portfolio, how you will arrange the materials, and how you will present your portfolio to an employer are critical stages to gaining positive results.

Deciding on Content

Before you assemble your portfolio for presentation, you should determine how you will select the items to go into it. Up till now, you have collected as much evidence as possible to show an employer. When you are about to interview with a potential employer, you must select the evidence that is most valued by that employer. You should not show your entire collection to every employer. Not only will there be too much material for an employer to review, but much of it will not even be targeted to the specific job you are interviewing for.

You should plan your selection of portfolio items by focusing on evidence of skills that are industry specific, employer specific, and job specific.

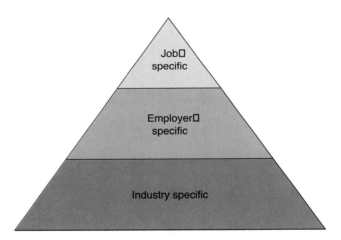

For example, in the hospitality industry, excellent customer service is an industry-specific skill. A particular hotel chain may require candidates to have an international experience because new hotel construction in the Pacific Rim is producing more jobs there than in the United States; in this case, international experience is an employer-specific skill. A job-specific skill then might be the ability to speak Japanese for a reservationist's position in the hotel's Tokyo location. While evidence of good customer service skills is extremely important, this job probably cannot be filled by someone who does not speak Japanese. In this case, it is critical to build a portfolio around international experience including any evidence of experience with cultures in the Pacific Rim, in particular Japanese culture.

For example, a nationally recognized food service employer in Rhode Island identifies work experience as the most valued credential an applicant can present. A worldwide beverage distributor, however, asks for prescreening of candidates by grade point average first. Although both of these employers basically value candidates with appropriate industry training, each employer goes one step further in identifying a specific credential as being most important.

A candidate applying to both of these companies for a job may, in fact, meet both of these criteria for employment but should concentrate primarily on emphasizing the credential each employer is most interested in. As a result, the candidate may not show transcripts to the first employer but would be sure to highlight good transcripts to the other.

The real key to making your portfolio effective is knowing how to move it from being industry specific to being employer specific for a job interview. The more time you spend getting to know how employers may evaluate you, the more effective your portfolio can be during the interviewing process.

Arranging Portfolio Materials

You should give some thought to the order in which you will present your materials in your portfolio to maximize the effect of your presentation to a prospective employer.

To arrange a winning portfolio, go through all of the materials you initially decided to include. Choose two pieces that are both evidence of your best work and different from what you think other candidates will have. Place one of these pieces on the opening page of your portfolio and one on the last page. The first should pique the employer's interest to go on to see more of your credentials. The last should leave the employer with a positive impression of you and your abilities.

One way to think about arranging the pieces in the middle of your portfolio is by theme, for example, international experience or community service/volunteerism. Your theme should be chosen keeping in mind the experience the employer is looking for and your own strengths. In each case, you would focus most of the entries in your portfolio on evidence demonstrating one of the above (international or community service work experience) as your strength or specialty area. This approach gives you the opportunity to focus your presentation on promoting a strength you know the employer is looking for.

If you do not have enough experience in one specialty area but do have lots of experience in many different areas, then show the diversity of your experiences as your strength.

Think carefully about how you arrange your portfolio so that it can make a maximum impact on a prospective employer.

Presenting Your Portfolio

Your time with an employer on an interview is limited, so manage your portfolio presentation well. You may have to narrate to provide both flow to the presentation and a coherent picture of your credentials to the employer, but be prepared to have only one or two succinct comments about each page you show. Plan what you will say to complement your interview, not monopolize it.

It is important for you to tell the employer at the beginning of the interview that you have your portfolio with you and will speak about it later in the interview. This alerts the interviewer that you are well prepared. The initial stage of the interview is the time for general discussion about the company, your career interests, and the type of position available. Once these topics have been covered, the interviewer will get into more specific questions about your experience and your qualifications for the job. This is the time to bring your portfolio forward. Use it to illustrate how you have already applied the skills you say you have. For example, when you are asked about your experience and skills, answer by first *describing* your skills and experience and saying that you have some examples that demonstrate your accomplishments and abilities (see Activity 5-5).

Finally, make sure you have created a memorable impression of yourself. Take a "leave-behind" piece from your portfolio on your interview. Remember to make a copy of something you can actually give to the employer to take with your résumé. And then, when you write a thank-you letter for the job interview, mail one more short sample of your work to continue to remind the employer of how qualified you are for the job.

ACTIVITY 5-5 • *Role-Play Your Portfolio Presentation*

Work with another person who can play the role of an interviewer. Summarize the skills and accomplishments you want to highlight to an employer, and select the evidence you have to demonstrate. Have the "interviewer" ask you about your skills and role-play your response to each question and the presentation of your portfolio.

It may take a few practice sessions to become familiar with promoting yourself this way, but it will be worth it when you convince a prospective employer you are a highly qualified candidate for the job.

Example

Interviewer Asks:
Can you give me an example of a situation in which you displayed leadership skills?

Sample Response 1:
Yes. As an officer of Future Business Leaders of America, I was responsible for motivating the membership to initiate an annual fundraiser for the homeless in our community. Let me show you some letters of appreciation from the mayor and the homeless shelter we worked with.

Sample Response 2:
Yes. In my research and design class, I led our work group in presenting our marketing proposal to a local business firm. Here is a copy of our proposal, which was accepted and implemented.

Portfolio Assessment

Your portfolio will evolve over time, with each new professional experience you build. It is helpful to have your portfolio assessed from time to time to help you determine whether or not you are building the best credentials for your career goal. The best evaluators of a portfolio are employers. Arrange to have an employer in your career field critique your portfolio at least twice during your academic experience. Career counselors and faculty members are also good resources for helping you assess your portfolio. When you have your portfolio assessed, you should focus on finding out what additional experiences you need to become better qualified to attain your career goal. You may show a lot of work experience but little evidence of community involvement. An employer may recommend more community involvement for you to help you demonstrate more of a balance in your life. Or all of your work experience may be in one industry segment, and an employer may recommend more work experience but in different aspects of your industry.

Another area of major importance to your portfolio assessment is consideration of what further training you need to become better qualified for a particular job. If you need further training, you will need to decide whether to obtain that training directly with an employer, on the job, or in school. An employer, career counselor, or faculty member can help you with this decision. Before you conduct any employment interviews, you should be able to tell an employer what further training you think you need to be effective and the plan you have for obtaining that further training.

Chapter Summary

This chapter is your personal guide to developing the critical skills employers will expect you to have when you interview for employment. The plan you develop will vary according to the specific industry, employer, and job you select. Regardless of what your career path is, it is essential that you use your educational experiences to build employment credentials so that you will be prepared to compete in a workplace where skills and credentials determine much of your future success.

Finally, presenting your unique credentials in a career portfolio will clearly demonstrate to an employer your focus, your unique qualifications, and your desire to start your career with a company where your skills are valued.

Part Two

Job Search
Techniques

Chapter Six

Sources of Job Information

Chapter Objectives

After completing this chapter, you will:

Understand the (hidden) nature of today's job market.

Be able to use published resources, referral services, the direct approach, and networking to obtain information and interviews in the visible job market.

Be able to use published resources, referral services, the direct approach, and networking to obtain information and interviews in the hidden job market.

Be able to use published resources, the direct approach, and networking to obtain information and interviews in the very hidden job market.

As the work world becomes more global and as more small entrepreneurial firms emerge, the job market is becoming more fluid than ever. Every day, hundreds of new jobs become available through company start-ups, corporate reorganizations, mergers, joint ventures, and acquisitions. The economy is a fast-moving target, and if you are not prepared to move with it, many jobs will pass right by you without your ever knowing it. To put you in control of uncovering a variety of job options, you need to understand that while some jobs are advertised in traditional ways, other jobs may never come to your attention if you are not creative and persistent in your job search.

One of your challenges is keeping informed about jobs that are available in your field. You may not be familiar with all the sources of jobs available to you or with ways to promote your availability for employment in everyday situations. Even if your school makes interviews available to you, you will want to seek out some companies on your own. Learning how to secure your own interviews will also be important to you once you are established in your career but wish to move on to a new job.

The Nature of Today's Job Market

It may seem to you that the job market is very visible. On a daily basis, you can scan classified ads in newspapers and magazines and on the Internet. Community bulletin boards and postings in the campus career services office, the department of unemployment security, and on companies' internal job-posting boards are but a few of the common places you may see notices of job openings.

Job hotlines now allow us to dial up jobs via the telephone 24 hours a day, and career days and job fairs are held regularly at schools and in the local community.

Although these should be your first sources of job information, they are only the beginning of a comprehensive job search. In fact, only 10 to 20 percent of the job market is visible through these sources. This means that 80 to 90 percent of available jobs are not obvious to you through traditional sources. Job leads that are uncovered from untraditional sources are considered to be part of the hidden job market and the very hidden job market. Some common sources of job information in these markets are published resources, referral services, a direct approach, and networking.

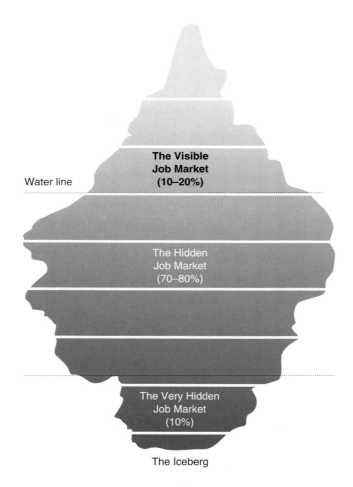

Water line

The Visible Job Market (10–20%)

The Hidden Job Market (70–80%)

The Very Hidden Job Market (10%)

The Iceberg

Developing techniques to learn about openings and get interviews is important to a successful job search, but it requires work on your part. Being aware of circumstances that can help you find out about jobs and acting on opportunities as they become available will help you maximize the number of job opportunities available to you.

The following sections tell you about some ways not to miss the visible job market and to uncover job information in the hidden and very hidden job markets.

The Visible Job Market

The visible job market consists of those sources that are the most obvious and easily accessible. For example, the newspaper, career fairs, and your school's placement office are sources you normally associate with finding job information. The following sections offer some ways to access the visible job market.

Published Resources

When employers want to solicit the widest range of responses to available positions, they publish these job openings in the printed resources most widely read by job seekers. These include the following.

Newspaper Classified Ads.   The newspaper is the most consistent source for published job openings. You should use the classified ads not only to look for specific jobs but also to note which companies seem to be running ads most often. The classified ads can bring to your attention the name of a company you are otherwise unfamiliar with. If you are seeking employment abroad, the classified section of newspapers from the country you wish to work in is the best indicator of current job openings and firms that are hiring. Whether in a domestic or international publication, classified ads are also an excellent source of information about qualifications for specific jobs. Reading the classifieds on a regular basis is essential to keeping current with the job market.

Job-Listing Bulletins/Newsletters.   Hundreds of independent publications list jobs weekly, monthly, or quarterly. Many colleges and universities publish job bulletins for their alumni. Like the classifieds, these bulletins and newsletters are good indicators of employers who are currently hiring. Some companies will maintain an ad over a long period of time to generate a pool of qualified candidates to choose from when an actual position becomes available. In any case, many job-listing bulletins are sold at newsstands and sometimes distributed in public places.

Placement Office Listings.   Whether on bulletin boards or in job books, current job opportunities are usually posted and maintained by school placement offices. Although you should not limit yourself to this source, you should start to find job information through your school's placement office. Once you are aware of how much information you can obtain there on a regular basis, you will know what you need to do to supplement that information.

Internship Directories.   Books that list the names and addresses of firms with formal internship programs can be found in most bookstores. Usually these books will list the contact for hiring and the types of internship that exist. These listings can help you gain an overview of the types of jobs available at specific companies.

Bulletin Board Postings.   Federal agencies, private employers, and community organizations all use bulletin boards to post job vacancies. Some communities use electronic bulletin boards to post information on jobs.

The Internet.   Internet employment services have become a popular means for firms to discover new talent. Most of the services provide classified job listings and advice on how to land a job.

Referral Services

Many employers prefer to use an outside source to screen and refer candidates to their companies. For entry-level recruits, college placement offices are the most commonly used source of candidate referrals. Referral services offered by college placement offices include the following.

Placement Office Résumé Referral Service.   Most schools offer employers the opportunity to ask for candidates to be prescreened by the placement office. In this case, the placement office prescreens candidates based on qualifications defined by the employer and refers only qualified candidates directly to the employer.

Job Hotlines.   Job hotlines are advertised in many magazines and newspapers, and many college and university placement offices are now using job hotlines to bring available jobs to students. Job hotlines allow job seekers direct access to job information via the telephone. These systems usually give employers the opportunity to call their job listings into a voice-mail system that can be accessed directly by job candidates. Hotlines are user friendly both to you and to employers because they are accessible 24 hours a day, far beyond the typical hours a placement office is open. The advantage of this system is that you can respond to the job opening much more quickly than in the traditional posting methods.

Placement Office Practical Training Binder.   For international students looking for a job at graduation to complete their practical training, some helpful information may be available in the placement office. It is important for international students to know where else to go for information on how to process the paperwork necessary to obtain a work permit for their practical training. On many campuses, the placement office works with the international student office to assist students in this area. The placement office is responsible for directing international students to firms interested in hiring them for practical training.

Direct Approach

Many companies provide students with opportunities to meet with them directly to discuss potential job openings. Perhaps the only time in your career when employers will come to you to speak about career opportunities is while you are in school. Common school recruiting programs in which employers participate include the following.

Campus Interviews. Some schools invite companies to conduct job interviews for graduates at the school. This type of on-campus recruiting program is one of the most direct ways to secure an interview through your placement office.

Open Houses/Industry Nights. Many companies precede their day of interviews at the school with an open house for students who will be interviewed. The purpose of the open house is to provide information about the company's training programs, corporate structure, history, expansion plans, and career opportunities. Since this may be the first meeting you have with the industry representative(s) from a particular company, you must make a positive first impression. Dress professionally when attending all open houses. Make an extra effort to ask questions during the question-and-answer period, and after the program introduce yourself to the industry representative(s). All of these things will help make you more visible to the employer.

Job Fairs/Career Days. Many schools hold some type of career day to bring employers and students together. Although career days are mostly aimed at providing career information to students, the contacts you make with industry representatives during these programs are another source of job interviews for you. Many schools hold regional job fairs in conjunction with other schools in the area; these fairs bring a number of schools and their students together with major employers, and both employers and students benefit from a greater pool of jobs and job applicants. Most communities also host local job fairs for the general public in such facilities as the local civic or convention center. The Internet has even created its own job fair for job seekers.

Networking

Networking is the process of communicating your career goals to others who may be able to provide you with professional contacts you may need to help you reach your goals. As a student, the more obvious professionals available to you for networking include the following.

Teachers and Counselors and Personal References. Teachers and counselors and personal references all can provide you with insight about jobs and offer advice about the jobs best suited for you. They can also refer you to career publications that will help you find out more about jobs in your field and tests that help you understand what jobs best fit your interests and personality.

Current Employer. If it is appropriate to do so, you can speak with your current employer about other job leads in or outside the company.

Cooperative Education/Internship Employer. Your cooperative education or internship employer can advise you on jobs available in his or her industry and company. He or she may also tell you the best way to find out about these jobs.

ACTIVITY 6-1 • *Accessing the Visible Job Market*

Accessing the visible job market takes some knowledge of the resources available to you and some planning on how you will utilize these resources to uncover as many job leads as you can.

Review the types of resources available to you in the visible job market. Check (√) one resource within each type you think you will use and describe why you think these resources will work best for you.

Types of Resources

Published
Newspaper classified ads   (   )
Job-listing bulletins/newsletters   (   )
Placement office listings   (   )
Internship directories   (   )
Bulletin board postings   (   )
The Internet   (   )

Referral Services
Placement office résumé referral service   (   )
Job hotlines   (   )
Placement office practical training binder   (   )

Direct Approach
Campus interviews   (   )
Open houses/industry nights   (   )
Job fairs/career days   (   )

Networking
Teachers, counselors, and personal references   (   )
Current employer   (   )
Cooperative education/internship employer   (   )

Describe the reasons for your choices:

_____

_____

_____

_____

_____

The Hidden Job Market

The hidden job market consists of sources of jobs that may be less obvious to you and may therefore require more of your initiative to find. For example, sourcing job information through professional associations or your local community may involve some planning on your part because you might not automatically think of these sources. The following are some ways to access the hidden job market.

Published Resources

There are many published resources that either post jobs or provide lists of potential employers that you might not ordinarily think about when you begin your job search. Knowing where to locate these resources can help you explore the hidden job market. The publications listed below are usually found in libraries and may be available in your school's placement office.

How People Find Jobs

Generally, there are four basic ways to find a job. Informal job-seeking methods are by far the most successful. But you can also find a job through want ads, employment agencies, and other methods. By looking below at a pie graph and lists of activities for each of these job-seeking methods, you can determine how to best use your time and energy in your own job search.

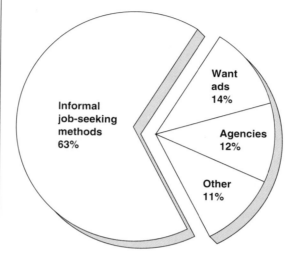

Informal job-seeking methods 63%

Want ads 14%

Agencies 12%

Other 11%

Informal (63%)
- Direct contact with employers
- Identifying possible employers through networking with family, friends, teachers, neighbors, and acquaintances
- Contact previous employers for possible leads
- Job club or support group

Want Ads (14%)
- Answer ads in newspapers
- Answer ads in trade or professional journals
- Place ads to "sell yourself"
- Answer storefront signs

Agencies (12%)
- Job service
- Private employment agencies
- School placement offices
- Local, state, and federal government personnel offices
- Chamber of Commerce
- Small Business Administration

Other (11%)
- Civil service tests
- Local labor unions
- Local community organizations
- Phone directories
- U.S. Armed Forces recruiting offices
- Professional organizations
- Women's organizations
- Political organizations
- Church groups
- Industrial directories and informal pamphlets (check your local library)

Source: U.S. Department of Labor.

Magazines and Trade Journals.   Some magazines and trade journals have a section dedicated to classified ads. This can be a particularly helpful source of information if you are looking for a job abroad. If you don't have a contact who can send you this information regularly, you can probably access international publications at your public or local university library.

Professional and Trade Association Job Finders.   Many professional and trade associations provide job information to their members. Many will also act as a referral source for members who are looking to fill vacant positions by passing on

résumés from candidates. Whether you are a member looking to hire or be hired, you should inquire as to whether this service is available in your association or professional organization.

Business Directories.   Business directories are good sources of information about companies' business standing. Before deciding to seek job information from a company, you will want to know that it is stable and has a solid future. Business directories are also a great way to resource smaller successful firms that you may not otherwise know about.

Company Literature/Annual Reports.   If you choose to go directly to a company for job information, you can learn a lot about the type of jobs that exist in the firm just by reading the company's literature and annual report. For example, an annual report with information about a company's products, customers, and future growth is a good indicator of existing jobs and new jobs that may emerge.

Referral Services

You may not be aware of the referral services listed below. They can, however, be an excellent source of available jobs and an indicator of which employers are hiring and what career fields are growing.

Employment Agencies.   Agencies are especially helpful to you once you have a few years of work experience. Some agencies are able to assist with entry-level positions, but most deal with advanced positions requiring at least two to three years' experience. It won't hurt to select one or two reputable employment agencies to submit résumés to during an entry-level job search. If you do have a lot of experience, use them more heavily. Just do not fall into the trap of depending solely on the agency to find you a job. And remember, be sure to ask if the employer will pay the placement fee if you are hired.

Government Employment Offices.   In many countries outside the United States, jobs are not advertised in the same way as in the states. Job information may be centralized with government employment offices. International students wishing to pursue a career in their home country can do so through these offices.

Professional Associations.   Some of the professional associations in your career field are listed in Section A of the Career Handbook. They can be extremely valuable sources of information to you throughout your career. For more contacts like this refer to the *Encyclopedia of Associations* in the reference area at your local library. Some professional associations publish job bulletins; some actually provide placement services and some do not. The only way you will know is to write and ask. If you are a member of the Future Business Leaders of America or the Distributive Education Clubs of America, write and ask for advice and any career literature they may have.

Direct Approach

A direct approach to uncovering jobs in the hidden job market involves your taking the initiative to contact companies on your own about possible job openings when the company has not invited you to inquire through company job postings, classified ads, and so on. The following are some ways to use the direct approach.

Walk-In.   Going into a company's human resource department for job information does not require an appointment. You may ask what jobs are currently available and obtain an application and company literature. Remember, the purpose is to obtain information; the walk-in approach is not a preferred way to obtain an interview.

Telemarketing Campaigns.   Get on the telephone and do some preliminary work for your job search. Call companies directly to see if they are actively seeking applicants

in any particular area. Find out the name, title, and address of the person who may be responsible for hiring. You can create a job for yourself over the telephone if you are smart. When you call, know what you are going to say and be prepared to announce your qualifications and what you have to offer the company, rather than just asking if there are any jobs available. Many times employers will call a candidate in for an informational interview if it sounds like the candidate might fit into the company somewhere. When you speak to someone on the telephone, you have an opportunity to create an impression that you cannot produce on a résumé or a job application.

Volunteer, Temporary, or Part-Time Work. Volunteer, temporary, and part-time jobs are excellent sources of job information. They give you an opportunity to gain firsthand knowledge about certain jobs without requiring you to make a permanent commitment to the job. You have the opportunity to observe others in different positions and broaden your knowledge about careers in the company or industry you are in. Often these situations can provide you with job leads or even become full-time jobs.

Networking

There are some contacts we all have that we often overlook as possible sources of job leads. Although some people do not readily seek these people out to discuss job search and possible career opportunities, you can pursue networking opportunities for jobs with the following.

Club and Organization Members. Speaking with members of clubs and organizations can help you learn about trends occurring in your industry and how these trends are affecting jobs. You can also learn about the companies that sponsor the club or organization and explore job information with them.

Mentors. If you are fortunate enough to have a mentor, this person can share much information with you about his or her own career. In addition, your mentor can introduce you to other industry professionals that can be a useful source to you.

Relatives. Family members can provide job information to you because of the experiences they have had with their own jobs and because of what they can tell you about the companies they have worked for. They also may be able to refer you to other family members who can help you.

Friends and Neighbors. Friends can share information with you about their jobs or what they have learned through their own job or what they have learned through their own job search. By exchanging information about each of your experiences you can both learn about the job market and talk about which jobs appeal to you the most and why. Even as an informal process, this can help you sort out where your interests lie and what direction your job search may take.

Classmates. Your classmates can be helpful to network with because they are probably experiencing the same anxiety, excitement, frustration, and sense of challenge that you are. They can share job information they have obtained through their experiences.

Community. Contacts in your community can provide information about what companies might be moving into your area and what type of jobs they may bring. Community contacts are also helpful with explaining what type of jobs may exist with nonprofit organizations. Some community contacts might include the local chamber of commerce, your church, and local politicians.

ACTIVITY 6-2 • *Accessing the Hidden Job Market*

Accessing the hidden job market takes some knowledge of the resources available to you and some planning on how you will utilize these resources to uncover as many job leads as you can.

Review the types of resources available to you in the hidden job market. Check (√) one resource within each type you think you will use and describe why you think these resources will work best for you.

Types of Resources

Published
Magazines and trade journals   ( )
Professional and trade associations job finders   ( )
Business directories   ( )
Company literature/annual reports   ( )

Referral Services
Employment agencies   ( )
Government employment offices   ( )
Professional associations   ( )

Direct Approach
Walk-in   ( )
Telemarketing campaigns   ( )
Volunteer, temporary, or part-time work   ( )

Networking
Club and organization members   ( )
Mentors   ( )
Relatives   ( )
Friends and neighbors   ( )
Classmates   ( )
Community   ( )

Describe the reasons for your choices:

_____
_____
_____
_____
_____
_____
_____
_____

The Very Hidden Job Market

The very hidden job market consists of opportunities that are usually overlooked as sources of job information. It includes existing sources you may not normally think about such as listing a want ad for yourself, or networking with colleagues at your country club.

Published Resources   With the very hidden job market, you must use creative techniques to access possible openings. For example, by taking published lists of addresses of businesses in

your career field, you can initiate your own mailing lists or telemarketing campaigns to make firms aware of your credentials and availability for employment.

Telephone Directory.   The yellow pages in your telephone directory are a great way to obtain a focused list of companies in your area by type of business.

Computerized Mailing Lists.   Through professional associations, the chamber of commerce, or catalogs that specialize in job search products and resources, you may sometimes purchase mailing lists of companies by industry.

Lists of New Firms with 100 Employees or Less.   Small companies are probably the most overlooked source of job information because many of them are unknown and many job seekers assume the best information comes from larger corporations. Your chamber of commerce can supply you with lists of smaller companies that are operating in your area. In fact, as mentioned earlier, more jobs will be available with smaller companies than with large organizations over the next 6 to 10 years.

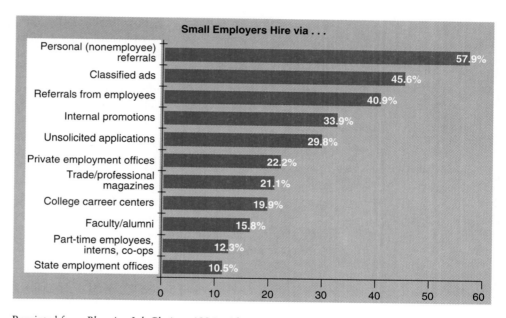

Reprinted from *Planning Job Choices: 1996,* with permission of the National Association of Colleges and Employers, copyright holder.

Direct Approach

In the very hidden job market, you need to be particularly assertive with your outreach to prospective employers to uncover job leads and promote yourself as a candidate for employment. To market yourself directly to employers you can utilize the following resources.

Mass Mailings.   At first, you may think mass mailings are a waste of time, but your chances of unearthing the job you want at a company you really never thought of are good through this method. Visit your placement office, go to the library, use the yellow pages—do a variety of things to find lists of potential employers. Then identify at least 20 that you may really be interested in, and from there it's up to you. Mailing out 200 résumés and cover letters is not a bad idea if your field is especially competitive. When using the mass-mailing campaign, you may want to adjust your cover letter to suit particular types of employers.

Want Ads for Yourself. It is possible that you are in a field where job leads are not as abundant as in another, or perhaps you are involved in marketing or advertising and want to stand out to a prospective employer. Today, some job candidates are sourcing job leads by placing ads about their qualifications in the Job Wanted section of the classifieds.

Former Employers. If you left a previous job in good standing, it can be helpful for you to contact your former employer for job information. You may be interested in returning to work at that company, or you may simply ask a former boss if he or she can refer you to a colleague for job information.

Networking

The least obvious groups of people in the least obvious settings can create tremendous networking opportunities. With a little forethought and creativity on your part, you can take advantage of the following opportunities to tap in to the very hidden job market.

Sporting Events. Although a sporting event is not the first thing that comes to mind as a source of job information, it can be one. Accepting an invitation from or extending one to a businessperson you would like to network with can result in a fun time that is also productive.

Country Clubs and Health Clubs. Joining a country club creates tremendous networking opportunities. Golf memberships are among the most popular with businesspeople. Health club memberships are also increasing in popularity with professionals because many companies now offer memberships as an employee benefit.

Fellow Job Seekers. Keeping informed about how others are doing with their job search can provide you with information about companies that are hiring, the person responsible for hiring, and qualifications sought for different jobs. Perhaps someone you know may turn down a job offer, opening up the possibility for you to apply for that job yourself.

Fellow Employees. You may learn that a fellow employee is leaving your company or being promoted, creating a job lead for you to act upon. Or you can simply learn about different job responsibilities from your co-workers.

Chamber of Commerce. Your chamber of commerce can be an excellent source of job information if you take the initiative to find out about all of the services and information it provides. In addition to listings of company names and addresses, your chamber of commerce probably sponsors events for the local business community. These may include monthly "business after hours" receptions where professionals meet to discuss issues affecting their businesses and network with each other on an informal basis. Some chambers sponsor a state leadership institute to heighten businesspeople's awareness of issues facing their community. Any organized events like this that bring businesspeople together for a common reason are great networking opportunities.

ACTIVITY 6-3 • *Accessing the Very Hidden Job Market*

Accessing the very hidden job market takes initiative and creativity on your part, along with some planning on how you will utilize these resources to find as many job leads as you can.

Review the types of resources available to you in the very hidden job market. Check (√) one resource within each type you think you will use, and describe why you think these resources will work best for you.

Types of Resources

Published Resources
Telephone directory   (   )
Computerized mailing lists   (   )
Lists of new firms with 100 employees or less   (   )

Direct Approach
Mass mailings   (   )
Want ads for yourself   (   )
Former employers   (   )

Networking
Sporting events   (   )
Country clubs and health clubs   (   )
Fellow job seekers   (   )
Fellow employees   (   )
Chamber of commerce   (   )

Describe the reasons for your choices:

_____

_____

_____

_____

_____

_____

_____

_____

INTERNATIONAL CAREER DIRECTIONS

Sourcing International Jobs

Sourcing international jobs can be an interesting experience that exposes you to the global marketplace and creates new career choices for you to consider. Although traditional sources of jobs such as trade journals and newspaper classified ads may be highly effective in helping you find international job leads, the electronic revolution has opened up the most diverse and direct access to information about international employment. On-line information services made possible by the technological advances in telecommunications and personal computers have created easier access to job information across the globe.

A host of on-line services exist locally, nationally, and internationally. The most well-known source for international jobs is the Internet's World Wide Web. The World Wide Web attracts literally millions of new users to the Internet each month, for a total of as many as 50 million people.

Popular job listings on the Web currently include the Monster Board, E-Span, Career Mosaic, and Career Web. Most of these services provide classified job listings and advice on how to find a job. Recruiters who use the Net generally give it high grades. They say it is effective and, when compared with other means of recruiting, inexpensive. The Internet is currently the most widely used electronic source of jobs in the United States and across the globe.

ACTIVITY 6-4 • *Learning to Source International Job Leads Electronically*

If you are not familiar with how to access the Internet, ask a course instructor, librarian, or someone else you know with experience on the Internet to show you how to access the different job resources available to you.

Scan the Monster Board, E-Span, Career Mosaic, and the Career Web. Select the one that currently has the most international job leads. Review the types of jobs, skills required, and geographic locations for jobs in your career field.

Make a list of the on-line services you find to be the most helpful leads for international jobs:

1. _____   4. _____

2. _____   5. _____

3. _____   6. _____

Develop the habit of scanning existing on-line services for international jobs and exploring new on-line services as they become available. Fully utilizing on-line services as a source of international job leads is the most comprehensive way to stay abreast of what is happening globally in your career field.

Chapter Summary

Any good job search begins with a thorough understanding of what jobs exist in your field and what resources are available for sourcing jobs that might interest you. Even with all the published materials pertaining to jobs and the many well-advertised career fairs, there is still a majority of the job market not accessible through these traditional means. Your ability to access the hidden job market is critical because you want to be sure to explore as many options as possible to obtain career information and create job leads. By acting on the many existing opportunities to enter the hidden job market, you put yourself in better control of the career decisions you will make.

Résumés and Job Applications

Before attempting to apply for any job, you should be able to prepare a professional résumé and a concise job application. Both are very often the first impression a potential employer has of you.

Today there are many alternatives to the traditional paper résumé, largely driven by new technology. Automated résumé systems allow employers a precise approach to résumé search and retrieval, and offer you ways to become a part of the fast-moving trend to locate and apply for jobs directly through on-line employment services.

Résumés

A résumé is both a factual presentation of yourself and an opportunity for self-promotion. Employers will use your résumé to see whether you have the educational background, previous work experience, and professional objectives needed to be successful in the job for which you are applying. Since employers like to be able to scan résumés quickly to determine applicants' eligibility for a job, your résumé should be brief, to the point, and formatted for easy reading. Although the length and style will depend on how much work experience you have, your résumé should be a concise, error-free, attractive outline of your relevant job experiences, skills, accomplishments, and academic credentials. While your résumé should be personalized to reflect your qualifications and professional interests, it should fit on one page, or be no more than two.

Although the traditional paper résumé is still the most commonly used, some employers are starting to rely on the different types of résumé presentations made possible by new technologies. Nontraditional résumés may include electronic résumés, disk résumés, interactive résumés, video résumés, audio résumés, and other creative résumés. The following sections discuss both traditional and nontraditional résumés.

Traditional Résumés

Two basic types of traditional résumés are used most frequently in a job search: the functional résumé and the chronological résumé.

The *chronological résumé* lists your work experience and educational history in chronological order, that is, by date. This type of résumé is excellent if you are entering the job market for the first time or are changing jobs within a given career field, because it highlights the education and work experience you have in your field. Sometimes your education is more important than your work experience when you are seeking a new job, especially if your education emphasizes for the employer the career direction you wish to take and your work experience is unrelated or minimal.

The *functional résumé* organizes your experience according to specific skills or functions. This format is appropriate if you are changing careers or reentering the workforce after a period of absence, because it emphasizes your skills and abilities and downplays any gaps in employment or any unrelated work experience. This résumé is especially effective if you have a lengthy work history. Most employers value previous work experience, both in and out of the field. Experience reflects your work ethic and commitment to improving professional skills.

Organization of a Traditional Résumé

Traditional résumés usually organize information into the following categories.

Identification.   Print your first name, middle initial, and last name at the top of the page.

Address.   A correct address is critical information. A potential employer may want to send you a job offer or communicate with you for some other reason. Receiving that information will be extremely important to you. If you are not currently living at your permanent address, list both your temporary and permanent addresses.

Telephone Numbers.   Like your address, your telephone number is critically important. Always include your area code. Do not assume the caller will know it. If you have no telephone or have an unlisted number that you prefer not to give out, leave the telephone number of a very reliable person who is home much of the time and can take messages for you without damaging your credibility. During your job search, check with that person regularly for messages. If you use an answering machine, be sure your greeting is professional and positive. If you have a fax machine, include your fax number.

Professional Objective.   Some employers suggest that a professional objective is not required on a résumé because it may limit your chances of being considered for a wide range of jobs. On the other hand, there are those who feel your professional objective is an important part of your résumé and should be included whether you are just starting out or making a next step in your career. Properly done, a professional objective indicates direction to an employer. You've gone to the trouble of deciding what you want to do; now you want to show the employer that you *know* what you want. A professional objective can be stated most clearly in one sentence, or no more than two sentences. Your objective should reflect your short- and long-term career goals and a realistic attitude. It should be broad enough to give you some flexibility but specific enough not to make it appear that you are floundering with your career direction.

The following are examples of good professional objectives:

- An entry-level job as an information coordinator leading to a career doing market research in the travel industry.
- An entry-level job as a store manager trainee leading to a career in retail operations.

The following are examples of poor professional objectives:

- An entry-level job as a store manager trainee leading to a retail buying career. (This is inappropriate because it is not a correct career path. If a buying track is what you want, you must start off on a buying track, as opposed to a management track.)
- An entry-level position in a growing company with an opportunity for advancement. (This is too general; it does not indicate that you have thought about any real direction.)

Use the short-term and long-term goals you developed in Chapter 2, "Self-Assessment," to develop an effective professional objective.

Education.   Don't leave anything out. You want to account the best you can for how you have spent your time. If you attended a school but did not complete a diploma, certificate, or degree, then list it as a place you attended. Only list your high school if you participated in a vocational program that is relevant to your career field.

Courses.   Courses are especially helpful to list if you are an entry-level applicant without a lot of work experience and if you have taken highly specialized courses that will help you on the job.

Special Skills.   You should list any special skills you have that are relevant to the job you are seeking. Business writing and computer skills are two examples. You don't want to list personal characteristics in this area. Save talking about your personality for the cover letter.

Work Experience.   Don't make assumptions for employers and leave out certain experiences because you think they won't be valuable. Chances are, if you think this way, an employer won't value them either. It is important not to leave big gaps of time on your résumé. You should list most of the experiences you have had and be prepared to convince an employer that you have learned from each one of them. Whether these experiences have been part-time or full-time jobs, it is vital for you to examine what you might have gained from each experience. So many times an employer sees someone who has worked as a waitperson for three summers and subsequently asks about the job. The employer then waits for the applicant to talk about

his or her experiences as a waitperson—working with the public, working under pressure, working nights, weekends, and holidays—only to find the applicant apologizing for lack of work experience related to his or her chosen career. Certainly if you worked to support your college education, that should be noted on your résumé. For example, stating "Earned 80 percent of college tuition through part-time employment" spells initiative, determination, and responsibility.

Work experience gained through internships, externships, or a cooperative education program may also be included in the Work Experience section of your résumé. Since the purpose of participating in one of these programs is to gain employment skills, you should be sure to write out all of the responsibilities you had as part of your job, just as you do when listing a part-time, full-time, or summer job. Too often, students overlook how valuable these experiences are to a prospective employer. Many students list these experiences in the Education section. It is much more effective to include your internship, externship, or cooperative education experience under Work Experience.

International Experience.   Usually international experience is described in the section of the résumé where the experience belongs (i.e., Education, Work Experience, etc.) as opposed to being listed in a separate section. It is acceptable to add a section called International Experience with a summary of your different jobs if you know that an employer is specifically looking for someone with such experience.

Extracurricular Activities/Hobbies.   Your extracurricular activities and hobbies demonstrate leadership potential, interpersonal skills, initiative, creativity, and ability to plan and organize. They also show that when there's nothing to do, you choose to make valuable use of your time rather than seeing it as an opportunity to do nothing. This may be an important characteristic to the manager who wants a secretary who will take initiative when he or she is away.

References.   You should always be prepared to list references. Have the courtesy to call or write to the person you'd like to be a reference for you. It is not essential to actually list references on your résumé, but you should at least add the line "References available upon request." When you do this, type up your list of references on a separate sheet of paper headed "References for _____ (your name)." This does not have to be mailed out with your résumé, but you should take it with you on a job interview.

Special Distinctions (Optional).   Special distinctions may include honors and awards you have received, competitions you have won, work that you have had published, press releases about any media appearances you have made, or a foreign language you speak. If any of these accomplishments are part of your background, you may add a Special Distinctions section to your résumé. This would normally be placed after the Work Experience section.

Community Service/Volunteer Work.   If you have participated in any type of community service or volunteer work, you should include a description of such work on your résumé. Many employers now look at this involvement as important because of the initiative and commitment it demonstrates. Many companies also are conscious of their social responsibility in the community and want employees who will represent them through community service and volunteer work. Remember to write the description of your experience using action words to describe the employment skills you used to perform the work you did. Your description of community service or volunteer work may be placed after the Work Experience section.

The following pages give formats and samples for both chronological and functional résumés.

Format for a Chronological Résumé

YOUR NAME

Permanent Address:
Street address
City, State, Zip
Phone number (w/area code)
Fax number (w/area code)

Temporary Address:
Street address
City, State, Zip
Phone number (w/area code)
Fax number (w/area code)

Professional Objective:
State the type of position you are applying for and your long-term goal. You may include indications of wanting growth and challenge in your objective.

Education:
List professional training and/or college(s) you graduated from first. If you attended a college but did not complete the program you were in, you may list the college and date attended without indicating a degree. List your high school only if you were in a special program of some kind (honors, tech-prep, etc.).

Courses: (*Optional*)
List no more than six; list only those that have something to do with the position for which you are applying.

Special Skills: (*Optional*)
Skills you have developed may be *technical* (word processing, desktop publishing, shorthand), *interpersonal* (team player, teaching, public speaking), or *thinking skills* (creativity, problem solving, decision making).

Work Experience:
Include part-time, full-time, and summer work, as well as internships, externships, and cooperative education experience, with brief descriptions and dates of employment. List the most recent job first and work down. If your employment history includes many short-term miscellaneous jobs, use the following rules:
1. List those relevant to the position for which you are applying.
2. List those you held for the longest periods of time.

Community Service/Volunteer Work: (*Optional*)

International Experience: (*Optional*)

Special Distinctions: (*Optional*)

Extracurricular Activities/Hobbies:
List any organizations individually along with your responsibilities. Then list hobbies and special interests that might be pertinent to the position for which you are applying. Also list others that seem less relevant as well, as they will indicate your diversity in a variety of areas.

References: (*Optional*)
State "References are available upon request." On a separate sheet of paper, list at least three. Be sure to get permission in advance. List teachers, friends, or former employers (but not relatives). Include names, titles, addresses, and telephone numbers with area codes.

Portfolio:
If you have a career portfolio, state "Portfolio available upon request."

Sample Chronological Résumé

JENNIFER M. GORDON

Permanent Address: **Temporary Address:**
64 Potter Street   5 Washington Avenue
Sodus, NY 14551   Providence, RI 02905
Phone: (315) 585-6609   Phone: (401) 598-0101
Fax: (315) 585-4434   Fax: (401) 598-1010

Professional Objective:
To obtain a sous-chef position in a large-volume restaurant leading to an executive chef's position for an upscale theme restaurant.

Education:
Johnson & Wales University, Providence, RI 02905
A.S. Culinary Arts, May 1996

Wayne Morgan High School, Sodus, NY 14551
Tech-prep program, Diploma 1994

Special Skills:

Garde-manger	Menu design	Purchasing and receiving
Wood grilling	Ice carving	Food cost control

Work Experience:

1995–present | Goldenquill Restaurant, East Providence, RI 02906
Line Cook.
Assist sous chef at sauté and fry station and with grilling and broiling in 100-seat seafood restaurant.

Summer 1995 | Acres Country Club, Cape Cod, MA 03421
Prep Cook.
Rotated among garde-manger, sauce, and grilling stations. Supervised four dishwashers and two kitchen workers. Received and purchased food products.

March 1995–June 1995 | Salina Foodservice Corporation, Dallas, TX 43431
Cooperative Education Experience
Line Cook.
Assisted head cook with preparing meals for corporate dining room at downtown Dallas bank. Prepared daily "heart healthy" menus. Did cooking demonstrations for spouses' program during bank's annual meeting.

Sept. 1994–March 1995 | Johnson & Wales University, Providence, RI 02903
Pasta Place Restaurant.
Prepared pasta menus for students' lunches and dinners at university student dining facility.

Community Service/Volunteer Work:

Sept. 1994–March 1995 | Meals on Wheels, Providence, RI 029056
Cook.
Cooked dinners for clients needing special assistance with meal preparation.

Special Distinctions:
- Employee of the Month, May 1995, Salina Foodservice Corporation
- Distinguished Visiting Chef Scholarship recipient
- 3rd place, National High School Recipe Contest

Extracurricular Activities/Hobbies:
Secretary, Chippers Club
Vice president, VICA (Vocational Industrial Clubs of America)

References available upon request.
Portfolio available upon request.

ACTIVITY 7-1 • *Chronological Résumé Worksheet*

Before you write your chronological résumé, you should have a clear picture of what you can include in each section. Fill in all of the information that best describes the experiences you have had; then select those you will include on your chronological résumé.

YOUR NAME

Jorge _____ Albert _____ Ortega _____
(First name)   (Middle initial)   (Last name)

Permanent Address:

918 W62 PL
(street)

Los Angeles CA, 90044
(city, state, zip code)

323-778-5039
(area code) telephone number

_____
(area code) fax number

Temporary Address:

_____
(street)

_____
(city, state, zip code)

_____
(area code) telephone number

_____
(area code) fax number

Professional Objective:

To use the skills that I have obtained ~~to~~ for the benefit of the company

Education:

College name United Education Institute

College address Los Angeles CA.

Degree received _____

High school name Verdugo Hills H.S.

High school address Tujunga CA.

Diploma received G.E.D

Courses: (*Optional*)

_____

_____

_____

Special Skills: (*Optional*)

_____

_____

Work Experience:

Dates of employment: _Currently Employed_

Company name: _Starbucks_

Company address: _____

Position held: _Barista_

Position description: _Count registers, take drink orders,_

_____

_____

_____

Dates of employment: _____

Company name: _____

Company address: _____

Position held: _____

Position description: _____

_____

_____

_____

Dates of employment: _____

Company name: _____

Company address: _____

Position held: _____

Position description: _____

_____

_____

_____

Dates of employment: _____

Company name: _____

Company address: _____

Position held: _____

Position description: _____

_____

_____

_____

Community Service/Volunteer Work: (*Optional*)

_____

_____

_____

International Experience: (*Optional*)

_____

_____

_____

Special Distinctions: (*Optional*)

_____

_____

_____

Extracurricular Activities/Hobbies:

_____

_____

_____

References: (*Optional*)

Name and title: _____

Company name: _____

Street address: _____

City, state, zip code: _____

(Area code) phone number: _____

Name and title: _____

Company name: _____

Street address: _____

City, state, zip code: _____

(Area code) phone number: _____

Name and title: _____

Company name: _____

Street address: _____

City, state, zip code: _____

(Area code) phone number: _____

Format for a Functional Résumé

YOUR NAME

Permanent Address:	**Temporary Address:**
Street address	Street address
City, State, Zip	City, State, Zip
Phone number (with area code)	Phone number (with area code)
Fax number (with area code)	Fax number (with area code)

Professional Objective:
State the type of position you are applying for and your long-term goal. You may include indications of wanting growth and challenge in your objective.

Professional Experience and Skills:
List (and discuss, if necessary) *all* of the professional skills you can bring to an employer as a result of the different experiences you have had. These may include personal and interpersonal skills that are helpful to your career but should also stress your technical skills. Think about all of the skills you have acquired and focus on those you think are transferable to other jobs.

Employment History:
List the jobs you have had, including your present position, in order by date, starting with your most recent job. You may omit any jobs you held for just a few months or any that are completely unrelated to the job you are seeking. It is not necessary to provide a detailed description of the jobs you held, but do list your job titles and place of employment along with the dates employed. (Remember, the information should be presented in such a way that the reader can focus first on your professional experience and skills.)

Community Service/Volunteer Work: (*Optional*)

Family Care/Household Management Experience: (*Optional*)

International Experience: (*Optional*)

Special Distinctions: (*Optional*)

Education:
List professional training and/or college(s) first and then high school attended, with date of graduation along with degree and major. Underline names of schools. List most recent program first and work backward, in order.

Courses: (*Optional*)
If listing courses helps clarify some of your specific skills, then list them following the same rule as noted in a chronological résumé. Most skills can be listed in the section on professional experience and skills.

References: (*Optional*)
(Follow the rule noted on the chronological résumé.

Portfolio:
Follow the rule noted on the chronological résumé.

Sample Functional Résumé

ROSE MARTINSON

PERMANENT ADDRESS:

43 Racine Avenue
Skokie, Illinois 60076
(847) 546-7898
Fax: (847) 546-7022

PROFESSIONAL OBJECTIVE:
To obtain an executive secretarial position within a major corporation which will benefit from my administrative, communication, and interpersonal skills.

RELEVANT EXPERIENCE & SKILLS:
Production
- Generated all personal and business correspondence via IBM word processor.
- Processed over 25,000 full- and part-time job opportunities annually.
- Arranged hotel and travel accommodations for executive staff.
- Demonstrated ability to type 75 wpm and take shorthand at 120 wpm.
- Gained knowledge of desktop publishing, WordPerfect, and Lotus 1-2-3.

Planning/Promotion
- Coordinated daily schedules of management staff.
- Supervised four clerical assistants.
- Initiated and implemented new filing system and interoffice communication procedural manual.
- Assisted in formulation of marketing strategies.
- Aided in generation of promotional materials serving as liaison among professional photographers, printers, and media personnel.
- Coordinated the planning and execution of a one-day conference on stress management.

EMPLOYMENT HISTORY:

1994–present	Northwestern University, Evanston, IL
	Administrative Assistant to Placement
1992–94	The Field Foundation, Chicago, IL
	Administrative Assistant to Director of Office Services
1990–92	Howard T. Mack, Inc., Skokie, IL
	Administrative Assistant to Associate Personnel Director

EDUCATION:

1990	Bryant & Stratton Business Institute, Buffalo, NY
	A.S. Administrative Management

References available upon request.

Portfolio available upon request.

ACTIVITY 7-2 • *Functional Résumé Worksheet*

Before you write your functional résumé, you should have a clear picture of what you can include in each section. Fill in all of the information that best describes the experiences you have had, and then select those you will include on your functional résumé.

YOUR NAME

_____
(First name)   (Middle initial)   (Last name)

Permanent Address: **Temporary Address:**

_____   _____
(street)   (street)

_____   _____
(city, state, zip code)   (city, state, zip code)

_____   _____
(area code) telephone number   (area code) telephone number

_____   _____
(area code) fax number   (area code) fax number

Professional Objective:

_____

_____

_____

Professional Experience & Skills:

_____

_____

_____

_____

_____

Employment History:

Company name: _____

Company address: _____

Position held: _____

Company name: _____

Company address: _____

Position held: _____

Company name: _____

Company address: _____

Position held: _____

Company name: _____

Company address: _____

Position held: _____

Company name: _____

Company address: _____

Position held: _____

Company name: _____

Company address: _____

Position held: _____

Community Service/Volunteer Work: (*Optional*)

_____

_____

_____

_____

Family Care/Household Management: (*Optional*)

_____

_____

_____

_____

International Experience: (*Optional*)

_____

_____

_____

_____

Special Distinctions: (*Optional*)

_____

_____

_____

_____

Education:

College name: _____

College address: _____

_____

Degree received: _____

High school name: (optional) _____

High school address: _____

_____

Diploma received: _____

Courses: (*Optional*)

_____

_____

_____

References: (*Optional*)

Name: _____

Company name: _____

Street address: _____

_____

_____

City, state, zip code: _____

(area code) phone number: _____

Name: _____

Company name: _____

Street address: _____

_____

_____

City, state, zip code: _____

(area code) phone number: _____

Name: _____

Company name: _____

Street address: _____

_____

_____

City, state, zip code: _____

(area code) phone number: _____

Writing Your Own Résumé

Power Words That Describe Your Skills

The following is a list of action verbs and personal traits organized to help you emphasize particular sets of skills on your résumé. Note that these words are meant to describe your accomplishments in a lively and specific way. Also note that the list is arranged according to the skills discussed in Chapter 5.

Basic Skills

Math	Interviewed	Drafted	**Speaking**	Negotiated
Added	Figured	Edited	Addressed	Participated
Balanced	Reconciled	Formulated	Arbitrated	Persuaded
Billed	Subtracted	Published	Convinced	Presented
Calculated	Tabulated	Translated	Debated	Presided
Cashed	Tallied	Wrote	Directed	Promoted
Compared			Enlisted	Publicized
Compounded	**Writing**	**Reading**	Influenced	Recruited
Computed	Arranged	Edited	Interpreted	Represented
Counted	Authored	Proofread	Lectured	Sold
Divided	Corresponded	Reviewed	Moderated	Spoke
	Developed	Scanned		

Thinking Skills

Creative Thinking	Introduced	**Decision Making**	Predicted	Implemented
Authored	Improvised	Concluded	Envisioned	Investigated
Conceived	Invented	Recommended	Imagined	Rectified
Composed	Launched	Evaluated	Projected	Reduced
Created	Marketed	Determined	Planned	Risked
Designed	Originated			
Developed	Piloted	**Know How to**	**Problem Solving**	**Reasoning**
Devised	Planned	**Learn**	Analyzed	Concluded
Directed	Prepared	Interpreted	Assessed	Connected
Enhanced	Produced	Understand	Corrected	Deduced
Established	Proposed	Analyzed	Diagnosed	Determined
Formulated	Set up	Applied	Discovered	Judged
Illustrated	Structured	Recalled	Diverted	Proved
Improved	Wrote	Studied	Examined	Summarized
Initiated	Resourced		Fixed	
		Visualization	Identified	
		Anticipated		

Personal Qualities

Responsibility	Handled	**Self-Management**	Performed	**Self-Esteem**
Earned	Hired	Managed	Planned	Initiated
Fired	Ran	Organized	Prioritized	Risked
Financed	Took charge	Overcame		Strengthened

Integrity
Defended
Protected
Preserved

Sociability
Aided
Assisted
Attended
Counseled
Encouraged
Helped
Volunteered

Honesty
Admitted
Credited

Financial Responsibility
Borrowed
Earned
Financed
Paid
Saved

Technical Skills
Assembled
Built
Coded
Computed
Constructed
Designed
Dispatched
Displayed

Drafted
Engineered
Fed
Filed
Fitted
Fixed
Manufactured
Measured
Located
Logged
Operated
Overhauled
Packaged
Packed
Programmed
Rebuilt
Reconstructed
Remodeled
Repaired
Routed
Serviced
Stored
Transported
Typed
Upgraded

Academic Achievement
Accomplished
Achieved
Completed
Improved

Performed

Leadership and Management
Administered
Analyzed
Assigned
Authorized
Chaired
Consolidated
Contracted
Controlled
Coordinated
Delegated
Developed
Directed
Evaluated
Enacted
Established
Exceeded
Executed
Expanded
Guided
Headed
Implemented
Improved
Incorporated
Increased
Initiated
Instituted
Investigated
Launched

Led
Maintained
Managed
Mediated
Negotiated
Organized
Oversaw
Performed
Planned
Prioritized
Produced
Proposed
Recommended
Reduced
Repositioned
Retained
Reviewed
Scheduled
Revised
Sorted
Strengthened
Supervised

Professionalism
Committed
Dependable
Loyal
Presentable
Punctual
Reliable

References
Recommended
Referred

Special Distinctions
Awarded
Earned
Honored
Recognized
Won

Global Perspective
Adaptable
Flexible
Multi-lingual
Open
Patient
Sensitive
Tolerant
Understanding

Role Models and Mentors
Emulate
Learn

Career Planning
Assessed
Focused
Planned

Career Management
Assessed

Job Search Skills
Organized
Packaged
Planned
Promoted
Sold

Other Skill Areas

Financial Management
Allocated
Analyzed
Appraised
Audited
Balanced
Budgeted

Calculated
Forecast
Managed
Marketed
Planned
Projected a budget

Teaching
Advised

Clarified
Coached
Communicated
Encouraged
Evaluated
Explained
Guided
Influenced

Informed
Instructed
Interpreted
Lectured
Persuaded
Stimulated
Trained

Human Resources
Advised
Assessed
Clarified
Coached
Collaborated
Consulted
Counseled

Diagnosed	Represented	Compared	Identified	Retrieved
Educated	Sponsored	Compiled	Implemented	Reviewed
Employed	Strengthened	Completed	Inspected	Scheduled
Grouped	Trained	Computed	Interpreted	Screened
Guided	**Clerical and**	Critiqued	Interviewed	Summarized
Handled	**Research**	Decreased	Investigated	Surveyed
Hired	Arranged	Diagnosed	Monitored	Systemized
Integrated	Automated	Dispatched	Operated	Tabulated
Mediated	Budgeted	Distributed	Organized	Validated
Monitored	Calculated	Evaluated	Prepared	Verified
Motivated	Cataloged	Examined	Processed	
Negotiated	Classified	Executed	Purchased	
Recruited	Collected	Generated	Recorded	

ACTIVITY 7-3 • *Choosing Power Words for Your Résumé*

Review the experience(s) you chose to stress on your résumé (education, work, community service/volunteer work, international, military, family care/household management—recall Chapter 5).

Review the primary skill sets and the related skill sets listed within each type of experience. Then, using the list of power words for résumés arranged by skill sets, find the lists of skill sets that match the experience you are going to describe and the list of possible skills to include in the descriptions of your experience.

Community Service/Volunteer Work   ← Experience
                                                           ← Skill sets
Primary Skill Sets:
Leadership and Management
Personal Qualities
Teaching

Related Skill Sets: ← Skill sets
Human Resource Skills
Clerical and Research Skills

Power Words

Leadership and Management	**Teaching**
Administered	Advised
Analyzed	Clarified
Assigned	Coached
(etc.)	(etc.)

Fill in your list of experience and the skill sets that go with it.

← Experience →

_____ **Primary Skill Sets:** **Related Skill Sets:**	_____ **Primary Skill Sets:** **Related Skill Sets:**

For each of the skill sets above, review the list of power words for résumés and write down the words you think best describe some of your skills.

Example:

Your skill set: ___Teaching_____   Your skill set: _____

Your skills: ___Advised_____   Your skills: _____

_____   _____

_____   _____

_____   _____

Your skill set: _____   Your skill set: _____

Your skills: _____   Your skills: _____

_____   _____

_____   _____

_____   _____

Your skill set: _____   Your skill set: _____

Your skills: _____   Your skills: _____

_____   _____

_____   _____

_____   _____

Your skill set: _____   Your skill set: _____

Your skills: _____   Your skills: _____

_____   _____

_____   _____

_____   _____

Matching Résumé Format to Skills and Experience

Each type of experience develops different sets of skills. Primary skills sets are the predominant ones and related skills are the additional ones developed through each experience. Use the following guide to help you match the best résumé format to the type of experience and skills you have.

Experiences	Recommended Résumé Format

Educational Experience
Primary Skill Sets:
  Basic Skills
  Thinking Skills
  Personal Qualities
  Academic Achievement
  Professionalism
  Technical Skills
Related Skill Sets:
  Financial Responsibility
  References
	Chronological

Work Experience
Primary Skill Sets:
  Basic Skills
  Thinking Skills
  Personal Qualities
  Technical Skills
  Professionalism
  Leadership and Management Skills
  Financial Responsibility
Related Skill Sets:
  Career Planning
  Job Search Tech
  Human Resource Skills
  Career Management
  Financial Management
  Clerical and Research Skills
	Chronological or functional

Community Service/Volunteer Work
Primary Skill Sets:
  Leadership and Management
  Personal Qualities
  Teaching
Related Skill Sets:
  Human Resource Skills
  Clerical and Research Skills
	Functional

International Experience
Primary Skill Set:
  Global Perspective
Related Skill Set:
  Personal Qualities
	Functional

Military Experience
Primary Skill Sets:
  Leadership and Management Skills
  Technical Skills
  Teaching Skills
  Human Resource Skills
	Chronological or functional

Experiences	Recommended Résumé Format
Related Skill Sets: Clerical and Research Skills Personal Qualities	
Family Care/Household Management Primary Skill Sets: Thinking Skills Personal Qualities Financial Responsibility Teaching Financial Management Related Skill Set: Leadership and Management	Functional

Most of us gain our experience at school or work, in the community or at home. Some also gain experience through the military or international travel. Before deciding the type of résumé you will use and the skills you should stress on it, you should assess what experiences you have to emphasize the most on your résumé.

ACTIVITY 7-4 • *Assessing Your Experience*

Which of the following most clearly represents the experience upon which you are basing your résumé? Place a *1* in the area(s) from which you have gained the most experience, a *2* in the area(s) from which you have gained some experience, and a *3* in the area(s) from which you have gained little or no experience.

☐ Education/academic achievement   ☐ International experience

☐ Community service/volunteer work   ☐ Family care/household management

☐ Work experience   ☐ Military

Review your assessment. The areas you have numbered 1 or 2 are the experiences on which you will build your résumé. After reviewing the above text and checklist, which résumé format will you use? Why?

_____

_____

_____

_____

_____

ACTIVITY 7-5 • *Résumé Preparation Checklist*

Before printing the final copy of your résumé, review this résumé preparation checklist to be sure your résumé is ready to present to a prospective employer.

Place a check (✔) next to the steps you have already completed.

☐ My most current address and phone number are listed.

☐ My professional objective is clearly stated.

☐ My résumé is no more than two pages.

☐ I've chosen the proper format for my résumé.

☐ I've used the appropriate action verbs or personal qualities to describe my qualifications.

☐ I have emphasized all my strengths.

☐ All of my major accomplishments are listed.

☐ I have used numbers, percentages, and other details to describe how my accomplishments will add value to a company.

☐ My résumé can be easily scanned to pick up key words (see p. 131).

☐ I've chosen white, off-white, blue, or gray résumé paper of good stock.

☐ Someone else has proofread my résumé.

☐ My résumé contains at least one or two special skills or special distinctions that help me stand out among other applicants.

If one or more of the above steps has not been taken, do not print and distribute your résumé. Complete all missing steps, and you will feel confident about your final product.

Nontraditional Résumés

Perhaps the greatest impact the electronic age has had on your job search is the shift from using paper résumés to using résumés created, stored, and transmitted by various forms of electronic technology. Résumés can be sent electronically into employment databases around the world, along with an image of you or a sample of your work. Audio and video résumés help to personalize your self-presentation to prospective employers. In addition to developing an excellent traditional résumé, you should explore which nontraditional résumés best represent you. The following are some of the choices you have.

Electronic Résumés

An electronic résumé is one that is put on-line through an employment service offered on the Internet. The résumé can be sourced on the system by an employer who can communicate directly to the candidate electronically.

Disk Résumés

Many companies using electronic résumé tracking systems actually prefer to receive a résumé that has been stored on a disk. The disk can be inserted directly into the tracking system for future retrieval. Having a disk résumé in addition to your traditional résumé will help you stay in the running for jobs with companies that rely solely on electronic tracking systems for candidate identification. Résumé disks are easy to store, update, and place in the mail to a prospective employer.

Interactive Résumés

A marketing firm in Columbus, Ohio, talks about the most creative résumé it has seen to date. The interactive résumé was received in the mail on a diskette with a cover letter wrapped around it. The "résumé" included an animated 3-D rendering of the job candidate's face, a portfolio of his illustrations, and a list of work experience and references that could be printed out. The job candidate was a college graduate seeking a job as a multimedia designer. His interactive résumé was so impressive it generated 75 inquiries and 30 job offers.[1]

Video Résumés

A professionally prepared video of yourself can be an effective alternative to a traditional résumé if used properly. Your video may show you demonstrating a skill (teaching, speaking in public, making a culinary or pastry arts presentation, etc.) or showing and explaining the contents of your career portfolio. If you must mail your résumé to a prospective employer and you have a comprehensive portfolio to support it, a video can easily make your portfolio portable. A videotape of your portfolio presentation obviously should be done only if you can effectively portray confidence, professionalism, and skill through this medium.

Audio Résumés

An audiotape can be prepared on which you describe your background, credentials, and career goal verbally to a prospective employer. This can be particularly effective for job candidates who wish to demonstrate public speaking skills, foreign language and translation skills, or sales skills. There are companies that can package your audiotape so that there is a picture of you on the package cover and a short written summary of your qualifications on the inside cover. An audiotape can also become a part of your career portfolio.

Creative Résumés

Certain professions lend themselves more to nontraditional styles of résumés than others do. For example, creativity is an important skill in the fields of advertising, culinary arts, and retail management. An advertising graduate may send a prospec-

[1]*USA Today,* September 30, 1994.

tive employer a "display ad" of skills and credentials; a culinary arts graduate may present a four-sided résumé in a menu format; and a retail graduate may present a four-sided résumé in the form of a catalog of skills.

Before considering using a creative résumé, however, you should be sure that this is appropriate for your field. Certainly, video, audio, and disk résumés are great alternatives for job candidates in highly creative fields, but candidates applying for a job in the fields of accounting, business management, or education should use a more traditional approach to their résumé.

Scannable Résumés

Résumé scanning software and automated applicant tracking systems are being used by leading employers worldwide. Computerized résumé searches do all of the following:

1. Read résumés with a scanner.
2. Categorize applicants by job possibilities.
3. Rank applicants.
4. Generate letters of rejection or interview offers.
5. Store information for future openings.
6. Store actual résumé images.[2]

Restrac and Resumix are two popular automated applicant tracking systems being used by companies today. When résumés arrive at a company using such a system, they are fed through a scanner. The scanner sends a picture of the document to a computer. The computer "reads" each résumé quickly; identifies keywords; and, based on the keywords it reads, stashes the résumé in an appropriate database file. When a job opening occurs, an employer tells the applicant tracking system the keywords associated with the position and instructs it to find the résumés that contain matching keywords. What is important for you, as the job candidate, to know is that a scannable résumé is built more on nouns than on the action words or verbs stressed in a traditional résumé. These nouns usually describe as many of the candidate's specific skills as possible so that those keywords are readily identified in the scanner.

A Sampling of Keywords from a Software Database

Word Processor	Retail Marketer
Ability	Inventory turns
Display write 5	Point of sale
Lotus Manuscript	UPC scanner
Microsoft Word	Sell-through
Ready Set Go	Negotiate commercial terms
Unix Editor	Evaluation training programs

The following pages offer an example of how a traditional functional résumé is turned into a scannable functional résumé.

[2]From *Small Business News.*

Sample Functional/Traditional Résumé

ROSE MARTINSON

43 Racine Avenue
Skokie, Illinois 60076
(847) 546-7898
Fax: (847) 546-7022

PROFESSIONAL OBJECTIVE:
To obtain an executive secretarial position within a major corporation which will benefit from my administrative, communication, and interpersonal skills.

RELEVANT EXPERIENCE & SKILLS:
Production
- Generated all personal and business correspondence via IBM word processor.
- Processed over 25,000 full- and part-time job opportunities annually.
- Arranged hotel and travel accommodations for executive staff.
- Demonstrated ability to type 75 wpm and take shorthand at 120 wpm.
- Gained knowledge of desktop publishing, WordPerfect, and Lotus 1-2-3.

Planning/Promotion
- Coordinated daily schedules of management staff.
- Supervised four clerical assistants.
- Initiated and implemented new filing system and interoffice communication procedural manual.
- Assisted in formulation of marketing strategies.
- Aided in generation of promotional materials serving as liaison among professional photographers, printers, and media personnel.
- Coordinated the planning and execution of a one-day conference on stress management.

EMPLOYMENT HISTORY:

1994–present	Northwestern University, Evanston, IL
	Administrative Assistant to Placement
1992–94	The Field Foundation, Chicago, IL
	Administrative Assistant to Director of Office Services
1990–92	Howard T. Mack, Inc., Skokie, IL
	Administrative Assistant to Associate Personnel Director

EDUCATION:

1990	Bryant & Stratton Business Institute, Buffalo, NY
	A.S. Administrative Management

References available upon request.

Portfolio available upon request.

Sample Scannable Functional Résumé

ROSE MARTINSON

PROFESSIONAL OBJECTIVE:

Keywords

Administrative Assistant.	Administrative skills.
Communication skills.	Interpersonal skills.
Generated correspondence.	IBM word processor.
Desktop publishing.	WordPerfect.
Lotus 1-2-3.	Arranged accommodations.
Typing 75 wpm.	Shorthand 120 wpm.
Coordinated schedules.	Supervised staff.
Initiated.	Implemented new system.
Marketing strategies.	Promotional materials.
Liaison.	Planned conference.
A.S. Administrative Asst.	Bryant & Stratton Business Institute.
Reference.	Portfolio.

PROFESSIONAL EXPERIENCE & SKILLS:

Production

Generated all personal and business correspondence via IBM word processor.
Processed over 25,000 full- and part-time job opportunities annually.
Arranged hotel and travel accommodations for executive staff.
Typing 75 wpm.
Shorthand 120 wpm.
Knowledge of desktop publishing, WordPerfect, and Lotus 1-2-3.

Planning/Promotion

Coordinated daily schedules of management staff.
Supervised four clerical assistants.
Initiated and implemented new filing system and interoffice communication procedural manual.
Assisted in formulation of marketing strategies.
Aided in generation of promotional materials serving as liaison among professional photographers, printers, and media personnel.
Coordinated the planning and execution of a one-day conference on stress management.

EMPLOYMENT HISTORY:

1994–present	Northwestern University, Evanston, IL Administrative Assistant to Placement
1992–1994	The Field Foundation, Chicago, IL Administrative Assistant to Director of Office Services
1990–1992	Howard T. Mack, Inc., Skokie, IL Administrative Assistant to Associate Personnel Director

EDUCATION:

1990	Bryant & Stratton Business Institute, Buffalo, NY A.S. Administrative Management

REFERENCES: Available upon request

PORTFOLIO: Available upon request

INTERNATIONAL CAREER DIRECTIONS

Curriculum Vitae

For job candidates who are applying for a job outside the United States with a foreign-based firm, it is wise to prepare a curriculum vitae. The curriculum vitae is a very detailed résumé. In contrast to briefer U.S.–style résumés, the best of which are outcome oriented and achievement focused, the curriculum vitae can be as long as four pages. Employers in different cultures emphasize different qualifications as being important in a job applicant. For instance, although work experience is certainly valuable to an international job search, your education and your own personality and background are very important. The fact that you have a particular career path in mind is important to you, but career tracking as we know it does not exist outside the United States. Because in many countries jobs are appointed to individuals by the government or influential people in the country, self-promotion and previous work experience do not play as much of a role in the hiring process. Job appointments are made according to available positions, not according to the candidate's preference.

Outside the United States, more emphasis is given to a detailed chronology of academic and formal work experiences, and awards and recognitions, and less to the professional objective and special skills.

If you are dealing with a U.S. firm overseas, go ahead and use your American résumé. If the company is foreign based, prepare a curriculum vitae using the following guidelines.

Tips to Turn Your American Résumé into a Curriculum Vitae

1. For a non-English-speaking country, have your curriculum vitae translated into the appropriate language. Send both the English and native-language version.

2. Use the first page or two for personal information and education, followed by a career objective identifying the position you seek, and then pages of detailed work histories.

3. Personal information can include relevant facts such as dual citizenship, foreign language fluency, passport number and date of expiration, previous overseas experiences, security clearance, foreign travel experience, student temporary work permits, and personal interests and hobbies that suggest you'll easily adapt to an overseas environment. Unless untrue, say you have excellent health.

4. Work histories can be followed by bulleted accomplishments, highlighting what you achieved for your employer.

5. Include your photograph. Unlike in the United States, it is common to attach a passport-size photo of yourself to your curriculum vitae. Although a photo is not required, some employers prefer it because it helps them remember you. However, if you do not have a recent, clear, black-and-white or color photo of just your face, do not send a photo.

A current book on working abroad offers further advice for preparing your curriculum vitae:

• Use good-quality European-sized (21 2 29.7 cm) white paper. If you cannot get European-sized paper, use the American 8 1/2≤ 2 11≤ paper.

• Use the same sized paper for both your curriculum vitae and your cover letter. If you are having your résumé printed on American paper and then moving abroad, be sure to pack enough blank American paper and envelopes to continue your job search.

- Do not use colored paper, even a pale shade.
- Do not write CV or Curriculum Vitae as a title at the top of the page. It is obvious what it is.
- Do not write a title in another language before your name—for example, Monsieur, Madame, or Mademoiselle in French—on your résumé or cover letter.
- Don't use American abbreviations for state names or the name of your school.
- Don't include street addresses of former employers; just list the city, state, and country.[2]

Sample Format for a Curriculum Vitae

YOUR NAME

Permanent Address: **Temporary Address:**
Street address   Street address
City, State, Zip code   City, State, Zip code
  (Country)   (Country)
Phone (country code)   Phone (country code)
  (city code) number   (city code) number
Fax (country code)   Fax (country code)
  (city code) number   (city code) number

PERSONAL DATA: (Optional, but preferred in some countries)
Nationality:
Marital status:
Date of birth:
Driver's license:
Work permit:
Visa: Yes   No   Type of Visa:_____
Passport number:

OBJECTIVE:

EDUCATION:
In many countries outside the United States, education is weighed just as heavily as work experience when considering a candidate for a job. It is very important to list the schools you attended. List your most recent school first and continue to list others in order; include dates attended and degrees/diplomas received. Educational honors/awards should also be listed in this section. Be sure to highlight any study-abroad experience.

WORK EXPERIENCE:
Include part-time, full-time, and summer work, as well as internships, externships, and cooperative educational experience with brief descriptions and dates of employment. List the most recent job first and work down. If your employment history includes many short-term miscellaneous jobs, use the following rules:
1. List those relevant to the position for which you are applying.
2. List those you held for the longest periods of time.
3. List all international work experience you have had.

[2]From Carol Pineau and Maureen Kelly, *Working in France* (Boston, MA: Frank Books, 1991).

DIVERS: (This is sort of a catchall term that includes everything other than education and work.)

Awards:	Cite any awards you have received. Remember to list educational awards in the education section and work experience awards in the work experience section.
Published work:	List any articles, papers, or books you have personally written that have been published. Published work is a highly regarded credential in most countries throughout the world.
Hobbies/interests:	List your special interests and hobbies.

INTERNATIONAL TRAVEL:

List places throughout the world where you have traveled for either business, pleasure, or an educational experience. If you lived in another country for a period of three months or more, state that.

LANGUAGE(S) SPOKEN:

List all languages you can speak fluently. If you can read some languages well, but not speak the language fluently, state that.

REFERENCES:

List all references' names, titles, addresses, and phone numbers here. You should list three to five names. References of employers and instructors are particularly valuable, as are those of any government officials.

(A **photo** of yourself is optional but is preferred.)

Portfolio available upon request. (Include if you have a career portfolio.)

American Résumé

SUZANNE LECLAIRE

Permanent Address:
8496 Orange Trail
Baltimore, MD 66681
(401) 623-8401
(401) 623-9223

Temporary Address:
210 Weybosset Street
Cleveland, OH 58629
(616) 555-1412

PROFESSIONAL EXPERIENCE
1993–present
Director of Marketing, The Sports Attic, Cleveland, OH
- Oversaw marketing campaigns for chain of 45 Midwest sporting goods stores.
- Developed special promotional campaigns to tie in with gift-giving seasons.
- Coordinated newspaper advertising in-house, creating an annual savings of $230,000.

1990–1993
Regional Manager, The Ski Hut, Cleveland, OH
- Responsible for 18 area stores in national chain of 320 ski equipment stores.
- Organized six ski-school racing camps in the Midwest.
- Increased regional sales by 35% in first two years.
- Won Top Regional Manager award at company's national meeting, 1991 and 1992.

1988–1990
Assistant Manager (1988), Store Manager (1989–90), The Ski Hut, Columbus, OH
- Hired, trained, assisted, and motivated employees.
- Created weekly work schedules for staff.
- Handled all bookkeeping and banking.
- Made presentations at national sales conference.

EDUCATION
Case Western Reserve University, Cleveland, OH

1995   Master of Business Administration
Areas of specialty: Marketing and Finance

1991   Bachelor of Arts, graduated cum laude
Major in Economics, minor in French
Dean's list all semesters

COMMUNITY SERVICE/VOLUNTEER WORK
1992–1994   American Red Cross, Cleveland Chapter
As fund-raising chairperson, raised $75,000 through a variety of community projects.
Managed projects and organized volunteers.

1991   Small Business Association, Columbus, OH
Served as secretary.

1990   Supervised U.S. student groups at ski-racing school in Val d'Isere, France.

Portfolio available upon request.

Sample Curriculum Vitae*

SUZANNE LECLAIRE

Permanent Address:
8496 Orange Trail
Baltimore, MD 66681
U.S.A.
(401) 623-8401
(401) 623-9223

Temporary Address:
91-63 Montparnasse
Paris
France
(1) 45.55.01.15
(1) 45.56.12.26

Personal Data:
Nationality: American
Marital status: Single
Date of birth: 8/15/73
Driver's license: MD License # 9284633810
Work permit: Yes, 6/95–6/96
Visa: Yes
Passport number: 004692398

EDUCATION:

1995   Case Western Reserve University, Cleveland, OH
       Master of Business Administration
       Areas of specialty: Marketing and Finance

1991   Bachelor of Arts, graduated cum laude
       Major in Economics, minor in French
       Dean's list *all* semesters

WORK EXPERIENCE:

1993–present   **Director of Marketing**
               The Sports Attic
               Cleveland, OH
               • Oversee marketing campaigns for chain of 15 Midwest sporting goods stores.
               • Developed special promotional campaigns to tie in with gift-giving seasons.
               • Coordinated newspaper advertising in-house, creating an annual savings of $230,000.

1990–1993   **Regional Manager**
               The Ski Hut
               Cleveland, OH
               • Responsible for 18 area stores in national chain of 320 ski equipment stores.
               • Organized six ski-school racing camps in the Midwest.
               • Increased regional sales by 35% in first two years.
               • Won Top Regional Manager award at company's national meeting, 1991 and 1992.

*This is the curriculum vitae of an American student who, after graduation, moved to France to get a job.

1988–1990	**Assistant Store Manager** (1988)
	Store Manager (1989, 1990)
	The Ski Hut
	Columbus, OH

- Hired, trained, assisted, and motivated employees.
- Created weekly work schedules for staff.
- Handled all bookkeeping and banking.
- Made presentations at national sales conference.

1988	**Sales Associate Intern**
	Galeries Lafayette
	Hausmann
	Paris, France

Divers:

1992–1994	American Red Cross, Cleveland Chapter
	As fund-raising chairperson, raised $75,000 through a variety of community projects. Managed projects and organized volunteers.

1991	Small Business Association, Columbus, OH
	Served as secretary.

1990	Supervised U.S. student groups at ski-racing school in Val d'Isere, France.

Languages: Speak French fluently.

References: Mr. Joseph Corrigan
Vice President
Ski Hut
Columbus, OH

Phone: (703) 924-6368
Fax: (703) 924-6463

Ms. Carolyn Ellsworth
Store Manager
The Sports Attic
Cleveland, OH

Phone: (701) 724-9293
Fax: (701) 724-3439

Professor Paul Horbrath
School of Arts & Sciences
Case Western Reserve University
Cleveland, OH

Phone: (701) 724-0895
Fax: (701) 725-9119

Portfolio available upon request.

ACTIVITY 7-6 • *American Résumé versus Curriculum Vitae*

Read carefully the content of the sample curriculum vitae on pp. 138–39. Then read the American résumé on p. 141. Make a list of the differences between the two.

American Résumé   **Curriculum Vitae**

_____   _____

_____   _____

_____   _____

_____   _____

Once you have thoroughly listed the differences between the two, make a list of the changes you will make to turn your résumé from an American résumé to a curriculum vitae or vice versa.

_____

_____

_____

_____

_____

_____

Job Applications

Completed job applications are commonly required by employers as part of the job search process. They are used by human resource departments for candidates who apply for a job in person at a company. Job applications are often used during interviews conducted at your school. When you are asked to complete a job application prior to an interview, you should submit your résumé along with it, to be sure that your qualifications are presented in the best light. One purpose of the job application is to obtain factual information about you (e.g., social security number, emergency information, family relationships) that can be used for payroll or health insurance. Although the other purpose of the job application is to obtain information about your employment history, your professional qualifications are usually expressed better in your résumé.

On a job application you are simply presenting information an employer needs to see to determine whether you should be considered for a particular job. The job application is a screening device. It does not get you the job. Sometimes you will be asked to complete a job application after you've been hired so that the actual information about you needed by the human resources department can be recorded and used to process the necessary paperwork to start you as a new employee. You will want to ensure that your job application is the best one an employer sees.

The following are the main parts of a typical job application:

Identification

Name
Social security number

Personal Data

Alien registration number or immigration status
Address
Telephone number
Citizenship
Emergency information

Health

General health
Disabilities and physical limitations
Emotional and mental disorders
Family illness
Worker's compensation
Attendance

Educational History

Education and formal training
Future schooling

Job Interest

Position desired
Salary desired
Availability
Transportation

Experience

Work experience
Military experience
Volunteer activities
Certification, registration, and licenses
Professional associations
Clubs and organizations
Hobbies, interests, and leisure-time activities
Other skills

Miscellaneous

Future plans
References
Convictions (if applicable)

Points to Remember When Completing a Job Application

Name. Be sure to *print* your name where asked on the application and *sign* neatly on the signature line. You should carefully read and verify all statements on the application before signing it. Never list a nickname. Always use your complete legal name.

Social Security Number. Be sure to print your social security number so that it is readable and *correct!* Many companies use their employees' social security numbers in filing and computer systems. An error in your social security number could cause problems with your payments, benefits, taxes, retirement, and unemployment ac-

count. If you do not have a social security number, you should apply now at the nearest social security office or post office.

Address.   Before you list your address, read instructions. Then be prepared to put all your data in the correct spaces. If the application does not ask for a certain order, list in the following order: your street address, rural route or box number, city, state, and zip code. Consider your answer when asked how long you have lived at a certain address. This information will give employers an impression of your stability.

Telephone Number.   A source of frustration for an employer is wanting to reach a good candidate and not being able to do so because the candidate has either forgotten to leave a telephone number or has left an incorrect one. List a phone number that is likely to be answered during the day. If no one will be answering your phone, or if you do not have a phone, list the number of someone who can accept messages for you. Choose someone who will be polite, take your message accurately, and get the message to you very quickly. If you are using an answering machine to accept your messages, be sure to create a positive impression on the caller by recording a professional sounding message.

Date and Place of Birth.   You may be asked to give the date of your birth on some applications. It is important that you give the right information. This date is used to compute your insurance and retirement plans after you are hired. You can be fired for falsifying information on a job application. Remember that the law will be on your side if you are *denied* a job because of your age.

Proof of Age.   You may be asked to prove your age for some employers. Most employers accept a driver's license as proof of age. If you do not have a driver's license, get a copy of your birth certificate or any legal document that shows your age.

Citizenship.   You may be asked to indicate whether or not you are a citizen of the United States. Noncitizens are usually asked to list their visa type and number.

General Health.   It will benefit you the most if you can list your health as excellent. If you have a health problem that will not affect your ability to do the job you want, do not note any negative information on your application. Leave the health sections blank if necessary and be prepared to discuss your health during an interview. If you have a health problem, ask your doctor if it will in any way impair your ability to perform your job. If your doctor thinks the problem would be limiting, ask for advice on how to handle this on a job application.

Education and Formal Training.   You should be able to account for all the time you spent in school or in training. This information could be important in explaining gaps in your employment history. It will also clearly indicate to employers whether or not you meet one of the primary requirements for the job that is available.

Salary Desired.   If you have not recently researched the job market, be careful how you answer this question. You do not want to undersell yourself or ask for such a high salary that you rule yourself out of the competition. You can research the job market by following these suggestions:

Read want ads that list salaries for similar positions.

Call your local employment office or job placement office and ask the salary range for the type of job you are seeking.

Talk with people who do the kind of work you want.

You may list a specific salary, give a high-low range, or leave the space blank. Another alternative is to respond with the word *open*. This is a positive word. It will not commit you to a future either too low or too high. When considering a salary offer, don't forget to consider the benefits as well as the base salary. Added benefits can make one salary more valuable than a slightly higher one without benefits. Mentally adjust your desired salary according to the benefits, then state the salary you want.

Work Experience.   You should be well prepared to list your work history. List the data for your most recent job first. List your next most recent job in the next form, and so on. If you have no work experience, leave the spaces blank and be prepared to offset this during an interview.

Professional Organizations.   Employers may be interested in the professional organizations to which you belong. Such membership is especially important if the organization and job are directly related.

Hobbies, Interests, and Leisure-Time Activities.   What you do with your free time tells an employer much about your interests and drive. An employer may have a special interest in you if your hobby relates closely to your job.

References.   Consider the following people to be your references:

Former employers, supervisors, and co-workers.

Former teachers, instructors, and professors.

Your minister, priest, or rabbi.

Acquaintances who have job titles indicating responsibility.

Long-time acquaintances.

Many job-seekers think that employers do *not* contact references. This is a myth. Employers *often* contact references—especially when the job includes significant responsibility.

How to Complete a Job Application

Use a Pen.   Do not use a pencil; use only a black or blue pen. Your pen should let you print neatly without blobs, smudges, or smears. You may want to use a fine-point pen. This kind of pen makes it easier to print small when you must write in small blanks or boxes. It is wise to carry a spare pen with the same ink color and line width as your first pen.

Bring Your Résumé.   If you prefer, you may carry an extra résumé with you to use as a reminder of important information as well. In fact, it is wise to be prepared to present a résumé should you obtain an immediate interview.

Follow Instructions.   Be sure to read all the instructions before writing anything on an application. Many applications begin with general instructions, such as "Print in ink," or "To be handprinted in ink," or "Typewritten." Separate instructions may tell you not to put any data in certain spaces.

   Following instructions is important. Employers want to hire people who can follow instructions on the job. Employers will not have a high regard for your dependability and skill if you cannot follow instructions on an application.

The Dash.   Some application questions *will not apply to you.* Make a short dash (—) after each of these questions. The dash is simple; it tells the employer you have read the question but it does not apply to you.

Blank Spaces.   It is sometimes better to leave a blank space on your application. An application will not necessarily get you a job, but it can keep you from being considered for a job. If an honest answer to an application question is negative or can easily be misunderstood, leave this item blank. Do not even make a dash in this space.

ACTIVITY 7-7 • *Sample Job Application*

Study the following job application for employment to get an idea of what a typical job application looks like. Fill in each section accurately. Make sure you understand the questions you are required to answer, and be sure you feel comfortable with each response.

Once you have completed the job application, give it to someone to review. Discuss which sections you had the most difficulty with and why. Get input from others how to handle any sections about which you are uncertain.

XYZ CORPORATION
Application for Employment

INCOMPLETE APPLICATIONS WILL NOT BE CONSIDERED

NAME (Last First Middle)				Date	
Permanent Address	City	State	Zip	Area Code Phone Number	
Temporary Address	City	State	Zip	Area Code Phone Number	
Birth Date Male ☐ Female ☐				Social Security Number	

Are you applying for: Full Time ☐   Part Time ☐   Seasonal ☐   Other ☐

EDUCATIONAL HISTORY

School	Name and Location	Major	Grades			Circle Highest Grade Completed	Type of Degree or Certificate Recvd.	Date of Leaving
			High	Good	Aver.			
High						9 10 11 12		
Trade						1 2 3 4		
College						1 2 3 4		
Post-grad						1 2 3 4		

Other training or skills (factory or office machines operated, special courses)

Shorthand   WPM   Typing

WE ARE AN EQUAL OPPORTUNITY EMPLOYER

EMPLOYMENT HISTORY

READ CAREFULLY: Starting with your present or most recent job, working backwards, account for all time, including periods of unemployment (include five-year employment history)

Name, Address, Phone		Dates		Position, Duties, Supervisor	Base Wage/Salary	Reason for Leaving
		Month	Year			
	From				Starting	
	To				Final	
	From				Starting	
	To				Final	
	From				Starting	
	To				Final	
	From				Starting	
	To				Final	

Person to notify in case of emergency	Name	Address	City	State	Zip	Area Code/ Phone

JOB INTEREST

Have you ever been employed by XYZ Corporation?	Yes	No
Have you ever applied with XYZ Corporation?	Yes	No

In what types of work are you interested?   Starting wage expected?
$ per

How were you referred?   If by newspaper or agency, give name

Can you work:
Saturday ☐ Yes   Sunday ☐ Yes   Weekdays ☐ Yes   Evening ☐ Yes   Holidays ☐ Yes   Day ☐ Yes
☐ No   ☐ No   ☐ No   ☐ No   ☐ No   ☐ No
or Night hours? ☐ Yes
☐ No

PERSONAL DATA

Citizen of USA?   Yes ☐   No ☐   Alien Registration No. or Immigration Status:

Do you have any physical condition that may limit your ability to perform the job applied for?   Yes ☐   No ☐

Have you ever collected Worker's Compensation?   Yes ☐   No ☐   State of health: Fair ☐   Good ☐   Excellent ☐

Have you ever been convicted of any crime other than a minor traffic violation?   Yes ☐   No ☐

If yes, when, where, and disposition?

Do you have any relatives or acquaintances employed by XYZ Corporation?   Yes ☐   No ☐   Location:

If yes, give names:

PERSONAL INTERESTS

| Hobbies or interests, special skills: |
| Extracurricular activities (scholastic or athletic): |
| Honors or awards, leadership positions held: |
| What languages, other than English, do you speak fluently? |

MILITARY HISTORY

U.S. Military Service	Branch of Service	Duties
From Mo. Yr.	To Mo. Yr.	
Type of Discharge	Rank at Discharge	Draft or Reserve Status

If requested by the Company, I agree to submit to a physical examination before being finally accepted for employment and I also agree that, in the event I shall be employed by the Company, I will submit to further physical examinations when requested by the Company. I hereby authorize any physician, surgeon, practitioner, or other person (and any hospital, including veterans administration or governmental hospital, or any medical service organization), any insurance company or other institution or organization to release to the Company and to each other any medical or other information acquired, including benefits paid or payable concerning the undersigned.

I further agree to forfeit my statutory rights to ownership of any lost or abandoned personal property found by me on the Company's property.

I authorize my former employers and other individuals to give information concerning me, whether or not it is on their records, and I release them and their companies from any liability whatsoever. I certify that all statements given on this application are correct, and realize that falsification or misrepresentation of this or any other personnel record may result in my discharge. In the event of employment, I agree to abide by all present and subsequently issued rules of the Company.

PLEASE BE SURE YOU HAVE SIGNED: DATE

We appreciate your interest and the time you have taken to prepare the application. THANK YOU

You can explain the blank in the interview if necessary. In this way, the blank will not automatically be used to screen you from a job for which you might otherwise qualify.

Expect employers to ask you questions about blank spaces. If a blank space is not mentioned in the interview, be sure to mention it after you are offered the job. This will prevent the possibility of your being accused later of withholding information. An alternative to leaving a space blank is to write "Will explain in interview." Decide for yourself which way is better for you. But *do* be prepared to explain it.

Chapter Summary

A professionally prepared résumé is essential to any job search. For many years it has been the most widely used tool by employers to evaluate the qualifications of job candidates. However, in today's job market, many employers prefer to access candidate information through nontraditional résumés. You should consider what types of nontraditional résumés will best support your candidacy, taking care to choose alternatives that complement the industry segment and the employer you are interested in. The electronic résumé and the disk résumé are two options you should be prepared to use, because they will probably be the more prevalent style of résumé through the year 2005.

Chapter Eight

Letters

Chapter Objectives

After completing this chapter, you will:

Understand how to write effective job search letters.

Know the kinds of letters you may write during your job search.

Understand the function of job search letters.

Be able to write your own job search letters.

During your job search, letter writing is an important form of communicating with an employer. By corresponding directly with an employer over time, you demonstrate a sustained interest in the job and reveal something about your personality and professional goals.

The prime reason for writing a letter as you initiate your job search is to secure a job interview. If your background and work experience are comparable to those of other candidates, it is your cover letter that will really distinguish you from everyone else. The cover letter reveals the reason you want to work for the company and gives you an opportunity to talk about your positive traits and what you can bring to the employer. The clarity, conciseness, and professionalism of your letter can make a positive first impression on an employer who has not yet met you.

Guidelines for Writing Job Search Letters

Writing letters as part of the job search can be one of your most valuable efforts. It can also be one of the most difficult. The following are some basic guidelines to remember:

- Be brief and to the point.
- Use a standard business-letter format.
- Make sure you address the letter to the proper individual and use his or her proper title.
- Make absolutely *no* errors in grammar, punctuation, spelling, or typing. An error could automatically rule you out of consideration.

Be Brief and to the Point.   Think about what you want to say before you compose your letter. Be sure to think about presenting information about yourself that will really spark interest in you as a serious job candidate. Don't repeat the detailed experience listed in your résumé; summarize it. In your résumé, *what* you write is important; in your cover letter, *how* you write the highlights from your résumé is important.

It takes practice to create a well-written letter. Don't get frustrated if writing doesn't come easily to you and you have trouble with your cover letter at first. Seek out some help from your teacher, parents, or professional contacts and you will be sure to end up with a document you are proud of.

Use Standard Business-Letter Format.   Your cover letter should be like a professional business letter. There are sample formats for you to follow in this chapter. If you are not accustomed to business writing, these formats provide good basic guidelines for you to follow. There are many reference books available in the library on effective business-letter writing that give helpful hints on how to compose a letter that has a proper business format and elicits interest in the reader. By reviewing the sample formats in this chapter and completing the activity at the end, you will be able to structure your cover letter properly.

Address Letter to the Proper Individual; Use Proper Title.   It is important to personalize your letter by addressing it directly to the appropriate individual. You may find this person's name and title listed in a classified ad, a job vacancy bulletin, or a business directory. If the name of the contact person is not listed, or if you have heard about the job from another source, you should call the company and ask for the name and title of the person to write to. You may also want to ask for the person's proper address because he or she may not be located at the main address listed for the company; many times a company has offices or buildings spread out in different locations. At all costs, avoid writing cover letters that begin with *Dear Sir or Madam* or *To Whom It May Concern.* This type of general salutation may cause the reader to feel you have not taken much time to research the company or that you are not seriously considering that particular company in your job search. We all like to be acknowledged by name and we all like our name to be spelled correctly; your prospective employer is no different.

Make Absolutely No Errors.   Your cover letter must be perfect. Most employers view the quality of your cover letter as a reflection of your own professionalism, attention to detail, and written communication skills; therefore, even one error can cause an employer to pass on your application. Do not depend only on your own eye to proofread your letter. Have one or two other people read your letter and make necessary corrections. You may be too close to your own work to see your mistakes. If you use a word processor to prepare your letter, do not totally depend on the spell-checker. A wrong word that is spelled properly but used out of context in your letter will be accepted by the spell-checker, and will leave you with a mistake you could have avoided with your own eye.

Letters You May Write during Your Job Search

Cover Letters

A cover letter is a letter that accompanies your résumé. It is the main letter used in a job search. The purpose of the cover letter is to promote your qualifications to an employer so that you will obtain an interview. Employers can receive hundreds of résumés for a single job opening, depending on the type of job it is and on how many people are unemployed or looking to change their current jobs. When the résumés received show similar backgrounds among many candidates, employers look for some way to narrow down the number of applicants to be interviewed. A well-prepared cover letter can make you stand out favorably among other applicants and lead to your being selected for an interview.

Look at the sample format for cover letters. By using this as a guide for preparing your own cover letters, you will be sure to convey all of the important information your prospective employer needs to know.

Format for Cover Letters

Return address

Inside address

Mary Jones, Vice President
American Insurers
2500 Brook Avenue
Boston, MA 00215

Date

July 8, 1996

Salutation

Dear Ms. Jones:

First paragraph:
Your reason for
writing

In your initial paragraph, state the reason for the letter, name the specific position or type of work for which you are applying, and indicate from which resource (placement office, news media, friend, employment service) you learned of the opening.

Second
paragraph:
Your
qualifications

Indicate why you are interested in the position, the company, its products or services—above all, what you can do for the employer. If you are a recent graduate, explain how your academic background makes you a qualified candidate for the position. If you have some practical work experience, point out your specific achievements or unique qualifications. Try not to repeat the same information the reader will find in the résumé.

Third paragraph:
Refer to enclosed
résumé or
application

Refer the reader to the enclosed résumé or application form which summarizes your qualifications, training, and experiences.

Final paragraph:
Indicate your
plan for
follow-up

In the closing paragraph, indicate your desire for a personal interview and your flexibility as to the time and place. Repeat your phone number in the letter and offer any assistance to help in a speedy response. Finally, close your letter with a statement or question that will encourage a response. For example, state that you will be in the city where the company is located on a certain date and would like to set up an interview. Or, state that you will call on a certain date to set up an interview. Or, ask if the company will be recruiting in your area, or if it desires additional information or references.

Closing

Sincerely,

Your written
signature
Your name typed

Thomas L. Smith

There are three types of cover letters. They are the letter of application for a specific position, the letter of inquiry, and the letter in response to a blind box ad. The first is used when sending your résumé in response to a specific position you know is available through the classified ads, through a job posting system at work, or by word of mouth. The second type is used when you are inquiring about the availability of employment at a firm. The third is used when you are applying for a specific job but do not know the particular company (some companies deliberately run blind ads). In each case, the cover letter is your tool for promoting your qualifications for employment. You would approach writing these letters in slightly different ways.

Letter of Application for Specific Position.   This letter states your specific qualifications for the job for which you are applying. You should always begin by addressing the letter to a specific person, using his or her full title. Be sure to enclose a typed copy of your résumé and say in the letter that you did so. State the position for which

---

Your address

Date

Inside address
(If possible, use individual's name.)

Dear _____:

I am writing in response to your ad in the *Boston Globe* on Sunday, August 4, 1996, for an administrative assistant for your executive offices.

Your company interests me because of your worldwide reputation and excellent history of stability. I have read about your plans to expand your business into the Southeast, and those plans for growth convince me that XYZ Corporation is a progressive company.

Enclosed is my résumé. My typing speed is 75 wpm, shorthand 120, and I am proficient with machine transcription. I ranked second among the secretarial graduates in my class and completed an internship with your firm last year.

I look forward to an interview and will call you shortly to arrange a convenient time.

Sincerely,

(written signature)

Your name typed

you are applying and mention where you found out about the job (placement office, newspaper, etc.). Relate how your education has made you qualified for this position. State what you can offer rather than what you hope to gain. Unless requested to do so in the ad, do not mention a salary requirement in your letter because by being too high, or even too low, you can eliminate yourself from an interview. If the ad requires that you state a salary requirement, use the guidelines given in Chapter 7 for filling that space in a job application. Request an interview at the employer's convenience, and follow up in approximately one week with a telephone call.

Letter of Inquiry.   Use this letter if a mass-mailing campaign is part of your job search. It is similar to a "cold call" in sales. You are writing to inquire whether or not the company needs someone with your background. To your knowledge, there is not a specific position available. Address your letter to a specific person and use his or her full title. You may need to call the company in order to know the correct person's name and title. Enclose a copy of your résumé and say that you did so in the letter. State your interest in the company, referring to it by name. Briefly state how your background may benefit the company, mentioning your education and skills gained through outside activities or part-time jobs. Ask for the opportunity to discuss your qualifications in person, at the employer's convenience.

Your address

Date

Inside address
(If possible, use individual's name.)

Dear _____ :

I am writing to inquire about a career opportunity in marketing with your company.

At a recent career day held on my campus, I learned that XYZ Bank is expanding its branches throughout the Northeast. I have read about your profits over the past five years and see that XYZ Bank is a growth-oriented organization with a solid history.

My résumé is enclosed for your information and highlights my work experience in the marketing field. My phone number is also listed.

I look forward to an interview with you to further discuss how I think I can contribute to XYZ Bank.

Sincerely,

(written signature)

Your name typed

Letter in Response to a Blind Box Ad. This letter is similar to the letter of inquiry except for the second paragraph. Usually you will know the type of position that is available, but you will not be able to refer to your interest in a particular company with this type of ad. Instead, use the second paragraph to emphasize more of your specific skills and experience and to relate them to the available position.

Your address

Date

Inside address

Dear _____ :

I am writing in response to the classified ad for a cost accountant that appeared in the *Boston Globe* on Sunday, April 4, 1996.

My experience and education make me a well-qualified candidate for the job.

My résumé is enclosed for your information. My phone and fax numbers are listed.

I look forward to an interview to further discuss the contributions I think I can make to your company.

Sincerely,

(written signature)

Your name typed

ACTIVITY 8-1 • *Preparing Your Cover Letter*

Preparing your own cover letter is easy if you take the time to organize your thoughts about what you want to say in each part of the letter.

Select an employer to write to concerning your interest in employment. Write in what you think best represents what you want to say to your prospective employer in your letter.

Fill in each section to create your own cover letter.

Return
address

Date

Inside
address

Salutation

First paragraph:
Your reason for
writing

Second paragraph:
Your qualifications

Third paragraph:
Refer to enclosed
résumé/application

Final paragraph:
Indicate your plan for
follow-up

Closing

Your written
signature

Your name typed

Letter to Request a Recommendation

This letter is written to persons who will be able to recommend you satisfactorily for a position. Make a personal call in addition to writing the letter. Choose people you are sure will recommend you favorably. Identify yourself by name and make mention of how you know the person. If your name has changed since the time you first knew this person, mention the name by which he or she knew you. Ask permission to use this person's name as a reference in your job search. Make the contact friendly, but convince the person that this is important to you.

Send a copy of your résumé to each person you would like to serve as your reference, and send updates as you make them. This will enable the person to be more comfortable and/or specific when talking about you to an employer. In addition to having someone write you a letter of recommendation to a specific employer, you may also want to ask each person for an open letter of recommendation that can be used right away if you need it.

Your address

Date

Inside address
(Always use individual's name.)

Dear _____ :

I am currently conducting a job search and would like permission to give your name as a reference to some prospective employers.

I value the experience I gained when working for you last summer. Since you were my direct supervisor, you have firsthand knowledge of my skills, dependability, and ability to work well with others. Would you be willing to share your thoughts about my work performance with another employer by telephone or by writing a letter of reference for me to present on my interviews?

I can be reached at (telephone number, including area code). My current address is _____ . Thank you in advance for your cooperation.

Sincerely,

(written signature)

Your name typed

Thank-You Letter Following an Interview

This letter is written after the interview to acknowledge the interviewer's time and cooperation. This is a good way to ensure that your interviewer will remember you. Be sure to send the letter right after the interview and thank the interviewer for his or her time. Restate the position for which you applied, and give the date and/or place of the interview. In your letter mention one positive thing that happened during your interview. Express your interest in the opportunities offered in an enthusiastic way. Be sure to include your telephone number and return address. Without this information, an employer may not be able to contact you and you could lose out on a job offer.

To help in writing the thank-you letter, make sure you keep current and accurate records of every interview: the date, time, location, interviewer, and any special information concerning the company or job itself.

Your address

Date

Inside address
(Always use individual's name.)

Dear _____ :

I appreciated the opportunity to talk with you on (date). The information you shared with me about (company name) was excellent, and I am excited about the possibility of applying my education and experience to the position we discussed.

If I can provide you with any additional information, please let me know. I look forward to hearing from you soon.

Sincerely,

(written signature)

Your name typed

Letter Accepting a Position

This letter is written after you have agreed to accept a specific position. Whether a job offer comes to you verbally or in writing, answer the offer immediately. Be direct about accepting and restate the specific position you have accepted. Be sure to express your appreciation for the opportunity your employer has given you and express your eagerness to begin your new job.

Resist the temptation to sound either overly grateful or reticent about your abilities to fulfill the job requirement. A straightforward, pleasant, confident response is all that is needed.

Your address

Date

Inside address
(Always use individual's name.)

Dear _____ :

I am very pleased to accept your offer (state offer) as outlined in your letter of (date). (Include all details of offer—location, starting salary, starting date.)

(Mention enclosures—application, résumé, employee forms, or other information—and any related commentary.)

I look forward to meeting the challenges of the job, and I shall make every attempt to fulfill your expectations.

Sincerely,

(written signature)

Your name typed

Letter Refusing a Position

This letter is written after you have definitely decided not to accept the particular position offered. You should always write this letter to an employer, because by doing so you make a favorable impression. Someday you may again be applying for a job at that company, and it is good to be remembered as a professional person. Answer the offer immediately. Don't be embarrassed to tell the employer that you have decided not to accept the job offer. Be direct with the answer, but soften your tone to show appreciation for the offer. Be concise and make the letter simple. Express your thanks, remembering that you may want to reapply for a future position with the same company.

Your address

Date

Inside address
(Always use individual's name.)

Dear _____ :

Thank you for your letter of (date) offering me the position of (state position).

After considerable thought, I have decided not to accept your offer of employment as outlined in your letter. This has been a very difficult decision for me. However, I feel I have made the correct one for this point in my career.

Thank you for your time, effort, and consideration. Your confidence in me is sincerely appreciated.

Sincerely,

(written signature)

Your name typed

Thank-You Letter for a Plant Visit or an Office Visit

Address these letters to the specific person or people who hosted you. State your appreciation for their valuable time. Comment on what impressed you the most and on what you learned from the visit.

Your address

Date

Inside address
(Always use individual's name.)

Dear _____ :

Thank you for the tour you provided to our office careers class on Wednesday.

It was interesting to see how some of the new word processing equipment is being used at a large company like yours. I was impressed by the teamwork among the office staff in your customer service department. This must be a real asset to your customers.

While I was there, Ms. Crane mentioned that there was a part-time job open for an administrative assistant in your human resources department. I am interested in the job and have enclosed a copy of my résumé for your consideration.

Sincerely,

(written signature)

Your name typed

Application Letter for Cooperative Education/ Internship Program

Address the letter to the hiring authority and/or person involved in the selection process. Enclose a typed copy of your résumé and include references if typed separately. State why you would like to be considered for the program. State the kind of professional experience you hope to gain and how you will use this experience to reach your career goal. Finally, state what qualifications you can bring to the employer.

Your address

Date

Inside address
(If possible, use individual's name.)

Dear _____ :

I am writing this letter to apply to the (name of school's cooperative education or internship program).

This program offers me an opportunity to strengthen my current work history by giving me more focused experience in my career field. I feel this would give me an advantage over other students when I seek full-time employment.

Enclosed is my résumé. I am available for an interview at your request. I look forward to the opportunity to meet with you.

Sincerely,

(written signature)

Your name typed

Below is a list of the types of cover letters discussed in this chapter. Place a check next to the type of letter you would like to practice writing, and fill in each section of the accompanying letter format.

- ☐   Letter of application for a specific position
- ☐   Letter of inquiry
- ☐   Response to a blind ad
- ☐   Request for a recommendation
- ☐   Thank-you letter following an interview
- ☐   Letter accepting a position
- ☐   Letter refusing a position
- ☐   Thank-you letter for a plant visit or an office visit
- ☐   Application letter for cooperative education/internship program
- ☐   Letter for an international job search

Return address

Date

Inside address

Salutation

First paragraph: Your reason for writing

Second paragraph: Your qualifications

Third paragraph: Refer to enclosed résumé/application

Final paragraph: Indicate your plan for follow-up

Closing

Your written signature

Your name typed

Have someone critique your letter for content and for grammar, punctuation, and spelling.

Letters for an International Job Search

The types of letters that apply to a job search in America also apply to a job search abroad. Write your letter in English. Many countries accept handwritten cover letters if they are neatly constructed and written with a quality black pen. However, it is more professional to type your letters, as you do your résumé.

Although fax machines are certainly a plus to business communications throughout the world, it is best not to fax résumés and cover letters as a general rule. The quality of the document received by your prospective employer is diminished when it is received as a fax. Also, when you send your résumé and cover letter by fax it may imply that you did not prepare your application package far enough in advance for it to be sent by mail. Of course, if you are unexpectedly responding to a position that needs a quick response, the fax may be the way to go. Certainly, if an employer asks you to send the fax, do so. The safest way to handle your international correspondence is to send it via traditional mail and invite the employer to respond to you by fax.

Look at the sample for cover letters applied to an international job search situation.

3465 Alexander Drive
San Francisco, CA 92340

April 10, 1996

Mr. Jean Montagne
President
Citibank
11 Champs D'Elysée
Paris, FRANCE

Dear Mr. Montagne:

I am interested in an accounting position at one of your Citibank locations in Paris. I have just received my B.S. in accounting and have successfully completed a six-month cooperative education work experience at your Citibank location in New York.

In this position, I gained experience working with international clientele being serviced by your New York office.

My computer skills are extensive. I have effective writing and verbal communication skills including speaking French fluently. Enclosed are some articles from my school newspaper about presentations I have given to student groups on campus and two articles I wrote for the newspaper.

I am available for an interview since I will be in Paris the first week in May. I look forward to meeting with you and continuing my career with Citibank.

Sincerely,

John Simmons

Electronic Letters

Just as you can source job information on the Internet and transmit your résumé to companies on electronic employment services, so can you transmit your cover letter or letter of application via electronic mail. Like your résumé, your cover letter can be scanned into applicant tracking systems, allowing keywords in the letter to help sort your qualifications into the pool of other available candidates. The selection of keywords on the cover letter is critical to its usefulness. A cover letter takes as much electronic storage as a résumé and is usually stored with your résumé. The letter needs some distinctive terminology in order for it to be retrieved. Like your electronic résumé, your electronic cover letter will be retrieved by recruiters on the basis of keywords. Keywords to include in your electronic cover letter may be taken from the help wanted ad you are responding to or may be tied to someone who referred you for the job. For example, listing the name of the newspaper in which the ad appeared, along with some of the same words used in the ad, would cause your cover letter to be directly retrieved for that job. This is because most recruiters use systems where they can select a source for the résumé. That source would be a school, an employment agency, a professional association, a newspaper, or a job fair. The point is to write your cover letter using as many keywords as you can predict will be important. Then retrieval becomes easy and your chances of being in the final cut of candidates is increased.

Chapter Summary

The letters you create during your job search are critical because they sell your résumé and ultimately help differentiate you from other candidates with similar backgrounds. Letters give you the opportunity to emphasize your work experience, highlight your interest in an individual company, and express your unique personality. In many ways, the letters you write are the most critical elements of a successful job search because they can reveal more about you as a person than your résumé can. Whether on paper or on the information highway, a well-put-together letter during your job search can draw the favorable attention you need to obtain a job interview.

Successful Interviews

The job interview is the most widely used process for screening job candidates and hiring new employees. In many ways, it provides the most direct information about the candidate's background, personality, and style. Understanding how to best prepare for and follow up on interviews is critical to your success. New technology provides alternative ways to bring candidates and employers together for the interviewing process. Regardless of the medium used, the basic guidelines for a successful interview remain the same. Remember, the purpose of a successful job interview is to receive a job offer.

Securing a Job Interview

There are several ways to secure a job interview, but basically you either initiate the process yourself or have someone else do it for you. It is best to learn how to secure your own job interviews because by doing so you demonstrate initiative to a potential employer and put yourself in control of your own career.

To begin the process of securing your own interviews, review all of the sources of jobs discussed in Chapter 6. Choose to pursue several of the sources that are most available to you and that you feel most comfortable with. While you may have looked at these resources initially as a good way to obtain information about available jobs, you can now use these same resources as a means of actually pursuing a job interview. The key to your success will be to take the initiative to act on these resources and know what to ask for.

The following sections present some ways to obtain a job interview using the resources available to you.

Telephone Calls

Use the telephone yourself to:

- Respond to classified ads where telephone calls are being accepted.
- Follow up on a cover letter and résumé you have already sent.
- Make inquiries about available positions that may be unadvertised.

You should plan ahead what you will say once you've initiated the call.

Others as Resources

There are times when it simply may be better to have someone else initiate a call for you. For example, your placement office may be able to get through to an employer directly more readily than you can; a friend who already works at a company you are applying to may help make the employer aware of your expertise; an employment agency may be more successful with setting up an interview for you directly because this may be what the employer has requested. Recognize when it might be helpful to have someone else initiate a request for a job interview for you, but be ready to follow up properly on your own immediately after the contact has been made. In the end, the interview and, of course, the job offer will come to you because of your initiative, not someone else's.

Types of Interviews

Interviews fall into two basic categories: informational and traditional. Informational interviews may help you explore a career or practice your interviewing skills. The traditional job interview is the real thing; rather than seeking information, you are seeking a job offer.

Informational Interviews

An informational interview is designed to help you gather more information about an industry, a specific employer, or a type of job. There are two types of informational interviews. The first involves your interviewing an employer about what jobs are generally available for someone with your background and finding out more about the company itself. You may obtain more knowledge about the career paths in your field and the qualifications sought by a particular company.

The second type of informational interview involves your speaking to someone who is already working in your chosen career and has the job you think you want. During this interview you can clarify your career goal and gain a better understanding of the day-to-day responsibilities of a particular job.

Informational interviews are helpful because they provide you with an up-to-date perspective on your industry and on your desired job. By having a general feeling for what is happening in these areas, you will be better prepared for your job interviews.

Procedures for Arranging and Conducting Informational Interviews

- Compile a list of employers for the occupations in your career field. Use business directories, the *Encyclopedia of Associations,* the yellow pages of cities across the United States, the *College Placement Annual,* or other sources. Note employers' locations, phone numbers, types of businesses, product lines, and other relevant information. Include alumni from your school on your list. Check with your alumni or placement office for names of past graduates who would be willing to help you out.

- Review your list of employers and mark those you consider the most attractive.

- If possible, compare employer locations with other members of your class. Coordinating trips to visit the same city with a classmate may reduce travel costs.

- On your list, mark those employers located where you are able to travel and visit.

- Draft a separate list of employers to contact for arranging interviews. Base your new list on the occupations you are considering the most seriously, the new employers that appear the most attractive to you, and your ability to travel.

- Before contacting employing organizations, consider the following issues:

  When can the interviews be conducted? Other commitments may conflict or need to be rescheduled. Interviews should be scheduled to allow more than adequate time to locate destinations, accommodate delays, conduct the interviews, and take advantage of invitations to extend your visit or tour employers' facilities.

  What people are available for interviews? This can be checked by telephoning the employer to explain your needs. Public relations or personnel offices are good sources of this information.

  How can you know if the person you ask for an interview is able to give you the kind of information you are seeking? Verify that the person you contact actually works in the occupation you are assessing. Clearly explain your needs and objectives before requesting an interview.

  Where should the interviews be conducted? Request that interviews be conducted in locations allowing privacy and freedom from distraction. The people you interview may agree to provide tours of their workplaces. Your interviews should be conducted close enough to actual work settings for you to be able to observe them at some point during your visits.

- Schedule your informational interviews. Whenever possible, make your arrangements directly with the people you plan to interview. Explain the nature of your search and your reasons for requesting an interview. You should find most people open to talking with you about their occupation.

- Leave your phone number or address so your interview subjects are able to contact you if rescheduling becomes necessary.

- If you have not had experience in interviewing for information, you may want to practice mock interviewing with a classmate, friend, or relative.

- You should be familiar enough with the questions you want to ask so that you will not continually need to refer to a list during the interviews. This will help you achieve a more natural, relaxed, and spontaneous conversation with your interview subjects. This style of interview is likely to provide more honest, candid, and complete information than a straight question-and-answer interview format.

- Reconfirm interview times, dates, and locations on the day before each scheduled interview.

- At the conclusion of each visit, ask your subject for the names of other people who can provide information about the occupations in your targeted range of occupations. Obtaining permission to use your subjects' names can help in arranging future interviews.

- After each interview, take time to send a thank-you letter to your subject. Courtesy is a good habit, and you want to be remembered favorably by your subjects' organizations.

ACTIVITY 9-1 •   *Conducting an Informational Interview*

The following questions are for you to ask an employer on an informational interview. They give you an idea of the kind of information you can obtain from an employer about the career and job you think you are interested in. You can actually use this form to collect information when conducting an informational interview with an employer.

Questions for Informational Interviews

Occupation: _____

Person to be interviewed: _____

Write comments and additional interview questions in the spaces provided.

What do you like about your occupation? Why?

_____

_____

_____

_____

_____

What are the activities and responsibilities connected with your job? Could you describe your job routine for a typical day or week?

_____

_____

_____

Do the activities and responsibilities of your occupation vary depending on the employer, or are they generally the same? In what ways could your job situation be different from those of others in your occupation?

_____

_____

_____

Do the number of responsibilities in your occupation remain constant or increase over time?

_____

_____

_____

What skills are necessary to perform your job activities?

_____

_____

What training and education does your occupation require?

_____

_____

_____

Do the training requirements for your occupation vary from employer to employer?

_____

_____

_____

How much variety is connected with your work routine?

_____

_____

_____

How would you describe your actual work setting or workplace?

_____

_____

_____

What opportunities are there in your job for sharing ideas, acquiring new skills, and learning from your co-workers or supervisors?

_____

_____

_____

How competitive is entry into your field? What is the outlook for openings in your field over the next few years?

_____

_____

_____

What is the usual progression of jobs and assignments for people in your occupation? What career paths can people follow?

_____

_____

_____

Is yours considered a staff (management) or a line (support) position? If a line position, what other people do you supervise?

_____

_____

_____

What qualities do employers look for in job applicants who want to enter your occupation?

_____

_____

_____

What are the goals of your organization? How would you describe its overall philosophy and objectives?

_____

_____

_____

This interview began with the question "What do you like about your occupation?" What do you *not* like about your occupation? What job frustrations and negative points should I know about before deciding whether to enter this field?

_____

_____

_____

To what extent are the advantages and disadvantages of your particular job attributable to your particular place of employment?

_____

_____

_____

Do you know the names of employers other than your own who hire people in your occupation? Do you know of any sources I could consult to locate still more employers?

_____

_____

_____

Can you recommend the names of other people I can consult to find out more about your field? May I use your name to introduce myself?

_____

_____

_____

Traditional Job Interviews

A traditional job interview is one where you meet your interviewer, in person, to be interviewed for an actual job. This may occur at your school, on-site at the company, or on-site at a job fair. While the goal of an informational interview is to practice your interviewing skills, the goal of a traditional job interview is to obtain an actual job offer.

Multiple Interviews

When you interview with a company, you may be asked to participate in more than one interview if you become a strong candidate for a particular job. Your initial interview is the most critical because it is your first time to generate serious interest in you from the employer. When you succeed in making a favorable impression on an initial interview, an employer may ask you to visit the company for a second or third interview. The focus of each of these interviews will be a little different as you move from gaining an employer's initial interest in you to convincing the employer that your qualifications are better than those of any other candidates. Multiple interviews are usually common for candidates who are being seriously considered by a prospective employer to fill a position.

The Initial Interview.   The accompanying table is a summary of the five stages of an initial interview, detailing the topics the interviewer will cover in each and what the interviewer will be looking for from you.

Stages and Topics Covered during the Initial Interview

Stages	Interviewer Topics	Interviewer Looks for
First impressions	Introduction and greeting Small talk about traffic conditions, the weather, the record of the basketball team	Firm handshake, eye contact Appearance and dress appropriate to the business, not college, setting Ease in social situations, good manners, poise
Your record	**Education**	

	Interviewer Topics	Interviewer Looks for
	Reasons for choice of school and major Grades, effort required for them Special areas of interest Courses enjoyed most and least, reasons Special achievements, toughest problems Value of education as career preparation Interaction with instructors High school record, important test scores	Intellectual abilities Breadth and depth of knowledge Relevance of course work to career interests Special or general interest Value placed on achievement Willingness to work hard Relation between ability and achievement Reaction to authority Ability to cope with problems Sensible use of resources (time, energy, money)

Work Experience

Interviewer Topics	Interviewer Looks for
Nature of jobs held Why undertaken Level of responsibility reached Duties liked most and least Supervisory experience Relations with others	High energy level, vitality, enthusiasm Leadership, interest in responsibility Willingness to follow directions Ability to get along with others Seriousness of purpose Ability to motivate oneself to make things happen Positive "can do" attitude

Activities and Interests

Interviewer Topics	Interviewer Looks for
Role in extracurricular, athletic, community, and social service activities Personal interests—hobbies, cultural interests, sports	Diversity of interests Awareness of world outside the classroom Social conscience, good citizenship

Stages and Topics, Covered during the Initial Interview (*concluded*)

Stages	Interviewer Topics	Interviewer Looks for
Your career goals	Type of work desired Immediate objectives Long-term objectives Interest in this company Other companies being considered Desire for further education, training Geographical preferences and limitations Attitude toward relocation Health factors that might affect job performance	Realistic knowledge of strengths and weaknesses Preparation for employment Knowledge of opportunities Seriousness of purpose: career-oriented rather than job-oriented Knowledge of the company Real interest in the company Work interests in line with talents Company's chance to get and keep you
The company	Company opportunities Where you might fit in Current and future projects Major divisions and departments Training programs, educational and other benefits	Informed and relevant questions Indicators of interest in answers Appropriate, but not undue, interest in salary or benefits
Conclusion	Further steps you should take (application form, transcript, references) Further steps company will take, outline how application handled, to which departments it will be sent, time of notification of decision Cordial farewell	Candidate's attention to information as a sign of continued interest

Second and Third Interviews. Second and third interviews are sometimes conducted by a prospective employer in order to become more familiar with which candidates best fit the job.

Second interviews are conducted to allow the candidate and prospective employer the opportunity to discuss in greater detail the available job and whether or not the candidate's qualifications and career goals match the job opportunity. A second interview helps both the employer and the candidate to determine if they are the right match for each other. Second interviews are conducted in different ways. As the job candidate, you may be asked back to speak with your first interviewer again or to interview with others in the company. For example, if your first interviewer was from the human resources department, your second interview may be with the head

of the department in which you would be working. Very often, the human resources department screens potential candidates for department heads to interview, and the department head actually makes the hiring decision.

On your second interview you may be interviewed both one-on-one and with a group of other candidates. This method is sometimes used to determine how well you interact with others. Bringing in a group of applicants is also a way for some companies to show the candidates the company and talk about its history or future. During the second interview, you should be prepared to ask a lot of the more detailed questions you didn't discuss the first time. It is more appropriate to discuss salary and benefits during a second interview than during the first interview.

Third interviews are not the norm, but many companies conduct them with the one or two top candidates for the job in order to make a final decision. By the third interview, many employers feel familiar enough with the candidate to extend a job offer. Benefits and salary are almost always discussed in detail during a third interview because by this time the employer is dealing with only the most serious candidates.

Telephone Interviews

Occasionally, you may be in a situation where your interview will be conducted by telephone. This sometimes happens when there is not enough time to wait to interview in person or when travel expenses are too costly to bring the interviewer and interviewee together in the same place. Although most job candidates are not hired after having a telephone interview only, this type of interview often precedes or follows an in-person interview for the reasons described above.

While making a positive first impression in person is sometimes challenging, it is even more challenging to make a positive first impression through a telephone interview because in this case the employer does not have the benefit of observing your physical appearance or your body language, both of which play a major role in creating someone's impression of you.

To make your telephone interview successful, focus on these three things: voice quality, preparation, and attention to detail.

Voice Quality. When speaking on the telephone, be sure to project your voice, speak slowly, enunciate clearly, and sound enthusiastic.

Preparation. Try to be where you know you will be uninterrupted during your telephone interview. It would be helpful if you had access to a fax machine in the room or in a nearby room because you may be asked to fax another copy of your résumé, a letter of reference, or another document pertinent to your interview. You should have two copies of your résumé with you, one handy for the fax machine and one for you to refer to as you describe your skills, experiences, and employment dates over the phone. You should also prepare some notes of keywords or key points about yourself that you want to be sure to interject during the interview. Also prepare a list of questions you will want to ask the employer and have it available to refer to.

Attention to Detail. Because you are not in the interviewer's office, you cannot be handed copies of information or business cards that give you the correct spelling, title, address, telephone, and fax number of your interviewer. You need this information in order to send him or her a thank-you letter. It is probably best to get all of that detail after the interview from a receptionist or secretary at the company, but be prepared to take the information from your interviewer if the situation arises. As a follow-up to your telephone interview, mail or fax a thank-you letter immediately and stress your willingness to meet in person.

Interviewing Technology

Many employers are using some new interviewing techniques made available through changing technology. For example, video conferencing is one form of long-distance interviewing. Just as companies can conduct meetings and make presentations through video conferencing, many conduct interviews this way. As a job candidate you may look out for opportunities to pursue such an interview at your school, at area job fairs, or through special job programs sometimes sponsored by area hotels equipped with video conferencing equipment.

Some colleges and universities as well as some corporate human resource departments are purchasing desktop video conferencing systems to provide direct links between graduates and employers so that no one has to leave the campus or the home office.

This is just one example of how new applications of technology can broaden your opportunities for interviews without you incurring the cost of long-distance travel, in terms of both money and time.

For example, after an early October campus visit, a recruiter from consumer products giant Procter & Gamble in Cincinnati then held a second round of interviews a few weeks later for two December graduates via a video connection. The long-distance interviews resulted in a job offer for one of the students in the company's finance department.

Source: *Information Week*, January 23, 1995.

Preparing for a Job Interview

Successful interviews are the result of good preparation. Preparation gives you not only the information and the appearance you need but, more important, the confidence to succeed.

Think of preparing for an interview like preparing for a final exam. If you start studying well in advance, it helps. If you get enough of a head start on studying, you may not have to cram the night before. What this means is that you can get to sleep on time, and you can probably get up in time to have breakfast and freshen up properly so that you will arrive on time and feel good when you sit down for the exam. There will be an air of calmness and confidence that will help you think straight throughout the exam. You will leave knowing that regardless of the outcome, you gave it your best shot—you did the best you could. If you give the same preparation to an interview, you will gain the same satisfaction.

Preparing for an Interview

The three keys to interviewing success:

1. Preparation   Know yourself
2. Preparation   Know your career goals
3. Preparation   Know your employer

Self-Preparation

The various forms of preparation for your interview are situational knowledge, mental preparation, physical preparation, and written preparation.

Situational Knowledge

- Do you know where the company is located?
- Do you know how long it will take you to get there?
- Do you know where you will park?
- Do you know what office to go to?
- Do you know the name and title of the person with whom you will be interviewing?
- Do you have the phone number of the company so that you can call if you are going to be late for any reason?
- Do you know if you will be interviewing with more than one person?

Mental Preparation.   Mental preparation for a job interview involves several areas. It involves your knowledge of the company, the position for which you are applying, and the career path you wish to follow, as well as your mental attitude about work in general, your expectations about the job, and your confidence in your ability to do the job.

You have seen the kind of information you should research about the company with which you are to interview. Knowledge about the company serves many purposes on a job interview. *First,* it confirms your real interest in working for the company. *Second,* it provides you with a frame of reference for the interview. For example, if you are extremely nervous about your interview, you may want to jot down some questions about the information you read. Maybe it is to clarify something you did not really understand, or maybe it is to find out something you want to know that could not be found in the literature. By having a frame of reference from which to ask questions on the interview, you will feel more relaxed. You will be able to pick up the ball when there is a lag in conversation during the interview or have something to respond to if the interviewer asks you if you have any questions. The interview should be a *conversation* between two people. You shouldn't let yourself be talked at because you are too shy to ask questions. Remember, this is an investment for both you and the company. You have as much right to evaluate the opportunities being discussed as the interviewer has to evaluate you.

Third, having knowledge of the company before the interview puts you in a convincing position that shows the employer you really want to work with that company. Equipped with the proper knowledge, you can bring the company name into your responses and conversations. You can clearly and specifically state the reasons you want to work for that company and the reasons you would be an asset to the company. This is most difficult to do without being able to incorporate specific information about the company. You already learned how to use the sales process on a job interview. *Convincing* is the key word. *Genuinely convincing* is most important.

Part of mental preparation for an interview is having a clear understanding about the job for which you are interviewing. Time after time, interviewers comment that applicants don't really understand the nature of the job for which they are applying. Typically, the employer may ask, "What do you see yourself doing every day as a (*title of the job*)?" The one area in which applicants fall short is lack of specific information available to really answer questions effectively. And yet, isn't it critical to know what you are getting into when you choose a career field? The information provided in Sections A and C of the Career Handbook should give you the information you need about the job for which you are interviewing. You used this information once in deciding on your career goal; use it again to make

yourself more convincing on your job interview. Be able to speak comfortably about the job you are applying for as it relates to your career field and the professional objectives you have developed. Let the interviewer know that you have thought about the big picture and that the decisions you are making are a part of an overall plan. Employers like to see applicants who have *career direction.*

Next, your mental attitude about work will be evaluated in your interview. You should be enthusiastic about the challenges your career presents to you, as opposed to the person who does not see the value of work beyond the paycheck. If you emanate motivation and enthusiasm about work, the employer will see that you might be able to make some valuable contributions to the company. Your work ethic is important.

The employer will evaluate your expectations about the job as well. Demonstrate realistic attitudes about the responsibilities and authority you hope for as well as the starting salary you expect to earn. Be confident in your ability to do the job.

Physical Preparation.   Physical preparation for a job interview reinforces your mental preparation. You could have spent a lot of time thinking through all you will be discussing on the interview, but if you feel sick, tired, or sloppy, your mental attitude and alertness will be diminished.

The following are some important guidelines:

- Start with good hygiene and good grooming.
- Get proper rest the night before.
- Eat breakfast.
- Wear a professional outfit that still relates your own personal style.
- Present a professional image—enhance it! Along with the clothing you wear, bring your résumé and references in a leather-bound folder. Properly arrange your portfolio if this is part of your presentation; have a pen with you and bring extra copies of your résumé. Also have with you a small index card with all the pertinent data to allow you to quickly and efficiently complete a job application if you are required to do so.
- Wear little jewelry, just enough to enhance your presentation of yourself but not so much that it becomes the focus of attention. The same applies to makeup.
- Do not wear perfume.
- Remember to have clean hair, neatly and stylishly groomed.
- Arrive 15 minutes early.
- Relax. If you are nervous and worried about what to do with your hands, put some paperclips in your pocket. Unobtrusively playing with them can help reduce nervousness and eliminate restless hand movements.
- Smile.
- Be energetic.

Written Preparation.   Make sure you have the proper street directions to the company. It is not inappropriate to bring notes with you on an interview. Bring notes from your company research in case you need them. Prepare a brief list of questions to have with you. Write down any miscellaneous information that does not appear on your résumé that you feel might be worth bringing up at the interview. Summarize the details of the job as you perceive them from the ad you read or the information you researched. This information should not prove to be a distraction during the interview but rather a help should you need it. Remember how important eye contact is as an indicator of listening and interest level.

Finally, as a wrap-up to preparation in general, review the Proof by Example Exercise in Chapter 2. The information you have outlined through this simple exercise is the most valuable information you can impart during your interview.

Study it.

Review it.

Rehearse it mentally.

Rehearse the information in a conversational style that is clear, confident, and convincing.

Self-Preparation Summary

- Is my goal clear to me? If not, it will not be clear to an employer. Repeat the steps in the career planning process until you can answer this question comfortably.
- Have I decided if and where I am willing to relocate?
- Have I decided how much I need to earn to meet my living expenses?
- Have I researched the company so that I know the company's:

  Relative size.

  Plans or potential for growth.

  Array of product lines or services.

  Potential new products, services, location.

  Competition. What makes this company different?

  Age and style of management.

  Number of plants and stores or properties.

  Geographic locations, including location of home office.

  Parent company or subsidiaries.

  Structure of the training program.

  Recruiter's or department manager's name.

- Can I now explain to an employer why I want to work for this company?
- Can I also explain to an employer why the company should hire me?
- Do I have the proper outfits to wear on my interviews?
- Will I be well groomed, alert, and on time for my interview?
- Is my résumé ready?
- Have I developed a positive attitude so that the interview will be successful?

How to Research a Company

Company Standings. Look at the company's annual financial report and determine the following: Private or publicly owned? What information can I obtain from privately owned companies? Growth rate? Expansion? Analyze the competition: Who's the leader? How much competition? Reputations?

Organizational Framework. Look at the company's organizational chart thoroughly and determine: Degree of individual responsibility? Centralized or decentralized? What is the chain of command? What is the system for promotions within the company?

Philosophies and Policies.   Consider the philosophies of the company: Are they practiced as stated? Do you agree with what is practiced? Is the company production or people oriented? Is the management traditional or progressive? Are you allowed to read the company's policies? Do you agree with them?

Geographic.   Where is the company's market (international/national)? Direction and rate of expansion? Do you know where you will be located? How often is relocation required for promotion? How much travel is involved?

Management Development.   How much training is provided by the company? Is continuing education endorsed? Does the company have a human resources program? What support groups are available?

Salary and Benefits.   How open is the company about salary? How does it compare with the industry average? How are raises determined? What is the maximum earning potential?

Read the company's benefits and consider the following: insurance package (reputation of insurance company), travel pay, sick leave, training pay, overtime, vacation, family leave, relocation fee, holidays, continuing education, profit sharing, and retirement. On the average, benefits will equal about 25 to 30 percent of the salary. Remember, benefits are nontaxable.

Miscellaneous Advice.   Talk to someone employed by the company who is where you would like to be in two years, and ask:

How honest has the company been?

How strictly are policies followed?

Any questions your interviewer avoided or was unable to answer.

References and Resources. There are many ways to obtain pertinent information about a potential employer. The business resources you become familiar with as a job candidate will also benefit you once you are established in your career. Some of these resources are industry trade publications, business magazines and newspapers, periodicals, and reference volumes. Some suggested industry trade publications are listed for you in this book in Section A, "Career Paths," in the Career Handbook. You may also obtain information from the company's:

Financial reports.

Charts of corporate structure.

Company literature.

Other sources of information include:

Professors.

Employees of the company.

Alumni.

Journals.

Finally, one of the best ways to learn about a company is to thoroughly read its annual report.

Electronic Sources. Technology is creating new ways for you to research current information about companies in your career field. For example, by scanning the Internet you can access detailed information about worldwide businesses as you prepare for your job interviews.

CD-ROM technology also is catching on among campus recruiters. Prudential Insurance Company of America, the nation's largest insurer, tours some schools with a multimedia presentation based on CD-ROM that is intended to acquaint job candidates with Prudential's management training program. The presentation mixes animation and video clips with music, photographs, and text. Prudential officials believe that mixing media in this way helps create a better feeling for Prudential's corporate culture. Just as you realize you need to creatively market yourself to employers, employers also know that to stay competitive in the eyes of new professionals, they need to develop creative recruiting technology.

20 Questions Typically Asked by Interviewers

1. What kind of company or work environment are you looking for?
2. What kind of job or duties/responsibilities are you looking for?
3. Tell me a little bit about professional training and/or your college experience.
4. Describe some of the part-time/summer jobs you've had in the past.
5. What is your academic/school record up till now?
6. Describe some of your extracurricular/student activities.
7. What do you consider some of your strong points?
8. What are some of your short- and long-term job goals?
9. Tell me about your past employers.

10. What do you know about this company?

11. What led you to choose your major field of study?

12. Why did you select your institution for your education?

13. What are the three most important accomplishments thus far in your life?

14. What is the most difficult assignment you have tackled, and how did you resolve it?

15. Why should I hire you?

16. How would a friend/former employer/instructor describe you?

17. Will you relocate and/or travel for your job?

18. Give an example of your ability to work with a team.

19. What are your salary expectations?

20. Are you willing to spend at least six months as a trainee?

You should also be aware that there are some questions that are not appropriate for an employer to ask on an interview. The table following summarizes what is appropriate and inappropriate for an employer to ask in a preemployment interview regarding a number of personal subjects.

Guide to Appropriate Preemployment Inquiries

Subject	Acceptable	Unacceptable
Experience	Applicant's work experience. Applicant's military experience in armed forces of United States, in a state militia (U.S.), or in a particular branch of U.S. armed forces.	Applicant's military experience (general). Type of military discharge.
Character	"Have you ever been *convicted* of any crime?" If so, when, where, and disposition of case?	"Have you ever been *arrested*?"
Relatives	Names of applicant's relatives already employed by this company. Name and address of parent or guardian if applicant is a minor.	Marital status or number of dependents. Name or address of relative, spouse, or children of adult applicant. "With whom do you reside?" "Do you live with your parents?"
Notice in case of emergency	Name and address of *person* to be notified in case of accident or emergency.	Name and address of *relative* to be notified in case of accident or emergency.

Guide to Appropriate Preemployment Inquiries (*continued*)

Subject	Acceptable	Unacceptable
Organizations	Organizations, clubs, professional societies, or other associations of which applicant is a member, excluding any names the character of which indicates the race, religious creed, color, national origin, or ancestry of its members.	List all organizations, clubs, societies, and lodges to which you belong.
References	"By whom were you referred for a position here?"	Requirement of submission of a religious reference.
Physical condition	"Do you have any physical condition which may limit your ability to perform the job applied for?" Statement by employer that offer may be made contingent on passing a physical examination.	"Do you have any physical disabilities?" Questions on general medical condition. Inquiries as to receipt of worker's compensation.
Miscellaneous	Notice to applicant that any misstatements or omissions of material facts in his application may be cause for dismissal.	Any inquiry that is not job related or necessary for determining an applicant's eligibility for employment.
Race or color	*(None.)*	Complexion, color of skin, or other questions directly or indirectly indicating race or color.
Photograph	Statement that photograph may be required after employment.	Requirement that applicant affix a photograph to his application form. Request applicant, at his option, to submit photograph. Requirement of photograph after interview but before hiring.
Citizenship	Statement by employer that, if hired, applicant may be required to submit proof of citizenship.	Whether applicant or his parents or spouse are naturalized or native-born U.S. citizens. Date when applicant or parents or spouse acquired U.S. citizenship.

Guide to Appropriate Preemployment Inquiries (*continued*)

Subject	Acceptable	Unacceptable
		Requirement that applicant produce his naturalization papers or first papers. Whether applicant's parents or spouse are citizens of the United States.
National origin or ancestry	Languages applicant reads, speaks, or writes fluently.	Applicant's nationality, lineage, ancestry, national origin, descent, or parentage. Date of arrival in United States or port of entry; how long a resident. Nationality of applicant's parents or spouse; maiden name of applicant's wife or mother. Language commonly used by applicant; "What is your mother tongue?" How applicant acquired ability to read, write, or speak a foreign language.
Education	Applicant's academic, vocational, or professional education; schools attended.	Date last attended high school.
Name	"Have you worked for this company under a different name?" "Have you ever been convicted of a crime under another name?"	Former name of applicant whose name has been changed by court order or otherwise.
Address or duration of residence	Applicant's place of residence. How long applicant has been resident of this state or city.	
Birthplace	*(None.)*	Birthplace of applicant. Birthplace of applicant's parents, spouse, or other relatives. Requirements that applicant submit a birth certificate, naturalization, or baptismal record.

Guide to Appropriate Preemployment Inquiries (*concluded*)

Subject	Acceptable	Unacceptable
Age	"Can you, after employment, submit a work permit if under 18?" "Are you over 18 years of age?" "If hired, can you furnish proof of age?" or statement that hire is subject to verification that applicant's age meets legal requirements.	Questions which tend to identify applicants 40 to 64 years of age.
Religion	*(None.)*	Applicant's religious denomination or affiliation, church, parish, pastor, or religious holidays observed. "Do you attend religious services or a house of worship?" Applicant may not be told "This is a Catholic/ Protestant/Jewish/atheist organization."
Work days and shifts	Statement by employer of regular days, hours, or shift to be worked.	

ACTIVITY 9-2 • *Answering the 20 Questions Typically Asked by Interviewers*

Perhaps the most important part of preparing for your job interview is knowing how you will answer each question an employer may ask you.

In the spaces below, write down some key words or phrases that you will use to help you deliver a strong response to each question.

1. What kind of company or work environment are you looking for?

_____

_____

2. What kind of job or duties/responsibilities are you looking for?

_____

_____

3. Tell me a little bit about professional training and/or your college experience.

_____

_____

4. Describe some of the part-time/summer jobs you've had in the past.

_____

_____

5. What is your academic/school record up till now?

_____

_____

6. Describe some of your extracurricular/student activities.

_____

_____

7. What do you consider some of your strong points?

_____

_____

8. What are some of your short- and long-term job goals?

_____

_____

9. Tell me about your past employers.

_____

_____

10. What do you know about this company?

_____

_____

11. What led you to choose your major field of study?

_____

_____

12. Why did you select your institution for your education?

_____

_____

13. What are the three most important accomplishments thus far in your life?

_____

_____

14. What is the most difficult assignment you have tackled, and how did you resolve it?

_____

_____

15. Why should I hire you?

_____

_____

16. How would a friend/former employer/instructor describe you?

_____

_____

17. Will you relocate and/or travel for your job?

_____

_____

18. Give an example of your ability to work with a team.

_____

_____

19. What are your salary expectations?

_____

_____

20. Are you willing to spend at least six months as a trainee?

_____

_____

Assess which questions you are having the most difficulty preparing responses for. Meet with your instructor, your career counselor, or an employer you feel comfortable with to discuss how you can develop a powerful response to these questions. Remember, the time to think about what you want to say is before the interview, not during the interview.

Mock Interviews

A mock interview is simply a practice interview. It is conducted by someone other than a potential employer.

If you are in a class with others interested in a mock interview, you may want to have your instructor demonstrate one with you or a member of your class. If you have a portfolio, use the mock interview as an opportunity to practice your verbal presentation of the portfolio (see Chapter 5).

There is also tremendous value to videotaping mock interviews. If you are the person being videotaped, you will later have the chance to critique the responses you gave and the image you portrayed throughout the interview. In this way, you can gain self-confidence with the interviewing process. By watching someone else's video of his or her mock interview you can observe what that person did right and what needs to be improved to result in a more effective interview.

Information interviews and mock interviews are excellent resources for helping you prepare for your actual job interview.

ACTIVITY 9-3 • *Mock Interview Practice*

Ask someone to give you a mock interview: an instructor, a friend, a relative, or, of course, a member of your school's placement office. First, go through the following steps:

- Review the 20 questions typically asked by interviewers.
- Rehearse the answers mentally.
- Review the Proof by Example exercise in Chapter 2.
- Look over your résumé.

Give the person who will interview you the list of questions most frequently asked on an interview. Let them conduct the interview and evaluate you by using the following Mock Interview Evaluation form. Go through as many mock interviews as you think necessary to master the interviewing process.

Mock Interview Evaluation

	Outstanding	Very Good	Good	Needs Improvement	Unsatisfactory
Communication skills					
Appearance					
Proof by Example					
Enthusiasm					
Initial impression/clothing					
Poise/confidence					
Preparation					
Comments and evaluation					

Interviewed by:

_____

Date:

_____

Conducting a Successful Interview

Interview Strategies

When you meet the recruiter, shake his or her hand firmly, maintain eye contact, offer a pleasant but professional smile, and say, "Hello, I'm (*your name*). It's good to meet you (*Mr., Ms., or Mrs. recruiter's name*)." Wait for the recruiter to indicate you should sit down, or wait for him or her to sit down before you do so.

During the interview maintain:

A positive attitude.

Good posture.

An interested manner.

A good appearance.

A pleasant look on your face.

Eye contact with the recruiter.

Confidence.

Be yourself. This is what recruiters look for! The recruiter will be assessing:

Why this kind of employment?

Ultimate goal.

Relocation.

Social, civic activities.

Future career goals.

Job or career.

Reason for wanting to work for the company.

Quality of professional training.

Past experiences.

How you heard about this company.

Don't forget to make the interview a two-way conversation: Ask questions, as well as answering them.

What to Find Out during an Interview

- The exact job: its title and responsibilities, as well as the department in which you would work.
- The fit of the department into the company structure: its purpose, its budget, and other departments with which it works.
- Reporting structure: Would you have one or more bosses?
- Type of formal or informal training you would be given.
- Working on your own or as a member of a team.
- Will skills you learn on this job prepare you for higher-level jobs?
- How job performance is measured.
- What your opportunities for advancement are and where those who previously held your position are now.
- What the salary for this position is.

After the Interview

A successful interview does not end simply when you leave the interviewer's office. It is important to follow up with certain steps that will help you understand how the employer is evaluating you and how you are evaluating the company.

The Company's Postinterview Evaluation

Your evaluation by the employer continues after you leave the interview. Most interviewers have interview evaluation forms they complete on each job candidate. This helps the interviewer evaluate the candidate's qualifications for the job, compare each candidate's qualifications to those of all other job applicants, and remember important details about each individual interviewed.

Means by Which Companies Rate Applicants

Evidence of ability	⟶	Grades
Desire to work	⟶	Part-time and summer jobs
Ambition	⟶	Future career plans
Ability to communicate	⟶	Interview
Acceptable personality	⟶	Interview

Words Employers Use to Rate Applicants

Appearance and manner		Well groomed
		Professional presence
		Considerate
		Polite
Personality	⟶	Warm and friendly
		Attractive or repellent
		Attentive
		Responsive
		Enthusiastic
Intelligence	⟶	Mental organization
		Alertness
		Judgment
		Understanding
		Imagination
Attitude	⟶	Loyal
		Tactful
		Constructive
		Cooperative
		Reasonable
Self-expression	⟶	Clear and interesting
		Convincing
		Pleasant voice
Effectiveness	⟶	Reliable
		Trustworthy
		Industrious

Employer's Interview Evaluation

Appearance

Grooming	__ A	__ B	__ C
Posture	__ A	__ B	__ C
Dress	__ A	__ B	__ C
Manners	__ A	__ B	__ C

Preparation for Interview

Asked pertinent questions	__ A	__ B	__ C
Résumé	__ A	__ B	__ C

Verbal Communication

Conversational ability	__ A	__ B	__ C
Expression	__ A	__ B	__ C

Direction

Well-defined goals	__ A	__ B	__ C
Confidence level	__ A	__ B	__ C
Realistic and practical	__ A	__ B	__ C

Maturity

Responsible	__ A	__ B	__ C
Self-reliant	__ A	__ B	__ C
Decisive	__ A	__ B	__ C
Leader—school	__ A	__ B	__ C
Leader—work	__ A	__ B	__ C

Sincerity

Genuine attitude	A		B C
Artificial attitude	A		B C

Personality

Enthusiastic	A		B C
Extrovert	A		B C
Motivation	A		B C
Aggressive	A		B C
Unresponsive	A		B C
Noncommittal	A		B C

Qualifications

Academic preparation	A		B C
Work experience	A		B C
Position match	A		B C

Overall Evaluation

Long-range potential	A		B C
Drive and ambition	A		B C
Ability and qualifications	A		B C

    A—Outstanding
    B—Average
    C—Below average

INTERNATIONAL CAREER DIRECTIONS

Interviewing Techniques for International Employment

At times, students may need to recognize cultural differences that exist between different countries so that they can communicate more effectively when interviewing with a prospective employer. The information provided below is only a general comparison of some differences that may exist between U.S. and international employers.

Interviewing for a Job Outside the United States: Cultural Differences in the Interviewing Process

In the United States	Some Countries Outside the United States*
Self-Promotion • Assertiveness • Confidence in openly discussing goals and accomplishments. • Appropriate dress.	• Unless presented as part of a group activity, citing accomplishments and skills is viewed as boastful, self-serving, and too individualistic. • Asking employer directly about status of application is rude.
Directness in Communication • Open and direct responses to questions. • Eye contact with interviewer and relaxed posture are appropriate.	• Appearance of criticism must be avoided to save face. • Eye contact, especially with persons of higher status (e.g., employer, interviewer), is disrespectful.
Self-Disclosure • Personal descriptions of experiences, hobbies, strengths, weaknesses. • Answers to questions related to personality (e.g., leadership style, problem-solving abilities).	• Personal questions about likes, dislikes, and so on are considered an invasion of privacy and are discussed only with close friends and family.
Career Self-Awareness • Demonstrating knowledge of self, career goals, and how they relate to the job. • Discussion of long-range career plans.	• Jobs are assigned by government or family. • Questions about role in a company indicate potential disloyalty. • Company assigns work responsibilities. • Individual must be flexible to accept whatever job becomes available.
Individual Responsibility in Finding Employment • Use a wide variety of resources for identifying jobs (friends, family contacts, associations, career services, academic mentors, etc.).	• Jobs are found through government or family.

In the United States	Some Countries Outside the United States*
• Networking.	• Dependency on relationships in job search are fostered. One resource (e.g., academic adviser, employment agent) will find appropriate work for the job seeker.
Informality in the Interview Process	
• Congenial interviewing environment that encourages openness, some joking, exchange of information.	• Sitting with person of higher status requires deference. The job applicant is very polite and does not ask any questions or provide information that may indicate lack of respect for interviewer's position.
	• Handshaking, touching, using first name, crossing legs, and so on are inappropriate.
Punctuality	
• Arrive 5 to 15 minutes before appointment.	• Personal relationships are more important than time. Lateness anywhere from 15 minutes to two hours from agreed time is not insulting.
Individual Equality	
• Race, sex, age should not affect interview relationship.	• Males are expected to assume dominance in interactions with females.
	• Younger persons defer to older ones.
Preparation about Organization	
• Obtain as much information as possible about job and organization before interview.	• Research about organization may indicate excessive and undesirable initiative or independence.
• Demonstrate awareness of organization in letter of application and during interview.	

*These factors are not indigenous to one particular society, such as the Japanese, but represent a cross section of countries and continents. These differences may pertain to some specific cultures and may not necessarily represent all cultures, but because cultural differences may exist you should find out what these differences are for the specific country in which you are seeking a job. The book *Do's and Taboos,* by R. Axtell (New York: John Wiley & Sons, 1990) explains the customs in a large variety of countries and may be a helpful resource in learning more about this topic.

Follow-Up Strategies

How you follow up after the interview is just as important as the preparation you did beforehand.

Follow-up begins as you end your interview with the employer. If it is unclear to you what will happen next, *ask.* The employer may indicate that he or she will get back to you in two or three weeks or by a certain date. If that is the case, you may want to ask whether you will be contacted by telephone or in writing. If by telephone, you will want to be sure to leave a number where you can be easily reached.

If the employer says that he or she would like you to get back to him or her after thinking about the interview to pursue things further, *do it!* The employer is not giving you the runaround but may be testing your initiative and your genuine interest in the company. The employer may even ask that you visit one of the company's locations before pursuing a second interview if you have not done so already. This is to be sure that you will understand the company style and the type of environment in which you may be working. If you are unsure of your interest in the company, this visit could be a deciding factor for you. In that case, it is a benefit to both you and the employer.

If an employer asks you to take initiative in any way, *do it!* If you are absolutely sure the job or the company is not right for you, don't waste the employer's time by taking the next step, but *do* send a thank-you letter acknowledging the time given to your first meeting. You do not want to burn any bridges as you move through your career. If an employer says nothing about follow-up, *ask* what you should do or expect next. If an employer does not get back to you in the time indicated, call. Be sure to wait for the designated amount of time to go by before calling.

When you go home after an interview, write down all the questions you can remember and what your response was. This will help you remember what the employer told you and what you told the employer, in case any questions arise about what was communicated during the interview.

Always send a thank-you letter immediately after an interview. If you are interested in the job, the letter will jog the employer's mind about you as an applicant and will relate your interest in the job. If you are not interested in the job, still send a thank-you letter for the time the employer took with you. A few years from now, that employer may be one you want to work for, and you would not want to have created a negative first impression of your professionalism.

Sample Thank-You Letter of Interest after a Job Interview

Your address

Date

(Employer's name, title, address)

Dear (Ms. or Mr.) (Last name):

It was a pleasure meeting with you yesterday. My interview with you confirmed my interest in the international credit analyst's position at Finance Bank, Inc., and confirmed my belief that I have the qualifications to do the job.

I am further interested in working at Finance Bank, Inc., after observing the professional, results-oriented attitude in everyone I spoke with.

The international credit analyst's position would allow me to apply my strengths in computer programming, customer relations, and accounting procedures while at the same time expanding my knowledge of international banking. My ability to speak Spanish fluently should be particularly helpful in communicating with your new customers in Madrid.

I am very enthusiastic about joining the Finance Bank, Inc., team and contributing to the development of your customer base in Europe. I have enclosed some more samples of financial models I have worked on and a copy of the customer service award I received from my co-op employer, NNC Bank in Boston.

If you have any further questions, please do not hesitate to contact me. I look forward to hearing from you soon.

Sincerely,

John L. Coburn

ACTIVITY 9-4 • *Postinterview Company Evaluation*

An important part of your follow-up after an interview is to evaluate how much the company's philosophy and needs match your own professional interests. By completing the Postinterview Company Evaluation you can gain an understanding of the company that should be useful as you compare it to other firms you interview with. If you receive a job offer, this is one tool to help you decide whether or not to accept it.

Company name _____

Company Standing	Yes	No	Comments
Is the company public?	____	____	_____
Is the company private?	____	____	_____
Is the company an industry leader?	____	____	_____
Is the company growing?	____	____	_____
Does the company have a positive reputation?	____	____	_____

Organizational Framework

	Yes	No	Comments
Is the management mainly centralized?	____	____	_____
Is the management mainly decentralized?	____	____	_____
Is the company's advancement	____	____	_____
Vertical?	____	____	_____
Horizontal?	____	____	_____
Frequent?	____	____	_____

Philosophies and Policies

	Yes	No	Comments
Do I agree with the company philosophy?	____	____	_____
Is the company production oriented?	____	____	_____
Is the company people oriented?	____	____	_____
Is the company's management traditional?	____	____	_____
Is the company's management progressive?	____	____	_____

Geography

	Yes	No	Comments
Is the job in a desired location?	____	____	_____
Is relocation required?	____	____	_____
Is travel required?	____	____	_____

Management Development

	Yes	No	Comments
Is there a formal training program?	____	____	_____
Is the majority of training "hands on"?	____	____	_____
Is there a continuing education program?	____	____	_____
Is there a remedial training program?	____	____	_____
Is the evaluation system used as a management tool?	____	____	_____
Are there criteria to be met before salary increases are given?	____	____	_____
Are salary increases given on the basis of merit?	____	____	_____
Is there a maximum earning level?	____	____	_____
Does the company provide			
Health insurance?	____	____	_____
Dental insurance?	____	____	_____
Sick leave?	____	____	_____

The Interview Hall of Fame . . . and Shame

The Interview Hall of Fame and Shame depicts examples of some interviews that were successful and some that were not so successful. These stories demonstrate that certain things, when taken to an extreme, can hurt your chances of leaving an employer with a favorable impression. On the other hand, given the right balance between creativity and professionalism, you can develop some unique ways to stand out in a positive way when interviewing for a job.

For the best results, however, check first with your placement office to see if your strategies to impress an employer on your interview have a good chance of working.

Hall of Fame Case 1: John— Sous-Chef

John was about to graduate from a two-year culinary arts program. He loved his profession, and it showed in the quality of his work. John had received good grades in school, had four years of part-time work experience in the food service industry, and had represented his school well by earning several gold and silver medals in national food competitions. At graduation, John was interviewing for his first full-time job with many companies visiting his campus. For one interview, John came to the placement office, properly dressed and with résumé in hand. He also carried with him a black box. The placement director offered to store the box for John while he went on his interview. He declined the offer, stating he needed to bring it with him on his interview.

John was the last interviewee of the day. He went into the interviewing room, introduced himself, and before the interviewer could begin to ask questions, John opened the black box, producing the makings for a flaming dessert coffee. He said to the interviewer, "I know you've had a long day and that I am your last interview. I thought you'd like to sit back and relax a moment. While I prepare you some coffee, feel free to begin my interview." The interviewer smiled and immediately said, "You're hired."

Hall of Fame Case 2: Susan— Advertising Assistant

Susan was about to graduate from a two-year program in advertising and public relations. In addition to the job interviews she secured through her school's placement office, Susan arranged her own interview with a top advertising firm in Manhattan. Susan realized the competition would be stiff because there were many applicants.

Susan decided to use her expertise in her field to create a unique approach for her interview. Two weeks before her scheduled interview, Susan sent a portfolio by mail to her prospective interviewer, asking that it be reviewed prior to her interview. Her portfolio contained samples of two promotional brochures she had designed for her advertising class. Also enclosed were a copy of an ad she had created for the company where she had completed her internship and other samples of her writing.

That same week, Susan remembered the name of a graduate of her school who worked for the company with which she would be interviewing. Susan telephoned that person, introduced herself, and informally acquired some information about the company. Finally, one week before her interview, Susan had a classmate videotape her class presentation on how to design an effective promotional brochure and mailed it to her prospective employer. By the time Susan arrived for her interview, she felt comfortable because she knew a little about the company and her interviewer knew something about her.

Susan's preparation allowed more time during the interview to discuss the details of the job. The originality Susan demonstrated in her job search, combined with her qualifications, led to a job offer, which she accepted. Employers appreciate creativity that is professional yet unique. This approach told the employer that Susan really wanted the job and that she had initiative and creative skills to bring to the company.

**Hall of Fame
Case 3: Kirsten—
Corporate Travel
Agent**

After receiving her diploma in travel/tourism from a local travel school, Kirsten decided to continue at her job as a receptionist for a travel agency where she had worked while in school. After working there full-time for two months, Kirsten was fired because of a personality conflict she had with a co-worker that led Kirsten to refuse to work on several projects with her. Before interviewing for her next job, Kirsten sought advice from her school's placement office on how to explain the fact that she had been fired from her job.

Part of Kristen's corrective action was to complete a professional development workshop on teamwork and to obtain some temporary work, from which she received a positive evaluation on her ability to work with others. Equipped with demonstrated proof that she had addressed her problem, Kristen began interviewing again for full-time employment.

When her next interviewer asked Kirsten why she had left her job, Kirsten said that she had been fired because she had had differences with a co-worker and that led her to be uncooperative several times. Kirsten explained that there were no problems with her individual work performance and that she had taken steps in learning to be a good team worker.

Kirsten went on to discuss the positive side of the job she had and emphasized her accomplishments. She stated that she had sought advice from her school's placement office and now realized that despite her individual talents, her success depended on working well with others. Kirsten expressed sincere interest in the corporate travel agent's position and said she was ready to learn how to work better with others.

**Hall of Shame
Case 1: Dennis—
Systems Consultant**

The placement director at XYZ Business School was successful in getting Digital Corporation to recruit XYZ graduates for the first time. Five of the top students from the computer program were selected to interview with Digital Corporation.

Dennis, one of the candidates, appeared to have the best qualifications. He was in his last year of the program, academically was one of the top five graduates in his major, had part-time job experience as a systems analyst, had successfully completed a computer internship, and was a lab assistant on campus. Dennis was articulate and projected a professional image. At the interview, Dennis was asked, "What type of environment do you like to work in?" The question was intended to determine how much supervision Dennis needed and if he could work well in a fast-paced environment. Dennis responded to the question as follows: "See this suit I have on? I never wear these. I program best in my jeans with a six-pack of beer." Thoroughly confused, the interviewer commented that Dennis seemed to have the appearance of one person and the personality of another. She decided he was not a match for their company because he did not appear ready to adapt to the corporate environment at Digital Corporation.

When the placement director asked Dennis why he responded this way, he answered, "I went to your professional development seminar, and you said to always be honest on an interview." Four years later, Dennis was hired to work at Digital, after realizing that portraying a professional image is necessary in most corporate environments.

**Hall of Shame
Case 2: Larry—
Retail Management**

Larry was a Retail Management major from Brooklyn. He came to the placement office with a request to interview with Abraham & Straus department store for a buying position in their jewelry department. Larry first came to the placement office wearing a ring on every finger, expressing his desire to be a jewelry buyer because he liked jewelry. The placement director advised Larry to investigate the role of a buyer, explaining that it entailed excellent quantitative skills and business management expertise. She told Larry that if he tried to promote himself on the basis of his interest in jewelry, he would not be perceived as someone who really understood what the job entailed. Larry convinced the placement director that he understood and was scheduled for an interview.

On the day of the interview, Larry came to the placement office dressed professionally and seemingly well prepared for his interview. Later, the interviewer came to the placement director to tell her that Larry would not be called back for a second interview, the reason being that Larry had an unrealistic viewpoint of what a retail buyer does. In fact, before entering the interviewing office, Larry had slipped his rings on and proceeded to tell the interviewer he liked jewelry and wanted to be a jewelry buyer. Larry did not get a job in the retail field that year. After trying two or three jobs, Larry established a career as a sales representative for a local manufacturing company. Having a clear understanding of what a job entails day to day is critical.

Hall of Shame Case 3: Cheryl— Administrative Assistant

Cheryl saw a job posting in the placement office for an administrative assistant at a bank. Since this was what she had trained to do at her school, Cheryl saw this job as a good opportunity to launch her career. A good student, Cheryl received A's and B's in almost all her classes. She did not have much part-time job experience. The only jobs she had had for the past two summers were as a waitress and a retail sales clerk.

When Cheryl began preparing for her interview, she reviewed the checklist given to her in her professional development class. The checklist reminded her to wear her best dress or suit. Cheryl selected the new dress she had worn at her class formal the previous week. It was a straight, black dress with a low V back and sheer, long sleeves. She wore black hose and shoes and added a pearl necklace to complete her outfit.

When Cheryl went on her interview at the bank, she felt confident she would get the job. When she did not, she went to discuss with the placement director what might have gone wrong. The placement director called the personnel representative at the bank who had interviewed Cheryl and asked for her feedback on Cheryl's interview. The interviewer thought that Cheryl had interviewed well, but they were looking for a "different type" of person, one who would fit into the professional environment at their company. Cheryl had made the mistake of thinking that the dress appropriate for a social occasion was also best for her interview. The message we give by our appearance is powerful on an interview.

Chapter Summary

The interviewing process is a necessary and important part of your job search; it is a key factor in most hiring decisions. Although you cannot reliably predict the outcome of every interview, you stand the best chance of receiving a job offer if you have demonstrated initiative and preparation to the prospective employer.

Knowing what to expect on an interview, having specific information about the employer and the job available, and organizing your self-presentation thoroughly will all help you interview successfully. The real key to your success will lie in your ability to stand out from other job candidates because of both your unique credentials and your ability to promote yourself.

Mastering effective interviewing techniques early on will also enable you to make successful moves throughout your career. A job offer is worth the effort.

Accepting or Rejecting a Job

Congratulations! You have received one or more job offers. You now need to decide whether or which one you will accept. Accepting a job is a big step. It is a commitment. You must decide if the job represents the right match between you and your prospective employer. You must also consider whether or not the job brings you closer to your long-term career goal. As part of that process you will need to review what you offer the employer, what the employer offers you, how much you will earn, and how that salary compares to the cost of living in the geographic location you will be in.

What You Offer the Employer

You should be prepared to wait a while before receiving the job offer you want. The economy, geographic location, supply and demand, your experience, and how well you interview in your field will affect both how long it takes for you to receive a job offer and the number of job offers you receive. In some cases, you will find it better to accept a job that you do not consider ideal to get the experience you need and to demonstrate a realistic attitude about your readiness to fill certain positions. It takes some people longer than others to find the job they really want.

When you do receive a job offer, it is always good to review what you can bring to this job. This step is important because if you don't feel that what you have to offer matches what the employer is looking for, you probably will not be happy in your job.

A review of what you offer the employer will help you decide which job offer is right for you. You should review the skills you have that can benefit the company. You will want to be sure that you have the opportunity to use at least some of your skills on the job. This will help you practice and improve your skills so that you become more valuable to your company and better prepared to accept new responsibilities throughout your career. You may also offer the company a positive and realistic attitude about the level of responsibility you will have in the job. Being realistic about what you expect in your job is important to your employer because it means you can be focused on and satisfied with your current job for a period of time. This means you will not be overly concerned with a promotion or salary increase before the appropriate time for these changes. Consider whether the job offered can be a stepping-stone to more responsibility in that job or in your next job. You should also offer your employer the reassurance that you can be committed to this job for at least a one- to two-year period.

Finally, in considering your job offer, you can express to an employer that this job offers you the chance to learn new skills and techniques and contribute to the company those you already have. Your willingness to learn from as well as contribute to the company is important to an employer because it means you are willing to grow to become a more valuable asset to the company. By thinking about what you offer the employer and the job, you can make a better decision about whether or not this opportunity is the right one for you.

What the Employer Offers You

Among the things to consider when deciding on a job offer is what the employer can offer you. To determine if this is the right career opportunity for you, consider how much you can learn and grow professionally (professional development), the current standing of the company (how is it doing?), and the compensation package.

Key Immediate and Long-Range Factors to Consider

Factor	Immediate	Long-Range
Job content	Type of work	Opportunity for growth
Development	Training	Continuing education
Direction	Supervision	Quality of management
Work climate	Work environment	Company values
Compensation	Pay and benefits	Compensation philosophy

Reprinted from *Planning Job Choices: 1996*, with permission of the National Association of Colleges and Employers, copyright holder.

Professional Development

The very first thing you should think about is what you can learn in your new job. This is especially true when accepting your first job, because you will want this job to prepare you for future career opportunities. Many students underestimate the value of selecting a job based on the learning it can offer. You should consider the first job a stepping-stone in your career and focus primarily on how it will help you grow professionally. You can learn directly on the job or through training programs offered by the company. On the job, you will learn new skills and techniques, how to work better with others, and how to work better independently. By observing your co-workers and those in management or leadership positions, you can learn how the company operates and how certain situations are handled.

Training Programs

Training programs vary from company to company. Before accepting a job, find out about any formal training the company may have. You should know the duration of the program, salary during the training phase, location of the training (on site, home office, etc.), and what type of ongoing training will occur.

If training is done on the job, as opposed to in a formal program, this is fine in most cases. Just be sure to ask enough questions to get a feel for whether or not the training will be structured enough for your needs. If an employer offers you a lower salary to begin training on the job and says that it will increase to a certain amount after your training period, ask how long that will be. If you are accepting this as a condition of employment, you should be able to measure the time frame within which the change should occur. This will be important to you from a financial standpoint. You will then have an idea as to how long you will be working within a particular budget and be able to plan your personal and financial responsibilities based on that knowledge. On-the-job training and formal training programs can help you do a better job and will better prepare you for new opportunities that may interest you later on.

Promotional Opportunity

Some companies have more predictable promotional routes than others. Some move employees through different grades or levels of jobs based on their seniority with the company. Others base promotions strictly on performance. The large ones may offer many employees the chance to move up, while smaller companies have less room at the top. Many have a formal internal job posting system to which employees may respond by applying for posted positions. Other companies fill positions by going directly to employees selected on the basis of good performance. Knowing the promotional procedures at a company before you accept a job will help you understand your chances for advancement within that company.

Company Standing

Before you accept a job, you should feel comfortable about the company's current status. This means knowing about such things as the financial stability of the company, plans for growth or expansion, reputation and standing with the competition, involvement with employees, and stability of the workforce. You can find this information in company's corporate brochure and annual reports, in financial sections of many newspapers, or in business reference volumes like Moody's or Dun and Bradstreet. Your local chamber of commerce may also be able to provide you with some of this information.

Financial Stability.   You should know enough about the company to be reasonably sure it is financially healthy and will be in business in the future. When you've started your new job, you don't want to have to worry about whether your company will be around in a few years.

Growth or Expansion.   A company that is growing or expanding may have a wider offering of long-term career opportunities than one that is stagnant. You want to know that the position you take will be made interesting and challenging because the company is active and growing. If the company is expanding, this may raise questions in your mind about possible future relocation or changes in responsibilities.

Reputation and Standing with the Competition. Knowing if the company has a reputation for good business practices is important because you want to be proud to be associated with your employer. Knowing how well the company stands with its competition may tell you something about its ability to stay in business despite competition from other companies. If the company continues to perform well in comparison to its competitors, you may feel more secure about the company's ability to stay in business and about your ability to keep your job

Involvement with Employees and Stability of the Workforce. Some companies communicate with and involve employees in the company more than others do. Employees may be involved in providing ideas to improve the work environment or customer service, to cut costs, or to implement a new program. Working in a company that encourages employee participation can be interesting and professionally rewarding.

A company's low employee turnover may tell you that employees are generally happy with their jobs. A stable workforce usually indicates the company is a good one to work for.

ACTIVITY 10-1 • *What's Important to You in a Job?*

1. Review the items in Column 1 and, in the blanks, add any other factors you might use in deciding about a job.
2. In Column 2, check off the items that would influence your decision about a job offer.
3. Use Column 3 to prioritize the factors you've checked off; give each a letter.

> A = I *must have* this (most important).
>
> B = I *really* want this (important).
>
> C = This would be nice to have (least important).

Column 1	Column 2	Column 3
Fulfilling work	_____	_____
Variety of work	_____	_____
Responsibility	_____	_____
Recognition	_____	_____
Autonomy	_____	_____
Challenge	_____	_____
Advancement opportunity	_____	_____
Schedule	_____	_____
Working conditions	_____	_____
Customer contact	_____	_____
Type of customers	_____	_____
Salary	_____	_____
Fringe benefits	_____	_____
Training program	_____	_____
Location of job	_____	_____
Commuting distance	_____	_____
Size of institution	_____	_____
Reputation of institution	_____	_____
Friendliness of staff	_____	_____

Column 1	Column 2	Column 3
Friendliness of co-workers		
Evaluation system		

Benefits

When considering a job offer, you need to evaluate how well the compensation package meets your needs. Understanding the many different types of compensation programs that exist will help you make a good career decision. You want to have a sense of financial security and know that your personal needs are being met. This sense of security will leave you free to concentrate on your job performance and professional development.

The first thing to be aware of is that compensation does not consist of salary alone, but is *the combination of both the salary and the benefits offered to you.* This is important because if you are tempted to accept a job that pays a high salary and has few benefits, you may be required to pay a substantial amount of money for the benefits you need. You need to understand the value of the benefits offered to you, and then, by relating that to the salary, you can determine if this is the best compensation package for you. For example, the average cost paid by a company for a health insurance plan is approximately $3,000 per employee. If you were offered a job that paid $23,000 per year at a company that did not pay for your health insurance, instead of $20,000 elsewhere, that extra $3,000 would not be an advantage to you. Not only would you have to pay your own health insurance with it, but you would also be taxed more on the higher salary. There are many other types of benefits. Some are financially beneficial and some provide you personal or professional assistance, while others simply offer a convenience or enjoyment of some kind.

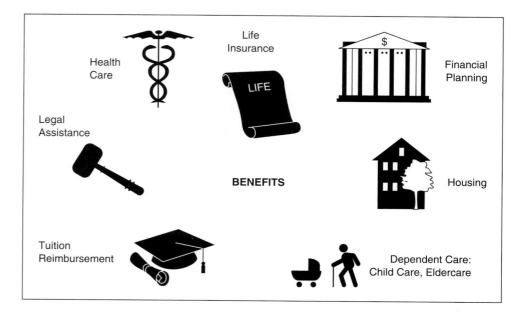

Health Benefits.   Health benefits vary from company to company. Some firms pay this benefit in full; others provide partial payment, with the employee contributing the remaining portion; and some companies offer no health care coverage. Be sure to ask what is available and how extensive the coverage is so that you will know if you need to plan for any of this expense on your own.

Life Insurance.   Life insurance is usually available in most companies. The purpose of life insurance is to provide your dependents financial support in the event of your death.

Education and Training.   Education and training benefits may be available through a variety of programs. In addition, *tuition reimbursement* is frequently available. This is a great benefit for employees who wish to continue their formal education while working. The economic value of tuition reimbursement is tremendous, as the cost of education remains relatively high. *Seminars* or *conferences* are also popular forms of education and training in many companies. Offered for periods from as little as a few hours to a week or more, these are good vehicles for providing new skills to staff or keeping them updated in current issues and techniques in their field.

Housing, Meals, and Transportation.   Housing, meals, and transportation are often referred to as living expenses. These costs are frequently covered in full for employees who must relocate temporarily or travel regularly for their jobs.

Travel.   Travel opportunities are often presented as benefits to employees. When travel is required for the job, companies usually reimburse employees for travel-related expenses. Sometimes trips are given away as a bonus or reward for top performance.

Financial Counseling.   Financial counseling provides employees the opportunity to learn how to better manage their own personal finances. For example, advice may be given on budgeting, investing, or computing personal income tax returns. In some companies, employees have the option of buying stock in the company that earns a monetary return for the individual based on how well the company does financially.

Time Off.   Time off with pay is usually available through paid vacations. Most companies also allow a certain amount of sick leave, which is to be used in times of illness. Generally, sick days are not to be used to supplement vacation time, because they have the exclusive purpose of being available only if needed for sickness. Paid holidays are another form of time off with pay. Although you should not seem primarily interested in time off, before accepting a job it is good to ask enough questions to be sure you thoroughly understand the company's position on time off. This will allow you to plan your time well and not overextend yourself with more time off than is acceptable to the company.

Family Care.   Family care services are often available to support employees in caring for children or older family members. These may include such things as day care or summer camps for children or elders.

Other Benefits.   Fitness and wellness programs may be available on the company's premises, or support may be provided for participating in off-site programs. Additional types of benefits may include a company car, club memberships, or discounts on products or services. These are usually referred to as "perks." Perks (short for the word *perquisites*) are benefits offered to provide a convenience, entertainment, or comfort of some kind. Although these are usually not as important to your final decision as the other benefits listed, when they do exist such extras may entice you to take the job.

ACTIVITY 10-2 • *Benefits Checklist*

Review the following list of benefits that may be offered to you by a prospective employer and rank which benefits you think are most important. Begin by placing a number *1* next to the benefit most important to you and end with a number *10* next to the benefit that is least important to you.

☐ Salary

☐ Health benefits

☐ Life insurance

☐ Education and training

☐ Seminars or conferences

☐ Housing, meals, and transportation

☐ Travel

☐ Financial counseling

☐ Time off

☐ Family care

Discuss your choices with others in your class to see where each of you match or differ. You may find that choices will vary according to age, family situations, or current financial status.

Keep in mind that although this variety of benefits may be available to you, you must consider which ones you need at this point in your life to determine if the compensation package is for you.

Salary

The salary offered you is certainly important; everyone likes to know they are paid what they are worth in the marketplace. Like benefits, the geographic location of the job can affect the total value of that salary, because in each area of the country living expenses vary. This means the same salary does not always have the same worth in different parts of the country. You may be willing to relocate and decide to take a job because it pays more than another, but the American Chamber of Commerce Researchers Association recommends: Don't jump at a high salary unless you know what it is really worth!

Bonuses. Some companies have a bonus system in addition to the regular salary plan. If you earn a bonus, it is usually in addition to an annual salary increase. A bonus is usually a monetary reward paid to an individual for outstanding performance.

Cost of Living and Budgeting

Computing Cost of Living

The following information will help you weigh the value of the salary you've been offered in a particular geographic area. The chart will enable you to do your own city-by-city comparisons of national cost-of-living differences. All index numbers are based on the composite prices of groceries, housing, utilities, transportation, health care, clothing, and entertainment in each city listed, with 100.0 as the national average. To calculate your approximate purchasing power in various areas, use the salary comparison equation.

Salary Comparison Equation

$$\frac{\text{(City 1)}}{\text{(City 2)}} \times \text{Salary} = \$ \underline{\hspace{2cm}}$$

• What is the Seattle equivalent of a $25,000 salary in New Orleans?

$$\frac{\text{Seattle}}{\text{New Orleans}} \quad \frac{111.9}{93.5} \times \$25,000 = \$29,920$$

• What is the New Orleans equivalent of a $35,000 salary in San Diego?

$$\frac{\text{New Orleans}}{\text{Seattle}} \quad \frac{93.5}{111.9} \times \$25,000 = \$20,889$$

Source: ACCRA, 4232 King St., Alexandria VA 22302–1507.

ACCRA Cost of Living Index

Average City, USA	100.0	**Florida**		**Iowa**	
Alabama		Jacksonville	98.2	Cedar Rapids	97.4
Birmingham	101.4	Miami/Dade County	112.2	Des Moines	99.6
Huntsville	99.1	Orlando	100.6	**Kansas**	
Alaska		Tampa	98.3	Lawrence	92.9
Anchorage	129.1	West Palm Beach	114.7	Wichita	95.5
Arizona		**Georgia**		**Kentucky**	
Phoenix	101.7	Atlanta	100.1	Lexington	98.1
Tucson	104.2	Augusta	100.4	Louisville	93.6
Arkansas		Columbus	93.1	**Louisiana**	
Little Rock	95.1	**Hawaii**		Baton Rouge	99.1
California		Hilo	137.3	New Orleans	93.5
Fresno	118.4	**Idaho**		**Maryland**	
Los Angeles/Long Beach	124.6	Boise	98.0	Hagerstown	100.8
Palm Springs	119.4	**Illinois**		**Massachusetts**	
Riverside	111.3	Champaign/Urbana	101.0	Framington-Natick	134.8
Sacramento	106.1	Peoria	102.6	Worcester	121.1
San Diego	128.5	Rockford	105.2	**Michigan**	
San Jose	135.6*	Schaumburg	124.0	Grand Rapids	108.9*
Colorado		Springfield	98.2	Lansing	103.4
Colorado Springs	93.8	**Indiana**		Midland	103.5
Denver	100.0	Bloomington	99.0	**Minnesota**	
Delaware		Evansville	91.5	Minneapolis	104.6*
Wilmington	108.8	Indianapolis	97.2	St. Paul	99.6
District of Columbia		Lafayette	103.6		
Washington, DC	131.7	South Bend	92.4		

*Cities marked with an asterisk show a second-quarter figure.

ACCRA Cost of Living Index *(concluded)*

Mississippi		**North Dakota**		**Texas**		
Hattiesburg	90.2	Fargo	96.3	Austin	99.2*	
Missouri		**Ohio**		Corpus Christi	92.9	
Kansas City	97.0	Cincinnati	105.8	Dallas	104.7	
St. Louis	97.7	Cleveland	114.3	El Paso	96.4	
Montana		Columbus	107.3	Fort Worth	93.4	
Missoula	96.9	**Oklahoma**		Houston	102.6	
Nebraska		Oklahoma City	96.0	San Antonio	93.1	
Omaha	89.9	Tulsa	94.7	**Utah**		
Nevada		**Oregon**		Salt Lake City	93.8	
Las Vegas	110.3*	Eugene	100.6	**Vermont**		
New Hampshire		Portland	108.0	Montpelier/Barre	109.7	
Manchester	115.5	**Pennsylvania**		**Virginia**		
New Mexico		Harrisburg	103.4	Richmond	113.6	
Albuquerque	99.1	Lancaster	110.6	Roanoke	96.8	
Santa Fe	107.3	Philadelphia	127.2	Virginia Beach	104.6	
New York		Wilkes-Barre	102.3	**Washington**		
Albany	105.7	**South Carolina**		Seattle	111.9	
Binghamton	101.0	Charleston	101.4	Spokane	97.1*	
Buffalo	112.7*	Columbia	97.1	**West Virginia**		
Nassau/Suffolk	147.9	**South Dakota**		Parkersurg	95.4	
New York City	213.3	Rapid City	97.2	Wheeling	93.9*	
Syracuse	103.2	**Tennessee**		**Wisconsin**		
North Carolina		Knoxville	94.4	Green Bay	97.0	
Chapel Hill	106.9	Memphis	94.5	La Crosse	95.2*	
Charlotte	100.1	Nashville	91.7	Milwaukee	103.4	
Greensboro	98.9			**Wyoming**		
Raleigh-Durham	96.4			Casper	99.3	
Winston-Salem	98.3					

Reprinted with the permission of the ACCRA, 4232 King St., Alexandria VA 22302–1507. The Cost of Living Index, produced by ACCRA, is updated quarterly and reflects the cost of housing, transportation, health care, and various consumer items, but excludes taxes. The cities included in the survey are those whose Chamber of Commerce or similar organization volunteers to participate. If a major city isn't listed, it didn't participate in the survey. Data are specific to a midmanagement standard of living.

Budgeting Your First Salary

After you have viewed your salary offer with respect to the cost of living, you may want to actually calculate your potential budget based on that salary. After reviewing this potential budget, you will be able to see how your salary might be allocated to suit your individual financial needs.

Savings Plans. Put yourself at the top of the list. Charles Lefkowitz, chairman of the International Association for Financial Planning, recommends, "You should put

away . . . 5 percent to 20 percent of every paycheck before you do anything else. If you can learn that discipline early on, you'll be way ahead." Payroll deduction plans are a great way to do this. Because the money never touches your hands, the temptation to spend it is not there. Also, some employers offer special benefits—such as IRAs, 401(k)s, or matching programs—to savers by means of payroll deductions.

Reserve Funds.   Have your own slush fund. Having at least a month's salary in a liquid, money-market-type account works well.

Avoiding Debt.   Get out of debt as soon as possible after you graduate. Paying off student loans early gives you the opportunity to invest your money. Be moderate with other debts you might incur. Never incur any debt unless you are sure you can afford to do so.

Tax Planning.   Plan a good tax strategy. Seeking professional help in this area may pay off. Keeping track of what is and is not fully deductible is the job of a professional. The key for you is to find out what deductions you are entitled to as well as the limitations involved. A free information packet, including a state-by-state directory of certified financial planners, is available from the International Association of Financial Planning (IAFP), 2 Concourse Parkway, Suite 800, Atlanta, GA 30328. A typical consultant's fee is $250. Depending on your needs and interests, the fee may be well worth the return.

Investments.   Invest early in your career. Investments in the stock market, mutual funds, or other sources won't be as important as your initial basic investments such as clothing and a car. Exercise discipline and pay off these debts as soon as possible. A working wardrobe and a vehicle are investments because they will get you to the job on time, looking good—leverage that you will need at the beginning of your career.

ACTIVITY 10-3 • *Compute Your Net Cash Flow*

Fill in the appropriate amounts for each income or expense item as it relates to your own personal finances. At the end, you can compute your monthly net cash flow.

Monthly Income

Wages and salary _____

Interest on savings, CDs, bonds _____

Other _____

   Total monthly income _____

Monthly Expenses

Rent or mortgage _____

Automobile loans _____

Personal loans (student loans) _____

Charge accounts _____

Income taxes _____

Social Security _____

Savings and investments _____

Contributions _____

Household maintenance _____

Furniture _____

Gas	_____
Electricity	_____
Telephone	_____
Water	_____
Transportation	_____
Food	_____
Clothing	_____
Medical	_____
Entertainment	_____
Other expenses	_____
Total monthly expenses	_____
Total monthly income	_____
Minus total monthly expenses	_____
Discretionary monthly income	_____

Source: International Association of Financial Planning.

Accepting the Right Job

Accepting the right job for the right reasons is critical to your career success and your personal happiness. If you select a job only for the benefits offered to you, you may not always be accepting the job that offers you the challenge or professional experience you need to move ahead in your career. To recognize a good job offer you should first evaluate what you can learn. Continuing to learn with each job you take will keep your career moving in a positive direction.

Beyond professional growth, there are lifestyle considerations that impact your decision. For example, your normal working hours and vacation time may be important to you if you want to keep a good balance between work and family and friends. If you have family responsibilities, child care or elder care services may be important to you. With the rising costs of health benefits, you may choose a job with good health benefits over one with a bigger salary. Early on in your career, frequent business travel may appeal to you, whereas you may prefer less business travel at later stages in your life and your career. You must assess your own personal and professional needs each time you consider a job offer. Your life's circumstances are likely to change over time, causing you to develop different priorities at different points in your life.

As discussed throughout this chapter, when making a decision on your first job, you will want to consider the type of position, the salary, and the location of the job. As you seek your first job, it is not likely that you will get your first choices in all three areas. If your main concern is to stay in a particular geographic area, your salary may be less than what you could earn somewhere else. If your main concern is to get a certain type of position, you may have to be willing to relocate anywhere for that opportunity. Your first job will involve a choice.

ACTIVITY 10-4 • *Making the Best Job Choice*

On the lines below, prioritize these three components—location, type of position, salary—in order of their importance to you.

1. _____

2. _____

3. _____

These will change throughout your career, but also as you gain experience, your chances of getting your first choice in all three areas will be better. Make this decision first before accepting a job.

Review the following two job offers available to a new college graduate with a degree in marketing.

Job 1: Sales Representative	Job 2: Telemarketing Representative
Responsible for developing a new customer base for new food product	Responsible for developing a new customer base for new food product
Frequent travel	Company training program
Company car	Two weeks paid vacation
Two weeks paid vacation	Salary: $23,000
Base salary: $20,000	Tuition reimbursement
Bonus potential: $5,000	

List the pluses and minuses of each job.

Job 1: Sales Representative		Job 2: Telemarketing Representative	
Pluses	Minuses	Pluses	Minuses

Complete the following, indicating which job you would take and why:

☐ Job 1

☐ Job 2

Your reasons: _____

_____

_____

Communicating Your Decision

Once you have made your decision of which job you will accept and which you will not, respond immediately to each employer. For the job you will accept, you should first call the person who extended the job offer. Tell the person you are pleased to accept the position, and ask what day and time you are to begin. If you are not sure of the location, ask your employer to forward directions. Follow up by sending a letter accepting a job offer (see Chapter 8).

If you are rejecting a job offer, you should call the employer directly and express thanks for the job offer if you can do so positively. Remember that it is important to maintain a good relationship with all employers. There may be a time, later in your

career, when you will reapply to one of these companies and you will want to have made a favorable impression. Follow up your phone call with a letter refusing the job offer (see Chapter 8).

Chapter Summary

Many factors can influence your decision to accept or reject a job offer. What is most important is that you base your decision foremost on what you can learn from the job. If you identify that you can further your training with the job, you can then begin to weigh the other factors that are important to your decision. Each job you take should help you build another set of skills that bring you closer to your ultimate career goal.

Dealing with Rejection

Understanding the various factors that may cause you not to get the job you want is a key to dealing with any feelings of rejection associated with this experience. Knowing which factors are in your control and which are not is the first step to overcoming the rejection. Once you know the reasons why you were not able to obtain the job you wanted when you wanted it, you can develop a plan for moving forward with your career.

Playing to Win

Any job search puts you into a competitive situation. When you are graduating, you are mainly competing with your fellow graduates for your first job. Once you are in the world of work and decide to change jobs, you are competing with possibly hundreds of other professionals in your industry. Think of the job search like a major sports competition.

A basketball team must physically and mentally prepare for *every* game it plays. Even on a winning streak, the team members can never assume they will win the next game. And after losing a game, the team members must meet to examine the game to see what mistakes they made, to learn how to correct those efforts, and to get their spirits up for the next game. The players know that every competition is just a little different from the one before and that, while some factors are in their control, many are not.

Factors That Most Often Lead to Rejection

Most employers have found that certain indicators in job candidates often result in unsuccessful performance on the job. Employers look for these indicators during job interviews to form impressions about job candidates' potential for success with their company. The following table lists some of the factors that cause job candidates not to be hired and the potential impact these factors have in the workplace.

Factor	Impact
1. Poor attendance	May indicate candidate will not be reliable on the job
2. Poor grades without a reasonable explanation	May indicate skills are not adequately developed or motivation is low
3. Lack of goals/objectives	May indicate candidate does not know interests, is indecisive, or has no career plans
4. Lack of enthusiasm	May indicate a lack of initiative or drive
5. Inability to express himself or herself	May indicate poor communication skills or lack of confidence
6. Lack of interest in type of business	May indicate candidate is focused only on getting a job as opposed to finding the right company to build a career
7. Unrealistic salary demands	May indicate candidate is more interested in salary than opportunity or is unwilling to begin in a job at his or her appropriate skill level
8. Poor personal appearance	May indicate a lack of pride in self or in work to be performed
9. Lack of maturity	May indicate inability to assume responsibility or handle difficult situations on the job
10. Lack of extracurricular activities	May indicate limited experience with leadership roles or opportunities to develop teamwork and interpersonal skills
11. Failure to get information about company	May indicate lack of interest in or seriousness about the company or job search itself
12. Objection to travel or relocation	May not be able to respond to career opportunities as they arise
13. Excessive interest in security and benefits	May indicate more of an interest in what the company offers than in what the candidate offers the company
14. Inadequate background for type of work	Indicates inappropriate preparation for the position available

What You Can and Cannot Control

In any job search, some factors are clearly within your control and others are not. The important thing to remember is to take charge of what you can control and learn to deal positively with things over which you have no control.

Factors You Can Control

Each job you apply for is like a new game. An important part of your preparation is to mentally and verbally rehearse your presentation of the unique skills you can bring to the employer. It is also necessary to research the particular company you are interviewing with to be prepared to apply your skills to the company's needs. Such preparation is in your control and can improve your chances of being offered a job with that company. Other factors in your control include the following:

- The professional image you portray in writing or in person.
- The positive attitude you bring to the interview.
- Your follow-up after sending a résumé or attending an interview.
- Your ability to sell your school training and previous work experience.
- Your flexibility to start where the company needs you most (type of position, geographic location, etc.).

Factors You Cannot Control

Many factors in the job search process are not in your control and may lead to rejection rather than a job offer. Some factors that are not in your control are the following:

- The number of other applicants.
- The qualifications of the other applicants.
- Company policy to try to promote from within first.
- The skill level of the interviewer.
- The screening process used by the company.

In basketball competitions, the unique combination of factors in the team's control and those out of the team's control impacts the results of each game differently. The same is true with your job search. Sometimes you win and sometimes you lose, but whether playing in a basketball championship or competing for a job, you must always play to win! And an important part of your follow-up is to learn what action you can take to make your next performance better. By understanding some of the reasons why employers do not choose some job candidates you can better prepare for future job interviews.

Cutting Your Losses

So you've given a 100 percent effort and still did not succeed. Being turned down for a job is *not* the end of the world. It *is* an opportunity for you to reevaluate yourself professionally and create new employment options with other employers. When the job search is going slower than you would like and you are turned down for a number of jobs, there are some ways to handle the situation to your benefit. *Do not limit your options!*

Take a Good Look at Yourself

Below are some suggestions accompanied by real-life examples of how to handle rejection in your job search.

- Keep your options open.
- Try again. Many applicants view a turndown for one job with a company as a permanent turndown by the company. It is certainly worth reapplying to a company you really want to work for, whether for the same type of position or another type of work sometime down the road.

Example.   Frank was about to graduate with his B.S. degree in fashion merchandising and retail management. For the entire four years he was in college, his goal was to work as a buyer for Abraham & Straus in Brooklyn, New York. The company came to his campus to recruit graduates every year. When Frank signed up for his on-campus interviews, he set up only one appointment, an interview with Abraham & Strauss. In April of his senior year, Frank went on the interview. Sometime later the placement office could not reach Frank to see how his job search was going. After doing some investigating, the placement director discovered Frank had stopped going to classes just six weeks before graduation. It turns out he had received a rejection letter from Abraham & Straus and decided there was no use finishing school if he couldn't get a job at the company he had always wanted to work for. Frank made a serious mistake in limiting his options in his job search, so much so that it sent him into a depression when he felt he had failed in his efforts to realize his career goal. With the help of the placement office and his faculty, Frank got back on track, finished school, and got a job with another leading retail employer. A year later Frank reapplied to Abraham & Straus and got the job. To combat possible rejection from a preferred employer, create many options for yourself.

Plan Your Next Move

- Try to get feedback from the employer about what qualifications you are missing or what other reason(s) led to the decision not to hire you.
- Focus on the interviews and the job offers you are getting. Many times, you may be so determined to work for a particular company that you overlook great opportunities with other employers who have made an offer to you. Be open to a wide range of employment opportunities.
- Do something! If you are actually unemployed and competing for the right job, secure temporary employment, do volunteer work, or become active in a professional association or club in your field. Being involved in any one of these activities helps you keep an upbeat attitude and provides you with excellent networking opportunities.

Example.   Gail completed her internship assignment as a paralegal in training with a local law firm. She enjoyed the job and felt she had grown professionally as a result of her work experience. When Gail graduated, she went back to the law firm and applied for a full-time position as a paralegal, but she was not hired. Assuming she had left the firm in good standing, Gail called her previous supervisor and asked her for feedback on why she did not get the job. She was told that the position required someone with more experience than she had. Gail applied for three other paralegal positions and was not hired for any of them for the same reason. Angry, Gail felt that she would not see the return on her educational investment and felt she was not qualified for the profession she had trained for. However, she was not a quitter. She telephoned each employer to find out what specific areas she needed to master better and found that they all agreed on the same two or three areas in which Gail lacked experience. Gail took temporary assignments at other law firms and each time told her supervisor what she needed to learn from the job she had. After three months of temporary assignments in legal firms, Gail could promote the fact that she now had work experience in her field and had improved upon her weaknesses. Within three months of graduation, Gail had a permanent position as a paralegal.

A large part of Gail's success lies in her abilities to remain *committed* to her goal and to identify what *further training* she needed.

Maintain a Positive Attitude

Above all, keep a positive attitude. Remember that most successful careers are built on the right match between employer and employee. If that match is not there, it is best to find out as soon as possible. If an interview does not result in a job offer, there are some things you can do to avoid depression and maintain a positive attitude. For example, maintain a proper diet, exercise, and get enough sleep. This helps reduce stress and helps you focus mentally. Remember that it is important to bring a positive attitude to your next interview.

Example.   Sarah, a graphics designer, went well prepared to her annual performance review. She knew she had some difficulties with her job performance, but overall she felt ready for the next challenge. Although she could not get others in her department to work together as a team, her own work had earned her a national award. Sarah felt well qualified to move into a leadership role and become the new department head overseeing the work of six other graphic designers.

During her review, Sarah told her boss she wanted a promotion so that she could run the department. As they discussed her performance, it became clear that Sarah had not yet been able to lead her team members in several projects, even though her own personal work on those projects was exemplary.

Sarah did not receive a promotion. Her company hired a department head from outside the firm and started to give Sarah the special design projects for their key accounts.

At first, Sarah felt rejected and assumed her boss did not understand her value to the company. She met with him to discuss her disappointment. Her boss told her that her performance as a manager was not satisfactory but that her strengths lay in the creative work she did for the company. Although Sarah felt like she had failed, she knew it would be best for her to focus on her job as a graphic designer and not try to move into a management role. Sarah did an honest self-assessment and realized that she had automatically considered the management role more important than the creative role she played as a graphics designer. Her perception of professional growth and accomplishment was limited to upward movement. She learned through this experience that rejection can sometimes help you define the right fit between you and your career.

Chapter Summary

The experience of being rejected for a job you really want can be an opportunity for setting a new career direction or revising your plan to achieve your original goal. The most important part of this experience is what you learn about yourself and what you do with that knowledge.

Part Three

Career Management

Your First Months on the Job

Your first months on the job set the stage for your long-term success with your job and your company. Even before you arrive, you will probably receive literature to describe the company's benefits and/or an employee manual or handbook. The first few days offer several opportunities for you to become well established. A more in-depth training period, usually lasting one to three months, will follow. Some companies also implement a probationary period of one to three months to help confirm you are the right match for the job. Perhaps the most significant indicators and guides to knowing how well you are doing in your new job are periodic performance reviews and assessments. All of these programs are in place to help you and your employer establish a productive and successful relationship.

Before Arrival on the Job

Your orientation actually begins with your pre-arrival period. Use the time between acceptance of the job offer and the first day of employment to maintain contact with the company. Be sure you have taken care of as many final arrangements as you can before your first day. For example, ask if any benefit forms can be completed, and be sure to ask if there are any organizational procedures you should be aware of before you start your job. Most often the company will provide you with literature that describes the company's benefits or otherwise welcomes you to the company. Read all of this material carefully, and ask any questions you may have so there will be fewer questions on your first day. Know where and to whom to report on your first day.

Your First Day

You can relieve the anxiety usually associated with your first day on the job by following some basic guidelines. Arrive a little early so that you are sure you are reporting to the right place. You may still have some paperwork to fill out before you start work, and an early arrival can give you more time to do this properly. Someone in the company will probably be responsible for guiding you through the day. While you should focus more on listening the first day, don't be afraid to ask any questions you may have.

Part of your day will probably be spent touring the area you are working in and meeting people in the organization. Focus on remembering the names of the people you will be working with most often. You may also be shown your work area and where and how to access the resources and supplies you need to get your job done. Someone may offer to take you to lunch as part of your welcome. If so, be sure to stick to your scheduled lunch time and avoid overindulging in food or drinks, so that you will still feel alert throughout the afternoon. You will probably get a feeling for the company and the people who work there by the end of the first day. If something left you feeling unsure or uncomfortable, don't panic. This is normal. There is so much to get used to in a new job that you certainly won't feel totally adjusted after your first day. While you should feel excited about all that lies ahead, be sure to keep your goals and expectations realistic and stay focused on learning.

Employee Handbook

Most companies publish an employee handbook to help employees understand their relationship with the company in a variety of areas. The major objectives of an employee handbook are to present information on company policies and practices and to explain company standards for performance. By pointing out the company's strong reputation and commitment to its employees, the employee handbook can help build morale and team spirit. Finally, an employee handbook can answer routine questions and can be designed to comply with certain legal and procedural requirements. Some of the topics often covered in an employee handbook are the following:

Introduction to the company.	Discharge procedures.
General communication.	Work rules and standards.
Hiring policies.	Pay policies.
The disciplinary program.	Benefits.
Performance appraisals.	

While the employee handbook is a good introduction to the company, it is also a handy reference guide for employees throughout their time with the company. The employee handbook is the most comprehensive tool used by employers to communicate company values and policies to employees.

Orientation and Training Programs

First Few Days and Weeks

After your first day, your orientation may last anywhere from a couple of days to a few weeks, depending on the company. Some examples of information provided during these extended orientation periods are on-the-job safety instructions; an overview of the company's background, present operations, and products or services; and how to get involved with employee programs (employee of the month, recognition programs, contests). Remember that your orientation period is mostly focused on getting you acquainted with your new environment and how it works. This differs from actual training programs, which may be longer (30–90 days) and aimed at giving you the tools to actually perform your job better.

For your employer, a well-run orientation program can help reduce employee turnover. For example, Corning is a company that has successfully implemented an employee orientation program. Corning's primary objectives were to reduce early career turnover by 17 percent and to shorten by one month the time it takes a new person to learn the job.

First One to Three Months

Training programs may be administered individually for new employees as they are hired or may be conducted periodically for small groups of employees who begin their new jobs at approximately the same time. Training may be hands-on to teach or refine technical skills (drafting, machine operations), or classroom style to reinforce interpersonal skills (teamwork, customer service). The following box is a sample of a basic retail training program.

Sample Training Program

Designed to help our management trainees achieve company objectives and identify individual store needs, our eight-month, three-phase training program is comprised of the following:

- Phase I, II, and III participant manual
- Product knowledge manuals
- Supplemental videos
- Management resource books
- Support materials (tests and evaluations)
- Graduation certificate

Phase I

This 30- to 60-day intensive program trains participants in the fundamentals of salesmanship, customer service, in-depth product knowledge, and basic store operating procedures. Trainees will learn skills ranging from the proper methods of greeting customers, determining customer needs, and overcoming objections to footwear fitting techniques.

Phase II

Reinforcing the basics begun in Phase I, this 90-day period gives the trainee hands-on experience in various aspects of retail store operations. During this phase most trainees will attain the position of assistant store manager and will take an active role in sales floor management. Skills covered include: recruiting and hiring techniques, coaching for improved sales productivity, visual merchandising, training techniques, and advanced store operating procedures, including loss prevention, bookkeeping, and accounting.

Phase III

Under the guidance of our most experienced store leader—the manager-trainer—trainees receive 90 to 120 days of hands-on experience in managing a total retail store operation. The skills taught during this phase are designed to fine-tune the MIT (manager-in-training) in the areas of communication, customer relations, delegation skills, recruiting and training, leadership, marketing, merchandising, and maximizing profits.

This program is divided into weekly lessons, each with clearly defined goals, discussion questions, and practice assignments. The objective of each lesson is reached through daily interaction on the sales floor and through one-on-one training with the store manager. The lessons are outlined in the *Management Training Development Manuals*.

Upon successful completion of this program, trainees can expect to attain a store management position in the near future.

Probationary Periods (One to Three Months)

Some companies have a period of formal probation for new employees. A probationary period is meant to give you the opportunity to demonstrate your skills, abilities, and overall fit with the company. Probationary periods may range from 30 to 90 days, depending on company policy. If your job involves this testing period, use it as an opportunity to demonstrate your abilities and positive attitude.

Periodic Review and Assessments

During your first three to six months on the job, it would be helpful to you for your employer to conduct periodic reviews and assessments of your job performance. This will help you know whether or not you are on the right track and give both you and the employer a chance to discuss your strengths and weaknesses so that you can set immediate goals for improvement. Periodic reviews and assessments can help you adjust to your job during the first few months by setting and keeping you on a successful course. If these are not formally planned by your employer, you might want to ask your immediate supervisor to conduct these sessions because you think they may be helpful to both of you.

Look at the example of a typical performance appraisal checklist used by an employer to evaluate a staff member.

PERFORMANCE APPRAISAL

(Sample)

Company Name:_____

Job Title: _____

Department:_____

Directions: In Parts I and II, check all items relevant to the employee's position. Using the scale below, rate each item on a scale of one to five and circle the number at the right.

Scale:
1 = Needs much improvement
2 = Needs some improvement
3 = Satisfactory
4 = Very good
5 = Excellent

PART I: General Work Habits and Attitudes   **Scale**

A.	Attendance/punctuality/professional appearance	1	2	3	4	5	
B.	Meets deadlines	1	2	3	4	5	
C.	Cooperates with others	1	2	3	4	5	
D.	Accepts suggestions and criticism	1	2	3	4	5	
E.	Manages work schedule	1	2	3	4	5	
F.	Uses equipment properly	1	2	3	4	5	

Comments:_____

_____

PART II: Job Performance   **Scale**

A.	Quality of work	1	2	3	4	5
B.	Ability to solve problems	1	2	3	4	5
C.	Uses original ideas	1	2	3	4	5
D.	Communicates well	1	2	3	4	5
E.	Time management	1	2	3	4	5
F.	Technical/professional knowledge	1	2	3	4	5
G.	Interpersonal skills	1	2	3	4	5
H.	Learns new duties quickly	1	2	3	4	5
I.	Ability to apply job knowledge	1	2	3	4	5

Comments:_____

_____

_____

What are this person's greatest strengths and weaknesses? _____

_____

_____

Suggestions to improve weaknesses:_____

_____

_____

What further training does this employee need?_____

_____

_____

What contribution has this person made to the company, department, or division beyond normal requirements of the position? _____

_____

_____

What is your overall evaluation of this employee?_____

_____

_____

Reviewed by:_____   Date: _____

Employee signature:_____   Date: _____

ACTIVITY 12-1 • *Appraise Your Own Performance*

Directions: Using this sample performance appraisal as your guide to how you may be evaluated at your next job, rate your own work performance for the most recent posistion you held. In Parts I and II, check all items relevant to your position. Using the scale below, rate each item on a scale of one to five and circle the number at the right.

Scale:

1 = Needs much improvement	4 = Very good
2 = Needs some improvement	5 = Excellent
3 = Satisfactory	

PART I: General Work Habits and Attitudes   Scale

A.	Attendance/punctuality/professional appearance	1 2 3 4 5
B.	Meets deadlines	1 2 3 4 5
C.	Cooperates with others	1 2 3 4 5
D.	Accepts suggestions and criticism	1 2 3 4 5
E.	Manages work schedule	1 2 3 4 5
F.	Uses equipment properly	1 2 3 4 5

Comments: _____

_____

PART II: Job Performance   Scale

A.	Quality of work	1 2 3 4 5
B.	Ability to solve problems	1 2 3 4 5
C.	Uses original ideas	1 2 3 4 5
D.	Communicates well	1 2 3 4 5
E	Time management	1 2 3 4 5
F.	Technical/professional knowledge	1 2 3 4 5
G.	Interpersonal skills	1 2 3 4 5
H.	Learns new duties quickly	1 2 3 4 5
I.	Ability to apply job knowledge	1 2 3 4 5

Comments: _____

_____

_____

What are your greatest strengths and weaknesses? _____

_____

_____

Suggestions to improve weaknesses: _____

_____

_____

What further training do you need? _____

_____

_____

What contribution have you made to the company, department, or division beyond normal requirements of your position? _____

Chapter Summary

Getting off to the right start can make a big difference to both you and your employer. If you learn early what is important to functioning well in your organization, the chances of your feeling comfortable and doing well may be greater.

During your first months on the job you should be familiar with how the company operates, how to perform your job well, how you will be evaluated, and how well you are doing. The goal is to use this time to become a productive member of the company. You should focus on your contribution to company goals and objectives as well as on your own professional development.

Growing with Your Job

Once you have completed your adjustment period to your new job and company, you can focus on your professional development. Professional development is the process of establishing yourself in your career. This may include building your professional relationships, changing job responsibilities, improving your effectiveness on the job, and building job skills that can survive economic swings.

Building Professional Relationships

Throughout your career, you will be required to interact with people at different levels in your organization and with those outside the company. This interaction will range from dealing with your boss and associates to dealing with customers. Each of these situations always requires professionalism, but each requires a slightly different approach.

Your Relationship with Your Boss

A positive and productive working relationship with your boss can enhance your personal development as well as your professional growth. The following should help you:

- *Loyalty* sets the stage for trust. You can be loyal to your boss and to yourself even when you don't both agree. Be up-front and discuss the issue honestly with him or her only.
- Don't talk negatively about your boss or the company you work for to other people.
- Don't waste your boss's time.
- Be aware of your boss's priorities.
- Help your boss get promoted. It may help you in the same way.
- Incorporate the boss's point of view in your decision making. Try to see his or her point of view, and you may make better decisions.
- Accept criticism from your boss as a learning experience. Criticism should not be interpreted as a threat. It should be seen as a desirable challenge.
- Admit your mistakes.
- Ask for feedback.
- Don't ever upstage your boss.
- Avoid presenting your boss with bad news early or late in the day or week.
- No surprises—keep your boss informed.

Remember you are part of the management team regardless of what position you hold. Your relationship with your boss should be mutually beneficial. You should foster an environment of cooperation so that you help each other achieve personal and company goals. Being a team player with your boss makes both of your jobs more productive and meaningful.

Handling Problems with Your Boss.   Problems with your boss can stem from a variety of sources but most often will lie with your boss, with you, or a combination of both.

Common problems that lie with the boss include his or her inability to do the job, lack of experience with the job, poor communication skills, insecurity, or poor leadership skills. If you think your boss has one of these problems, you should be professional in your approach to resolving or improving the situation. First, you should avoid being disloyal and talking about the problem to others before you have the chance to talk directly to your boss about it. Before meeting with your boss, ask yourself what you expect from the meeting. Maybe you are looking for more direction, more authority, more responsibility, more involvement, or simply more support from your boss. Try to pin down the reason for your frustration so that you are able to tell your boss how the situation may be negatively impacting your productivity or morale. Also be ready to ask how the situation can be improved. Very often differences between bosses and workers are the result of different expectations. Always take the high road and let your boss know that you are anxious to improve your relationship and try to agree on a plan that will help both of you benefit from your meeting.

Your Relationship with Your Associates

Imagine that you are at the top of your graduating class and are used to being number one. You've earned the job you have now, but something is different. You've been hired along with a lot of other "number ones," and suddenly the skills and talents that once put you on top now put you in competition. Yes, there are other people who are smarter, who can do it better, and who will challenge you. Learning to work with others and to respect their opinions, talents, and contributions to your organization can be difficult. Perhaps one of the hardest things you will face in your career is having to work with people you really don't like. Learn to separate your personal feelings and preferences about people and situations from your professional life. The person you dislike the most might be an important link in your team. Tomorrow's jobs require the ability to get things done with other people. You will actually be measured on team efforts as well as your individual accomplishments. You will be treated the way you treat other people. The following tips should help you learn to become part of a team:

- Be a team player.
- Build working relationships with those at your level and in other departments.
- Realize the power of praise. Compliment people for a job well done.
- Say thank you.
- Listen to what other people have to say.
- Respect other people the way you want them to respect you.
- Be objective; if there is a problem, ask yourself, "What's wrong? Am I part of the problem? What can I do about it?"
- Deal with pressure. Control your temper and emotions and remain level headed when the going gets rough. You may say or do something you'll be sorry for.
- Look at competition as an opportunity to do the best job you can. Above all, play fair as you compete to reach whatever goal you have set for yourself.
- Use common sense.
- Develop a genuine interest in other people. Show that you are sensitive to their individual needs.
- Be courteous.
- Cooperate. Work is more difficult when the climate is tense. Cooperation builds spirit and is often more productive than individual effort.
- Be humble. If you are humble, you will still receive the credit you deserve. Don't be caught up in always having to win, to have the best idea, or to be number one. You have a long career ahead of you, and if these are your goals, you will be disappointed many times.

Handling Problems with Your Associates. A large part of your professional development will depend on your ability to handle conflicts with co-workers. Problems with your co-workers are best dealt with immediately and professionally. You should focus on the person involved in the conflict with you. Go directly to that person and ask for a meeting to discuss the situation. You may want to do this over lunch so as not to interrupt your work. Also, being in a neutral environment usually helps to diffuse a tense situation. In your discussion, take the initiative to state the problem between you and what you think the cause is. Do not place blame on the other person. Direct your comments toward the situation, not the person. Then ask for the other person's viewpoint. This is very important because if you listen carefully you may learn that the other person's perceptions are much different than you thought. Active listening is important to any conflict resolution, so work hard at it. After you have both explained your viewpoints, state that your goal is to come up with a resolution that is agreeable to both of you. Discuss what that might be and resolve to make it happen. If the problem continues after you have truly tried to resolve it, seek the advice of your boss or another proper person at the company.

Your Relationship with Culturally Diverse Co-Workers

Cultural diversity is the coming together of people from different races and ethnic backgrounds. Cultural diversity in the workplace is increasing as the number of people with varied backgrounds increases rapidly throughout the United States. Building relationships with people from diverse backgrounds may take an understanding of their culture and require different communication skills or motivational techniques based on those differences. In the workplace, we cannot communicate with everyone the same way and expect the same results. Sensitivity to differences helps to foster positive relationships between diverse groups. You need to become familiar with the people in your workplace and develop an understanding of how to relate to them. Many of the relationships you build throughout your career are important because the people you interact with form impressions about you and the company by how you deal with them. Relating to others in a positive way helps them build a positive image of you, which is important to your credibility as a professional person.

One way to build successful relationships with co-workers from different cultures is to practice the skills of an effective cross-cultural communicator. Some of these skills include showing respect, tolerating uncertainty, relating to the person not just the task, being nonjudgmental, showing empathy, and being persistent.

Show Respect. We all like to be respected by others. You express respect for others when you listen to their ideas and acknowledge their accomplishments regardless of whether you agree with them or not. While it is certainly acceptable to express your difference of opinion, respect ensures that you do not ignore the other person's viewpoint or try to impose your ideas on him or her. Respect for others from different cultures is important because what is right or true in one culture is not necessarily right or true in another.

Tolerate Uncertainty. When you are uncertain of or unfamiliar with a situation that is different from your personal experiences, try to react to new, different, and at times unpredictable situations with little visible discomfort or irritation. Exaggerated discomfort often leads to frustration and hostility and is not conducive to effective communication.

Relate to the Person Not Just the Job. In the workplace we are usually concerned with the job at hand. When transferring knowledge about your job or skills to a co-worker from another culture, expect that there may be differences in performance even if you have showed that person how to do the job just as you do it. For example, a person from a culture where people do not work at the same pace as you may go slower to accomplish a task. That person should not necessarily be judged negatively as a slow worker. When working with culturally diverse co-workers, focus not only on how much gets done but also on making people feel like they are important contributors to the completed product.

Be Nonjudgmental. The ability to withhold judgment and remain objective until you have enough information requires an understanding of other people's point of view.

Show Empathy. Showing empathy involves really putting yourself in another person's shoes. Most individuals enjoy communicating with those who attempt to understand things from their point of view.

Be Persistent. Sometimes your first attempts to communicate effectively may not produce the result you hoped for. It may take several interactions, in which you practice some of the above communication skills, to break through cross-cultural barriers.

Your Role as a Leader

If you are in the position to lead a team, then your human relations skills will determine your success. People want to be led, not managed. You manage projects, things, and your time. You lead people.

Leadership can be developed if you know its essential ingredients and have a real desire to lead. The strong desire is important, because leadership requires much time, energy, commitment, and skill; and if you really don't want the responsibility, you will give up easily. If you really don't want a leadership role, don't accept it. You won't do yourself justice, nor will it be fair to the people looking for leadership. If you do think the leadership challenge is for you, here are some qualities of a good leader that you should master:

Vision.	Courage.
Self-starting.	Risk-taking.
Positive attitude.	Energy level.
Intelligence.	Enthusiasm.
Character.	Ability to motivate others.
Integrity.	Ability to plan and organize.

Leaders create an atmosphere in which others can grow and develop their abilities. Effective leadership focuses on putting the people in your responsibility area first. Here are some guidelines for leaders:

- Recognize the power of people in your area.
- Empower commitment and loyalty by example.
- Recognize individual accomplishments as well as team efforts.
- Combine monetary rewards with other benefits such as free time, a new opportunity, or additional authority.

Your Relationship with Customers

Good customer service is a major factor in allowing a company to remain competitive and stay in business. To provide good customer service, employees need to think about what the customer wants and how the customer wants to be treated. Being responsive to customers requires excellent communication skills (listening and speaking). Being able to talk with customers about their needs and preferences is helpful to the company in developing programs and products. If you are in a position that involves contact with customers, keep in mind that your reputation and your company's reputation are largely based on the customers' impression of you.

| Teamwork | More and more companies are encouraging teamwork, as well as individual performance, as a means of professional development and as a technique for achieving company goals. As a member of a team, you are usually responsible for performing a specific role to help the team be successful. For example, the team's goal may be to win the perfect attendance award for its department during the month of September. For that to happen, everyone must have perfect attendance. If one person on the team does not fulfill his or her role, the team will not succeed. Teamwork is important because it is a way of bringing together individual ideas and opinions to create new ideas or solve a problem. In some cases, teamwork is more effective than individual effort. Teamwork is also intended to foster relationships among the team members by opening their minds to different perspectives. |

| Total Quality Management (TQM) | You might find that your company has a total quality management (TQM) program. TQM programs are designed to deliver superior performance to the customer by giving employees more ownership in the day-to-day operations of the company. This means that if a customer has a particular problem with a product or service, employees at many different levels are able to take action to resolve that customer's problem or make recommendations to the company on how to improve something so the problem will not recur. TQM programs bring employees together to solve customer problems and provide input to the company on how to do things better. Being part of a TQM program can give you the opportunity to demonstrate your initiative, creativity, and problem-solving skills. |

Improving Your Effectiveness

You can be more effective in your job if you have good planning and presentation skills, exercise good meeting behavior, manage your time and organize your work well, and focus your performance on results.

| Planning Skills | Planning is preparing for what lies ahead. If you know that you will assist with showing the company's office procedures to the new secretarial staff, you may set a goal now to prepare a procedures manual for that purpose. As an assistant sales manager, you may be required to help project the next year's sales in your area and establish strategies for reaching those goals. Being a good planner helps you set direction for your job and keep yourself focused. |

| Presentation Skills | Good presentation skills help you to be convincing about your ideas because they help the listener(s) be attentive to what you are saying. Many people feel nervous at the thought of making a presentation even to a small group. You can reduce your anxiety about making a presentation and increase your effectiveness by following these guidelines: Decide on the main point you wish to convey. Develop convincing information (articles, statistics, etc.) to use to illustrate your point. This will help you address any questions. Prepare a brief outline on index cards. Do your homework. Spending enough time preparing your presentation will help you be more confident about what you say. Look confident. Dress professionally, look alert and well groomed, and show enthusiasm for what you say. |

| Proper Meeting Behavior | How you interact at company meetings reflects an image of you to others. Among the actions you can take to help to create a positive image are the following: |

- Arrive on time. It is wise to arrive 10 to 15 minutes before the start of any meeting. This will give you time to become oriented to the room and the meeting agenda, and to avoid having to sit on the perimeter of the room because all the best seats are taken.

- Introduce yourself to participants you may not know prior to the beginning of the meeting. Also, introduce yourself when you speak at the meeting if there are some attendees who may not know you.

- If the meeting is delayed, turn to someone and begin an informal conversation. You should be relaxed and prepared enough not to have to worry about any last-minute details by this time. This may give you an opportunity to communicate with someone you don't see on a regular basis.

- Arrive prepared. Don't count on being able to make last-minute copies or notes within 10 or 15 minutes before the meeting. Be prepared when you leave your own office.

- Rehearse your remarks well if you are to make a presentation. Bring a one-page list of key points you want to make at the meeting so you will be sure not to leave any out.

- Sit straight. Look interested, alert, and ready to participate.

- Pay attention, even when topics don't relate directly to you; don't shift to converse with others when the topic shifts. You should always listen to everyone who is speaking. Not only is this professional courtesy, but you may learn something important.

- Avoid interrupting. If you have questions or comments when someone else is speaking, try to wait until he or she has finished making the main point.

- Don't monopolize the time. Be concise and to the point with your remarks. You will be more effective this way and will leave others the opportunity to speak.

- Ask for clarification if you don't understand something. Don't be afraid of appearing stupid. If you don't ask for clarification, you may base an important decision on the wrong facts.

- Be positive and tactful when disagreeing. Even though it is right for you to express your disagreement with someone, make sure you make it clear that you are attacking the issue, not the person.

- Use *we* instead of *I* when talking to a group; *we* signifies being part of the group.

- Think before you speak. It is more important to focus on the quality of what you say at meetings than on the frequency of times you speak.

- Don't smoke in a room where it is not permitted. Not only would you violate a company policy, but you also may alienate some participants who may be bothered by smoking.

- Pour soft drinks into a cup. Never drink from a can at a business meeting; it looks unprofessional.

- Say thank you quietly and leave at the end of the meeting or when the chairperson indicates you should leave.

- After the meeting, congratulate anyone who performed exceptionally well in his or her presentation.

Time Management and Organizational Skills

Improving your ability to manage your time and organize your work will help you become more productive and effective. It can also help you be recognized as someone who may be able to assume more job responsibilities.

Assess your workload and schedule on a weekly, then daily, basis. Be sure to identify the most important things you must get done during the work week. Then look at your schedule for any meetings, appointments, or sales calls that might take away from the quality time you will have to work on important projects. To ensure that you can get to work on those projects, reserve at least two days during the week to devote large chunks of time for your work. Try to set aside 30 minutes a day to organize and complete some of your work in between lunches, meetings, and appointments. Create files for your projects and important information. Use the computer as much as you can to store information and finish projects. Keep a daily to-do list and check off tasks as you complete them. Know when to say no! Keep a daily calendar. Plan on arriving

at work on time every day. Be flexible enough to work through lunch, stay late, or come in for a few hours on Saturday morning to keep on top of your work.

There are great payoffs for being organized and managing your time well. Personally you will reduce your stress and receive greater satisfaction from your work. Professionally you will develop the image of a professional who is serious about getting things done and moving on to the next challenge.

Focus on Results

In every job you have, you can increase your effectiveness by knowing what's important for you to do. Jobs exist because certain functions need to be performed and certain results are expected. For example, imagine that your job as a telemarketer involves selling cable TV service by telephone. You decide that you want to do better today than you did yesterday. Yesterday you made 25 calls and convinced eight clients to buy the service. You might decide to make 35 calls today, but what's really important is not making more calls but selling more cable subscriptions than you did yesterday. Therefore, a better goal might be to convince 10 clients to buy the service regardless of how many calls it takes. The workplace is becoming more and more structured toward individual workers having yearly objectives, thus creating more accountability for job performance.

There will be many times during your daily job routine when the hectic pace and multitude of tasks that need to get done become overwhelming. By using good planning and presentation skills, exercising proper meeting behavior, managing your time effectively, and keeping focused on results, you can get things done both independently and with others.

Promotions

As you progress in your job, you may demonstrate the ability and desire to take on other responsibilities in the company. This is a great way to build your career, because assuming new roles makes you more versatile and more valuable to your company. These growth opportunities can involve a new job or more responsibilities than you have in your current job. The following information and guidelines will help you establish and achieve your goals for promotion.

Job Enlargement versus Job Enrichment

You may be asked to perform more tasks at the same level of difficulty. This is job enlargement. Or you may be asked to assume more responsibility (for example, supervising other people). This is job enrichment. Either of these two instances could be described as a promotion.

The reason it is important to be aware of these two different types of promotion is that at some point you need to decide what type of growth opportunity is best for you. If you enjoy the hands-on work you do and would be challenged by doing more of it, you may choose this as a way to grow professionally. Sometimes people who prefer to continue in their same job but expand upon it a little more don't see these additional responsibilities as a promotion. A promotion does not always have to involve supervising others or moving up to the next-higher job title and level of responsibility. For some people this works very well, while others do better growing in the existing job. What is most important about either of these forms of promotion is that you feel properly challenged in a job that suits your skills and personality. You and your employer are the best judges of which route suits you best.

Mentors

A mentor is someone with more experience than you who is willing to provide helpful advice for your professional development. If at all possible, find a mentor early in your career. This person can be a big help in setting and achieving your professional goals.

Selecting both a role model and a mentor can keep you on the right track with your personal and professional development. The one thing both have in common is previous experience and success. Role models can be selected from any walk in life, can be living or dead, or can be famous or unknown. Mentors are usually selected from within your career field, are living success stories, are usually employed within your own company, and are not necessarily famous people. You may or may not be able to consult with your role model, but you will be able to actually work with your mentor on an ongoing basis. In many ways your role model helps you believe in yourself and serves as your inspiration, while your mentor helps you develop hands-on strategies for success in the workplace and is a partner with you in your career success.

Selecting a mentor is a most important challenge. Look for candidates who possess the "hallmarks of master mentors":

- Strong interpersonal skills.
- Organizational knowledge.
- Exemplary supervisory skills.
- Technical competence.
- Personal power and charisma.
- Status and prestige.
- Willingness to be responsible for someone else's growth.
- Ability to share credit.
- Patience and risk taking.

What a Mentor Is	What a Mentor Is Not
Friend	Preacher
Role model	Dictator
Adviser	Financier
Committed listener	Policeman
Confidante	Judge
Teacher	Boss
Enlightener	Meddler
Tipster	Spy
Orientor	Baby sitter
Encourager	Hoverer
Defender	Rescuer
Advocate	Smotherer
Guide	Case manager
Inspirer	Tattle-tale

Source: *Leader Digest,* 1993

ACTIVITY 13-1 • *Selecting a Mentor*

As you set goals for your own personal development, it will be helpful to choose someone who can be your mentor. While a student, you may consider someone from the company where you have a part-time or summer job, an internship, or a cooperative education assignment.

Think about some people who are possible mentors for you and write their names down.

Names   **Reasons Why**

_____   _____

_____   _____

_____   _____

_____   _____

_____   _____

_____   _____

Performance Reviews

Although you may have a three- or six-month assessment on your first job, performance reviews are conducted once a year in most companies. You should view your performance review as a chance to assess your professional strengths and weaknesses and to set goals for improvement. It is helpful to do your own pre–performance review prior to the actual scheduled time for your meeting with your supervisor. You should review the major responsibilities of your job, evaluate how many of those responsibilities you have met, evaluate the quality of the work involved, and think about why you were not able to fulfill some of your job responsibilities if this applies. You should also jot down a list of any of your unplanned accomplishments; these may range from winning an award to being asked to take charge of a special project. Be honest with yourself. By taking the time to reflect on your performance prior to your formal review, you accomplish two things: you reduce the chances of there being any surprises with your performance review, and you prepare yourself to discuss action steps for improvement. Even when your performance is satisfactory to both you and your employer, there is always room for improvement.

Recession-Proofing Your Job

In tough economic times, many businesses are faced with the decision to reduce their workforce. If you are properly prepared, you can handle these times should you become unemployed.

The key is to try to remain marketable to an employer. You can do this by having experience with a broad scope of responsibilities in your field, by being willing to take on many tasks, and by remaining flexible. You should also become comfortable with a little risk or uncertainty, because in a job transition you cannot be sure where you will end up or how long it will take to get there. Many times, a company may be willing to work at finding you a new role within the company, but there may be a long period of uncertainty in the process. Be patient and be open to a variety of job options.

ACTIVITY 13-2 • *Assess Your Transferable Skills*

Below is a partial listing of transferable skills that employers value. The more transferable skills you develop, the easier it will be to move to another job and perhaps even change careers during downturns in the economy.

People Management
Supervision
Teaching
Training

Sales & Marketing
Selling
Negotiating

Operation Management
Planning
Organizing
Budgeting

Communication
Public speaking
Writing
Foreign language

Leadership
Coaching
Direction setting
Inspiring

Technical
Computer
Desktop publishing

After reviewing the above partial listing of transferable skills, list the ones you currently have:

_____   _____
_____   _____
_____   _____
_____   _____

Now review the list again and list the transferable skills you would like to acquire:

_____   _____
_____   _____
_____   _____
_____   _____

Write out a plan to develop each of the transferable skills you want to acquire.

Skill	Plan
Example: Selling	I will complete a sales training program offered next weekend on campus.
_____	_____
	_____
	_____
_____	_____
	_____
	_____
_____	_____
	_____
	_____
	_____
_____	_____
	_____

Build an account of all the transferable skills you have. Transferable skills are those that are acquired in one set of circumstances that can also be applied to a new set of circumstances. Examples of some transferable skills include organizational, budgeting, or interpersonal skills. Being able to show that you have talents to bring to a new situation and that you are willing to do so can help you keep your current job or be hired by a new employer. If you are laid off or fired from a company due to an overall staff reduction and have maintained a positive relationship with your employer, the company may provide you with outplacement assistance.

Factors That Enable You to Recession-Proof Your Career

- Broad responsibilities.
- Many skills.
- Flexibility.
- Ability to deal with risk or uncertainty.
- Transferable skills.
- Positive attitude.

Successful Career Moves

There are points in your career when you need to evaluate whether your current position within the company is where you should be at this time in your professional development. If you decide that you are not receiving the challenge, compensation, or recognition you really need, it may be time to leave the company and pursue a new career opportunity. When you decide to do this, do it right. Give proper notice to your employer that you are leaving. Depending on your job and the company, anywhere from two weeks' to two months' notice may be appropriate. It is better not to leave your job until you have a new one. Not only does this ensure a steady source of income for you, but, in general, prospective employers would rather interview candidates who are currently employed. This is because employed people tend to be more current with their skills and active in their profession. Always leave your job on good terms with your employer. Hopefully, both you and your employer have gained something from your professional relationship, causing your departure to be amicable. Remember that the company you leave may serve as a reference for you later on, so you want to leave a positive image of yourself. Every career change can be a new beginning for you if you approach it professionally and with a positive attitude.

If you decide to resign from your job, you should write a letter of resignation to your supervisor aimed at informing your employer of your decision to leave and stating the benefit of your experience with the company (see the following sample).

June 2, 1996

Ms. Carol Faulkner
Director of Management Information Systems
TechCorp
1818 Tech Parkway
Boston, MA 02982

Dear Ms. Faulkner:

This letter is to confirm my decision to leave TechCorp on June 30, 1996. My family is relocating to California the first week in July.

My experience with TechCorp has been an asset to my career. I have learned technical skills and developed new, improved leadership skills through my work with members of the operations team.

Thank you for the career opportunity TechCorp has provided me. Best wishes!

Sincerely,

Richard D. Eaton

Chapter Summary

Positive relationships with others on the job will help you grow professionally and create new opportunities for you. This is because organizations are made of people and much of the success and failure of a company is contingent upon the ability of its people to achieve company goals. When you are viewed as someone who can work well with your peers, your supervisor, those you supervise, and—most of all—customers, you become a valuable company resource.

In addition, learning how to improve your own personal production and effectiveness helps you grow toward greater responsibility and greater personal satisfaction with your career.

Contemporary Issues in the Workplace

Chapter Objectives

After completing this chapter, you will:

Be familiar with health-related issues and how they are affecting the workplace.

Be familiar with family-care issues and how they are affecting the workplace.

Understand the role of ethics in the workplace.

Evaluate how you will deal with these issues in the workplace.

The world of work is changing toward increasing integration between personal and professional areas of life. The overlap of personal and professional interests is a result of changing personal value systems. For example, there is a trend for workers to value free time more than ever before, and for some people alcoholism or drug addiction affects performance in the workplace.

Changes in society also influence contemporary issues in the workplace. For example, career women who want to raise families are now faced with conflicts in priorities. Drug testing, AIDS testing, and a renewed emphasis on ethics in the workplace are a direct response to larger societal concerns, resulting in some behavioral problems in the workforce. Because contemporary issues in the workplace affect the way we live and work, you should be aware of some that will affect you during your career.

Health-Related Issues

Substance abuse, AIDS, the smoke-free workplace, wellness and health education programs, and the Americans with Disabilities Act are some of the health-related issues you should know about. By being better informed on these issues, you can understand why certain company policies are in place and what assistance is available to you to help you deal with these issues personally or with co-workers.

Health-related issues affect employees in the workplace in many ways. Substance abuse may affect an employee's productivity and attitude and can result in increased absenteeism. AIDS (acquired immune deficiency syndrome) has employees concerned about how the disease can be transmitted and how to relate well to a co-worker who has contracted the virus (human immunodeficiency virus, HIV) that causes it. Laws requiring more accommodations are opening up new career opportunities for special-needs employees. And companies that have implemented a "smoke-free" workplace are encouraging smokers to become nonsmokers and all employees to become more conscious of their personal health habits. As a result of the emergence of these health-related issues, more companies are committed to formal health education programs for their employees.

Substance Abuse

Overuse of some drugs and alcohol can produce behavioral problems for employees that disrupt either their own productivity or the environment they work in. An increasing number of employers —including the U.S. Postal Service, General Motors, Alcoa, the New York Times, and American Airlines—are requiring pre-employment urine or blood tests to screen for the presence of cocaine, barbiturates, amphetamines, marijuana, and opiates.

The effects of substance abuse problems are profound on both the employer and the employee, and that is why they have become a major focus of attention. Employers report higher incidence of problems with productivity, accidents, medical claims, absenteeism, and employee theft among employees with substance abuse problems. These all result in higher costs to the employer. As a job candidate or an actual employee, you can be affected by these problems whether you are a substance abuser or not.

In fact, 64 percent of recovering drug abusers admitted that drugs adversely affected their performance, while 44 percent of them admitted selling drugs to employees. If you test positive for drugs when looking for a job, you will almost certainly not be hired. Once you are employed, detection of drug or alcohol use can cause you to be fired if you show any kind of work-related problem because of it.

Some companies attempt to help an experienced employee overcome the problem. It is often more cost effective for the company to do that because there really is no guarantee that a new worker won't have the same problem. Through employee assistance programs (EAPs), companies offer on-site or off-site confidential counseling and treatment. Other companies' insurance plans cover drug programs, and some offer paid leaves of absence. When AT&T evaluated its EAP after three years, it found that 86 percent of those who had been treated were completely rehabilitated.

AIDS

The prevalence of the AIDS virus has led to much discussion about the potential effects of being HIV-positive on the employee's productivity and on attitudes of co-workers. Most companies have weighed these issues and developed company policies regarding the employment of HIV-positive workers and job candidates. In most companies, guidelines state that physical disabilities and chronic health conditions are not to be considered in hiring and promotion decisions unless they interfere directly with performance. This means that HIV-positive workers are no less productive than other employees because of the infection.

Why Employees Seek Help from EAPs

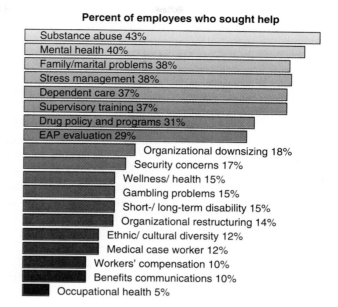

Percent of employees who sought help

Substance abuse 43%
Mental health 40%
Family/marital problems 38%
Stress management 38%
Dependent care 37%
Supervisory training 37%
Drug policy and programs 31%
EAP evaluation 29%
Organizational downsizing 18%
Security concerns 17%
Wellness/ health 15%
Gambling problems 15%
Short-/ long-term disability 15%
Organizational restructuring 14%
Ethnic/ cultural diversity 12%
Medical case worker 12%
Workers' compensation 10%
Benefits communications 10%
Occupational health 5%

Source: Charles D. Spencer and Associates Inc., "Employee Benefit Plan Review," December 1994. Reprinted in *The CQ Researcher* 5, no. 16 (April 28, 1995).

A different concern regarding this issue may be transmission. The question among fellow employees and the employer may be whether or not workers will be safe. Except for professions involving exposure to blood, there should be no concern for transmission due to exposure in the work environment. Despite this truth, many HIV-positive workers today face fear and prejudice from colleagues, friends, and even family, and as a result can lose their jobs, their insurance, and other work-related benefits. Education of the workforce is the answer to this problem; and many companies, such as Levi Strauss & Co., offer education on this workplace issue to their employees.

Health Education

As a result of some of these health-related issues, there is an increased effort to provide health education in the workplace. Many employers have implemented such programs to familiarize employees with how their substance abuse or that of their co-workers can affect them on the job. The programs are also aimed at prevention. Health education programs can inform workers how to interact with co-workers who have tested HIV-positive and help to correct misconceptions about the virus.

Another major component of health education involves wellness programs, which promote overall good nutrition and exercise as a way of life. These wellness programs instruct employees on how to keep fit and may recommend individual fitness programs as well. For companies, the major reasons for offering wellness programs are that they are cost effective (their cost often is outweighed by savings in health care costs), are responsive to employees' demand, and offer a sense of social responsibility. For the employee, participation can result in reduced absenteeism because of improved physical health and mental attitude, reduced expenses from joining outside fitness programs, stress reduction, and assurance that one's work life can be a positive factor contributing to an overall healthy lifestyle.

Smoke-Free Workplace

The predominance of the smoke-free workplace is a direct result of health hazards caused from smoking and pollutants in the work environment. Heavy pressure to

forbid smoking in more and more work sites continues. Local ordinances continue to be enacted that require employers to provide a smoke-free workplace. When executives were asked to choose between two job candidates with equal qualifications, and only one smoked, they were 15 times more likely to hire the nonsmoker. Accountemps, a temporary service for the accounting industry, surveyed 100 corporate vice presidents and human resources managers. Results indicated that smoking during a job interview may reduce your chances of being hired. Employees who smoke cost their companies a substantial amount of money. In addition, negative social reactions are attached to smoking in the workplace.

Accommodations for Special-Needs Employees

The Americans with Disabilities Act (ADA) has required employers to make accommodations for employees with special needs. The act bars employment discrimination against the disabled and mandates access for the disabled to public spaces. Companies that fail to meet these standards are subject to civil actions for noncompliance. The Americans with Disabilities Act makes it easier for job candidates and employees to get to and from work and move about safely in the workplace.

Family Care Issues

Parental leave for child care and leave for elder care are the two fastest-emerging work–family conflicts. Caring for the family often means taking care of older parents as well as children. This, coupled with job demands, puts tremendous pressure on many workers, who often experience stress trying to keep everything balanced.

Parental Leave

The Family Medical Leave Act (FMLA) of 1993 requires companies to allow eligible employees up to 12 weeks' leave during any 12-month period for (1) childbirth, adoption, or foster child care; (2) serious illness of a spouse, child, or parent; or (3) a personal serious health condition. Many leaves are nonpaid although employees are entitled to continue their company-provided medical coverage during their leave. Despite the strong interest many men and women have in staying home to care for their children, many of them simply cannot afford to. Some studies interpret the low number of men taking leave as a lack of interest, when it appears likely that the absence of pay is the real issue. In Sweden, a parent-insurance benefit program was established by law in 1974. Men are paid up to 90 percent of their salaries during their leaves. Today, according to Sheila Kamerman, Ph.D., a professor at the Columbia University of Social Work, about 25 percent of eligible men make some use of the parent insurance. Perhaps if American men knew that their jobs would not be threatened and they could be paid for their time off, more would ask for leave.

Child Care

"Seventy-seven percent of women and 73 percent of men surveyed report that they take time away from work attending to their children—making phone calls or ducking out for a long lunch to go to a school play. That alone translates into hundreds of millions of dollars in lost output for U.S. corporations," says John P. Fernandez, manager of personnel services at AT&T. Dana Friedman, senior research associate at The Conference Board, says, "Child care is likely to be the fringe benefit of the 1990s because what's good for employees becomes good for business."

The quality of day care varies enormously. States license and monitor the private for-profit and not-for-profit centers. In some states, important matters such as learning activities or the teacher–child ratio are ignored. The tremendous amount of time being spent by workers on child care and the inconsistent quality of day care centers are creating a new push toward the corporate on-site day care center. There are ad-

vantages to such centers. Parents can drop in anytime. Companies benefit in the recruitment and retention of employees. One of the most innovative efforts recently made was by Levi Strauss & Co. When children get sick, traditional day care centers are not the answer for working parents, because sick children are not allowed in day care centers. To enable parents of sick children not to miss work, Levi Strauss & Co. funded a 17-bed children's infirmary that is attached to an independent day care center in San Jose, California.

Chicken Soup is a sick-child day care operation in Minneapolis. First Bank System, a Minneapolis bank holding company, pays 75 percent of the $26.26 a day for each employee's child who checks into Chicken Soup. First Bank loses $154 a day if a $40,000-a-year middle manager misses work to take care of a sick child. Chicken Soup saves the company 87 percent, or almost $135 a day.

Companies are realizing the advantages of day care centers. About 3,000 companies offer subsidized day care centers, financial assistance for child care, or child care referral services.

Elder Care

Elder care (caring for older parents or relatives) is an issue affecting the workplace because, with more women working and not at home on a full-time basis to respond to elders' needs, employers need to make accommodations for workers faced with this responsibility. Employers can offer them reduced work hours, time off without pay, or rearranged work schedules as needed so that employees do not have to quit their jobs. Although, to date, more women than men have been affected by the elder care issue, it is expected that men may share this responsibility to the same degree as child care responsibilities as the need develops.

You should be aware that most companies are willing to accommodate some of your special needs, especially the need for a more flexible work schedule, to properly care for elderly family members. As child care and elder care become a concern for you, you should plan on meeting with your employer to discuss your unique situation and make arrangements that will satisfy both of you. The fact that these options are available to you demonstrates companies' commitment to attracting and retaining competent workers by assisting them with family issues that may directly impact their work life. This should reduce the number of workers who need to quit working for extended periods of time to take care of their family responsibilities.

Elder Care Affects the Workplace

According to survey information compiled by Work/Family Directions, a Boston consulting firm, employees caring for elderly or dependent adults miss an average of five workdays annually, and they experience the following difficulties:

Care-Related Problem	Percentage of Employees Experiencing It
Distracting phone calls	91
Expropriation of vacation time	74
Stress from unexpected time off	74
Unscheduled time off	58
Tardy arrival at and early departure from work	47

Reprinted with permission, *Inc.* magazine (September 1995). Copyright 1995 by Goldhirsh Group, Inc., 38 Commercial Wharf, Boston, MA 02110.

Ethics

Although the practice of good business ethics has always been important, as we look to the 21st century we must make a stronger commitment to both the practice and enforcement of ethics. The prevalence of unethical behavior in the workplace, and in society, requires stricter enforcement of laws against such behavior in order to stop it. Many individuals or companies have become comfortable with behavior with which they should be uncomfortable. Theft, fraud, discrimination, and harassment are a few examples of unethical behavior that exist in today's workplace.

Equal Employment Opportunity (EEO)

Fairness in hiring practices is the goal of the Equal Employment Opportunity Act. Companies that maintain a policy of nondiscrimination in all phases of employment must also comply in full with all applicable laws. The following practices ensure that companies properly implement their nondiscrimination policy. The company will:

* Recruit, advertise, hire, transfer, and promote without regard to race, religion, color, national origin, physical handicap, sex, age, or any other legally protected classification.
* Base all employment decisions on candidates' qualifications to do the job.

Despite the widespread attention given to this issue nationwide, few U.S. corporations can be proud of their minority hiring and promotion records to date. This is because issues not related to performance keep entering the hiring process and prevent us from realizing equal employment opportunity. As the number of available minority workers will be increasing over the years, measures must be taken now to revisit this issue and set the law in practice. Minority workers may find more attention given to this effort in future years as the potential workforce continues to include more minority candidates.

Affirmative Action

Today's American workplace looks much different than it did in the 1960s when blacks and other minorities were often discriminated against in the hiring process and in the daily work environment. Women were also often discriminated against when seeking employment or working outside the home.

The affirmative action law was instituted to improve the participation of more minority and female workers in the workplace. Today, attitudes about affirmative action range from extremely supportive to slightly opposed. Those in favor believe that because of affirmative action, women and members of racial and ethnic minority groups play a larger role in the workplace. Those opposed say that as affirmative action has evolved there is now too much emphasis on meeting "goals and timetables" for hiring or promoting women and minorities. Results of a 1995 survey in the *Los Angeles Times* indicate that over the past four years, there has been a rise in opposition to affirmative action programs for minorities.

Most employers are engaged in some sort of affirmative action program. As they implement these programs, employers must be careful to maintain a balance in their hiring practices first for hiring the most qualified candidates and then ensuring there is a good mix of workers from all backgrounds in their workplace.

Sexual Harassment

Awareness of sexual harassment in the workplace has been heightened by recent incidents that have been publicized nationally. As a result, companies are reviewing their policies on sexual harassment and setting in place programs to teach people what it is and what harm it can do.

Sexual harassment policies in many companies read as follows: "All unwelcome sexual advances, requests for sexual favors, and other such verbal or physical conduct is prohibited by the company." These policies exist so that all employees can share a work environment free of potentially harmful comments or actions. Employees who

Rising Opposition to Affirmative Action

Most people support affirmative action, but opposition has risen in the past four years, according to a national poll. Respondents were asked: Generally speaking, do you favor or oppose affirmative action programs for minorities?

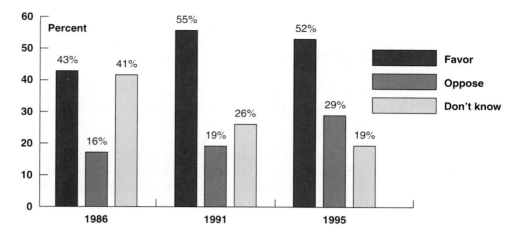

Source: *Los Angeles Times* poll, Survey No. 356, March 1995. Reprinted in *The CQ Quarterly* 5, no. 16 (April 28, 1995).

feel they have been harassed usually have the option of complaining to someone in the company (human resources department, supervisor's boss, etc.) other than the harasser. This provides them a more comfortable form of communication.

Tips for Dealing with Sexual Harassment

1. Tell the harasser to stop the offensive behavior.
2. Document all incidents of harassment.
3. Notify your supervisor or other appropriate person of the harassment.
4. Know your company or school policy on sexual harassment and follow its procedures.
5. Consider filing a forward grievance or complaint if the above steps do not remedy the situation.
6. Stay on the job.
7. Find support from family, friends, or other groups to help you through the situation.

Abuse of Privilege

Abuse of privilege occurs when someone takes a privilege that is given them, such as a company expense account, and extends its use beyond what is acceptable or expected by the company. In this case, an individual may use a company expense account to be reimbursed for personal expenses that are not company related.

Most companies have policies prohibiting the removal of company property without written permission from the supervisor responsible for the property in question. Company property can include tools or equipment; confidential literature; computer disks, tapes, and other storage media; or information identified as proprietary or a trade secret.

Removing or attempting to remove company property without permission can be grounds for disciplinary action. If you are not sure whether an action will be considered an abuse of privilege, review any written company policies in your employee handbook or ask a responsible person in the company about the proper use of company policy or property. If you are still not sure whether you are acting appropriately, do not take the risk of making a mistake that could negatively affect your reputation and possibly your career.

Conflict of Interest

Conflicts of interest sometimes occur between company and personal interest or goals. A drafter who has a private consulting business outside of the job with his or her employer may experience a conflict of interest if trying to consult during the employer's work hours.

Most companies expect all employees to avoid activities that create conflicts of interest with their responsibilities to the company. Employers may ask employees to refrain from activities that may conflict or interfere with company operation or with others with whom the company does business. Conflicts of interest include, but are not limited to the following:

1. *Outside employment:* A second job with a competitor is usually prohibited because of the danger that exists for sharing procedures, business plans, and product development techniques, especially if the second company is competing for the same customers.
2. *Gifts and entertainment:* There are some companies that have strict policies prohibiting employees from accepting gifts of more than nominal value from people or companies that do business, or want to do business, with the company.
3. *Legal issues:* All companies prohibit employees from doing anything in the conduct of business that would violate any local, state, or federal law.
4. *Fair competition:* Companies generally encourage their employees to conduct business fairly and ethically with consideration given to the needs of customers, fellow workers, and suppliers.

5. *Political and religious activities:* Most companies prefer employees to limit their political and religious activity to their own time, with no use of company facilities.

These are some examples of situations that can create possible conflicts of interest for an employee. Each company usually spells out its policies regarding these issues in the employee handbook and addresses questions about those policies during employee orientation.

Preferential Treatment

Preferential treatment is when an employee shows special treatment to certain groups of people or takes shortcuts for one person and not another. An example would be an account representative at a bank who processes a loan for a friend without following the prescribed waiting period for approval or without checking all of the necessary references.

These are just some examples of how day-to-day work activities can lead an individual into an ethical dilemma. When faced with an ethical decision, most people follow their own personal code of behavior, as opposed to the behavior of others or any formal company policy. Ultimately, you are in control of your own actions.

Chapter Summary

Workplace issues are continuing to evolve into complex situations for both the employer and employee. You should first know your own position on each of these issues and then be sure that your thinking is relatively compatible with your employer's policies regarding them. This compatibility is an important part of fitting into and ultimately being successful in a company. Being aware of these issues is also important to you if you are thinking of starting or operating your own business. As an employer, you will need to be sure that you are able to create a business environment in which these workplace issues can be dealt with properly. Your ability to manage issues related to health, family care, and ethics will be critical to your success.

Career Handbook

The Career Handbook is a practical guide to help you manage your career throughout your lifetime.

    Section A, "Career Paths," shows you the many career areas that exist in your chosen field of study. Some of the actual jobs available in each of these career areas are outlined to show you how your chosen career may progress over the years. Section B, the "Glossary of Terms Used in Job Descriptions," defines some of the key words commonly found in job descriptions. This will help you use Section C, the "Index of Job Descriptions," which is a comprehensive list of actual job descriptions defining the job titles presented in "Career Paths." These three sections work together to present you with a better understanding of the day-to-day job responsibilities in your chosen career and can be referred to periodically when making career decisions. Section D, "Career Resources," provides you with additional sources of career information that will help you guide your own job search and enhance your professional development.

    Section A, "Career Paths," is designed to help you decide how you want to apply your degree after graduation and then provides you direction for future career moves. It is useful for self-assessment and goal setting as you conduct periodic reviews of your own career. In almost any career field, there is a wide variety of jobs that suit different interests, abilities, and personalities. The job titles listed range from high people-oriented to high task-oriented jobs. They show you that you may change jobs to try many different types of work without changing the career field you have chosen. The salary ranges listed vary according to geographic location, type of industry and employer, the overall state of the economy, and your own experience level, and should always be weighed against the relative cost of living in a given area. Understanding the overview of career paths in your career field can also help you communicate to an employer that you know your long-term professional goal, that you know the series of jobs you may need to hold before getting there, and that you realize it is necessary to start any career with an entry-level job.

    In addition to helping you understand the terminology used in job descriptions, the "Glossary of Terms Used in Job Descriptions" is also a helpful tool for constructing your résumé. When used in conjunction with "Power Words for Résumés" in Chapter 7, it provides an additional resource for identifying words that best describe on your résumé what you bring to an employer. It is also good to review this chapter when preparing for a job interview so that you will be able to describe your specific skills to the interviewer.

    Once you are aware of the career paths available to you and understand the main terms used in job descriptions, you should find that the "Index of Job Descriptions" will explain the responsibilities of the job(s) you are interested in. This information is useful in clarifying whether your perception of what a job entails is accurate and should be critical to helping you decide on your career goal. Being able to articulate to an employer, during an interview, a proper understanding of the job available to you may be important to the success of your interview. This is because employers frequently find that job candidates misunderstand what many jobs entail until an explanation is provided by the employer.

    Finally, you can use Section D, "Career Resources," when seeking your first job or to sharpen your career strategies from time to time as you progress in your career. Some of the resources included can help you find information on prospective employers, refine your job search skills, and improve your professional skills.

    The Career Handbook is something you will find useful at many points in your career, long after your first job.

Career Paths

In this section, you will become aware of the many career choices available to you, learn how to choose a career area, and learn how to map out a plan in order to make successful career moves. If there was ever a time to do the work that you really love, to do the kind of work that you are really attracted to, it's now. Your career training enables you to choose a variety of traditional career paths. It also opens doors to many of the new and exciting career paths emerging in the workplace.

Take some time to think about any and every career direction that exists for you. When you do this, you will feel more confident about the decisions you make because you will know that you have considered all of your options. In this age of change, it will be necessary for you to consider new options periodically. Learning to be flexible now will be helpful as your world of work changes.

You have already made your first step in choosing a career area by deciding on your major or program. Unfortunately, many times students do not have access to all the information they need to decide how to best apply their professional training in the workplace. Focusing on your career means selecting an area within your field that interests you the most.

For example, if you are a retailing major, you may choose to become involved in management, buying, distribution, visual merchandising, or sales within the retail field. As a business administration/management student, you may put your professional training to work in banking, insurance, finance, human resources, retailing, advertising, production, or distribution. Your first step, then, is to look at career areas directly related to your major or program.

Don't stop there. Your talents can go to work in many other areas as well. For example, if you are pursuing professional training in accounting, you may first look into private and public accounting firms, but you should also consider accounting work in a retail firm or a hotel as possibilities. If you

are pursuing a degree in secretarial sciences, you may consider secretarial work in any type of business or industry that is of interest to you. You may also want to explore jobs that allow you upward mobility into management or sales.

Most important to choosing your career area is really understanding the jobs in each area. Without a clear understanding of what a job involves, you cannot really know if it's what you want, nor can you convince a potential employer that you are right for that job. Job titles don't tell us what we need to know. They are only a start. Every day, people perform in the jobs that we think we want someday. What the job really consists of or how we would spend our time every day on the job is often something we're not familiar with. Then how can we be sure this is what we really want to do? One way to find out is to become familiar with job descriptions. Once employed in the workplace, you'll then be likely to say, "There's more to this job than you think there is."

The next section presents you with over 600 job titles representing 18 different career areas. The actual job descriptions for each job title can be found in the "Index of Job Descriptions," Section C. Follow these steps (illustrated on the accompanying table) to make most effective use of this section.

1. Consider the different career areas available in the field as presented in the overview.

2. Review the entry, mid-management/specialists, and management positions and their related salary ranges.

3. Focus on the area(s) in which you have the most interest.

4. Look down that column of job titles and ask yourself what each one represents. You may wish to ask yourself, "What does a merchandise analyst do every day?"

How to Use "Career Paths"

Fashion and Retail Management—Career Overview

Level	Career Areas Management	Buying	Distribution	Sales
Entry ($$$$)	Job titles	Job titles	Job titles	Job titles
Mid-management/specialists ($$$$)	Job titles	Job titles	Job titles	Job titles
Management ($$$$)	Job titles	Job titles	Job titles	Job titles

➤ Recommended Pre-Professional Part-Time/Summer Experience

5. Review the corresponding job description in the "Index of Job Descriptions" if you are unclear about the responsibilities of a particular job title. This index also opens up a whole variety of jobs available to you about which you may have had no previous knowledge.

6. Look at the recommended pre-professional part-time/summer experience for your career area to gain insight into the kinds of part-time work employers see as valuable in order to obtain an entry-level professional position.

After each career overview, the following information is presented (see details in the accompanying box).

- Experience needed.
- Salaries.
- Qualifications.
- Where the jobs are.
- Trade publications.
- Professional associations.

"Career Paths" is your beginning to understanding your own career options. *Don't stop there!* After you have obtained your first job, you will need to refer to this information periodically to decide on your next move. By understanding the jobs in the mid-management/specialists and management segments of your career, you can create a clear vision of where you are going and how long it might take to get there.

Important Points to Remember about Career Paths

- The salaries listed represent only an average range for the country as a whole in 1995. In general, *salaries vary according to geographic location, types of industries and employers, the overall state of the economy, and your own experience level.* You should always weigh a salary that is offered to you with how it compares to these variables.

- Under "Qualifications" you will find the most common and necessary traits you need to be successful in tomorrow's jobs. Those common qualifications often include:

  Positive attitude
  Enthusiasm
  Effective written and verbal skills
  Well-groomed appearance
  Ability to work on a team
  High energy level
  Flexibility
  Ability to learn
  Brightness
  Technical skills

- In "Where the Jobs Are," the most common industries where jobs exist in each career area are outlined. The industries listed are those in which entry-level jobs are most available. There may be many more types of employers depending on your level of experience and future trends in business.

- Because a successful career includes keeping up-to-date on current trends in your field and adapting to those trends, it is important to be aware of the basic "trade publications and professional associations" appropriate for your career.

- It should become obvious by studying the career paths outlined here that each career area is made up of a *planned sequence of related jobs.*

Accounting

Level	Public Accounting	Private/Mgt. Accounting	Government
1. Entry ($18,000–$23,000)	Staff Accountant Junior Accountant	Junior Accountant	Revenue Officer
2. Mid-management/ specialists ($22,000–$37,000)	Accountant Senior Accountant	Accountant Senior Accountant General Accountant Chief Internal Auditor Department Manager Tax Accountant Cost Accountant	Accountant Internal Auditor
3. Management ($30,000–$60,000+)	Manager Partner	Vice President Treasurer Controller Chief Financial Officer	Chief Internal Auditor

Recommended Pre-Professional Part-Time/Summer Work Experience
Inventory Clerk, Data Entry Clerk, Accounts Payable/Receivable Clerk, General Office Clerk, Proofreader, Teller, Cashier, CRT Clerk, File Clerk, Salesclerk, Accounting Clerk

Public Accounting

Level	Job Title	Experience Needed
Entry	Staff or Junior Accountant	Professional training
2	Accountant	1–3 years
2	Senior Accountant	3–4 years
3	Manager	5–7 years
3	Partner	8+ years

Salaries in Public Accounting

Level	Salary	Firm Size
Entry	$18,000 to $21,000	Medium-size firm
	$20,000 to $23,000	Large firm
2	$22,000 to $26,000	Medium-size firm
	$24,000 to $27,500	Large firm
2	$27,000 to $35,000	Medium-size firm
	$28,000 to $37,000	Large firm
3	$37,000 to $46,000	Medium-size firm
	$40,000 to $60,000	Large firm

Salaries vary with the size of the firm and are higher for 2- to 4-year college graduates, CPAs, and those with graduate degrees.

Qualifications

Personal   Good communication and concentration skills. Accuracy and attention to detail. Flexibility. Objectivity. Ability to judge and make decisions. Reliability.

Professional   Writing and communication skills. Exceptional mathematical ability. Commitment to professional standards. Ability to work independently.

Where the Jobs Are
CPA firms.
Public accounting is divided into two tiers: the "Big Six," and other national, regional, and local practices.

The "Big Six"

Arthur Andersen & Company, Chicago, IL
Coopers & Lybrand, New York, NY
DeLoitte & Touche, New York, NY
Ernst & Young, Cleveland, OH
KPMG Peat Marwick, New York, NY
Price Waterhouse & Company, New York, NY

These companies have branches throughout the country.

Private Management Accounting

Level	Job Title	Experience Needed
Entry	Junior Accountant	Professional training
2	Accountant	1–3 years
2	Senior Accountant	3–4 years
2	General Accountant	4–8 years
	Department Manager	4–8 years
	Chief Internal Auditor	4–8 years
3	Vice President	15+ years
	Treasurer	15+ years
	Controller	15+ years
	Chief Financial Officer	15+ years

Salaries in Private/Management Accounting

Level	Salary	Firm Size
Entry	$20,000 to $22,000	Medium-size firm
	$20,000 to $23,000	Large-size firm
2	$23,000 to $29,000	Medium-size firm
	$26,000 to $31,000	Medium-large-size firm
	$28,000 to $33,000	Large-size firm
3	$30,000 to $36,000	Medium-size firm
	$36,000 to $56,000	Large-size firm

Salaries vary with the size of the firm and are higher for 2- or 4-year college graduates, CPAs, those with graduate degrees, and accountants whose jobs require extensive travel.

Qualifications

Personal   Reliability. Ability to work independently. Flexibility. Discipline.

Professional   Understanding of business and the marketplace. Willingness to increase knowledge of practical accounting techniques.

Where the Jobs Are
Private corporations
Consulting

Government

Level	Job Title	Experience Needed
Entry	Revenue Officer	Professional training
2	Accountant	1–3 years
2	Internal Auditor	1–3 years
3	Chief Internal Auditor	3–5 years
3	Chief Accountant	5–7 years

The goal of the accounting department of a typical government agency is to function within the budgetary constraints mandated by legislative action. The IRS is the largest employer of accountants in the United States.

Salaries in Government
Positions are comparable to salaries in private industry, and much of the work performed is the same. Salary rates are based on varying grade levels.

Qualifications

Personal   Reliability. Ability to work independently. Flexibility. Discipline.

Professional   Knowledge of standard accounting procedures; ability to design accounting techniques; interest in publishing work in professional journals.

Where the Jobs Are
Department of Agriculture
Department of Defense audit agencies
Department of Energy
Department of Health and Human Services
Department of the Air Force
Department of the Navy
Department of the Army
General Accounting Office
Treasury Department (includes the Internal Revenue Service)

Special Certifications

C.M.A. (Certificate in Management Accounting) The C.M.A. exam is sponsored by the National Association of Accountants and tests decision-making capability and knowledge of business law, finance, and organization.

C.I.A. (Certificate in Internal Auditing) The C.I.A. exam is sponsored by the Institute of Internal Auditors and tests the theory and practice of internal auditing. Both exams are open to graduating seniors, but work experience is required for certification. Multiple certification is permissible and encouraged.

C.P.A. (Certificate in Public Accounting) The advantages of holding the C.P.A. are many, as it serves as tangible proof of your skill and your commitment to the profession. Public accounting firms, particularly the largest, often expect their accountants to receive certification as quickly as state law allows. Beyond the entry level, the C.P.A. is often a requirement for advancement. Information on how to prepare for the C.P.A. exam, as well as test dates, is available through C.P.A. review courses.

Trade Publications

CPA Journal (monthly)
New York Society of
Certified Public Accountants
600 Third Avenue, New York, NY 10016

Government Accountant's Journal (quarterly)
Association of Government Accountants
727 South 23rd Street, Arlington, VA 22202

Journal of Accountancy (monthly)
American Institute of
Certified Public Accountants
1211 Avenue of the Americas
New York, NY 10036

Management Accounting (monthly)
Warren, Gorham, and Lamont, Inc.
210 South Street, Boston, MA 02111

The Practical Accountant (monthly)
Warren, Gorham, and Lambert, Inc.
210 South Street, Boston, MA 02111

The Wall Street Journal (daily)
23 Cortland Street, New York, NY 10007

Professional Associations

American Institute of Certified Public Accountants
1211 Avenue of the Americas
New York, NY 10036

American Society of Women Accountants
35 East Wacker Drive
Chicago, IL 60601

Association of Government Accountants
727 South 23rd Street
Arlington, VA 22202

Institute of Internal Auditors
249 Maitland Avenue
Altamonte Springs, FL 32701

National Association of Accountants
919 Third Avenue
New York, NY 10022

Business Administration

Level	Banking	Insurance	Finance	Human Resources
1. Entry ($20,000–$25,000) Management Trainee	Bank Officer Trainee Systems Trainee	Adjuster Trainee Claims Examiner Underwriter Trainee Actuarial Trainee Beginning Agent	Registered Representative	Employment Recruiter Interviewer Personnel Assistant Job Analyst
2. Mid-management/ specialists ($24,000–$38,000)	Assistant Loan Officer Loan Officer Department Manager Supervisor Systems Analyst Systems Consultant Senior Systems Consultant Branch Manager Loan Manager	Assistant Underwriter Underwriter Specialist Senior Underwriter Assistant Actuary Actuary Senior Claims Adjuster	Investment Banker Trader Purchasing Agent Research Analyst Trust Officer Financial Analyst Portfolio Manager Credit Manager	College Recruiter Training Manager Employment Manager Corporate Recruiter Personnel Manager Wage and Salary Administrator Benefits Coordinator Labor Relations Specialist Plant Safety Specialist EEO Coordinator
3. Management ($35,000–$76,000)	Manager Division Manager Vice President President	Underwriting/ Supervisor Office Manager Chief Actuary Agent Regional Vice President Vice President	Treasurer/Controller Vice President President	Director of Human Resources Vice President of Human Resources

Level	Retailing	Advertising	Production	Distribution
1. Entry ($20,000–$25,000) Management Trainee	Department Manager Store Manager Trainee Buyer Trainee	Junior Copywriter Media Buyer Project Coordinator Account Executive Trainee	Expeditor Assistant Buyer Assistant Purchasing Agent Production Planner Assistant Quality Assurance Manager	See Careers in Fashion and Retail Management
2. Mid-management/ specialists ($24,000–$38,000)	Assistant Store Manager Sales Representative Display Coordinator Distribution Coordinator Merchandise Analyst Assistant Buyer	Copywriter Senior Copywriter Media Planner Media Department Head Project Director Research Account Director Associate Research Director Account Executive Senior Account Executive	Purchasing Agent Purchasing Manager Traffic Manager Inventory Manager Quality Assurance Manager Buyer	

Level	Retailing	Advertising	Production	Distribution
3. Management ($35,000–$76,000+)	Merchandise Manager Buyer Store Manager Operations Manager Vice President/Operations Sales Manager	Accounts Supervisor/ Manager Department Manager Copy Chief Creative Director Director of Media Advertising Research Director	Plant Manager Materials Manager Manufacturing Manager Regional Manager Operations Research Analyst Vice President/ Production	

Recommended Pre-Professional Part-Time/Summer Work Experience

Salesclerk, Cashier, Messenger, Data Entry Clerk, General Office Clerk, Inventory Clerk, File Clerk, Accounting Clerk, Receptionist, Teller, Typist, CRT Clerk, Proofreader, Waitperson, Shipper/Receiver

Banking

Level	Job Title	Experience Needed
Entry	Bank Officer Trainee	Professional training
Entry	Systems Trainee	Professional training
2	Assistant Loan Officer	1–2 years
2	Supervisor	1–2 years
2	Systems Analyst	2 years
2	Systems Consultant	3 years
2	Department Manager	3–5 years
2	Loan Officer	3–5 years
2	Branch Manager	3–5 years
2	Senior Systems Consultant	5 years
2	Loan Manager	5–6 years
3	Division Manager	6+ years
3	Manager	6+ years
3	Vice President	8–10 years
3	President	10+ years

Salaries are higher for those with 2- or 4-year college degrees.

Qualifications

Personal   Strong analytical skills. Strong negotiation skills. Strong interpersonal skills. Ability to work under pressure. Ability to work with figures.

Professional   Familiarity with business applications of software and hardware. Ability to analyze financial statements and do creative financial planning. Good business judgment.

Where the Jobs Are

Credit lending
Trusts
Operations
Systems

Salaries in Banking

Level	
Entry	$20,000 to $25,000
2	$24,000 to $31,000
2	$29,000 to $35,000
3	$35,000 to $50,000
3	$50,000+

Insurance

Level	Job Title	Experience Needed
Entry	Adjuster Trainee	Professional training
Entry	Claims Examiner	Professional training
Entry	Underwriter Trainee	Professional training
Entry	Actuarial Trainee	Professional training
Entry	Sales Trainee*	Professional training
2	Assistant Underwriter	1–2 years
2	Assistant Actuary	1–2 years
2	Underwriter Specialist	2–4 years

Qualifications

Personal   Enthusiasm. Self-motivation. Attention to detail. Good analytical skills. Excellent communication skills. Good quantitative skills. Confidence.

Professional   Accurate thinking and writing skills. Ability to write concisely. Aptitude for computers. Ability to supervise.

Level	Job Title	Experience Needed	Where the Jobs Are
2	Agent	2–4 years	Home offices/headquarters
2	Actuary	3–5 years	Branch offices
2	Senior Underwriter	3–5 years	Independent agencies
2	Senior Claims Examiner	4–6 years	Private corporations
3	Underwriting Supervisor	6+ years	Real estate
3	Office Manager	5+ years	
3	Chief Actuary	6+ years	
3	Regional Director	5+ years	
3	Vice President	8+ years	

Salaries in Insurance
See Salaries in Banking.

*New sales workers earn about $2,000 a month during the first six months of training. Most sales workers are paid on commission. The size of the commission depends on the type and amount of insurance sold. Insurance sales workers generally pay their own automobile and travel expenses. Independent sales workers must also pay office rent, clerical salaries, and other operating expenses out of their own earnings. Salaries are higher for those with 2- and 4-year college degrees.

Finance

Level	Job Title	Experience Needed	Qualifications
Entry	Registered Representative*	Professional training	
Entry	Manager Trainee	Professional training	
2	Trader	1–2 years	
2	Financial Analyst	2–3 years	
2	Research Analyst	3–5 years	
2	Investment Banker	3–5 years	
2	Purchasing Agent	3–5 years	
2	Portfolio Manager	5–6 years	
2	Credit Manager	5–6 years	
2	Trust Officer	6–8 years	
3	Treasurer/Controller	6+ years	
3	Vice President	8–12 years	
3	President	12–15 years	

Qualifications

Personal   Interest in economic trends. Ability to handle frequent rejection. Ability to work independently. Good grooming. Good communication skills.

Professional   State licensing and successful completion of exams prepared by securities exchanges or NASD (National Association of Securities Dealers, Inc.).

Where the Jobs Are
Financial institutions
Banks
Private corporations
Consulting firms
Government
Securities exchanges

Salaries in Finance
See Salaries in Banking.

*Trainees are usually paid a salary until they meet licensing and registration requirements. During training, sales workers earn $900–$1,200 a month. After licensing, earnings depend on commission from sales of stocks, bonds, life insurance, or other securities.

Salaries are higher for those with 2- or 4-year college degrees.

Human Resources

Level	Job Title	Experience Needed
Entry	Interviewer	Professional training
Entry	Employment Recruiter	Professional training
Entry	Personnel Assistant	Professional training
Entry	Job Analyst	Professional training
2	College Recruiter	1–3 years
2	Training Manager	2–4 years
2	Corporate Recruiter	3–5 years
2	Benefits Coordinator	1–3 years
2	Plant Safety Specialist	3–5 years
2	Equal Employment Opportunity Coordinator	1–3 years
2	Labor Relations Specialist	4–6 years
2	Wage and Salary Administrator	4–6 years
2	Employment Manager	4–6 years
2	Personnel Manager	5–7 years
3	Personnel Director	5–7 years
3	Vice President of Human Resources	7–10 years

Salaries in Human Resources

Entry	$20,000 to $23,000
2	$24,000 to $33,000
2	$28,000 to $38,000
3	$33,000 to $55,000
3	$55,000 to $76,000+

Salaries are higher for those with 2- and 4-year college degrees.

Qualifications

Personal Excellent communication skills, listening skills especially important. Ability to speak and write effectively. Ability to work under pressure.

Professional Fair-mindedness. Good decision-making skills. Ability to enforce policies.

Where the Jobs Are

Private corporations
Education
Government agencies
Consulting firms
Independent businesses

Retailing

See Careers in Fashion and Retail Management.

Advertising

Level	Job Title	Experience Needed
Entry	Assistant Media Planner	Professional training
Entry	Junior Copywriter	Professional training
Entry	Project Director	Professional training
Entry	Account Executive Trainee	Professional training
2	Copywriter	1–3 years
2	Account Executive	1–3 years
2	Research Account Executive	1–3 years
2	Media Planner	3–5 years
2	Associate Research Director	3–8 years
2	Senior Account Executive	5–8 years
2	Associate Media Director	5–7 years
2	Research Director	7–10 years
2	Senior Copywriter	7–10 years
2	Media Director of Planning	7–10 years

Salaries in Advertising

Entry	$20,000 to $22,000
2	$22,000 to $24,000
2	$24,000 to $26,000
2	$26,000 to $30,000
2	$30,000 to $33,000
2	$33,000 to $38,000
3	$38,000 to $41,000
3	$41,000 to $47,000
3	$47,000 to $62,000
3	$62,000 to $75,000+

Salaries are higher for those with 2- or 4-year college degrees.

Qualifications

Personal Strong interpersonal skills. Ability to work with a team. Problem-solving mentality.

Professional Good writing skills, knowledge of the media. Sales ability. Negotiation skills.

Level	Job Title	Experience Needed	Where the Jobs Are
3	Accounts Supervisor/ Manager	10–13 years	Advertising agencies Media
3	Department Manager	10+ years	Private corporations
3	Copy Chief	10+ years	Consulting
3	Creative Director	10+ years	Freelancing
3	Director of Media Advertising	10+ years	
3	Research Director	10+ years	

Production

Level	Job Title	Experience Needed	Salaries in Production
Entry	Expeditor	Professional training	See Salaries in Banking
Entry	Assistant Buyer	Professional training	
Entry	Assistant Purchasing Agent	Professional training	
Entry	Production Planner	Professional training	
Entry	Assistant Quality Assurance Manager	Professional training	
2	Purchasing Agent	1–3 years	
2	Purchasing Manager	3–5 years	
2	Traffic Manager	2–4 years	
2	Inventory Manager	2–4 years	
2	Quality Assurance Manager	3–5 years	
2	Buyer	4–6 years	
3	Plant Manager	5–6 years	
3	Materials Manager	5–6 years	
3	Manufacturing Manager	5–6 years	
3	Regional Manager	6–8 years	
3	Operations Research Analyst	6–8 years	
3	Vice President/Production	7–10 years	

Qualifications

Personal   Good organizational skills. Aptitude for figures. Ability to plan and make quick decisions. Flexibility.

Professional   Ability to interpret computer data. Ability to supervise and think ahead.

Where the Jobs Are
Manufacturing
Distribution
Private corporations

Distribution

See Careers in Fashion and Retail Management.

Trade Publications

Advertising Age (weekly)
Crain Communications, Inc.
740 North Rush Street, Chicago, IL 60611

Adweek (weekly)
Adweek Publications
820 Second Avenue, New York, NY 10017
(regional editions for East, Southeast, West, Southwest, and Midwest)

ABA Banking Journal (monthly)
345 Hudson Street, New York, NY 10014

American Banker (daily)
One State Street Plaza, New York, NY 10014

The Banker's Magazine (bimonthly)
Warren, Gorham, and Lamont, Inc.
210 South Street, Boston, MA 02111

Bank News (monthly)
912 Baltimore Avenue, Kansas City, MO 64105

Professional Associations

The Advertising Council
825 Third Avenue
New York, NY 10022

Advertising Research Foundation
Information Center
3 East 54th Street
New York, NY 10022

American Advertising Federation
1400 K Street, N.W.
Suite 1000
Washington, DC 20005

American Association of Advertising Agencies
200 Park Avenue
New York, NY 10017

Association of National Advertisers
155 East 44th Street
New York, NY 10017

American Bankers Association
1120 Connecticut Avenue, N.W.
Washington, DC 20036

Consumer Bankers Association
1725 K Street, N.W.
Washington, DC 20006

National Association of Bank Women
111 East Wacker Drive
Chicago, IL 60601

United States League of Savings Association
111 East Wacker Drive
Chicago, IL 60601

American Management Association
135 West 50th Street
New York, NY 10020

Computer Systems

Level	Programming	Operations	Marketing/Sales	Support Services
1. Entry ($20,000–$25,000)	Systems Consultant Systems Analyst	Tape Librarian Data Entry Supervisor Computer Operator	Sales Representative	Instructor Product Support Representative Service Representative
2. Mid-management/ specialists ($25,000–$34,000)	Lead Consultant Lead Analyst	Supervisor/Systems Operators Peripheral Systems Operator MIS Supervisor Systems Analyst	Account Representative	Training Manager Documentation Specialist District Manager
3. Management ($30,000–$75,000+) MIS Director	Senior Systems Consultant Senior Analyst	Operations Manager EDP Auditor Manager/Systems Analysis	Account Supervisor Vice President/ Account Services	Consultant Regional Manager Vice President President

Recommended Pre-Professional Part-Time/Summer Work Experience
CRT Clerk, Typist, Data Entry Clerk, Coder, Salesclerk, File Clerk, Cashier, General Office Clerk

Programming

Level	Job Title	Experience Needed	Salaries in Programming	
Entry	Systems Consultant	Professional training	Entry	$20,000 to $22,000
Entry	Systems Analyst	Professional training	Entry	$22,000 to $24,000
2	Lead Consultant	1–3 years	2	$25,000 to $28,000
2	Lead Analyst	1–3 years	2	$28,000 to $34,000
			3	$34,000 to $40,000

Salaries are higher for those with 2- or 4-year college degrees.

Level	Job Title	Experience Needed
3	Senior Systems Consultant	3–5 years
3	Senior Analyst	3–5 years
3	MIS Director	6–8 years

Qualifications

Personal   Patience. Persistence. Ability to work with extreme accuracy. Ability to work under pressure and with deadlines. Good written and verbal communication skills.

Professional   Ability to think logically. Capable of doing highly analytical work. Problem-solving ability. Decision-making skills. Team worker.

Where the Jobs Are
Manufacturing firms
Data processing service organizations
Government
Banks
Insurance
Education

Operations

Level	Job Title	Experience Needed
Entry	Tape Librarian	Professional training
Entry	Data Entry Supervisor	Professional training
Entry	Computer Operator	Professional training
2	Systems Operator Supervisor	1–2 years
2	Peripheral Equipment Operator	1–2 years
2	Systems Analyst	2–4 years
2	MIS Supervisor	2–4 years
3	Operations Manager	3–6 years
3	EDP Auditor	3–6 years
3	Manager of Systems Analysis	6–8 years
3	MIS Director	6–10 years

Salaries in Operations
See Salaries in Programming.

Qualifications

Personal   Patience. Persistence. Ability to work under pressure. Flexibility. Good communication skills. Detail oriented. Manual dexterity. Interest in learning new procedures.

Professional   Ability to make quick decisions and supervise others. Analytical skills essential. Team worker.

Where the Jobs Are
Manufacturing
Data processing service organizations
Government
Banks
Insurance
Education

Marketing/Sales

Level	Job Title	Experience Needed
Entry	Sales Representative	Professional training
2	Account Representative	1–3 years
3	Account Supervisor	3–6 years
3	Vice President/ Account Services	6–10 years

Salaries in Marketing/Sales
Level	Salary
Entry	$20,000 to $24,000
2	$24,000 to $26,000
3	$26,000 to $34,000
3	$34,000 to $54,000
3	$54,000 to $75,000+

Salaries are higher for those with 2- or 4-year college degrees.

Qualifications

Personal   Excellent verbal communication skills. Confidence. Enthusiasm. Well-groomed. Ability to work independently. Self-motivated. Flexibility.

Professional   Product knowledge. Perception of customer needs. Willingness to learn.

Where the Jobs Are
Computer service organizations
Consulting
Computer manufacturers
Government

Support Services

Level	Job Title	Experience Needed
Entry	Product Support Representative	Professional training
Entry	Service Representative	Professional training
2	Training Manager	2–4 years
2	Documentation Specialist	1–2 years
2	District Manager	3–5 years
2	Academic Department Head	3–5 years
3	Consultant	5+ years
3	Regional Manager	5–8 years
3	Vice President	8–10 years
3	President	8–10+ years

Qualifications

Personal Excellent communication skills. Self-motivated. Well-groomed. Patience. Ability to work independently. Confidence.

Professional Product knowledge. Perception of customer needs. Team worker. Ability to make decisions.

Where the Jobs Are
Computer service organizations
Computer manufacturers
Consulting
Education
Banks
Insurance
Manufacturing

Salaries in Support Services

Level	Salary
Entry	$20,000 to $25,000
2	$22,000 to $26,000
2	$24,000 to $30,000
3	$30,000 to $35,000
3	$35,000 to $55,000+

Salaries are higher for those with 2- or 4-year college degrees.

Trade Publications

Byte (monthly)
70 Main Street, Peterborough, NH 03458

Computer Decisions (monthly)
50 Essex Street, Rochelle Park, NJ 07662

Computer Design (monthly)
11 Goldsmith Street, Littleton, MA 01460

Computer Times
P.O. Box 13918, Philadelphia, PA 19101

Computer and Electrical Engineering (quarterly)
Pergamon Press, Maxwell House, Fairview Park
Elmsford, NY 10523

Computer and People (bimonthly)
Berkley Enterprises, Inc.
815 Washington Street
Newtonville, MA 02160

Computerworld (weekly)
CW Communications, Inc.
Box 880, 375 Cochituate Road,
Framingham, MA 01701

Datamation (monthly)
Technical Publishing Company
666 Fifth Avenue, New York, NY 10103

Data Processor
IBM Corporation
1133 Westchester Avenue, White Plains, NY 10604

Information Systems News (bimonthly)
333 East Shore Road, Manhasset, NY 11030

Software News (monthly)
5 Kane Industrial Drive
Hudson, MA 01749

Professional Associations

American Foundation of Information Processing
Societies
1815 North Lynn Street
Suite 800
Arlington, VA 22209

American Society for Information Science
1010 Sixteenth Street, N.W.
Washington, DC 20036

Association for Computational Linguistics
c/o Dr. D. E. Walker
SRI International
Menlo Park, CA 94025

Association for Computer Programmers and Analysts
294 Main Street
East Greenwich, RI 02818

Association for Systems Management

24587 Bagley Road
Cleveland, OH 44138

Microcomputer Software Association
1300 North 17th Street, No. 300
Arlington, VA 22209

Women in Data Processing
P.O. Box 8117
San Diego, CA 92102

Court Reporting and Related Careers

Level	Court Reporting	Hearing Reporting	Legislative Reporting	Conference Reporting	Freelance Reporting
1. Entry ($20,000–$25,000)	Court Reporter	Hearing Reporter	Legislative Reporter	Conference Reporter	Freelance Reporter
2. Mid-management/ specialists ($23,000–$42,000)	See Paralegal Careers				
3. Management ($42,000–$60,000)					

Recommended Pre-Professional Part-Time/Summer Work Experience
Typist, CRT Clerk, General Office Clerk, Messenger, File Clerk, Court Clerk, Coder, Research Assistant, Law Clerk

Court Reporting and Related Careers

Level	Job Title	Experience Needed
Entry	Court Reporter	Professional training
Entry	Hearing Reporter	Professional training
Entry	Legislative Reporter	Professional training
Entry	Conference Reporter	Professional training
Entry	Freelance Reporter	Professional training
2	Paralegal	2–4 years (with further education)
2	Legal Assistant	2–4 years
2	Legal Technician	2–4 years
2	Paralegal Instructor	2–4 years
2	Proofreader	2–4 years
2	Marketing Representative	2–4 years
2	Sales Representative	2–4 years
2	Paralegal Supervisor	4–6 years
2	Senior Legal Assistant	4–6 years
2	Research Assistant	5–8 years
2	Information Specialist	5–8 years
2	Litigation Paralegal	5–8 years
2	Placement Director	5–8 years
2	Editor	5–8 years
2	Systems Programmer	5–8 years
3	Law Office Administrator	8–10 years

Level	Job Title	Experience Needed
3	Lawyer	8–10 years (with further education)
3	Law Office Administrator	8–10 years
3	Law Library Manager	8–10 years
3	Program Director	8–10 years
3	Consultant/Adviser	8–10 years
3	Marketing Analyst	8–10 years

Salaries in Court Reporting and Related Careers

Entry	$20,000 to $25,000
Entry	$22,000 to $26,000
2	$26,000 to $30,000
2	$28,000 to $34,000
2	$34,000 to $42,000
3	$42,000 to $60,000+

Qualifications

Personal Strong concentration. Physical stamina. Manual dexterity. Detail-oriented. Professional appearance. Ability to work under pressure.

Professional Accurate thinking and spelling. Transcription skills. Familiarity with legal terminology. Excellent written and verbal communication skills. Positive attitude. High energy level.

Where the Jobs Are
Courts
Legal firms/departments
Freelancing

Business and industry (meetings and conferences)
Conventions
Sales
Stockholders' meetings

Trade Publications

American Bar Association Journal
750 N. Lake Shore Drive, Chicago, IL 60611

National Shorthand Reporters Association
118 Park Street, Southeast, Vienna, VA 22180

Professional Association

National Shorthand Reporters Association
118 Park Street, Southeast
Vienna, VA 22180

Criminal Justice

Level	City	County	State	Military	Federal Services
1. Entry ($20,000–$30,000)	Patrol Officer Traffic Officer	Deputy Sheriff	Private Private First Class	Military Police	Parole Officer Probation Officer Corrections Officer Postal Inspector Border Patrol Agent Polygraph Operator Document Examiner Watchmen Bank Guard Railroad Police
2. Mid-management/ specialists ($25,000–$50,000)	Detective	Sheriff	Corporal Sergeant Crime Lab Technician Motor Vehicle Registration Coordinator	Air Police Off. Shore Patrol Off.	IRS Agents Customs Agent Federal Food Inspector Consumer Product Commission Inspector Intelligence Specialist Lab Technician Insurance Investigation Specialist Loss Prevention Specialist INS Investigator Forensic Scientist Secret Service
3. Management ($35,000–$100,000)	Criminal Investigator	Investigator	Chief of Police Lieutenant Captain Colonel	Military Investigator	U.S. Marshal

Recommended Pre-Professional Part-Time/Summer Work Experience
Summer Clerk, Law Clerk, File Clerk, Receptionist, Legal Secretary, Computer Operator, Research Clerk, Messenger

City

Level	Job Title	Experience Needed
Entry	Patrol Officer	Professional training
Entry	Traffic Officer	Professional training
2	Detective	3–5 years
3	Criminal Investigator	5–7 years

Salaries in Cities

Level	Salary
Entry	$20,000 to $30,000
2	$25,000 to $40,000
3	$40,000 to $55,000

Salaries vary widely according to geographical location. This national average figure includes many smaller towns and less populated communities.

Qualifications

Personal Maturity. Perception. Good judgment. Adaptability. Good written and verbal communication. Emotional stability. Integrity. Reliability. Sobriety. Physical agility.

Professional Leadership. Confidentiality. Ethical. Cultural awareness. Problem solving.

Where the Jobs Are
Police departments
Crime labs

County

Level	Job Title	Experience Needed
Entry	Deputy Sheriff	Professional training
2	Sheriff	4–5 years
3	Investigator	5–10 years

Salaries in Counties

Level	Salary
Entry	$20,000 to $25,000
2	$25,000 to $40,000
3	$45,000 to $55,000

Salaries vary widely according to geographic location and longevity in most positions.

Qualifications

Personal Maturity. Perception. Good judgment. Adaptability. Emotional stability. Integrity. Reliability. Flexibility. Sobriety.

Professional Leadership. Problem solving. Critical thinking. Cultural awareness.

Where the Jobs Are
Sheriff's departments
Courthouses

State

Level	Job Title	Experience Needed
Entry	Private	Professional training
	Private First Class	Professional training
2	Corporal	4–5 years
2	Sergeant	5–8 years
2	Crime Lab Technician	4–5 years
2	Motor Vehicles Registration Coordinator	4–5 years
3	Chief of Police	8–10 years
3	Lieutenant	8–10 years
3	Captain	8–10 years
3	Colonel	8–10 years

Salaries with the State

Level	Salary
Entry	$22,000 to $26,000
2	$26,000 to $35,000
2	$35,000 to $50,000
3	$50,000 to $75,000
3	$75,000 to $100,000

Salaries vary widely according to geographic location, rank, and longevity in many positions.

Qualifications

Personal Physical ability. Maturity perception. Good judgment. Good oral and written communication. Emotional stability. Integrity. Sobriety. Reliability.

Professional Leadership. Ethical. Cultural awareness. Problem-solving. Confidentiality.

Where the Jobs Are
Police department
State crime lab
Registry of motor vehicles
State regulatory agencies

Military

Level	Job Title	Experience Needed
Entry	Military Police	Professional training
2	Air Patrol Officer	2–4 years
2	Shore Patrol Officer	2–4 years
3	Military Investigator	4–8 years

Salaries with the State

Level	
Entry	$22,000 to $26,000
2	$26,000 to $32,000
3	$32,000 to $50,000

Salaries vary widely among different branches in the military and ranking systems for positions.

Qualifications

Personal   Self-discipline. Maturity. Perception. Good judgment. Good written and oral communication. Adaptability. Emotional stability. Integrity. Reliability. Sobriety.

Professional   Leadership. Teamwork. Mechanical aptitude. Computer skills. Foreign language.

Where the Jobs Are
Military police
Naval investigative service
Military bases
Office of Special Investigations

Federal Services

Level	Job Title	Experience Needed
Entry	Parole Officer	Professional training
Entry	Probation Officer	Professional training
Entry	Corrections Officer	Professional training
Entry	Postal Inspector	Professional training
Entry	Border Patrol Agent	Professional training
Entry	Polygraph Operator	Professional training
Entry	Document Examiner	Professional training
Entry	Watchman	Professional training
Entry	Bank Guard	Professional training
Entry	Railroad Police Officer	Professional training
2	IRS Agent	2–4 years
2	Customs Agent	2–5 years
2	Federal Food Inspector	4–7 years
2	Consumer Product Safety Commission Investigator	4–7 years
2	Intelligence Specialist	4–7 years
2	Lab Technician	4–7 years
2	Insurance Investigation Specialist	4–7 years
2	Loss Prevention Specialist	4–7 years
2	INS Investigator	4–7 years
3	Forensic Scientist	8–12 years
3	Secret Service Agent	10–12 years
3	U.S. Marshal	10–12 years

Salaries in Federal Services

Level	
Entry	$20,000 to $23,000
Entry	$23,000 to $25,000
2	$25,000 to $35,000
2	$35,000 to $50,000
3	$50,000 to $65,000
3	$65,000+

Qualifications

Personal   Maturity. Adaptability. Good written and oral communication. Perception. Reliability. Integrity. Sobriety.

Professional   Knowledge of federal regulations. License to operate certain equipment. Cultural awareness. Problem-solving. Ethical. Confidentiality.

Where the Jobs Are
Federal agencies
Correctional facilities
Crime rehabilitation centers

Trade Publications

Journal of Criminal Justice
Pergamm Press
Fairview Park
Elmsford, NY 10523

Criminology
American Society of Criminology
1314 Kinnear Road, Suite 212
Columbus, OH 43212

Journal of Police Science and Administration
IACP
1110 North Glebe Road, Suite 200
Arlington, VA 22201

Criminal Justice International
Office of International Criminal Justice
University of Illinois at Chicago
715 S. Wood
Chicago, IL 60612

Law & Order
Hendon, Inc.
1000 Skokie Boulevard
Wilmette, IL 60091

Professional Associations

International Association of Chiefs of Police
1110 North Glebe, Suite 200
Arlington, VA 22201

American Society of Criminology
Ohio State University Research
1314 Kinnear Road, Suite 212
Columbus, OH 43212

Lambda Alpha Epsilon
American Criminal Justice Association
P.O. Box 61047
Sacramento, CA 95860

National Council on Crime and Delinquency
77 Maiden Lane
San Francisco, CA 94108

Fraternal Order of Police
5613 Belair Road
Baltimore, MD 21206

National Sheriff's Association
1400 Duke Street
Alexandria, VA 22314

Data Entry

Level	Operations
1. Entry ($18,000–$20,000)	Data Entry Operator Keypunch Operator Tape Librarian
2. Mid-management/ specialists ($20,000–$25,000)	Computer Operator Peripheral Equipment Operator Supervisor of Data Entry Services
3. (See Careers in Computer Systems: Programming, Operations, Marketing/Sales, and Support Services)	

Recommended Pre-Professional Part-Time/Summer Work Experience
Keypunch Operator, CRT Clerk, Typist, General Office Clerk, Word Processing Operator

Operations

Level	Job Title	Experience Needed	Salaries in Data Entry	
Entry	Data Entry Operator	Professional training	Entry	$18,000 to $20,000
Entry	Tape Librarian	Professional training	2	$20,000 to $25,000
2	Computer Operator	2–4 years	3	(See Salaries in Computer Systems)

Level	Job Title	Experience Needed
2	Peripheral Equipment Operator	2–4 years
2	Supervisor of Data Entry Services	4–6 years

Qualifications

Personal   Attention to detail. Good attention span. Ability to do repetitive work. Ability to work under close supervision. Patience. Manual dexterity.

Professional   Positive attitude. Enthusiasm. Team worker. Ability to make decisions. Problem-solving skills. Excellent communications skills.

Where the Jobs Are
Insurance companies
Research organizations
Education
Hospitals
Government
Computer service organizations
Banks

Trade Publications

See Careers in Computer Systems.

Professional Associations

See Careers in Computer Systems.

Dental Assistant

Level	Private Practices, Hospitals, Health Maintenance Organizations	Education	Marketing/Sales
1. Entry ($18,000–$22,000)	Dental Assistant	Instructor	Sales Representative
2. Mid-management/ specialists ($22,000–$26,000)	Clinical Dental Assistant Administrative Dental Assistant Dental Hygienist (with further education) Claims Examiner Claims Representative Research Assistant	Academic Department Head	Sales Manager
3. Management ($26,000–$35,000)	Office Manager Research Analyst Dentist (with further education)	School Director Administrator/Education	Director of Marketing and Sales

Recommended Pre-Professional Part-Time/Summer Work Experience
Receptionist, File Clerk, Typist, CRT Clerk, Sales, Accounting Clerk

Private Practices, Hospitals, Health Maintenance Organizations

Level	Job Title	Experience Needed			
Entry	Dental Assistant	Professional training	2	Administrative Dental Assistant	1–2 years
2	Clinical Dental Assistant	1–2 years	2	Dental Hygienist	*Further education*
			2	Medical Claims Examiner	1–2 years

2	Medical Claims Representative	1–2 years
2	Research Assistant	2–4 years
3	Office Manager	4–6 years
3	Research Analyst	4–6 years
3	Dentist	*Further education*

Salaries in Private Practices, Hospitals, Health Maintenance Organizations

Entry	$18,000 to $22,000
2	$21,000 to $25,000
2	$25,000 to $27,000
3	$27,000 to $30,000
3	$30,000 to $36,000

Salaries are higher for those with 2- or 4-year college degrees.

Qualifications

Personal   Patience. Concentration. Good grooming and hygiene. Manual dexterity. Congenial personality. Ability to work with people who may be under stress.

Professional   Knowledge of medical terminology. Ability to learn on the job. Familiarity with billing procedures and health plans.

Where the Jobs Are
Private practices
Hospitals
Health maintenance organizations
State and local public health departments
Government (hospitals and dental clinics of the U.S. Public Health Service and the Veterans Administration)

Education

Level	Job Title	Experience Needed
Entry	Instructor	Professional training and/or college degree
2	Academic Department Head	4–5 years
3	Administrator/ Education	6–8 years
3	School Director	8–10+ years

Salaries in Education
See Salaries in Teacher Education.

Qualifications

Personal   Patience. Good communication skills. Ability to manage.

Professional   Awareness of policies and laws in the health care field. Planning and organizational skills. Ability to work with budgets.

Where the Jobs Are
Dental schools
Hospital dental departments

Sales/Marketing

Level	Job Title	Experience Needed
Entry	Sales Representative	Professional training
2	Sales Manager	3–5 years
3	Director of Marketing/Sales	5 + years

Salaries in Sales/Marketing
See Salaries in Careers in Marketing.

Qualifications

Personal   Positive attitude. Good communication skills. Ability to work independently. Self-motivated. Tolerance for rejection. Confidence.

Professional   Product knowledge. Perception of customer needs. Familiarity with medical terminology.

Where the Jobs Are
Medical suppliers
Dental suppliers

Trade Publications

The Dental Assistant
American Dental Assistants Association
Suite 1130, 666 N. Lake Shore Drive
Chicago, IL 60611

Dental Assisting
P.O. Box 7573, Waco, TX 76714

Dental Products
Readers Service Center
P.O. Box 2610, Clinton, IA 52735

Dental Management
7500 Old Oak Blvd., Cleveland, OH 44130

Dental Economics
P.O. Box 3408, Tulsa, OK 74101

The Journal of Dental Education
American Association of Dental Schools
1625 Massachusetts Ave., NW
Washington, DC 20036

Dental Abstracts
American Dental Association
211 East Chicago Avenue, Chicago, IL 60611

Professional Associations

American Dental Assistants Association
Suite 1130
666 N. Lake Shore Dr.
Chicago, IL 60611

National Association of Dental Assistants
3837 Plaza Drive
Fairfax, VA 22030

Commission on Dental Accreditation
American Dental Association
211 E. Chicago Ave.
Suite 1814
Chicago, IL 60611

Dental Assisting National Board, Inc.
666 North Lake Shore Dr.
Suite 1136
Chicago, IL 60611

Drafting

Level	Operations	Support Services	Education
1. Entry ($20,000–$24,000)	Junior Drafter	Junior Drafter	Instructor
2. Mid-management/ specialists ($24,000–$29,000)	Senior Drafter	Junior Consultant	Academic Department Head
3. Management with further education ($29,000–$50,000+)	Engineer Designer Architect	Senior Consultant	Program Director School Director

Recommended Pre-Professional Part-Time/Summer Work Experience
CRT Clerk, Data Entry Operator, Runner for Architectural, Engineering, or Construction Firm

Operations

Level	Job Title	Experience Needed
Entry	Junior Drafter	Professional training
2	Senior Drafter	4–6 years
3	Engineer	With further education
3	Designer	With further education
3	Architect	With further education

Salaries in Operations

Level	Salary
Entry	$20,000 to $24,000
2	$24,000 to $29,000
3	$29,000 to $50,000+

Salaries are higher for those with 2- or 4-year college degrees.

Qualifications

Personal   Good eyesight. Manual dexterity. Attention to detail. Patience. Ability to work independently. Accuracy. Neatness. Excellent communication skills. Ability to work under pressure.

Professional   Ability to do free-hand drawings of three-dimensional objects. Artistic ability. Ability to conceptualize. Ability to meet deadlines. Team worker.

Where the Jobs Are

Engineering and architectural firms
Durable goods and manufacturing industries (*machinery, electrical equipment, and fabricated metals*)
Construction
Transportation
Communications
Utilities industries

Support Services

Level	Job Title	Experience Needed
Entry	Junior Drafter	Professional training
2	Senior Drafter	4–6 years
2	Junior Consultant	6–8 years
3	Senior Consultant	8–10 years

Salaries in Support Services
See Salaries in Operations.

Qualifications

Personal   Positive attitude. Enthusiasm. High energy level. Excellent communication skills. Professional appearance.

Professional   Technical knowledge. Perception of customers' needs. Team worker. Ability to work independently. Strong marketing and sales skills.

Where the Jobs Are
See "Where the Jobs Are" in Operations.

Education

Level	Job Title	Experience Needed
Entry	Instructor	Professional training and/or college degree
2	Academic Department Head	4–6 years
3	Program Director	6–8 years
3	School Director	8–10 years

Salaries in Education
See Salaries in Teacher Education.

Qualifications

Personal   Positive attitude. Enthusiasm. High energy level. Excellent communication skills. Listening skills. Flexibility. Ability to work under pressure.

Professional   Ability to organize and plan. Technical knowledge. Managerial skills. Ability to work with budgets. Team worker.

Where the Jobs Are
Technical schools
Vocational schools
Drafting departments

Trade Publication

Design and Drafting News
American Institute for Design and Drafting
966 Hungerford Drive, Suite 10-B
Rockville, MD 20854

Professional Associations

American Institute for Design and Drafting
966 Hungerford Drive
Suite 10-B
Rockville, MD 20854

American Institute of Technical Illustrators
Association
2513 Forest Leaf Parkway
Suite 906
Ballwin, MO 63011

Coordinating Council for Computers in Construction
1221 Avenue of the Americas
New York, NY 10020

National Association of Trade and Technical
Schools
2021 K Street, N.W.
Washington, DC 20006

Electronics

Level	Repair	Research	Support Services	Production	Education
1. Entry ($20,000–$24,000)	Electronics Technician	Electronics Technician	Sales/Field Representative Customer Service Representative	Electronics Technician	Instructor
2. Mid-management/ specialists ($22,000–$28,000)	Robotics Technician Broadcast Technician Engineering Technician Communications/ Equipment Technician Computer Technician Digital Technician Office Machine Repairer Commercial/ Industrial Technician Medical Technician Health Technician Service Technician	Design Technician Research Technician	Production Technician Instructor Sales/Service Manager Training Supervisor	Production Technician	Academic Department Head
3. Management ($28,000–$40,000+)	Electronics Engineer (*with further education*)	Director of Research and Development	Consultant Administrator Director of Marketing and Sales	Production Manager	Program Director School Director

Recommended Pre-Professional Part-Time/Summer Work Experience
Assistant Technician, Repair Person, CRT Clerk, Computer Operator, Data Entry Operator

Repair

Level	Job Title	Experience Needed
Entry	Electronics Technician	Professional training
2	Robotics Technician	1–3 years
2	Broadcast Technician	1–3 years
2	Engineering Technician	1–3 years
2	Communications Equipment Technician	1–3 years
2	Medical Technician	1–3 years
2	Health Technician	1–3 years
3	Service Technician	1–3 years
3	Electronics Engineer	*With further education*

Salaries in Repair

Level	Salary
Entry	$20,000 to $22,000
2	$22,000 to $25,000
2	$25,000 to $28,000
3	$28,000 to $35,000
3	$35,000 to $40,000+

Salaries are higher for those with 2- or 4-year college degrees.

Qualifications

Personal Ability to do detailed work. Ability to work independently. Accuracy. Manual dexterity. Good communication skills.

Professional Aptitude for mathematics and science. Perception of customers' needs. Problem-solving ability. Team worker.

Where the Jobs Are
Defense contractors
Private corporations
Government
Education
Broadcasting
Computer service organizations
Research organizations
Radio and TV stations

Research

Level	Job Title	Experience Needed
Entry	Electronics Technician	Professional training
2	Design Technician	3–5 years
2	Research Technician	3–5 years
3	Director of Research and Development	6–10 years *With further education*

Salaries in Research

Level	Salary
Entry	$20,000 to $24,000
2	$22,000 to $25,000
2	$25,000 to $28,000
3	$28,000 to $35,000
3	$35,000 to $40,000+

Salaries are higher for those with 2- or 4-year college degrees.

Qualifications

Personal Ability to do detailed work. Ability to work independently. Accuracy. Good communication skills. Resourcefulness. Flexibility. Analytical skills.

Professional Aptitude for mathematics and science. Aptitude for technical work. Ability to interpret and predict. Familiarity with computer. Problem-solving ability. Team worker. Ability to conceptualize.

Where the Jobs Are
Defense contracts
Private corporations
Government
Education

Support Services

Level	Job Title	Experience Needed
Entry	Sales/Field Representative	Professional training
Entry	Customer Service Representative	Professional training
2	Instructor	1–3 years
2	Sales/Service Manager	2–5 years
2	Training Supervisor	2–5 years
3	Consultant	5–7 years

Salaries in Support Services
See Salaries in Careers in Marketing and Teacher Education.

Qualifications

Personal Positive attitude. Enthusiasm. Good communication skills. Well-groomed appearance. Self-motivated. Ability to work independently. Confidence. Tolerance for rejection.

Level	Job Title	Experience Needed	Where the Jobs Are
3	Administrator/Educator	6–8 years	Defense contractors
3	Director of Marketing and Sales	7–10 years *With further education*	Private corporations
			Government
			Education
			Manufacturers of electronic equipment

Professional Product knowledge. Perception of customers' needs. Effective marketing and sales skills.

Production

Level	Job Title	Experience Needed
Entry	Electronics Technician	Professional training
2	Production Technician	2–4 years
3	Production Manager	5–7 years

Professional Ability to plan, organize, coordinate, and supervise. Concern for quality. Team worker. Knowledge of safety procedures. Aptitude for figures, finances, inventories, and quotas.

Salaries in Production
See Salaries in Electronics Repair.

Where the Jobs Are
Manufacturing

Qualifications

Personal Accuracy. Good communication skills. Manual dexterity. Ability to do detailed work. Positive attitude. Enthusiasm. Ability to work under pressure.

Education

Level	Job Title	Experience Needed
Entry	Instructor	Professional training and/or college degree
2	Academic Department Head	4–6 years
3	Program Director	6–8 years
3	School Director	8–10 years

Professional Ability to organize and plan. Technical knowledge. Managerial skills. Ability to work with budgets. Team worker.

Where the Jobs Are
Technical schools
Vocational schools
Electronic departments

Salaries in Education
See Salaries in Teacher Education.

Qualifications

Personal Positive attitude. Enthusiasm. High energy level. Excellent communication skills. Listening skills. Flexibility. Ability to work under pressure.

Trade Publications

EDN
Cahners Publishing Company
Cahner Building, 275 Washington Street
Newton, MA 02158

Electronics
Lake Publishing Corp.
Box 159, 17730 West Peterson Road
Libertyville, IL 60048

Electronics
McGraw-Hill Publications
1221 Avenue of the Americas
New York, NY 10020

Professional Associations

International Society of Certified Electronic
Technicians
2708 W. Berry
Suite 3
Fort Worth, TX 76109

Jets Inc.
345 East 47th Street
New York, NY 10017

Fashion and Retail Management

Level	Management	Buying	Distribution	Visual Merchandising and Design	Sales
1. Entry ($20,000–$24,000)	Manager Trainee Department Manager Assistant Store Manager Customer Service Representative	Buyer Trainee	Merchandise Planner	Window Trimmer Display Coordinator	Sales Representative
2. Mid-management/ specialists ($24,000–$32,000)	Assistant Store Manager Area Manager Group Manager Divisional Manager Personnel Assistant Training Specialist Credit Manager	Junior Buyer Merchandise Analyst Fashion Coordinator	Administrative/ Analyst Planner MIS Specialist Coordinator of Scheduling Traffic Manager Production Coordinator Inventory Coordinator Transportation Specialist	Display Director Freelancer Fashion Writer Design Assistant (with further education) Fashion Display Specialist	Sales Manager District Sales Manager
3. Management ($32,000–$70,000+)	Store Manager Personnel Manager Operations Manager Director of Training Director of Human Resources Vice President/ Human Resources Vice President Operations	Buyer Merchandise Manager Vice President/ Merchandising	MIS Director Transportation Manager Administrative Manager Inventory Control Manager Distribution Manager Warehousing/ Operations Manager Vice President/ Operations	Consultant Fashion Designer (with further education)	Regional Sales Manager Vice President/ Sales Vice President/ Manufacturing

Recommended Pre-Professional Part-Time/Summer Work Experience

Sales, Shipping/Receiving, Cashier, Waitperson, Inventory Clerk, Posting Clerk, Data Entry Clerk, CRT Clerk, Telephone Sales, Demonstrators, General Office Clerk

Management

Level	Job Title	Experience Needed
Entry	Manager Trainee	Professional training
Entry	Department Manager	Professional training
Entry	Assistant Store Manager	Professional training
Entry	Customer Service Representative	Professional training
2	Assistant Store Manager*	1–3 years
2	Area Manager	1–3 years
2	Group Manager	2–4 years
2	Divisional Manager	3–5 years
2	Personnel Assistant	3–5 years
2	Training Specialist	3–5 years
2	Credit Manager	5–6 years
3	Personnel Manager	6–8 years
3	Operations Manager	1–10 years
3	Store Manager*	3–8 years
3	Director of Training	5–7 years
3	Director of Human Resources	7–9 years
3	Vice President/ Operations	9+ years
3	Vice President/Human Resources	9+ years

*Varies greatly depending on size and type of retail operation.

Salaries are higher for those with 2- and 4-year college degrees and vary greatly with the size and type of retail operation.

Salaries in Management

Level	Salary
Entry	$20,000 to $24,000
2	$19,000 to $30,000
3	$30,000 to $45,000+

Qualifications

Personal Enthusiasm. Positive attitude. Ability to learn quickly. Flexibility. Willingness to work weekends, nights, and holidays. Willingness to relocate helpful. Diplomacy.

Professional Demonstrated leadership ability. Aptitude for dealing with figures, finances, inventories, and quotas. Team worker.

Where the Jobs Are

Department stores
Specialty stores
Bookstores
Grocery/supermarkets
Boutiques
Computer sales centers
Government surplus organizations

Buying

Level	Job Title	Experience Needed
Entry	Buyer Trainee	Professional training
2	Junior Buyer	1–3 years
2	Merchandise Analyst	3–5 years
2	Fashion Coordinator	1–3 years
3	Buyer	5–7 years
3	Merchandise Manager	5–7 years
3	Vice President of Merchandising	7–10 years

Salaries in Buying

Level	Salary
Entry	$20,000 to $22,000
2	$20,000 to $25,000
2	$22,000 to $29,000
3	$25,000 to $60,000
3	$35,000 to $70,000+

Salaries are higher for those with 2- or 4-year college degrees and vary greatly depending on the size and type of retail operation.

Qualifications

Personal Ability to make quick decisions. Ability to work at a fast pace. Ability to conceptualize. Good written and verbal communication. Creativity. Risk taker. Negotiation skills. Willingness to travel extensively.

Professional Product knowledge. Aptitude for dealing with figures, finances, inventories, and quotas. Marketing and sales skills.

Where the Jobs Are

Department stores
Specialty stores buying offices
Resident buying offices

Distribution

Level	Job Title	Experience Needed
Entry	Merchandise Planner	Professional training
2	Inventory Coordinator	1–2 years
2	Production Coordinator	1–2 years
2	Traffic Manager	2–4 years
2	Transportation Specialist	2–4 years
2	Administrative/Analyst Planner	3–5 years
2	Coordinator of Scheduling	3–5 years
2	MIS Specialist	3–5 years
3	Distribution Manager	4–6 years
3	Transportation Manager	4–6 years
3	Administrative Manager	4–6 years
3	Inventory Control Manager	4–6 years
3	Warehousing/Operations Manager	4–6 years
3	MIS Director	6–10 years
3	Vice President/ Operations	6–10 years

Salaries in Distribution

Entry	$20,000 to $22,000
2	$22,000 to $25,000
2	$25,000 to $30,000
2	$28,000 to $32,000
3	$32,000 to $36,000
3	$36,000 to $40,000
3	$40,000 to $50,000+

Salaries are higher for those with 2- or 4-year college degrees.

Qualifications

Personal Ability to write and speak effectively. Patience. Listening skills. Ability to get along with people. Attention to detail. Organizational skills. Initiative. Good decision-making skills.

Professional Familiarity with computers. Ability to plan and supervise. Aptitude for figures, finances, inventories, and quotas.

Where the Jobs Are

Distribution centers
Manufacturing firms
Carriers
Public warehouses
Material handling equipment manufacturers and dealers
Consulting firms
Education
Print media
Communications
Government
Computer service organizations

Visual Merchandising and Design

Level	Job Title	Experience Needed
Entry	Window Trimmer	Professional training
Entry	Display Coordinator	Professional training
2	Fashion Display Specialist	1–3 years
2	Display Director	3–5 years
2	Freelancer	2–5 years
2	Fashion Writer	2–5 years
2	Design Assistant	*With further education*
3	Consultant	5–7 years
3	Fashion Designer	*With further education*

Salaries in Visual Merchandising

Entry	$18,000 to $20,000
Entry	$20,000 to $23,000
2	$22,000 to $25,000
2	$25,000 to $30,000
3	$30,000 to $35,000
3	$35,000 to $50,000
3	$50,000 to $65,000+

Salaries are higher for those with 2- or 4-year college degrees.

Qualifications

Personal Ability to conceptualize. High energy level. Ability to make quick decisions. Ability to work under pressure.

Professional Ability to work with budget restrictions. Willingness to travel. Willingness to work long hours including nights, weekends, and holidays. Familiarity with current trends and events.

Where the Jobs Are
Manufacturers' showrooms
Design houses
Retail stores

Advertising agencies
Magazines
Consulting
Apparel manufacturers

Sales

Level	Job Title	Experience Needed
Entry	Sales Representative	Professional training
2	Sales Manager	2–5 years
2	District Sales Manager	4–6 years
3	Regional Sales Manager	5–8 years
3	Vice President of Sales	7–10 years

Salaries in Sales
See Salaries in Marketing Careers.

Qualifications

Personal Positive attitude. Enthusiasm. High energy level. Ability to take rejection. Ability to work independently. Self-motivated. Negotiation skills. Confidence. Excellent communication skills. Tolerance for rejection.

Professional Product knowledge. Perception of customer needs. Willingness to learn. Diplomacy. Good grooming.

Where the Jobs Are
Clothing manufacturers
Design houses
Apparel manufacturers
Resident buying offices
Computer manufacturers

Trade Publications

Advertising Age (weekly)
Crain Communications
740 North Rush Street, Chicago, IL 60611

Journal of Retailing (quarterly)
New York University
202 Tisch Building
New York, NY 10003

Stores Magazine (monthly)
National Retail Merchants Association
100 West 31st Street, New York, NY 10001

Women's Wear Daily (daily)
Fairchild Publications, Inc.
7 East 12th Street, New York, NY 10003

Professional Associations

American Marketing Association
250 South Wacker Drive
Chicago, IL 60606

American Retail Federation
1616 H Street, N.W.
Washington, DC 20006

Association of General Merchandise Chains
1625 I Street, N.W.
Washington, DC 20006

National Retail Merchants Association
100 West 31st Street
New York, NY 10001

Food Service

Level	Production	Support	Control	Service
1. Entry ($20,000–$24,000)	Sauce Cook Roasting Cook Soup Cook Vegetable Cook Seafood Cook Pastry Cook Baker Garde Manger Rounds Cook/ Swing Cook Butcher Commis Line Cook Prep Cook Sous Chef Pantry Person	Food Service Salesperson Sanitation Supervisor	Purchasing Assistant Manager Trainee	Bartender Assistant Steward Waiter
2. Mid-management/ specialists ($24,000–$38,000)	Chef Pastry Chef Assistant Chef Assistant Pastry Chef Kitchen Manager Catering Manager Cafeteria Manager Food Production Manager Banquet Manager	Product Development Technologist Menu Planner Chef Instructor Director of Recipe Development Nutritionist Administrative Dietitian Quality Assurance Specialist Research and Development Specialist Sales and Marketing Specialist Packaging Specialist Home Economics Teacher Food Service Engineer Account Executive Training Manager Personnel Director Sales Manager Director of Marketing and Advertising Marketing and Promotion Manager Facilities Designer Real Estate Manager	Assistant Manager Merchandising Supervisor Storeroom Supervisor Purchasing Agent Accountant Computer Specialist Assistant Food and Beverage Manager Production Manager Food Service Manager Unit Manager Vending Manager Purchasing Manager Quality Control Manager Restaurant Manager	Wine Steward Head Bartender Dining Room Manager Hostperson Head Waiter Dining Room Captain Banquet Captain

Level	Production	Support	Control	Service
3. Management ($38,000–$60,000+)	Executive Chef Chef de Cuisine	Educator/Administrator Food Service Consultant	Food and Beverage Manager Controller Regional Vice President District Manager Owner/Operator General Manager	Beverage Manager Food Service Director Maitre d'Hotel

Recommended Pre-Professional Part-Time/Summer Experience

Cook, Grill Person, Prep Cook, Baker, Dishwasher, Checker and Cashier, Receiver, Storeroom Clerk, Barback, Waitperson, Counterworker, Hostperson, Busperson, Dining Room Attendant

Production

Level	Job Title	Experience Needed
Entry	Sauce Cook	Professional training
Entry	Roasting Cook	Professional training
Entry	Soup Cook	Professional training
Entry	Vegetable Cook	Professional training
Entry	Seafood Cook	Professional training
Entry	Pastry Cook	Professional training
Entry	Baker	Professional training
Entry	Garde Manger	Professional training
Entry	Rounds Cook/ Swing Cook	Professional training
Entry	Butcher	Professional training
Entry	Commis	Professional training
Entry	Line Cook	Professional training
Entry	Prep Cook	Professional training
Entry	Sous Chef	Professional training
Entry	Pantry Person	Professional training
2	Assistant Chef	2–4 years
2	Assistant Pastry Chef	2–4 years
2	Chef	4–6 years
2	Pastry Chef	4–6 years
2	Kitchen Manager	5–7 years
2	Catering Manager	5–7 years
2	Cafeteria Manager	5–7 years
2	Banquet Manager	5–7 years
2	Food Production Manager	6–8 years
3	Chef de Cuisine	8+ years
3	Executive Chef	8+ years

In all career areas in the food service industry it is important to note that the experience needed to progress to different positions varies widely according to the size, type, and volume of the operation.

Salaries in Production*

Entry	$20,000 to $22,000
2	$22,000 to $27,000
2	$27,000 to $38,000
3	$38,000 to $45,000
3	$45,000 to $60,000+

*Some positions, including Kitchen Managers, Banquet Chefs, Banquet Managers, and Sales Personnel, earn bonuses and/or commissions based on sales volume. Chefs' salaries are frequently based on food cost percentages and labor cost percentages.

Salaries vary widely according to the size, type, and location of the food service operation. In many large or fine-dining establishments and luxury hotels, top management positions are salaried over $100,000.

Special combinations of bonus, housing, meals, clothing allowance, company car, etc., are often in addition to salary.

Qualifications

Personal Positive attitude. Enthusiasm. High energy level. Confidence. Diplomacy. Accuracy and attention to detail. Reliability. Excellent communication skills. Ability to work under pressure. Ability to handle stress. Good grooming and hygiene habits. Professional appearance.

Professional Knowledge of and commitment to professional standards. Team worker. Perception of customer needs. Creative talent. Ability to conceptualize. Aptitude for finances, figures, inventories, and budgets.

Where the Jobs Are
Restaurants
Hotels
Motels
Resorts
Private businesses
Institutional food service operations (schools, universities, in-plant, hospitals, health care facilities, etc.)
Clubs
Transportation
Education

Catering firms
Fast-food operations
Franchises*
Contract food operations
Government

*Franchising is a form of licensing by which the owner (the franchisor) obtains distribution through affiliated dealers (the franchisee). Franchise agreements call for the parent company to give an independent businessperson rights to a successful restaurant concept and trademark, plus assistance in organizing, training, merchandising, and management.

Support Services

Level	Job Title	Experience Needed
Entry	Food Service Salesperson	Professional training
Entry	Sanitation Supervisor	Professional training
2	Menu Planner	1–3 years
2	Chef Instructor	1–3 years
2	Nutritionist	1–3 years
2	Home Economics Teacher	1–3 years
2	Administrative Dietitian	1–3 years
2	Quality Assurance Specialist	3–5 years
2	Product Development Technologist	3–5 years
2	Research and Development Specialist	3–5 years
2	Sales and Marketing Specialist	3–5 years
2	Packaging Specialist	3–5 years
2	Food Service Engineer	3–5 years
2	Quality Assurance Specialist	3–5 years
2	Account Executive	3–5 years
2	Facilities Designer	3–5 years
2	Training Manager	5–7 years
2	Sales Manager	5–7 years
2	Marketing Manager	5–7 years
2	Marketing and Promotion Manager	5–7 years
2	Real Estate Manager	5–7 years
2	Director of Recipe Development	6–8 years
2	Personnel Director	6–8 years
2	Director of Marketing and Advertising	6–8 years
3	Educator/Administrator	8–10+ years
3	Food Service Consultant	8–10+ years

Salaries in Support Services

Level	Salary
Entry	$20,000 to $24,000
2	$24,000 to $28,000
2	$28,000 to $35,000
2	$35,000 to $40,000
3	$40,000 to $50,000
3	$50,000 to $60,000+

Qualifications

Personal   Positive attitude. Enthusiasm. Excellent verbal and written communication skills. Ability to judge and make decisions. Accuracy and attention to detail. Well groomed. Ability to work independently.

Professional   Knowledge of and commitment to professional standards. Technical knowledge. Product knowledge. Strong marketing and sales skills. Perception of customer needs. Creative talent. Ability to conceptualize. Team worker.

Where the Jobs Are

Restaurants
Hotels
Motels
Resorts
Private businesses
Institutional food service operations (schools, universities, in-plant, hospitals, health care facilities, etc.)
Clubs
Transportation
Education
Catering firms
Fast-food operations
Franchises*
Contract food operations
Consulting
Wholesalers
Restaurant equipment suppliers
Manufacturers of food products
Government

*See note regarding franchises under Production heading.

Control

Level	Job Title	Experience Needed
Entry	Purchasing Assistant	Professional training
Entry	Manager Trainee	Professional training
2	Assistant Manager	2–4 years
2	Accountant	2–4 years
2	Purchasing Agent	2–4 years
2	Computer Specialist	2–4 years
2	Merchandising Supervisor	3–5 years
2	Storeroom Supervisor	3–5 years
2	Assistant Food and Beverage Manager	3–5 years
2	Production Manager	4–6 years
2	Food Service Manager	4–6 years
2	Unit Manager	4–6 years
2	Vending Manager	4–6 years
2	Purchasing Manager	5–7 years
2	Quality Control Manager	5–7 years
2	Restaurant Manager	5–7 years
3	Food and Beverage Manager	6–8 years
3	Controller	8–10 years
3	District Manager	8–10 years
3	Regional Vice President	8–10 years
3	Owner/Operator	8–10 years
3	General Manager	8–10 years

Qualifications

Personal Positive attitude. Enthusiasm. Ability to make quick and accurate decisions. Attention to detail. Excellent written and verbal communication skills. Confidence. Ability to handle pressure.

Professional Demonstrated leadership ability. Aptitude for dealing with figures, finances, inventories, and quotas. Team worker. Product knowledge. Perception of customers' needs. Planning and organizational skills. Ability to work with budgets.

Where the Jobs Are

Restaurants
Hotels
Motels
Resorts
Institutional food service operations (schools, universities, in-plant, hospitals, health care facilities, etc.)
Clubs
Catering firms
Fast-food operations
Franchises
Contract food operations
Lounges
Drinking establishments
Government

Salaries in Control

Level	Salary
Entry	$20,000 to $23,000
2	$23,000 to $26,000
2	$26,000 to $32,000
2	$32,000 to $38,000
3	$38,000 to $45,000
3	$45,000 to $60,000+

Service

Level	Job Title	Experience Needed
Entry	Bartender	Professional training
Entry	Assistant Steward	Professional training
Entry	Professional Waiter	Professional training
2	Hostperson	1–3 years
2	Wine Steward	1–3 years
2	Head Bartender	1–3 years
2	Dining Room Manager	2–5 years
2	Head Waiter	2–5 years
2	Dining Room Captain	2–5 years

Salaries in Service*

Level	Salary
Entry	$20,000 to $22,000
2	$20,000 to $25,000
2	$25,000 to $30,000
3	$30,000 to $35,000
3	$35,000 to $45,000+

*In many service positions, especially at the entry level, tips and gratuities constitute a portion of the salary. Salaries involving tips and gratuities vary according to the volume and type of operation.

Level	Job Title	Experience Needed
2	Banquet Captain	2–5 years
3	Beverage Manager	4–6 years
3	Food Service Director	5–7 years
3	Maitre d'Hotel	7–10 years

Where the Jobs Are

Restaurants
Hotels
Motels
Resorts
Lounges
Drinking establishments
Transportation
Clubs
Franchises
Institutional food service operations (*in-plant*)
Contract food operations
Government

Qualifications

Personal Positive attitude. Enthusiasm. High energy level. Good communication skills. Ability to work under pressure. Well groomed. Professional appearance. Flexibility.

Professional Product knowledge. Perception of customer needs. Team worker. Demonstrated leadership ability. Commitment to professional standards. Ability to supervise others. Good organizational and planning skills.

Trade Publications

Nations Restaurant News
Lebhar-Friedman
425 Park Avenue, New York, NY 10022

Restaurants and Institutions
Cahners Publishing Co.
Cahners Plaza, 1350 East Touhy Avenue
P.O. Box 5080, Des Plaines, IL 60018

Restaurant Business
633 Third Avenue, New York, NY 10017

Restaurant Management
Harcourt, Brace, Jovanovich
7500 Old Oak Blvd., Cleveland, OH 44130

Professional Associations

American Culinary Federation (ACF)
Box 3466
St. Augustine, FL 32084

National Restaurant Association (NRA)
311 First Street, N.W.
Washington, DC 20001

Council on Hotel, Restaurant and Institutional Education (CHRIE)
Henderson Blvd., S-208
University Park, PA 16802

International Food Service Executives Association
111 East Wacker Dr.
Chicago, IL 60601

Hospitality

Level	Rooms Division	Food and Beverage Services	Support
1. Entry ($20,000–$25,000)	Guest Services Agent Reservationist Information Specialist Head Cashier Concierge Front Desk Supervisor Inspector Assistant Manager (Front Office) Assistant Housekeeper Housekeeper Team Leader (Floor Supervisor)	See Food Service Careers— Production, Control, and Service	See Food Service Careers— Support Accountant Night Auditor Sales Trainee Sales Representative

Career Handbook   291

Level	Rooms Division	Food and Beverage Services	Support
2. Mid-management/ specialists ($25,000–$42,000)	Front Office Manager Rooms Attendant Executive Housekeeper Superintendent of Service Rooms Division Supervisor	See Food Service Careers— Production, Control, and Service	See Food Service Careers— Support See Travel/Tourism Careers— Hotels, Motels, Resorts Sales Director Group Sales Manager Area Sales Manager Auditor Corporate Account Executive Association Account Executive International Account Executive Tour and Travel Account Executive
3. Management ($38,000–$65,000+)	Resident Manager Assistant Hotel Manager Vice President/Operations General Manager	See Food Service Careers— Production, Control, and Service	See Food Service Careers— Support See Travel/Tourism Careers— Hotels, Motels, Resorts Chief Accountant Vice President/Finance Vice President/Marketing

Recommended Pre-Professional Part-Time/Summer Work Experience
Room Clerk, Starter, Telephone Operator, Messenger, Bellhop, Lobby Porter, Maid, Linen Room Attendant, Cashier, Seamstress, Doorperson, Cook, Waitperson, Busperson, Pantry Worker

Rooms Division

Level	Job Title	Experience Needed	Salaries in Rooms Division*	
Entry	Guest Services Agent	Professional training	Entry	$20,000 to $24,000
Entry	Reservationist	Professional training	2	$24,000 to $28,000
Entry	Information Specialist	Professional training	3	$28,000 to $38,000
Entry	Head Cashier	Professional training	3	$38,000 to $43,000
Entry	Concierge	Professional training	3	$43,000 to $46,000
Entry	Front Desk Supervisor	Professional training	3	$46,000 to $65,000+
Entry	Inspector/ress	Professional training		
Entry	Assistant Manager (Front Office)	Professional training		
Entry	Assistant Housekeeper	Professional training		
Entry	Housekeeper	Professional training		
Entry	Team Leader (Floor Supervisor)	Professional training		
2	Front Office Manager	1–2 years		
2	Rooms Attendant	1–2 years		
2	Executive Housekeeper	2–4 years		

*Salaries in Rooms Division vary widely according to the type of hotel. In many large or luxury hotels, top management positions are salaried over $100,000. Special combinations of bonus, housing, meals, clothing allowance, company car, etc., are often in addition to salary. For details on salaries in the Hospitality Industry, consult the Roth Young Hospitality Industry Wage and Salary Review.

Qualifications

Personal   Positive attitude. Enthusiasm. High energy level. Diplomacy. Courtesy. Confidence. Ability to make quick decisions and work independently. Good grooming and professional appearance. Ability to handle pressure. Excellent communication skills.

Level	Job Title	Experience Needed
2	Superintendent of Service	4–6 years
2	Rooms Division Supervisor	4–6 years
3	Resident Manager	6–8 years
3	Assistant Hotel Manager	6–8 years
3	Vice President/ Operations	8–10 years
3	General Manager	8–10 years

Professional Computer knowledge helpful. Aptitude for figures, finances, inventories, and quotas. Knowledge of and commitment to professional standards. Team worker. Ability to plan, organize, and forecast.

Where the Jobs Are

Hotels
Motels
Resorts
Inns
Bed and breakfast operations

Food and Beverage Service

Level	Job Title	Experience Needed
Entry	See Food Service Careers—Control and Services	Professional training
2	See Food Service Careers—Control and Services	Professional training
3	See Food Service Careers—Control and Services	Professional training

Qualifications

See Qualifications in Food Service Careers—Production, Control, and Service.

Where the Jobs Are

Hotels
Motels
Resorts
Inns
Bed and breakfast operations

Salaries in Food and Beverage Services

See Salaries in Food Service Careers—Production, Control, and Service.

Support

Level	Job Title	Experience Needed
Entry	See Food Service Careers—Support	Professional training
Entry	Accountant	Professional training
Entry	Night Auditor	Professional training
Entry	Sales Trainee	Professional training
Entry	Sales Representative	Professional training
2	See Food Service Careers—Support See Travel/Tourism Careers—Hotels, Motels, and Resorts	
2	Auditor	2–4 years
2	Group Sales Manager	2–4 years
2	Area Sales Manager	3–5 years
2	Corporate Account Executive	2–4 years
2	International Account Executive	3–5 years
2	Tour and Travel Account Executive	3–5 years
3	See Food Service Careers—Support See Travel/Tourism Careers—Hotels, Motels, and Resorts	

Level	Job Title	Experience Needed
3	Chief Accountant	5–8 years
3	Vice President/ Finance	8–10 years
3	Vice President/ Marketing	8–10 years

Salaries in Support

See Salaries in Food Service Careers—Support and Salaries in Travel/Tourism Careers—Hotels, Motels, and Resorts.

Qualifications

See Qualifications in Food Service Careers—Support and Qualifications in Travel/Tourism Careers—Hotels, Motels, and Resorts.

Where the Jobs Are

Hotels
Motels
Resorts
Inns
Bed and breakfast operations

Trade Publications

Hotel & Motel Management
545 Fifth Ave., New York, NY 10017

Lodging Hospitality
1100 Superior Ave., Cleveland, OH 44114

Hotel & Motel Red Book
American Hotel Association Directory
Corporation
888 Seventh Ave., New York, NY 10019

Cornell Hotel and Restaurant Administration Quarterly
School of Hotel Administration
Cornell University, Ithaca, NY 14853

Nations Restaurant News
Lebhar-Friedman, Inc.
425 Park Ave., New York, NY 10022

Restaurant and Institutions
Cahners Publishing Co.
Cahners Plaza, 1350 East Touhy Ave.
P.O. Box 5080, Des Plaines, IL 60018

Professional Associations

American Hotel and Motel Association
888 Seventh Avenue
New York, NY 10019

Council on Hotel, Restaurant, and Institutional
Education (CHRIE)
Henderson Bldg., S-208
University Park, PA 16802

Hotels Sales and Marketing Association
International
1400 K St., N.W., Suite 810
Washington, DC 20005

National Executive Housekeepers Association
1001 Eastwind Dr., Suite 301
Westerville, OH 43081

Foodservice and Lodging Institute
1919 Pennsylvania Ave., NW
Washington, DC 20006

American Bed and Breakfast Association
6811 Kingwood Drive
Falls Church, VA 20042

Club Managers Association of America
7615 Winterberry Place
Bethesda, MD 20817

National Restaurant Association
311 First St., N.W.
Washington, DC 20001

International Food Service Executives' Association
111 East Wacker Drive
Chicago, IL 60601

Marketing

Level	Sales/Management	Market Research	Telemarketing	Retailing
1. Entry ($20,000–$23,000)	Sales Representative Customer Service Representative	Coder-Editor Junior Analyst Associate Analyst	Telemarketing Representative Junior Account Executive	Buyer Trainee Sales Representative
2. Mid-management/ specialists ($24,000–$50,000)	Sales Supervisor Branch Sales Manager District Sales Manager Regional Sales Manager Central Region Sales Manager Advertising Manager	Analyst Senior Analyst Research Manager Product Manager	Telemarketing Trainer Account Executive Telemarketing Communicator Script Writer Supervisor Telemarketing Center Manager	Assistant Buyer Sales Manager Buyer Merchandise Manager

Level	Sales/Management	Market Research	Telemarketing	Retailing
3. Management ($35,000–$65,000+)	National Sales Manager Vice President/Marketing and Sales President	Market Research Director Vice President President	Executive Administrator	Executive

Recommended Pre-Professional Part-Time/Summer Work Experience

Sales, Telemarketing, General Office, Demonstrator, Messenger, Research Clerk, Coder, Data Entry Clerk, CRT Clerk, Waitperson

Sales/Management

Level	Job Title	Experience Needed
Entry	Sales Representative	Professional training
Entry	Customer Service Representative	Professional training
2	Sales Supervisor	1–2 years
2	Branch Sales Manager	2–4 years
2	District Sales Manager	3–5 years
2	Regional Sales Manager	5+ years
2	Central Region Sales Manager	6–8 years
2	Advertising Manager	6–8 years
3	National Sales Manager	7–9 years
3	Vice President/Marketing and Sales	7–9 years
3	President	8–10 years

Qualifications

Personal   Positive attitude. Enthusiasm. Flexibility. High energy level. Good listening skills. Ability to speak and write effectively. Tolerance for rejection. Initiative. Self-motivation. Resourcefulness. Goal orientation.

Professional   Logic. Product knowledge. Perception of customer needs. Time management skills. Commitment. Good grooming. Professional social skills.

Where the Jobs Are

Private industry
Advertising
Insurance
Financial services
Retailing
Computer services
Publishing houses
Equipment suppliers
Product manufacturers

Salaries in Sales/Management

Level	Salary
Entry	$20,000 to $23,000
2	$24,000 to $35,000
2	$35,000 to $50,000
3	$50,000 to $65,000
3	$65,000+

Salaries are higher for those with 2- or 4-year college degrees.

Market Research

Level	Job Title	Experience Needed
Entry	Coder-Editor	Professional training
Entry	Junior Analyst	Professional training
Entry	Associate Analyst	Professional training
2	Analyst	2–4 years
2	Senior Analyst	4–6 years
2	Research Manager	4–6 years
2	Product Manager	6–8 years
3	Market Research Director	7–9 years
3	Vice President	7–9 years
3	President	10 years+

Salaries in Market Research

Level	Salary
Entry	$20,000 to $23,000
2	$23,000 to $25,000
2	$23,000 to $27,000
2	$26,000 to $32,000
2	$32,000 to $40,000+
3	$35,000 to $40,000
3	$40,000 to $50,000+

Salaries are higher for those with 2- or 4-year college degrees.

Qualifications

Personal Detail-oriented. Good communication skills. Good organizational skills. Initiative. Patience. Resourcefulness. Ability to handle confidential information.

Professional Familiarity with computers. Aptitude for figures. Analytical thinking. Problem solving. Ability to conceptualize. Ability to evaluate and predict.

Where the Jobs Are
Private industry
Government

Telemarketing

Level	Job Title	Experience Needed
Entry	Telemarketing Representative	Professional training
Entry	Junior Account Executive	Professional training
2	Telemarketing Trainer	2–4 years
2	Account Executive	2–4 years
2	Telemarketing Communicator	2–4 years
2	Script Writer	2–4 years
2	Supervisor	5–7 years
2	Telemarketing Center Manager	5–7 years
3	Executive/Administrator	7–10 years

Salaries in Telemarketing

Entry	$20,000–$22,000
2	$22,000 to $35,000
2	$35,000 to $50,000
3	$50,000+

Salaries are higher for those with 2- or 4-year college degrees.

Qualifications

Personal Positive attitude. Good listening skills. Enthusiasm. Goal orientation. Self-motivation. Tolerance for rejection.

Professional Product knowledge. Perception of customers' needs.

Where the Jobs Are
Private industry
Education
Government
Telemarketing
Consulting
Advertising agencies
Computer service organizations
Publishing houses

Retailing

See Careers in Fashion and Retail Management.

Trade Publications

Telemarketing Magazine
17 Park Street, Norwalk, CT 06854

Teleprofessional Magazine
Box 123, Del Mar, CA 92014

Telemarketing Insiders Report
470 Main Street, Suite 108, Keyport, NJ 07735

Professional Associations

Telemarketing Recruiters, Inc.
114 East 32nd Street
New York, NY 10016

Telemarketing Council
Direct Marketing Association
6 East 43rd Street
New York, NY 10017

American Telemarketing Association
104 Wilmot Street
Deerfield, IL 60615

Medical Assistant

Level	Private Practices, Hospitals, Health Maintenance Organizations	Education	Medical Suppliers
1. Entry ($20,000–$23,000)	Medical Assistant	Instructor	Sales Representative
2. Mid-management/ specialists ($23,000–$28,000)	Claims Examiner Claims Representative Research Assistant Clinical Medical Assistant Administrative Medical Office Assistant	Department Head Medical Librarian	Sales Manager
3. Management ($28,000–$35,000+)	Medical Records Administrator Office Manager Nurse *(with further education)* Research Analyst Doctor *(with further education)*	School Director Administrator/ Education	Director of Marketing and Sales

Recommended Pre-Professional Part-Time/Summer Work Experience
Office Clerk, Receptionist, General Office Clerk, Lab Assistant, Nurse's Aide, Volunteer

Private Practices, Hospitals, Health Maintenance Organizations

Level	Job Title	Experience Needed
Entry	Medical Assistant	Professional training
2	Claims Examiner	1–3 years
2	Claims Representative	2–5 years
2	Claims Medical Assistant	1–3 years
2	Administrative Medical Office Assistant	3–5 years
3	Medical Records Administrator	5–7 years
3	Nurse	*With further education*
3	Research Analyst	7–10 years
3	Doctor	*With further education*

Qualifications

Personal   Listening skills. Courtesy. Neat, well-groomed appearance. Patience.

Professional   Ability to train on the job. Confidentiality. Computer and word processing skills. Good organizational and management skills.

Where the Jobs Are
Physicians' group practice
Physicians' independent practice
Clinics
Free-standing emergency centers
Hospitals
Nursing homes
Health care centers
Rehabilitation centers
Health maintenance organizations

Salaries in Private Practices, Hospitals, Health Maintenance Organizations

Level	
Entry	$20,000 to $23,000
2	$23,000 to $25,000
2	$25,000 to $28,000
3	$28,000 to $31,000
3	$31,000 to $35,000+

Salaries are higher for those with 2- or 4-year college degrees.

Education

Level	Job Title	Experience Needed	
Entry	Instructor	Professional training and/or college degree	
2	Academic Department Head	4–5 years	
2	Medical Librarian	4–5 years	
3	Administrator/ Education	6–8 years	
3	School Director	8–10+ years	

Qualifications

Personal
Patience. Good communication skills. Ability to manage.

Professional   Awareness of policies and laws in the health care field. Planning and organizational skills. Ability to work with budgets.

Where the Jobs Are
Career schools
Hospitals
Medical assistant departments

Salaries in Education
See Salaries in Teacher Education.

Medical Suppliers

Level	Job Title	Experience Needed
Entry	Sales Representative	Professional training
2	Sales Manager	3–6 years
3	Director of Marketing and Sales	7–10 years *(may need further education)*

Professional   Product knowledge. Perception of customer needs. Familiarity with medical terminology.

Where the Jobs Are
Medical supply companies
Pharmaceutical houses

Salaries with Medical Suppliers
See Salaries in Careers in Marketing.

Qualifications

Personal   Positive attitude. Good communication skills. Ability to work independently. Self-motivated. Tolerance for rejection. Confidence.

Trade Publication

Professional Medical Assistant
American Association of Medical Assistants,
20 North Wacker Drive, Chicago, IL 60606

Professional Associations

The American Association of Medical Assistants
20 North Wacker Drive
Suite 1575
Chicago, IL 60606

American Medical Technologists
Registered Medical Assistants
710 Higgins Rd.
Park Ridge, IL 60068

Paralegal

Level	Private Practices, Community Legal Services, Government Agencies	Corporation	Law Libraries	Education	Legal Publishing Houses	Computer Firms
1. Entry ($19,000–$24,000)	Summer Clerk Paralegal Assistant Legal Assistant	Paralegal	Legal Technician	Paralegal Instructor	Paralegal	Sales Representative
2. Mid-management/ specialists ($24,000–$40,000)	Litigation Support Manager Paralegal Supervisor Legal Assistant Manager Litigation Real Estate Probate Paralegal Recruiting Coordinator/ Administrator	Paralegal Coordinator Senior Legal Assistant Corporate Paralegal	Research Assistant Information Specialist	Placement Director	Editor	Systems Programmer Litigation Support Consultant
3. Management ($40,000–$55,000+)	Law Office Administrator Lawyer *(with further education)* Case Manager	Law Office Administrator Paralegal Manager	Law Library Manager Law Librarian	Program Director	Consultant/ Adviser	Marketing Analyst

Recommended Pre-Professional Part-Time/Summer Work Experience
General Office Clerk, Messenger, Library Clerk, Research Assistant, Coder, Legal Secretary, Court Reporter, Sales, Telemarketing, and Summer Clerk

Private Practices, Community Legal Services, Government Agencies

Level	Job Title	Experience Needed
Entry	Summer Clerk	Professional training
Entry	Paralegal Assistant	Professional training
Entry	Paralegal	Professional training
Entry	Legal Assistant	Professional training
2	Paralegal Supervisor	2–5 years
2	Litigation Support Manager	2–5 years
2	Litigation Paralegal	2–5 years
2	Real Estate Paralegal	2–5 years
2	Probate Paralegal	2–5 years
2	Legal Assistant Manager	4–6 years
2	Recruitment Coordinator/ Administrator	4–7 years

Salaries in Private Practices, Community Legal Services, Government Agencies

Entry	$20,000 to $24,000 (10–25% for overtime)
2	$24,000 to $34,000
2	$34,000 to $40,000
3	$40,000 to $55,000+

*After two years on the job, paralegal salaries often increase by more than 20 percent.

Qualifications

Personal Courtesy. Proven written and verbal communication skills. Interest in current events and history. Detail-oriented. Patience.

Professional Familiarity with legal terminology Research and investigative skills. Ethics. Confidentiality. Logic. Team worker.

Where the Jobs Are
Community legal service projects
Government agencies
Private practices

Corporations

Level	Job Title	Experience Needed
Entry	Paralegal	Professional training
2	Paralegal Coordinator	2–5 years
2	Senior Legal Assistant	2–5 years
2	Corporate Paralegal	2–5 years
3	Paralegal Manager	5–7 years
3	Corporate Paralegal	5–8 years

Salaries in Corporations
See Salaries in Private Practices, Community Legal Services, and Government Agencies.

Qualifications

Personal Positive attitude. Professional appearance. Enthusiasm. Detail-oriented. Proven written and verbal communication skills.

Professional Familiarity with legal terminology. Research and investigative skills. Ethics. Confidentiality. Logic. Team worker.

Where the Jobs Are
Private corporations
Public businesses

Law Libraries

Level	Job Title	Experience Needed
Entry	Legal Technician	Professional training
2	Research Assistant	3–6 years
2	Information Specialist	4–7 years
3	Law Library Manager	7–10 years
3	Law Librarian	7–10 years

Salaries in Law Libraries
See Salaries in Private Practices, Community Legal Services, and Government Agencies.

Qualifications

Personal Positive attitude. Detail-oriented. Patience. Interest in current events and history.

Professional Familiarity with legal terminology. Research and investigative skills. Ethics. Confidentiality.

Where the Jobs Are
Law libraries

Education

Level	Job Title	Experience Needed
Entry	Paralegal Instructor	Professional training
2	Placement Director	3–5 years
3	Program Director	6–10 years

Salaries in Education
See Salaries in Teacher Education.

Qualifications

Personal Leadership qualities. Excellent communication skills. High energy level. Positive attitude. Enthusiasm. Patience.

Professional Ethics. Knowledge of subject matter. Team worker. Well organized. Willingness to retrain.

Where the Jobs Are
Education
Private corporations
Consulting

Legal Publishing Houses

Level	Job Title	Experience Needed
Entry	Paralegal	Professional training
Entry	Proofreader	Professional training
Entry	Marketing Representative	Professional training
2	Junior Editor	3–5 years
3	Senior Editor	6–8 years
3	Consultant/Adviser	8–10 years

Salaries in Legal Publishing Houses

Level	Salary
Entry	$19,000 to $24,000
Entry	$24,000 to $26,000
2	$26,000 to $30,000
3	$30,000 to $37,000
3	$37,000 to $50,000+

Qualifications

Personal   Positive attitude. Enthusiasm. Detail-oriented. Proven written and verbal communication skills. Initiative. Professional appearance.

Professional   Problem-solving ability. Analytical thinking. Ability to conceptualize. Decision-making skills. Familiarity with legal terminology.

Where the Jobs Are
Legal publishing houses

Computer Firms

Level	Job Title	Experience Needed
Entry	Sales Representative	Professional training
2	Litigation Support Consu.	3–5 years
2	Systems Programmer	3–5 years
3	Marketing Analyst	5–8 years

Salaries in Computer Firms

Level	Salary
Entry	$18,000 to $22,000
2	$20,000 to $24,000
2	$25,000 to $28,000
3	$29,000 to $35,000

Qualifications

Personal   Excellent verbal communication skills. Confidence. Enthusiasm. Professional appearance. Ability to work independently. Self-motivated. Flexibility.

Professional   Product knowledge. Perception of customer needs. Willingness to learn. Problem-solving skills. Decision-making skills.

Where the Jobs Are
Computer manufacturers
Computer sales firms
Research organizations
Consulting
Computer service organizations

Trade Publications

National Paralegal Reporter
National Federation of Paralegal Associations
P.O. Box 40158, Overland Park, KS 66204

American Association for Paralegal Education Newsletter
American Association for Paralegal Education
P.O. Box 40244, Overland Park, KS 66204

Bulletin of the American Association for Paralegal Education
American Association
for Paralegal Education
P.O. Box 40244, Overland Park, KS 66204

International Legal Practitioner
International Bar Association
Two Harewood Place, Hanover Square
London WIR 2HB, England, United Kingdom

Professional Associations

National Association of Legal Assistants
1601 S. Main Street, Suite 300
Tulsa, OK 74119

National Paralegal Association
P.O. Box 406
Solebury, PA 18963

National Association for Independent Paralegals
585 Fifth Street West
Sonoma, CA 95476

American Bar Association
750 N. Lake Shore Drive
Chicago, IL 60611

American Paralegal Association
P.O. Box 35233
Los Angeles, CA 90035

National Federation of Paralegal Associations
104 Wilmot Road, Suite 201
Deerfield, IL 60015-5195

Secretarial Sciences

Level	Administration	Information Processing	Specialization
1. Entry ($17,000–$24,000)	Receptionist Secretary Administrative Secretary Executive Secretary	Word Processor Page Creator Editor Coder Proofreader	Legal Secretary Medical Secretary Technical Secretary School Secretary Membership Secretary Sales Secretary Travel Secretary Social Secretary International Group Secretary Statistical Typist City Mortgage and Real Estate Secretary
2. Mid-management/ specialists ($24,000–$29,000)	Administrative Assistant Conference and Meeting Coordinator Department Manager	Information Packager Systems Administrator Information Broker Information Manager Coding Clerk Supervisor	Paralegal Legal Assistant Personnel Clerk Medical Records Technician Customer Service Representative
3. Management ($29,000–$40,000+)	Executive Assistant Private Secretary Office Manager	Production Planner Financial Analyst Marketing Director Research Analyst (See Careers in Word Processing)	Personnel Assistant Sales Assistant Manager Trainee Office Manager (See Paralegal Careers)

Recommended Pre-Professional Part-Time/Summer Work Experience
Sales, File Clerk, CRT Clerk, Typist, Receptionist, Word Processor, Data Entry Operator, Inventory Clerk, Computer Operator, Library Assistant, General Office Clerk, Messenger

Administration

Level	Job Title	Experience Needed
Entry	Receptionist	Professional training
Entry	Secretary	Professional training
Entry	Administrative Secretary	Professional training
Entry	Executive Secretary	Professional training
2	Administrative Assistant	1–3 years
2	Conference and Meeting Coordinator	2–4 years
2	Department Manager	3–5 years
3	Executive Assistant	4–6 years
3	Private Secretary	5–7 years
3	Office Manager	5–7 years

Salaries in Administration

Entry	$17,000 to $24,000
2	$24,000 to $29,000
3	$29,000 to $40,000+

Qualifications

Personal Positive attitude. Enthusiasm. Detail-oriented. Excellent communication skills. Flexibility. Ability to work well under pressure. Self-starter. Dependable.

Professional Good typing, spelling, and grammar skills. Decision-making skills. Professional appearance. Responsible. Team worker. Resourcefulness. Ability to work independently.

Where the Jobs Are

Insurance
Banking
Hotels
Travel corporations
Education
Law offices
Medical offices
State and local government
Federal government
Manufacturing
Private corporations

Information Processing

Level	Job Title	Experience Needed
Entry	Word Processor*	Professional training
Entry	Page Creator	Professional training
Entry	Editor	Professional training
Entry	Coder	Professional training
Entry	Proofreader	Professional training
2	Information Packager	2–4 years
2	Systems Administrator	2–4 years
2	Information Broker	2–4 years
2	Information Manager	3–5 years
2	Coding Clerk Supervisor	3–5 years
3	Production Planner	4–6 years
3	Financial Analyst	5–7 years
3	Marketing Director	7–10 years
3	Research Analyst	7–10 years

*See Careers in Word Processing.

Salaries in Information Processing

Entry	$17,000 to $22,000
2	$23,000 to $27,000
3	$27,000 to $33,000+

Qualifications

Personal Positive attitude. Enthusiasm. Detail-oriented. Excellent written communication skills. Ability to work well under pressure. Ability to meet deadlines.

Professional Proofreading skills, ability to edit texts effectively. Good typing, spelling, and grammar. Ability to work independently. Team worker. Professional appearance.

Where the Jobs Are

Insurance
Banking
Education
Publishing houses
Advertising agencies
Media
Law offices
State and local government
Federal government
Private corporations

Specialization

Level	Job Title	Experience Needed
Entry	Legal Secretary	Professional training
Entry	Medical Secretary	Professional training
Entry	Technical Secretary	Professional training
Entry	School Secretary	Professional training
Entry	Membership Secretary	Professional training
Entry	Sales Secretary	Professional training
Entry	Travel Secretary	Professional training
Entry	Social Secretary	Professional training
Entry	International Group Secretary	Professional training
Entry	Statistical Typist	Professional training
Entry	City Mortgage and Real Estate Secretary	Professional training
2	Paralegal*	3–5 years
2	Legal Assistant	3–5 years
2	Personnel Clerk	3–5 years
2	Medical Records Technician	3–5 years
2	Customer Service Representative	3–5 years
3	Personnel Assistant	5–7 years
3	Sales Assistant	5–7 years
3	Management Trainee	5–7 years
3	Office Manager	6–8 years

*See Paralegal Careers.

Salaries in Specialization

Entry	$17,000 to $22,000
2	$22,000 to $27,000
3	$27,000 to $35,000+

Qualifications

Personal Positive attitude. Enthusiasm. Excellent verbal and written communication skills. Flexibility. Ability to work well under pressure. Dependable.

Professional Good typing, spelling, and grammar skills. Decision-making skills. Professional appearance. Team worker. Resourcefulness. Ability to work independently. Knowledge of specialized terminology.

Where the Jobs Are

Law offices
Hospitals
Medical offices
Travel corporations
Hotels
Real estate companies
Insurance
Banking
Education
State and local government
Federal government

Travel/Tourism

Level	Travel Agencies	Corporate Travel	Tourist Bureaus/ Offices	Convention and Visitors' Bureaus
1. Entry ($18,000–$22,000)	Travel Counselor Reservationist Travel Agent Receptionist	Reservationist Travel Agent Receptionist Travel Counselor	Information Coordinator	Coordinator/Travel Information Center Coordinator of Membership Sales
2. Mid-management/ specialists ($22,000–$26,000)	Incentive Travel Specialist Outside Sales Agent Employment Interviewer	Travel Specialist	Attractions Specialist Research Analyst Surveyor Assistant Marketing Director Interpreter	Destinations Promoter Public Relations Specialist Convention Sales Manager Convention Center Manager Finance Manager Director of Transportation

Level	Travel Agencies	Corporate Travel	Tourist Bureaus/Offices	Convention and Visitors' Bureaus

3. Management ($26,000–$45,000+)	Travel Director
	Travel Agency
	  Manager
	Personnel
	  Manager
	Owner/Operator
		Travel Director
		Corporate Travel
		  Manager
			Director of Marketing
			  and Sales
			State Travel Director
			Chief Tourism Officer
			Deputy Commissioner
			  of Tourism Development
			Commissioner of Tourism
				Executive Director
				Vice President/
				  Sales and
				  Marketing

Level	Chambers of Commerce	Department of Economic Development	Education	Tour Operations

1. Entry ($18,000–$20,000)	Membership
	  Coordinator
		Information
		  Coordinator
			Instructor	Tour Guide
				Tour Escort
				Tourist Information
				  Assistant

2. Mid-management/ specialists ($19,000–$24,000)	Sales Manager
	Research Analyst
	Program
	  Coordinator
		Economic
		  Development
		  Coordinator
		Demographer
		Urban Planner
		Director of Public
		  Safety
			Academic
			  Department
			  Head
				Tour Operator
				Director of Escort
				  Services
				Director of Tour
				  Guides
				Tour Director

3. Management ($24,000– $45,000+)	Executive Director
	Vice President/
	  Marketing
	  and Sales
		Executive
		  Director
			Education
			  Consultant
				Manager of
				  Tour Operations

Recommended Pre-Professional Part-Time/Summer Work Experience

Sales, Receptionist, General Office Clerk, Volunteer, Coder, Telephone Salesperson, Waitperson, Travel Assistant

Level	Associations	Conference and Meeting Planning	Hotels, Motels and Resorts	Public Relations

1. Entry ($18,000–$19,000)	Sales
	  Representative
	Coordinator of
	  Membership Sales
		See Careers in Hotels,
		  Motels, and Resorts
			Reservationist
			Reservations
			  Manager
			Reception
			  Manager
			Front Desk Clerk
			Concierge
				Account
				  Representative

2. Mid-management/ specialists ($19,000–$24,000)	Public Relations
	  Specialist
	Research Analyst
	Meeting Planner
	Special Events
	  Coordinator
	Sales Manager
			Meeting Planner
			Conference Planner
			Convention Planner
			Front Office
			  Manager
			Mail and
			  Information
			  Coordinator
			Special Events
			  Coordinator
			Conference Service
			  Coordinator
				Account Manager
				Speaker
				Informer
				Research and
				  Evaluator
				Special Events
				  Coordinator
				Press
				  Coordinator
				Communications
				  Technician

Level	Associations	Conference and Meeting Planning	Hotels, Motel and Resorts	Public Relations
3. Management ($24,000–$45,000+)	Director of Marketing and Sales Executive Director Vice President/ Marketing and Sales		Group Sales Manager Convention Sales Manager	Account Executive Director of Public Relations Vice President/ Communications

Level	Travel Writing	Airlines/Airports	Car Rental Agencies	Cruiselines
1. Entry ($18,000–$19,000)	Travel Writer	Reservationist Customer Service Representative Flight Attendant Ticket Agent Sales Representative	Customer Service Agent Rental Sales Representative	Sales Representative Reservationist
2. Mid-management/ specialists ($19,000–$24,000)	Proofreader Coder Freelancer	Airport Operations Agent Passenger Service Agent Ramp Agent Customs Inspector	Station Manager Lead Agent	Activities Coordinator Health Club Director Recreation Director
3. Management ($24,000–$45,000+)	Travel Editor	Supervisor of Gate Services Airline Schedule Analyst Airport Manager Airport Security Officer Schedule Planning Manager	City Manager	Cruise Director Director of Sales and Marketing

Recommended Pre-Professional Part-Time/Summer Work Experience
Sales, Receptionist, General Office Clerk, Volunteer, Coder, Telephone Salespersons, Waitperson, Travel Assistant

Travel Agencies

Level	Job Title	Experience Needed
Entry	Travel Counselor	Professional training
Entry	Reservationist	Professional training
Entry	Travel Agent	Professional training
Entry	Receptionist	Professional training
2	Incentive Travel Specialist	1–2 years
2	Outside Sales Agent	1–2 years
2	Employment Interviewer	2–4 years
3	Travel Director	4–6 years
3	Travel Agency Manager	4–6 years
3	Personnel Manager	4–6 years
3	Owner/Operator	Varies

Salaries in Travel Agencies

Entry	$18,000 to $20,000
Entry	$20,000 to $22,000
2	$22,000 to $25,000
3	$25,000 to $28,000+

Qualifications

Personal   Positive attitude. High energy level. Enthusiasm. Ability to work with budgets. Negotiation skills. Good communication skills. Effective interpersonal skills. Flexibility. Patience.

Professional   Familiarity with computers. Familiarity with geographic areas and destinations. Strong marketing and sales skills.

Where the Jobs Are

Travel agencies
Department stores

Corporate Travel

Level	Job Title	Experience Needed
Entry	Reservationist	Professional training
Entry	Travel Agent	Professional training
Entry	Receptionist	Professional training
Entry	Travel Counselor	Professional training
2	Travel Specialist	1–3 years
3	Travel Director	3–5 years
3	Corporate Travel Manager	3–5 years

Salaries in Corporate Travel

Level	Salary
Entry	$18,000 to $22,000
Entry	$22,000 to $24,000
2	$24,000 to $26,000
2	$26,000 to $28,000
3	$28,000 to $31,000
3	$31,000 to $35,000+

Qualifications

Personal Good communication skills. Effective interpersonal skills. Professional appearance. Positive attitude. Enthusiasm. Articulate. Initiative. Flexible.

Professional Awareness of product knowledge. Strong sales and marketing skills.

Where the Jobs Are
Corporate travel firms
Private industry
Government

Tourist Bureaus/Offices

Level	Job Title	Experience Needed
Entry	Information Coordinator	Professional training
2	Attractions Specialist	Professional training
2	Research Analyst	1–3 years
2	Surveyor	1–3 years
2	Assistant Marketing Director	3–5 years
2	Interpreter	3–5 years
3	Director of Marketing and Sales	5–8 years
3	State Travel Director	5–8 years
3	Chief Tourism Officer	8–10 years
3	Deputy Commissioner of Tourism Development	8–10 years
3	Commissioner of Tourism	8–10 years

Salaries in Tourist Bureaus/Offices

Level	Salary
Entry	$18,000 to $20,000
2	$19,000 to $21,000
2	$21,000 to $23,000
2	$23,000 to $25,000
3	$25,000 to $27,000
3	$27,000 to $34,000
3	$34,000 to $50,000+

Qualifications

Personal Positive attitude. Enthusiasm. Resourcefulness. Ability to communicate well. Effective interpersonal skills. Flexibility. Detail-oriented. Well groomed.

Professional Ability to interpret, predict, and organize. Knowledge of area lodging, restaurants, attractions. Strong marketing and sales skills. Familiarity with computers. Attention to national trends. Successful completion of civil service exam.

Where the Jobs Are
Research division
Promotion division
Information division
News division
Public affairs division

Convention and Visitors' Bureaus

Level	Job Title	Experience Needed
Entry	Coordinator/Travel Information Center	Professional training
Entry	Coordinator of Membership Sales	Professional training

Salaries in Convention and Visitors' Bureaus
See Salaries in Travel/Tourism—Tourist Bureaus/Offices.

Level	Job Title	Experience Needed	Qualifications
2	Destination Promoter	1–3 years	
2	Public Relations Specialist	1–3 years	
2	Convention Sales Manager	3–5 years	
2	Convention Center Manager	3–5 years	
2	Finance Manager	3–5 years	
2	Director of Transportation	3–5 years	
3	Executive Director	5–7 years	
3	Vice President of Sales and Marketing	7–10 years	

Qualifications

Personal Positive attitude. Enthusiasm. Accurate writing skills. Detail-oriented. Flexibility. Good communication skills. Effective interpersonal skills. Well groomed. Resourcefulness.

Professional Ability to conceptualize. Strong marketing and sales skills. Good organizational skills. Knowledge of area attractions, services, lodging, and restaurants.

Where the Jobs Are
Convention and visitors' bureaus

Chambers of Commerce

Level	Job Title	Experience Needed
Entry	Membership Coordinator	Professional training
2	Sales Manager	3–5 years
2	Research Analyst	1–3 years
2	Program Coordinator	1–3 years
3	Executive Director	5–7 years
3	Vice President/ Marketing and Sales	7–10 years

Qualifications

Personal Positive attitude. Enthusiasm. Resourcefulness. Ability to communicate well. Flexibility. Detail-oriented. Well groomed.

Professional Awareness of area businesses. Ability to coordinate and plan. Strong marketing and sales skills.

Where the Jobs Are
Sales
Research
Promotion

Salaries with Chambers of Commerce
See Careers in Travel/Tourism—Tourist Bureaus/Offices.

Department of Economic Development

Level	Job Title	Experience Needed
Entry	Information Coordinator	Professional training
2	Economic Development Coordinator	1–3 years
2	Demographer	2–4 years
2	Urban Planner	2–4 years
2	Director of Public Safety	3–5 years
3	Executive Director	5–7 years

Qualifications

Personal Detail-oriented. Ability to work independently. Accurate writing skills. Resourcefulness.

Professional Familiarity with computers. Ability to evaluate, plan, coordinate, and interpret data. Awareness of local and national economic trends.

Where the Jobs Are
Promotion
Research

Salaries with Departments of Economic Development
See Salaries in Travel/Tourism—Tourist Bureaus/Offices.

Education

Level	Job Title	Experience Needed
Entry	Instructor	Professional training and/or college degree
2	Academic Department Head	4–5 years
3	School Director/ Administrator	6–8 years
3	Education Consultant	8–10 years

Salaries in Education
See Salaries in Careers in Teacher Education.

Qualifications

Personal   Listening skills. Patience. Enthusiasm. Positive attitude. Detail-oriented. Flexibility. High energy level. Good communication skills.

Professional   Familiarity with computers. Broad knowledge of Travel/Tourism industry. Good organizational skills.

Where the Jobs Are
Schools
Consulting firms
Travel companies

Tour Operations

Level	Job Title	Experience Needed
Entry	Tour Guide	Professional training
Entry	Tour Escort	Professional training
Entry	Tourist Information Assistant	Professional training
2	Tour Operator	1–2 years
2	Director of Escort Services	3–5 years
2	Director of Tour Guides	3–5 years
2	Tour Director	3–5 years
3	Manager of Tour Operations	5+ years

Qualifications

Personal   High energy level. Enthusiasm. Positive attitude. Effective interpersonal skills.

Professional   Problem-solving ability. Leadership skills. Ability to settle complaints and give advice. Background in geography.

Where the Jobs Are
Tour operators
Attractions
Government
Private industry

Salaries in Tour Operations
See Salaries in Travel/Tourism—Travel Agencies.

Associations

Level	Job Title	Experience Needed
Entry	Sales Representative	Professional training
Entry	Coordinator of Membership Sales	Professional training
2	Public Relations Specialist	1–3 years
2	Research Analyst	1–3 years
2	Meeting Planner	1–3 years
2	Special Events Coordinator	1–3 years
2	Sales Manager	3–5 years
3	Director of Sales and Marketing	5–7 years
3	Executive Director	5–7 years
3	Vice President/Marketing and Sales	7–10 years

Salaries with Associations
See Salaries in Travel/Tourism—Tourist Bureaus/Offices.

Qualifications

Personal   Good communication skills. Enthusiasm. Positive attitude. Initiative. Detail-oriented. Accurate writing skills.

Professional   Strong marketing and sales skills. Familiarity with computers. Awareness of local and national business interests. Ability to supervise.

Where the Jobs Are
Professional associations
Chambers of commerce

Conference and Meeting Planning

See Careers in Travel/Tourism—Hotels, Motels, and Resorts.

Where the Jobs Are
Company or corporate meeting planners

Associations (or similar and usually not-for-profit organizations)
Independent meeting planners

Hotels, Motels, and Resorts

Level	Job Title	Experience Needed
Entry	Reservationist	Professional training
Entry	Reservations Manager	Professional training
Entry	Reception Manager	Professional training
Entry	Front Desk Clerk	Professional training
Entry	Concierge	Professional training
2	Meeting Planner	1–2 years
2	Conference Planner	1–2 years
2	Convention Planner	1–2 years
2	Front Office Manager	1–2 years
2	Mail and Information Coordinator	1–2 years
2	Special Events Coordinator	3–5 years
2	Conference Service Coordinator	3–5 years
3	Group Sales Manager	5+ years
3	Convention Sales Manager	5+ years

Salaries in Hotels, Motels, and Resorts

Entry	$20,000 to $22,000
2	$22,000 to $25,000
2	$25,000 to $29,000+
3	$29,000 to $33,000
3	$33,000 to $35,000+

Qualifications

Personal   Positive attitude. High energy level. Patience. Confidence. Good grooming. Professional appearance. Flexibility. Excellent interpersonal skills.

Professional   Negotiation skills. Sales and marketing skills. Ability to supervise.

Where the Jobs Are
Hotels
Motels
Resorts

Public Relations

Level	Job Title	Experience Needed
Entry	Account Representative	Professional training
2	Account Manager	1–3 years
2	Speaker	2–4 years
2	Informer	2–4 years
2	Researcher and Evaluator	2–4 years
2	Special Events Coordinator	2–4 years
2	Press Coordinator	3–6 years
2	Communications Technician	3–6 years
3	Account Executive	6–8 years
3	Director of Public Relations	6–8 years
3	Vice President of Communications	8–10 years

Qualifications

Personal   Excellent written and verbal communication skills. Effective interpersonal skills. Detail-oriented. Positive attitude. Enthusiasm. High energy level. Flexibility. Ability to work under pressure.

Professional   Ability to meet deadlines. Strong sales and marketing skills. Ability to supervise.

Where the Jobs Are
Convention and visitors' bureaus
Hotels, motels, and resorts
Civic centers
Tourist bureaus/offices
Chambers of commerce
Conference and meeting planning
Departments of economic development

Salaries in Public Relations
See Salaries in Careers in Marketing—Advertising/Public Relations.

Travel Writing

Level	Job Title	Experience Needed
Entry	Travel Writer	Professional training
2	Proofreader	1–2 years
2	Coder	1–2 years
2	Freelancer	2–4 years
3	Travel Editor	5–8 years

Salaries in Travel Writing
Salaries can pay well but will vary. Many publications feel that travel is a perk and pay less—even one-third—for travel stories than for other features.

Qualifications

Personal
Excellent writing skills. Detail-oriented. High energy level.

Professional
Ability to conceptualize. Knowledge of subject matter. Ability to meet deadlines.

Where the Jobs Are
Travel journals
Publishing houses
Magazines
Public relations departments
Advertising agencies
Research organizations

Airlines/Airports

Level	Job Title	Experience Needed
Entry	Reservationist	Professional training
Entry	Custom Service Representative	Professional training
Entry	Flight Attendant	Professional training
Entry	Ticket Agent	Professional training
Entry	Sales Representative	Professional training
2	Airport Operations Agent	1–3 years
2	Passenger Service Agent	1–2 years
2	Ramp Agent	1–2 years
2	Customs Inspector	1–3 years
3	Supervisor of Gate Services	3–5 years
3	Airline Schedule Analyst	3–5 years
3	Airport Manager	5–8 years
3	Airport Security Officer	3–5 years
3	Schedule Planning Manager	5–7 years

Salaries in Airlines/Airports

Level	Salary
Entry	$18,000 to $20,000
2	$20,000 to $23,000
2	$23,000 to $25,000
3	$25,000 to $28,000
3	$28,000 to $32,000
3	$32,000 to $39,000+

Qualifications

Personal Positive attitude. Enthusiasm. Good communication skills. Effective interpersonal skills. Well groomed. Willingness to work nights, holidays, and weekends. Flexibility.

Professional Awareness of airline/airport policies and procedures. Familiarity with computers. Supervisory skills. Planning skills.

Where the Jobs Are
Airlines
Airports

Car Rental Agencies

Level	Job Title	Experience Needed
Entry	Customer Service Agent	Professional training
Entry	Rental Sales Representative	Professional training
2	Station Manager	1–3 years
2	Lead Agent	1–3 years
3	City Manager	3–5 years

Salaries with Car Rental Agencies

Level	Salary
Entry	$18,000 to $22,000
2	$22,000 to $24,000
3	$24,000 to $35,000
3	$35,000 to $50,000+

Qualifications

Personal Positive attitude. Enthusiasm. High energy level. Good communication skills. Effective interpersonal skills.

Professional Ability to work with figures. Negotiation skills. Knowledge of geographic areas helpful. Resourcefulness.

Where the Jobs Are
Car rental agencies
Airports
Hotels
Major shopping malls

Cruiselines

Level	Job Title	Experience Needed	Qualifications
Entry	Sales Representative	Professional training	
Entry	Reservationist	Professional training	
2	Activities Coordinator	1–3 years	
2	Health Club Director	2–4 years	
2	Recreation Director	2–4 years	
3	Cruise Director	5–8 years	
3	Director of Sales and Marketing	7–9 years	

Qualifications

Personal   Positive attitude. High energy level. Enthusiasm. Good communication skills. Effective interpersonal skills. Flexibility.

Professional   Knowledge of safety policies and procedures. Strong marketing and sales skills.

Where the Jobs Are
Cruiselines (on board)
Cruiselines (on land)

Salaries with Cruiselines*

Level	Salary
Entry	$18,000 to $22,000
Entry	$22,000 to $25,000
2	$25,000 to $28,000
2	$28,000 to $32,000
3	$32,000 to $38,000+

*Most sales positions pay 25% in incentive pay and bonuses.

Trade Publications

Meeting News
1515 Broadway, New York, NY 10036

Travel Weekly
One Park Avenue, New York, NY 10016

International Travel News
2120-28th Street
Sacramento, CA 95818

Travelhost
8080 N. Central Exp., 14th Floor, Dallas, TX 75206
Courier

National Tour Association
546 East Main Street, Lexington, KY 40058

Professional Associations

National Tour Association
546 East Main Street
Lexington, KY 40058

Travel Industry Association of America
Suite 600
1899 L St., NW
Washington, DC 20036

Association of Travel Marketing Executives
804 D St., NE
Washington, DC 20002

Travel and Tourism Research Association
Box 8066
Foothill Station
Salt Lake City, UT 84108

International Association of Convention & Visitor Bureaus
Box 758
Champaign, IL 61820

American Society of Travel Agents
4400 MacArthur Blvd., NW
Washington, DC 20007

Word Processing

Level	Corporations	Education	Vendor Companies	Consulting	Employment Agencies
1. Entry ($17,000–$20,000)	Word Processor Lead Word Processing Operator	Instructor	Sales Representative	Training Specialist	Instructor
2. Mid-management/ specialists ($20,000–$24,000)	Coordinator/ Scheduler Records Manager Proofreader Trainer	Academic Department Head	Marketing Support Representative Sales Manager	Consultant	Employment Counselor
3. Management ($24,000–$28,000+)	Administrative Support Manager Night Shift Supervisor Word Processing Center Manager	Program Director Consultant	Director of Marketing and Sales Vice President/ Marketing and Sales	President/Owner	Owner/ Manager

Recommended Pre-Professional Part-Time/Summer Work Experience

Data Entry Operator, Clerk Typist, Messenger, Word Processing Operator Trainee, File Clerk, CRT Clerk

Corporations

Level	Job Title	Experience Needed
Entry	Word Processor	Professional training
Entry	Lead Word Processing Operator	Professional training
2	Coordinator/Scheduler	1–3 years
2	Records Manager	3–5 years
2	Proofreader	1–3 years
2	Trainer	3–5 years
3	Administrative Support Manager	5–7 years
3	Night Shift Supervisor	4–6 years
3	Word Processing Center Manager	5–7 years

Salaries in Corporations

Level	Salary
Entry	$17,000 to $20,000
2	$20,000 to $22,000
2	$22,000 to $24,000
3	$24,000 to $26,000
3	$26,000 to $28,000+

Qualifications

Personal   Positive attitude. Detail-oriented. Ability to work independently. Ability to make accurate decisions. Confidence. Enthusiasm.

Professional   Ability to type. Good spelling, punctuation, and grammar. Ability to handle advanced electronic equipment. Team worker.

Where the Jobs Are

Law departments
Personnel
Claims area
Records department
Communications
Medical department
Word processing center

Education

Level	Job Title	Experience Needed
Entry	Instructor	Professional training and/or college degree
2	Academic Department Head	4–5 years
3	Program Director	6–8 years
3	Consultant	8–10 years

Salaries in Education
See Salaries in Teacher Education.

Qualifications

Personal   Patience. Good communication skills. Ability to manage. Detail-oriented.

Professional   Knowledge of various types of word processing equipment. Willingness to retrain as needed.

Where the Jobs Are
Schools
Consulting firms

Vendor Companies

Level	Job Title	Experience Needed
Entry	Sales Representative	Professional training
2	Marketing Support Representative	1–3 years
2	Sales Manager	3–5 years
3	Director of Sales and Marketing	5–7 years
3	Vice President of Marketing and Sales	7–10 years

Salaries with Vendor Companies
See Careers in Marketing—Sales/Management.

Qualifications

Personal
Positive attitude. High energy level. Initiative. Self-motivated. Enthusiasm. Ability to work independently.

Professional
Product knowledge. Perception of customer needs. Strong sales and marketing skills.

Where the Jobs Are
Word processing manufacturing firms
Office equipment suppliers

Consulting

Level	Job Title	Experience Needed
Entry	Training Specialist	Professional training and/or college degree
2	Consultant	1–5 years
3	President/Owner	6+ years

Salaries in Consulting
See Salaries in Computer Systems—Support Services.

Qualifications

Personal   Positive attitude. Enthusiasm. Ability to work independently. Effective written and verbal communication skills. Flexibility.

Professional   Product knowledge. Perception of customer needs. Strong marketing and sales skills.

Where the Jobs Are
Freelancing
Education
Equipment manufacturers
Private corporations

Employment Agencies

Level	Job Title	Experience Needed	Qualifications
Entry	Instructor	Professional training	
2	Employment Counselor	1–3 years	
3	Owner/Manager	3–6 years	

Qualifications

Personal Assertiveness. Ability to work under pressure. Good communication skills. Effective interpersonal skills. Positive attitude. Enthusiasm. Persistence. Patience. Risk taker. High energy level.

Professional Ability to assess clients' needs. Strong business ethics. Good business judgment. Ability to manage. Strong marketing and sales skills.

Salaries in Employment Agencies

Vary but are usually based on a base salary plus commissions on the number of candidates successfully placed in jobs. Percentages of commission progress with salary amounts; however, compensation in employment agencies also can include bonuses and travel reimbursement. As an owner, compensation is earned after all of the overhead costs for running the business (rent, salaries, equipment, etc.) are paid.

Where the Jobs Are

Temporary employment agencies
Permanent placement agencies

Trade Publications

Information Management and
Processing Association
P.O. Box 16267, Lansing, MI 48901

The Word
Office Technology Management Association
9401 West Beloit Road, Suite 101
Milwaukee, WI 53227

Professional Associations

Information Management and Processing
Association
P.O. Box 16267
Lansing, MI 48901

National Association of Professional Word
Processing Technicians
110 W. Byberry Road
Philadelphia, PA 19116

Office Technology Management Association
9401 W. Beloit Road
Suite 101
Milwaukee, WI 53227

Word Processing Society, Inc.
P.O. Box 92553
Milwaukee, WI 53202

Glossary of Terms Used in Job Descriptions

accept   To receive with consent; to take without protest.

accountability   The state of being subject to judgment for an action or result which a person has been given authority and responsibility to perform.

act   To exert one's power so as to bring about a result; to carry out a plan or purpose. (See **execute, implement,** and **perform.**)

add   To affix or attach; to find the sum of figures.

administer   To direct the application, execution, use, or general conduct of.

adopt   To take and apply or put into action.

advise   To give recommendations to. (See **propose** and **recommend.**) To offer an informed opinion based on specialized knowledge.

affirm   To confirm or ratify.

align   To arrange or form in a line.

amend   To change or modify.

analyze   To study the factors of a situation or problem in order to determine the outcome or solution; to separate or distinguish the parts of a process or situation so as to discover their true relationships.

anticipate   To foresee events, trends, consequences, or problems in order to deal with them in advance.

apply   To adjust or direct; to put in use.

appraise   To evaluate as to quality, status, or effectiveness of.

This glossary was developed in 1981 by Richard B. Shore and Patricia Alcibar for American Management Associations. Used by permission.

From: JoAnn Sperling, *Job Descriptions in Human Resources* (New York: Amacom [A Division of American Management Association], 1985).

approve   To sanction officially; to accept as satisfactory; to ratify thereby assuming responsibility for. (*Used only in the situation where the individual has final authority.*)

arrange   To place in proper or desired order; to prepare for an event. (See **prepare.**)

ascertain   To find out or learn with certainty.

assemble   To collect or gather together in a predetermined order or pattern. (See **collect, compile,** and **coordinate.**)

assign   To give specific duties to others to perform. (See *delegate.*)

assist   To lend aid or support in some undertaking or effort. (*No authority over the activity is implied.*)

assume   To take upon oneself; to undertake; to take for granted.

assure   To confirm; to make certain of. (See **ensure.**)

attach   To bind, fasten, tie, or connect.

attend   To be present for the purpose of listening or contributing.

audit   To examine and review a situation, condition, or practice, and conclude with a detailed report on the findings.

authority   The power to influence or command thought, opinion, or behavior.

authorize   To empower; to permit; to establish by authority.

balance   To arrange or prove so that the sum of one group equals the sum of another.

batch   To group into a quantity for one operation.

calculate   To ascertain by mathematical processes; to reckon by exercise of practical judgment.

cancel   To strike or cross out.

carry   To convey through the use of the hands.

center   To place or fix at or around the center; to collect to a point.

chart   To draw or exhibit in a graph.

check   To examine for a condition; to compare for verification. (See **control, examine, inspect, monitor,** and **verify.**)

circulate   To distribute in accordance with a plan. (See **disseminate.**)

classify   To separate into groups having systematic relations.

clear   To get the agreement or disagreement of others.

close   To terminate or shut down.

code   To transpose words or figures into symbols or characters. (Also **encode.**)

collaborate   To work or act jointly with others.

collate   To bring together in a predetermined order.

collect   To gather facts or data; to assemble; to accumulate. (See **assemble** and **compile.**)

compile   To collect into a volume; to compose out of materials from other documents.

compose   To make up, fashion, or arrange.

concur   To agree with a position, statement, act, or opinion.

conduct   To lead, guide, or command the efforts of others toward producing a chosen result.

confer   To converse with others to compare views. (See **consult, discuss,** and **negotiate.**)

consolidate   To combine separate items into a single whole.

construct   To set in order mentally; to arrange.

consult   To seek advice of others; to confer.

control   To exert power over in order to guide or restrain; to measure, interpret, and evaluate for conformance with plans or expected results.

cooperate   To work jointly with others. (See **collaborate.**)

coordinate   To bring into common action or condition so as to harmonize by regulating, changing, adjusting, or combining. (See **assemble.**)

copy   To transfer or reproduce information.

correct   To rectify; to make right.

correlate   To establish a mutual or reciprocal relationship; to put in relation to each other.

cross foot   To add across, horizontally.

cross off   To line out, strike out.

cross out   To eliminate by lining out.

date stamp   To affix or note a date by stamping.

decide   To choose from among alternatives or possibilities so as to end debate or uncertainty.

delegate   To entrust to the care or management of another; to authorize or empower another to act in one's place. (See **assign, authorize,** and **represent.**)

delegation   Assigning to a subordinate the responsibility and commensurate authority to accomplish an objective or specific result.

delete   To erase; to remove.

design   To conceive and plan in the mind for a specific use; to create, fashion, execute, or construct according to a plan. (See **develop, devise, formulate,** and **plan.**)

determine   To make a decision; to bring about; to cause; to decide and set limits to, thereby fixing definitely and unalterably. To find out something not before known as a result of an intent to find defined and precise truth.

develop   To conceive and create; to make active, available, or usable; to set forth or make clear, evident, or apparent.

development   The result of developing.

devise   To come up with something new, especially by combining known ideas or principles. (See **design, develop, formulate,** and **plan.**)

direct   To lead, guide, or command the efforts of others toward producing a chosen result. (See **conduct, manage,** and **supervise.**)

direction   Guidance or supervision of others.

disassemble   To take apart. (Also **dissemble.**)

discover   To find out something not known before as a result of chance, exploration, or investigation. (See **ascertain** and **determine.**)

discuss   To exchange views for the purpose of convincing or reaching a conclusion.

dissemble   To take apart. (Also **disassemble.**)

disseminate   To spread information or ideas. (See **circulate, distribute, issue,** and **release.**)

distribute   To divide or separate into classes; to pass around; to allot; to deliver to named places or persons. (See **circulate, disseminate, issue,** and **release.**)

divide   To separate into classes or parts subject to mathematical division.

draft   To compose or write papers and documents in preliminary or final form, often for the approval or clearance of others.

duty   Assigned task.

edit   To revise and prepare for publication.

endorse   To express approval of; to countersign.

ensure   To make safe or certain. (See **assure.**)

establish   To set up or bring into existence on a firm basis.

evaluate   To ascertain or determine the value of.

examine   To investigate; to scrutinize; to subject to inquiry by inspection or test.

execute   To put into effect; to follow through to the end.

exercise   To employ actively, as in authority or influence.

expedite   To accelerate the movement or progress of; to remove obstacles.

facilitate   To make easy or less difficult.

feed   To supply material to a machine.

figure   To compute.

file   To lay away papers, etc., arranged in some methodical manner.

fill in   To enter information on a form.

find   To locate by search.

flag   To mark distinctively.

follow up   To check the progress of; to see if results are satisfactory.

formulate   To develop or devise a plan, policy, or procedure; to put into a systemized statement.

furnish   To give or supply. (See **provide**.)

goal   An objective.

guidance   Conducting or directing along a course of action.

implement   To carry out; to perform acts essential to the execution of a plan or program; to give effect to.

inform   To instruct; to communicate knowledge.

initiate   To originate; to introduce for the first time.

insert   To put or thrust in.

inspect   To examine carefully for suitability or conformance with standards. (See **check, control, examine, monitor,** and **verify**.)

instruct   To impart knowledge to; to give information or direction to; to show how to do.

instructions   To furnish with directions; to inform.
Specific: Precise and detailed directions that closely limit what can be done or how it can be done.
General: Directions that are merely outlined, hence do not closely limit what can be done or how it can be done.

intensive   Exhaustive or concentrated.

interpret   To explain or clarify; to translate.

interview   To question in order to obtain facts or opinions.

inventory   A list of items; stock on hand.

investigate   To study closely and methodically.

issue   To distribute formally.

itemize   To set or note down in detail; to set by particulars.

line   To cover the inside surface of; to draw lines on.

list   To itemize.

locate   To search for and find; to position.

maintain   To keep up-to-date or current; to keep at a given level or in working condition.

manage   To control and direct; to guide; to command the efforts of others toward producing a chosen result. (See **supervise**.)

measure   To find the quality or amount of; to ascertain dimension, count, intensity, etc.

merge   To combine.

mix   To unite or blend into one group or mass.

monitor   To observe or check periodically for a specific purpose.

multiply   To perform the operation of multiplication.

negotiate   To exchange views and proposals with an eye to reaching agreement by sifting possibilities, proposals, and pros and cons.

nonroutine   Irregular or infrequent situations that arise relating to business or official duties. Characteristic of higher-level jobs.

note   To observe, notice.

notify   To give notice to; to inform.

objective   A desired result. (See **goal**.)

observe   To perceive, notice, watch.

obtain   To gain possession of; to acquire.

open   To enter upon; to spread out; to make accessible.

operate   To conduct or perform activity.

organization   Individuals working together in related ways within a specific structure toward a common end.

organize   To arrange in interdependent parts; to systematize.

originate   To produce as new; to invent.

outline   To make a summary of the significant features of a subject.

participate   To take part in.

perform   To carry out; to accomplish; to execute.

place   To locate an employee in a job.

plan   To devise or project a method or course of action.

policy   A definite course or method of action selected from among alternatives and in light of given conditions, to guide and determine present and future decisions.

position description   A document that describes the purpose, scope, duties, responsibilities, authorities, and working relationships associated with a position or entity to be occupied and performed by one person.

position specification   A document that describes the physical characteristics, knowledge, skill, experience, and education requirements of a person who would be ideally suited to perform a specific job.

post   To announce by public, written notice; to transfer or carry information from one record to another.

practice   To work repeatedly to gain skill.

prepare   To make ready for a special purpose.

principle   A governing law of conduct; a fundamental belief serving as a responsible guide to action; a basis for policy.

procedure   A particular way of accomplishing something or of acting; a series of steps followed in a regular, definite order; a standardized practice.

proceed   To begin or carry out.

process   To subject to some special treatment; to handle in accordance with prescribed procedures.

program   A series of planned steps toward an objective.

promote   To act so as to increase sales or patronage; to advance someone to a higher level or job.

propose   To offer for consideration or adoption; to declare an intention.

provide   To supply for use; to make available; to furnish.

purchase   To buy or procure.

purpose   Something set up as an objective or end to be attained; a reason.

rate   To appraise or assess; to give one's opinion of the rank or quality of.

receive   To take something that is offered or sent.

recommend   To advise or counsel a course of action or to suggest for adoption a course of action.

reconstruct   To restore; to construct again.

record   To register; to make a record of.

refer   To direct attention to.

register   To enter in a record or list.

release   To authorize the publication of, dissemination of.

remit   To transmit or send money as payment.

render   To furnish, contribute.

report   To supply or furnish organized information.

represent   To act for or in place of; to serve as a counterpart of; to substitute in some capacity for.

request   To ask for something.

require   To demand as necessary or essential.

requisition   A document making a request.

research   Inquiry into a specific subject from several sources.

responsibility   The quality or state of being accountable for.

responsible for   Having caused; accountable for.

review   To examine, usually with intent to approve or dissent; to analyze results in order to give an opinion.

revise   To change in order to make new, to correct, to improve, or bring up-to-date.

route   To prearrange the sending of an item to the location to which it is to be sent.

routine   Regular procedure, or normal course of business or official duties.

scan   To examine point by point; to scrutinize.

schedule   To plan a timetable; to set specific times for.

screen   To examine so as to separate into two or more groups or classes, usually rejecting one or more.

search   To look over and through for the purpose of finding something.

secure   To get possession of; to obtain; to make safe.

select   Chosen from a number of others of a similar kind.

separate   To set apart from others for special use; to keep apart.

serve   To hold an office; to act in a capacity; to discharge a duty or function.

sign   To authorize by affixing one's signature.

sort   To put in a definite place or rank according to kind, class, etc.

stack   To pile up.

standard of performance   A statement of the conditions that will exist when a job is acceptably done. Whenever possible, the elements of the statement include specific reference to quantity, quality, cost, and time.

stimulate   To excite, rouse, or spur on.

study   To consider attentively; to ponder or fix the mind closely upon a subject.

submit   To present information for another's judgment or decision.

subtotal   An interim total.

subtract   To deduct one number from another.

summarize   To give only the main points.

supervise   To oversee a work group—leading, guiding, or commanding its efforts to produce a chosen result.

support   To provide service, assistance, or supplies to another person or department.

survey   To ascertain facts regarding conditions or the condition of a situation usually in connection with the gathering of information.

tabulate   To form into a table by listing; to make a listing.

trace   To record the transfer of an application or document; to copy as a drawing.

train   To increase skill or knowledge by capable instruction.

transcribe   To make a typed copy from shorthand notes or dictated record; to write a copy of.

transpose   To transfer; to change the usual place or order.

underline   To emphasize or identify by drawing a line under the characters or subject.

verify   To prove to be true or accurate; to confirm or substantiate; to test or check the accuracy of.

Index of Job Descriptions

Academic Department Head Administers affairs of an academic department. May administer department's budget and recruit academic personnel. Conducts meetings to discuss current teaching strategies and obtains recommendations for changes within the department.

Account Executive Responsible for the development of and service of a customer account. Brings business to the firm. Consults with the client and collaborates with associates to find best strategies for servicing clients.

Account Executive (Advertising) Meets with clients. Participates in meetings with other departments on the ideas for a campaign. Plans overall strategy for clients. Keeps up-to-date on media rate changes and new media outlets. Serves as a link between the agency and the clients.

Account Executive (Food Service) Initiates and signs new customers, which includes scouting new business, helping survey clients' needs, writing formal request letters, and making formal presentations, usually accompanied by management representative(s). Representative of the food service contractor who deals directly with the liaison designate of the client.

Account Executive (Public Relations) Meets with clients to determine needs for public relations program. May review company strategies and goals, current customer base, and reputation with the public. Recommends public relations program. Keeps up-to-date on new and existing programs and policies. Serves as a link between the public relations firm and the clients.

Account Executive (Telemarketing) Organizes and manages a program internally once it has been brought in by a telemarketing representative. Coordinates script writing, script testing, list preparation, forms design (to record sales and customer data), and client reports. Monitors the project and provides regular reports for the client.

Account Executive Trainee (Advertising) Fields material from other departments. Takes calls from clients. Keeps in touch with traffic department on schedules for ads and spots.

Account Manager Develops an efficient coverage pattern for the territory. Decides on the call frequency for major accounts. Develops a sales plan for the territory. Promotes, sells, and services product line. Reviews customer-call reports. Coordinates activities at individual key customer locations.

Account Representative (See **Account Executive**)

Account Supervisor (See **Account Manager**)

Accounts Supervisor/Manager (See **Account Manager**)

Accountant Helps businesses and individuals set up financial recordkeeping. Examines, analyzes, and interprets accounting records for the purpose of giving advice or preparing statements. Estimates future revenues and expenditures to prepare budget.

Accountant (Food Service) Prepares and analyzes financial reports that furnish up-to-date financial information. Accountants employed by large restaurant firms may travel extensively to audit or work for clients or branches of the firm.

Accountant (Hospitality) Sets up the financial recordkeeping for the hotel or other lodging facility. Estimates future revenues and expenditures to prepare the operation's budget for each year.

Activities Coordinator (Cruiselines) Plans and implements activities for passengers on cruiselines.

Actuarial Trainee Works for insurance companies analyzing statistics to determine probabilities of accident, death, injury, earthquake, flood, fire, etc., so that the rates charged for insurance policies will bring in profits for the company while still being competitive with those of other insurance carriers.

Actuary   Uses mathematical skills to predict probabilities of events that will be used for insurance plans and pension programs.

Adjuster   Investigates and settles claims of losses suffered by policyholders of all kinds of insurance.

Adjuster Trainee   Assists with investigations and settling claims of losses suffered by policyholders of all kinds of insurance.

Administrative Analyst/Planner   Responsibilities include developing any new systems and setting up any long-range planning systems; responsible for the planning group, which actually plans each day's shipment to distribution centers. Works on product allocation and inventory control. Responsible for anything that might affect the distribution area.

Administrative Assistant   An administrative support job performed with little or no supervision, and one that is a step higher than an executive secretary. Handles dissemination of contract information or works with a chief officer of a company in preparing corporate reports. Often involves supervision of others.

Administrative Dental Assistant   Checks office and laboratory supplies; maintains waiting, reception, and examination rooms in a neat and orderly condition; answers telephones; greets patients and other callers; records and files patient data and medical records; fills out medical reports and insurance forms; handles correspondence, schedules appointments, and arranges for hospital admission and laboratory services. May transcribe dictation and handle the bookkeeping and billing.

Administrative Dietitian   Responsible for training and supervision of food service supervisor and assistants in food preparation and formulating policies, enforcing sanitary and safety regulations. Buys food, equipment, and other supplies, so must understand purchasing and budgeting.

Administrative Manager   Provides maximum support to all divisions through the regional or district distribution centers and ensures that timely, cost-effective service is provided to those units and their customers. Supervises personnel, equipment, materials, facilities, product handling, inventory control, building services, customer relations, order processing, office services, and district operations.

Administrative Medical Office Assistant   (See **Administrative Dental Assistant**)

Administrative Secretary   Handles everything except dictation and typing. Duties range from filing and setting up filing systems, routing mail, and answering telephones to more complex work such as answering letters, doing research, and preparing statistical reports.

Administrative Support Manager   (Word Processing) Responsible for the operation of the entire word processing center.

Administrator (Education)   Directs the administration of an educational institution, or a division of it, within the author-

ity of the governing board. Develops or expands programs or services. Administers fiscal operations such as budget planning, accounting, and establishing costs for the institution. Directs hiring and training of personnel. Develops policies and procedures for activities within area of responsibility.

Administrator (Education)   Involved with curriculum and program development and directing teaching personnel of the school system. Confers with teaching and administrative staff to plan and develop curriculum designed to meet needs of the students. Visits classrooms to observe effectiveness of instructional methods and materials. Evaluates teaching techniques and recommends changes for improving them. Conducts workshops and conferences for teachers to study new classroom procedures, new instructional materials, and other aids to teaching.

Advertising Manager   Plans and executes advertising policies of an organization. Confers with department heads to discuss possible new accounts and to outline new policies or sales promotion campaigns. Confers with officials of newspapers, radio, and television stations and then arranges billboard advertising contracts. Allocates advertising space to department. May authorize information for publication.

Agent (Insurance)   Sells traditional life insurance to clients. May also sell mutual funds and other equity-based products. Many agents also qualify as financial planners after obtaining certification. Explains financial products in detail to prospective clients. Processes necessary paperwork when closing a sale.

Air Patrol Officer   Patrols areas, by air, where the military is located.

Airline Schedule Analyst   Reviews schedules for all incoming and outgoing flights. Makes recommendations for changes in schedules to ensure maximum service while still maintaining strict procedures.

Airport Manager   Responsible for operating a safe facility and for fund raising. Keeps the public informed on safety decisions affecting the area surrounding the airport.

Airport Operations Agent   Customer service agent responsible for assigning boarding times, lifting tickets; coordinates baggage service; announces flight arrivals to main desk.

Airport Security Officer   Notes suspicious persons and reports to superior officer. Reports hazards. Inspects baggage of passengers. Assists passengers with lost luggage claims. Directs passengers to appropriate boarding areas. Warns or arrests persons violating ordinances. Issues tickets to traffic violators. Maintains overall security of the airport.

Analyst (Marketing)   (See **Market Research Analyst**)

Architect   Involved with all aspects of the planning, design, and construction of buildings. Prepares proposals that include illustrations and scaled drawings. Draws the structural system as well as the other elements that go into the project. Provides advice about choosing contractors.

Area Manager (Retail) Manages a selling center within a store. This would include a small group of departments carrying related merchandise.

Area Sales Manager (Hospitality) Responsible for sales promotion for a group of hotel properties in a specified geographic area.

Assistant Actuary (See **Actuary**)

Assistant Buyer (Production) (See **Buyer-Production**)

Assistant Chef (See **Chef**)

Assistant Club Manager (See **Club Manager**)

Assistant Food and Beverage Manager (See **Food and Beverage Manager**)

Assistant Hotel Manager Assists with supervising the operations of the different departments of a hotel: food service, housekeeping, front office, and maintenance. Ensures the smooth functioning and profitability of the hotel by maintaining the property and quality guest service.

Assistant Housekeeper (See **Housekeeper**)

Assistant Loan Officer (See **Loan Officer**)

Assistant Manager (Food Service) Performs supervisory duties under the manager's direction. Must be capable of filling in when the manager is absent, thus needs good management skills and knowledge of the operation.

Assistant Manager (Front Office) (See **Front Office Manager**)

Assistant Manager Trainee (Recreation) (See **Assistant Club Manager**)

Assistant Marketing Director (Travel) Assists with the development of competitive strategies for clients. Reviews services and products being offered and evaluates client's market position. Assists companies with monitoring themselves to make sure they are delivering what is promised.

Assistant Media Planner Learns to interpret rate cards of various media. Analyzes audience ratings. Writes letters and memos. Compares media alternatives. Prepares and delivers presentations to clients. Talks with sales representatives from various media. Evaluates media buying.

Assistant Pastry Chef (See **Pastry Chef**)

Assistant Professor A designation of faculty rank used to refer to faculty members with some, but not extensive, teaching experience in their area of expertise. (See **Professor**)

Assistant Purchasing Agent (See **Purchasing Agent**)

Assistant Quality Assurance Manager (See **Quality Assurance Manager**)

Assistant Store Manager (See **Store Manager**)

Assistant Travel Editor (See **Travel Editor**)

Assistant Underwriter (See **Underwriter**)

Assistant Wine Steward (See **Wine Steward**)

Associate Analyst (Marketing) (See **Market Research Analyst**)

Associate Media Director Makes decisions on media buying. Reviews alternative selections and results of ratings to determine decision.

Associate Professor A higher designation of faculty rank than assistant professor; used to refer to faculty members with more extensive teaching experience in their area of expertise. Often, this ranking is also marked by research work, publications, or industry experience. (See **Professor**)

Associate Research Director (Advertising) Evaluates information published by government, trade, or other groups as relates to individual ad campaigns. Evaluates suggestions and findings of the research account executive to determine best approach to each ad campaign. Keeps campaigns operating within specified guidelines.

Association Account Executive (Hospitality) Responsible for the development of and service of professional or trade association business coming into the hotel or other related facility.

Attractions Specialist Has specific knowledge of local attractions and how to promote them. Provides input on target population for promotional effort.

Auditor (Hospitality) Examines and analyzes accounting records of hotel or food service operation and prepares reports concerning its financial status and operating procedures. Analyzes data to check for duplication of effort, extravagance, fraud, or lack of compliance with management's established policies.

Baker Prepares all the baked items that are not desserts, such as breads, rolls, muffins, danish, and croissants for use in dining rooms of hotels and restaurants and related facilities. Depending on the size of the staff and the operation, may also make pies, cakes, and some pastry items.

Bank Guard Responsible for security in banks.

Bank Manager Manages, directs, and coordinates activities of workers engaged in accounting and recording of financial transactions, setting up trust or escrow accounts, probating estates, and administering trust or mortgage accounts. Develops relationships with customers, business, community, and civic organizations to promote goodwill and generate new business.

Bank Officer Trainee Gains experience in the main functions of the banking business. These include the trust department, where money is invested for families, institutions, or other businesses; the credit department, where decisions are made on loaning money to customers; and operations where all of the normal business functions (data processing, personnel, public relations, and accounting) are monitored.

Banquet Captain May greet the host, hostess, and guests. Ensures that everything is as ordered. Ensures that all party rooms are in order at all times and checks before and after a function to make sure that the patrons are satisfied. Presents the bill for signature or payment when the function is over. Pays employees at the end of the function.

Banquet Manager   Arranges banquet and food service functions. Arranges banquet details after they have been agreed upon by the catering manager and the customer. Prepares and updates banquet menus. Reports inventory needs to purchasing agent and storeroom, and may supervise the scheduling of staff to work the functions.

Bartender   Mixes and serves alcoholic and nonalcoholic drinks for patrons of a bar following standard recipes. Mixes ingredients, such as liquor, soda, water, sugar, and bitters to prepare cocktails and other drinks. Serves wine and draught or bottled beer. Collects money for drinks served. Orders or requisitions liquors and supplies. Places bottled goods and glasses to make an attractive display. May slice and pit fruit for the garnishing of drinks. May prepare appetizers, such as pickles, cheese, and cold meat.

Benefits Coordinator   Administers various employee benefit programs such as group insurance—life, medical, and dental; accident and disability insurance; pensions; investment savings; and health maintenance organizations. Initiates medical and option forms and/or affidavits; arranges for their completion and submission within time limits. Implements new benefit programs; arranges and conducts employee information presentations and enrollments. Ensures program compliance with governmental regulations.

Beverage Manager   Responsible for compiling statistics of liquor costs, sales, profits, and losses. Inventories the bar as needed, sometimes daily, and prepares the daily consumption report that is forwarded to the auditing office. Issues merchandise to all bar areas, but usually does not buy liquor. Instead, forwards purchase orders to a central purchasing agent, who may order for several hotels in a chain.

Border Patrol Officer   Responsible for guarding all U.S. points of entry to detect and prevent illegal entry into the United States. Inspects commercial carriers, terminals, and traffic checkpoints to stop those who attempt to enter the country without proper clearance. Also responsible for deportation actions.

Branch Manager   Plans, coordinates, controls the work flow, updates systems, strives for administrative efficiency, and is responsible for all functions of a branch office.

Branch Sales Manager   Makes a direct sales effort to the customers in the area to sell a product line. Provides management with sales and booking forecasts on a monthly, quarterly, and annual basis. Keeps abreast of prices and performance of competitors' products in his or her territory. Handles service and related problems as they arise. Trains and supervises sales staff.

Broadcast Technician   Performs the work of an electronics technician, specifically on various types of broadcast equipment. (See **Electronics Technician**)

Butcher   Responsible for cutting, boning, and otherwise caring for and preparing meats for cooking.

Buyer (Production)   Responsible for placing orders, expediting back orders, and processing paperwork for stock and nonstock supplies. This includes processing requisitions, researching products, clarifying specifications, typing purchase orders, following up on back orders, selecting vendors, maintaining up-to-date product information files, and utilizing computer terminals and hand-held order entry devices to place order.

Buyer (Retail)   Selects the goods to be sold by retail stores or wholesale outlets. Buyers also help to plan the selling programs for the goods they have purchased. They normally specialize in one type of goods such as men's clothing, housewares, or accessories.

Buyer Trainee (Retail)   Assists supervising buyer. Places orders and speaks with manufacturers by telephone. Supervises the inspection and unpacking of new merchandise and overseeing its distribution.

Cafeteria Manager   In charge of a unit with as few as 1 employee to as many as 70 or more. Oversees all employees, sometimes giving limited on-the-job training. Has hiring and firing responsibilities. Purchases what is needed for unit, usually from a central purchasing office, and keeps records of the same.

Camp Manager   Directs and coordinates activities of workers concerned with preparation and maintenance of buildings and facilities in residential camp; coordinates through staff or personally directs staff in preparing and maintaining such camp facilities as dining halls, etc., used by resident employees. Schedules purchase and delivery of food supplies. Enforces safety and sanitation regulations.

Captain   An officer ranking above a first lieutenant and below a major.

Case Manager   Organizes a case's pleadings, oversees the mechanics of producing documents and maintaining documents library. Experience as a litigation paralegal usually required.

Catering Manager   Works with the Executive Chef on menus, food quality, or service problems. Responsible for arranging any catered functions held at the establishment, from weddings to conventions, from banquets to dances. Draws up necessary contracts. Helps customers select menu, decorations, and room arrangement and transmits these requirements to various departments for execution.

Central Region Sales Manager   Responsible for sales function in the central region. (See **Regional Sales Manager**)

Chef   Supervises, coordinates, and participates in activities of cooks and other kitchen personnel engaged in preparing foods for a hotel, restaurant, cafeteria, or other establishment. Estimates food consumption, and requisitions or purchases foodstuffs. Receives and checks recipes. Supervises personnel engaged in preparing, cooking, and serving meats, sauces, vegetables, soups, and other foods. May employ, train, and discharge workers. In small establishments, may maintain time and payroll records.

Chef de Cuisine (Maitre de Cusine)   In complete charge of food services. Reports to the Food and Beverage Director in large operations or to the owner or manager in smaller operations; may assume duties of the Food and Beverage Director as well when needed.

Chef Instructor Brings a chef's perspective to the "lab" classroom and teaches hands-on cooking techniques. (See **Instructor**)

Chief Accountant Responsible for the supervision and control of the general accounting functions. This includes general ledger, payables, payroll, property, budget reporting, and statistical accumulation. Responsible for financial statement and report preparation and budget reviews. Supervises and trains employees in accounting, payroll, and accounts payable.

Chief Accountant (Hospitality) Responsible for the supervision and control of the general accounting functions of the hotel. This includes night audit functions, general ledger, payables, payroll, property, budget reporting, and statistical accumulation. Responsible for financial statement and report preparation and budget reviews. Supervises and trains hotel employees in accounting, payroll, and accounts payable.

Chief Actuary Oversees the calculation of probabilities of death, sickness disability, injury, property loss, fire, and other hazards. Evaluates and analyzes relevant statistics. Determines the rate of expected losses due to the issuance of various types of policies. Determines the various provisions contained in insurance policies.

Chief Financial Officer Develops corporate financial objectives. Establishes policies and procedures for the effective recording, analyzing, and reporting of all financial matters. Directs the controller, treasury, and corporate financial services activities to ensure that each of these functions meets established goals and provides effective service to the corporation as a whole.

Chief Internal Auditor   (See **Internal Auditor**)

Chief Tourism Officer Oversees the staff engaged in tourism development for a particular area. Works within established budgets. Approves promotional campaigns.

City Manager Responsible for managing inbound business for a car rental company.

City Mortgage and Real Estate Secretary Works with real estate investment officers and provides secretarial support for an investment team. Prepares commitment letters and various reports, maintains files, and handles telephone communications.

Claims Examiner Analyzes insurance claims to determine extent of insurance carrier's liability and settles claims with claimants in accordance with policy provisions. Investigates questionable inquiries.

Claims Representative Reviews insurance claim forms for completeness; secures and adds missing data; and transmits claims for payment or for further investigation.

Clinical Dental Assistant Reviews patients' records and presents them to the dentist; obtains information needed to update medical histories; takes patient X rays; assists the dentist in examining patients; instructs about medications.

Clinical Medical Assistant Receives patients' height, weight, temperature, and blood pressure; obtains medical histories; performs basic laboratory tests; prepares patients for examination or treatment; assists the physician in examining patients. Instructs patients about medication and self-treatment, draws blood, prepares patients for X rays, takes EKGs, and applies dressings.

Club Manager Estimates and orders food products and coordinates activity of workers engaged in selling alcoholic and nonalcoholic beverages for consumption on the premises. May manage staff involved in operating club with recreational facilities for private groups or the general public. Responsible for grounds and buildings, payroll, and promotion.

Coder Converts routine items of information obtained from records and reports into codes for processing by data typing using predetermined coding systems.

Coder-Editor Synthesizes the results of questionnaires or mail or telephone surveys. The results are then reviewed by the research analyst.

Coding Clerk Supervisor Supervises and coordinates activities of workers engaged in converting routine items of information from source documents into codes to prepare records for data processing. Modifies, revises, or designs forms and initiates procedures to develop more efficient methods of data input.

Cold Cook (Garde Manger) Responsible for cold hors d'oeuvres, cold plates, salads, buffets, ice and vegetable carvings, tallow and butter sculpturing, etc. (See **Garde Manger**)

College Recruiter Interviews college graduates on campus. Works in conjunction with the policies and standards approved by the Employment Manager.

Colonel A military officer ranking above a lieutenant colonel and below a brigadier general.

Commis A professional assistant in the kitchen or dining room.

Commissioner of Tourism Promotes overall tourism efforts. Generates new sources for funding. Interfaces with businesses in the community to gain support for tourism development.

Communications Equipment Technician Performs the work of an electronics technician specifically on various types of communications equipment. (See **Electronics Technician**)

Communications Technician May direct activities of production, circulation, or promotional personnel. May prepare news or public relations releases, special brochures, and similar materials. Assigns staff member, or personally interviews individuals and attends gatherings to obtain items for publication, verify facts, and clarify information.

Computer Operator Operates computer equipment to ensure that tasks are processed in accordance with a schedule of operations. Maintains and completes daily logs. Maintains an accurate report of equipment and/or software malfunctions.

Concierge Handles guests' problems in a hotel, makes reservation requests with restaurants and transportation facilities, arranges tours, procures theater tickets, and handles a host of other activities.

Conference and Meeting Coordinator Coordinates the planning and execution of conferences and meetings on and off site. Notifies attendees of details. Makes necessary facilities arrangements. Makes travel arrangements if required. Oversees the function and conducts postmeeting evaluation.

Conference Planner Compiles list of individuals or groups requesting space for activities and schedules needed facilities. Notifies program participants of locations assigned. Maintains schedules and records of available space, space used, and cancellations. Requisitions needed equipment. Arranges for services during the conference. Follows up with client after the conference for evaluation of services provided.

Conference Reporter Attends conferences at the request of the conference coordinator. Records minutes of the meetings and activities that occur during the conference. Types up summaries and distributes to requesting parties.

Conference Service Coordinator Books meetings, services them, and follows up with a postmeeting evaluation.

Consultant Consults with client to determine need or problem, conducts studies and surveys to obtain data, and analyzes data to advise on or recommend a solution. Advises client on alternate methods of solving problem or recommends a specific solution. May negotiate contract for consulting service.

Consultant/Advisor (Paralegal) Assists the legal publisher in planning new kinds of books to be written either about the paralegal profession or the procedures utilized by paralegals in law offices.

Consumer Product Safety Commission Investigator Responsible for enforcing compliance with all regulations that protect the consumer against unsafe products.

Controller Directs financial affairs of an organization. Prepares financial analyses of operations for guidance of management. Establishes major economic objectives and policies for the company. Prepares reports that outline company's financial position in areas of income, expenses, and earnings based on past, present, and future operations. Directs preparation of budgets and financial forecasts.

Convention Center Manager Manages the building, does marketing and public relations for events at the center. Responsible for entire budget for the center and supervises personnel.

Convention Planner Arranges space and facilities for convention. Keeps exhibitors and attendees informed of procedures and policies for participation. Assigns troubleshooters to be available to provide needed services during the convention and minimizes situations that may result in a safety, legal, or logistical problem.

Convention Sales Manager Responsible for generating convention business at hotel, civic center, or other appropriate facility. Oversees sales staff. Approves advertising and rate packages. Handles projections on business and expected income. Works within established budgets.

Cook Prepares, seasons, and cooks soups, meats, vegetables, desserts, and other foodstuffs for consumption in hotels and restaurants. Reads menu to estimate food requirements and orders food from supplier or procures it from storage. Adjusts thermostat controls to regulate temperature of ovens, broilers, grills, and roasters. Measures and mixes ingredients according to recipe, using a variety of kitchen utensils and equipment, such as blenders, mixers, grinders, slicers, and tenderizers to prepare soups, salads, gravies, desserts, sauces, and casseroles. Bakes, roasts, broils, and steams meat, fish, vegetables, and other foods. Observes and tests foods being cooked by tasting, smelling, and piercing with fork. Carves meats, portions food on serving plates, adds gravies or sauces, and garnishes servings to fill orders.

Coordinator of Membership Sales Maintains prospect lists for membership in travel clubs or travel associations. Coordinates marketing programs to solicit new membership. Explains membership policies and benefits and receives payment of membership dues. Makes decisions on appropriateness of membership.

Coordinator/Scheduler (Word Processing) Sees that there is an even flow of work to the word processor.

Coordinator of Scheduling (Retail) Prepares production schedules. Determines type and quantity of material needed to process orders. Issues work orders. Calculates costs for manufacturing.

Coordinator/Travel Information Center Supervises and coordinates activities of workers engaged in greeting and welcoming motorists at state highway information center. Provides information, such as directions, road conditions, and vehicular travel regulations. Provides maps, brochures, and pamphlets to assist motorists in locating points of interest or in reaching destination. May direct tourists to rest areas, camps, resorts, historical points, or other tourist attractions.

Copy Chief Supervises one or more copywriters in an advertising agency, department, or service, whose function it is to assign the work of preparing the textual matter for advertisements; supervises the actual writing and transmits the completed work in accordance with the existing traffic arrangement in the firm. Coordinates copywriting activities with the layout, art, and production departments of the organization.

Copywriter Writes original advertising material about products or services for newspapers, magazines, radio and television, posters, or other media.

Corporal The lowest-ranking non-commissioned officer, just below a sergeant.

Corporate Account Executive (Hospitality) Responsible for the development of and service of corporate (business and industry) business coming into the hotel.

Corporate Paralegal Drafts minutes, forms and dissolves corporations, works with the Securities and Exchange Commission (SEC), reviews Blue Sky laws, oversees mergers and acquisitions, assists with leveraged buyouts.

Corporate Recruiter Recruits corporate-level staff for the organization. Works in conjunction with the policies and standards approved by the Employment Manager.

Corporate Travel Manager Sets up travel budget, establishing policies for employees to follow; acts as a liaison with an outside travel agency that actually handles the arrangements; also involves personnel relocation as well as meetings and convention planning. May administer corporate aircraft, transportation to training programs, the car pool, and possibly group recreational trips or vacations for employees; may also negotiate discounts with travel suppliers.

Correctional Officer Responsible for maintaining security in prison facilities and overseeing the safety of the inmate population.

Court Reporter Makes accurate records of what is said during proceedings of all types. Memorizes and then reproduces the appropriate symbols involved in shorthand and machine reporting. All types of recordings—manual, machine, and tape—are transcribed accurately and typed in the required format.

Creative Director Develops basic presentation approaches and directs layout design and copywriting for promotional material. Reviews materials and information presented by client and discusses various production factors to determine most desirable presentation concept. Confers with heads of art, copywriting, and production departments to discuss client requirements and scheduling, outlines basic presentation concepts, and coordinates creative activities.

Credit Manager Responsible for the collection of accounts deemed to be delinquent and for determining when the accounts should be referred to an outside agency for further collection efforts. Generates reports on a daily and monthly basis. Posts cash on a daily basis.

Crime Lab Technician Collects and examines evidence from crime scenes and submits results to be used as evidence in criminal cases.

Criminal Investigator Conducts investigations of collusion, bribery, conflicts of interest, thefts from government jurisdictions, and offenses specified in the acts protecting government personnel and procedures.

Cruise Director Supervises all activity on board the cruise-line. Responsible for overall safety and service of passengers. Oversees staff on board.

Customer Service Agent (Travel) Arranges for car rental on-site at rental company by phone with travel agent or in person with individual customer. Processes contracts and arranges billing upon return of the rental vehicle.

Customer Service Manager (Retail) Responsibilities include making certain that shipments take place as scheduled. Acts as a liaison between customers and the sales force. Spends most of the time on administrative duties, including reviewing performance standards. Also trains personnel.

Customer Service Representative Responds to customer inquiries and performs a variety of duties related to customer service. Works with customers to offer alternatives to unresolvable problems. Receives, researches, and answers customer inquiries and requests regarding accounts, products, rates, and services. Develops and maintains company's image and corporate philosophy in the community.

Customer Service Representative (Airlines) Duties include booking onward flight reservations, securing hotel and car rental reservations, and ticketing passengers in flight.

Customer Service Representative (Retail) Resolves customer complaints and requests for refunds, exchanges, and adjustments. Provides customers with catalogs and information concerning prices, shipping time, and costs. Approves customers' checks and provides check-cashing service according to exchange policy. Issues temporary charges. Keeps records of items in layaway, receives and posts customer payments, and prepares and forwards delinquent notices.

Customs Agent Examines incoming travelers' luggage, registers weights of incoming vessels, and enforces approximately 400 laws and regulations for the federal government. Ensures that revenue is paid for incoming goods and prevents prohibited goods from entering or leaving the country.

Data Entry Operator Operates keyboard machine to transcribe data onto magnetic tape for computer input. Examines codes on forms and source documents to determine work procedures.

Data Entry Supervisor Accountable for quality, productivity, cost effectiveness, and timeliness of work to ensure efficient and effective conversion and verification of data into computer readable forms. Directs distribution of work; prioritizes allocation of resources to meet schedules. Sets performance standards and reviews policies for data entry personnel.

Dean Develops academic policies and programs for college or university. Directs and coordinates activities of academic department heads within the college. Participates in activities of faculty committees and in the development of academic budgets. Serves as a liaison with accrediting agencies that evaluate academic programs.

Demographer Plans and conducts demographic research and surveys to study the population of a given area and affecting trends.

Dental Assistant Helps dentist during the examination and treatment of patients. Sets up and maintains instruments, arranges appointments, and keeps records of patients.

Dental Hygienist   Licensed to clean teeth under the supervision of a dentist. Instructs patients in dental care, diet, and nutrition for proper mouth care.

Dentist   Helps patients take care of their teeth and gums, either to correct dental problems or to advise patients on ways to prevent future cavities and gum problems.

Department Manager (Office)   Directs and coordinates departmental activities and functions utilizing knowledge of department functions and company policies, standards, and practices. Gives work directions, resolves problems, prepares work schedules, and sets deadlines to ensure completion of operational functions. Evaluates procedures and makes recommendations for improvements. Assigns or delegates responsibility for specific work.

Department Manager (Retail)   Supervises and coordinates activities of personnel in one department of a retail store. Assigns duties to workers and schedules lunch, breaks, work hours, and vacations. Trains staff in store policies, department procedures, and job duties. Evaluates staff. Handles customer complaints. Ensures that merchandise is correctly priced and displayed. Prepares sales and inventory reports. Plans department layout. Approves checks for payment and issues credit and cash refunds.

Deputy Commissioner of Tourism Development   Establishes goals, policies, and procedures of tourism development for a given area.

Deputy Sheriff   Performs patrol services and investigates offenses. Serves as bailiff in the courtroom. Serves orders or civil papers of the county courts, including subpoenas, show-cause orders, property seizures, and garnishments. Collects legal fees assigned by the courts.

Design Assistant   Researches colors by contacting color forecasting services. Visits color forecasters to see presentations. Finds new garments on the market and in stores. Contacts fabric salespeople by phone for fabric samples. Keeps records, does patterns, and keeps design room organized.

Design Technician   Tests and assists in the design of all kinds of electronics equipment developed by Electronics-Design Engineers. Performs the work of an electronics technician. (See **Electronics Technician**)

Designer (Drafting)   Makes design drawings to assist in developing experimental ideas evolved by research engineers, using specifications and sketches, and employing knowledge of engineering theory and its applications to solve mechanical and fabrication problems.

Destination Promoter   Sells meeting and convention planners, tour operators, and wholesalers on the idea of choosing a destination for their program. Services individual travelers with information and products that will make their business or pleasure trips more satisfying.

Detective   Continues investigative work started by patrol officers, identifies and apprehends offenders, recovers stolen properties and completes official reports, and prepares testimony and evidence for court presentation.

Dining Room Captain   Works under the general supervision of the dining room manager; in charge of one section of the dining room. Instructs, supervises, and gives help to the staff working the area when needed. Watches all the tables in given jurisdiction to detect any dissatisfaction; may make adjustments in response to complaints.

Dining Room Manager   Supervises all dining room staff and activities, including staff training, scheduling of staff working hours, keeping time records, and assigning workstations. Should be capable of working in a formal public atmosphere.

Director of Escort Services   Responsible for the hiring, training, and assignment of tour escorts. Trains the escorts in the areas for which they will be responsible.

Director of Human Resources   Oversees the day-to-day activities of the human resources staff. Ensures that staff complies with policies set and approved by the Vice President of Human Resources and senior management. (See **Vice President of Human Resources**)

Director of Marketing and Sales   Supervises sales department. Coordinates sales and marketing departments to develop and implement an effective marketing effort. Responsible for increasing sales volume through direct sales efforts and by assisting sales reps in the field. Coordinates future market growth plans with regard to products, services, and markets. May plan and implement advertising and promotion activities.

Director of Marketing/Sales (Cruiselines)   Develops pricing strategies for packages sold to groups and individuals. Establishes advertising and promotion programs. Reviews competition's strategies for attracting clients and implements competitive strategies.

Director of Marketing and Advertising (Food Service)   Plans and carries out advertising and promotional programs. Works with company's top-level management to prepare an overall marketing plan. Arranges with various suppliers regarding schedule and cost of brochures, menus, advertisements, etc., being promoted. Responsible for the advertising budget.

Director of Media Advertising   Defines corporate media objectives. Provides media information and advice to the company. Measures media costs against industry standards. Searches for new, creative ways to use media. Recommends controls, quality, and cost of media purchases.

Director of Public Relations   Plans, directs, and conducts public relations program designed to create and maintain a public informed of employer's programs, accomplishments, and point of view.

Director of Public Safety   Responsible for the safety of the people and equipment in a city, town, or state.

Director of Recipe Development   Creates new recipes for the menus of larger restaurants or restaurant chains.

Requires thorough knowledge of food preparation and the ability to apply this knowledge creatively.

Director of Research and Development   Directs and coordinates activities concerned with research and development of new concepts, ideas, basic data on, and applications for organization's products, services, or ideologies. Reviews and analyzes proposals submitted to determine if benefits derived and possible applications justify expenditures. Develops and implements methods and procedures for monitoring projects. May negotiate contracts with consulting firms to perform research studies.

Director of Sales and Marketing   (See **Director of Marketing and Sales**)

Director of Tour Guides   Responsible for the hiring, training, and assignment of tour guides.

Director of Training   Oversees training function for an entire company at all locations. Responsible for approval of recommended programs and proposed budgets. (See **Training Manager**)

Director of Transportation   Responsible for getting convention goers from their hotels to and from the center; trafficking trucks in and out of the building; working with the city to make sure street lights are working; dealing with city's Taxi and Limousine Commission to ensure there are adequate services for the center.

Display Coordinator   Designs and implements the window decorations and interior displays that are so important in promoting sales. Must work well within limitations of time, space, and money.

Display Director   Supervises the display of merchandise in windows, in showcases, and on the sales floor of retail stores. Schedules plans for displays and ensures staff follows store plan. Often responsible for several stores within a designated division.

Distribution Manager (Retail)   Oversees the routing of merchandise from one branch store to another on the basis of sales. Analyzes reports of stock on hand and kind and amount sold.

District Manager   Manages personnel for an assigned district, ensuring the development and accomplishment of established objectives. Trains, develops, and motivates staff. Recruits new hires. Maintains good business relationships with customers through periodic contacts and proper handling of administrative functions.

District Manager (Food Service)   Supervises smaller facilities in certain areas. Purchasing, negotiation, and supervision of area personnel are main responsibilities.

District Sales Manager   Actually carries out "cold calls," maintains reporting forms and proper business files, holds periodic meetings with sales staff.

District Sales Manager (Travel)   Administers city ticket and reservations offices and promotes and develops airline passenger and cargo traffic in the district.

Divisional Manager (Banking)   Responsible for the activities of a related group of departments in a bank, such as all departments involved with customer service versus operations or systems.

Divisional Manager (Retail) Retail executive responsible for the activities of a related group of selling departments or divisions.

Doctor (Medical)   Examines patients, orders or executes various tests and X rays to provide information on patient's condition. Analyzes reports and findings of tests and of examinations and diagnoses condition. Recommends treatment.

Document Examiner   Helps resolve criminal cases by using a variety of skills and tools to examine evidence such as handwriting samples.

Documentation Specialist   Makes computer technology accessible to people who have no computer background. Translates the technology into plain, comprehensible English. Writes promotional brochures and advertising copy.

Drafter   Develops detailed design drawings and related specifications of mechanical equipment according to engineering sketches and design-proposal specifications. Often calculates the strength, quality, quantity, and cost of materials. Usually specializes in a particular field of work such as mechanical, electrical, electronic, aeronautical, structural, or architectural drafting.

Drafter (Computer Assisted—CADD)   Drafts layouts, drawings, and designs for applications in such fields as aeronautics, architecture, or electronics, according to engineering specifications, using the computer. Locates file relating to projection database library and loads program into computer. Retrieves information from file and displays information on cathode ray tube (CRT) screen using required computer languages. Displays final drawing on screen to verify completeness, after typing in commands to rotate or zoom in on display to redesign, modify, or otherwise edit existing design. Types command to transfer drawing dimensions from computer onto hard copy.

Economic Development Coordinator   Directs economic development planning activities for city, state, or region. Negotiates with industry representatives to encourage location in an area. Directs activities, such as research, analysis, and evaluation of technical information to determine feasibility and economic impact of proposed expansions and developments.

Editor   Reads the rough drafts and manuscripts of authors and other writers that are to be published in a magazine, book, or newspaper. Corrects grammatical errors and makes suggestions for improving readability and consistency of style.

Editor (Word Processing)   Helps design the overall package and rough out the information to be contained on each page of a videotext display. Once the information is set up, the page creator takes over.

EDP Auditor   Monitors computer functions of the entire company and operational procedures and reports findings back to top management with recommendations for improvements. EDP Auditors make specific recommendations for improved accuracy, procedures, and security.

Education Consultant   Develops programs for in-service education of teaching personnel. Reviews and evaluates curricula used in schools and assists in adaptation to local needs. Prepares or approves manuals, guidelines, and reports on educational policies. Conducts research into areas such as teaching methods and strategies.

Educator/Administrator   (Food Service) Designs and teaches courses tailored to students of food service, such as sanitation, food service management, and nutrition. Develops curriculum and hires staff. Works with designated budget to purchase equipment and materials needed to operate the school. Seeks support from industry with instruction and funding.

Electronics Engineer   Works on research and development, production, and quality control problems. Highly specialized; may work in a specific area such as the design and implementation of solid-state circuitry in radar, computers, or calculators.

Electronics Technician   Repairs and maintains machines and equipment used in processing and assembly of electronic components. Starts equipment or machine. Reads blueprints and schematic drawings to determine repair procedures. Dismantles machine. Removes and sets aside defective units for repair or replacement. Starts repaired or newly installed machines and verifies readiness for operation.

Employment Agency Owner   Manages employment services and business operations of private employment agency. Directs hiring, training, and evaluation of employees. Analyzes placement reports to determine effectiveness of employment interviewers. Investigates and resolves customer complaints.

Employment Counselor   (Word Processing) Screens and places word processing professionals in available jobs.

Employment Interviewer   (See **Interviewer**)

Employment Manager   Oversees the recruiting function. This includes soliciting qualified applicants through various sources including advertising and college recruiting. Oversees screening, interviewing, and selection procedures. Responsible for overseeing the hiring of all personnel.

Employment Recruiter   Matches job seekers with job openings that employers have listed with placement firms, employment agencies, or governmental employment offices.

Engineer   Applies the theories and principles of science and mathematics to practical technical problems. Designs and develops consumer products. Determines the general way the device will work, designs and tests all components, and fits them together in an integrated plan. Evaluates overall effectiveness of the new device, as well as its cost and reliability.

Engineering Technician   Develops and tests machinery and equipment, applying knowledge of mechanical engineering technology, under direction of engineering and scientific staff.

Equal Employment Opportunity Coordinator   Monitors and enforces governmental regulations concerning equal employment practices in all levels of the organization. Maintains required records to verify adherence to approved affirmative action plan.

Executive Administrator   (Education) Makes projections for future needs; oversees curriculum and policy decisions. Hires and supervises personnel; prepares school budget. Works with local groups to ensure the best interest of the community is being met.

Executive Chef   Coordinates activities of and directs indoctrination and training of chefs, cooks, and other kitchen personnel engaged in preparing and cooking food. Plans menus and utilization of food surpluses and leftovers, taking into account probable number of guests, marketing conditions, and population, and purchases or requisitions foodstuffs and kitchen supplies. Reviews menus, analyzes recipes, determines food, labor, and overhead costs, and assigns prices to the menu items. Observes methods of food preparation and cooking, sizes of portions, and garnishing of foods to ensure food is prepared in prescribed manner. Develops exclusive recipes and varied menus.

Executive Director   Develops and coordinates an administrative organization plan and staff to carry out the plan. Delegates authority and responsibility for the execution of the organization's many departments and functions. Establishes operating policies and procedures and standards of service and performance. Involved with fund-raising. Serves on various civic committees.

Executive/Administrator   (Telemarketing) Directs the planning and operations of telemarketing function. Sets goals and objectives for telemarketing programs and establishes budgets as well as sales goals. Guides development of telemarketing programs and evaluates available systems applications.

Executive Assistant   Member of the management team that is responsible for overseeing the overall administrative functions of an office. Ensures productivity of office staff. Makes recommendations for improved systems. Supervises staff. Handles special projects and confidential materials. Assists executive. Represents the company at professional and community events on a regular basis. Often acts as a spokesperson for the executive.

Executive Director, Associations   Directs and coordinates activities of professional or trade associations in accordance with established policies to further achievement of goals, objectives, and standards of the profession or association. Directs or participates in the preparation of educational and informative materials for presentation to membership or public in newsletters, magazines, news releases, or on radio or television.

Executive Director, Chamber of Commerce   Directs activities to promote business, industrial, and job development, and civic improvements in the community. Administers programs of departments and committees which perform such functions as providing members with economic and marketing information, promoting economic growth and stability in the community, and counseling business organizations and industry on problems affecting local economy. Coordinates work with that of other community agencies to provide public services. Prepares and submits annual budgets to elected officials for approval. Studies governmental legislation, taxation, and other fiscal matters to determine effect on community interests, and makes recommendations based on organizational policy.

Executive Director, Convention Bureau   Directs activities of convention bureau to promote convention business in the area. Administers promotional programs. Coordinates efforts with local hotels, restaurants, transportation companies, exhibit centers, and other related facilities. Works within specified budgets. Serves on various civic and community boards to enhance the position of the bureau.

Executive Director, Department of Economic Development   Directs activities of the department. Ensures that demographic and economic information is maintained. Decides on research projects to be conducted. Directs publications prepared for public information. Works in conjunction with local and national agencies.

Executive Housekeeper   Supervises housekeeping staff. May hire and train new employees. Orders supplies, takes inventories and keeps records, prepares budgets, sees to needed repairs, draws up work schedules, inspects rooms. May be in charge of interior decoration.

Executive Secretary   Schedules meetings, takes minutes at meetings, and then transcribes and types them; composes letters; evaluates priority of incoming mail and telephone calls. Organizes and executes special projects and reports. May prepare budget reports. Works with a minimum of supervision; initiates much of own work according to office priorities.

Expeditor   Ensures that merchandise and supplies that have been ordered are received when and where needed.

Facilities Designer   Plans and designs utilization of space and facilities for hotels, food service operations, and other related properties. Draws design layout, showing location of equipment, furniture, work spaces, doorways, electrical outlets, and other related facilities. May review real estate contracts for compliance with regulations and suitability for occupancy. Suggests decor that is both practical and attractive to suit the purpose of the facility as well as maximize client business.

Fashion Coordinator   Offers advice to the buying staff in large department stores on changing tastes, trends, and styles. Works with buying staff to be sure that the store's merchandise is completely up-to-date.

Fashion Designer   Creative specialist responsible for designing coats, suits, dresses, as well as other lines of apparel. Adapts higher-priced merchandise to meet the price range of the customers.

Fashion Display Specialist   Responsible for designing display windows and display units within department or clothing stores. May have supervisory responsibilities as a coordinator for chain of stores.

Fashion Writer   Writes articles on the subject of fashion. Writes press releases and complete public relations projects. Writes about projected fashion trends, designers, new store openings. Writes newsletters for stores and buying offices. Covers fashion shows and does research.

Federal Food Inspector   Responsible for enforcing compliance with all regulations that ensure food safety for the consumer.

Finance Manager   Directs activities of workers engaged in performing such financial functions as accounting and recording financial transactions. Establishes procedures for control of assets, records, loan collateral, and securities.

Financial Analyst   Performs the quantitative analysis required for strategic planning and investments. Evaluates the financing and refinancing of certain projects and lines of credit. Prepares various reports for management. Collects data for financial comparisons with similar companies and securities.

Flight Attendant   Directly responsible for making passengers' flight comfortable, enjoyable, and safe. Ensures cabin is in order and that supplies and equipment are on board. Greets passengers as they board the plane. Helps passengers with carry-on luggage and with finding their seats. Instructs passengers before take-off in the location and proper usage of oxygen masks and other emergency equipment and exits. Serves meals and beverages.

Food and Beverage Manager   Responsible for compiling statistics of food and liquor costs, sales, and profits and losses. May also develop the procedures of portion control and item usage. May inventory bars as needed and prepare daily consumption reports that are forwarded to the auditing office. Takes inventory of foodstuffs with the chef, and works closely with the chef on matters of buying and producing.

Food Director (Recreation)   Responsible for all food service areas at a particular theme park, amusement park, arcade, or other type of recreational facility. Supervises the procurement and preparation of food and drinks for concession stands, snack bars and dining halls, and rooms. Hires and trains staff. Maintains control of food costs and inventories. Deals directly with suppliers in ordering and paying for all food products. Enforces sanitation policies and health department codes throughout all food service facilities.

Food Production Manager   Responsible for all food preparation and supervision of kitchen staff. Must possess leadership skills and have knowledge of food preparation techniques, quality, and sanitation standards and cost control methods.

Food Service Consultant   Advises clients on site selection for food service operation, menu design and selection, interior decor, equipment, and overall design and layout of dining facility. Advises owner/operator of expected food and beverage costs, and helps to develop effective pricing strategy for all menu items.

Food Service Director   Exercises general supervision over all production areas in one or more kitchens. Also responsible for all the service that may be needed on counters and in the dining rooms. Responsible for the buying of food, its storage, its preparation, and the service necessary to handle large groups.

Food Service Engineer   Analyzes and creates efficient and cost-effective production processes, designs manufacturing equipment, or operates a plant's physical systems.

Food Service Manager   Responsible for the operation's accounts and records and compliance with all laws and regulations, especially those concerning licensing, health, and sanitation.

Food Service Salesperson   Tells customers how a given item performs against the competition, how it will benefit the buyer, and ultimately, how it can increase profits and encourage repeat business. Demonstrates new products, gives customers actual product samplings, advises on menu ideas and serving suggestions, and even helps work out portion costs.

Forensic Scientist   Responsible for determining facts surrounding a crime based on physical evidence analysis.

Freelancer (Travel)   Submits articles to travel editor for publication. Works independently. Initiates own stories and also writes specific articles or stories for publications upon request.

Freelancer (Visual Merchandising)   Initiates own designs and plans and offers services to Designers and Display Directors.

Freelance Reporter (Court Reporting)   Reporters who are in business for themselves. Develop their own contracts, follow up on recommendations of those for whom they may already have worked, and generally initiate their own assignments.

Front Desk Clerk   Responsible for direct personal contact with the guests, handling reservations, special needs, check in and check out. Familiarizes guests with a facility as well as the surrounding area. Prepares status reports on available rooms for manager. Receives guests' complaints and makes appropriate decisions about how to resolve them.

Front Desk Supervisor (Hospitality)   Directs the front desk operations in the hotel. Oversees those responsible for guests' reservations, special needs, checkin, and checkout. Reviews status reports on available rooms. Ensures that guests' complaints are handled promptly and properly.

Front Office Manager (Hospitality)   Supervises front office operations of the rooms division of a hotel or motel.

Garde Manger (Cold Cook)   Prepares and works with all cold meat, fish, and poultry dishes. Prepares appetizers and hors d'oeuvres such as canapes. Makes all salad dressings and mayonnaise according to recipe. Works with leftover foods to make appetizing dishes. Prepares and serves pâté maison. Makes ice and vegetable carvings.

General Accountant   Handles daily business needs, such as payroll, budgeting, accounts receivable, accounts payable, general ledger, and financial statements. Must pay close attention to all laws and regulations affecting daily business operations. Involved in sending out all payments, royalties, dividends, rents, and other necessary expenditures.

General Manager (Food Service)   Acts as overseer to all phases of a particular group, working with the management team to plan future accounts and solve day-to-day problems.

General Manager (Hospitality)   Establishes standards for personnel administration and performance, service to patrons, room rates, advertising, publicity, credit, food selection and service, and type of patronage to be solicited. Plans dining room, bar, and banquet operations. Allocates funds, authorizes expenditures, and assists in planning budgets for departments.

Group Manager (Retail)   Supervises many departments within a retail operation.

Group Sales Manager   Concentrates on managing group sales efforts, including planning and forecasting sales and supervising sales staff. Identifies target markets and assigns specific groups to specific sales personnel. Devises and implements promotions and training programs.

Group Sales Representative (Travel)   Promotes sale of group season tickets for sports or other entertainment events. Telephones, visits, or writes to organizations, such as chambers of commerce, corporate employee recreation clubs, social clubs, and professional groups, to persuade them to purchase group tickets or season tickets to sports or other entertainment events, such as baseball, horseracing, or stage plays. Quotes group ticket rates, arranges for sale of tickets and seating for groups on specific dates, and obtains payment. May arrange for club to sponsor sports event, such as one of the races at horseracing track.

Guest Services Agent (Hospitality)   Works as a liaison between hotel guests and party providing desired services. Informs guests on services available to them in the hotel facility and assists them with making the proper connections. Concerned with any requests that guests may have and with providing answers to questions that concern guests.

Head Bartender   In charge of the entire bar. Responsible for stocking and dispensing. Responsible for hiring and firing. Must know how to mix all drinks served in the bar. Establishes drink formulas and sets up portion controls for each drink. Coordinates inventory, requisitioning, and stocking needed items, proper accounting, and receipt of proper payment for bar items.

Head Cashier (Hospitality)   Oversees the duties of the hotel's cashiers, which include receiving guests' payments when checking out of the hotel. Approves the cashing of guests' checks and the processing of certain loans. Responsible for security of the safe deposit box.

Head Waitperson   Supervises and coordinates the activities of dining room employees engaged in providing courteous and rapid service to the diners. Greets the guests and escorts them to tables. Schedules dining reservations. Arranges parties for patrons. Adjusts any complaints regarding the food or service. Hires and trains the dining room employees. Notifies the payroll department regarding work schedules and time records. May assist in preparing menus. May plan and execute the details of a banquet.

Health Club Director (Cruiselines)   Oversees uses of the health club on cruiseline. Ensures passenger understanding of use of the equipment and exercise available. Ensures safety and cleanliness of equipment. Supervises staff and approves recommended programs.

Health Technician (Electronics)   Performs the work of an electronics technician, specifically on various types of health equipment. (See **Electronics Technician**)

Hearing Reporter   Follows up and records all that is said during various types of proceedings, whether they be court trials or informal meetings. Hearings are presided over by a commissioner and there is no jury. Hearings may be conducted by various governmental agencies and departments with differing functions and responsibilities.

Home Economics Teacher   Teaches everything from balancing menus to hygiene to food journalism.

Hostperson   Supervises and coordinates the activities of the dining room personnel to provide fast and courteous service to the patrons. Schedules dining reservations and arranges parties or special services for the diners. Greets the guests, escorts them to tables, and provides their menus. Adjusts complaints of the patrons.

Housekeeper   Ensures clean, orderly, attractive rooms in the hotel or related facility. Inventories stock to ensure adequate supplies. Issues supplies and equipment to workers. May record data and prepare reports concerning room occupancy, payroll expenses, and department expenses.

Incentive Travel Specialist   Travel specialists responsible for developing special packages for trips that have been won as a prize or premium.

Information Broker (Word Processing)   Responsible for formulating specifications on the basis of which information is pulled from the database and then relayed to the client company.

Information Coordinator (Travel)   Coordinates organization and communication of travel information as needed. Responsible for providing accurate information to telephone inquirers and visitors about a destination, attraction, activity, or program. Participates in and conducts surveys.

Information Manager   Involves specializing in database management. Besides having a general knowledge of how organizations work and how information flows through them, knowledge of how to set up and improve information systems is important. Knowledge of library referencing and indexing systems is applied. Helps a technical expert set up an electronic filing system or corporate database. Sorts and updates database files, advises how to design the automated office system that would best fit with the organization's style, workflow, and procedures.

Information Packager   Edits word processing systems and their software, applies working knowledge of word processing and text, and finds imaginative opportunities in which to further apply that knowledge and those related skills.

Information Specialist (Hospitality)   Provides specific information on area attractions and services to guests staying at the hotel. May work in conjunction with the Concierge in providing guests with information on restaurants, shopping areas, museums, historical sites, theater, and local entertainment. Is well informed on the history of the area and information available at the area's Chamber of Commerce and Visitor and Convention Bureau.

Information Specialist (Paralegal)   Consolidates legal information after research for easy accessibility. Lists resources for future research by subject and sets up reference library to maintain information in sequential order. Advises users on how to extract the information they need quickly and efficiently.

Informer   Person assigned by an organization as the contact person for the press or other media for obtaining desired information on an as-needed basis.

INS Investigator   Reviews applications for visas, determines whether aliens may enter or remain in the country, and gathers all information for the administrative hearings and criminal prosecution of immigration law violations.

Inspector   Supervises cleaning staff and inspects hotel guest rooms, corridors, and lobbies. Assigns work to cleaning staff and trains personnel in housekeeping duties. Posts room occupancy records. Adjusts guests' complaints regarding housekeeping service or equipment. Writes requisitions for room supplies and furniture renovation or replacements.

Instructor (Education)   Instructs students in commercial subjects (typing, accounting, computer systems), communications courses (reading and writing), and personality development in business schools, community colleges, or training programs. Instructs students in subject matter, utilizing various methods, such as lecture and demonstration, and uses audiovisual aids and other materials to supplement presentation. Prepares or follows teaching outline. Administers tests. Maintains discipline.

Insurance Agent   (See **Agent, Insurance**)

Insurance Investigation Specialist   Examines insurance claims made by individuals and businesses to ensure that the

claims being made are legitimate. Investigates false claims and determines appropriate course of action.

Intelligence Specialist   Conducts background clearances and work on security personnel matters.

Internal Auditor   Conducts independent appraisal from within the organization by analyzing, criticizing, and recommending improvements to internal financial practices. Ensures the safety and profitability of investments and assets, and seeks to uncover sources of waste and inefficiency.

International Account Executive (Hospitality)   Responsible for the development of and service of international client business coming into the hotel. May also be responsible for referring clientele to international properties in other countries. May assist with providing information to client on the foreign country, its currency, passport and customs regulations, and overall familiarization with the area.

International Group Secretary   Provides secretarial support for a team headed by an account executive. Duties include transcribing letters and memos from dictaphone tapes and typing comprehensive multicountry proposals for clients, preparation of travel arrangements, and assisting with clients, brokers, and foreign visitors.

Interpreter   Translates spoken word from one language to another. Provides consecutive or simultaneous translation between languages. Usually receives briefing on subject area prior to interpreting session.

Interviewer   Interviews job applicants to select persons meeting employers' qualifications. Searches files of job orders from employers and matches applicants' qualifications with job requirements and employer specifications.

Inventory Control Manager   Ensures that all stock units are in adequate supply, both components and finished goods. Responsible for overall quality of the product. Maximizes customer service levels, inventory investment, and manufacturing efficiencies.

Inventory Coordinator   Prepares reports of inventory balance, prices, and shortages. Compiles information on receipt or disbursement of goods and computes inventory balance, price, and costs. Verifies clerical computations against physical count of stock and adjusts errors in computation or count. Investigates and reports reasons for discrepancies.

Inventory Manager   Supervises compilation of records of amount, kind, and value of merchandise, material, or stock on hand in establishment or department of establishment. Compares inventories taken by workers with office records or computer figures from sales, equipment shipping, production, purchase, or stock records to obtain current theoretical inventory. Prepares inventory reports. Makes planning decisions.

Investigators   Investigates civil offenses within a city, county, or state and makes recommendations for appropriate action for the violators.

Investment Banker   Analyzes the needs of clients and makes recommendations to them on the best way to obtain the money they need. Obtains permission from each of the state governments to sell the issue in their state.

IRS Agent   Responsible for examining taxpayers' records to determine tax liabilities and investigating cases involving tax fraud or evasion of tax payments.

Job Analyst   Reviews all job functions within the company to continuously maintain updated details on job requirements, specific functions, and qualifications needed.

Junior Accountant   (See **Accountant**)

Junior Account Executive (Telemarketing)   (See **Account Executive—Telemarketing**)

Junior Analyst (Marketing)   (See **Market Research Analyst**)

Junior Buyer (Retail)   Performs duties of buyer trainee and also becomes involved in deciding on products for purchase and evaluating the store's needs. Learns to study the competition on a regular basis so as to evaluate and predict decisions.

Junior Consultant   (See **Consultant**)

Junior Copywriter   Studies clients from printed materials and past correspondence. May answer phone, type, file, or draft simple correspondence. May write some descriptive copy and come up with concepts for new ad campaigns. Works with the art department on presentations.

Junior Drafter   Copies plans and drawings prepared by drafters by tracing them with ink and pencil on transparent paper or cloth spread over drawings, using triangles, T-square, compass, pens, or other drafting instruments. Makes simple sketches or drawings under close supervision.

Keypunch Operator   Operates alphabetic and numeric keypunch machine, similar in operation to electric typewriter, to transcribe data from source material onto magnetic tape and to record accounting or statistical data for subsequent processing by automatic or electronic data processing equipment.

Kitchen Manager   Supervises all the production personnel in the kitchen area. Oversees the buying, storing, and preparation of all food. Takes inventory and reorders when necessary. Usually employed in operations where chefs are not employed.

Labor Relations Specialist   Responsible for being fully knowledgeable of current contracts or established policies affecting the working environment of all personnel including such areas as hiring requirements, pay policies, performance standards, leave of absence authorizations, and disciplinary procedures. When dealing with bargaining units, negotiates contracts as needed.

Law Librarian   Ensures books and other legal materials are updated periodically. Conducts legal research as needed, frequently accessing database information.

Law Library Manager   Manages the ordering and organizing of all materials to be housed in the law library. Responsible for keeping up-to-date on changes in the law and

for obtaining new literature describing most current laws. Supervises staff. Trains staff and library users on how to use the library. Oversees telephone information service.

Law Office Administrator   Designs, develops, and plans new procedures, techniques, services, processes, and applications in the office; plans, supervises, and assists in the installation and maintenance of relatively complex office equipment; plans production, operations of service for the efficient use of manpower, materials, money, and equipment in the office.

Lawyer   Conducts civil and criminal law suits; draws up legal documents, advises clients as to legal rights, and practices other phases of the law.

Lead Agent (Travel)   A car rental agent responsible for answering customers' questions.

Lead Analyst   Assists higher level personnel in analytical studies of complex and important problems involving existing and proposed systems and their costs. Develops, examines, and implements reporting systems and procedures which provide significant contributions in terms of time saved and increased efficiency or reduced costs.

Lead Analyst   Assists in developing the data processing procedures for solving business or mathematical problems. Assists in analyzing and evaluating proposed and existing systems.

Lead Consultant   Develops flowcharts to establish logic of execution. Codes logic in programming language. Writes program language to initiate and control the program in the hardware. Reviews existing programs and effects changes as requested. Solves production hang-ups in existing system. Writes operating instructions for computer personnel. Reviews output for the user. Supervises other programmers and gives final approval on the programs they have written. Ensures senior management receives information as requested.

Lead Word Processing Operator   Coordinates work priorities and assigns work to word processors. May train and supervise word processors. Ensures quality of work output.

Legal Assistant   Oversees the work of other paralegals in a firm. Delegates work, handles personnel-related problems, writes appraisals of other paralegals, and supervises the hiring of paralegals when needed. Works on special projects.

Legal Assistant Manager   Acts as a liaison between management and legal assistants; responsible for hiring, supervision, review, and dismissals, if necessary, as well as budgetary responsibilities. Also assigns case work to ensure work distribution, quality and timeliness.

Legal Secretary   Schedules appointments, court appearances; prepares documents, billing, bookkeeping, and recordkeeping. Handles subpoenas, mortgages, deeds, closings, pleadings, briefs, wills, proxies, and abstracts. May also review law journals and assist in other ways with legal research.

Legal Technician   Initiates and composes standardized legal forms routinely as needed for specific legal actions. Accepts service of legal documents, reviews for correct form and timeliness, annotates case files and status records to reflect receipt

and due dates for responses. Establishes, maintains, and closes out case files or systems of legal records. Maintains tickler system, coordinates schedules with court clerks, notifies witnesses of appearances, and reminds attorneys of court appearances and deadlines for submitting various actions or documents.

Legislative Reporter   Records events, speeches, and debates that take place in the different state legislatures. Attends and reports committee meetings.

Line Cook   Responsible for any duties necessary in order to prepare and produce menu items efficiently. Duties may include cutting and portioning, cooking, and serving items.

Litigation Paralegal   Assists attorneys at trial, prepares for trial, digests or summarizes depositions, indexes or organizes documents, prepares simple pleadings and discoveries such as interrogatories.

Litigation Support Consultant   Provides consulting services in litigation support. Consultation areas include analyzing the project, designing a database structure, developing a database building plan, creating coding sheets, and writing report programs.

Litigation Support Manager   Responsible for computerized litigation support. Consults with attorneys about whether a certain case will require automation and, if so, how to design the document retrieval database.

Loan Manager   Supervises loan personnel and approves recommendations of customer applications for lines of credit when loan officer is not able to do so. Communicates changes in policies and regulations regularly to loan personnel and customers.

Loan Officer   Interviews applicants applying for loans. Prepares loan request paper, obtains related documents from applicants. Investigates applicants' background and verifies credit and bank references. Informs applicants whether loan requests have been approved or rejected. Processes the loans.

Loss Prevention Specialist   Guards the internal security of a business to prevent employee thefts and inventory loss.

Mail and Information Coordinator   Coordinates the information and mail services, usually at the front desk. Responsible for ensuring that outgoing and incoming mail for the facility as well as for guests is properly routed. Advises guests on most efficient procedures for receiving or sending important mail. Ensures that messages get to hotel personnel and guests on a timely and accurate basis. May also provide guests with general information about the facility and the area.

Maître d'Hôtel   In charge of the dining room in a hotel or restaurant. Supervises a team of captains, waitpersons, and junior waitpersons.

Manager (Accounting)   Organizes and directs all general accounting activities. Maintains accounting systems that ensure the proper accounting and recording of company resources; provides financial statements, analysis, and other key management reports.

Manager (Banking)   (See **Bank Manager**)

Manager (Recreation)   Manages recreation facilities, such as tennis courts, golf courses, or arcades, and coordinates activities of workers engaged in providing services of the facility. Determines work activities necessary to operate facility, hires workers, and assigns tasks and work hours accordingly. Initiates promotion to acquaint public with activities of the facility. Maintains financial records.

Manager of Systems Analysis   Evaluates advances in computer equipment and software capabilities in light of the company's future system requirements. Coordinates the formulation of short- and long-range technical systems development plans, with special emphasis on technical feasibility. Organizes, schedules, and conducts training programs for data processing personnel and users of computer services.

Manager of Tour Operations   Supervises support functions related to the execution of a successful tour. Areas of responsibility include the bookkeeping, secretarial, telex, and computer operations areas.

Manager Trainee   Performs assigned duties, under direction of experienced personnel, to gain knowledge and experience needed for management position. Receives training and performs duties in various departments to become familiar with personnel functions and operations and management viewpoints and policies that affect each phase of the business.

Manager Trainee (Finance)   Works with financial manager while gaining an overall exposure to all aspects of the finance function of the company. Assists with budgets, purchase options, and expenses. Helps review financial reports for different product lines and assists with consolidating financial data for updated reports. May interview other department heads, customers, vendors, and other key people dealing with the finance area.

Manager Trainee (Food Service)   Assists with all functions of the area assigned. Learns the overview of the entire operation before specializing. If in a large operation, may rotate within one area of the facility, such as the production or purchasing area, to learn all of its functions if that is the area of specialty. Usually trains by rotating among various stations in the kitchen itself and among related areas such as purchasing, the storeroom, front of the house, etc.

Manager Trainee (Retail)   Works with store manager organizing and managing the store on a daily basis. Spends time on the selling floor, learning customer service techniques and computerized systems. Assists with managing, merchandising, and analyzing stock. Directs and physically puts stock out on the floor and presents merchandise. May work with buyer learning financial planning, vendor negotiations, and branch store communications.

Manufacturing Manager   Coordinates all manufacturing operations to produce products of high quality and reliability at optimum cost and in accordance with customer shipping schedules. Participates in the preparation of the manufacturing budget. Ensures safety of employees in their exposure to varied manufacturing process hazards. Resolves various manufacturing and production problems.

Market Manager (Food Service)   Responsible for compiling information on the age, sex, and income level of restaurants' potential clientele and their dining habits and preferences. Marketing managers consider customer preferences in order to suggest appropriate sales advertising techniques. This information provides the basis for success/failure projections in certain demographic areas.

Market Research Analyst   Researches market conditions in local, regional, or national area to determine potential sales of product or service. Examines and analyzes statistical data to forecast future marketing trends. Gathers data on competitors and analyzes prices, sales, and methods of marketing and distribution. Formulates surveys, opinion polls, or questionnaires.

Market Research Director   Oversees market research for a company. Sets goals and objectives for projects. Sets timetables for completion and assigns personnel to projects. Keeps appropriate administrators informed on findings and makes recommendations and proposes marketing strategies based on results.

Marketing Analyst (Paralegal)   Examines and analyzes statistical data to forecast future marketing trends in the paralegal field. (See **Market Research Analyst**)

Marketing Director   Directs and coordinates the development of marketing programs assigned to attain maximum penetration in the required market segments. Directs the creation, writing, and publishing of market and product plans. Explores development of product line offerings.

Marketing and Promotion Manager (Food Service)   Supervises any advertising or sales promotion for the operation. Works with food production staff to create menus and promotions with customer appeal. Often coordinates these activities with an advertising agency.

Marketing Representative (Paralegal)   Promotes and sells law-related books. Works in the marketing division of legal publishing companies.

Marketing Support Representative   Backs up the sales force by demonstrating the equipment and working with the customers after the equipment is installed; teaches the customers' word processing specialists to use the equipment and helps them find the best methods of doing the company's particular tasks.

Materials Manager   Studies receiving or shipping notices, requests for movement of raw materials and finished products, and reports of warehousing space available to develop schedules for material-handling activities. May confer with supervisors of other departments to coordinate flow of materials or products. Supervises activities of shipping and receiving personnel.

Media Director of Planning   Plans media relations in line with company goals. Reports and analyzes industry media trends. Communicates with product development to determine product market plans as they relate to media proposals and media scheduling. Oversees Media Planners.

Media Planner   Plans and administers media programs in advertising department. Confers with representatives of advertising agencies, product managers, and corporate advertising staff to establish media goals, objectives, and strategies within corporate advertising budget. Studies demographic data and consumer profiles to identify target audiences of media advertising.

Medical Assistant   Works in hospitals or clinics cleaning and sterilizing equipment, performing various tests, and helping to maintain records.

Medical Claims Examiner   Claims examiner for the medical field. (See **Claims Examiner**)

Medical Claims Representative   Claims representative for the medical field. (See **Claims Representative**)

Medical Librarian   Records, arranges, and makes medical information available to people. Handles books, films, periodicals, documents, and other media related to the medical field.

Medical Records Administrator   Plans, develops, and administers medical record systems for hospital, clinic, health center, or similar facility to meet standards of accrediting and regulatory agencies. Assists medical staff in evaluating quality of patient care and in developing criteria and methods for such evaluation. Develops and implements policies and procedures for documentation, storing, and retrieving information and for processing medical/legal documents.

Medical Records Technician   Gathers all information on patient's condition and records it on permanent files that become the history and progress of treatment of a patient's illness or injury. Accumulates the results of a physician's examinations, information on laboratory tests, and electrocardiograms, and records these results in the records. Accuracy is particularly important because much of this information is referred to during malpractice cases, and it is also vital when processing insurance claims.

Medical Secretary   Processes many kinds of complex health insurance forms. Responsible for patient billing, records management, medical and office supply organization, and appointments. Takes dictation and transcribes on dictaphone. Deals with medical supply vendors and pharmaceutical houses. Prepares correspondence and assists physicians with reports, speeches, articles, and conference proceedings.

Medical Technician (Electronics)   Performs the work of an electronics technician, specifically on various types of medical equipment. (See **Electronics Technician**)

Meeting Planner   Establishes objectives of the meeting, selects the hotel site and facilities, negotiates rates, sets budgets, makes air and hotel reservations, chooses speakers, plans food and beverages, arranges for all audiovisual equipment.

Arranges meeting registration, exhibits, promotion and publicity scheduling, and room set-up, and arranges postmeeting evaluation. Planners are involved with negotiations that save the organization money.

Membership Coordinator   Solicits membership for club or trade association. Visits or contacts prospective members to explain benefits and costs of membership and to describe organization of club or association. May collect dues and payments for publications from members.

Membership Secretary   Compiles and maintains membership lists, records the receipt of dues and contributions, and gives out information to members of the organizations and associations. Sends out newsletters and other promotional materials on a regular basis. Answers telephone inquiries and coordinates mass mailings.

Menu Planner   Works with the Executive Chef to select all items offered on menus. Must know food service costs, preparation techniques and equipment, customer trends and preferences.

Merchandise Analyst   Evaluates available merchandise in different locations and identifies when transfers might be appropriate. Evaluates quality of merchandise from the vendors for price paid with the buyer.

Merchandise Manager   Takes charge of a group of departments, usually organized by merchandise. Coordinates and oversees the efforts of the buyers. Develops merchandise plans, divides up the buyers' merchandise assignments, and reviews their selections. Visits the manufacturers' showrooms and travels abroad.

Merchandise Planner   Allocates merchandise from distribution point to stores as requested by buyers and merchandise managers. Ensures that merchandise is shipped properly and on a timely basis from the distribution center.

Merchandising Supervisor (Food Service)   Plans and carries out promotional programs to increase sales. Works with printers, artists, writers, and other suppliers. Must know employer's food service operations thoroughly and be able to apply market research techniques as well as budgeting and planning skills.

Military Investigator   Investigates all matters pertaining to military personnel and programs to monitor and/or discover illegal activities within the military. Also investigates outside threats to military personnel and programs.

Military Police   Operates on military bases, patrols areas where the military is located. Are generally limited in their jurisdiction to military personnel, or to persons involved in illegal activities aimed toward military personnel.

MIS Director   Recommends and initiates programs and/or systems that support the desired corporate profit objectives. Issues business data and management information that facilitate the businesses' planning and decision-making process at all levels. Responsible for total information service provided to user departments.

MIS Manager Responsible for coordinating the short-term planning for MIS/EDP efforts in systems development and computer processing; for establishing guidelines for measurement of division activity to these plans; and for monitoring Division MIS/EDP performance to ensure that information is made available to all levels of management on a complete, reliable, economic, and timely basis.

MIS Specialist Has specific knowledge of and provides service to a specialized area in the company. May concentrate on such areas as accounting, sales, production, or any other function requiring the services of the MIS department to meet its particular need.

MIS Supervisor Ensures timely and accurate processing of incoming orders through the order preparation and data processing areas to assist in achieving a high level of customer service. Maintains external relationship with vendors of paper supplies and forms, equipment manufacturers, equipment maintenance representatives, and leasing companies. Maintains contact with all company departments using the services of the MIS department.

Motor Vehicle Registration Coordinator Coordinates all aspects of motor vehicle registration and follow-up, including motor vehicle inspections and driver and licensing examinations.

National Sales Manager (Marketing) Devises and implements sales strategies, forecasts sales, supervises in-house salespeople; establishes and attains sales goals; trains and develops sales personnel. Develops and implements marketing and advertising strategy.

Night Auditor (Hospitality) Brings all of the establishment's accounts up-to-date so that a day's revenue report can be made to upper management. (*In a hotel, a revenue report includes such items as a detailed account of room revenues, number of rooms occupied, average room revenue, percentage of occupancy figures, and the like.*) The night audit process is usually augmented by a computerized system. The night auditor often plays the role of the night manager.

Night Shift Supervisor (Word Processing) Supervises work of word processing department during the night shift. Schedules the staff for the shift. Prioritizes work that must be completed. Responsible for maintaining the equipment and resolving routine problems that may occur in processing.

Nurse Cares for ill, injured, convalescent, and handicapped persons in hospitals, clinics, private homes, sanitariums, and similar institutions. Observes patient and reports adverse reactions to medical personnel in charge. Administers specified medications, and notes time and amount on patient's chart. Performs routine laboratory work.

Nutritionist Identifies the kinds and amounts of nutrients in food, translates this knowledge for schools and health care menus and restaurants and hotels; develops new foods and ingredients.

Operations Assistant (Recreation) Responsible for assisting with overseeing the general operation of a recreational facility. Solves problems that arise concerning facilities and grounds. Contacts vendors, contractors, and equipment repair technicians as needed. Obtains and renews necessary licenses and permits.

Office Manager (See **Department Manager, Office**)

Operations Manager (Computer Systems) Ensures that all jobs adhere to established conventions and may cancel any job that deviates from these conventions. Controls the processing of jobs and is responsible for obtaining the maximum utilization of the computer.

Operations Manager (Retail) Oversees all functions of store operations, which include personnel, credit, payroll, shipping and receiving, customer service, warehousing and distribution, security, and maintenance.

Operations Research Analyst Conducts analyses of management and operational problems and formulates mathematical or simulation models of the problem. Analyzes problems in terms of management information and conceptualizes and defines problems. Studies information and selects plan from competitive proposals that affords maximum profitability or effectiveness in relation to cost or risk.

Outside Sales Agent (Travel) Brings new business to an agency on a referral basis.

Owner/Manager (Employment Agency) An owner who also manages the agency. (See **Employment Agency Owner**)

Owner/Operator (Food Service) Coordinates all employees; may be responsible for buying food and supplies; may help with menu planning; keeps the restaurant within health and sanitation guidelines; oversees payroll function. In small restaurants, may oversee marketing and promotion effort.

Owner/Operator (Travel Agency) Delegates responsibilities to qualified managers. Encourages creative marketing and sales activities. Manages budget for the overall operation.

Packaging Specialist Develops packaging to fit specific products for industry needs.

Page Creator (Word Processing) Composes actual pages of catalogs relayed to home television or telephones. Involves word processing, text editing, and formatting, together with computer graphics. The system plus its computer graphics is called videotex.

Pantry Person Draws from the storeroom all the raw materials needed to prepare all the fruit or vegetable salads, seafood cocktails, canapes, and other cold dishes. Serves these items to waiters and waitresses. May slice and portion cold meats and cheeses. Serves desserts and side dishes such as bread and butter. Makes sandwiches and prepares garnishes for other departments.

Paralegal Assists a lawyer with routine legal assignments. Maintains legal volumes to make sure they are up-to-date; assists with legal research. Helps administer estates, draft wills and trusts, complete federal and state tax returns, pre-

pare initial and amended articles of incorporation, stock certificates, and other securities. Helps prepare court-related forms. Performs a variety of related duties upon request of the attorney.

Paralegal (Publishing House)   Assists the general counsel in the company's legal department with the areas of law that affect publishing, such as contract law and copyright law. May assist the legal publisher in planning new books about the paralegal profession or the procedures utilized by paralegals in the office.

Paralegal Assistant   Assists paralegals in large scale litigation with such duties as organizing and indexing documents, summarizing simple depositions, and performing assignments that enhance the overall organization of the case.

Paralegal Coordinator   Responsible for paralegal workload management, both as a resource for attorneys needing paralegal assistance and to ensure fairly divided workloads among paralegals on staff.

Paralegal Instructor   Teaches paralegal students the legal procedures used by paralegals in the law office.

Paralegal Manager   Responsible for hiring, performance reviews, salary administration, budgets, and work assignments.

Paralegal Supervisor   Oversees work of paralegal responsible for researching law, investigating facts, and preparing documents to assist lawyers.

Parole Officer   Helps clients find a place to live or work after being conditionally released from prison; must enforce the specific conditions of the client's release at all times.

Partner (CPA Firm)   Responsible for major audit accounts. Solves complex accounting problems for clients, using standard accounting principles. Also responsible for quality of client service and volume of new business brought in to the firm. Achieves objectives through the effective management of the technicians and sales staff in the firm.

Passenger Service Agent   Provides passengers with information; assists passengers with information, assists passengers when boarding the plane.

Pastry Cook   Prepares desserts (both hot and cold), ices, and cakes for both daily use and for special occasions.

Pastry Chef   Oversees the bread and pastry needs of all kitchens and departments in a large hotel, club, or restaurant. Supervises pastry cooks and bakers. Requires ability to coordinate the activity of others. Supervises the preparation of desserts, pastries, frozen desserts, fondants, fillings, and fancy sugar decorations. Creates new recipes and produces delicate items that require mastery of fine techniques.

Peripheral Equipment Operator   Operates on-line or off-line peripheral machines, according to written or oral instructions, to transfer data from one form to another, print output, and read data into and out of digital computer. Mounts and positions materials, such as reels of magnetic tape or paper tape onto reader-sorter. Sets, guides, keys, and switches according to instructions to prepare equipment for operations. Separates and sorts printed output forms.

Personnel Assistant   Performs diversified duties in the processing and monitoring of employee benefits programs and maintenance of all employee personnel files. Sets up files on new employees. Records changes on all employee status as necessary and forwards to payroll department.

Personnel Clerk   Prepares job postings and determines eligibility to bid and successful bidder(s). Prepares monthly absenteeism reports. Prepares monthly accident reports. Assists applicants with filling out employment applications appropriately. Acts as a backup for the department secretary; performs a variety of basic personnel and clerical functions.

Personnel Director   Supervises the hiring and firing of company employees. Prepares performance reports and sets up personnel policies and regulations. In a large corporation, oversees the entire personnel function.

Personnel Manager   Responsible for developing, implementing, and coordinating policies and programs covering the following: employment, labor relations, wage and salary administration, fringe benefits administration, indoctrination and training, placement, safety, insurance, health benefits, and employee services.

Placement Director (Paralegal)   Responsible for employment orientation and job development, and may act as a liaison between the employer and the paralegal graduate seeking a position.

Plant Manager   Responsible for manufacturing of products in the required quantity and quality and for performing this function safely at a minimum cost. Recommends improvements in manufacturing methods. Sets up and approves production schedules. Regularly reviews inventories of required materials. Directs and approves all requisitions for maintenance and repair of building and equipment and for machine parts and manufacturing supplies.

Plant Safety Specialist   Coordinates safety programs. Communicates policies, programs, and regulations to appropriate personnel. Ensures compliance with governmental regulations. Enforces safety policies for chemical use, fire codes, equipment, and ventilation systems. Ensures proper guarding of machinery to avoid operator injury. Maintains records as well.

Police Patrol Officer   Responsible for the enforcement of laws and ordinances for the protection of life and property in an assigned area during a specific period. Conducts preliminary investigations, assists in the apprehension of criminals.

Polygraph Operator   Tests victims, suspects, witnesses and others through the use of a lie detector machine.

Portfolio Manager   Manages nontrust accounts, such as the pension fund of a corporation or a university endowment. Decides what stocks should be bought and sold within the portfolio.

Postal Inspector Investigates losses and thefts of the mail or property owned by the post office. In addition, investigators and security force personnel protect postal buildings and installations.

Prep Cook Responsible for any duties necessary in order to prepare food items for production.

President Plans, develops, and establishes policies and objectives of the business organization in accordance with the board of directors and corporate charter. Plans business objectives and develops policies to coordinate functions between departments. Reviews financial statements to determine progress and status in attaining objectives. Directs and coordinates formulation of financial programs to provide funding for new or continuing operations to maximize return on investments. May preside over board of directors. Evaluates performance of company executives.

President/Owner Acts as president of a business and owns and operates it as well. (See **President**)

Press Coordinator Arranges meetings and special events with the press. Contacts press either by phone or mail to detail upcoming events.

Private An enlisted man of either of the two lowest ranks in the U.S. Marine Corps.

Private First Class An enlisted man ranking just below a corporal in the U.S. Army and just below a lance corporal in the U.S. Marine Corps.

Private Secretary As the executive's administrative partner, duties vary according to the size of the organization and the executive's responsibilities. May outline day's work for the office, schedule duties to be performed by all who work in the office; keeps everything on schedule despite interruptions. Greets callers, handles mail, keeps track of financial records, and processes data.

Probate Paralegal Oversees probate proceedings from beginning to end, prepares federal tax forms, assists at the sales of assets, and drafts wills and trusts.

Probation Officer Responsible for compiling the presentence investigation for the court. Makes formal court reports and recommendations to the judge for case deposition. Works with caseloads of individuals to assist them with counseling, job placement, and traditional social work–oriented functions while at the same time enforcing the rules imposed on the client by the court.

Product Development Technologist Technologist working in the food service industry conducting experiments to improve flavor, texture, shelf life, or other product characteristics; develops new products or packaging materials; compares competitive products; ensures that every item meets quality standards, and interprets and solves the problems of the food service operator.

Product Manager Oversees the research, development, and production of a particular product. Assesses need for modifications on the product based on input from market research.

Estimates timely and cost-effective procedures for implementing periodic modifications. Ensures that quality of product is maintained.

Product Support Representative (Computer Systems) Acts as the customer's liaison with the computer manufacturer. Assists with familiarizing the customer with the computer. Acts as part trainer, part salesperson, and part adviser to the customer.

Production Coordinator Coordinates flow of work within or between departments of manufacturer to expedite production. Reviews master production schedule and work orders, establishes priorities and availability or capability of workers, parts, or material. Confers with department supervisors to determine progress of work. Compiles reports on the progress of work.

Production Manager Supervises and coordinates activities of those who expedite flow of materials, parts, and assemblies and processes within or between departments.

Production Manager (Food Service) Takes leadership position in such production operation areas as engineering, scheduling, purchasing, quality control, inventory control, distribution, and human relations.

Production Planner Ensures that inventories of stock items are maintained at reasonable levels and that orders for non-stock items are processed in a timely, effective manner. Works with plant supervisor to establish manning levels that are appropriate based on current and projected levels of activity. Requisitions all raw materials and supplies required to manufacture products.

Production Technician Assists engineer in preparing layouts of machinery and equipment, work-flow plans, time and motion studies, and analyses of production costs to produce the most efficient use of personnel, materials, and machines.

Professional Waitperson Serves meals to the patrons according to the established rules of etiquette. Presents a menu to the diner, suggesting dinner courses and appropriate wines, and answering questions regarding the food preparation. Writes the order on a check or memorizes it. Relays the order to the kitchen and serves the courses from the kitchen and service bars. Garnishes and decorates the dishes preparatory to serving them. Serves the patrons from a chafing dish at the table, observes the diners to fulfill any additional requests and to perceive when the meal has been completed. Totals the bill and accepts payments. May carve the meats, bone the fish and fowl, and prepare flaming dishes and desserts at the patron's table.

Program Coordinator Oversees programs after the planning stage. Takes appropriate action to initiate planned programs, service them while in progress, and arrange for program evaluation. May assist with recommending speakers, agendas, room setup, and promotional efforts.

Program Director Plans and develops methods and procedures for implementing programs; directs and coordinates program activities, and exercises control over personnel ac-

cording to knowledge and experience in area with which the program is concerned. Prepares program reports. Controls expenditures.

Program Director (Education) Supervises the development of a variety of academic programs or other programs related to an educational institution. Such programs might involve parents, student organizations, industry, or other special interest groups. (See **Program Director**)

Project Director Plans, directs, and coordinates activities of designated project to ensure that aims, goals, or objectives specified for project are accomplished in accordance with set priorities, timetables, and funding. Develops staffing plan and establishes work schedules for each phase of the project. Prepares project status reports for management.

Proofreader Reads typeset (original copy) or proof of type setup to detect and mark for corrections and grammatical, typographical, or compositional errors. Reads proof against copy, marking by standardized codes errors that appear in proof. Returns marked proof for correction and later checks corrected proof against copy.

Proofreader (Paralegal) Reviews the content of law-related manuscripts to verify facts needed in case preparation. Also can act as person who checks for improper usage or spelling or grammar errors in legal copy.

Proofreader (Word Processing) Checks the work of the correspondence secretary and word processor for accuracy of copy.

Public Relations Specialist Writes news releases, directs advertising campaigns, or conducts public opinion polls. Tries to create favorable attitudes about a client or its products.

Purchasing Agent Responsible for buying the raw materials, machinery, supplies, and services necessary to run a business.

Purchasing Agent (Food Service) Purchases foodstuffs, kitchen supplies, and equipment. Makes large contracts for several products. Purchases all supplies with the exception of capital goods such as furniture and fixed equipment.

Purchasing Assistant (See **Purchasing Agent**)

Purchasing Manager Responsible for the management of the procurement functions of the company. Establishes practices and procedures to be followed by buyers and other department personnel. Negotiates price and delivery. Selects vendors, assesses vendor capabilities, develops alternate sources, and evaluates vendor performance. Ensures that department records are maintained.

Purchasing Manager (Food Service) Responsible for the actual purchase of all supplies and equipment, usually coordinated through the Executive Chef or Cook. Required to monitor and control costs and to maintain accurate inventories. Supervises purchasing agents responsible for a particular product line.

Quality Assurance Manager Develops and maintains a system to assure that all products manufactured by the organization meet customer specifications and achieve superior quality and reliability levels. Revises and updates quality control manual. Meets with vendors, customers, and quality representatives to discuss and resolve quality problems as required.

Quality Assurance Specialist (Food Service) Analyzes ingredients and finished products and checks standards of production, packaging, and sanitation. May be assigned to a particular type of product or food item.

Quality Control Manager (Food Service) Travels to various units to inspect those units and make sure they adhere to company and state standards. Usually responsible for more than one operation.

Railroad Police Responsible for safety and security on the railroads.

Ramp Agent Supervises baggage area to be sure baggage is sent to proper destinations.

Real Estate Manager (Food Service) Supervises the negotiations for the acquisition and disposition of properties. Supervises staff engaged in preparing lease agreements, recording rental receipts, and performing other activities necessary to efficient management of company properties, or in performing routine research on zoning ordinances and condemnation considerations. Directs appraiser to inspect properties and land under consideration for acquisition and recommends acquisitions, lease, disposition, improvement, or other action consistent with best interests of the company. Negotiates contracts with sellers of land and renters of property.

Real Estate Paralegal Prepares loan documents, oversees transactions from beginning to end, drafts and reviews leases, works closely with escrow and title companies, reviews surveys, and prepares closing binders.

Reception Manager Supervises all activities of guest services, including registration of incoming guests and checkout of departing guests; provides guests with information about functions at the hotel and about the general area where the hotel is located; takes messages for guests and provides wake-up calls; handles guest relations, problems with rooms, billing, or any other routine difficulty.

Receptionist Greets people who come into an office and directs them to the proper department. They may also do other tasks such as answering the phone and some typing. Learns the departments and key personnel in the company and what functions they perform.

Records Manager Examines and evaluates records-management systems to develop new or improve existing methods for efficient handling, protecting, and disposing of business records and information. Reviews records retention schedule to determine how long records should be kept.

Recreation Director (Cruiselines) Develops safe recreation programs suitable for a cruiseline. Ensures adherence to established standards and policies. Ensures staff is properly certified for instruction when needed. Makes recommendations to activities coordinator for recreation schedules.

Recruiting Coordinator/Administrator Works with the firm administrator and the recruiting or hiring committee to hire new attorneys. Coordinates Summer Clerk interviewing.

Regional Director May oversee a group of regional managers. (See **Regional Manager**)

Regional Manager Responsible for overseeing the activities of all operations in a particular geographical area of the country.

Regional Sales Manager Recruits in-house personnel, recruits general agents, and assists when needed with training new sales staff with "cold calling." Holds periodic sales meetings to strengthen competitive position and explain strategies for market penetration.

Registered Representative (Account Executive or Broker) Buys or sells securities for customers. Relays the order to members of the firm who are stationed on the exchange floors; if the security is not traded on the exchange, sells it directly in the over-the-counter market. Advises customers on the timing of the purchase or sale of securities. Counsels customers about tax shelters, mutual funds, and other investments.

Regional Vice President (Food Service) Deals with new business development; senior management contact, both internal and external; pricing analysis; proposal development and presentation; and contract negotiations. Works with planning and achieving marketing objectives within the responsible geographic territory.

Rental Sales Representative Negotiates car rental rates with travel agents, corporate businesses, and other commercial accounts and individual clients so as to remain competitive in the market.

Research Account Executive (Advertising) Researches printed literature. Drafts reports from research. Gets competitive bids from suppliers. Sits in on planning sessions. Suggests new methods of data gathering. Helps design surveys.

Research Analyst Evaluates research findings and determines their applicability to specific projects within the company. Recommends needed research projects. Compares research findings with similar studies or surveys to determine reliability of results. Uses statistical data and measurement to examine and apply findings.

Research Analyst (Financial) Researches and sells their research to institutional investors. Recommends portfolio managers to the stocks they believe should be bought and sold.

Research Assistant Compiles and analyzes verbal or statistical data to prepare reports and studies for use by professional workers in a variety of areas. Searches sources, such as reference works, literature, documents, newspapers, and statistical records, to obtain data on assigned subjects. May interview individuals to obtain data or draft correspondence to answer inquiries.

Research Assistant (Paralegal) Performs legal research by operating a computer-assisted legal research system.

Research and Development Specialist (Food Service) Conducts research on new product lines and equipment for the food service industry. May work with food products in test kitchens or with new equipment in operating food service establishments. Reports findings to manufacturers of food products and equipment and publicizes results in trade publications to inform the industry about the possible alternatives the findings may provide for food service professionals.

Research Director May supervise a group of research projects at a given time. (See **Project Director**)

Research Manager (See **Project Director**)

Research Technician (Electronics) Performs research to evaluate new methods for the electronics technician. Tests findings. May pass recommendations on to research and development. Upon request, works with other researchers and engineers to test findings.

Researcher and Evaluator (Travel) Investigates and evaluates public relations efforts of the organization. Responsible for making recommendations on public relations programs based on goals and objectives and competition's position in the marketplace. Evaluates needs for expanding public relations efforts. Researches and recommends best strategy.

Reservationist Sells reservations and other travel products such as tours, hotel accommodations, car rentals; operates computer reservations equipment; assists passengers in solving their travel needs.

Reservationist (Cruiselines) Books cruises for individual clients and groups. Sells the cruise by telephone to inquirers. Explains details of the trip and accepts payment.

Reservationist (Hotel) Responsible for confirming room reservations, either by mail or by telephone, and for writing or typing out reservation forms. Works with computer to keep guest reservations current and for billing procedures. May assist guests with other reservations for local transportation, dining, or entertainment, depending on the staff size of the hotel.

Reservations Manager Supervises and coordinates activities of personnel engaged in taking, recording, and canceling reservations in front office of hotel. Trains front office staff. Reviews daily printouts listing guests' arrivals and individual guest folios received by room clerks. Approves correspondence going to groups and travel agents to answer special requests for rooms and rates. Evaluates computer system and manual record procedures for efficiency.

Resident Manager (Hospitality) Lives on the premises to manage the day-to-day operations of a hotel or other lodging facility.

Restaurant Manager Responsible for efficiency, quality, and courtesy in all phases of a food service operation. In large organizations, may direct supervisory personnel at the next

lower level. In smaller operations, might supervise kitchen and dining room staffs directly. Knowledge of the responsibilities of all restaurant staff is essential to this position.

Revenue Officer   Investigates and collects delinquent federal taxes and secures delinquent tax returns from individuals or business firms according to prescribed laws and regulations. Recommends civil penalties when necessary. Writes reports on all actions taken.

Roasting Cook   Responsible for all meat preparation that is made to order. Also responsible for all items that are deep fried, shallow fried, sautéed, or broiled.

Robotics Technician   Performs the work of an electronics technician, specifically on various types of robotic devices. (See **Electronics Technician**)

Rooms Attendant   Coordinates service for a block of rooms in a hotel. Ensures room service operations are running smoothly. Arranges for any special requests from guests concerning accommodations. Checks the room rack and key rack frequently. Oversees the operation of switchboard and messages going to guests.

Rooms Division Supervisor   Directs all activities involved with the rooms division of the hotel. This includes staffing, housekeeping, occupancy, service, and promotion.

Rounds Cook   Replaces every member of the kitchen brigade who may be absent from each station. Must be efficient and versatile in cooking techniques.

Sales Assistant   Responsible for successful management of a selling area. Involves supervision of a selling area and customer service functions. In a large department store, may also direct inventory control and merchandise presentation and increasing the sales growth and profitability of an area.

Sales Director (Hospitality)   Responsible for research and analysis, short-term and long-range planning, determination of marketing strategies and tactics, setting of goals and objectives, budgeting, the booking of individual as well as group business, and the securing of business for the food and beverage department as well as for the rooms division.

Sales/Field Representative (Electronics)   Advises customers on installation and maintenance problems and serves as the link between the manufacturer and the customer.

Sales Manager   Coordinates sales distribution by establishing sales territories, quotas, and goals, and advises dealers and distributors concerning sales and advertising techniques. Directs staffing, training, and performance evaluations to develop and control sales programs. Prepares periodic sales reports showing sales volume and potential sales. May recommend or approve budget, expenditures, and appropriations for research and development work.

Sales Manager (Food Service)   Responsible for the development and operation of the sales department. Maintains files on past group business. Works with the social director and

promotion office on contacts and may do some traveling to other areas to bring new business into the establishment. Also trains and supervises sales representatives and some account executives.

Sales Manager (Retail)   Oversees the various sales departments in wholesale and retail companies. Directs promotional sales campaigns for their merchandise or services.

Sales and Marketing Specialist (Food Service)   Plans, researches, promotes, and sells products to the food service industry.

Sales Representative   Secures orders from existing and potential customers by means of visiting the customer facility or calling by phone. Follows up on quotations submitted to customers. Submits weekly activity/call reports concerning customer quotes, orders, or problems. Provides a territory sales forecast on a monthly basis.

Sales Representative (Computer Systems)   Calls on prospective clients to explain types of services provided by establishment, such as inventory control, payroll processing, data conversion, sales analysis, and financial reporting. Analyzes data processing requirements of prospective clients and draws up prospectus of data processing plan designed specifically to serve client's needs. May also sell computers and related equipment directly.

Sales Representative (Hospitality)   Follows initial lead on a prospective client. Responsible for explaining hotel's services to government, business, and social groups to generate interest in the facility as a site for a major function. Sales representative conducts "cold calls" as well as calls to a selected prospect list. The sales representative may pass the interested client on to an account executive, who will actually set up, service, and maintain the account.

Sales Secretary   Types drafts of newsletters; keeps track of company's dealings with outside printers, suppliers, and creative people. Types, files, answers telephones, and routes mail. Takes orders, books events, or handles whatever customer request comes in for the product or service being sold.

Sales/Service Manager (Electronics)   Oversees both the sales and service efforts of a branch or many branch operations of a company. Ensures that the quality and customer service levels are maintained in the field. Receives feedback from customers through the sales and service staff. Determines what action should be taken with repeated problems.

Sales Supervisor   (See **Sales Manager**)

Sales Trainee (Hospitality)   Usually begins with front office experience to learn client relations and total product line offered by the hotel. May go on sales calls with sales representatives or assist an account executive with servicing an account.

Sales Trainee (Insurance)   Attends sales strategy sessions as an observer, or "tails" an experienced agent on calls. Assists established agents to service accounts.

Sanitation Supervisor (Food Service) Supervises porters, dishwashers, kitchen persons, and pot washers. Ensures that dishes, cooking utensils, equipment, and floors are kept clean. Ensures that kitchen always meets health department regulations and standards.

Sauce Cook Responsible for all preparation of sauces to be used on main items on the menu. In a middle-sized operation, the sauce cook is also the Sous Chef.

Schedule Planning Manager (Travel) Approves and enforces scheduling recommendation for all air traffic coming and going into and out of the airport.

School Director Plans, develops, and administers education programs. Confers with administrative personnel to decide scope of programs to be offered. Prepares schedules of classes and rough drafts of course content to determine number and background of instructors needed. Interviews, hires, trains, and evaluates work performance of education department staff. Assists instructors in preparation of course descriptions. Prepares budget for education programs and directs maintenance of records of expenditures, receipts, and public and school participation in programs.

School Director/Administrator (See **School Director** and **Administrator**)

School Director (Vocational) Directs and coordinates schools with vocational training programs. Confers with members of industrial and business community to determine manpower training needs. Reviews and interprets vocational educational codes to ensure that programs conform to policies. Prepares budgets and funding allocation for vocational programs. Reviews and approves new programs. Coordinates on-the-job training programs with employers and evaluates progress of students in conjunction with program contract goals.

School Secretary Handles secretarial duties in elementary and secondary schools; may take care of correspondence, prepare bulletins and reports, keep track of money for school supplies and student activities, and maintain a calendar of school events.

Script Writer Provides the creative support in a telemarketing agency. Writes all material that is to be read by the telemarketing representative.

Seafood Cook Prepares all seafood dishes, mousses, soufflés, etc. Also prepares the fish for cold display or for hors d'oeuvres and then sends to the garde manager for final decoration.

Secret Service Agent Protects the president and vice president of the United States, along with their families, and protects the coins and securities of the government by enforcing laws pertaining to counterfeiting.

Secretary Performs secretarial duties for a supervisor. Takes and transcribes dictation with speed and accuracy. Maintains correspondence and data files, arranges appointments, answers routine inquiries, and handles general office duties. Often assists in performing administrative details using initiative and judgment. Requires thorough knowledge of company policies, the organization, and how to operate in the channels of the organization. As part of the management team, must be ready to make decisions and provide relevant information to staff members on a daily basis.

Secretary (Food Service) In large food service operations, performs a variety of administrative duties; works with customers on group business and with vendors on orders and supplies. Frees the employer to work on other areas outside the property.

Senior Accountant (See **Accountant**)

Senior Account Executive (See **Account Executive**)

Senior Analyst (See **Lead Analyst**)

Senior Analyst (Marketing) (See **Market Research Analyst**)

Senior Claims Examiner (See **Claims Examiner**)

Senior Consultant (See **Consultant**)

Senior Copywriter (See **Copywriter**)

Senior Drafter Gives final approval to the plans drawn up by other drafters before presenting the plan to client. (See **Drafter**)

Senior Legal Assistant Oversees the work of paralegals and legal assistants in the firm. (See **Paralegal** and **Legal Assistant**)

Senior Systems Consultant Provides specialized advice on programming languages and documentation. Maintains up-to-date knowledge of all programming language. Makes provisions for the orderly processing of changes, updatings, and modifications of programs. Coordinates all company programming efforts. (See **Systems Consultant**)

Senior Underwriter (See **Underwriter**)

Sergeant U.S. Marine Corps, U.S. Army, a noncommissioned officer of the fifth grade, ranking above a corporal and below a staff sergeant.

Service Representative Goes out into the field upon customer's request to service problems with purchased equipment. May diagnose the problem, correct and test the equipment to see if it is working properly. Reports problem to research and development. Tells owners and dealers about new products, service techniques, and developments in maintenance.

Service Technician (Electronics) (See **Service Representative**)

Sheriff A constitutional officer who is an elected official. Supervises deputies and plain clothes investigators. Responsible for the administration of the county jail. Serves civil papers and orders of the county courts and transports prisoners.

Shore Patrol Officer Patrols areas, on shore, where the military is located.

Social Secretary Arranges social functions, answers personal correspondence, and keeps the employer informed about all social activities.

Soup Cook Responsible for all soups, both cold and hot, plus garnishes, stocks, etc.

Sous Chef Principal assistant of the Chef de Cuisine. In a large operation, will assist the Chef de Cuisine in general administrative and supervisory duties and will implement every order given. Must have the same professional background as the chef but not necessarily the same number of years of experience.

Special Events Coordinator Performs basic function of the meeting planner and also is directly responsible for the advertising and promotion of the event, for the budget for the event, and for identifying the appropriate target market. Works with the press and media on promotion. Acts as the liaison between all participating parties.

Speaker Person elected by an organization to present its views, policies, or decisions.

Staff Accountant Oversees the general ledger of a firm. Reviews cost center and chart of accounts structure. Makes recommendation as to cost center/account structure which will identify the nature of expenses to their proper areas; assists in controlling annual expenditures. Reconciles daily cash flow statements and reconciles to monthly bank statements. Reconciles payroll and cash disbursement accounts. Reviews accounts payable aging and vendor statements for problems.

State Travel Director Promotes visitor traffic within the destination, whether for pleasure, business, or convention purposes, and from within or from without the state.

Station Manager Supervises a car rental business.

Statistical Typist Works in all types of businesses typing statistical data from source material such as: company production and sales records, test records, time sheets, and surveys and questionnaires.

Stenographer Takes dictation in shorthand of correspondence, reports, and other matter, and operates typewriter to transcribe dictated materials.

Stewardess (Food Service) Supervises and coordinates activities of the pantry, storeroom, and noncooking kitchen workers, and purchases or requisitions the foodstuffs, kitchen supplies, and equipment. Inspects the kitchens and storerooms to ensure that the premises and equipment are clean and in order and that sufficient foodstuffs and supplies are on hand to ensure efficient service. Establishes controls to guard against theft and waste.

Store Manager An executive responsible for the profitable operation of the store. Has broad merchandising responsibilities, develops staff, contributes to the store's public relations effort, and supervises the maintenance of the store. Spends significant amount of time on the selling floor and supplies other areas of management with detailed information on the operation of the store.

Storeroom Supervisor (Food Service) Responsible for supervising, receiving, inspecting, counting, and storing of all food and other articles delivered to the storeroom. Responsible for filling out all requisitions and, under the instructions of the house auditor, for keeping a journal in ledger of all goods received and delivered. Records names of purveyors, the costs and descriptions of articles, and other required information. Supervises monthly inventories with the auditor.

Summer Clerk A law school student who works for a law firm during the summer break usually so both parties can learn more about each other in making potential employment decisions.

Superintendent of Service (Hospitality) Responsible for overseeing all functions providing guest services in the hotel. This may include the front office and housekeeping as well as food service operations. Ensures quality service while keeping informed about any client-centered problems that may affect new or repeat business. Solves problems related to guest services.

Supervisor (Banking) Responsible for improving the overall productivity of a department or area, motivating staff, and staying within budget. Oversees production, product development, marketing, and systems functions in the bank.

Supervisor of Data Entry Services Directs all data input activities serving the users of centralized data input facility. Directs the development of data input procedures, performance standards, and controls. Directs the evaluation of new data entry equipment. Ensures accurate and timely completion of projects.

Supervisor of Gate Services Observes staff to ensure that services to passengers are performed courteously and correctly. Supervises and coordinates the activities of staff engaged in admitting passengers to airplanes and assisting passengers disembarking at terminal exits of commercial flights. Reviews flight schedules, passenger manifests, and information obtained from staff to determine staffing needs. Recommends alternate procedures if needed. Evaluates performance of staff.

Supervisor (Telemarketing) Manages groups of telemarketing communicators and is directly responsible for their performance. May also be responsible for training and scheduling of staff.

Surveyor Interviews people and compiles statistical information. Asks questions following a specified outline on questionnaire and records answers. Reviews, classifies, and sorts questionnaires. Compiles results in a format that is clear and concise and highlights findings relevant to the objective of the survey.

Swing Cook (See **Rounds Cook**)

Systems Administrator (Word Processing) Involves systems maintenance and management and systems analysis and design.

Systems Analyst   Prepares detailed instructions for assigned programming systems or components enabling qualified personnel to proceed with implementation. Evaluates procedural and/or programming systems required to operate and support programs and systems. Solves the problems of adapting computer hardware and software to end-users' needs. Determines how the company can save money by adapting existing equipment. Coordinates and supervises the efforts of many computer professionals. Maintains quality control by assessing the system once it has been implemented.

Systems Consultant   Advises clients on developing, implementing, and maintaining automated programs for clients and for in-house use; on selecting hardware, writing software, and consulting with user/client when special programs must be developed. Writes the codes that make up a computer program, tests their programs, debugs them (eliminates errors), and sometimes writes the accompanying documentation that tells others why the program was written the way it was.

Systems Operators Supervisor   Directs operations for optimum use of computer and peripheral equipment. Coordinates between users and other data processing functions in establishing and maintaining processing schedules. Recommends hardware changes and directs the installation of new equipment.

Systems Programmer   Prepares the computers to understand the language that the applications programmers will be using and tells the computer what peripheral equipment, such as printers and automatic teller machines, it will be controlling.

Systems Trainee (Banking)   Works in programming or part of a systems team project, refining the use of current equipment or developing systems for as yet unmet needs.

Tape Librarian   Documents and allots hardware space for all computer and peripheral equipment for schedules; produces debugging statistics and other statistical reports for the department management personnel.

Team Leader (Floor Supervisor)   Responsible for supervision of a floor in a hotel. Oversees the maintenance and upkeep, the repair and security of all rooms on an assigned floor. Supervises housekeeping staff assigned to that floor and coordinates the group to work efficiently. Submits work reports to Executive Housekeeper if requested.

Technical Secretary   Assists engineers or scientists. In addition to the usual secretarial duties, may prepare much of the correspondence, maintain the technical library, and gather and edit materials for scientific papers.

Telemarketing Center Manager   Responsible for executing the program once components have been assembled and the script written. This involves either making or receiving the calls in a way that achieves each client's objective.

Telemarketing Communicator   Delivers what everyone else sells. Coordinates or manages the allocation of the product to the proper sales and delivery channels.

Telemarketing Representative   Sells a product or "qualifies" customers for the field sales force by telephone.

Telemarketing Trainer   Instructs communicators about the product or services and how to use the scripts. Trainers also teach telemarketing efficiency, listening skills, and sales techniques.

Ticket Agent   Sells tickets to airline passengers at the airport and city ticket office; promotes and sells air travel; gives air travel and tour information; makes the flight and tour reservations; computes fares; prepares and issues tickets; routes baggage; and prepares cash reports.

Tour Director   Conducts the actual tour. Accompanies travelers as an escort throughout the trip. Solves problems and settles complaints. Has alternative plans set for the group so that tour will be successful even under adverse conditions. Coordinates the group to stay together and encourages questions about the area being visited.

Tour Escort   Assists passengers; generally assists with tours; accompanies the tour from start to finish; often handles large sums of money; makes necessary changes in group's accommodations or itinerary as needed.

Tour Guide   Does complete narration; has specialized knowledge of a particular region or country; hired to accompany a tour only while it visits the area of special expertise.

Tour Operator   Puts together all the elements of a trip: transportation, accommodations, meals, sightseeing, and the like; negotiates rates and block space; coordinates details of the itinerary; markets the product.

Tour and Travel Account Executive   Responsible for the development and service of group tour business coming into the hotel. Brings travel and tour groups to the hotel. Consults with the tour operators and travel agents and collaborates with the hotel staff to find best strategy for servicing the group.

Tourist Information Assistant   Provides information and other services to tourists at state information centers. Greets tourists, in person or by telephone, and answers questions and gives information on resorts, historical sights, scenic areas, and other tourist attractions. Assists tourists in planning itineraries and advises them of traffic regulations. Sells hunting and fishing licenses and provides information on fishing, hunting, and camping regulations. Composes letters in response to inquiries. Maintains personnel, license sales, and other records. Contacts motel, hotel, and resort operators by mail or telephone to obtain advertising literature.

Trader   Matches buyers and sellers of securities.

Traffic Manager   Negotiates price and service issues of all modes of transportation carrier contracts and determines the appropriate transportation mode to be utilized. Develops, maintains, and disseminates logistical data.

Traffic Officer   Directs and controls the flow of traffic for both motor vehicles and pedestrians. Enforces parking regulations. Tracks stolen or wanted automobiles. Investigates traffic accidents. Provides motorists' assistance, escort duty, crowd handling, and rerouting traffic.

Trainer (Word Processing) Trains correspondence and word processing secretaries to make fewer errors by checking their work.

Training Manager Develops ongoing training programs for new and experienced personnel. Conducts training seminars. Writes and coordinates training manuals, working with specialists for specified details. Prepares training videotapes and/or films; maintains library of video and film training aids. Notifies employees of training sessions. Introduces topic specialists at the beginning of the program and the program agenda. Develops means of measuring the effectiveness of programs through testing.

Training Specialist Develops and conducts training programs for specialized functions within the company upon the approval of the training manager. (See **Training Manager**)

Training Supervisor May supervise training manager(s) as well as the entire training function for the company. Responsibilities might include overseeing training programs at various divisions and performing all budgetary responsibilities pertaining to the programs. Also may evaluate existing programs and make recommendations for modifications or new or additional programs. (See **Training Manager**)

Transportation Manager Responsible for all aspects of transportation including inbound, between facilities, and outbound. Supervises various functions and personnel. Negotiates rates with warehouses and transportation companies. Plans, monitors, and implements the distribution department's fiscal budget. Establishes the most beneficial routing of company shipments for satisfactory customer service. Determines price levels. Plans for the department on a quarterly, yearly, and five-year basis.

Transportation Specialist Advises industries, business firms, and individuals concerning methods of preparation of shipments, rates to be applied, and mode of transportation to be used. Consults with clients regarding packing procedures and inspects packed goods for conformance to shipping specifications to prevent damage, delay, or penalties. Files claims with insurance company for losses, damages, and overcharges of shipments.

Travel Agency Manager Supervises the day-to-day operations of the agency. Prepares sales reports and dictates office policies. Decides on promotion and pricing of packages. Supervises, hires, and trains employees. Attends trade shows to keep informed on latest computer systems, rates, and promotions being offered by the airlines, hotels, and other related services. Initiates advertising for the agency and keeps budget.

Travel Agent Plans itineraries and arranges accommodations and other travel services for customers of the travel agency. Plans, describes, and sells itinerary package tours. Converses with customers to determine destination, mode of transportation, travel dates, financial considerations, and accommodations required. Books customer's mode of transportation and hotel reservations. Obtains travel tickets and collects payment. May specialize in foreign or domestic service, individual or group travel, or specific geographical areas.

Travel Counselor Advises clients on best ways to travel, destinations, costs, and safety issues. Offers advice to clients on packages available, preparation for a trip, or availability of transportation or accommodations. Researches information requested by the client.

Travel Director Client-contact person who actually goes out with the incentive groups and on site, coordinating sightseeing trips and trouble-shooting.

Travel Editor Buys articles submitted by freelance writers; selects unsolicited articles for publication; selects letters from readers to publish; replies to readers' letters of comment or criticism; works with layout and make-up of travel pages. May assign staff to stories almost anywhere in the world. Reviews manuscripts submitted by travel writers for content and readability. Chooses manuscripts for publication.

Travel Secretary Coordinates all aspects of the travel function. Researches options to maintain an economical, efficient travel program. Schedules personnel for approved travel on corporate jets. Schedules personnel from approved travel authorizations on commercial flights. Makes hotel reservations. Performs clerical and secretarial duties pertaining to all travel arrangements.

Travel Specialist Develops specialized expertise about a particular area of travel. May work for a travel agency, tour operator, publications department, or other related areas using information mastered about a specialized area of travel. May specialize in a geographic area, type of destination, or any other specific area in the travel industry.

Travel Writer Provides practical guides, directories, and language books and brochures. Contributes feature stories to travel sections of large newspapers.

Treasurer Directs and coordinates organization's financial programs, transactions, and security measures according to financial principles and government regulations. Evaluates operational methods and practices to determine efficiency of operations. Approves and signs documents affecting capital monetary transactions. Directs receipt, disbursement, and expenditures of money or other capital assets.

Treasurer/Controller Has combined responsibilities of both the Treasurer and the Controller. (See **Treasurer** and **Controller**)

Trust Officer Manages money and securities as well as real estate and other property. Decides how assets will be managed.

Underwriter Reviews applications, reports, and actuarial studies to determine whether a particular risk should be insured. Specializations are usually in life, property, and liability, or health insurance.

Underwriter Specialist Specializes as an underwriter in life, property, and liability, or health insurance. (See **Underwriter**)

Underwriter Trainee Assists the underwriter. Usually spends much time on the telephone gathering information and verifying what has been reported before the underwriter makes final decisions. (See **Underwriter**)

Underwriting Supervisor Oversees the underwriting department. Ensures staff is working within appropriate guidelines and regulations when reviewing submitted materials. Evaluates performance of the staff and hires new underwriters as needed.

Unit Manager Representative of a food service contractor who is permanently assigned to one particular client installation.

Urban Planner Works with city or state officials to produce plans for future building and construction projects. Must be able to project an area's future population and its needs and design facilities to meet those needs.

U.S. Marshal Responsible for executing and enforcing commands of federal courts; processing federal prisoners; seizing property under court order; and protecting federal judges, witnesses and juries.

Vegetable Cook Prepares all garnishes such as potatoes, vegetables, egg dishes, etc.

Vending Manager Independent businessperson who places own machines in various installations in a community or facility. Responsible for locating new machine sites, developing good public relations for the firm by handling complaints, maintaining quality control of the product and proper functioning of the machines. Handles cash funds and keeps required records.

Vice President Plans, formulates, and recommends for approval of the President basic policies and programs which will further the objectives of the company. Executes decisions of the President and Board of Directors. Develops, in cooperation with the President and supervisors, an annual budget, and operates within the annual budget upon approval. Recommends changes in the overall organizational structure to the President. Approves public relations programs.

Vice President of Account Services Oversees the promotion, sales, and service of a product line to a variety of customers within a defined geographical area. Develops and seeks out business of a highly complex nature and of importance to the company. Ensures efficient servicing of all accounts, once obtained. Prepares programs for training and development of the field managers and other new and experienced personnel.

Vice President of Communications Ensures the development and execution of advertising, public relations, public affairs, and members' relations' programs, together with effective internal and external communications to promote understanding, acceptance, and support of corporate activities and objectives by employees and the subscribing public.

Vice President of Finance Acts under authority and responsibility delegated by corporate executive office. Conducts management studies, prepares workload and budget esti-

mates for specified or assigned operation, analyzes operational reports, and submits activity reports. Develops and recommends plans for expansion of existing programs, operations, and financial activities.

Vice President of Human Resources Develops Human Resources policies and programs for the entire company. The major areas covered are organizational planning, organizational development, employment, indoctrination and training, employee relations, compensation, benefits, safety and health, and employee services. Originates Human Resources practices and objectives which will provide a balanced program throughout all divisions. Coordinates implementation through Human Resources staff. Assists and advises senior management of Human Resources issues.

Vice President of Marketing (Hospitality) In addition to overseeing the sales function, also coordinates the advertising, public relations, publicity, and community relations for the hotel. (See **Vice President of Marketing**)

Vice President of Marketing/Sales Represents the marketing function's needs in the development of corporate policy. Formulates sales goals, marketing plans, and strategy and directs the execution of these areas for the achievement of corporate marketing objectives. Manages the sales force to achieve marketing and sales goals for assigned products.

Vice President of Merchandising Manages several divisions of merchandise. Responsible for planning and giving buyers both fashion and financial direction. Plans sales, inventory, and marketing by store, based on the turnover desires. Plans markups and ensures that inventory supports sales efforts.

Vice President of Operations Directs the formulation of corporate policies, programs, and procedures as they relate to distribution, operations, research, production, engineering, and purchasing. Maximizes group and divisional short- and long-range growth and profitability.

Vice President of Production Plans, directs, and controls production and related support functions to provide timely manufacturing and delivery of output at lowest possible costs. Manages, controls, and reviews all assigned resources: staff, technical, material, and financial. Manages budgets and expense control to ensure effective meeting of operating objectives.

Vice President of Sales Responsible for the selling of the output of several different manufacturing facilities. Must develop effective sales policies which result in each plant's producing the optimum profit. Determines final prices and works closely with the sales staff, the production, scheduling, and traffic staffs and research and development personnel. After the initial sale is made, the sales staff assumes continuing sales effort to such accounts.

Wage and Salary Administrator Maintains files of updated job descriptions. Ensures that responsibilities are appropriately compensated according to established standards.

Participates in and reviews local and national salary surveys to set current salary standards and pay rates for each position within the organization. Processes salary increases or other changes for personnel according to established policies.

Warehousing/Operations Manager Determines and develops distribution strategies and practices that will support the corporate objective. Responsibilities include: identifying areas within the company that offer some opportunity for improvement; optimizing investments in all locations, in inventory, facilities, and people; and matching the corporate distribution support capabilities to the outgoing marketing, business, and operational needs. Makes use of financial and computer expertise in evaluating projects and allocation of resources.

Watchman Responsible for security in buildings and grounds.

Window Trimmer Displays merchandise in windows or showcases of retail stores to attract attention of prospective customers. Originates display ideas or follows suggestions or schedule of manager. Arranges mannequins, furniture, merchandise, and backdrop according to prearranged or own ideas. Constructs or assembles prefabricated displays.

Wine Steward Administers scheduling of all bar personnel, both on regular shifts and for catering work, and keeps records of their hours. Responsible for hiring, firing, and training all bar personnel, keeping customer account files, maintaining liquor and wine storage, setting standards, and ensuring that they are maintained.

Word Processing Center Manager Responsible for word-processing support given to a function or a number of departments. Trains and motivates personnel; maintains good working regulations with departments being serviced, and administers basic first-line management responsibilities. Develops new procedures, keeps records, and orders supplies.

Word Processor Uses computers and specialized word processing equipment to enter, edit, store, and revise correspondence, statistical tables, reports, forms, and other materials. Word processing systems include keyboard, a cathode ray tube (CRT) for display, and a printer. Some equipment also has telecommunications hookups and scanners to ready manuscripts.

Section D

....

Career Resources

Books

Corwen, Leonard. *Your Resume: Key to a Better Job.* 4th ed. New York: Prentice Hall, 1991.

Duncan, Melba J., with Kathleen Moloney. *How to Succeed in Business as an Executive Assistant.* New York: Macmillan Publishing Co., 1989.

duPont, M. Kay. *Business Etiquette and Professionalism.* Los Altos, CA: Crisp Publications, 1990.

Ettinger, Blanche. *Opportunities in Customer Service Careers.* Lincolnwood, IL: NTC Publishing Group, 1992.

Eyler, David R. *Job Interviews That Mean Business.* New York: Random House, 1992.

_____. *Résumés That Mean Business.* New York: Random House, 1992.

Field, Shelly. *100 Best Careers for the Year 2000.* New York: Prentice Hall, 1992.

Fruehling, Rosemary T. *Working at Human Relations.* 2nd ed. Eden Prairie, MN: Paradigm, 1991.

Fry, Ron. *Your First Interview.* Hawthorne, NJ: The Career Press, 1991.

Girard, Joe, with Robert Casemore. *How to Sell Yourself.* New York: Warner Books, 1992.

Gordon, Barbara. *Opportunities in Commercial Art and Graphic Design Careers.* Lincolnwood, IL: NTC Publishing Group, 1992.

Hansen, Katharine. *Dynamic Cover Letters.* Berkeley, CA: Ten Speed Press, 1990.

Haynes, Marion E. *Effective Meeting Skills.* Los Altos, CA: Crisp Publications, 1990.

Irish, Richard K. *Go Hire Yourself an Employer.* 3rd ed. New York: Doubleday, 1987.

Jackson, Carole, with Kalia Lulow. *Color for Men.* New York: Ballentine Books, 1984.

Krannick, Ronald L., and Caryl Rae. *Networking Your Way to Career Success.* Manassos, VA: Import Publications, 1989.

Lauber, Daniel. *Government Job Finder.* River Forest, IL: Planning/Communications, 1992.

Lock, Robert D. *Job Search: Career Planning Guide, Book II.* 2nd ed. New York: Brooks/Cole Publishing Co., 1991.

_____. *Student Activities for Taking Charge of Your Direction and Job Search, Book III.* 2nd ed. New York: Brooks/Cole Publishing Co., 1991.

Maddux, Robert B., and Dorothy Maddux. *Ethics in Business.* Los Altos, CA: Crisp Publications, Inc., 1990.

Marano, Hara Estroff. *Style Is Not a Size.* New York: Bantam Books, 1991.

Shea, Gordon F. *Mentoring.* Los Altos, CA: Crisp Publications, 1990.

Stevens, Mark. *The Big Six.* New York: Simon & Schuster, 1991.

Zemke, Ron. *The Service Edge: 101 Companies That Profit from Customer Care.* New York: Penguin Books USA, 1989.

Magazines

The Black Collegian. Black Collegiate Services, Inc., New Orleans, LA.

The Career Choices Newsletter. Career Choices Newsletter Co., Forest Hills, NY.

Careers and the Disabled. Equal Opportunity Publications, Inc., New York.

EEO Bimonthly: Technical and Business Career Opportunities. CRS Recruitment Publications/CASS Communications, Inc., Northbrook, IL.

Vitality. Vitality, Inc., Dallas, TX.

Working Woman. Working Woman, Inc., New York.

Reference Books

CPC Annual. Bethlehem, PA: College Placement Council.

Dictionary of Occupational Titles. 4th ed. Indianapolis, IN: U.S. Department of Labor, Employment and Training Administration. The JIST Search People, JIST Works, Inc., 1991.

Encyclopedia of Careers and Vocational Guidance. 8th ed., 4 vols. Largo, FL: Careers, Inc., 1990.

Section E

Bibliography

Books

Carnevale, Anthony P. *America and the New Economy*. U.S. Department of Labor Employment and Training Administration. Alexandria, VA: The American Society for Training and Development, 1991.

Carnevale, Anthony P.; Leila J. Gainer; Janice Villet; and Shari L. Holland. *Training Partnerships: Linking Employers and Providers*. U.S. Department of Labor Employment and Training Administration. Alexandria, VA: The American Society for Training and Development, 1990.

Crosby, Philip B. *Let's Talk Quality*. New York: McGraw-Hill, 1989.

Elsea, Janet, G. *The First Four Minutes. First Impression, Best Impression*. New York: Simon & Schuster, 1984.

Goldenkoff, Robert, and Dana Morgan. *Federal Jobs for College Graduates*. New York: Prentice Hall General Reference, 1991.

Harkavy, Michael. *101 Careers: A Guide to the Fastest-Growing Opportunities*. New York: John Wiley & Sons, 1990.

Hirsh, Sandra, and Jean Kummerow. *Life Types*. New York: Warner Books, 1989.

Kaponya, Paul. *How to Survive Your First 90 Days at a New Company*. Hawthorne, NJ: The Career Press, 1990.

Mollay, John T. *Dress for Success*. New York: Warner Books, 1988.

Petras, Kathryn, and Ross Petras. *Jobs '95*. New York: Prentice Hall, 1995.

Pollan, Stephen M., and Mark Levine. *Your Recession Handbook (How to Thrive and Profit during Hard Times)*. New York: William Morrow and Company, 1991.

Scheetz, Patrick L. *Recruiting Trends 1991–92*. 21st ed. East Lansing: Michigan State University, 1991.

Strasser, Stephen, and John Sena. *From Campus to Corporation*. Hawthorne, NJ: The Career Press, 1990.

U.S. Department of Labor and Bureau of Labor Statistics. *Occupational Outlook Handbook*. 1994–95 ed. Indianapolis: 1994 JIST Works, Inc., 1990.

Articles

Garber, Janet. "Workplace 1992." *Careers and the Disabled*. Greenlawn, NY: Equal Opportunity Publications, Inc., February 1992, pp. 14–17.

Gold, Carolyn. "Harness Your Stress." Company newsletter. Boston: The Sheraton Corporation, pp. 91–94.

Katz, Robert L. "Human Relations Skills Can Be Sharpened. People: Managing Your Most Important Asset." *Harvard Business Review,* 1990.

Special Edition: "Riding the Tide of Change." *The Wyatt Communicator,* Winter 1991, pp. 4–11.

Schlosberg, Jeremy. "Job Opportunity Index." *Career Futures,* Fall 1991, pp. 2–7.

U.S. Bureau of Labor Statistics. *Occupational Projections and Training Data,* pamphlet (Washington, D.C.: U.S. Government Printing Office, 1990).

Weis, William L. "No Ifs, Ands, or Butts. Why Workplace Smoking Should be Banned." *Best of Business Quarterly,* Summer 1986.

Index

Easy Steps to CHINESE

7 TEXTBOOK

轻松学中文

SIMPLIFIED
CHARACTERS
VERSION

Yamin Ma
Xinying Li

北京语言大学出版社
BEIJING LANGUAGE AND CULTURE
UNIVERSITY PRESS

图书在版编目 (CIP) 数据

轻松学中文: 英文版. 第 7 册 / 马亚敏, 李欣颖编著
– 北京: 北京语言大学出版社, 2010.7 (2016.11 重印)
ISBN 978-7-5619-2791-5

Ⅰ.①轻... Ⅱ.①马... ②李... Ⅲ.①汉语–对外汉语教学
– 教材 Ⅳ.①H195.4

中国版本图书馆CIP数据核字（2010）第111053号

书　　名　**轻松学中文**. 课本. 第 7 册
责任编辑　王亚莉　侯晓娟
美术策划　王　宇
封面设计　王　宇　王章定
版式设计　北京鑫联必升文化发展有限公司
责任印制　汪学发

出版发行　**北京语言大学出版社**
社　　址　北京市海淀区学院路15号　邮政编码：100083
网　　址　www.blcup.com

电　　话　编辑部 010-8230 3647/3592
　　　　　发行部 010-8230 3650/3591/3651/3080
　　　　　读者服务部 010-8230 3653/3908
网上订购　010-8230 3908　service@blcup.com
印　　刷　北京联兴盛业印刷股份有限公司
经　　销　全国新华书店

版　　次　2010年7月第1版　2016年11月第5次印刷
开　　本　787mm×1092mm　1/16　印张：15.25
字　　数　228千字
书　　号　ISBN 978-7-5619-2791-5/H.10166
　　　　　14800

© 2010 北京语言大学出版社

Easy Steps to Chinese (Textbook 7)
Yamin Ma, Xinying Li

Editor　　　　　Yali Wang, Xiaojuan Hou
Art design　　　Arthur Y. Wang
Cover design　　Arthur Y. Wang, Zhangding Wang
Graphic design　Beijing Xinlianbisheng Cultural Development Co. Ltd.

Published by
Beijing Language & Culture University Press
No.15 Xueyuan Road, Haidian District, Beijing, China 100083

Distributed by
Beijing Language & Culture University Press
No.15 Xueyuan Road, Haidian District, Beijing, China 100083

First published in July 2010

Printed in China
Copyright © 2010 Beijing Language & Culture University Press

Website: www.blcup.com

ACKNOWLEDGEMENTS

A number of people have helped us to put the books into publication. Particular thanks are owed to the following:

- 戚德祥先生、张健女士、苗强先生 who trusted our expertise in the field of Chinese language teaching and learning

- Editors 王亚莉女士、侯晓娟女士 for their meticulous work

- Graphic designers 王宏伟先生、闫海涛先生 for their artistic design

- Art consultant Arthur Y. Wang and artists 陆颖、顾海燕、龚华伟、袁林 for their artistic ability in the illustrations

- 付丽女士、王彤先生 who assisted with the sound recording

- And finally, members of our families who have always given us generous support.

INTRODUCTION

- *Easy Steps to Chinese* includes 8 books and has three stages: Stage 1–Books 1 and 2; Stage 2–Books 3, 4, 5 and 6; and Stage 3–Books 7 and 8. The primary goal of this series *Easy Steps to Chinese* is to help the students establish a solid foundation of vocabulary, knowledge of Chinese and communication skills through the natural and gradual integration of language, content and cultural elements. This series adopts a holistic approach, and is designed to emphasize the development of communication skills in listening, speaking, reading and writing.

- *Easy Steps to Chinese* comprises 8 colour textbooks, each of which is supplemented by a CD, a workbook (starting from Book 6, the textbook and workbook are combined into one book), a teacher's book with unit tests and a CD. Books 1–3 are also accompanied by picture flashcards, word cards and posters.

- 《轻松学中文》共八册，分为三个阶段。第一阶段为第一、二册；第二阶段为第三、四、五、六册；第三阶段为第七、八册。此套教材旨在帮助汉语为非母语的中、小学生奠定扎实的汉语学习基础。此目标是通过语言、话题和文化的自然结合，从词汇、汉语知识的学习及语言交流技能的培养两个方面来达到的。此套教材把汉语作为一个整体来教授，在教学过程中十分注重听、说、读、写四项交际技能的培养。

- 《轻松学中文》每册包括一本彩色课本（附一张CD），一本练习册（第六、七、八册课本与练习册合并成一册），一本教师用书（附单元测验试卷及一张CD），1–3册还配有词语卡片、图卡和教学挂图。

COURSE DESIGN

课程设计

The design of this series has achieved:

本套教材的课程设计力图达到：

- **A balance between authentic and modified language**
  All the oral and written materials have been modified and carefully selected to suit the students' level, so that a gradual development of the target language can be achieved.

- **A balance of focus on language and culture**
  This series provides ample opportunities for the students to experience the language and its culture in order to develop intercultural awareness and enrich their personal experience.

- **A balance between language knowledge and communication skills**
  Explicit knowledge of the target language is necessary and important for the students to achieve accuracy, fluency and overall communication skills. This series is designed to ensure that knowledge-based language learning is placed within a communicative context, resulting in the improvement of both linguistic knowledge and performance.

- **A balance between a broad and controlled course**
  This series serves as a core while offering a broad range of vocabulary, topics and various text types to meet the different needs of the students.

- 地道语言与调整语言的平衡
  为了使学生的汉语程度能循序渐进地提高，本套教材中的口语及书面语都经过严谨的选择，并作过适当的调整。

- 语言与文化的平衡
  为了培养学生的多元文化意识，丰富他们的经历，本套教材为学生接触汉语及中国文化提供了各种各样的机会。

- 语言知识与交际能力的平衡
  为了能在听、说、读、写四项技能方面准确并流利地运用汉语，学生对语言知识的掌握不仅是重要的，而且也是必要的。本套教材把语言知识的学习与语言技能的培养巧妙地结合在一起，力求使学生在增加汉语知识的同时提高运用语言的能力。

- 扩展与控制的平衡
  本套教材不仅可以作为汉语教学的"主

- **A balance between the "oral speech" and the "written form"**
  This series aims to balance the importance of both oral and written communication skills. The development of writing skills is embedded in the course, while oral communication skills are being developed from the outset.

This series covers:

- *Pinyin* is introduced to the students from the very beginning. The *pinyin* above the Chinese characters is gradually removed to ensure a smooth transition.

- Chinese characters are taught according to the character formation system. Once the students have a good grasp of radicals and simple characters, they will be able to analyze most of the compound characters they encounter, and to memorize new characters in a logical way.

- Grammar and sentence structures are explained in note form. The students are expected to use correct grammar and compound sentence structures in both oral and written forms to communicate when their overall level of Chinese has steadily improved over the years.

- Dictionary skills are taught once they have learned radicals and simple characters. The students are encouraged to use dictionaries whenever appropriate in order to become independent learners.

- Typing skills are taught when the students have learned some basic knowledge of Chinese.

- Listening practice is designed to help the students develop their ability to infer meanings of unfamiliar words and content.

- Speaking practice involves students using Chinese to communicate their thoughts spontaneously in real-life situations with accuracy and fluency.

- Reading skills are developed through regular reading of simple passages to suit the students' level. Gradually, they will develop skills and confidence when reading articles in newspapers, magazines or on the Internet in order to expand their vocabulary and knowledge of modern China, and to get in touch with the current issues emerging within China and around the world.

- Writing skills are gradually developed through a process of guided writing on topics familiar to the students. Writing tasks will become easier, as the students learn to organize their thoughts coherently and logically, and develop the skills to select appropriate vocabulary, sentence structures and genres to construct an effective written piece with accuracy and fluency.

线", 而且所提供的大量词汇、话题及各式各样的文体还可满足不同水平学生的需要。

- "语"与"文"的平衡
  本套教材力图使学生在口语及书面语两个方面同时提高。写作能力及口头交际能力的培养贯穿始终。

本套教材所包括的内容有:

- 拼音是初级阶段教学重点之一。附在汉字上面的拼音将逐渐取消以确保平稳过渡。

- 汉字是根据汉字的结构来教授的。学生一旦掌握了一定数量的偏旁部首和独体字,他们就有能力分析遇到的大部分合体字,并能有条理地记忆新汉字。

- 语法及句型是以注解的方式来解释的。经过几年有条不紊的学习,学生可望在口头及书面交流时运用正确的语法及复合句型。

- 查字典、词典的技能是在学生学会了部分偏旁部首及独体字后才开始培养的。为了培养学生的独立学习能力,教师要经常鼓励学生自己查字典、词典来完成某项功课。

- 打字技能的培养是在学生已经掌握了一些汉语基本知识后才开始的。

- 听力练习力图培养学生猜生词的意思及文章内容的能力。

- 口语练习设计旨在培养学生用准确、流利的汉语在现实生活中跟人即兴沟通、交流。

- 阅读练习旨在鼓励学生养成每天阅读简短篇章的习惯,从而帮助学生提高阅读能力,树立阅读信心。高年级阶段,学生可望读懂报纸、杂志及因特网上的简短文章,以便扩大词汇量,增加对现代中国的了解。

- 写作能力的培养需要一个长期的过程。学生先在教师的指导下写他们所熟悉的话题,直到能够运用适当的词汇、语句、体裁,有条理地、准确地、恰当地、有效地交流思想。

The focus of each stage:

- Stage 1 (Books 1 and 2): ◆ *pinyin* ◆ strokes and stroke order ◆ the structures of Chinese characters ◆ tracing of characters ◆ radicals and simple characters ◆ dictionary skills ◆ typing skills ◆ listening skills ◆ speaking skills ◆ reading skills ◆ writing skills: guided writing assignments around 100 characters

- Stage 2 (Books 3, 4, 5 and 6): ◆ radicals and simple characters ◆ formation of phrases ◆ expansion of vocabulary ◆ grammar and sentence structures ◆ dictionary skills ◆ typing skills ◆ classroom instruction in Chinese ◆ listening skills ◆ speaking skills ◆ reading skills ◆ writing skills: guided writing assignments between 100–300 characters ◆ exposure to modern China and Chinese culture

- Stage 3 (Books 7 and 8): ◆ classroom instruction in Chinese ◆ expansion of vocabulary ◆ grammar and sentence structures ◆ dictionary skills ◆ typing skills ◆ listening and speaking skills through spontaneous interaction ◆ reading practice on a daily basis ◆ writing skills: independent writing assignments between 300-500 characters ◆ exposure to modern China and its culture ◆ contemporary topics: current issues around the world

每个阶段的教学重点：

- 第一阶段（第一、二册）：◆拼音 ◆笔画和笔顺 ◆字形结构 ◆描红 ◆偏旁部首和独体字 ◆查字典、词典 ◆打字 ◆听力 ◆口语 ◆阅读 ◆写作（100个字左右）

- 第二阶段（第三、四、五、六册）：◆偏旁部首和独体字 ◆词语构成 ◆词汇扩展 ◆语法及句型结构 ◆查字典、词典 ◆打字 ◆课堂用语 ◆听力 ◆口语 ◆阅读 ◆写作(100–300字) ◆接触现代中国和中国文化

- 第三阶段（第七、八册）：◆课堂用语 ◆词汇扩展 ◆语法及句型结构 ◆查字典、词典 ◆打字 ◆听力 ◆口语 ◆阅读 ◆独立写作(300–500字) ◆接触现代中国和中国文化 ◆时事

COURSE LENGTH

- This series is designed for non-Chinese background students at both primary and secondary levels. Book 1 starts with basic knowledge of Chinese. Primary school students in Grade 5 or 6, or secondary school students in Grade1 can start with Book 1.

- With three periods, of approximately three hours per week, most students will be able to complete one book within one academic year. Fast learners can spend less than a year completing one book. As the 8 books of this series are continuous and ongoing, each book can be taught within any time span.

课程进度

- 本套教材为非华裔中、小学生编写。因为第一册从最基本的汉语知识教起，所以学生不需要有任何汉语知识背景。学生可以从小学五、六年级开始使用第一册，也可以从中学一年级开始使用第一册。

- 如果每星期上三节课，每节课在一小时左右，大部分学生可在一年之内学完一册。如果有些学生学得比较快，他们可以加快进度，不到一年就学完一册书。由于本套教材是连贯的，老师可以在任何时段内根据学生的水平来决定教学进度。

HOW TO USE THIS BOOK

Here are a few suggestions as to how to use this book.

The teacher should:

- The text of each lesson should be studied thoroughly, and can also be used as a sample essay.

- The students should study the new words/phrases in the vocabulary list before listening to the recording of the text, and then study the text. After this, the students could carry out an oral practice guided by questions related to the topic.

- The section of "language points" in each lesson aims to help students review as well as learn new set phrases, sentence structures and grammar that appear in the text.

- An oral exercise in each lesson, which is accompanied by a sample dialogue and a set of sentences for reference, is designed to guide the students in carrying out their conversations or presentations.

- In order to help the students improve their reading comprehension skills, two pieces of reading passages are included in each lesson along with a variety of exercises.

- In each lesson, there are two types of writing exercises: one is an essay, which requires the use of a particular genre and the other is a written response.

- The book is filled with a variety of texts and reading passages that are related to everyday life so that the students can use Chinese to communicate appropriately and coherently.

- A wide variety of exercises can be modified or extended according to the students' levels.

- The text is on the CD attached to the book. The students can also scan the QR code on the front cover of the book to get the audio files. The symbol indicates the track number, for example, is track one.

Yamin Ma
July 2010, Hong Kong

怎样使用本册教材

以下是使用本册教材的一些教学建议，仅供教师参考。建议教师：

- 可以把每一课的课文当做精读来教，并把课文作为写作的范文。

- 在学每一课的课文之前，可以先教生词表中的字、词，然后让学生听课文录音。学完课文后，学生可以做"口语热身"中"根据课文回答问题"的练习，最后再做"根据实际情况回答问题"的练习。

- 每一课都配有"语言难点"，旨在帮助学生复习并掌握汉语的词语、句型及语法。

- 每一课配一个口语训练题，并附有对话范本及参考句子，旨在引导并帮助学生完成口语任务。

- 每一课配有两篇阅读理解文章，并配有不同类型的练习题，帮助学生提高阅读理解能力。

- 每一课配有两个写作训练，一个是有文体要求的作文，另一个是回应式作文。

- 整册书内容丰富，贴近现实生活，旨在培养学生运用汉语的综合能力。

- 在教学中，可以根据学生的能力及水平对一些练习作适当的调整或扩展，以符合学生的需要。

- 每一课的课文录音都附在CD里，亦可扫描封面正面二维码下载。课文录音部分均附有标记和轨迹编号，例如，表示轨迹1。

马亚敏
2010年7月于香港

CONTENTS 目录

[1] 尊敬的招生部主任：

您好！

我叫王月，在上海国际学校读十二年级。我申请到贵校的医学院学临床医学专业。

[5] 我父母都是医生。我父亲是心脏科专家，我母亲是儿科医生。自从上了中学以后，我开始对医学感兴趣。在学校，我选修了生物、化学和物理课程。我相信，通过我的努力，这三门课都会取得优异的成绩。除了学习这些课程以外，我还参加了好几项课外活动。

[10] 为了熟悉医生这个职业，我利用假期及课余时间到本地一家公立医院见习。我还订阅医学杂志，目的是想了解医学的最新动向。我在学校专门学了紧急救护课程，并取得了证书。学校每次举行越野赛跑、田径运动会、露营等活动，我总是紧急救护小组的一员。我从中

[15] 积累了不少经验，也更坚定了学医的决心。

我是一个学习勤奋、工作踏实的人。我自信、胆大、心细、有责任心。我追求完美，乐于接受挑战，而且能跟别人合作。从初中到高中，我当过班长、级长，

[20] 还负责并组织过学校的开放日、文化节、筹款等活动。

我坚信自己是学医的最佳人选，因为我出身于医生家庭，对医学有热情，而且

[25] 也为学医作好了一切准备。如果贵校能接受我的申请，我一定会加倍努力，把这门

第一单元
第1课

学科学好。我盼望贵校能给我面试的机会。

　　　　此致

[30] 敬礼!

　　　　　　　　　　　　　　　　　　王月

　　　　　　　　　　　　　　　2010年2月4日

生词

1. 招生 zhāoshēng enroll new students
*2. 贵（貴）guì your (respectfully)
3. 临（臨）lín be faced with
　临床 lín chuáng clinical
4. 医学 yī xué medical science
5. 父亲 fù qin father
*6. 脏（臟）zàng internal organs　心脏 xīn zàng heart
7. 专家 zhuān jiā expert; specialist
8. 母亲 mǔ qin mother
9. 儿科 ér kē (department of) paediatrics
10. 优异 yōu yì excellent; outstanding
11. 假期 jià qī vacation; holiday
12. 课余 kè yú spare time; leisure time
13. 公立 gōng lì public
14. 订阅 dìng yuè subscribe to (a newspaper, a periodical, etc.)
15. 动向 dòng xiàng trend
16. 紧急 jǐn jí urgent; emergent
　紧急救护 jǐn jí jiù hù first aid
17. 证书 zhèng shū certificate
18. 坚（堅）jiān firm　坚定 jiān dìng firm
19. 勤 qín diligent

20. 奋（奮）fèn exert oneself
　勤奋 qín fèn diligent
21. 踏 tā settle down
　踏实 tā shí steady and sure
22. 胆（膽）dǎn courage　胆大 dǎn dà bold
23. 细（細）xì thin; careful
　心细 xīn xì careful
24. 追 zhuī pursue　追求 zhuī qiú pursue
25. 完美 wán měi perfect
26. 班长 bān zhǎng class monitor
27. 开放 kāi fàng open　开放日 kāi fàng rì Open Day
28. 坚信 jiān xìn firmly believe
29. 佳 jiā good; fine　最佳 zuì jiā best
30. 人选 rén xuǎn candidate
31. 出身 chū shēn family background
32. 热情 rè qíng enthusiasm; enthusiastic
*33. 而且 ér qiě besides
34. 倍 bèi times　加倍 jiā bèi double
35. 盼 pàn hope　盼望 pàn wàng long for
36. 面试 miàn shì interview
37. 敬礼 jìng lǐ send greetings

3

口语热身

消化课文

1. 根据课文回答问题

1) 王月写这封信的目的是什么？

2) 王月是从什么时候开始对医学感兴趣的？为了考医学院，她选修了哪些课程？

3) 为了学医，王月作了哪些准备？举两个例子。

4) 通过参加紧急救护活动，王月有哪些收获？

5) 王月的性格怎样？列举三项。

6) 王月以前组织过哪些学校活动？

2. 根据实际情况回答问题

1) 你打算申请哪几所大学？你为什么对这几所大学感兴趣？

2) 你想在大学里学什么专业？你是从什么时候开始对这个专业感兴趣的？你是怎样在课余时间为学这个专业作准备的？

3) 你的性格有什么特点？你大学毕业后打算做什么工作？你觉得你适合做这种工作吗？为什么？

4) 你出身于什么样的家庭？你父母的工作对你有何影响？

5) 你今年选择了哪些课外活动？通过这些课外活动，你从中积累了哪些经验？

6) 你在学校负责过什么活动？你对今年学校的哪项活动最满意？你为这项活动做了什么？

7) 你见习过吗？在何时、何地做的见习？通过见习，你积累了什么经验？见习对你今后选择大学专业有什么帮助？

8) 假期你一般怎么过？如果让你选择，做义工或外出旅游，你会怎么选择？为什么？

1. 完成句子

Ⓐ 例子：我申请到贵校的医学院学临床医学专业。
(第3行)

我申请到贵公司 _____。

Ⓑ 例子：自从上了中学以后，我开始对医学感兴趣。(第6行)

自从这个学期以来，_____。

Ⓒ 例子：我相信，通过我的努力，这三门课都会取得优异的成绩。(第7行)

通过见习，_____ _____。

Ⓓ 例子：我到本地一家公立医院见习。(第11行)

本校是一所____。

Ⓔ 例子：我在学校专门学了紧急救护课程，并取得了证书。(第12行)

我组织了一个慈善活动，并_____。

Ⓕ 例子：我对医学有热情，而且也为学医作好了一切准备。(第24行)

我不但胆大、心细，而且_____。

2. 填空

Ⓐ 例子：我对医学感兴趣。(第6行)

Ⓑ 例子：我对医学有热情。(第24行)

对_____了解
对_____作简单的介绍

3. 选择其中一个短语造句

Ⓐ 例子：为了熟悉医生这个职业，我利用假期到本地一家公立医院见习。(第10行)

为了取得紧急救护证书/获得筹款

Ⓑ 例子：我乐于接受挑战，而且能跟别人合作。
(第17行)

跟……说汉语/聊天儿

4. 从课文中找反义词

1) 结束→(　　　)(第6行)　　4) 懒惰→(　　　)(第16行)

2) 必修→(　　　)(第7行)　　5) 胆小→(　　　)(第16行)

3) 私立→(　　　)(第11行)　　6) 冷淡→(　　　)(第24行)

口语训练

角色扮演

　　假设你写了一封大学入学申请信给某大学。今天招生部主任要对你进行面试。你的面试要谈及以下几点：

- 打算选择的专业
- 为选择这个专业作的准备，包括课程、课外活动等
- 你的性格
- 被录取后的打算

（注：可以把课文改编成对话。）

例子：

主任：你好！我是招生部主任。我姓黄。

你：黄主任，您好！谢谢您给我这个面试的机会。

主任：你是从什么时候开始对医学感兴趣的？

你：自从上了中学以后。我出身在一个医生家庭：我爸爸是心脏科专家，我妈妈是儿科医生。

主任：那你为学医做了哪些准备工作？

你：在高中阶段，我选修了生物、化学和物理课程。这些都是学医学的必修课，而且我的成绩一直都很优秀。

主任：你对医学有哪些认识？

你：我从前年开始订阅医学杂志，电视上有关医学的节目，我是一定要看的。我对心脏科特别感兴趣。现在的医学越来越发达，在心脏科方面有很多发展的空间。

主任：你参加过哪些课外活动？

你：我参加、组织过很多校级

活动。在学校，我专门学了紧急救护课程，并获得了证书。每次学校组织大型的活动，我都是急救小组的负责人。我还在本地一家公立医院见习。

主任：你的性格怎么样？

你：我是一个学习勤奋、工作踏实的人。我很自信，胆大、心细，有责任心。我还是个完美主义者，对自己的要求特别高。

主任：讲一讲你觉得我们为什么应该录取你，好吗？

你：我为学医作好了一切准备。在学习方面，我读了学医的必修课。我对医学的新动向很了解。经过在医院三个月的见习，我更坚定了学医的决心。

主任：如果你被录取了，有什么打算？

你：除了读必修课以外，我会选修心理学和汉语。第一年的暑假，我会去北京天坛医院见习，积累经验。

主任：谢谢你来面试。我们会在下周一通知你面试结果。

你：谢谢您给我这个机会。我对医学有热情，而且我已经准备好了。我一定不会让你们失望。

参考句子

a) 我从小酷(kù ài)爱音乐。我的理想是将来做一名小提琴家。

b) 除了读这六门课程以外，我还参加了 150 个小时的课外活动。我用中文写了一篇专题论文，题目叫"中国传统节日与文化"。

c) 通过这些活动，我学会了怎样跟别人合作，还认识到只有认真才能把工作做好。

d) 虽然我的学习负担很重，还有其他任务，比如做义工、参与各种慈善活动等，但是我在高中阶段学会了怎样有效、合理地管理时间。

e) 通过这些活动，我发现自己的性格比以前开朗多了，做事比以前更有信心了，自理能力也提高了。这些活动培养了我的责任心、爱心和团队精神。在参加这些活动的过程中，我也放松了自己，减轻了压力。

f) 我对教育事业很有热情。请相信我，我一定会加倍努力，争取成为一名好老师。

写作训练

1. 写正式的书信

假设你想去中国的一所大学参加汉语短训班。你从网上了解到了短训班的课程，但是你还有一些问题要问。请给这所大学的招生部主任写一封信，在信里你要提及：

- 你学汉语的经历及汉语水平
- 参加汉语短训班的理由
- 询问 (xún wèn) 有关课程、食宿等方面的问题

参考句子

a) 我从网上看到了你们学院开设的汉语短训班。我想咨询 (zī xún) 一下关于课程的一些问题。

b) 我已经学了五年汉语了。我平时在学校学汉语，除此以外，每个星期还有一次补习。我大概学了一千个汉字，能读一些简单的短文。

c) 我的听力和阅读能力比较强，我希望能进一步提高口语和写作水平。

d) 我觉得汉语很有用。我相信如果我会说汉语，以后找工作会容易一些。所以，我决心把汉语学好。我会继续努力，不断提高我的汉语水平。

e) 我想知道你们能否安排我住在本地人的家里。这样的话，除了上课，我平时还可以练习口语。短训班期间你们是否会组织观光、旅游？

f) 我还想知道参加这个短训班是否有入学考试，会考哪些内容。

2. 阅读下面的采访内容并写回应式作文

假设你现在在国外留学。你听说国内的一个朋友也正为出国留学作准备。写信告诉他/她应该为出国作哪些准备，并根据亲身体会提一些建议。

出国留学的挑战

（在上海的一家出国留学中心） [1]

各位同学，今天我们有幸请来了80年代走出国门留学的王美华女士，为在座的各位解答有关出国留学方面的疑问。请大家欢迎。

学生1：请问王女士，您认为学生出国以前一般要作哪些准备？

王：我觉得在国内时就要把英语练好，如有可能，掌握二外就 [5]
更有利。如果口语不过关，到了国外很难跟外国学生和老
师进行交流，不利于学习。还有，出国前要作好心理上的
准备。由于文化上的差异，国外的一些情况跟想象中的可
能不同。最后，要设法事先与那里的中国学生组织取得联
系，了解一些具体的情况。 [10]

学生2：请问到了国外怎样才能尽快适应环境？

王：这也是很多留学生出国后面临的第一个问题。到了国外，
除了要跟中国学生接触、交往之外，还要尽量融入非华
人的社交圈，这样就能很快地熟悉、了解当地的文化和习
俗。还有，在国外留学不能像在国内一样只管埋头读书， [15]
而要主动与周围不同文化背景的人交流。

学生3：请问拿到国外的学位后是否肯定能找到工作？

王：拿到了国外的学位并不等于你能找到工作。由于中国越来
越开放以及世界经济的全球化，接受过国际化教育、具
备不同文化背景的年轻人将是就业市场上的抢手人才。 [20]
同学们一定注意到了，如今在国内拥有国外学位的人越来
越多，就业市场竞争也越来越激烈。我建议同学们毕业后
尝试通过实习来寻找适合自己的就业方向。想考研的同
学不一定本科毕业后马上考，可尝试工作或实习一年，同
时考虑清楚将来自己到底想做什么。 [25]

9

阅读与理解

[1]　　人人都知道，热门专业确实吸引不少人去学，因为热门专业的毕业生比较容易找　①　，工作待遇好，社会地位高，工资也高。然而，在选　②　专业时学生一定要考虑以下两个　③　：

1. "热门" 是变化的

[5]　　如果某行业人才紧缺，用人单位就会用高薪聘请，所以就有很多人去学该专业，这就形成了热门专业。但是，几年后，学这个专业的人多了，就业市场不缺这方面的人才了，这个　④　也有可能成为冷门。所以，这几年的热门专业过几年可能就不再热门了。

2. "热门" 专业是否适合你

[10]　　有些热门专业不一定适合你，所以不要头脑发热去追赶潮流，而应该冷静考虑以下四个问题：

　　a) 该热门专业符合自己的　⑤　、爱好吗？如果你对该专业很感兴趣，即使这个专业将来不热门了，工作后你也会做得很好。

　　b) 该热门专业是否符合你的学习动机？如果是，你一定会为该专业奋斗。

[15]

　　c) 你有　⑥　学好这个专业吗？如果没有，那么你以后也不可能做好相应的工作。

　　d) 你的性格适合从事这个专业的工作吗？如果不适合，最好不要学习这个专业。

[20]　　当今世界，国际化程度越来越高，就业市场变化很快，没有人能准确断定三五年后什么专业会热、什么专业会冷。因此，选择适合自己的专业关系到你今后的前途。

从下面的方框里为短文选择最合适的词语填空

```
能力    方面    大学    专业
  问题   回答   工作   兴趣
```

1. _____   2. _____   3. _____

4. _____   5. _____   6. _____

B 从右边找到最适合的部分完成下列句子

1. 目前这个专业热门，□   A 读热门专业。

2. 如果一个人是做老   B 但不一定一直是热门专业。
   师的料，   □   C 将来哪个专业会变得热门。

3. 不是每个人都适合 □   D 他一定要读热门专业。

4. 谁也不知道   □   E 找工作可能会比较难。

                                    F 他将来很有可能成为一个好老师。

C 根据短文回答问题

1. 为什么现在的年轻人喜欢读热门专业？

2. 热门专业过几年为什么会变成冷门专业？

3. 选择专业时，高中毕业生为什么要考虑自己的兴趣爱好？

4. 如果一个人读了某一个热门专业，他今后有没有可能做不好这个专业
   的工作？为什么？

D 判断正误，并说明原因

1. 一般人认为学热门专业的大学毕业生比较容易找工作。 róng yì 对　错

   原因：＿＿＿＿＿＿＿＿＿＿＿＿＿＿＿＿＿＿＿＿＿＿＿ ＿　＿

2. 由于人才市场某一个专业的人才紧缺，那么这个专业会变 jǐn quē

   成热门专业。

   原因：＿＿＿＿＿＿＿＿＿＿＿＿＿＿＿＿＿＿＿＿＿＿＿ ＿　＿

3. 如果你的志向正好是现在的热门专业，你以后很有可能会 zhì xiàng

   学好这个专业，干好这一行。

   原因：＿＿＿＿＿＿＿＿＿＿＿＿＿＿＿＿＿＿＿＿＿＿＿ ＿　＿

4. 在选择读哪个专业时，学生不应该考虑自己的性格。

   原因：＿＿＿＿＿＿＿＿＿＿＿＿＿＿＿＿＿＿＿＿＿＿＿ ＿　＿

E 用短文中的动词填空

1. ＿＿＿＿＿＿（第1行）大学生　　　5. ＿＿＿＿＿＿（第7行）画家

2. ＿＿＿＿＿＿（第3行）就业问题　　6. ＿＿＿＿＿＿（第9行）当老师

3. ＿＿＿＿＿＿（第5行）校长　　　　7. ＿＿＿＿＿＿（第12行）兴趣

4. ＿＿＿＿＿＿（第6行）习惯　　　　8. ＿＿＿＿＿＿（第21行）专业

F 为短文配题目

☐ 1. 大学生大都读热门专业

☐ 2. 如何看待热门专业 kàn dài

☐ 3. 热门专业是就业市场的需要

☐ 4. 热门专业跟冷门专业之间的关系

12

90后大学生的特点

2009年9月，中国的高校终于向期待已久的90后大学生敞开了大门。90后大学生有些什么特点呢？　　　　　　　　　　　　　　[1]

他们中有些人从接到大学录取通知书那天起，就开始收到亲朋好友送来的红包以及各种实用的礼物，比如电脑、手机、数码相机及音乐播放器。这些装备在这一代人眼里已不算奢侈品了。　　　[5]

进入大学之前，90后的大学生提前作好了各种准备。他们有的在暑假期间考驾照、学外语，还有的外出打工赚钱。他们说打工并不仅仅是为了赚钱，重要的是通过这种方式接触社会，创造条件去适应社会，同时也锻炼自己的能力。还有的学生计划赚了钱后去外地旅游，见见世面。　　　　　　　　　　　　　　　　　　　　[10]

大部分即将入学的大学生为自己的未来生活定了一个明确的目标。有些学生表示，上了大学后，除了努力学习，还要多关注并参加学校及社会活动，如参加社团组织或环保等公益活动。他们心里明白，如今大学毕业生就业竞争十分激烈。将来找工作时，一个人的工作经验和能力有时比学历更重要。因此，他们认为考上大学只是人生　[15]
新里程的第一步。现在社会发展很快，每个人都要尽早培养能力，把握机会，这样才能争取日后成功。

针对90后的特点，一些专家提醒将要入学的大学生，第一，消费不要太超前，要学会理财，花钱不能大手大脚；第二，要自觉学习，并尝试做一个职业规划；第三，既要学会独立，又要学会如何与人　[20]
打交道，与人愉快合作。

13

1. 期待已久 (第1行) ^{qī dài} ☐ | A 将来的光景。

2. 奢侈品 (第5行) ^{shē chǐ} ☐ | B 很会花钱。

3. 未来 (第11行) ^{wèi lái} ☐ | C 已经盼望了很长一段时间。 ^{pàn wàng}

4. 人生新里程 (第15行) ^{lǐ chéng} ☐ | D 对人大方。

5. 花钱大手大脚 (第19行) ☐ | E 花费很多钱才能买到的东西。

| F 期望过高。 ^{qī wàng}

| G 人生中一个新的阶段。 ^{jiē duàn}

B 判断正误，并说明原因

1. 亲朋好友常常会用送礼的方式来祝贺那些被大学录取的学   对   错

   生。

   原因：_____ ___ ___

2. 上大学之前，有些学生已经拿到了驾驶执照。 ^{jià shǐ zhí zhào}

   原因：_____

3. 有些学生打工赚了钱后去国外游山玩水。 ^{zhuàn}

   原因：_____

4. 每个即将入学的大学生对未来生活都制订了一个目标。 ^{zhì dìng}

   原因：_____

5. 如今找工作时，一个人只要有学历就行了。

   原因：_____

1. 90后的大学生是_____出生的。
   a) 二十世纪九十年代
   b) 十九世纪
   c) 2009年

2. 亲朋好友送的礼物有_____。
   a) 手机、电脑、收音机
   b) 音乐播放器(bō fàng qì)、电脑、录像机
   c) 相机(xiàng jī)、手机、电脑

3. 有些大学生上大学时会_____。
   a) 外出旅游
   b) 参加各种各样的活动
   c) 学开车

4. 有些大学生购物不考虑_____。
   a) 式样
   b) 他们的经济能力
   c) 父母的感受

D 从短文中选出最合适的动词填空

1. 你被北大_____（第3行）了，我为你高兴。

2. 我最近_____（第8行）了大量(dà liàng)关于中国历史的资料。

3. 进入大学后，你应该为自己_____（第11行）一个计划。

4. 全社会应该_____（第12行）青年人的就业问题。

5. 我这个学期_____（第12行）了很多课外活动。

6. 近几十年来，中国的经济_____（第16行）很快。

E 根据短文回答问题

1. 已被大学录取的学生在入学前一般会作哪些准备？（列出两项）

2. 在大学期间，除了学习以外，他们还会做些什么？（列出两项）

3. 大部分新生怎样看待(kàn dài)考上大学这件事？

4. 在人际交往方面，一些专家给新生提出了什么建议？

第一单元
第2课

[1] 老师们、同学们：

你们好！

我希望大家听完我的演讲之后，对我有一个更全面的了解，并确信我是下一届学生会主席的最佳人选。

[5] 首先，我是同学们中的一员。你们关心的事就是我关心的事。作为学生，我们对学校的一些事情不太满意。很多同学抱怨学校餐厅里卖的食物品种少，而且绝大部分都很油腻，价钱也不合理。如果我当上了学生会主席，我会跟学校餐厅的负责人商讨，要求他们改进。我们学校的厕

[10] 所卫生状况也不够好，我会要求学校增加清洁的次数。除此以外，我会跟环保小组合作，经常开展节电、回收、美化校园等活动。还有，学校的娱乐活动不够丰富。学生会应该为同学们组织更多的活动，

[15] 比如周末主题舞会、歌唱比赛、话剧演出等。

其次，我参加和组织过很多活

[20] 动，积累了不少工作经验。我是一个诚实、工作踏实、有责任心、组织能力强的

[25] 人，而且周围有

16

很多能干的同学帮助我。我相信通过我们的合作和共同的努力，一定能实现大家的愿望。

最后，我善于跟人沟通。为了配合学校的工作，我会定期跟每个班级的学生会代表开会，听取他们的意见，并把同学们的想法 [30] 和建议及时转达给校方。如果大家给我这个机会，我会感到非常荣幸，并乐意为同学们服务。

谢谢大家！

生词

1. 演讲 yǎn jiǎng speech
2. 确（確）què surely
   确信 què xìn be sure
*3. 抱 bào hold
4. 怨 yuàn resentment
   抱怨 bàoyuàn complain
5. 品种 pǐn zhǒng variety
6. 绝（絕）jué most
   绝大部分 jué dà bù fen vast majority
7. 腻（膩）nì greasy
   油腻 yóu nì greasy
8. 商讨 shāng tǎo discuss
9. 状（狀）zhuàng state; shape
   状况 zhuàngkuàng condition
10. 增 zēng increase
    增加 zēng jiā increase
11. 次数 cì shù frequency
12. 开展 kāi zhǎn carry out

13. 美化 měi huà beautify
14. 校园 xiàoyuán campus
15. 舞会 wǔ huì dance; ball
16. 歌唱 gē chàng sing (a song)
17. 话剧 huà jù stage play
18. 诚（誠）chéng honest; sincere
    诚实 chéng shí honest
19. 能干 nénggàn capable; competent
20. 共同 gòngtóng common
21. 实现 shí xiàn realize; achieve
22. 愿望 yuànwàng desire; wish
23. 善于 shàn yú be good at
24. 定期 dìng qī regularly
25. 班级 bān jí class
26. 想法 xiǎng fǎ idea; opinion
27. 及时 jí shí timely
28. 转达 zhuǎn dá pass on
29. 荣（榮）róng honour　荣幸 róngxìng be honoured

17

口语热身

消化课文

1. 根据课文回答问题

1) 同学们对学校的哪些事情不满意？列出至少两项。

2) 演讲者从哪几个方面来说服同学们他是学生会主席的最佳人选？

3) 同学们对学校的餐厅有哪些不太满意的地方？

4) 如果能当上学生会主席，演讲者会在环保方面做些什么工作？

5) 如果能当上学生会主席，演讲者将怎样丰富同学们的课余生活？

6) 如果能当上学生会主席，演讲者将怎样跟学生及校方沟通？

2. 根据实际情况回答问题

1) 你们学校组织学生会选举吗？选举在每年的什么时候举行？哪个年级的学生可以参与学生会主席的选举？

2) 今年谁是你们学校的学生会主席？你觉得他/她是最佳人选吗？为什么？

3) 你们学校的学生会主席主要负责哪些活动？列出至少两项。

4) 你们学校的餐厅受学生欢迎吗？学生们对餐厅的服务满意吗？他们经常抱怨什么？

5) 你们学校的卫生状况好不好？平时教室里干净吗？有哪些需要改进的地方？

6) 你们学校经常开展哪些节电、回收及美化校园的活动？你参加过哪些活动？在环保方面，你觉得还有哪些需要改进的？

7) 你们学校每年都举行哪些大型的活动？哪些活动最受欢迎？你参加并组织过学校的哪些活动？从中学到些什么？

8) 你能跟周围的同学合作吗？假如你今年做了学生会主席，你会为学校做些什么？

1. 填空

Ⓐ例子：我希望大家听完我的演讲之后，对我有一个更全面的了解。（第3行）

我们对学校的一些事情不太满意。（第6行）

Ⓑ例子：我会跟环保小组合作。（第11行）

对_____熟悉

对_____要求很高

对_____满意

跟_____见面

跟_____联络

2. 用带点的词语模仿例子造句

Ⓐ例子：首先，我是同学们中的一员。（第5行）

其次，我参加和组织过很多活动。（第18行）

最后，我善于跟人沟通。（第28行）

Ⓑ例子：如果我当上了学生会主席，我会跟学校餐厅的负责人商讨，要求他们改进。

（第8行）

继父把我当做自己的亲生女儿。

3. 完成句子

例子：学生会应该为同学们组织更多的活动。

（第12行）

学校应该为学生开设_____。

4. 从课文中找反义词

1) 片面→(　　)（第3行）　　4) 减少→(　　)（第10行）

2) 不满→(　　)（第6行）　　5) 单调→(　　)（第12行）

3) 清淡→(　　)（第8行）　　6) 首先→(　　)（第28行）

5. 用课文中的动词填空

1) _____次数（第10行）　　4) _____经验（第20行）

2) _____活动（第13行）　　5) _____愿望（第27行）

3) _____比赛（第18行）　　6) _____意见（第29行）

实际运用

角色扮演

在这个口语练习中有三个角色：学生会主席，学生1和学生2。学生会主席顺利获选（huò xuǎn），他/她跟他/她的团队商量学生会应该怎样安排今后的工作。他们的讨论要谈及以下几点：

- 帮助改善（gǎi shàn）餐厅的食品供应（gōngyìng）
- 帮助改善厕所卫生
- 开展节约用电、用水活动
- 开展回收、利用活动
- 绿化、美化校园
- 组织丰富多彩的娱乐活动
- 配合学校的工作
- 定期召开（zhào kāi）学生代表会，听取意见和建议，并及时转达给校方

例子：

学生1：恭喜你成功当选（dāngxuǎn）为学生会主席。

主席：谢谢大家。没有大家的支持，我肯定选不上。我还需要你们继续支持。我们还有很多工作要做。

学生2：别担心，我们会一起合作、一起努力。我相信我们一定能把工作做好。

主席：我们先计划一下今年有哪些事情要做。

学生1：我认为现在头等（tóu děng）重要的事是同学们的健康，所以我们要尽快（jǐn kuài）跟学校餐厅沟通，让他们赶快改善食物供应。

主席：你说得对。我觉得学校的厕所卫生状况也很差，我们应该建议学校每天增加清洁厕所的次数。

学生2：还有，午饭过后我们发现教室里和餐厅里都很脏，垃圾到处都是。学校的回收箱也不够，学生浪费水、电的现象比

20

较严重。我们应该定一个目
标，比如说下个月节约10%
的水电费。

主席：　在绿化、美化学校方面，我
们应该在学校周围植树、种
花，把餐厅的旧桌椅换成新
的，把餐厅的墙壁粉刷一
下。这样学生的学习、生活
环境就更好了。

学生1：我们每个月应该为低年级的
同学组织一次周末主题舞
会，为他们提供社交、娱乐
的机会。

学生2：我很赞成你刚才说的。我还
觉得学生会应该定期跟每个
班的班长开会，听听他们的
意见和想法，并及时转告给
校方。

学生1：我们也应该常跟家长教师协
会联系，听听他们对学校有
什么看法及建议。学生会一
定要跟校方、家长教师协会
密切合作，积极配合学校的
工作。

主席：　看来，我们今年有很多工作
要做。

……

参考句子

a) 下个月我们学校要举办义
卖会，我们得赶快动手准
备。学生会每年都负责组
织学生表演、有奖比赛、
募捐、美食摊等活动，我
们应该想办法把今年的义
卖会办得更好。

b) 学生会成员可以分成几个
小组，有人负责做广告、
宣传工作；有人负责布置
学校；有人负责安排当天
的食物义卖；有人组织学
生乐队表演、歌唱比赛、
时装表演等；有人组织
每个班级的摊位；还有人
安排当天的清理工作。

c) 我们可以要求每个班级在
一年内至少开展一次慈善
活动，比如义卖糕饼、二
手货义卖等。

d) 高年级的同学应该为低年
级的同学多组织一些丰富多
彩的课外活动，一方面丰
富低年级同学的课余生活，
另一方面可以培养高年级
同学的组织、领导能力。

写作训练

1. 写电邮

写一封电邮给你在远方的朋友，告诉他/她你对学校的一些事情不满意，并表示自己有意参选（yǒu yì cān xuǎn）下一届学生会主席。你的电邮要提及以下几个方面：

- 对校长、学生会工作不满意
- 有意参选下一届学生会主席的理由（lǐ yóu）
- 希望听听朋友的意见

参考句子

a) 好久没有跟你联络了。你近来怎么样？

b) 我不太喜欢我们学校的新任校长，有不少同学也不喜欢他/她。他/她的有些想法、做法不太现实（xiàn shí），有时候太严格（yán gé）。他/她还规定（guī dìng）所有的高中生都要穿校服到学校。

c) 现任学生会主席很少跟其他学生会会员开会。他们在选举时保证要做的事都没有做到。有些学生会会员的组织能力和办事（bàn shì）能力挺强的，但是他们之间的合作不好。学生会主席挺能干的，但是靠他一个人也是办不好事情的。

d) 我在这个学校已经有五年了。如果我能当选学生会主席，是有能力领导学生会的，并能跟所有成员合作。我还会经常跟校方及家长教师协会（xié huì）沟通。

e) 我们是多年的老朋友，你对我最了解了。我很想听听你的看法和建议。

2. 阅读短文并写回应式作文

写一封申请信，表示你想参加第一届中国青年领袖大会，并说明为什么想参加，然后根据你的实际情况提出一些具体问题。

第一届中国青年领袖大会

由五位北京大学政法系毕业生倡导并组织的第一届中国青年 [1]
领袖大会将于2010年12月9日至12日在北京大学召开。此大会计划
每年举行一次，其目的是为关心国家及世界大事的有志青年大学
生提供一个平台，培养他们的领导才能。

第一届中国青年领袖大会期望吸引200~300名大学生参加。以 [5]
下是五天的议程安排：

第一天：参观北京市人民政府办公厅，并与政府官员讨论
全球化对中国的影响以及如何保持中国的文化传统。

第二天：分析中国目前的环境污染问题及环境保护措施，并
对今后如何更好地做好环保工作交换建议和看法。 [10]

第三天：参观外交学院，并跟外交学院专家就中国在国际舞台
上的地位、与各国之间的关系及最近发生的国际重大事件进行讨论。

第四天：对中国的法律条款，比如死刑、反贪污法等进行讨
论并交换看法。

第五天：拜访知名教育家，跟他们一起讨论、分析中国目前 [15]
的高考制度、高等教育、就业等问题并交换建议及看法。

申请方法：有意者（年级不限）需在2010年10月10日之前写一
封申请信，并附上个人简历以及所在大学的推荐信。入选者将收到
大会组织者的回复。

报名方式：发电邮(ylchelpdesk@gmail.com) [20]

或传真(0086-10-2659 4740)

联 系 人：林小姐

电 话：0086-10-2659 4738/4739

报 名 费：人民币1500元。（来京参会的往返交通费用自理。）

食宿安排：入住北大招待所，两人一间，提供三餐。 [25]

阅读一

如何丰富大学生活

第一段 [1]　各位老师、同学：

第二段　　　　大家好！

第三段　　　　如何度过未来四年的大学生活是每个大学新生都要面对的一个问题。对这个问题的不同认识和态度将影响到四年之后的人生道路。不[5]同的人生理想和规划将带来不同的结果。

第四段　　　　大学是人生中一个关键的阶段。从入学的第一天起，我们每个人就应当对大学生活有一个正确的认识和规划，应当制订　①　自己的目标，使四年的生活过得充实、丰富。

第五段　　　　我早已为自己的四年大学生活定了计划。第一，从大一　②　我就努[10]力学习，争取各门功课都　③　优异的成绩。我认为，在大学阶段学习仍然非常重要。我还要培养自己的自学能力，因为大学跟中学是不同的，在大学里，学习主要靠自己。第二，我还要　④　学汉语。我相信掌握一门外语对今后工作很有利。我计划大学毕业后到中国去进修或者读硕士。第三，除了学习以外，我还要尽自己所能担任一定的职务，多　⑤　、[15]参加一些校园及社会活动，这样既可以锻炼组织能力和语言表达能力，又可以增强自信及适应社会的能力。第四，在现代社会，人际关系很重要。如果我能多参加活动，多与别人　⑥　，就能提高自己的　⑦　能力。第五，我要继续保持自己良好的品质。现在，企业用人首先　⑧　的是一个人的品质，例如吃苦耐劳、正直诚实、具有团队合作精神等。

第六段 [20]　　大学生活马上就要开始了。我既兴奋又紧张。我坚信我的大学生活将过得丰富多彩。四年后，我再向在座的老师、同学汇报！

第七段　　　　谢谢大家！

从下面的方框里为短文选择最合适的词语填空

```
适合    取得    影响    开始    结束
    继续    组织    沟通    考虑    接触
```

1. _____   2. _____   3. _____   4. _____

5. _____   6. _____   7. _____   8. _____

B 根据短文选择正确答案

1. "未来四年"(第3行)的意思是
   _____。

   a) 在过去的四年里
   b) 在今后的四年里
   c) 在四年的时间里

2. "进修"(第13行)的意思是
   _____。

   a) 见习
   b) 工作
   c) 继续读书

3. "担任一定的职务"(第14行)的
   意思是 _____。

   a) 做义工
   b) 负责做一些事或工作
   c) 做一个职员

4. "在座的老师"(第21行)的意思
   是 _____。

   a) 坐在下面听演讲的老师
   b) 没有座位,只能站着的老师
   c) 教过自己的老师

C 根据短文找出四个正确的句子

☐ 1. 演讲者四年大学毕业后有可能留在学校教书。

☐ 2. 演讲者是一个事先定计划,做事有条理的人。

☐ 3. 演讲者是一个不诚实的人。

☐ 4. 这是一篇演讲稿。

☐ 5. 演讲者是一个刚上大学的新生。

☐ 6. 演讲者已经大学毕业四年了。

☐ 7. 演讲者有信心把四年大学生活过得充实、丰富。

1. "我"在四年大学期间会重视各科学习。 对 错

原因：＿＿＿＿＿＿＿＿＿＿＿＿＿＿＿＿＿＿＿＿＿＿ ＿ ＿

2. 在大学里，"我"会抽出时间去读一个硕士学位。

原因：＿＿＿＿＿＿＿＿＿＿＿＿＿＿＿＿＿＿＿＿＿＿ ＿ ＿

3. "我"相信多组织、参加各种活动能锻炼组织能力。

原因：＿＿＿＿＿＿＿＿＿＿＿＿＿＿＿＿＿＿＿＿＿＿ ＿ ＿

4. "我"认为一个品德高尚的人将来比较容易找工作。

原因：＿＿＿＿＿＿＿＿＿＿＿＿＿＿＿＿＿＿＿＿＿＿ ＿ ＿

E 从短文中找反义词

1. 过去→( )(第3行)   4. 虚伪→( )(第19行)

2. 次要→( )(第12行) 5. 平静→( )(第20行)

3. 古代→( )(第16行) 6. 轻松→( )(第20行)

F 从右边的段落大意中找出最合适的

1. 第一、二段 □ | A 演讲者对新生的一次讲话。

2. 第三段 □ | B 演讲的结束语。

3. 第四段 □ | C 演讲者大学毕业后的计划。

4. 第五段 □ | D 演讲的开场白。

5. 第六段 □ | E 演讲者四年大学生活的具体规划。

6. 第七段 □ | F 一个适当的规划保证大学生活过得充实。

| G 演讲者有信心四年大学后将用漂亮的"答卷"作为汇报。

| H 对大学生活不同的认识和态度将会产生不同的结果。

模拟联合国（MUN）
mó nǐ lián hé guó

"模拟联合国"的活动源自美国，在欧美已有60多年的历史。在世界上，模拟联合国很受学生的喜欢。自诞生至今，模拟联合国已吸引了全球超过20万名大学生和高中生。全世界每年举办近400个模拟联合国会议。90年代中期，模拟联合国进入了中国。

[1] 第一段

模拟联合国关注的问题很广，大都是当今各国面临的热点问题。话题主要包括：和平与安全、恐怖主义、人权、环境、贫穷与发展、全球化、公共卫生等。在模拟联合国会议上，学生们扮演各个国家的外交官，按照类似联合国会议的规则和程序进行发言、辩论、谈判，最后达成共识。

[5] 第二段

模拟联合国为学生们打开了一扇窗，提供了一个舞台，让青年人关心世界，用国际眼光来思考问题，讨论问题。青年们通过深入分析国际时事来增强对世界的关注、加深对重大事件的理解。通过了解和参与模拟联合国活动，学生们能认识自己祖国之外的广大的世界，从中培养领导能力。模拟联合国大会让参与者学会以多元化的思维来思考问题，从一名"世界公民"的角度去思考国际争端。通过在模拟联合国中的实战，参与者运用谈判技巧，充分表达自己的观点。

[10]第三段

[15]

当然，在模拟联合国会议上，青年人对世界的认识还很不成熟，他们在会场上的讨论大多是运用从书本上学到的知识或受媒体的影响，无法像真正的外交家、法官那样去解决国际纠纷。但是通过这些会议的平台，青年人能够看清自己的不足，认清今后的努力方向。

第四段

[20]

1. 第一段　　☐

2. 第二段　　☐

3. 第三段　　☐

4. 第四段　　☐

A 模拟(mó nǐ)联合国(lián hé guó)活动关心的问题及会议(huì yì)形式。

B 通过参加模拟联合国活动，学生对自己的能力及未来的努力方向更清楚了。

C 模拟联合国活动深受每个国家学生的喜爱。

D 模拟联合国活动的起源(qǐ yuán)及在全球的规模(guī mó)。

E 模拟联合国活动的不足之处。

F 模拟联合国活动作为一个平台(píng tái)，学生从参与中得到了锻炼。

B 根据短文找出四个正确的句子

☐ 1. 最初的模拟联合国活动是从美国开始的。

☐ 2. 在世界各地，每年都有几百场模拟联合国会议召开。

☐ 3. 在模拟联合国会议上，青年人有机会锻炼他们的口头表达(biǎo dá)能力。

☐ 4. 通过参加模拟联合国活动，青年们对本国的事务(shì wù)更关心了。

☐ 5. 在中国也有模拟联合国活动。

☐ 6. 只有高中生才能报名参加模拟联合国活动。

☐ 7. 在模拟联合国会议上，青年人很少有机会扮演(bàn yǎn)不同的官员(guānyuán)。

C 从短文中选出最合适的动词填空

1. 模拟联合国活动＿＿＿＿（第2行）了很多大学生参加。

2. 模拟联合国活动给学生＿＿＿＿（第10行）了锻炼表达能力的好机会。

3. 全社会应该＿＿＿＿（第11行）青少年的成长。

4. 青年人应该＿＿＿＿（第12行）父母为什么对他们管得严。

5. 在参加模拟联合国活动的过程中，我＿＿＿＿（第13行）了不少朋友。

6. 国际纠纷(jiū fēn)很难＿＿＿＿（第19行），需要各国的合作。

1. "自诞生至今"（第2行）的意思
   是 _____。

   a) 成立已经很久了

   b) 今天诞生

   c) 自从成立到今天

2. "近"（第3行）的意思是 _____。

   a) 超过

   b) 不到

   c) 最近

3. "打开了一扇窗"（第10行）的意
   思是 _____。

   a) 提供了解世界的机会

   b) 为进入大学读书创造了机会

   c) 为进入联合国工作提供方便

4. "世界公民"（第15行）的意思是
   _____。

   a) 联合国的工作人员

   b) 外交官

   c) 生活在地球上的一员

1. 模拟联合国活动　　　□

2. 中国从90年代中期　　□

3. 在模拟联合国会议上，□

4. 青年人通过　　　　　□

A 参与者有机会充分发表他们的观点。

B 和平与安全、人权、环境等问题。

C 才开始有模拟联合国活动。

D 在美国已经有60多年的历史了。

E 认清今后的努力方向。

F 参与模拟联合国活动认识了外面的
  世界。

1. 参加了模拟联合国活动后，学生看问题的眼光会有什么变化？

2. 在模拟联合国会议上，学生们是通过什么方式达成共识的？

3. 通过参加模拟联合国活动，参与者提高了哪方面的能力？

4. 在模拟联合国会议上，为什么参与者对国际问题的看法不成熟？

第一单元 第3课

[1] 尊敬的张先生：

我昨天从晚报上看到了贵公司招聘汉语夏令营辅导员的广告，因此我写信申请这份工作。

我即将从上海国际中学毕业。我一直在国际学校读[5]书。我的同学来自世界各地，所以我对不同的文化一点儿都不陌生。假期里，我经常去世界各地旅游。我到过北京不止一次，还去过中国其他大城市，比如天津、广州、深圳等。

在学校，我是学生会的干事。我们学校每年都举行[10]校级活动，比如文化节、开放日、募捐活动日等，我一直是主要负责人之一。我还做过低年级学生露营级长，参加过话剧表演，是合唱团的指挥。我兴趣很广，擅长戏剧表演，在音乐和体育方面都有特长。由于我在英国和法国分别

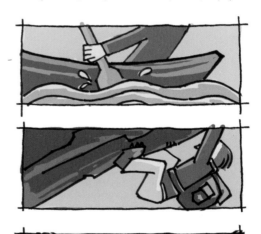

[15]住过几年，所以我英语和法语都说得很流利。我汉语基础也很好，各门科目成绩优异。我是个正直的人，性格外向、自信，还挺幽默。我有责任心，[20]善于跟人沟通、合作，办事灵活，组织能力强。

从贵公司的网站上我得知参加汉语夏令营的学生来自世界各地。由于我特殊的生活和[25]学习背景、能力和经验，我认

30

为自己很适合这份工作，也相信自己能胜任这份工作。我也一定会珍惜这次宝贵的工作机会。如果需要推荐信，请跟我的学校联系。

　　盼望早日得到答复。

　　此致

[30] 敬礼！

黄兴

五月十四日

生词

1. 晚报 wǎnbào evening paper
2. 聘 pìn employ; hire　　招聘 zhāo pìn recruit
3. 即将 jí jiāng soon
4. 陌 mò road　　陌生 mò shēng unfamiliar
5. 不止 bù zhǐ more than
6. 天津 tiān jīn Tianjin (one of the four municipalities directly under the Central Government in China)
7. 广州 guǎngzhōu Guangzhou (provincial capital of Guangdong Province)
8. 深圳 shēnzhèn Shenzhen (a city in Guangdong Province)
9. 干事 gàn shì person in charge
10. 举行 jǔ xíng hold
11. 募 mù raise; collect
　　募捐 mù juān make or take up a collection
12. 合唱团 hé chàngtuán choir
13. 挥（揮）huī wave　　指挥 zhǐ huī conduct
14. 擅 shàn be good at　　擅长 shàncháng be good at
15. 特长 tè cháng strong point; merit
16. 分别 fēn bié respectively
17. 流利 liú lì fluent
18. 础（礎）chǔ plinth　　基础 jī chǔ foundation
19. 正直 zhèng zhí morally upright
20. 外向 wài xiàng extrovert
21. 幽默 yōu mò humourous
22. 灵（靈）líng quick; smart
　　灵活 líng huó quick; flexible
23. 得知 dé zhī get to know
24. 殊 shū different　　特殊 tè shū special
25. 背景 bèi jǐng background
26. 胜任 shèng rèn competent; qualified
27. 珍 zhēn value highly
*28. 惜 xī cherish　　珍惜 zhēn xī cherish
29. 宝贵 bǎo guì valuable
30. 推 tuī push; elect
31. 荐（薦）jiàn recommend
　　推荐 tuī jiàn recommend
32. 答复 dá fù reply

31

消化课文

1. 根据课文回答问题

1) 黄兴从哪儿得到的招聘夏令营辅导员的信息？

2) 黄兴一直在什么样的学校里读书？这对他有什么好处？

3) 他在学校负责过哪些大型活动？

4) 他有哪些特长？他学习成绩怎么样？

5) 他性格怎么样？请列出三项。他的语言技能怎么样？

6) 黄兴为什么觉得他适合这份工作？

2. 根据实际情况回答问题

1) 你做过暑期工吗？是什么时候、在哪儿做的？有哪些收获？

2) 你的同学大都喜欢做什么样的暑期工？你觉得学生该不该做暑期工？为什么？

3) 你从小到大在哪些学校就读过？你最喜欢或最不喜欢哪所学校？请说一说其中的一所学校。

4) 你在音乐、美术或体育方面有什么特长？你擅长做什么？得过什么奖或证书？

5) 你会说几种语言？你觉得学习语言重要吗？为什么？你其他科目的成绩怎么样？

6) 你们学校每年举行哪些慈善、募捐、义卖等活动？你每次都参加吗？你认为今年的哪次活动办得最成功？为什么？

7) 你今年参与并组织了什么大型活动？你为此活动做了什么？你对你的工作满意吗？为什么？

8) 你们学校每年有哪些校级表演/演出？你参加过什么表演/演出？

1. 完成句子

Ⓐ 例子：我昨天从晚报上看到了贵公司的广告，
因此我写信申请这份工作。（第2行）

Ⓑ 例子：在音乐和体育方面，我都有特长。（第13行）

我能说一口流利的
汉语，因此＿＿＿。

在口语方面，＿＿＿

＿＿＿＿＿。

2. 用所给词语造句

Ⓐ 例子：我即将从上海国际中学毕业。（第4行）
我校将于7月20日至26日举办汉语夏
令营。

Ⓑ 例子：由于我在法国住过几年，所以我法语
说得很流利。（第14行）

即将　上大学

将　面试

由于……，
所以……

3. 选择其中一个短语造句

Ⓐ 例子：我对不同的文化一点儿都不陌生。（第5行）
对……发火/印象很深/满意

Ⓑ 例子：在学校，我是学生会的干事。（第9行）
在家里/电脑上

4. 从课文中找反义词

1) 熟悉→(　　　)（第6行）　　4) 死板→(　　　)（第20行）

2) 高 → (　　　)（第11行）　　5) 弱 → (　　　)（第21行）

3) 内向→(　　　)（第18行）　　6) 普通→(　　　)（第24行）

5. 用课文中的动词填空

1) ＿＿＿＿老师（第2行）　　4) ＿＿＿＿汉语（第16行）

2) ＿＿＿＿表演（第11行）　　5) ＿＿＿＿沟通（第20行）

3) ＿＿＿＿合唱团（第12行）　6) ＿＿＿＿这份工作（第26行）

口语训练

小组讨论

讨论学生怎样才能找到适合自己特长和兴趣爱好的暑期工。讨论的内容应包括以下几点：

- 看看自己有哪些特长、爱好以及办事的能力
- 怎样找到合适的暑期工
- 面试时要注意什么

例子：

学生1：我今年想找一份暑期工，可是我从来没做过，所以不知道怎么去找，也不知道怎样准备面试。

学生2：最近，我在报纸上看到一则招聘设计助理的广告。你画画儿画得好，又在学校学过设计课程，我觉得你可以试试申请这份工作。

学生1：那好吧，我先写封申请信寄去。我觉得你很容易就能找到暑期工。你中英文都说得很流利，而且你的数理化学得都好。我建议你去做家教。

学生3：我敢肯定孩子们一定会喜欢你，因为你很幽默，办事灵活，而且有爱心。你可以从早补到晚，赚大把的钱。

学生2：这不把我累死！我相信只要做喜欢的事，我一定能做好。但是，我也不希望整个暑假都打工，我还是希望有一点

34

儿自己的时间。

学生3：我在音乐、戏剧表演方面有特长，所以想去一个音乐主题夏令营当辅导员。我认为暑期工要适合自己的特长和兴趣，这样才能从中获益。

学生1：除了看报纸，我们还可以从哪儿得到招聘暑期工的信息？

学生2：你可以上网找，但是网上的信息不一定可靠。申请之前，一定要先打电话或亲自去用人单位看看，千万别上当、受骗。

学生3：你也可以问问熟人或父母的同事。

学生1：听说申请暑期工的人挺多，面试要有技巧。你们能不能给我一些建议？

学生2：去面试一定要提前到，不能迟到。面试那天，要穿比较正式的衣服，要尽量把自己的优点说出来。

学生3：推荐信很重要。你要找一个了解你的人写推荐信。

a) 做暑期工最主要的是在工作中锻炼自己，学会怎样跟人沟通、合作。通过做暑期工，我们能提高处理、解决问题的能力。最后，我们还能赚一些零用钱。

b) 我也想去夏令营做辅导员。我的特长是体育，特别是野外活动，比如爬山、划船、露营等。

c) 如果能把做暑期工跟见习结合在一起，那是最理想的。比如说，我今后想做律师，我可以在暑假里一边打工赚钱，一边积累工作经验，那真是一举两得。

d) 我建议你找一份自己喜欢的工作。如果一个人只是为了赚钱，做他不喜欢的工作，那么我觉得这是浪费时间。

e) 我将来想做会计师。今年暑假我想去会计事务所见习。如果我喜欢会计工作，我就继续往这个方向发展。所以说，做暑期工是一个尝试的好机会。

写作训练

1. 写申请信

写一封申请信申请见习。在信中你要提及以下几个方面:

- 见习的目的
- 见习的内容
- 见习的时间
- 期望达到的目标 *qī wàng*
- 盼望对方考虑你的申请

参考句子

a) 我今天写信想申请到贵公司见习。

b) 我见习的目的是想多了解一下金融这个行业,因为我在大学里想学金融专业。 *jīn róng*

c) 我对外科特别感兴趣,希望能观摩一些手术,比如心脏手术、脑手术等。如果不能安排我去外科,您能否把我安排到儿科,因为我对儿科也挺感兴趣的。一切都听从您的安排。 *guān mó*

d) 我的见习时间最好是七月到十月,每个星期一次,每次 4~5 个小时。

e) 我希望通过见习开开眼界,对我将来想学的专业有比较全面的了解。这样,我就可以为想学的专业作好准备。

f) 我希望您能认真考虑我的申请,并盼望早日得到您的肯定答复。非常感谢!

g) 如果需要面试,请安排在 6 月 15 日后,因为之前我不在上海。

2. 阅读短文并写回应式作文

假设你想在大学毕业后开办自己的公司。读了这篇短文后，你受到了一些启发(qǐ fā)。请写一篇日记，写下初步(chū bù)的想法，并打算说服你的父母。

年轻人创业

很多人认为我们这一代年轻人不负责任、好吃懒做(hào chī lǎn zuò)、没有人生目标。自从上了高中后我就想用实际(shí jì)行动证明(zhèngmíng)这种说法是片面(piànmiàn)的。 [1]

大学毕业后的第一年，我开始着手(zhuóshǒu)开办一家茶叶出口(chá yè chū kǒu)公司。中国是茶叶之乡，茶叶品种丰富，质量上乘(shàngchéng)。可惜的是中国的茶叶还没有在世界上得到应有的地位(dì wèi)，没有被更多的消费者(xiāo fèi zhě)认识。我 [5]
把这个想法告诉了经商(jīng shāng)的父亲，他答应在资金(zī jīn)上支持我办公司。

我利用大学期间的几个假期对中国好几个茶叶产地(chǎn dì)进行了实(shí)
地考察(dì kǎo chá)。我对茶叶的生产(shēngchǎn)过程、包装(bāozhuāng)、广告、销售(xiāoshòu)等各个方面进
行了了解，对商业运作也作了充分的准备。我的公司于2009年1月1
日开张(kāi zhāng)了。经过半年的努力，我的公司先后在印度(yìn dù)、新加坡(xīn jiā pō)、菲(fēi) [10]
律宾(lù bīn)等亚洲国家建立(jiàn lì)了分销网络(fēn xiāo wǎng luò)。一年里，我的公司不但没有亏(kuī)
本(běn zhuǎn)，反而赚了十几万人民币。这比我的预期(yù qī)要好。

我的茶叶公司的成功让一家茶叶生产商大吃一惊(dà chī yì jīng)，这正是他
们想做的，但是一直没有实现。于是这位生产商表示愿意支付(zhī fù)100
万人民币，收购(shōugòu)我的公司，我没有答应。 [15]

通过办公司，我的体会是，如果想办公司，资金当然是最重
要的，但是除此以外，创业者一定要执著(zhí zhuó)，肯花工夫，在各方面
要提前作好充足的准备。创业者还要有乐观的一面，也要对风险
有充分的心理准备，做好最坏的打算。

刚过了23岁生日的我，可以代表中国新一代的年轻人自豪(zì háo)地 [20]
告诉人们，我们是有创业精神、追求上进、富有创意的一代。

阅读与理解

阅读一

第一段 [1]	每个高中毕业生都将面临大学专业选择的难题。怎样才能找到最适合自己的大学专业呢？请听以下几位高中见习生的见习心得。
第二段	见习生1：这次见习使我对自己喜欢的职业有了更进一步的认识，今后的学习、发展也有了更明确的方向。
第三段 [5]	见习生2：我发现，通过见习我提升了自己，还获得了宝贵的工作经验。我没想到自己在见习期间成长得特别快，各方面的能力也提高了不少。
第四段	见习生3：见习之后，我发现在学校学的知识跟社会的要求还有距离。我认为，通过见习我们不仅可以缩小这个距离，而且可以
[10]	获得实际的工作经验，为今后找到理想的专业作了准备。
第五段	见习生4：我觉得通过见习可以了解一个行业的发展情况和前景，重要的是我也更清楚了自己喜欢做什么，擅长做什么。还有，见习之后我对理工科更感兴趣了。
第六段 [15]	见习生5：我发现用人单位非常重视见习生的动手能力、创新能力、人际交往能力、分析能力和表达能力。我现在才体会到了这些能力越早培养越好。我今后会在这些方面下工夫。
第七段	见习生6：我发现见习单位十分关注一个人的品德、工作和学习态度等。还有，用人单位喜欢综合能力较强的学生。
第八段 [20]	总之，接受采访的高中见习生对见习的态度都很积极。他们都认为通过见习对自己更了解了，也提高了工作能力，积累了经验，对未来要读的专业也有了初步的了解。他们都说见习确实是正确选择大学专业的一个重要、有效的途径。

A 判断正误，并说明原因

1.对高中毕业生来说，选择大学专业是件容易的事。   对   错

原因：_____   ___   ___

2.见习生1以前对自己喜欢的职业一点儿都不了解。

原因：_____   ___   ___

3.见习生4本来就对理工科感兴趣。

原因：_____   ___   ___

4.见习生6认为综合能力强的学生受工作单位的欢迎。

原因：_____   ___   ___

B 用短文中的动词填空

1. _____ (第1行) 工作   5. _____ (第16行) 科学家

2. _____ (第5行) 金奖   6. _____ (第17行) 环境问题

3. _____ (第7行) 能力   7. _____ (第19行) 见习生

4. _____ (第14行) 品德教育   8. _____ (第20行) 市场

C 从短文中选出最合适的词语填空

1.我_____ (第3行) 医学专业有了初步的了解。

2.见习不仅丰富了我的工作经验，_____ (第4行) 让我交到了几个朋友。

3._____ (第5行) 见习，我发现自己需要提高动手能力。

4.见习了两个星期后，我_____ (第12行) 了解自己了。

5.我花了一个月时间_____ (第15行) 找到了一份暑期工。

6.见习单位喜欢学习态度好的学生，_____ (第18行)，他们很看重一
个人的品德。

39

D 为短文配题目

☐ 1. 见习与职业的关系

☐ 2. 如何选择见习单位
<small>dān wèi</small>

☐ 3. 高中生对职业见习的感 想
<small>gǎn xiǎng</small>

☐ 4. 重新认识自己
<small>chóng xīn</small>

E 根据短文选择正确答案

1. "面临" (第1行)的意思是
<small>miàn lín</small>
   _____。

   a) 面前

   b) 面对

   c) 临走

2. "心得" (第2行)的意思是
<small>xīn dé</small>
   _____。

   a) 工作和学习中的体会、认识

   b) 心里难受

   c) 得了心病

3. "下工夫" (第16行)的意思
   是 _____。

   a) 花时间，努力

   b) 练武术

   c) 多花钱

4. "初步" (第21行)的意思是
<small>chū bù</small>
   _____。

   a) 进一步

   b) 初中

   c) 开始阶段的

F 根据短文回答下列问题

1. 见习生5回校后可能会有哪些行动？

2. 被采访的见习生对见习的态度怎么样？

3. 见习的好处有哪些？

40

"环球文化村"嘉年华

2009年3月21日，由全球最大的国际学生组织AIESEC（国际经济学商 学学生联合会，简称"联合会"）主办的亚太青年领袖发展与交流会议在香港正式开始。当日，开幕典礼及"环球文化村"嘉年华在香港的尖沙咀星光大道上举行。来自超过十六个国家和地区的约两百名不同肤色、不同民族的优秀大学生，穿上各国民族服饰，配合摊位展示及表演，与香港市民互相交流自己国家或地区的文化特色和风俗。

今年的会议以"梦想今天，成就将来"为主题。在接下来的一个星期里，各国青年学子参加了各种活动，包括世界时事讨论、领袖训练工作坊等。除了体验跨国文化、了解文化差异，与会者还向香港三十多位企业高层管理人员请教经验，拓展领导才能。此外，他们还走进香港社会，亲身感受了这个国际大都会的魅力。

联合会成立于1948年，被联合国确认为全球最大的国际学生组织，现在会员已遍布一百多个国家和地区。该组织由大学生来负责运作，是一个国际性、非政府、非盈利的独立机构。这个组织每年为大学生提供4000多个海外实习机会，并在世界各地举办了300多场国际会议。联合会又是一个国际交流平台，让青年人建立个人人际网络，发现并发挥自己的潜能。

香港的联合会成立于1967年，先后在6所大学设立了分会。自2002年联合会在中国内地正式成立以来，已有30多所大学设立了分会。2008年，中国内地有700多名大学生通过该组织参加了海外实习。

[1] 第一段

[5]

第二段

[10]

第三段

[15]

第四段

[20]

41

1. 亚太青年领袖发展与交流会议开幕典礼于2009年3月21日在香港星光
   大道＿＿＿＿＿＿（第4行）。

2. 为了＿＿＿＿＿＿（第5行）"环球文化村"嘉年华，市政府还组织了丰富
   多彩的文化活动。

3. 不同民族的学生聚在一起＿＿＿＿＿＿（第6行）参加嘉年华的体会。

4. 在北京的交换生家里待了半年，我亲身＿＿＿＿＿＿（第9行）了独特的中国
   文化传统及习俗。

5. 你一定要来上海＿＿＿＿＿＿（第11行）一下这个国际大都市。

6. 中国交响乐团＿＿＿＿＿＿（第12行）于1956年。

7. 如果你来我公司实习，我们将＿＿＿＿＿＿（第15行）住宿。

8. 国际经济学商学学生联合会最近几年在中国内地发展得很快，已在
   30余所大学＿＿＿＿＿＿（第18行）了分会。

☐ 1. 联合会是由大学生负责运作的，是个不赚钱的机构。

☐ 2. 参加亚太青年领袖发展与交流会议的学生来自十多个国家和地区。

☐ 3. 香港市民也可以报名参加各种工作坊。

☐ 4. 联合会是联合国确认的一个国际性学生组织。

☐ 5. 在嘉年华期间，香港市民组织了各种摊位和时装表演。

☐ 6. 联合会在香港的六所大学里有30个分会。

☐ 7. 参加会议的各国青年人与香港社会接触，都感受到了香港是个动
   感国际大都市。

C 判断正误，并说明原因

1. 2009年的亚太青年领袖发展与交流会议在香港的尖沙咀星   对   错
光大道上举行了开幕典礼。

原因：_____ __ __

2. 联合会的会员来自全世界的一百多个国家和地区。

原因：_____ __ __

3. 青年人可以通过联合会这个国际平台互相交流、建立人
际网络，并发挥各自的才能。

原因：_____ __ __

4. 从2002年起，中国内地每一所大学都有了联合会分会。

原因：_____ __ __

5. 2008年，联合会帮助700多名中国大学生去海外实习。

原因：_____ __ __

D 从右边的段落大意中找出最合适的

1. 第一段   ☐ | A 联合会的性质、规模、作用及运作方式。
2. 第二段   ☐ | B 联合会在香港和中国内地的分布及作用。
3. 第三段   ☐ | C 2009年亚太青年领袖发展与交流会议的主题及
4. 第四段   ☐ | 活动。
                 | D 联合会这个独立机构的特色。
                 | E 联合会为培养青年领袖所作的贡献。
                 | F 2009年亚太青年领袖发展与交流会议在香港开
                    幕当天的盛况。

43

单元复习

生词

第1课

招生　*贵　临床　医学　父亲　心脏　专家　母亲
儿科　优异　假期　课余　公立　订阅　动向
紧急救护　证书　坚定　勤奋　踏实　胆大　心细
追求　完美　班长　开放日　坚信　最佳　人选
出身　热情　*而且　加倍　盼望　面试　敬礼

第2课

演讲　确信　抱怨　品种　绝大部分　油腻　商讨
状况　增加　次数　开展　美化　校园　舞会　歌唱
话剧　诚实　能干　共同　实现　愿望　善于　定期
班级　想法　及时　转达　荣幸

第3课

晚报　招聘　即将　陌生　不止　天津　广州　深圳
干事　举行　募捐　合唱团　指挥　擅长　特长　分别
流利　基础　正直　外向　幽默　灵活　得知　特殊
背景　胜任　珍惜　宝贵　推荐　答复

自从……后　对……感兴趣/有热情　通过努力　取得优异的成绩

参加好几项课外活动　为了熟悉这个职业　利用假期及课余时间

目的是想了解医学的最新动向　专门学了……　取得证书

积累了不少经验　坚定了学医的决心　学习勤奋、工作踏实的人

坚信自己是最佳人选　出身于医生家庭　接受申请　加倍努力

对……有全面的了解/（不）满意　首先……，其次……，最后……

当上了学生会主席　要求改进　增加清洁的次数　跟……合作

开展节电活动　为……组织活动　参加活动　组织能力强　实现愿望

通过合作和共同的努力　善于跟人沟通　配合学校的工作　听取意见

把想法和建议转达给……　感到荣幸　乐意为……服务

招聘辅导员的广告　即将毕业　来自世界各地　对……不陌生

到过北京不止一次　举行活动　兴趣很广　擅长表演

在……方面有特长　英语说得流利　汉语基础好　成绩优异

善于跟人沟通、合作　办事灵活　特殊的生活背景　胜任这份工作

珍惜工作机会　跟……联系　盼望早日得到答复

**第二单元
第4课**

[1] 各位同学：

你们好！

今天我来介绍一下中国的家庭。

中国的传统家庭一般是三世或四世同堂，也就是说

[5] 一家三代、四代住在一起。在中国的传统家庭里，长辈爱
护、照顾晚辈，晚辈尊敬、孝顺长辈。"尊老爱幼"一直
是中国人的传统美德。

但是，在现代中国社会里，三世或四世同堂的家庭
已经很少了。自从二十世纪八十年代初以来，中国实行了

[10] 独生子女政策，也就是说，在一般情况下，一对夫妇只能
生一个孩子。现在的年轻人结婚后一般不会跟父母住在一
起，老年人也不喜欢跟子女住在一起，因为他们有自己的
生活方式，所以现代家庭大都是由三口人组成的小家庭。

随着中国的改革开放，中国人的传统家庭观念也发生

[15] 了变化。近些年，离婚率上升了，单亲家庭也增加了。不
少年轻人选择不结婚，做单身贵族。还有一些年轻夫妻，
为了享受二人世界，婚后不生孩子。由此可见，中国的家
庭结构比以前
多样化了。

[20] 　　虽然长辈
不跟已婚子女
同住，但是他
们大多还会帮
助照看孙子、

[25] 孙女或外孙、

外孙女。长辈年老体弱时，晚辈也会通过各种方式照顾他们。在现代中国社会中，虽然家庭观念和结构发生了变化，但是中国人的传统美德还在继续发扬光大。

我的发言完了。谢谢大家！

生词

1. 晚辈 wǎn bèi younger generation
2. 美德 měi dé virtue
3. 世纪 shì jì century
4. 年代 nián dài decade of a century
5. 实行 shí xíng implement
6. 独生子女 dú shēng zǐ nǚ only child
7. 策 cè plan; strategy　政策 zhèng cè policy
8. 夫 fū husband　夫妇 fū fù married couple
9. 年轻 niánqīng young
   年轻人 niánqīng rén young people
10. 老年 lǎo nián old age
    老年人 lǎo nián rén old people; senior citizen
11. 方式 fāng shì way; mode
*12. 由 yóu by means of
    由……组成 yóu……zǔ zhèng be composed of
13. 随着 suí zhe along with; following
14. 革 gé change　改革 gǎi gé reform
15. 观念 guānniàn concept
16. 率 lù rate
17. 上升 shàngshēng rise

18. 单亲 dān qīn single parent
19. 单身 dān shēn single; unmarried
20. 贵族 guì zú noble
21. 妻 qī wife
    夫妻 fū qī husband and wife
22. 由此可见 yóu cǐ kě jiàn it can be concluded that...
23. 结构 jié gòu structure
24. 多样化 duō yàng huà diversify
25. 已婚 yǐ hūn married; be married
26. 大多 dà duō mostly
27. 照看 zhào kàn look after
28. 孙子 sūn zi grandson (son's son)
29. 孙女 sūn nǚ granddaughter (son's daughter)
30. 外孙 wài sūn grandson (daughter's son)
31. 外孙女 wài sūn nǚ granddaughter (daughter's daughter)
32. 扬（揚）yáng spread
    发扬 fā yáng promote; develop
    发扬光大 fā yángguāng dà bring to a great height of development
33. 发言 fā yán make a speech

消化课文

1. 根据课文回答问题

1) 在中国的传统家庭里，一般几代人在一起生活？

2) 中国人的传统美德是什么？

3) 中国的独生子女政策是何时开始实行的？请简单介绍这个政策。

4) 中国的现代家庭有哪些特点？

5) 在中国，年轻的夫妻有了孩子后，谁会帮助他们照看？

6) 在作者看来，虽然中国的家庭观念和结构发生了变化，中国人的传统美德会失去吗？

2. 根据实际情况回答问题

1) 你跟祖父母/外祖父母一起生活过吗？是什么时候？你跟他们合得来吗？

2) 在你们国家，现在有三世同堂或四世同堂的家庭吗？过去有吗？现在的家庭大多是几口之家？

3) 在你们国家，子女一般什么时候搬出去自己住？子女结婚后会跟父母一起住吗？父母年老体弱的时候由谁照顾？

4) 在你们国家，一般的家庭有几个孩子？母亲一般外出工作还是在家带孩子？如果母亲工作，孩子由谁照顾？

5) 你们国家的离婚率高吗？单身贵族多吗？

6) 在你们国家，爷爷、奶奶或外公、外婆会帮忙照看孙子、孙女、外孙、外孙女吗？你从小是由谁带大的？

7) 你经常去看望祖父母、外祖父母吗？他们现在住在哪儿？他们的身体怎么样？他们跟谁住在一起？

8) 你喜欢在大家庭里还是小家庭里生活？为什么？大家庭和小家庭各有什么好处和坏处？

1. 选择其中一个短语造句

Ⓐ例子：在现代中国社会里，三世或四世同堂的家庭已经很少了。（第8行）

在过去的五年里

在高中的两年里

在见习期间

Ⓑ例子：现在的年轻人结婚后一般不会跟父母住在一起。（第11行）

跟……通电话/借东西

2. 完成句子

Ⓐ例子：自从二十世纪八十年代初以来，中国实行了独生子女政策。（第9行）

Ⓑ例子：现代家庭大都是由三口人组成的小家庭。（第13行）

Ⓒ例子：随着中国的改革开放，中国人的传统家庭观念也发生了变化。（第14行）

Ⓓ例子：由此可见，中国的家庭结构比以前多样化了。（第17行）

自从中国改革开放以来，_____。爸爸再婚了。我的新家现在由_____。随着中国经济的快速发展，_____。由此可见，中国的出生率_____。

3. 从课文中找反义词

1) 古代→(　　　)（第8行）　　4) 双 → (　　　　)（第15行）

2) 很多→(　　　)（第9行）　　5) 平民→(　　　　)（第16行）

3) 下降→(　　　)（第15行）　　6) 停止→(　　　　)（第28行）

4. 用课文中的动词填空

1) _____（第6行）长辈　　　3) _____（第14行）变化

2) _____（第9行）政策　　　4) _____（第17行）生活

口语训练

小组讨论

学了课文"中国的家庭"以后，试讨论你们国家或地区的人们的家庭观念及结构有哪些特点，并谈谈你们的看法。讨论应包括以下几点：

- 家庭结构的变化
- 对大家庭和小家庭的看法
- 对独生子女政策的看法
- 对传统家庭观念的看法

例子：

学生1：我知道中国从上世纪80年代开始实行独生子女政策。现在中国的家庭大部分都是一家三口的小家庭。

学生2：在我们国家没有独生子女政策。一对夫妇想生几个孩子就生几个孩子。但是现在有些年轻夫妇选择不生孩子，做丁克一族，享受二人生活。

学生3：我觉得单身贵族的生活很自由。我大学毕业后不打算结婚。自己赚的钱自己花，自己想做什么就做什么。

学生4：我们国家的大家庭不少。我大学毕业后，肯定会结婚，生几个孩子，因为我喜欢小孩子。

学生2：我也喜欢大家庭。我们家祖父母跟我们一家六口住在一起。平时我们互相关心、互相照顾。爷爷、奶奶退休后没事

干，在家照看我弟妹。我父
母出去工作、挣钱。有时
候爷爷、奶奶身体不好，我
们也方便照顾他们。

学生1：我比较喜欢小家庭。小家庭
生活条件好。家里只有一个
孩子，生活负担轻。教育、
医疗条件好，因为父母把全
部精力放在一个孩子身上，
能培养孩子全面发展。

学生3：我不一定要大家庭，但我一
直希望有一个姐姐或妹妹。
我总觉得独生子女很孤独，
在家里没有伙伴可以玩儿，
父母也不可能每时每刻陪着
我。

学生4：我认为中国人比较重视家
庭。家庭成员之间关系比较
亲近。

学生2：你说得对。中国人过年、过
节一定会团聚在一起，一家
老小开开心心地庆祝。

学生1：我是美国人，我们也很重视
家庭。每年的圣诞节、感恩
节，我们也都赶回家，跟家
人一起庆祝。

参考句子

a) 中国的独生子女政策有利
也有弊。在独生子女家庭
里，一个孩子往往被宠坏
了，他们被叫做"小皇帝、
小公主"。但是独生子女长
大结婚后要照顾双方的父
母，他们的负担比较重。
独生子女政策还有其他负
面影响，比如说，独生子
女比较孤单。

b) 我认为中国的独生子女政
策有很多好处。最主要的
是中国的人口太多了。如
果不实行独生子女政策，
中国的人口现在可能是
十八九亿，而不是十三亿。
多生出几亿人口，吃饭、
住房、穿衣都会有问题。

c) 在全球化的影响下，各个
国家的家庭结构都在发生
变化，离婚率也越来越高。

d) 我还是喜欢传统的家庭观
念。小辈年幼时，长辈照
看小辈；长辈年老体弱时，
小辈又可以照顾他们。

写作训练

1. 写电邮

假设你最近跟父母发生了一些不愉快的事情，比如在学习和生活习惯、谈恋爱、大学专业的选择等方面有不同的看法。写一封电邮给父母，说出你的想法。在电邮中，你要提及以下几个方面：

- 写电邮的目的
- 你最近的烦恼
- 你们之间不愉快的事情
- 你希望怎样解决

参考句子

a) 我写电邮是为了跟你们说一说我的心里话。

b) 我最近很苦恼。在很多事情上，我们有不同的看法。我想在大学里读美术专业，但是你们希望我读经济学。

c) 我在家里没有权力决定自己的事情。我们经常吵架，有时候我们好几天不说话。有几次我真想离家出走，但是又觉得这样不能解决问题。

d) 我已经十八岁了，我有能力也有权力决定一些事情。

e) 我知道你们不喜欢我在中学阶段谈恋爱。但到目前为止，我觉得谈恋爱没有影响我的学习。我认为在中学阶段，通过谈恋爱可以积累跟异性交往的经验。

f) 我的文科不如理科。不管我怎么努力，我的文科成绩总是不太理想。

g) 我觉得我们应该经常沟通，互相理解。

2. 阅读下面的采访内容并写回应式作文

读了下列采访内容，你有一些感想。请写一篇日记，谈谈你的感想，并分析你父母对你教育的 成 败之处。

中国式的家庭教育

王：大家好，我是主持人王冬。今天我们有幸请到了教育司副司长 [1]
钟先生来给我们讲一讲中国式的家庭教育面临的挑战。钟先
生，您好！

钟：您好！教育确实关系到中国的未来，而家庭教育是关键。进入
二十一世纪，中国的未成年人口就有3亿多。 [5]

王：中国的家长对孩子有哪些期望？

钟：很多家长希望他们的孩子将来有出息，希望他们一生幸福、平
安，还希望他们将来拥有财富和地位。

王：那么，家庭教育是怎样影响孩子的成长的？

钟：绝大部分家长受孔子"学而优则仕"的影响，认为读书、考高 [10]
分、进名牌大学是孩子的唯一出路。可是，这样的孩子长大后
往往是"高分低能"，在当今社会中将面临种种挑战。还有些
家长也同意读书重要，但是一个孩子不但要有知识，还要有高
尚 的品格，包括诚实可靠、宽容善良、有合作精神、热爱和
平等。我认为这样的孩子才是我们国家需要的人才。 [15]

王：在家庭教育方面，您给家长们什么忠告？

钟：在某种 程度上，家长肩负着教育孩子的重任。孩子的发展一定
是多样化的，不可能每个孩子都成为科学家。不同的孩子有不同的
潜力，家长要给予他们针对性的教育，为他们 创 造条件，使其发
挥最大的潜力。孩子的积极性、自信心不是天生的，需要家庭的培 [20]
养、支持和鼓励。另外，家长要培养孩子优良的品德和做人的尊
严，这样他们长大后才能成为一个幸福、有所作为的人。

阅读一

[1]   客家是汉族民系中重要的一支。今天的客家人是世界上分布地区最广的民系之一。在中国，客家人在大陆聚居的省区有19个，而香港特别行政区有100多万客家人，台湾省大约有400多万。还有很多客家人居住在东南亚国家，比如在新加坡，客家人有20多万，是当地六个

[5]   主要华人族群之一。

    据考证，客家民系在历史上有过五次大迁移，从中原到南方，再从南方去海外，终于在中国的南方及海外地区形成了一个客家体系。

    客家人经过长期的历史发展，成为了汉民族中独特的群体。客家人的精神来自五千年的历史文化，来自艰苦环境的磨炼，来自祖辈一

[10]   代一代的言传身教。客家人的精神可以归纳如下：

1. 刻苦勤俭是客家人最突出的特色。在这方面，客家妇女表现得尤其突出。她们吃苦耐劳，勤俭持家。

2. 客家人具有开拓进取的精神。从古到今，他们外出谋生、经商，在各行各业都有杰出的客家人。

[15] 3. 客家人历来就重视文化学习。为了谋求生路、经商、做官，他们必须学习文化知识，也特别重视教育。

4. 客家人有浓厚的念祖思乡之情。他们无论生活在何处，都不会忘记祖辈、亲人。居住在海外的客家华侨很多都会返回祖国寻根。

[20] 5. 客家人特别爱国爱家。他们赚了钱后大都会赞助家乡的建设。

6. 客家人有尊老爱幼、团结互助的优良传统。他们的家庭、亲情观念也很重。无论遇到什么困难，他们都会互相帮助、克服困难。

1. "聚居"（第2行）的意思是 _____。

   a) 集中居住

   b) 移居

   c) 搬迁

2. "海外"（第7行）的意思是 _____。

   a) 地中海

   b) 国内

   c) 国外

3. "言传身教"（第10行）的意思是 _____。

   a) 教训

   b) 引导

   c) 言语和行动起到模范作用

4. "历来"（第15行）的意思是 _____。

   a) 在历史上

   b) 一直

   c) 将来

5. "寻根"（第19行）的意思是 _____。

   a) 投资

   b) 植树

   c) 寻找祖籍宗族

6. "赞助"（第20行）的意思是 _____。

   a) 拿出钱来帮助别人

   b) 花精力帮助

   c) 协助

☐ 1. 有很多客家人居住在香港。

☐ 2. 在中国的每一个省都有客家人居住。

☐ 3. 台湾省大约有20多万客家人。

☐ 4. 客家人有着五千年的文化历史。

☐ 5. 实际上，客家人也是汉族人。

☐ 6. 从古到今，客家人一直居住在中国的南方。

☐ 7. 客家人保持着互相帮助、团结友爱的中华民族的优良传统。

1. 历史上，客家人从中原直接去了海外。 对 错

原因：_____ ___ ___

2. 客家妇女善于管家理财，也很节俭。
   lǐ cái jié jiǎn

原因：_____ ___ ___

3. 客家人不怎么善于经商。

原因：_____ ___ ___

4. 客家人看重文化知识，但是他们不重视教育。
   zhòng shì

原因：_____ ___ ___

5. 客家人有了钱后总想为家乡的建设出力。
   jiàn shè

原因：_____ ___ ___

6. 客家人保持着中国的文化传统，比如尊敬长辈、爱护晚辈等。
   bǎo chí

原因：_____ ___ ___

D 为短文配题目

☐ 1. 客家精神

☐ 2. 客家人的历史

☐ 3. 客家人的经商之道

☐ 4. 客家人的生活习惯

E 用短文中的动词填空

1. _____ （第7行）风俗

2. _____ （第15行）环境保护

3. _____ （第16行）中国历史

4. _____ （第18行）痛苦的往事
   tòng kǔ

5. _____ （第18行）母校

6. _____ （第22行）麻烦

中国婚俗的变迁

中国人通常把婚姻看得很重，称婚姻是"终身大事"，那么中国人把婚礼办得既讲究又隆重也就不难理解了。

[1]第一段

从上个世纪的50年代到今天，中国婚俗的演变经历了几个阶段。20世纪的50至70年代，由于物质生活条件普遍比较差，中国人结婚只是发喜糖给亲戚朋友。到了80年代后期，大部分婚礼都在饭店举行，那时也开始时兴旅游结婚。从20世纪的最后十年到今天，婚俗简直起了翻天覆地的变化。

第二段 [5]

如今，年轻人的婚礼在格调和档次上都有很高的要求。婚纱的设计、新房的布置、家具的选购，这一切是最花心思和金钱的。新人拍结婚照可能要破费几万块钱。婚宴是整个婚俗的高潮。在豪华饭店办婚宴可以保证全方位的服务和一流的美食。婚宴上还有各种活动，既让新人和客人玩儿得尽兴，又给每个人留下美好的回忆。

第三段 [10]

当今中国的婚俗既有新意又保持了传统。有相当一部分新人会选择中式加西式的婚礼形式：新娘穿了旗袍再换婚纱，新郎穿了马褂再换西服。有的婚宴是中式酒席加西式糕点，有的却是西式的自助餐。但是，中国的婚俗还保留着独具风格的中国传统文化特征。中国人喜爱红色，认为红是吉祥的象征。所以，在中国的婚宴上新娘喜欢穿红衣服，放的鞭炮、宴会厅和新房的布置一般都用红色。亲朋好友一般会对新人说："祝你们幸福美满，白头偕老，早生贵子。"

第四段 [15]

随着时代的变迁，中国的婚俗发生了很多变化，但是有些传统的习俗仍然保留了下来，同时也增添了一些新的色彩。

[20]第五段

A　根据短文选择正确答案

1. "终身大事"（第1行）的意思
   是 _____。
   a) 人生第一件大事
   b) 一辈子最重要的事
   c) 健康大事

2. "喜糖"（第5行）的意思是
   _____。
   a) 白糖
   b) 红糖
   c) 结婚时招待（zhāo dài）亲友的糖果

3. "时兴"（shí xīng）（第6行）的意思是
   _____。
   a) 一时高兴
   b) 一时流行
   c) 令人兴奋（xīng fèn）

4. "翻天覆地"（fān tiān fù dì）（第7行）的意思
   是 _____。
   a) 巨大
   b) 很小
   c) 微不足道（wēi bù zú dào）

5. "新人"（第9行）的意思是
   _____。
   a) 已婚夫妇
   b) 新来的客人
   c) 新郎（xīn láng）、新娘（xīn niáng）

6. "玩儿得尽兴"（jìn xìng）（第12行）的意
   思是 _____。
   a) 玩儿得太多了
   b) 玩儿得痛快（tòngkuai）
   c) 玩儿得不开心

B　从右边的段落大意中找出最合适的

1. 第一段　☐
2. 第二段　☐
3. 第三段　☐
4. 第四段　☐
5. 第五段　☐

A 如今年轻人婚礼的格调（gé diào）和档次（dàng cì）都很讲究（jiǎng jiu）。

B 现在中国人的婚俗（hūn sú）既保留（bǎo liú）了中国传统文化特色，又融入（róng rù）了西方婚俗文化。

C 中国人心目中的婚姻（hūn yīn）大事。

D 中国的婚俗体现（tǐ xiàn）了中国的传统文化特征（tè zhēng）。

E 如今，中国的婚俗仍然保留着中式婚礼形式。

F 中国的婚俗随着时代的变迁（biànqiān）发生了很大变化。

G 从20世纪50年代至今，婚俗经历了几个阶段的演变（yǎnbiàn）。

H 西式婚俗在中国也很流行。

58

1. 20世纪60年代，那时候中国人生活还不富裕(fù yù)，结婚只发　　　对　　错
喜糖而已。

　　原因：＿＿＿＿＿＿＿＿＿＿＿＿＿＿＿＿＿＿＿＿＿＿　＿＿　＿＿

2. 如今，为了准备婚事，新人花很多时间、精力(jīng lì)和金钱(jīn qián)。

　　原因：＿＿＿＿＿＿＿＿＿＿＿＿＿＿＿＿＿＿＿＿＿＿　＿＿　＿＿

3. 如今在中国，新人拍结婚照一般都很便宜。

　　原因：＿＿＿＿＿＿＿＿＿＿＿＿＿＿＿＿＿＿＿＿＿＿　＿＿　＿＿

4. 在高档(gāo dàng)饭店办婚宴，食物好吃，但是服务质量没有保证(bǎo zhèng)。

　　原因：＿＿＿＿＿＿＿＿＿＿＿＿＿＿＿＿＿＿＿＿＿＿　＿＿　＿＿

5. 在婚宴上，亲朋好友会给新人献上美好的祝福。

　　原因：＿＿＿＿＿＿＿＿＿＿＿＿＿＿＿＿＿＿＿＿＿＿　＿＿　＿＿

D　从短文中选出最合适的动词填空

1. 人们很难＿＿＿＿＿＿（第2行）年轻人为什么要花费那么多钱办婚礼。

2. 在改革开放的几十年中，中国人＿＿＿＿＿＿（第3行）了几个发展阶段。

3. 如今，大部分年轻人＿＿＿＿＿＿（第13行）去饭店办婚宴。

4. 在中式婚礼上，新娘＿＿＿＿＿＿（第17行）穿红色的旗袍。

5. 在今天的中国，很多城市都＿＿＿＿＿＿（第20行）了很大的变化。

6. 在婚宴上，亲朋好友会参加各种活动，这＿＿＿＿＿＿（第21行）了喜庆的气氛。

李安的电影

[1] 李安是国际知名的华人电影导演。在国际影坛上，他曾经获得过多个国际电影奖。

李安出生于台湾，祖籍是江西。他从小不喜欢读书，因此两次都没有考上大学，最后进了台湾艺术大学学影剧专
[5] 业。1979年，李安去美国学戏剧及电影制作专业，并获得了学士和硕士学位。

李安拿到学位后，没能找到机会拍电影。他只能在家照看子女、做家务，靠妻子赚钱养家。但在这段时间里，李安接触到了不少西方的文化和电影。1991年，台湾的一家电影公司找
[10] 他拍《推手》。这部电影拍得很成功，李安也因此一举成名。

1995年，李安决定去好莱坞拍电影。2001年，他拍摄的《卧虎藏龙》获得了奥斯卡"最佳外语片"奖，并创造了美国有史以来外语片最高卖座纪录。在西方，外国人甚至通过看《卧虎藏龙》来了解东方文化。2005年，他拍摄的《断背
[15] 山》讲述了60年代美国西部牛仔的同性恋生活。这部影片也得到了西方影评界和观众的好评，并获得了奥斯卡"最佳导演奖"。

李安的电影为东西方文化架起了一座桥梁。在拍电影
[20] 时，他能充分接受西方的电影技巧。李安拍的电影有浓厚的现代感和生活感，同时，他对东西方文化有自己的体会。李安成功地把东西方文化结合在
[25] 一起，创造出了他自己独特的电影风格。

zhī míng
1. 知名 renowned

huá rén
2. 华人 Chinese; foreign citizens of Chinese origin or descent

tán
*3. 坛（壇）(sports or literary) circle; field

yǐng tán
影坛 movie world

céng
4. 曾 once

céng jīng
曾经 once

huò dé
5. 获得 gain; win

tái wān
6. 台湾（灣）Taiwan (a province of China)

jí
7. 籍 place of origin

zǔ jí
祖籍 ancestral home

jiāng xī
8. 江西 Jiangxi (a province of China)

xué shì
9. 学士 bachelor

shuò
10. 硕（碩）big; large　硕士 master

shuò shì

xué wèi
11. 学位 academic degree

qī zǐ
12. 妻子 wife

zhuàn
13. 赚（賺）make a profit

zhuàn qián
赚钱 make money

xī fāng
14. 西方 the West

bù
*15. 部 a measure word used for books or films

yì jǔ chéng míng
16. 一举成名 become famous overnight

hǎo lái wù
17. 好莱（萊）坞（塢）Hollywood

pāi shè
18. 拍摄 take a picture or shoot

cáng
19. 藏 hide

ào sī kǎ
20. 奥斯卡 Oscar

wài yǔ
21. 外语 foreign language

bìng
22. 并（並）in addition

zào
23. 造 make; create　创造 create

chuàng zào

yǒu shǐ yǐ lái
24. 有史以来 since the beginning of history

mài zuò
25. 卖座 draw large audiences

jì lù
26. 纪录 record

wài guó
27. 外国 foreign country

wài guó rén
外国人 foreigner

dōng fāng
28. 东方 the East

bèi
29. 背 back of the body

shù
30. 述 narrate　讲述 tell about

jiǎng shù

xī bù
31. 西部 western part

tóng xìng liàn
32. 同性恋 homosexuality

píng
*33. 评（評）comment

yǐng píng
影评 film review

jiè
34. 界 circle; field

zhòng
35. 众（眾）crowd

guān zhòng
观众 audience

hǎo píng
36. 好评 favourable comments

jià
*37. 架 put up

liáng
38. 梁（樑）beam; bridge

qiáo liáng
桥梁 bridge

nóng
39. 浓（濃）thick

nóng hòu
浓厚 (of interest) great

jié hé
40. 结合 combine

dú tè
41. 独特 unique

fēng gé
42. 风格 style

61

消化课文

1. 根据课文回答问题

1) 李安祖籍何处？他最初是在哪儿接触到电影和戏剧的？

2) 李安在哪儿获得了什么专业的学士和硕士学位？

3) 李安在美国拿到学位后做了哪些事情？

4) 李安拍的第一部电影叫什么？对他有什么影响？

5) 李安拍摄的《卧虎藏龙》获得了什么奖项？

6) 李安的电影有什么独特的风格？

2. 根据实际情况回答问题

1) 你最喜欢哪个名人？他/她为什么有名？你为什么会喜欢他/她？ 他/她为社会作了哪些贡献？

2) 你平时喜欢看什么电影？多久看一次电影？你最近看了一部什么电影？简单介绍一下这部电影。你喜欢这部电影吗？为什么？

3) 你看过中国电影吗？你喜欢看哪一类电影？你最喜欢哪一部电影？这部电影的导演是谁？这部电影获过什么奖项？

4) 在你们国家，最有名的电影导演是谁？他/她拍过哪些有名的电影？你最喜欢他/她的哪部电影？为什么？

5) 在你们国家，最有名的电影演员有谁？你最喜欢哪个演员？为什么？

6) 你最喜欢的体育明星是谁？他/她为什么有名？你每次都看他/她的比赛吗？上一次的比赛是什么时候？

7) 你平时喜欢看书吗？你最近在看什么书？你最喜欢的是哪本书？你为什么喜欢这本书？

8) 你平时喜欢听谁的歌？为什么？你最喜欢的一首歌叫什么名字？你为什么喜欢这首歌？

1. 选择其中一个短语造句

Ⓐ 例子：在国际影坛上，他曾经获得过多个国际
电影奖。（第1行）

在这段日子里

在学习汉语的过程中

Ⓑ 例子：李安的电影为东西方文化架起了一座
桥梁。（第18行）

为……作准备/办签证

2. 用所给词语造句

Ⓐ 例子：他曾经获得过多个国际电影奖。（第1行）　　曾经　住过

Ⓑ 例子：这部电影拍得很成功，李安也因此一
举成名。（第10行）　　因此　获奖

Ⓒ 例子：外国人甚至通过看《卧虎藏龙》来了解
东方文化。（第13行）　　通过　组织

3. 完成句子

Ⓐ 例子：李安出生于台湾。（第3行）　　我校成立于_____。

Ⓑ 例子：李安成功地把东西方文化结合在一起。　　救护车把_____。

（第23行）

4. 从课文中找反义词

1) 国内→( )（第1行)　　4) 最初→( )（第4行)

2) 去世→( )（第3行)　　5) 分离→( )（第24行)

3) 讨厌→( )（第3行)　　6) 普通→( )（第25行)

5. 用课文中的动词填空

1) _____学位（第2行)　　3) _____新的纪录（第12行)

2) _____电影（第7行)　　4) _____历史（第15行)

口语训练

口头报告

介绍一个你喜欢的名人，他/她可能是个影视明星、歌星、运动员、作家、商人等等。你的口头报告应包括以下几点：

- 他/她的姓名、长相、国籍、职业、婚姻（hūn yīn）状况、性格爱好等
- 你喜欢他/她的原因（yuán yīn）
- 他/她对你的影响

例子：

我今天要向大家介绍一位香港的歌星及影视明星。他叫刘德华。他的花名（huā míng）叫华仔，英文姓名叫"Andy Lau"。他是香港人，祖籍是广东。我很喜欢刘德华，因为他歌儿唱得好，而且他电影也演得好。

他的身高有1.74米，信佛教（fó jiào）。他长得很帅（shuài），而且身材（shēn cái）一直都保持（bǎo chí）得很好。跟他一起合作过的人都说他是个绅士。他心肠（xīn cháng）好，会体贴（tǐ tiē）人，很容易相处。他工作勤奋、敬业（jìng yè）。他总是很青（qīng）春，充满（chūn chōngmǎn）活力。

刘德华会说广东话、普通话、英语和泰语。他喜欢读书，喜欢打保龄球（bǎo líng qiú）、羽毛球和桌球（zhuō qiú）。他喜爱收集（shōu jí）古董（gǔ dǒng）、书画。刘德华还是个慈善家，他支持好几个慈善机构，并成立了"刘德华慈善基金会"，帮助贫困（pín kùn）儿童和伤（shāng）残（cán）人士。

上中小学时，刘德华就热心于参加校内的戏剧演出，还参与

64

幕后制作、负责编剧。刘德华在香港无线艺员培训班学习过，1981年第一次在一部电视剧中亮相。

从上个世纪90年代开始，刘德华在电影和音乐方面同时发展。在电影方面，他跟香港、内地、台湾以及新加坡的演员合作拍片。到今天他已演了超过120部电影。1985年，刘德华进军乐坛。他的第一张专辑叫《只知道此刻爱你》。从1991年开始，他被称为香港乐坛"四大天王"之一，也是香港及亚太地区最受欢迎的男歌星之一。到现在为止，刘德华一共发行过100多张专辑，全球总销量超过5000万张。他在世界各地举办过300多场演唱会，他自己能作曲并填词。

刘德华是我心目中的偶像。我是他忠实的粉丝。他开演唱会，我一定会去；他拍的每一部电影我一定会看。我希望他不断进步。

同时，我也会学习他与人为善的品格和勤奋、敬业的精神。

参考句子

a) 他富有同情心、乐于助人。他乐于挑战自己，十分喜爱运动。他的志向是做一个网球运动员。

b) 他从小酷爱音乐，希望将来能做他自己喜欢做的事。

c) 我跟他的性格很像。我们又有相同的爱好。

d) 他拍的电影曾经多次在国际电影节上获奖。

e) 他积极、热心地参加慈善活动，一有时间就为社区服务，为社会作贡献。

f) 他是一个世界知名的商人。他勤劳、节俭，又热心支持教育。他捐钱建学校，资助贫困儿童上学。

g) 她是一个华裔跳水运动员。她通过努力、刻苦的训练，曾获得过奥运会的跳水冠军。

h) 他是一个国际知名的赛车手。他聪明，而且懂几门外语。每次有他参加的比赛，总是有上万名的观众来看。

写作训练

实际运用

1. 写叙述文

请介绍一个从小到大对你影响最大的人。在文中你要提及以下几个方面：

- 他/她是谁
- 他/她的性格、长相、职业、爱好等
- 他/她对你有哪些影响

参考句子

a) 在我的成长过程中，我父亲对我的影响最大，尤其是在学习的态度上。他总是认真工作，不断进修。（jìn xiū）

b) 父母是我的榜样（bǎng yàng）。他们的一举一动都会影响我。我的很多好习惯都是从他们身上学来的。

c) 我祖母（zǔ mǔ）是一个正直的人。她一辈子（yí bèi zi）做人诚实，工作认真，从来都不马虎。她从来都不说假话，对自己的要求特别高。

d) 从小到大，我爸爸教育我要努力学习，争取最好的成绩。他还要求我要有礼貌，做一个诚实、善良的人。他经常对我说年轻人要有理想，要有目标，每天不断进步，朝着（cháo）自己的目标努力。

e) 我的外公常常教育我要关心别人，多做善事，长大成为对社会有用的人。

66

2. 阅读短文并写回应式作文

你早就听说过贝聿铭(bèi yù míng)这个名字，读了下面的短文后对他有了更多的认识。写一封电邮向你的朋友简单介绍贝聿铭先生。

美籍华人贝聿铭先生是一位世界级的现代建筑设计大师。他 [1]
父亲是中国银行的创始人之一。贝聿铭先生1917年出生于广州，
他的童年和少年时期是在风景如画的苏州(sū zhōu)和高楼林立(lín lì)的上海度过
的。他从小立志要当一名建筑师。贝聿铭1935年远渡重洋(yuǎn dù chóng yáng)，到美
国留学，学习建筑。他从美国的麻省理工学院(má shěng lǐ gōng)毕业后，又在哈佛(hā fó) [5]
大学取得了硕士学位。

在美国的许多大城市都有贝聿铭的作品。贝聿铭在美国各地
负责设计过博物馆、学院、商业中心、摩天大厦(mó tiān dà shà)等，由他设计的
大型建筑在百项以上。他负责设计并建造的肯尼迪(kěn ní dí)图书馆于1979年
落成，在美国建筑界引起轰动(hōng dòng)，被公认为美国建筑史上最佳杰作(jié zuò) [10]
之一。贝聿铭因此声名远扬(shēng míng yuǎn yáng)，成为世界级的建筑大师。

贝聿铭的作品不仅遍布美国，而且分布于全世界。1984年，
他为香港中国银行设计了一座70层、高315米的大厦，是贝氏所有
设计方案(fāng àn)中最高的建筑物。还有，北京西山有名的香山饭店融合(róng hé)
了中国古典园林(yuán lín)建筑的特色，设计别具一格。贝聿铭还应法国总(zǒng) [15]
统(tǒng)的邀请，完成了巴黎卢浮宫(lú fú gōng)的扩建设计。1988年，巴黎的卢浮
宫玻璃金字塔落成(luò chéng)。这项工程完成后，卢浮宫成为世界上最大的
博物馆。

贝聿铭的建筑设计曾获奖无数，最有名的当数相当于诺贝尔(nuò bèi ěr)
奖的普利兹(pǔ lì zī)建筑奖，是建筑界最高的荣誉(róng yù)。他的设计风格既优美 [20]
又有气魄(qì pò)，融合了科技、人性、自然与文化等元素(yuán sù)。贝聿铭坚信
建筑不是流行风尚(fēng shàng)，建筑是千秋(qiān qiū)大业，要对社会和历史负责。

67

阅读与理解

中国电影的发展

第一段 [1]　　1905年，中国的第一部电影在北京前门上^{shàng yìng}映。1931年，中国拍成了第一部有声电影。

第二段　　20世纪30年代的中国电影主题分为几类，有的反^{fǎn yìng}映农村悲^{bēi kǔ}苦的农民生活，如《春蚕^{cán}》；有的反映都市底层^{dū shì dǐ céng}人物的苦难境遇^{kǔ nàn jìng yù}，如《马路天使^{tiān shǐ}》**[5]**；有的反映小知识分子面临^{miàn lín}社会动荡^{dòng dàng}时矛盾^{máo dùn}的心理，如《十字街头》。

第三段　　20世纪40年代，中国电影进入了一个黄金^{huáng jīn}时期，电影艺术达到了新的高峰^{gāo fēng}，诞生^{dàn shēng}了一批经典^{pī jīng diǎn}之作，如《万家灯火》等。

第四段　　1949年新中国成立以后一直到"文化大革命^{gé mìng}"之前（1966年），**[10]**中国成立了一批电影基地^{jī dì}，如北京电影制片厂、上海电影制片厂等，制作了一批优秀的电影，如《早春二月》等。"文革"期间（1966~1976），电影受到了较大的影响，但20世纪70年代的一些电影仍然^{réng rán}受到人们的喜爱，如《闪闪^{shǎn shǎn}的红星》等。

第五段　　从1978年开始，中国实行改革开放政策，中国电影又走向了新的**[15]**高峰。20世纪80年代，陈凯歌^{chén kǎi gē}的《黄土地》、张艺谋^{zhāng yì móu}的《红高粱^{gāo liang}》让世界重新^{chóng xīn}认识了中国电影。90年代后，中国电影的综合^{zōng hé}实力开始增^{zēng}强^{qiáng}，多部影片进入了国际市场，例如张艺谋2002年导演的《英雄^{yīng xióng}》成为了第一部进入美国主流^{zhǔ liú}电影院放映^{fàng yìng}的中国电影。还有些电影不仅获得了国际大奖，而且票房收入^{piào fáng shōu rù}可观^{kě guān}。

第六段 [20]　　随着中国国家实力逐步^{zhú bù}增强，中国电影在技术^{jì shù}和人才^{rén cái}方面也都已具备了世界水准^{shuǐ zhǔn}。中国电影的潜力^{qián lì}将得到进一步开发，中国电影将创造新的辉煌^{huī huáng}。

1. "底层人物"(第4行)的意思
   是 _____。
   a) 社会最低的阶层
   b) 知名人物
   c) 大人物

2. "黄金时期"(第7行)的意思
   是 _____。
   a) 金钱时代
   b) 最繁华的、辉煌的时期
   c) 找到黄金的时候

3. "高峰"(第8行)的意思是
   _____。
   a) 时期　　　b) 阶段
   c) 比喻事情发展的最高点

4. "美国主流电影院"(第18行)的
   意思是 _____。
   a) 既是电影院又是剧场
   b) 对当地美国影片开放的电影院
   c) 有名的电影院

5. "票房收入"(第19行)的意思是
   _____。
   a) 演员的工资
   b) 卖电影票而赚到的钱
   c) 电影票价

6. "水准"(第21行)的意思是 _____。
   a) 品牌
   b) 标准
   c) 水平

1. 第一段　　☐
2. 第二段　　☐
3. 第三段　　☐
4. 第四段　　☐
5. 第五段　　☐
6. 第六段　　☐

A 中国电影事业前景美好。

B 中国电影在技术上已经达到了国际水平。

C "文化大革命"期间中国电影的发展。

D 20世纪30年代中国电影的类别。

E 20世纪30年代中国电影中的演技。

F 改革开放后中国电影在艺术上走向了一个新的
　高峰，并向国际市场发展。

G 新中国成立后至"文化大革命"结束中国电影
　的发展。

H 中国电影业的诞生。

I 20世纪40年代中国电影在艺术上达到了新的高峰。

判断正误，并说明原因

1. 到了20世纪40年代，中国才拍出了第一部电影。 对 错

   原因：_____ ___ ___

2. 《闪闪的红星》是在"文化大革命"期间拍的。
   shǎnshǎn

   原因：_____ ___ ___

3. 自从改革开放后，中国电影事业没有太大的发展。

   原因：_____ ___ ___

4. 中国电影曾经在国际上获得过电影大奖。

   原因：_____ ___ ___

5. 当今的中国有技术也有人才，一定能拍出国际水平的电影。

   原因：_____ ___ ___

D 从短文中选出最合适的动词填空

1. 最近张艺谋又_____（第1行）了一部古装故事片。
   zhāng yì móu

2. 中国电影的历史可以_____（第3行）四个阶段。

3. 中国电影已经_____（第7行）了国际市场，而且有几部电影票房收入

   相当可观。

4. 中华人民共和国于1949年_____（第9行）。

5. 李安拍摄的电影多少_____（第12行）了西方电影技巧的影响。

6. 这部武打片是陈凯歌_____（第17行）的。
   wǔ dǎ piàn chén kǎi gē

中国的民族乐器

中国的民族乐器历史悠久。从已经出土的文物可证实：远在先秦时期就有了多种多样的乐器。以下是最具代表性的几种中国民族乐器。 [1] 第一段

编钟是中国古代一种打击乐器，用青铜铸成。因为编钟能奏出歌唱一样的旋律，所以也被叫做"歌钟"。大小不同的扁圆钟按照音调高低的次序排列起来，挂在一个巨大的钟架上。用木锤敲击编钟便能奏出美妙的乐曲。通常编钟的钟体越小，音高就越高，音量也越小。编钟最早出现在商代，兴起于西周，盛行于春秋战国，自宋代以来渐渐衰退。在中国古代，编钟是上层社会专用的乐器，是等级和权力的象征。 第二段 [5]

古筝是一种古老的弦乐器。目前最常用的古筝规格是长163厘米左右，有21根弦。古筝常用于独奏、重奏、器乐合奏和歌舞、戏曲等的伴奏。因古筝的音域宽广，音色优美动听，所以被称为"众乐之王"，也称为"东方钢琴"。 [10]第三段

二胡又叫南胡，是中国最主要的拉弦乐器。在世界上，二胡被誉为"中国的小提琴"。二胡可以独奏，也可参加重奏或合奏，在民乐团中的重要性相当于管弦乐队里的小提琴。 第四段 [15]

笛子是中国广为流传的吹奏乐器。因为笛子用天然竹材制成，所以也称为"竹笛"。笛子是中国最具特色的吹奏乐器之一。笛子虽然短小简单，但它却有几千年的历史。笛子的表现力非常丰富，它既能演奏出不同的旋律，又能表现各种情调。除此以外，笛子还能表现大自然的各种声音，比如模仿各种鸟的叫声等。 第五段 [20]

根据短文找出四个正确的句子

☐ 1. 中国的民族乐器种类繁多。

☐ 2. 笛子是一种弦乐器。

☐ 3. 编钟是中国现代上层社会专用的乐器。

☐ 4. 人们一般称"古筝"为"东方钢琴"。

☐ 5. 编钟是用木头做成的。

☐ 6. 在古代，编钟是一种很普通的乐器。

☐ 7. 笛子是用竹子做的，有着几千年的历史。

☐ 8. 人们把二胡比作"中国的小提琴"。

B 判断正误，并说明原因

1. 远在中国的先秦时期，各种民族乐器就出现了。　　　　　对　错

　　原因：＿＿＿＿＿＿＿＿＿＿＿＿＿＿＿＿＿＿＿＿＿　＿＿　＿＿

2. 有人把编钟叫做"歌钟"。

　　原因：＿＿＿＿＿＿＿＿＿＿＿＿＿＿＿＿＿＿＿＿＿　＿＿　＿＿

3. 在春秋战国时期，编钟开始走下坡路。

　　原因：＿＿＿＿＿＿＿＿＿＿＿＿＿＿＿＿＿＿＿＿＿　＿＿　＿＿

4. 在中国古代，编钟是一种相当普遍、深受民众喜爱的乐器。

　　原因：＿＿＿＿＿＿＿＿＿＿＿＿＿＿＿＿＿＿＿＿＿　＿＿　＿＿

5. 最常见的古筝长16.3米，有21根弦。

　　原因：＿＿＿＿＿＿＿＿＿＿＿＿＿＿＿＿＿＿＿＿＿　＿＿　＿＿

6. 在中国的民乐团中，二胡的确起着很重要的作用。

　　原因：＿＿＿＿＿＿＿＿＿＿＿＿＿＿＿＿＿＿＿＿＿　＿＿　＿＿

7. 笛子是一种吹奏乐器，深受广大中国人的喜爱。

　　原因：＿＿＿＿＿＿＿＿＿＿＿＿＿＿＿＿＿＿＿＿＿　＿＿　＿＿

1. 笛子是一种很简单的乐器，⬜ ｜ A 比如鸟的叫声。

2. 古筝有21根弦，⬜ ｜ B 只能独奏。_{dú zòu}

3. 用笛子能吹奏出各种声音，⬜ ｜ C 但演奏起来表现力很强。_{yǎn zòu}

4. 编钟的钟体越小，⬜ ｜ D 音高就越高，音量也越小。

5. 古筝的音域很广，⬜ ｜ E 需要用铁锤敲击。_{tiě chuí qiāo jī}

6. 编钟在春秋战国时期 ⬜ ｜ F 相当流行。

｜ G 可以为歌舞伴奏。_{bàn zòu}

｜ H 音色美妙动听。_{měi miào}

D 根据短文选择正确答案

1. "悠久"（第1行）的意思是_{yōu jiǔ}

_____。

a) 年代久远

b) 很短

c) 不算长

2. "巨大"（第5行）的意思是_{jù dà}

_____。

a) 极高

b) 体积非常大_{tǐ jī}

c) 极小

3. "独奏"（第11行）的意思是_{dú zòu}

_____。

a) 交响乐_{jiāo xiǎng yuè}

b) 独唱

c) 由一个人用一种乐器演奏

4. "众乐之王"（第12行）的意思

是 _____。

a) 乐器中的王子

b) 在所有乐器中居首位

c) 最好的音乐

E 从短文中选出最合适的词语填空

1. _____（第4行）的玻璃瓶能奏出优美的音乐。_{bō li}

2. _____（第10行）的钟楼跟它周围的现代建筑融为了一体。_{róng}

3. 中国民族乐器二胡能奏出跟小提琴一样_____（第12行）的音乐。

4. 民乐团中的_____（第14行）乐器有二胡、笛子、古筝等。

5. 古筝是一种很有_____（第18行）的中国民族乐器。

73

第二单元
第6课

[1] 　　上个月，我以交换生的身份去中国的大连生活、学习了两个星期。在这两个星期里，我对中国文化有了进一步的了解，对西方文化也有了更深刻的体会。

　　在饮食方面，吃饭在中国人的日常生活中很重要。
[5] 中国人有时候午饭也要炒菜。中国人做菜时非常讲究，注重色、香、味、形，做出来的菜好像一件工艺品。西方人午饭大都吃三明治，做晚饭也不复杂。他们习惯吃烤的食物，还喜欢吃沙拉。

　　在称呼方面，中国人称呼亲戚以外的人时，也要分清
[10] 辈分，比如，叫男性长辈"爷爷"或者"叔叔"；叫女性长辈"奶奶"或者"阿姨"。年轻人称呼中老年人时，要在他们的姓前面加一个"老"字，表示尊敬；中老年人称呼年轻人时，则在他们的姓前面加一个"小"字，表示亲切。但是在西方，人们大都直呼其名。

[15] 　　在礼仪方面，中国文化和西方文化都非常重视人际交往，但在交往的观念和方式上有明显的差异。中国人热情
[20] 好客，喜欢问长问短，他们会询问有关别人的年龄、职业、收入、婚姻状况等问题。西方人则比较重视个人的隐私，尊重别
[25] 人的私生活。

74

在教育方面，我发现中国的学生读书普遍比较用功，学校、家长和学生都很看重学习成绩。中国人和西方人对待分数的态度也不同。大多数西方人都不太看重分数。

大连的生活、学习经历令我难忘。如果今后有机会，我还会去[30]中国，希望了解更多的中国文化和习俗。

生词

1. 差异 chā yì difference
2. 大连 dà lián Dalian (a city in northern China)
3. 深刻 shēn kè deep; profound
4. 饮食 yǐn shí diet
5. 究 jiū probe into　讲究 jiǎng jiū be particular about
6. 复杂 fù zá complicated
7. 称 (稱) chēng call
8. 呼 hū call　称呼 chēng hu call; form of address
9. 分清 fēn qīng distinguish
10. 辈分 bèi fen position in the family hierarchy; generation
*11. 性 xìng gender　男性 nán xìng male
　　女性 nǚ xìng female
12. 中年 zhōngnián middle age
　　中老年 zhōng lǎo nián middle and old age
13. 亲切 qīn qiè warm; close
14. 则 (則) zé indicating contrast
15. 直呼其名 zhí hū qí míng directly call one's name
16. 仪 (儀) yí ceremony　礼仪 lǐ yí courtesy
17. 重视 zhòng shì lay stress on

18. 人际 rén jì interpersonal
19. 显 (顯) xiǎn apparent; show up
　　明显 míngxiǎn obvious
20. 好客 hào kè hospitable
21. 问长问短 wèncháng wènduǎn take the trouble to make detailed inquiries
22. 询 (詢) xún inquire　询问 xún wèn ask about
*23. 有关 yǒu guān relate to
24. 收入 shōu rù income
25. 姻 yīn marriage　婚姻 hūn yīn marriage
26. 隐 (隱) yǐn privacy; hidden
　　隐私 yǐn sī privacy; secret
27. 尊重 zūn zhòng respect
28. 私生活 sī shēng huó private life
29. 普遍 pǔ biàn general; common
30. 看重 kàn zhòng regard as important; think highly of
31. 对待 duì dài treat
32. 分数 fēn shù mark; grade
*33. 令 lìng make; cause
34. 习俗 xí sú custom

75

消化课文

1. 根据课文回答问题

1) 作者是以什么身份去大连生活、学习的？她去了多久？有什么收获？

2) 中国人是怎样对待饮食的？中国人做菜时注重什么？西方人午饭、晚饭都吃些什么？

3) 中国人和西方人在称呼亲戚以外的人时有什么不同？

4) 在礼仪方面，中国人和西方人有哪些相同和不同的地方？

5) 中国人和西方人怎样对待子女的学习成绩？

6) 如果作者以后有机会再去中国，她会有什么期望？

2. 根据实际情况回答问题

1) 你和家人都注重饮食健康吗？在你们家，哪餐饭比较重要？你们经常全家人一起吃吗？

2) 你能说出几个中国菜的名字？你和家人常去哪一家饭店吃饭？你们一般吃什么？请简单介绍一下这家饭店。

3) 在你们国家，人们称呼亲戚以外的人时，要注意辈分吗？在这方面，你们跟中国人的习惯差不多还是差很多？

4) 在你们国家，学生平时读书用功吗？考试前他们是否会很紧张？学生们很看重考试成绩吗？

5) 在你们国家，家长是否很看重子女的学习成绩？为了子女能考上名牌大学，他们会做些什么？

6) 你最近有没有去过中国？去中国的目的是什么？有哪些收获？

7) 你在中国人家里住过吗？请讲一讲这个家庭给你留下了哪些印象。

8) 如果将来你有机会去中国人的家里生活一两个星期，你最希望去哪里？为什么？你希望得到哪些收获？

1. 完成句子

Ⓐ 例子：在这两个星期里，我对中国文化有了进一步的了解。（第2行）

Ⓑ 例子：吃饭在中国人的日常生活中很重要。

（第4行）

Ⓒ 例子：在礼仪方面，中国文化和西方文化都非常重视人际交往。（第15行）

Ⓓ 例子：在交往的观念和方式上有明显的差异。

（第17行）

在过去的两年里，

_____。

在学习汉语的过程中，_____。

在饮食方面，____

_____。

在环保问题上，

_____。

2. 选择其中一个短语造句

Ⓐ 例子：我发现中国的学生读书普遍比较用功。

（第26行）

我估计/相信/建议

Ⓑ 例子：大多数西方人都不太看重分数。（第28行）

绝大部分/一小部分/有些

3. 用带点的词语模仿例子造句

Ⓐ 例子：大连的生活、学习经历令我难忘。（第29行）

Ⓑ 例子：我希望了解更多的中国文化和习俗。

（第30行）

4. 从课文中找反义词

1) 马虎→(　　　)（第5行）　　4) 晚辈→(　　　)（第10行）

2) 东方→(　　　)（第6行）　　5) 公 → (　　　)（第25行）

3) 女性→(　　　)（第10行）　　6) 过去→(　　　)（第29行）

口语训练

小组讨论

各个国家、民族都有自己的文化和习俗。由于全球化，各国的传统文化及习俗正在相互影响，也在不断变化。试讨论你们国家或地区的传统文化和习俗都发生了哪些变化。讨论要包括以下几个方面：

• 饮食方面

• 称呼方面

• 礼仪方面

• 教育方面

• 其他方面

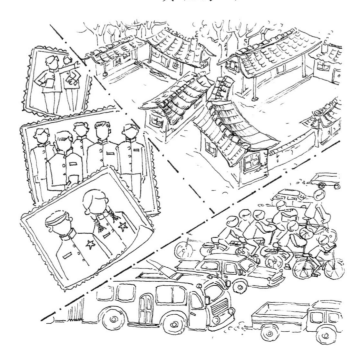

例子：

学生1：在饮食方面，我觉得中餐花样多，每个地区（dì qū）都有不同的菜式，菜的口味和做法也都不同。一个国家有那么多菜式，这在世界上是少有的。

学生2：我很同意你刚才说的。我在上海交换生的家里住了一个月。我很喜欢吃他们家做的上海菜。在上海的饭店里，你能吃到各种口味的饭菜。中餐太丰富了，真是中国文化的宝贵财富（cái fù）。

学生3：但是现在的中国人不但吃中餐，他们还能吃到各个国家的饭菜。

学生1：中国人称呼别人时，一般不直呼其名，要分清辈分，否则别人会认为你不尊重他/她，没有礼貌，没有家教（jiā jiào）。

学生2：但是现在在中国，有的人也对别人直呼其名。在一些公共场合，人们一般称男性"先生"，称女性"小姐"。这样

的称呼已经很国际化了。

学生3：我也注意到了。在礼仪方面，中国人的习俗也在改变。中国人还是热情好客，但是一般不再询问有关他人的收入、婚姻状况、年龄等个人隐私的问题了。

学生1：我觉得中国人特别重视教育，普遍看重分数，每个家长都希望子女能考上世界名牌大学。

学生2：我们国家也很重视教育。大部分家长都肯为子女花钱请家教、上补习班等。

学生3：我相信每个国家都重视教育。我父母为我请了几个家教，每个月为我花不少钱。可我感觉压力很大，因为父母希望我每门功课都拿高分。

学生1：在穿着方面，好像各国的年轻人穿的衣服都差不多。

……

参考句子

a) 近二三十年，中国人的饮食发生了很大的变化。现在食品比以前丰富多了。在超市里，你能买到各个国家的食品。很多人喜欢吃西式快餐、日餐、韩餐、东南亚风味餐等。

b) 现在也有越来越多的外国人喜欢吃中国的美食。世界各地都有中餐馆。

c) 现在全世界的年轻人穿着 chuānzhuó 都差不多，吊带背心 diào dài bèi xīn、牛仔裤非常流行。

d) 如今，很多中国家长送子女去外国留学、学英语，外国的家长也会送子女到中国学中文、学中国文化。

e) 现在全球化了，有些国家的习俗也被其他国家的人所接受。比如说西方人的圣诞节这一天，很多国家都有庆祝活动。在香港，过春节时西方人也发红包；过圣诞节时中国人也送圣诞礼物给亲朋好友。

写作训练

1. 写电邮

假设今年春节你去了中国，在一个中国朋友家里过春节，亲身体验了中国人过年的一些习俗。写一封电邮给你在国外的朋友，说说你亲眼看到、亲身体验到的一切。在电邮中，你要提及：

- 你所去的地方的简介
- 中国人过春节的习俗
- 建议他/她有机会去中国亲身感受中国人过春节的习俗

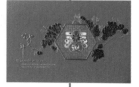

参考句子

a) 春节前，人们忙着办年货、贴春联、买年花等。人们买桃树是希望新的一年里有好运气；买盆橘是希望大吉大利；红色"福"字倒贴在门上、墙上，表示"福"到了。做这些都是希望在新的一年里吉利、平安。

b) 年夜饭人们一定会吃鱼，希望"年年有余"，还会吃年糕，希望"年年高升"，吃汤圆是希望"团团圆圆"。吃完年夜饭，全家人坐在一起守岁。十二点一到，人们一起放鞭炮、烟花，庆祝新年的到来。

c) 中国人过年的一些活动，比如舞龙、舞狮、放鞭炮等都是为了驱邪、保平安。过年时家人团聚，在一起吃年夜饭表示团团圆圆；而特别的食品、摆设都是为了求吉利。

d) 我建议你有机会去中国过春节，亲身体验中国人过春节的一些习俗。这样的经历一定会令你难忘。

2. 阅读短文并写作文

写一篇博客，介绍你居住的地区在全球化的影响下在哪些方面受到了其他文化和习俗的影响。

香港人文化习俗的演变

香港受英国统治长达150多年之久。今日的香港已经从一个人烟稀少的小渔村发展成为繁华的国际大都市，称得上是中西文化合璧的典范。 [1]

19世纪中期，英国人开始接管香港。当时，中、英人士语言、风俗及习惯不同，英国人依照自己的生活习惯生活，而中国人保持着中国的传统习俗。到了20世纪初，在香港的中国人开始受到西方生活方式和习俗风尚的影响。这些中国人主要有两种：一种是少数社会精英，他们接受过西式教育；第二种人是在日常工作与生活中接触到西方文化的人，比如在外国洋行工作的人。虽然他们受到西方文化和习俗的影响，但是基本上还保持着中国人的本色。慢慢地，香港的普通老百姓也开始受到西方文化和习俗的影响。150多年后的今天，香港已经被打造成为一个展示西方文明的窗口。在香港，现代化的企业和机构、严格的管理制度、干净的街道、秩序井然的社区使居民养成了文明的习惯，中西方文化和习俗完美地结合在一起。 [5] [10]

在香港的现代化进程中，中西方文化相互影响、相互交融。今天的香港犹如万花筒般多姿多彩，但是香港人仍然保持着自己的习俗和信仰。白领职员白天西装革履，翻阅英文报纸，晚上回到家中却搓麻将、看中文影视剧；还有一些香港人至今仍问卜算命，相信风水。 [15]

香港社会给予人们自由的生活空间。香港人在传统与现代、本土文化与西方文化的交汇中选择不同的生活方式。 [20]

81

阅读与理解

中国的少数民族

[1]　　中国自古以来就是一个多民族的国家。除了汉族以外，中国有55个少数民族，占全国人口的9.44%。以下将分别介绍人们比较熟悉的几个少数民族。

　　蒙古族是一个富有传奇色彩的民族，历史上出现过成吉思汗、

[5]　忽必烈等重要人物。蒙古族人主要集中在内蒙古自治区，过着游牧生活，但是现在大多数都定居下来了。每年七、八月举行的庆祝丰收的"那达慕"大会是蒙古族的传统节日。大会上有赛马、摔跤、射箭、棋艺、歌舞等比赛。

　　回族是中国少数民族中散居全国、分布最广的民族。清真寺是回

[10]　族穆斯林主要的宗教活动场所。回族人至今保持着中亚人传统的穿衣打扮：男子多戴小白帽，留大胡子；而女子多戴头巾，也叫盖头。回族人忌吃猪肉，他们喜欢的菜肴有：涮羊肉、手抓羊肉等。明代著名航海家郑和就是回族人。

　　藏族是中国古老的民族之一。有"世界屋脊"之称的青藏高原是

[15]　藏族人的主要聚居地。藏族普遍信奉藏传佛教，即喇嘛教。藏族的民间节日有藏历新年、酥油灯节、浴佛节等。藏族接待宾客时，要献上一条白色的丝织长巾，藏语称为"哈达"。

　　满族主要分布在中国的东北三省，其人口总数在中国55个少数民族中居第二位。满族人庆祝的重要节日跟汉族人的差不多。满族历史

[20]　悠久。满族人建立了清朝政权，清朝皇帝康熙、雍正、乾隆等都曾经在中国历史上作出过重大贡献。经改良的满族妇女的旗袍早已成了中国民族服装的代表之一。

1. 中国总共有多少个民族？

2. 中国的哪个少数民族擅长赛马？

3. 藏族人主要居住在哪儿？
   zàng zú

4. 旗袍最初是哪个少数民族的服装？

1. 中国是个_____的国家。

   a) 多民族

   b) 以少数民族为主

   c) 信奉佛教
   xìn fèng fó jiào

2. 回族女子戴的头巾叫 _____。
   huí zú

   a) 小白帽　b) 盖头
   gài tou

   c) 旗袍

3. 在中国历史上，_____建立了
   清朝政权。
   zhèngquán

   a) 蒙古族　b) 回族　c) 满族
   měng gǔ zú 　　　　_mǎn zú_

4. 回族穆斯林去_____进行宗教
   mù sī lín 　　　　　　_zōng jiào_
   活动。

   a) 那达慕　b) 哈达
   _nà dá mù_ 　_hǎ dá_

   c) 清真寺
   qīngzhēn sì

5. 满族人主要居住在_____。

   a) 西藏　b) 中国的东北

   c) 内蒙古自治区
   zì zhì qū

6. 汉族人口占全国总人口的_____。

   a) 9.44%　b) 90.56%

   c) 10%

1. 在清朝的皇帝中，人们_____（第2行）的有康熙、雍正和乾隆。
   kāng xī yōngzhèng qiánlóng

2. 在中国历史上，成吉思汗是个富有_____（第4行）的人物。
   chéng jí sī hán

3. 经过改良后的满族妇女的_____（第7行）服装成了今天的旗袍。
   gǎi liáng

4. 满族人_____（第10行）聚居在中国的东北三省。
   _jù jū_

5. 中国是一个_____（第14行）的文明国家。

6. 浴佛节是藏族人民的_____（第21行）节日。
   _yù fó_

83

D 判断正误，并说明原因

1. 在中国这块土地上，汉族人口最多。

   原因：_____

   对　错

   ──　──

2. 中国少数民族的人口占全中国总人口的一成以上。

   原因：_____

   ──　──

3. 每年七、八月份举行的"那达慕_{nà dá mù}"大会上有射箭_{shè jiàn}比赛。

   原因：_____

   ──　──

4. 中国各地都有回族人居住。

   原因：_____

   ──　──

5. 手抓羊肉是回族人喜爱的食物。

   原因：_____

   ──　──

6. 藏族人信奉的藏传佛教也叫"喇嘛教_{lǎ ma jiào}"。

   原因：_____

   ──　──

7. 满族人庆祝的节日跟汉族人的完全不同。

   原因：_____

   ──　──

E 根据短文找出四个正确的句子

☐ 1. 蒙古族人不是牧民_{mù mín}。

☐ 2. 著名的航海家_{háng hǎi jiā}郑和_{zhèng hé}是藏族人。

☐ 3. 藏族人接待客人时总是献上一条哈达_{hǎ dá}。

☐ 4. 康熙_{kāng xī}皇帝是满族人。

☐ 5. 回族人不吃猪肉和牛肉。

☐ 6. 满族是中国55个少数民族中人口总数居第二位的民族。

☐ 7. 人们一般把青藏高原称为"世界屋脊_{wū jǐ}"。

生活中的中国文化

什么叫文化？根据易中天先生的说法，"文化就是人类 生 存 和 ___①___ 的方式"。文化就是我们日常生活中最常见的、最普通的事。 `[1]`

文化体现在生活中，而中国文化就 ___②___ 在中国人生活中的方方面面。以下从三个方面来简单地 ___③___ 一下生活中的中国文化。

第一是亲情。中国人很注重家庭、亲情。俗话说"血浓于水"，在血缘关系中，最亲的是母子，其次是兄弟。在中国人的眼里，兄弟"情同手足"。即使没有血缘关系，乡情也是一种亲情。出门在外，老乡见了面就 ___④___ 特别亲切。所有这些关系又都跟吃有关，因为子女同吃母亲的奶，兄弟吃同一锅饭，乡亲吃同一口井里的水。 `[5]`

第二是饮食。中国人有句老话，叫"民以食为天"，也就是说中国人很 ___⑤___ 饮食。吃饭在中国人看来是头等重要的事。朋友们 ___⑥___ 在一起要吃饭；结婚要摆酒席请客吃饭；逢年过节、红白喜事、老人做寿、小孩满月、求人办事等等都要请客吃饭。对中国人来说，请人吃饭是很重情谊的表达方式，好像很多事情都可以在饭桌上 ___⑦___ 。 `[10]`

第三是面子。面子对中国人来说很重要。有的人虽然家里没钱，请人吃饭却一定要有大鱼大肉，摆阔气。 ___⑧___ 衣也要面子。中国人在重要场合要穿得体面、得体，否则就没面子。为什么那么看重面子呢？因为中国人是一个群体意识很强的民族。如果一个人不合群，失去了群体关系，得不到别人的认可，他就很难在社会上立足。 `[15]`

介绍 注重 发展 聚 解决 进步 体现 买 穿 感到

1. _____ 2. _____ 3. _____ 4. _____

5. _____ 6. _____ 7. _____ 8. _____

B 给下列词语配上最合适的解释

1. 头等 (第11行) ☐
2. 面子 (第15行) ☐
   kuò qì
3. 阔气 (第16行) ☐
4. 体面 (第17行) ☐
5. 得体 (第17行) ☐
6. 合群 (第18行) ☐
7. 立足 (第19行) ☐

shēng cún
A 站得住脚，能生存下去。

B 第一等；最高的。

róng qià
C 跟大家都合得来，关系融洽。

D 相当。

E 好看；有面子。

F 言语、行动合适。

háo huá   shē chǐ
G 豪华、奢侈。

xū róng
H 表面的虚荣。

I 身体。

C 根据短文选择正确答案

1. "血浓于水"(第5行)的意思是
   _____。
   xuè yuán
   a) 血缘关系是最亲的
   b) 乡情最亲
   c) 兄弟姐妹关系最亲

2. "血缘关系"(第6行)的意思是
   _____。
   a) 兄弟姐妹   b) 乡亲
   c) 父母子女、兄弟姐妹之间的关系

3. "民以食为天"(第10行)的意思
   是 _____。
   a) 不吃饭也可以
   b) 吃饭是最重要的一件事
   c) 吃不吃饭没关系

4. "红白喜事"(第12行)的意思是
   _____。
   shòusāng
   a) 男女结婚、高寿丧事
   b) 老人做寿   c) 小孩满月

D 判断正误，并说明原因

1. 兄弟之间的关系很亲，因为他们有血缘关系。　　　　　　　对　错

   原因：＿＿＿＿＿＿＿＿＿＿＿＿＿＿＿＿＿＿＿＿＿＿＿＿　＿＿　＿＿

2. 虽然同乡之间没有血缘关系，但是老乡一见面一定会感到非常

   亲热。

   原因：＿＿＿＿＿＿＿＿＿＿＿＿＿＿＿＿＿＿＿＿＿＿＿＿　＿＿　＿＿

3. 在中国，男女结婚一定要摆酒席^{bǎi jiǔ xí}请亲朋好友吃饭。

   原因：＿＿＿＿＿＿＿＿＿＿＿＿＿＿＿＿＿＿＿＿＿＿＿＿　＿＿　＿＿

4. 中国人通过请客吃饭来表示他们很看重情谊^{qíng yì}。

   原因：＿＿＿＿＿＿＿＿＿＿＿＿＿＿＿＿＿＿＿＿＿＿＿＿　＿＿　＿＿

5. 中国人不认为一个人在重要场合穿得随便^{suí biàn}会丢面子。

   原因：＿＿＿＿＿＿＿＿＿＿＿＿＿＿＿＿＿＿＿＿＿＿＿＿　＿＿　＿＿

6. 一个人要在社会上立足，他一定要得到别人的认可。

   原因：＿＿＿＿＿＿＿＿＿＿＿＿＿＿＿＿＿＿＿＿＿＿＿＿　＿＿　＿＿

E 从右边找到最适合的部分完成下列句子

1. 文化的定义是：　　　　　☐　　A 他就很难在社会上立足。
2. 如果一个人不合群，　　　☐　　B 事情就好办了。
3. 在重要场合，　　　　　　☐　　C 也要请客吃饭。
4. 求人办事　　　　　　　　☐　　D 人类生存和发展的方式。
5. 请人吃了饭，　　　　　　☐　　E 要给人面子。
　　　　　　　　　　　　　　　　F 中国人很讲究穿着^{chuānzhuó}得体。
　　　　　　　　　　　　　　　　G 事情还是可以商量的。

87

单元复习

生词

第4课

晚辈　美德　世纪　年代　实行　独生子女　政策
夫妇　年轻人　老年人　方式　由……组成　随着
改革　观念　率　上升　单亲　单身　贵族　夫妻
由此可见　结构　多样化　已婚　大多　照看　孙子
孙女　外孙　外孙女　发扬光大　发言

第5课

知名　华人　影坛　曾经　获得　台湾　祖籍　江西　学士
硕士　学位　妻子　赚钱　西方　*部　一举成名　好莱坞
拍摄　藏　奥斯卡　外语　并　创造　有史以来　卖座
纪录　外国人　东方　背　讲述　西部　同性恋　影评
界　观众　好评　*架　桥梁　浓厚　结合　独特　风格

第6课

差异　大连　深刻　饮食　讲究　复杂　称呼　分清
辈分　男性　女性　中老年　亲切　则　直呼其名
礼仪　重视　人际　明显　好客　问长问短　询问
*有关　收入　婚姻　隐私　尊重　私生活　普遍　看重
对待　分数　*令　习俗

长辈爱护、照顾晚辈　晚辈尊敬、孝顺长辈　实行独生子女政策

尊老爱幼　在一般情况下　生活方式　随着改革开放　离婚率上升

观念发生了变化　单亲家庭增加　享受二人世界　年老体弱

家庭结构比以前多样化　虽然……，但是……　通过各种方式

传统美德还在继续发扬光大

知名的华人导演　在国际影坛上　曾经获得……奖　获得学士/硕士学位

靠……赚钱养家　接触到西方的文化和电影　创造最高纪录

通过看《卧虎藏龙》来了解东方文化　讲述生活　得到观众好评

为东西方文化架起桥梁　充分接受西方的电影技巧　有现代感和生活感

对……有自己的体会　把……结合在一起　创造出独特的风格

以……身份……　对……有了进一步的了解　有了更深刻的体会

在饮食/称呼/礼仪/教育方面　在日常生活中　注重色、香、味、形

做出来的菜像一件工艺品　分清辈分　叫男性长辈"爷爷"

重视人际交往　询问婚姻状况　尊重别人的私生活/个人隐私

看重学习成绩　对待/看重分数　……经历令我难忘

网络的利与弊

[1] 尊敬的主席、评委、正方代表，在座的老师们、同学们：

大家好！

我方今天要辩论的题目是：对青少年来说，网络弊大于利。

[5]　　如今，网络发展很快。网络在青少年的日常生活中占有很重要的地位。一般人的看法是网络给我们带来了很多正面的影响。但同时，网络也给我们带来了不少负面影响。

第一，在网上，由于同类的信息太多，有时候人们花了很多时间找资料，但是收获不大。

[10]　　第二，网络上的信息不一定正确、可靠，有些信息会误导网民。由于青少年辨别是非的能力差，所以他们有时候很容易上当、受骗。

第三，有些青少年滥用网络。他们把作业答案和论文放在网上卖钱，还有些人通过网络欺负别人。在网络上，人们

[15] 不用提供真实的信息，这会使一些青少年养成说谎的习惯。

第四，现在的青少年大都通过网络跟人沟通、联络，因此他们跟人面对面沟通的机会少了。这使他们的交际能力下降了。

[20]　　第五，有些青少年非常依赖网络。他们上网成瘾，好像每时每刻都在上网。这些青

[25] 少年没有心思读书，也没有兴趣参加其他有利

90

于健康的活动。结果，他们不但学习成绩下降了，而且健康状况尤其是视力也变坏了。还有一些青少年整天生活在网络世界里，不关
[30] 心周围的事物。这对他们的成长没有好处。

所以我方的结论是：对青少年来说，网络弊大于利。谢谢大家！

生词

1. 网络 wǎng luò Internet
2. 委 wěi committee　评委 píng wěi judge
3. 正方 zhèngfāng (of debaters) those holding affirmative or positive views
4. 在座 zài zuò be present
5. 辩（辯）biàn debate　辩论 biàn lùn debate
6. 题目 tí mù topic
7. 青少年 qīngshàonián youth
8. 大于 dà yú more than
9. 如今 rú jīn nowadays
10. 占有 zhànyǒu occupy
11. 地位 dì wèi position
12. 看法 kàn fǎ opinion
13. 同类 tóng lèi of the same kind
14. 正确 zhèngquè correct
15. 可靠 kě kào reliable
16. 误导 wù dǎo mislead
17. 网民 wǎngmín netizen
18. 辨 biàn differentiate; distinguish
    辨别 biàn bié differentiate; distinguish

19. 是非 shì fēi right and wrong
20. 上当 shàngdàng be deceived
21. 骗（騙）piàn deceive　受骗 shòupiàn be deceived
22. 滥（濫）làn excessively　滥用 làn yòng abuse
23. 案 àn case　答案 dá àn answer
24. 欺 qī deceive　欺负 qī fu bully
25. 真实 zhēn shí true; real
26. 谎（謊）huǎng lie　说谎 shuōhuǎng tell a lie
27. 交际 jiāo jì communication
28. 依 yī depend on
29. 赖（賴）lài rely; depend　依赖 yī lài rely on
30. 成瘾 chéng yǐn become addicted
31. 每时每刻 měi shí měi kè all the time
32. 心思 xīn si thought
33. 有利 yǒu lì advantageous
34. 结果 jié guǒ result
35. 整天 zhěngtiān all day
36. 事物 shì wù thing
37. 成长 chéngzhǎng grow up
38. 结论 jié lùn conclusion

口语热身

消化课文

1. 根据课文回答问题

1) 发言者代表辩论会的哪一方？

2) 他对网络有什么总的看法？

3) 网络上的信息有什么特点？

4) 一些青少年是怎样滥用网络的？

5) 经常通过网络与人沟通、联络，结果会怎样？

6) 上网成瘾的后果是怎样的？

2. 根据实际情况回答问题

1) 你们学校经常组织辩论会吗？你参加过几次？辩论过什么题目？你做过正方代表还是反方代表？你们在辩论中赢了还是输了？

2) 你们中文班有没有组织过汉语辩论会？你参加了吗？你们辩论过什么题目？如果有机会让你参加汉语辩论会，你会参加吗？你觉得用汉语辩论有什么好处？

3) 你认为网络在你的生活中占什么地位？网络为你的学习和生活带来了哪些正面的影响？请举两个例子。

4) 你认为网络为你的学习和生活带来了哪些负面影响？请举两个例子。

5) 你每天上网上多长时间？你经常查哪方面的信息？在网上，你上过当、受过骗吗？你对低年级的同学有哪些忠告？

6) 你周围有没有人滥用网络？举一两个例子。

7) 你身边有没有人上网成瘾？请讲一讲他们的情况。你自己呢？请说一说。

8) 你同意本课发言者的观点吗？请讲一讲你对网络的看法。

1. 完成句子

Ⓐ例子：对青少年来说，网络弊大于利。(第3行)

Ⓑ例子：这些青少年没有心思读书……结果，他们的学习成绩下降了。(第24~28行)

Ⓒ例子：还有一些青少年整天生活在网络世界里……这对他们的成长没有好处。(第29行)

对我来说，＿＿＿＿。有些青少年整天上网。结果，＿＿＿＿。＿＿＿＿，这对他们的身体健康没有好处。

2. 选择其中一个短语造句

Ⓐ例子：如今，网络发展很快。(第5行)

目前/现在

Ⓑ例子：网络也给我们带来了不少负面影响。

(第7行)

给……发电邮/打电话/介绍一下

Ⓒ例子：现在的青少年大都通过网络跟人沟通、联络。(第16行)

跟……关系很好/交朋友/谈话

3. 用所给短语造句

Ⓐ例子：他们把作业答案和论文放在网上卖钱。

(第13行)

把意见转达给老师

Ⓑ例子：他们上网成瘾，好像每时每刻都在上网。

(第22行)

好像一天忙到晚

4. 从课文中找反义词

1) 反方→(　　　)(第1行)　　4) 正面→(　　　)(第7行)

2) 小于→(　　　)(第3行)　　5) 错误→(　　　)(第10行)

3) 利　→(　　　)(第3行)　　6) 虚假→(　　　)(第15行)

93

实际运用

小组讨论

　　网络已经成为现代人生活中的一个重要部分。你们讨论的题目是：网络对青少年的影响。你们的讨论应包括以下几点：

- 网络有哪些用途？
- 青少年应该怎样正确使用网络？
- 你们是否需要改掉一些使用网络的不良习惯？

例子：

学生1：我们的生活真的离不开网络，因为网络的用途很广，有好多事情可以通过网络来做。通过网络，我们能接触到各种各样的信息，从而扩大了我们的知识面，也开阔了眼界。

学生2：现在的青少年喜欢通过网络做事，比如说，我假期前就常常帮爸爸、妈妈在网上订机票、预订机位、订酒店、买电影票，还在网上购物。

学生3：网络上的东西应有尽有。我从网络上可以找到作业答案，也可以下载考卷。可是我也知道网络上的一些信息不一定真实，也不可靠，所以说我们青少年要有辨别是非的能力，避免上当、受骗。

学生1：网络在青少年的日常生活中占有很重要的地位，但是网络也给青少年带来了不少负面的影

响。为了安全，我常常在网上用假身份。时间长了，我怕自己会养成说谎的习惯。

学生2：我一到家第一件事情就是上网。我好像大多课余时间都在网上。结果，跟家人的沟通少了，跟人面对面交际的能力也差了，身体和视力都变坏了。

学生3：我身边有些朋友过分(guò fèn)依赖网络，上网成瘾，平时没有心思读书。我经常劝(quàn)他们不要每时每刻上网，要培养一些兴趣和爱好，这样有利于他们的身心健康。

学生1：你说得对。网络确实(què shí)给我们带来了很多方便，但是我们要时常提醒自己，不要整天上网。如果在网上看到不健康、不适合青少年的内容，不要去浏览。

学生2：我们千万不能滥用网络，在网上欺骗(qī piàn)别人，这样会犯法的。

参考句子

a) 通过电脑，我们很容易接触到不健康的网站。经常看这些不健康的内容，对我们的成长不利。我们应该自觉(zì jué)地不去看那些不健康的网站。

b) 现在有很多学生在电脑上玩儿虚拟(xū nǐ)世界的游戏。在虚拟世界里，他们可以造房子、买家具、养宠物等。玩儿这样的游戏浪费了他们不少宝贵的时间，我不认为他们有什么收获。

c) 网络方便了现代人的生活。很多年轻人通过网络联络、社交，有些人通过网络学习，还有些人通过网络做(zuò)生意(shēng yi)等。

d) 现在是信息爆炸(bào zhà)的时代。人们只要一点鼠标(shǔ biāo)，就可以看到五花八门、各种各样的信息。有时你在网上浏览了几个钟头，也没有什么收获，有时候不真实的信息甚至会误导你。

95

写作训练

1. 写辩论稿（gǎo）

写一份正方辩论稿：网络利大于弊。在辩论稿里，你要写到通过网络，青少年能够：

- 接触到丰富的信息
- 从大量的信息中挑选（tiāoxuǎn）出有用的信息
- 随时随地跟人联络
- 更方便地享受现代人的生活
- 享受网络提供的娱乐
- 做其他事情

文体：辩论稿

辩论稿的正文一般分三部分：

1. 开头应点明辩论题目；
2. 主体部分要突出主题，材料要典型，分析要有力，使听众赞同；
3. 结尾可归纳自己的见解，使听众有完整的印象。

基本格式：

各位评委、主席，各位老师、同学：

大家好！今天辩论的题目是"……"，我方坚决支持/反对……，原因有以下几点：

第一，……；第二，……；第三，……；最后，……。

以上几点已充分证明了……的观点是成立的/不能成立的！

谢谢大家！

参考句子

a) 在网络上，青少年可以接触到各种信息，他们可以从丰富的信息中选择他们需要的。

b) 在网络上，大部分信息是真实、可靠的。如果有不可靠的信息，青少年要学会辨别哪些信息是正确的、可以用的，这给青少年提供了提高辨别能力的好机会。

c) 网络使人们的沟通方便了很多。你随时随地可以给远方的朋友发电邮，也可以通过网络同时跟几个人通话。

d) 你能通过网络找工作、登（dēng）广告（guǎnggào）、做生意（zuòshēngyi）、购物、传文件等。

e) 网络提供各种娱乐形式，比如下棋、打牌，还可以教你弹吉他、吹笛子（chuī dí zi）等。

f) 由于从小就接触网络，现在的青少年见识广、头脑灵活，有丰富的想象力和创造力。

g) 所以我方的结论是：对青少年来说，网络利大于弊。

2. 阅读短文并写回应式作文

假设你认同网络媒体有很多优势，但是你的学习和生活也离不开传统媒体。写一篇网络日志，谈谈网络媒体和传统媒体如何影响你的学习和生活。

网络媒体与传统媒体

今天，网络媒体越来越普及，对传统媒体形成了巨大的冲击。传统媒体会不会在不久的将来被网络媒体代替？ [1]

传统媒体一般包括报刊、广播和电视。跟传统媒体相比，网络媒体有很多好处。第一，传统媒体只可以"一对多"单向传播，网络媒体实现了"一对一"、"多对一"和"多对多"的双 [5] 向传播，使传媒跟受众直接自由交流。第二，网络媒体可以通过互联网高速传播，还可以随时更新，速度快、效率高。第三，网络媒体的信息量大，内容丰富。第四，网络媒体具有全球性，通过互联网把全世界连在了一起。第五，网络使用者只需输入关键字就可以找到他们需要的信息，并可通过下载或打印的方式进 [10] 行复制。第六，网络媒体融合了文字、声音、图像、动画、视频等多种形式。

可见，网络媒体有它独特的优势，但是并不能完全代替传统媒体，因为网络上的信息有时候缺乏权威性和真实性。浏览互联网必须使用电脑或者手机，花费较高，而且还需要联网，这不是 [15] 所有人随时随地都能做到的。在网上寻找信息也可能要花费大量时间，因为网上垃圾内容多，重复的内容也多，这时，书籍、报刊、杂志就更有优势。作为传统媒体的电视，它仍然很受大众的喜爱。一家人围在一起观看电视节目会给人一种轻松、愉快、温馨的感觉。广播媒体也在一些特定的场合继续发挥着它独特的作 [20] 用。

阅读与理解

阿里巴巴

第一段[1]　　"阿里巴巴"集团成立于1998年，总部设在中国的杭州。"阿里巴巴"是目前全球最大的网上交易市场之一，也是全球企业中电子 商务 (B2B)做得最好的品牌之一。

第二段[5]　　马云先生是"阿里巴巴"集团的主要 创 始人之一，也是该公司的首席执行官。2001年，马云被世界经济论坛选为"全球青年领袖"，2005年被美国《财富》杂志评为"亚洲最具权力的25名商人之一"。2007年，美国《商业周刊》评选马云为"年度商业人物"。

第三段　　马云希望把"阿里巴巴"网发展成为普及实用、安全可靠的网络工具，让大众受惠。到2006年底，"阿里巴巴"已经成为拥有超过800 [10]万网商的电子商务网站，业务范围遍布200多个国家和地区，每天向全球提供800多万条商业信息，被称为"最受欢迎的B2B网站"。

第四段　　2003年，"阿里巴巴"集团 创 建了淘宝网。淘宝网现在已成为中国最大的网络零售网站，商品非常齐全，从收藏品到工艺品、电子产品、日用品，应有尽有。截至2009年年中，淘宝网的注册用户接近 [15]1.45亿。仅仅2009年上半年，淘宝网交易额就达809亿元人民币，相当于2009年上半年全中国消费品零售总额的1.4%。淘宝网已经成为人们网上购物的首选目的地。

第五段　　"阿里巴巴"集团快速发展，形成了自己特有的公司文化。在商业上，公司尽量满足客户的需要。公司要求员工做人诚实正直，并 [20]鼓励他们持续学习、积极参与，发扬团队精神。公司本身还不断 创 新，积极面对新的挑战。

第六段　　"阿里巴巴"已经向世人证 明了它是一个成功的企业，也已完成了它的核心使命：让全世界的商人轻松地做生 意。

1. 在国际上，马云是个什么样的商人？

2. 马云在公司担任什么职务？
   (dān rèn)(zhí wù)

3. 淘宝网是一个什么样的网站？在淘宝网上能买到手机和电脑吗？
   (táo bǎo)

4. 为了应对将来的挑战，公司正在做什么准备工作？

1. "阿里巴巴"集团_____。

   a) 在20世纪90年代末成立

   b) 的总部设在上海

   c) 只做网络零售，不做其他业务
   (líng shòu)

2. 马云希望把"阿里巴巴"网发展成为一个_____。

   a) 最受欢迎的网上购物中心

   b) 专门卖电子产品的网站

   c) 深受用户欢迎的安全、可靠的网络工具

3. "阿里巴巴"集团发展快速，公司要求_____。

   a) 员工诚实做人，继续进修
   (jìn xiū)

   b) 每天加班、加点

   c) 经常跟客户沟通

4. 淘宝网办得很成功，因为_____。

   a) 商户可以在淘宝网上谈生意

   b) 到2009年年中，使用淘宝网的用户有近1.45亿

   c) 淘宝网是全世界最大的一家网络零售网站

C 从右边的段落大意中找出最合适的

1. 第一段　□
2. 第二段　□
3. 第三段　□
4. 第四段　□
5. 第五段　□
6. 第六段　□

A "阿里巴巴"网已成为最受欢迎的电子商务网。

B "阿里巴巴"已经用事实证明它能让全球商人在网上轻松地做生意。

C "阿里巴巴"集团的性质及经营的业务。

D "阿里巴巴"已发展成为有独特公司文化的公司。

E "阿里巴巴"集团从创建到目前的发展。

F "阿里巴巴"集团的核心使命。

G 淘宝网的规模、功绩及在用户心目中的地位。

H 主要介绍马云以及公众对他的评价。

D 根据短文找出四个正确的句子

□ 1. 马云还担任"阿里巴巴"集团的董事长。

□ 2. "阿里巴巴"已经成为全球最大的网上交易市场之一。

□ 3. "阿里巴巴"电子商业网站使用户受惠，业务范围遍布200多个国家和地区。

□ 4. "阿里巴巴"网站上的信息多而且快，每天向全球提供800多万条商业信息。

□ 5. 淘宝网也叫电子商务网。

□ 6. 淘宝网办得非常成功，2009年上半年的交易额高达809亿元人民币。

□ 7. 从1998年至2009年年底，"阿里巴巴"有注册用户1.45亿。

E 从短文中选出最合适的词语填空

1. 网上购物现在已经相当_____（第8行）了。

2. 马云要求他的员工做人诚实、_____（第8行）。

3. 淘宝网上货品_____（第13行），小到一本相册大到大型机器。

4. 马云被公认为_____（第22行）的企业家。

网络游戏

目前，有相当一部分青少年热衷(rè zhōng)于网络游戏。他们特别喜欢玩儿虚拟(xū nǐ)世界的游戏，原因是玩儿这种游戏时他们可以脱离(tuō lí)现实生活环境，沉浸(chén jìn)在自己的世界里。 [1] 第一段

有些网络游戏平台(píng tái)在短时间内迅速发展。据说某一个受欢迎的游戏平台有"常住居民"几百万。这种网络游戏平台为青少年提供了十分有趣(yǒu qù)的虚拟社会环境。在这种虚拟的环境里，青少年有一个自由自在的生活空间(kōng jiān)和社交场所。在这个属于(shǔ yú)他们的世界里，他们可以自由地设定(shè dìng)自己的形象(xíng xiàng)和服装、领养(lǐng yǎng)宠物、设计居所、交朋友、管理自己的资产(zī chǎn)。有数据(shù jù)显示，每天有大约10万种虚拟物品在网上进行"交易(jiāo yì)"。 第二段 [5] [10]

了解到这个庞大(páng dà)的网络游戏市场，中国的一家网络游戏公司研发(yán fā)了一款立体网络游戏——海底世界。该游戏集互动性、游戏性、教育性为一体，特别适合青少年群体。在"海底世界"的社区内，用户可以选择成为一条鱼或者其他的海洋生物，然后可以探索(tàn suǒ)、闲逛(xián guàng)、玩耍(wán shuǎ)、交友、装饰(zhuāng shì)自己的小屋、造房筑路、参加海洋知识竞赛、体验集体(jí tǐ)游戏等。在这个虚拟游戏里，无暴力(bào lì)、无色情(sè qíng)，它为青少年提供了一个健康的交流平台和社交场合(chǎng hé)。家长们很放心让孩子玩儿这样的游戏，因为"海底世界"给了孩子们一个开心、丰富多样的世界，培养了他们的创造力和想象(xiǎng xiàng)力。 第三段 [15]

这类网络游戏虽然能够鼓励青少年发展个性，开发并培养他们的创造力，但是沉迷(chén mí)于游戏是不利于他们的学业和身心健康的，所以还得适可而止(shì kě ér zhǐ)。 [20] 第四段

101

1. 第一段　☐
2. 第二段　☐
3. 第三段　☐
4. 第四段　☐

A 网络游戏发展迅速(xùn sù)，因为在虚拟(xū nǐ)世界的游戏里，青少年可以自由自在地"生活"。

B 在庞大(páng dà)的网络市场上，游戏公司互相竞争。

C 网络游戏虽然对青少年发展个性有利，但是青少年也要有节制(jié zhì)。

D 青少年热衷(rè zhōng)于玩儿虚拟世界的游戏的原因。

E 家长们普遍鼓励青少年玩儿网络游戏。

F 具体介绍"海底世界"这款很受家长和孩子喜爱的网络游戏。

B　从短文中选出最合适的词语填空

1. 在虚拟_____（第2行）里，青少年可以设计自己的形象、管理资产(zī chǎn)等。

2. 网络游戏为孩子们创造了一个属于他们的生活_____（第2行）。

3. 在虚拟的环境里，青少年有一个自由自在的活动_____（第7行）。

4. 青少年可以通过网络跟他们的_____（第8行）交流、联络。

5. 现在的网络游戏_____（第11行）很混乱(hùn luàn)，需要监管(jiān guǎn)。

6. 网络给人们提供了一个_____（第17行）平台。

7. 有些网络游戏有助于青少年的_____（第20行）发展。

8. 教育专家认为经常玩儿网络游戏会对学生的_____（第21行）不利。

C　从短文中找反义词

1. 现实→(　　　　)（第2行）
2. 拘束(jū shù)→(　　　　)（第6行）
3. 平面→(　　　　)（第12行）
4. 普通→(　　　　)（第13行）
5. 个体→(　　　　)（第13行）
6. 烦恼→(　　　　)（第18行）

D 根据短文选择正确答案

1. "热衷于" (rè zhōng) (第1行)的意思是 _____。

   a) 流行
   b) 非常喜爱
   c) 十分热闹

2. "常住居民" (第5行)的意思是 _____。

   a) 非法的游戏者
   b) 成人居民
   c) 经常玩儿游戏的人

3. "庞大" (páng dà) (第11行)的意思是 _____。

   a) 非常大
   b) 不太大
   c) 最大

4. "适可而止" (shì kě ér zhǐ) (第22行)的意思是 _____。

   a) 禁止
   b) 做到适当的程度就应该停止 (tíng zhǐ)
   c) 开放

E 根据短文找出四个正确的句子

☐ 1. 现在只有一小部分青少年沉迷于网络游戏。 (chén mí)

☐ 2. 在网络游戏里，青少年可以购物、造房子等。

☐ 3. 在玩儿网络游戏时，青少年可以沉浸在他们自己的虚拟世界里。 (chén jìn) (xū nǐ)

☐ 4. "海底世界"是由政府出资研发的一种网络游戏。 (yán fā)

☐ 5. 在"海底世界"游戏中，游戏者可以选择成为一种海洋生物。

☐ 6. 家长不希望他们的孩子玩儿"海底世界"，因为在这个游戏里有色情内容。

☐ 7. "海底世界"为青少年打开了一个新天地，培养了他们的想象力。 (xiǎngxiàng)

F 根据实际情况回答问题

1. 你喜欢玩儿网络游戏吗？如果喜欢，你最喜欢的是什么游戏？请简单介绍一下这个游戏。

2. 你认为网络游戏有利于青少年的身心健康吗？请举例说明。

科技产品与生活

[1]　　21世纪科技发展迅速。丰富的科技产品不仅给人们的日常生活带来了方便，而且也提高了人们的生活质量。

　　高科技已经进入了人们生活的方方面面，科技产品无处不在。如今，家家户户都使用家电产品，如冰箱、自动洗

[5] 衣机等等，这节省了很多做家务的时间。手机已经成为最普遍的通讯工具。不管你在哪儿，都可以通过手机跟人联络，这缩短了人与人之间的距离。目前，时尚的笔记本电脑、数码相机不但轻巧而且功能多，很受青少年的喜爱。

　　高科技为人们的学习和娱乐创造了新天地。网络教育

[10] 现在越来越普及了。人们可以在网上学习远程课程，坐在家里也可以接受教育。通过网络，人们不用买音乐光碟就能听新歌，不用看电视就能知道天下大事，不用见面就能跟人聊天儿。现在，各种电脑软件发展也很迅速。很多青少年可以在电脑上建城市、造房子等，他们好像生活在虚拟

[15] 世界里。这种活动能培养青少年的想象力和创造力。自从机器宠物问世后，不少人选择养机器狗、机器猫，这不但省时而且省事。

　　此外，高速列车也使人们的生活更加便利

[20] 了。以前人们要坐一两天的火车才能到达一个边远的地方，现在只要在火车上睡一晚就能到达目的地了。

[25]　　科技的发展确实对

104

人们的生活产生了巨大的影响，但是人们对高科技产品也越来越依赖了。这是好事还是坏事，真是天知道！

1. 科技 kē jì science and technology
2. 产（産）chǎn produce　产品 chǎn pǐn product
3. 进入 jìn rù enter
4. 方方面面 fāngfāngmiànmiàn all sides; every aspect
5. 无处不在 wú chù bú zài everywhere
6. 家家户户 jiā jiā hù hù every family
7. 使用 shǐ yòng use
8. 家电 jiā diàn household electrical appliances
9. 自动 zì dòng automatic
10. 讯（訊）xùn message　通讯 tōng xùn communication
11. 缩（縮）suō shrink　缩短 suō duǎn shorten
12. 距 jù distance　距离 jù lí distance
13. 尚 shàng prevailing custom　时尚 shí shàng fashion
14. 笔记本电脑 bǐ jì běndiànnǎo laptop
15. 数码 shù mǎ digital
16. 相机 xiàng jī camera　数码相机 shù mǎ xiàng jī digital camera
17. 轻巧 qīngqiǎo light and ingenious
18. 天地 tiān dì the world
19. 普及 pǔ jí popular
20. 远程 yuǎnchéng long-distance

远程课程 yuǎnchéng kè chéng long-distance course
21. 光碟 guāng dié disc
22. 天下 tiān xià the world
23. 大事 dà shì major issue
24. 软（軟）ruǎn soft　软件 ruǎn jiàn software
25. 迅 xùn fast; swift
26. 速 sù fast; speed　迅速 xùn sù rapid
27. 虚 xū false　虚拟 xū nǐ virtual; fictious
28. 想象 xiǎngxiàng imagine
　　想象力 xiǎngxiàng lì imagination
29. 问世 wèn shì come out; be born
30. 省事 shěng shì save trouble
31. 高速 gāo sù high speed
*32. 列 liè row; line　列车 liè chē train
33. 便利 biàn lì covenient
34. 边远 biānyuǎn remote
35. 目的地 mù dì dì destination
36. 确实 què shí really; indeed
37. 产生 chǎnshēng produce
38. 巨 jù huge　巨大 jù dà huge
39. 好事 hǎo shì good deed
40. 坏事 huài shì bad thing

105

口语热身

消化课文

1. 根据课文回答问题

1) 一些家电产品给人们的生活带来了什么方便？

2) 人们的日常生活中少不了哪些高科技产品？

3) 网络在哪几个方面改变了人们的生活？

4) 如今，人们怎样创造出虚拟世界？

5) 在高速列车出现以前，人们需要多久才能到达远方的目的地？

6) 高科技产品在哪几个方面改变了人们的生活？

2. 根据实际情况回答问题

1) 请说一说你们家用哪些家电产品？你家现在最离不开什么家电产品？为什么？"科技发展对人们的生活产生了巨大的影响"，你同意这种说法吗？为什么？

2) 你每天用哪几样通讯工具？你觉得有了手机以后，你跟朋友之间的距离缩短了吗？

3) 你有数码相机吗？你是从什么时候开始用数码相机的？你见过、用过传统的照相机吗？传统的照相机跟数码相机有什么不同？

4) 你养过宠物吗？如果让你选择，你会养一般的宠物还是机器宠物？为什么？

5) 你一般用网络的哪些功能？你觉得网络给你的生活和学习带来了哪些方便？请举一两个例子。

6) 如果网上有紧急救护课程，你会选修该课程吗？为什么？你认为通过网络学习远程课程跟在教室里学习有什么不同？

7) 你乘坐火车旅行过吗？你最多坐过几个小时的火车？你有什么感受？

8) 你玩儿过虚拟世界的游戏吗？有些人玩儿虚拟游戏会上瘾，你会吗？为什么？

1. 完成句子

Ⓐ例子：丰富的科技产品给人们的日常生活带来了方便。（第1行）

Ⓑ例子：不管你在哪儿，都可以通过手机跟人联络。（第6行）

_____给我带来了很大的压力。

不管父母怎么反对，我还是_____。

2. 选择其中一个短语造句

Ⓐ例子：高科技已经进入了人们生活的方方面面。（第3行）

家家户户 = 每家每户

时时刻刻 = 每时每刻

Ⓑ例子：你可以通过手机跟人联络。（第6行）

通过这次活动/参加义卖会

跟……开玩笑/吵架/商量/合得来

3. 用带点的词语模仿例子造句

Ⓐ例子：丰富的科技产品不仅给人们的日常生活带来了方便，而且也提高了人们的生活质量。（第1行）

尽管空余时间不多，但是我还是抽空跟朋友一起出去玩儿。

因为我昨天没睡好觉，所以今天白天没有精神。

Ⓑ例子：网络教育现在越来越普及了。（第9行）

4. 从课文中找反义词

1) 降低→（   ）（第2行）

2) 手动→（   ）（第4行）

3) 浪费→（   ）（第5行）

4) 过时→（   ）（第7行）

5) 麻烦→（   ）（第19行）

6) 好事→（   ）（第27行）

107

口语训练

小组讨论

科技产品对你们的生活、学习有非常大的影响。你们的讨论内容应包括:

- 哪些科技产品对你们的生活、学习影响较大?
- 如果没有这些产品,你们的生活和学习会受到哪些影响?
- 你们觉得应该怎样正确地使用这些科技产品?

例子:

学生1: 对一个家庭来说,冰箱、洗衣机、自动洗碗机、吸尘器、烤箱和煤气炉最重要。如果没有这些科技产品的话,我们每天要花很多时间做家务。

学生2: 家电产品确实进入了家家户户,影响到我们生活的方方面面。但是,另一方面,现代人越来越不会做家务,越来越懒惰了。我不知道这是好事还是坏事。

学生3: 那当然是好事。对我来说,小汽车最重要。如果家里没有车,我来上学就得转几次车,我爸爸每天上、下班至少在路上要花三个小时。科技产品为我们带来了方便,既省时又省事。

学生1: 我觉得现代通讯工具,比如手机和电脑,对每个人的影响都很大。现代通讯缩短了人与人之间的距离。我们现在的

108

生活简直离不开手机和电脑了。

学生2：我很赞同你刚才说的。我现在几乎不买报纸，也不看电视，我从手机和网络上就能及时了解世界上发生的大事。

学生3：科技的迅速发展确实方便了我们现代人的生活，但是也给我们带来了挑战。我们应该正确、合理地使用科技产品，让它们更好地为我们服务。

学生1：我们应该善用科技产品。我认为有了车不等于我们不用走路了；有了计算器不等于我们不用心算了；有了电脑打字不等于我们不用写字了。有些事情一定要我们亲手去做，亲自去学。科技产品不可能完全代替人的大脑和手脚。

参考句子

a) 科技产品无处不在，但是我们不应该完全依赖它们。如果我们每天长时间开车、用电脑，我们的大脑、手脚功能都会退化。

b) 在现代生活里，各行各业都离不开电脑。如果你注意一下，会发现在一些地方，工作人员让你填了表格，然后再把你的资料输进电脑。这不是把一件事做了两遍吗？

c) 有些科技产品虽然能省时、省力、省事，但不环保，比如说洗碗机，费时、费水、费电。

d) 数码相机很轻巧，外出旅游很方便。数码相机样式又时尚，深受年轻人的喜爱。

e) 自从数码相机问世后，我们不用洗照片了，而且每次能拍上千张照片。

f) 有了网络，我们做事既省时又省事。我现在一般不去图书馆借书，在网上我可以查到需要的资料。

写作训练

实际运用

1. 写叙述文

你为学校网站写一篇文章，说说虽然电脑功能很多，已经成为一件必不可少的日用品，但是如果不善用电脑，它有可能给我们带来一些负面的影响。在文章中，你要提及：

- 电脑给我们带来了哪些负面的影响？
- 现在青少年用电脑时"一心多用"的现象表现在哪些方面？
- 我们应该怎样善用电脑？

参考句子

a) 在电脑上打字时，电脑能帮我们自动改错。如果长期用电脑打字，结果是我们的拼写(pīn xiě)和书写(shū xiě)能力会越来越差。我认为有些作业应该用手写。

b) 现在的学生每时每刻都在用电脑。很多同学一边做功课一边跟朋友在网上聊天儿，一边听音乐，一边上 YouTube，还随时上脸谱网(liǎn pǔ)。我认为这样做会分散(fēn sàn)注意力，影响学习效果(xiào guǒ)，因为我相信一心不可二用。

c) 电脑是学习的工具，需要时才打开电脑。网络上的资料不能随便抄袭(suí biàn chāo xí)，只能作为参考材料(cān kǎo cái liào)。

d) 有时候用电脑学习效果好，但也不是每一件事都需要用电脑做。所以我们要决定什么时候该用电脑，什么时候不该用。

e) 学生要学会自律，自己要限制(xiàn zhì)使用电脑的时间。

110

2. 阅读短文并写回应式作文

假设你们学校已开始要求每个学生都带电脑上学，你对此感到又高兴又担心。参照(cānzhào)下面的短文，为校报写一篇文章，谈谈你对此事的看法。

电脑是把双刃剑(shuāng rèn jiàn)

越来越多的学校要求每个学生都带电脑上学。带电脑上学有 [1]
好处，也有很多弊端(bì duān)。带电脑上学的好处，有些家长表示怀疑(huái yí)，
但也有些家长认为不会用电脑的孩子就相当于现代"文盲(wén máng)"。

支持上学用电脑的家长认为网上的一些测验、练习对学习有
帮助。有了自己的电脑，学生可以更专心地学习，老师也有时间 [5]
和精力照顾到每一个学生。经常用电脑，学生不但对电脑软件更
熟悉了，还能学会一些设计，能制作多媒体(duō méi tǐ)报告等。而且，学生
还可以随时上网查资料。

一些不支持带电脑上学的家长则认为电脑就像电子鸦片(yā piàn)。由
于中学生的自控(zì kòng)能力比较弱，带电脑到学校弊远大于利。他们 [10]
说，学生在家里、课下用电脑做功课、查资料、跟朋友沟通等已
经花去了很多时间。如今学生再带电脑到学校，课上也用电脑，
这样学生会过分依赖电脑，独立思考(dú lì sī kǎo)的空间(kōng jiān)也就少了。

更有一些家长强烈(qiáng liè)反对学校让学生带电脑上学。因为他们认
为网络游戏太刺激(cì jī)、紧张，有些学生玩儿了一场还想再玩儿。除 [15]
了课下和晚上玩儿游戏以外，学生们很有可能在课堂上也玩儿，
或者心里一直盼着下课铃(líng)快点儿响。这样，学生上课无法专心，
学习效果(xiào guǒ)一定会受到影响。而且，每个学生大多数时候都抱着一
部电脑，不再互相交流，他们的社交能力也会下降。用电脑太
久，对学生的身体和视力都不好。 [20]

看来，电脑走进教室是一种趋势(qū shì)。那么(nà me)，该怎样利用电脑这
把双刃剑，让电脑既能更好地为教学服务，又尽量减少对学生的
负面影响，将是一个令人头疼的问题。

111

阅读与理解

电子时代

第一段 [1]　　我们生活在电子时代。如果让你现在就关掉手机、关掉电脑，你会有什么感觉？你是否会觉得时间停顿了，生活没有意思了？如果你留意一下公交车上的乘客，是否有的人在看手机，____①____人在打电话，有的人在听音乐？如果你留心一下咖啡馆，是否看到大部分人不是在

[5]　笔记本电脑上发电邮、浏览信息，____②____在手机上发短信或者玩儿电子游戏？如今，24小时不关手机甚至不关电脑已经非常普遍了。

第二段　　没有人统计过我们每个人每天在电脑和手机上浪费了多少时间。但我们中有很多人已经很久没有去图书馆，很久没有用笔写信了，____③____电子产品给我们带来了太多的方便。上班族中的绝大部分人

[10]　每天早上一到单位____④____会打开电脑，随便在网上看看，时间就不知不觉地过去了，甚至有的人一上午几乎干不了什么。几乎每个中学生放学回到家做的第一件事就是打开电脑，在网上闲逛几个小时后____⑤____开始做作业。

第三段　　电子产品不断地改变着我们每个人的学习、工作和生活习惯。我

[15]　们也已经不知不觉地成了工具的工具。仔细想一想，我们每个人每天都依赖电子产品，其实我们多少都会有一些"电子产品依赖症"的症状。虽然我们的生活越来越电子化，电子产品也改善了我们的物质生活，带来了许多便利，但是我们在享受的同时也失去了很多。

第四段　　今天，让我们回到家就关掉手机、电脑、游戏机、音乐播放器

[20]　吧！让我们再像以前那样，跟朋友、跟家人欢聚，面对面地沟通，让生活重新变得____⑥____有意义吧。

有时　就是　就　才　更　虽然　因为　有的

1. ＿＿＿＿＿＿＿＿＿　　　2. ＿＿＿＿＿＿＿＿＿　　　3. ＿＿＿＿＿＿＿＿＿

4. ＿＿＿＿＿＿＿＿＿　　　5. ＿＿＿＿＿＿＿＿＿　　　6. ＿＿＿＿＿＿＿＿＿

B 根据短文选择正确答案

1. "留意"（第3行）的意思是

＿＿＿＿＿＿。

a) 注意

b) 检查

c) 去意大利留学

2. "上班族"（第9行）的意思

是 ＿＿＿＿＿＿。

a) 大学生

b) 一群人

c) 办公室职员

3. "单位"（第10行）的意思是

＿＿＿＿＿＿。

a) 一套住房

b) 单车停放位

c) 工作的地方

4. "不知不觉"（第10行）的意

思是 ＿＿＿＿＿＿。

a) 不知道就不睡觉

b) 自己没有意识到

c) 知道，也有感觉

C 根据短文回答问题

1. 如今，在咖啡馆里，你会看到什么景象？

2. 现在的中学生放学回家后一般先做什么？

3. 文中"工具的工具"（第15行）中第一个工具是指什么？

4. 作者认为哪些人有"电子产品依赖症"的症状？

1. 第一段　☐　A 人们过分依赖电子产品的后果。

2. 第二段　☐　B 电子产品为人们的生活带来了方便，也使人们

3. 第三段　☐　　浪费了大量时间。

4. 第四段　☐　C 电子化的生活给人们带来的各种疾病。

D 提醒人们该重温以往的美好生活。

E 电子产品是工具。

F 电子时代人们时刻依赖电子产品。

G 绝大部分现代人经常去图书馆、用手写信等。

1. 大部分人在乘坐公共交通工具时会使用电子产品。　　　　对　错

原因：_____　__　__

2. 如今人们的生活已经离不开手机、电脑。

原因：_____　__　__

3. 电子产品并没有给人们的学习、工作和生活习惯带来什么

变化。

原因：_____　__　__

4. 由于人们依赖电子产品，所以差不多每个人都有一些"电

子产品依赖症"的症状。

原因：_____　__　__

5. 跟过去相比，现在的人跟家人面对面的沟通变少了。

原因：_____　__　__

数码时代的青少年

数码时代对社会的各个方面都产生了巨大的影响。这种影响既有 [1]
积极的一面也有消极的一面。大多数人认为，积极的影响大大超过消
极的影响。网络、电子邮件、博客(bó kè)以及互动(hù dòng)和超现实(xiàn shí)的电子游戏将会
使年轻一代更聪明，更有知识，而且对国家的政治(zhèng zhì)以及国际事务有更
多的兴趣。不过，有些教育专家和社会学家却不太乐观，提醒人们数 [5]
码时代正在使年轻一代变成知识贫乏(pín fá)的一代。

在数码时代，年轻一代每时每刻都通过各种电子工具来消磨(xiāo mó)时
间。他们白天忙着用手机打电话、发短信、跟朋友聊天儿或查看留
言；晚上忙着写博客，设计有个人特色的网页，浏览朋友的网页或在
网上闲逛(xián guàng)。所有这些花去了他们大量的时间。他们中有些人只关心自 [10]
己及跟自己有关的社交小圈子(quān zi)。数码时代的电子工具正好为这一代青
少年提供了方便与可能。

如今，很多青少年不读书、不看报、不阅读文学作品，更不会去
博物馆。他们不关心发生在自己身边的其他事情，也不想了解历史或
是掌握实际(shí jì)的技能。虽然他们发电邮、写博客、在网上浏览一大堆信 [15]
息，但是他们的实际阅读和写作水平正在下降。

教育家和社会学家担心，如果社会、学校和家长对青少年不严格(yán gé)
要求，过于放纵(fàng zòng)和溺爱(nì ài)，最后的受害者还是年轻的一代。这些青少年
需要老师和家长的正确引导(yǐn dǎo)。只有这样，他们才能真正利用数码产品
的优势(yōu shì)，使自己变得更聪明，更有时代感。 [20]

从短文中找反义词

1. 消极→( )(第2行)   4. 麻烦→( )(第12行)

2. 丰富→( )(第6行)   5. 上升→( )(第16行)

3. 夜晚→( )(第8行)   6. 错误→( )(第19行)

B 根据短文找出四个正确的句子

☐ 1. 大多数人认为，数码时代为社会带来的消极影响很小。

☐ 2. 写电邮及博客(bó kè)可以提高一个人的阅读和写作水平。

☐ 3. 如今，年轻一代主要的休闲(xiū xián)活动都跟电子产品有关。

☐ 4. 在年轻的一代中，有些人对历史和实际的技能没兴趣。

☐ 5. 如今，绝大多数青少年在网上阅读古典名著(míng zhù)。

☐ 6. 有些教育家和社会学家不看好当代的青少年。

☐ 7. 青少年能自觉(zì jué)地善用(shàn yòng)数码产品。

C 从短文中选出最合适的动词填空

1. 电子产品对现代人的生活 _____(第1行)了很多影响。

2. 教师和家长应该经常_____(第5行)青少年善用电子产品。

3. 如今，大部分人看到电脑就想_____(第8行)电邮。

4. 电子工具为人们相互间的交流_____(第12行)了方便。

5. 通过学习，我更进一步_____(第14行)了这门学科。

6. 青少年一有时间就喜欢在网上闲逛(xián guàng)，_____(第15行)一大堆信息。

7. 课上，老师_____(第18行)学生认真听讲。

8. 他打算_____(第19行)暑假做专题论文。

D 从右边找到最适合的部分完成下列句子

1. 数码时代对社会 ☐
2. 教育专家担心 ☐
3. 如今，青少年 ☐
4. 现在年轻一代的写作水平 ☐
5. 善用数码产品 ☐
6. 只有真正利用数码产品
   的优势，_{yōu shì} ☐

A 年轻一代将来可能会很无知。

B 娱乐活动与电子产品无关。

C 产生了积极和消极的影响。

D 越来越差了。

E 对书籍、报纸没有兴趣。_{shū jí}

F 的青少年一点儿都不自私。

G 对青少年管教得太严。

H 能对青少年产生积极的影响。

I 青少年才会变得更聪明，有时代感。

E 根据短文选择正确答案

1. "乐观"（第5行）的意思是

   ＿＿＿＿。

   a) 对事物的发展充满信心

   b) 令人高兴

   c) 高兴地观看

2. "消磨"（第7行）的意思是
   _{xiāo mó}

   ＿＿＿＿。

   a) 留住

   b) 节约

   c) 度过时间

3. "社交"（第11行）的意思是

   ＿＿＿＿。

   a) 社区交通

   b) 人与人的交际往来

   c) 社团活动

4. "放纵"（第18行）的意思是
   _{fàngzòng}

   ＿＿＿＿。

   a) 不管教

   b) 严格要求
   _{yán gé}

   c) 管得严

5. "溺爱"（第18行）的意思是
   _{nì ài}

   ＿＿＿＿。

   a) 过分宠爱

   b) 爱得太少

   c) 缺少爱

6. "引导"（第19行）的意思是
   _{yǐn dǎo}

   ＿＿＿＿。

   a) 吸引

   b) 带领
   _{dài lǐng}

   c) 演讲

117

健康的饮食习惯

[1]　　从本周一开始，我校快餐食品，比如比萨饼、汉堡包等都涨价20%，但是荤素搭配的盒饭降价20%。奇怪的是，相对便宜、健康的盒饭没有吸引更多的学生去吃。喜欢吃快餐的学生照样吃快餐，因为他们习惯了。

[5]　　学校餐厅为什么要调整饭菜的价格呢？近年来，我校学生普遍偏食，而且越来越不重视饮食健康。他们特别爱吃快餐及各种垃圾食品。这些不良的饮食习惯影响了他们的身体发育和健康。校医指出，多吃快餐尤其是高糖及油腻食品，直接影响了学生的身体素质，有害健康。有些学

[10]生已经得了肥胖症、高血压、高血脂等疾病。虽然学校餐厅想了一些办法来吸引学生多吃健康食品，但是效果不明显。上学期末，校方、学生会跟餐厅商量并决定上调快餐的价格，希望吃快餐的

[15]学生改吃健康的盒饭。学生会今天分别采访了二十名七年级和十一年级的学生。采访的结果令人

[20]遗憾：多数学生表示，餐厅供应的盒饭不好吃，还有人说他们喜

[25]欢吃快餐，

就是贵一点儿也不在乎。

　　看来，盒饭不能够代替快餐，高价的快餐食品也不会吓跑学生。学校和学生会还得再跟餐厅商量，一方面不能增加学生午饭的花费，另一方面要"逼"学生少吃快餐，改吃健康食品，从而改掉 [30] 不良的饮食习惯。

（胡小丽报道）

生 词

1. 涨（漲）zhǎng rise　　涨价 zhǎng jià rise in price
2. 荤（葷）hūn meat or fish
3. 搭配 dā pèi mix in proportions
4. 降价 jiàng jià cut down the price
5. 怪 guài strange　　奇怪 qí guài unexpected; strange
6. 相对 xiāng duì relatively
7. 照样 zhào yàng as before; as usual
8. 价格 jià gé price
9. 偏 piān partial
   偏食 piān shí (have a) partiality for a particular kind of food
10. 发育 fā yù growth
11. 指出 zhǐ chū point out
12. 直接 zhí jiē directly
13. 素质 sù zhì quality
14. 害 hài harm　　有害 yǒu hài be harmful to
15. 症 zhèng symptom
    肥胖症 féi pàng zhèng obesity

16. 血压 xuè yā blood pressure
    高血压 gāo xuè yā high blood pressure
17. 血脂 xuè zhī blood fat
18. 疾 jí disease　　疾病 jí bìng disease
19. 效果 xiào guǒ result
20. 上调 shàng tiáo raise
21. 遗（遺）yí leave behind
22. 憾 hàn regret　　遗憾 yí hàn regretful
23. 供应 gōng yìng supply
24. 在乎 zài hu care about; mind
25. 能够 néng gòu can; be able to
26. 代替 dài tì replace
27. 高价 gāo jià high price
28. 吓（嚇）xià frighten; scare
29. 一方面……，另一方面…… yì fāngmiàn, lìng yì fāngmiàn on the one hand..., on the other hand...
30. 报道 bào dào report

消化课文

1. 根据课文回答问题

1) 这个星期，学校餐厅饭菜的价格有什么变化？结果怎样？

2) 学校的餐厅为什么要调整饭菜的价格？

3) 由于吃快餐过多，有些学生得了什么疾病？

4) 谁决定上调快餐的价格？

5) 学生会采访二十名学生的结果为什么令人遗憾？

6) 学校和学生会下一步想怎么做？他们想达到什么目的？

2. 根据实际情况回答问题

1) 你们学校有餐厅吗？餐厅都卖些什么食品？你一般午饭吃什么？吃一顿午饭，你一般要花多少钱？

2) 餐厅卖的饭菜价格怎么样？哪些食品比较贵？哪些食品比较便宜？如果快餐价格上调50%，你觉得吃快餐的人会减少吗？为什么？

3) 你们学校有没有想办法让学生们少吃快餐？想了什么办法？办法有效吗？

4) 如果学校餐厅停止供应垃圾食品，比如薯条、汉堡包、可乐等，学生们会怎么想？

5) 你们学校餐厅饭菜的价格是谁决定的？学生会的成员可以参与决定饭菜的价格吗？为什么？

6) 在你周围的同学当中，偏食、挑食的人多吗？他们喜欢吃什么？不喜欢吃什么？

7) 你认为现在大部分青少年的饮食习惯健康吗？为什么青少年特别喜欢吃快餐？

8) 你觉得你的饮食习惯健康吗？你怎样保持饮食的均衡？

1. 完成句子

Ⓐ 例子：从本周一开始，快餐食品涨价20%。(第1行)

从今天开始，＿＿＿。

Ⓑ 例子：奇怪的是，相对便宜、健康的盒饭没有
吸引更多的学生去吃。(第2行)

有趣的是，＿＿＿＿＿。

Ⓒ 例子：多吃快餐尤其是高糖及油腻食品，有害
健康。(第8行)

＿＿＿＿＿＿有害健康。

2. 选择其中一个短语造句

Ⓐ 例子：近年来，我校学生越来越不重视饮食健
康。(第5行)

上个学期/今年年初/二十一世纪

Ⓑ 例子：他们特别爱吃快餐及各种垃圾食品。

(第6行)

十分/非常/挺/最/相当

Ⓒ 例子：他们喜欢吃快餐，就是贵一点儿也不在乎。

(第24行)

离不开/少不了/不得了/舍不得

3. 用所给词语造句

例子：一方面不能增加学生午饭的花费，另一方
面要"逼"学生改吃健康食品。(第28行)

一方面　健康食品

另一方面　锻炼身体

4. 从课文中找反义词

1) 降价→(　　　)(第2行)　　4) 轻视→(　　　)(第6行)

2) 素 → (　　　)(第2行)　　5) 间接→(　　　)(第9行)

3) 正 → (　　　)(第6行)　　6) 少数→(　　　)(第20行)

121

口语训练

实际运用

角色扮演

在这个口语练习中有四个角色：校长、小卖部经理、家长代表和学生会主席。你们讨论小卖部应该怎样让学生少吃快餐，少喝饮料，多吃健康食品。你们讨论的内容应包括：

• 小卖部将采取哪些措施？ (cǎi qǔ) (cuò shī)

• 新菜单将试用多长时间？ (shì yòng)

• 希望有什么结果？

例子：

校长：最近学生会作了一项调查，发现学校餐厅卖的食品大都是西式快餐。这些食物都含有高蛋白、高盐、高糖和高脂肪。在校期间，学生不爱喝水，他们通常买饮料喝。这样的饮食习惯使学生上课时思想不能集中。调查还发现，超重的学生比以前多了，有些学生还得了肥胖症、高血压等疾病。

家长：我认为快餐食品直接影响了学生的身体素质和发育。为了学生的学习和身体健康，学校餐厅应该多卖健康食品，少供应快餐。在课间休息及午饭时间不卖糖果和饮料。我希望学校餐厅在这方面改进一下。

经理：学生的饮食习惯和健康状况不完全是小卖部的责任。为了让学生少吃快餐，我们已经上调了快餐的价格，希望高价的快餐能吓跑学生，可是很多学

122

生照样会吃。如果学校不让我们卖快餐，我们没有问题。可是如果学生要求我们卖快餐食品，那怎么办？

主席：学生确实喜欢吃快餐，这是事实。我们现在是要想办法，而不是责怪小卖部。我认为小卖部提供的食物既要荤素搭配又要有营养。

校长：小卖部应先起草一个菜单，有些食品要降价，有些还要涨价。看来，我们不得不减少快餐品种。

主席：我同意，但我觉得涨价了的快餐学生还是会买的。

家长：是啊！如果这样的话，小卖部就会从学生那里赚更多的钱。

校长：快餐的价格不能太高。新的菜单出来后，我们先试用一个月，看看效果怎么样，然后再开会讨论、商量。

经理：没问题。

参考句子

a) 上调快餐的价格是其中一个措施。我们还应该教育学生，使他们认识到吃太多的快餐会影响身体健康。

b) 小卖部应该停止供应快餐，只提供有营养的食品。

c) 要增加盒饭的品种，供应适合学生口味的盒饭，这样就能吸引更多的学生来买。

d) 我发现我们学校有一部分学生偏食，每天只吃煎炸食品、喝饮料。时间长了，他们的健康会受影响。

e) 我们学校有个奇怪的现象：高价快餐照样有人吃。这个现象令人遗憾。快餐食品一方面适合学生的口味，另一方面学生也买得起。所以，涨价不是解决问题的办法。

f) 我们决定下个月10号再开会，看看新菜单效果怎么样，是否吃快餐的学生人数会减少，吃盒饭的人数会增加。然后再决定下一步该怎么做。

123

写作训练

1. 写报道

你所居住地区的中小学为学生提供的午餐不太健康。本地政府拨款组织了一个"健康午餐"委员会，配合各学校餐厅的工作，力争为学生提供健康的午餐。请为某一份报纸写一篇报道，报道中要提及：

- "健康午餐"委员会是怎样跟各学校餐厅合作的？
- 学校餐厅提供的午餐有了哪些改变？
- 学生的饮食习惯有了哪些转变？

文体：报道

新闻报道的题目要醒目、点明主题，让读者对报道的内容一目了然。

报道多数为倒金字塔结构：
1. 开头一定先告诉读者4个主要元素，即人物、事件、时间、地点，也就是将最重要的内容放在最前面；
2. 然后按照事件重要程度先后排序，仔细描述事件过程；
3. 结语要求简洁、有力，强调该新闻的意义与影响。

全文要注重客观、可信的新闻性质和价值，突出真实性。

参考句子

a) 从今年的1月1日起，本地政府组织了一个"健康午餐"委员会。这个委员会的成员由营养师、校长代表、学校餐厅主管、学生代表组成。他们的首要任务是对本地区的每一所中小学提供的午餐作一个全面的调查，然后决定如何跟学校餐厅配合，争取为每一位中小学生提供健康的午餐。

b) 这个"健康午餐"委员会还特意聘请了几位营养厨师，为学校餐厅出谋划策。营养厨师还对每个学校餐厅的卫生情况及烹饪方法提出了改进的意见，并亲自掌厨，培训餐厅的厨师。

c) 现在，各所学校的餐厅再也不提供高糖、多盐、高脂肪和油腻的食品。午餐都是荤素搭配、营养丰富的饭菜，满足青少年身体发育的需要，保证他们健康成长。

2. 阅读短文并写回应式作文

写一封电邮给你国外的朋友，告诉他/她香港人饮茶是怎么回事以及饮茶在香港人的生活中如何重要。

香港人爱饮茶

饮茶是香港人生活的一部分。在香港，不论有钱人还是一般百姓都有饮茶的习惯，区别仅仅是酒楼的地点、名气、豪华程度以及点心的价格。香港人饮茶，不单是为了品茶、吃点心，更重要的是与朋友、同事以及家人一边闲聊，一边享受美食，共度美好时光。 [1]

港式饮茶一般分为早市、午市及下午茶，从早上七点到晚饭前都有地方可以饮茶。部分酒楼更会在下午茶时段提供优惠，例如特价点心或免茶水费等。每逢周末、节假日，茶楼、酒楼门口都有人群轮候位子。平时快节奏的香港人，只有在这时才真正慢下来。 [5]

待客人坐下后，便有侍应生送上热茶，当然客人也可以点喜欢的茶。香港人吃点心时通常喜欢喝普洱、铁观音、香片茶等等，以达到去油腻的效果，尤其是普洱，消脂去腻效果最佳。客人可以在固定的餐单上用笔在想吃的点心旁打勾，随后几分钟内点心就会送上来。客人也可以顺便跟推点心车的阿婶点。点完后送上饮茶单，由阿婶在上面盖上一个小戳。点心的品种有叉烧包、烧卖、萝卜糕等。除了这些咸点，还有甜点，比如奶皇包、麻球、芒果布丁等。这一餐茶可以饮到午后。 [10] [15]

老年人一般会一大早就到茶楼等开门，相熟的会坐在一围，称为"搭台"，天天如此。他们边看报纸边吃喝、交谈，约早上八九点钟就喝完第一轮。一家大小多数会晚些时候才去茶楼饮茶。

"得闲饮茶"，香港人经常这样相约。 [20]

125

台湾小吃

[1]　　台湾的小吃可以说是名扬天下。从台南、台中　①　台北，在每座城市的夜市上都有品种丰富、价廉物美（jià lián wù měi）而且很有特色的小吃。

　　珍珠（zhēn zhū）奶茶是台湾人发明的一种饮品。在台湾的任何一个奶茶摊位，你都能品尝到几十种甚至上百种不同口味的珍珠奶茶。珍珠奶茶

[5] 是在红茶里加入鲜奶及粉圆（fěn yuán）。珍珠奶茶香浓可口（kě kǒu），深受人们的喜爱。

　　炭烤臭豆腐（tàn kǎo chòu）也是一种流传（liú chuán）已久的台湾小吃。豆腐经过发酵（fā jiào）后，先用油炸，然后用炭烤，将多余（duō yú）的油逼出，外皮具有香酥（xiāng sū）的口感。外酥里嫩（nèn）的臭豆腐再配上酸甜、清脆（qīng cuì）的泡菜（pào cài），真是美味　②　。

　　台湾另一种小吃——大肠包小肠，可以说是最具人气的美食。其

[10] 实，大肠就是糯米（nuò mǐ）肠，小肠是指香肠。这种小吃的口味众多（zhòng duō），有原味、辣味、黑胡椒（hú jiāo）味等，相信总有一种是你喜欢的。

　　太阳饼是台湾的一种点心，其特点是：皮薄、酥香、馅儿（xiànr）软。饼皮有上百层，放在嘴里即刻就化。太阳饼吃起来不甜　③　不腻，口感很好，回味无穷（huí wèi wú qióng）。

[15]　　凤梨（fèng lí）酥是台湾最受欢迎的糕点之一。凤梨酥的馅儿是由菠萝、冬瓜和麦芽糖（mài yá táng）做成的，不黏牙（nián），甜而不腻，外皮酥香，吃起来既爽口（shuǎng kǒu）　④　有菠萝的香味。每个到台湾旅游的人　⑤　会买几盒凤梨酥带回家。

　　台湾的小吃多得数不清。最好的办法是亲自去一趟台湾，亲口尝一尝。你一定会惊叹（jīng tàn），台湾的小吃不但继承（jì chéng）了传统的中国小吃特

[20] 色，　⑥　还把中国的美食发扬光大。

又　极了　而且　也　但是　都　因此　到

1. _____ 2. _____ 3. _____

4. _____ 5. _____ 6. _____

B 根据短文找出四个正确的句子

☐ 1. 台湾的小吃好吃但是一般挺贵。

☐ 2. 台湾人用红茶做珍珠奶茶。 zhēn zhū

☐ 3. 用来配炭烤臭豆腐的泡菜又酸又辣。 tàn kǎo chòu

☐ 4. 大肠包小肠的口味多种多样。

☐ 5. 太阳饼的馅儿里有菠萝。 xiànr

☐ 6. 去台湾旅游的人都爱买凤梨酥带回家。 fèng lí sū

☐ 7. 台湾的小吃数都数不过来。

C 根据短文选择正确答案

1. "价廉物美"(第2行)的意思是 jià lián wù měi
   _____。

   a) 东西的价格贵但好看

   b) 好看的东西没有标价

   c) 东西的价钱低，质量高

2. "流传已久"(第6行)的意思是 liú chuán
   _____。

   a) 传下来或传播开很长时间了 chuán bō

   b) 流失了很久

   c) 刚刚出名

3. "最具人气"(第9行)的意思是
   _____。

   a) 很多人

   b) 最受欢迎

   c) 有人生气

4. "上百层"(第13行)的意思是
   _____。

   a) 正好100层

   b) 不到100层

   c) 100层以上

127

1. 只有很少一部分人知道台湾的小吃出名。　　　　　　　　　　对　错

原因：＿＿＿＿＿＿＿＿＿＿＿＿＿＿＿＿＿＿＿＿　＿　＿

_{zhēn zhū}
2. 珍珠奶茶的口味只有十几种。

原因：＿＿＿＿＿＿＿＿＿＿＿＿＿＿＿＿＿＿＿＿　＿　＿

_{tàn kǎo chòu}
3. 炭烤臭豆腐就是直接用炭烤臭豆腐。

原因：＿＿＿＿＿＿＿＿＿＿＿＿＿＿＿＿＿＿＿＿　＿　＿

_{nuò mǐ}
4. 大肠包小肠中的大肠是糯米做的。

原因：＿＿＿＿＿＿＿＿＿＿＿＿＿＿＿＿＿＿＿＿　＿　＿

5. 太阳饼的特点是甜而不腻。

原因：＿＿＿＿＿＿＿＿＿＿＿＿＿＿＿＿＿＿＿＿　＿　＿

_{fèng lí sū}
6. 凤梨酥在台湾小吃中是最受游客欢迎的。

原因：＿＿＿＿＿＿＿＿＿＿＿＿＿＿＿＿＿＿＿＿　＿　＿

1. 名扬天下（第1行）　☐　　A 立即；马上。

2. 多余（第7行）　☐　　B 没有钱。

_{jí kè}
3. 即刻（第13行）　☐　　C 非常出名。

_{wú qióng}
4. 无穷（第14行）　☐　　D 无时无刻。

_{jì chéng}
5. 继承（第19行）　☐　　E 不必要的。

　　　　　　　　　　　　_{yí liú}
　　　　　　　　　　F 接受前人遗留下来的东西。
　　　　　　　　　　_{xiàn dù}
　　　　　　　　　　G 没有限度。

中国的面条

中国人一直有吃面条的习惯。吃面条___①___能填饱肚子，还有民俗礼仪的意义，比如过生日时往往少不了吃面条。因为面条又长又细，细的意思是瘦，而瘦则与"寿"谐音，___②___过生日吃的面条又称长寿面。吃长寿面是中国的传统习俗。 [1]

中国的面条，有的细如丝线，有的宽如腰带，形式数不胜数。面条的制作方法又有很多种，有擀、切、削等等，___③___多种烹饪方法，如煮、炒、煎、炸等。吃面条的习俗有着悠久的历史，各地都有自己不同风味的面条。以下介绍几种有名的面条。 [5]

上海的阳春面用海米（上海人称为"开洋"）、葱油拌面条，所以阳春面___④___叫海米葱油拌面。一碗美味的阳春面讲究面条滑爽，海米鲜美，葱油喷香。阳春面的汤是用猪骨熬出来的，特别鲜美。 [10]

炸酱面是北京富有特色的面食。所配材料一般是黄瓜、豆芽等。炸酱的做法是把肉丁及葱姜等放在油里炒，___⑤___加入甜面酱。最后把煮熟的面条放在碗里，浇上炸酱，并拌以所配材料。炸酱面做起来很方便，面条里既有肉又有菜，深受以面食为主食的北方人的喜爱。 [15]

担担面是最具代表性的四川小吃。其做法是在煮熟的面条上浇上炒制的猪肉末。一碗地道的担担面讲究面条筋道、味道麻辣、色泽鲜红、香气扑鼻。

刀削面是山西人日常喜爱的面食。厨师一手拿刀直接把面条削进开水锅里煮。吃刀削面___⑥___可以配番茄酱、肉炸酱等，并配上应时蔬菜。吃刀削面可以饱口福，而观看刀削面的制作则饱了眼福。 [20]

从下面的方框里为短文选择最合适的词语填空

也　还有　所以　而且　时　再　因为　不仅

1. ＿＿＿＿＿＿＿＿　　2. ＿＿＿＿＿＿＿＿　　3. ＿＿＿＿＿＿＿＿

4. ＿＿＿＿＿＿＿＿　　5. ＿＿＿＿＿＿＿＿　　6. ＿＿＿＿＿＿＿＿

B　根据短文找出四个正确的句子

□ 1. 中国人有过生日吃面条的习俗。

□ 2. 中国的各个地区都吃同一种面条。

□ 3. 阳春面用的汤是海米汤。

□ 4. 做炸酱(zhá jiàng)面时要放肉丁、葱(cōng)、姜(jiāng)和甜面酱。

□ 5. 担担(dàn dàn)面吃起来又辣又香。

□ 6. 吃刀削(xiāo)面时只配炸酱，不用配菜。

□ 7. 中国的面条不仅形式多样，烹饪(pēng rèn)方法也很多。

C　根据短文回答问题

1. 中国面条的制作方法主要有哪几种？

2. 中国人烹饪面条的方法主要有哪几种？

3. 阳春面有什么特色？

4. 为什么炸酱面受北方人的喜爱？

5. 吃哪两种面时要配上蔬菜？

1.对中国人来说，面条只是一种能填饱肚子的食物。 对　错

　　原因：＿＿＿＿＿＿＿＿＿＿＿＿＿＿＿＿＿＿＿＿ ＿＿　＿＿

2.中国的面条只有两种，细面和宽面，但做法有多种。

　　原因：＿＿＿＿＿＿＿＿＿＿＿＿＿＿＿＿＿＿＿＿ ＿＿　＿＿

3.上海的阳春面是汤面，汤是将猪骨熬很长时间熬出来的。

　　原因：＿＿＿＿＿＿＿＿＿＿＿＿＿＿＿＿＿＿＿＿ ＿＿　＿＿

4.中国的北方人经常吃面食。

　　原因：＿＿＿＿＿＿＿＿＿＿＿＿＿＿＿＿＿＿＿＿ ＿＿　＿＿

5.吃担担面时，要先将面条炒熟，然后在上面浇上辣椒油。

　　原因：＿＿＿＿＿＿＿＿＿＿＿＿＿＿＿＿＿＿＿＿ ＿＿　＿＿

6.顾客看不到刀削面师傅把面条削进锅里去煮。

　　原因：＿＿＿＿＿＿＿＿＿＿＿＿＿＿＿＿＿＿＿＿ ＿＿　＿＿

E 给下列词语配上最合适的解释

1.数不胜数(第5行)　　□ ｜ A 真正的。

2.地道(第17行)　　　□ ｜ B 当地。

3.应时(第20行)　　　□ ｜ C 数也数不过来。

4.饱眼福(第21行)　　□ ｜ D 适合季节的。

　　　　　　　　　　　　｜ E 看着感到满足。

　　　　　　　　　　　　｜ F 流行。

单元复习

＜生词

第7课

网络　评委　正方　在座　辩论　题目　青少年　大于
如今　占有　地位　看法　同类　正确　可靠　误导
网民　辨别　是非　上当　受骗　滥用　答案　欺负
真实　说谎　交际　依赖　成瘾　每时每刻　心思
有利　结果　整天　事物　成长　结论

第8课

科技　产品　进入　方方面面　无处不在　家家户户
使用　家电　自动　通讯　缩短　距离　时尚　笔记本电脑
数码相机　轻巧　天地　普及　远程课程　光碟　天下
大事　软件　迅速　虚拟　想象力　问世　省事　高速　列车
便利　边远　目的地　确实　产生　巨大　好事　坏事

第9课

涨价　荤　搭配　降价　奇怪　相对　照样　价格
偏食　发育　指出　直接　素质　有害　肥胖症　血脂
高血压　疾病　效果　上调　遗憾　供应　在乎　能够
代替　高价　吓　一方面……另一方面……　报道

对青少年来说　占有重要的地位　弊大于利　带来负面的影响

不一定正确、可靠　误导网民　辨别是非的能力　提供真实的信息

由于……，所以……　容易上当、受骗　滥用网络　交际能力下降

跟人面对面沟通　依赖网络　上网成瘾　有利于健康　学习成绩下降

健康状况尤其是视力变坏了　生活在网络世界里　对成长没有好处

不仅……，而且……　带来方便　高科技进入生活的方方面面

节省时间　成为通讯工具　不管……，都可以……　缩短距离

不但轻巧而且功能多　受青少年的喜爱　创造新天地　接受教育

天下大事　生活在虚拟世界里　自从……问世后　不但省时而且省事

对……产生影响　对……越来越依赖

涨价20%　荤素搭配　奇怪的是……　相对便宜　吸引更多的学生去吃

照样吃快餐　普遍偏食　重视饮食健康　不良的饮食习惯影响发育

直接影响身体素质，有害健康　效果不明显　上调价格　代替快餐

采访的结果令人遗憾　贵一点儿也不在乎　再跟餐厅商量

增加午饭的花费　改掉不良的习惯

[1] ## 杭州简介：

杭州市位于中国东南沿海，是浙江省的省会。杭州市有600多万人口，是浙江省[5]的政治、经济、文化中心。杭州是中国七大古都之一，有2000多年的历史。杭州以美丽的西湖山水而闻名，人们经常用"人间天堂"来赞[10]美这座美丽的城市。

景点：

杭州有江、河、湖、山，自然风景优美，名胜古迹特别多。除了西湖风景区以[15]外，还有灵隐寺、六和塔等。

▼ 西湖   ▲ 灵隐寺

▲ 六和塔

léi fēng tǎ
◀ 雷峰塔

气候：

杭州气候温和，四季分明，年平均气温在16度左右。杭州的夏天很闷热，冬[20]天相当寒冷。每年3至4月是杭州旅游的最好季节。

美食、特产：

杭州的名菜很多，最著名的有东坡肉、龙井虾仁等。[25]等。杭州还有许多传统的工艺品和特产，比如丝绸、瓷器、龙井茶等。

租船、租自行车服务：

想游览西湖的美丽风[30]景，游客可以选择租游船，每小时80元，也可以租自行车，每小时15元。

住宿：

杭州有近百家不同风[35]格、设备齐全的宾馆，还有各类家庭旅馆，可以满足不同游客的需要。

交通：

游客可搭乘飞机、专线[40]火车或长途汽车到达杭州。杭州市区的公共交通十分方便，有空调公交车、电车、出租车等。

注意事项：

[45] 　　在旅行途中，游客要注意交通安全，保管好自己的行李及物品，还要注意饮食卫生。除此以外，游客还要注意保护景点的环境，不要乱扔垃圾。

　　杭州市旅游局

[50] 　　电话：86-571-86964321

　　电邮：hzinfo@yahoo.com.cn

　　网址：www.hangzhou.com.cn

▲ 东坡肉

▲ 龙井虾仁

1. 杭州 (hángzhōu) Hangzhou (provincial capital of Zhejiang Province)
2. 位于 (wèi yú) be located
3. 沿 (yán) along　沿海 (yánhǎi) coastal
*4. 省 (shěng) province　浙江省 (zhè jiāngshěng) Zhejiang Province
　　省会 (shěnghuì) provincial capital
5. 治 (zhì) rule; govern　政治 (zhèngzhì) politics
6. 古都 (gǔ dū) ancient capital
7. 湖 (hú) lake　西湖 (xī hú) West Lake
8. 山水 (shānshuǐ) scenery with hills and streams
9. 闻（聞）(wén) hear　闻名 (wénmíng) famous
10. 人间 (rén jiān) world; earth　11. 赞美 (zàn měi) praise
12. 寺 (sì) temple; mosque; monastery
　　灵隐寺 (líng yǐn sì) Lingyinsi Temple (in Hangzhou)
13. 塔 (tǎ) pagoda
　　六和塔 (liù hé tǎ) a famous pagoda in Hangzhou
14. 闷热 (mēn rè) hot and stuffy　15. 寒冷 (hánlěng) cold
16. 特产 (tè chǎn) special local product
17. 名菜 (míng cài) famous dish

18. 东坡 (dōng pō) a famous poet in Song Dynasty
　　东坡肉 (dōng pō ròu) a kind of pork dish named after a famous poet
19. 仁 (rén) kernel　虾仁 (xiā rén) shelled shrimp
20. 龙井 (lóngjǐng) Dragon Well tea (a kind of green tea)
　　龙井虾仁 (lóngjǐng xiā rén) shelled shrimps cooked with Dragon Well tea leaves
21. 绸（綢）(chóu) silk　丝绸 (sī chóu) silk
22. 游船 (yóuchuán) pleasure boat
23. 宾（賓）(bīn) guest　宾馆 (bīn guǎn) guesthouse
24. 搭乘 (dā chéng) travel by
25. 线（綫）(xiàn) route; line　专线 (zhuānxiàn) special line
26. 长途 (cháng tú) long-distance
27. 公交 (gōngjiāo) public transportation
28. 途中 (tú zhōng) on the way
29. 保管 (bǎoguǎn) take care of　30. 行李 (xíng li) luggage
31. 物品 (wù pǐn) articles; goods
32. 乱（亂）(luàn) mess up; random
33. 旅游局 (lǚ yóu jú) bureau of tourism

口语热身

消化课文

1. 根据课文回答问题

1) 杭州市在哪个省？一共有多少人口？

2) 杭州市是一个什么样的城市？以什么闻名？

3) 杭州市有哪些著名的旅游景点？

4) 杭州市的气候有什么特点？有什么特产？

5) 杭州市的交通方便吗？有哪些交通工具？游客可以租借什么交通工具游览西湖？

6) 如果你想去杭州市旅游，哪个季节去比较好？为什么？

2. 根据实际情况回答问题

1) 你知道中国的哪些大城市？请列出五个城市。你去过中国的哪些城市？你最喜欢哪一个？为什么？

2) 你去过北京吗？北京跟你居住的地方有哪些相同点和不同点？举例说明。

3) 你居住的地方有哪些名胜古迹？你都参观过吗？你最喜欢哪一个？请讲一讲。

4) 你居住的地方气候怎么样？如果你的朋友打算到你所在地旅游，你会建议他/她哪个季节来？为什么？

5) 你居住的地方有哪些特产？如果你的朋友来看你，你会带他/她去哪儿吃有特色的饭菜？吃什么？

6) 你居住的地方交通方便吗？有哪些交通工具？哪种交通工具最便宜？哪种最方便？

7) 在你所在地旅游，人们可以租汽车吗？可不可以租自行车或船？人们住宾馆、酒店方便吗？价钱怎么样？

8) 你居住的地方安全吗？游客一般要注意什么？

1. 用所给词语造句

例子：杭州市位于中国东南沿海。（第2行）

将于　成立

2. 完成句子

Ⓐ例子：杭州是中国七大古都之一。（第6行）

Ⓑ例子：杭州以美丽的西湖山水而闻名。（第7行）

Ⓒ例子：杭州的名菜很多，最著名的有东坡肉、龙井虾仁等。（第23行）

上海是_____之一。

北京以_____闻名。

最有趣的是_____。

3. 用带点的词语模仿例子造句

例子：除了西湖风景区以外，还有灵隐寺、六和塔等。（第14行）

无论我碰到什么困难，一定要把汉语学好。

我们不但可以游览杭州的美景，而且还可以品尝美食，真是一举两得。

4. 选择其中一个词语造句

例子：杭州年平均气温在16度左右。（第18行）

杭州有近百家不同风格、设备齐全的宾馆。（第34行）

大约/大概/超过/不到

5. 用课文中的动词填空

1)_____这座城市（第9行）　　4)_____飞机（第39行）

2)_____西湖（第29行）　　5)_____卫生（第44行）

3)_____需要（第36行）　　6)_____衣物（第46行）

口语训练

1.口头报告

请介绍中国的一个有名的旅游城市。你的介绍应包括：

- 地理位置、人口
- 气候、交通、住宿
- 旅游景点
- 美食、特产
- 旅游时应注意的事项

▲ 大闸蟹

▲ 碧螺春

▲ 苏绣

苏州园林

参考句子

a) 苏州位于江苏省内，人口大约800多万。苏州是一座历史悠久的文化名城，有4000多年历史。

b) 苏州以山水秀丽而闻名。苏州有"人间天堂""园林之城""东方水城"等美称。

c) 苏州四季分明，气候温和，雨水充足。苏州特产有碧螺春茶叶、阳澄湖大闸蟹等。苏州的传统工艺品有苏绣、丝绸等。

d) 苏州的园林是建筑、山水、花木、书画、雕刻等艺术的结合。最出名的园林有拙政园、狮子林等。

e) 游客可以搭乘飞机到上海，然后转乘专车直达苏州。每天有几十列火车及长途专线旅游巴士经过苏州。苏州市内的交通十分发达，公交车、出租车等非常方便。

f) 苏州有很多不同风格的宾馆，价钱合理，环境舒适。

2. 小组讨论

讨论的题目是：旅游的好处与坏处。你们的讨论内容应包括：

- 旅游的好处
- 旅游的坏处

例子：

学生1：旅游有很多好处。旅游可以开阔眼界，增长（zēng zhǎng）知识。我认为如果你想了解某（mǒu）一个国家，就应该去那个国家旅游一下，这样才能比较全面地了解那个国家的文化、习俗，同时也可以学习那个国家的语言。

学生2：我不赞成你的说法。假设你说的是对的，可是你有没有考虑过费用？我认为要了解一个国家不一定要到那个国家去旅游。如果你想学外语，在国内也可以学。

学生3：你们不要争了。旅游当然有很多好处，但是旅游也有坏处。有的人以为去国外旅游可以练习外语，但是大部分人去国外只是游山玩水。有的人还觉得通过旅游，可以学到很多东西。其（qí）实有很多东西从书本里、电脑里、电视上就能学到。

学生2：对。去国外旅游要花很多钱，还要花时间。我认为不值得。

学生1：我认为你们说得不对。从课堂上和书本里学到的东西跟亲身体会的是不一样的。我同意你们的部分观点。旅游的确（dí què）很花钱，但是值得。旅游能使一个人有国际视（shì）野，能增强（yě）（zēngqiáng）自信心，还能锻炼一个人的能力。

学生2：我周围有一些朋友每个假期都去国外旅游，但是我不认为他们比我的知识面广，比我更有国际视野，比我更自信。

……

写作训练

1. 设计小册子 (shè jì)

请你选择中国的一个城市，帮助旅游局为来华游学团设计一个小册子。在小册子里，你要提及：

- 游学内容简介
- 游学的目的
- 游学所在城市的景点、气候、住宿和交通情况
- 当地美食、特产
- 签证事宜 (shì yí)
- 其他注意事项

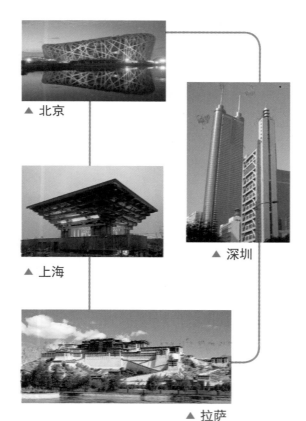

▲ 北京

▲ 上海

▲ 深圳

▲ 拉萨

参考句子

a) 我们会安排学生到当地家庭做客，亲身体验当地人的生活情况，了解该市的历史、文化及风俗习惯。学生可以利用这个机会练习汉语口语。这次游学一定会给学生留下难忘的印象。

b) 除了参观、访问、学习汉语，学生还有机会去市区逛街、购物，品尝当地的美食。我们还会安排自由活动时间。

c) 我们还可以组织各种活动，比如学习书法，看杂技表演、京剧、武术演出等。

d) 本市酒店环境清静、舒适，交通方便。

e) 团费包括食宿、门票、交通费，但是不包括保险 (bǎo xiǎn)、长途电话费。

f) 本市旅游旺季 (wàng jì) 是每年的三至十一月。冬天寒冷，不是旅游的好季节。

g) 如果提前报名可以享受八折优惠。

h) 本旅行社代办签证。签证费500元人民币。

2. 阅读短文并写回应式作文

假设你刚从九寨沟（jiǔ zhàigōu）旅游回来。写一封信给朋友，向他/她简单介绍九寨沟，并告诉他/她去那里旅游的最佳时间及在旅行中需注意的事项。

"人间仙境"（xiān jìng）九寨沟

　　九寨沟位于四川省阿坝（ā bà）州九寨沟县境内，距离成都市400多公里。九寨沟是一条长50余公里的山沟谷地，三条主沟组成英文字母的"Y"字形。九寨沟因周围有九个藏族村寨（zàng zú cūn zhài）而得名，总面积约620平方公里，大约有52％的面积是原始森林（yuán shǐ sēn lín）。20世纪70年代，九寨沟被一群偶然闯入（ǒu rán chuǎng rù）的伐木（fá mù）工人发现，1982年成为国家首批（shǒu pī）重点（zhòng diǎn）风景名胜区。 [1] [5]

　　九寨沟海拔（hǎi bá）约3000米，属高原湿润气候，山顶终年积雪（zhōng nián jī xuě）。九寨沟四季的景色（jǐng sè）都很迷人：春天的花草，夏天的流瀑（liú pù），秋天的红叶，冬天的白雪，都让游人流连忘返（liú lián wàng fǎn）。九寨沟的自然景观（jǐng guān）十分独特，那里有奇妙（qí miào）的湖泊（hú pō）、瀑布（pù bù），是名副其实（míng fù qí shí）的"中华水景之王"。那里有美丽的雪山、森林，组成神奇的景观。到过九寨沟的游人，都说那里是"童话世界""人间仙境"。 [10]

　　九寨沟的动植物资源（zī yuán）丰富，而且种类繁多（zhǒng lèi fán duō）。举世闻名的大熊猫、金丝猴（jīn sī hóu）、白唇鹿（bái chún lù）等珍稀（zhēn xī）动物都在此生活。在九寨沟这个植物王国里，生长着数以千计的药用植物。因此，九寨沟又是四川中药主产地之一。其中名贵的药材冬虫夏草就生长在周围的高山上。 [15]

　　到了九寨沟，别忘了品尝当地的民族风味食品：虫草鸭、烤全羊、手扒（bā）牛排、杂面、青稞（qīng kē）酒等。如果要买纪念品，当然少不了当地的藏族手工艺品，如藏饰、刺绣（cì xiù）、佛珠（fó zhū）等。

　　到九寨沟旅游，游客会有轻微（qīng wēi）的高原反应（fǎn yìng）。年老体弱者，有高血压、心脏病者前往九寨沟时要格外（gé wài）注意。春末至秋初前往九寨沟的游客最多，十月是最佳的旅游时间。 [20]

阅读与理解

丝绸之路

第一段 [1]　　丝绸之路，简称"丝路"，是西汉年间（约公元前202年~公元8年）由张骞（zhāngqiān）出使西域（xī yù）开辟（kāi pì）的、中国历史上一条横贯（héngguàn）欧亚大陆（dà lù）的贸易（mào yì）交通线。丝路以长安（今西安）为起点，经甘肃（gān sù）、新疆（xīn jiāng），到中亚、西亚，并连接地中海各国的陆上通道，有7000多公里长。由于从这条路西运的
[5]　货物中大多数是丝绸制品（zhì pǐn），因此被叫做"丝绸之路"。

第二段　　　丝绸之路促进（cù jìn）了欧亚一些国家在贸易、经济和文化方面的发展。中国古代的四大发明经丝路西传，加速（jiā sù）了西方国家的文明。中国的天文、医学、音乐、建筑等各个领域（lǐng yù）的知识也通过丝路介绍到了西方。中国商队通过丝路运出的铁器、金器、银器、镜子和其他豪华（háo huá）制品，丰富了西
[10]　方国家人民的生活。

第三段　　　丝绸之路第一次为中国认识世界和其他文明打开了一个窗口。通过丝路，西方世界的物质（wù zhì）文明和精神文明也传入了中国。大量新奇（xīn qí）的植物品种从中亚和西亚输入（shū rù）到中国，比如芝麻（zhī ma）、核桃（hé tao）、大蒜（suàn）、大葱（cōng）等。这些植物的输入对中国农业、畜牧业（xù mù yè）以及医药等各方面的发展，
[15]　都起了极大的作用。许多珍奇（zhēn qí）的动物品种也输入到中国，例如骆驼（luò tuo）、犀牛（xī niú）、孔雀（kǒng què）等。从丝路传入的还有各种宗教（zōng jiào），其中佛教（fó jiào）对中国的影响最大。

第四段　　　丝绸之路不仅是古代东西方之间的贸易之路，更重要的是古代中国文明通过它影响了世界文明的发展，同时，中国也从其他国家和地区吸
[20]　取（qǔ）了不同的文明营养。

1. 丝绸之路简称 _____。

    a) 丝路

    b) 中亚交通线

    c) 贸易之路

2. 丝绸之路的起点_____。

    a) 古时候叫西安

    b) 是今天的西安

    c) 是甘肃 (gān sù)

3. _____通过丝绸之路传入中国。

    a) 芝麻 (zhī ma)、核桃 (hé tao) 等植物品种

    b) 铁器、镜子等豪华制品 (háo huá zhì pǐn)

    c) 西方的医学、天文知识

4. _____对中国影响很大。

    a) 西方的文明

    b) 中亚的丝绸制品

    c) 佛教 (fó jiào)

1. 在中国古代，丝路从中国开始一直通到西亚、欧洲国家。   对   错

   原因：_____ ___ ___

2. 中国古代四大发明加速 (jiā sù) 了西方国家文明的发展。

   原因：_____ ___ ___

3. 除了丝绸制品，中国没有其他东西通过丝路运往欧亚其他

   国家。

   原因：_____ ___ ___

4. 西方的金器、银器等豪华制品丰富了中国人民的生活。

   原因：_____ ___ ___

5. 孔雀 (kǒng què) 是通过丝路输入中国的一种珍奇 (zhēn qí) 动物。

   原因：_____ ___ ___

6. 古代的中国文明影响了西方文明的发展。

   原因：_____ ___ ___

C 从右边的段落大意中找出最合适的

1. 第一段　☐
2. 第二段　☐
3. 第三段　☐
4. 第四段　☐

A 丝绸之路促进了欧亚国家在贸易、经济等方面的发展。

B 西方的宗教是通过丝绸之路传入中国的。

C 通过丝绸之路，中国及欧亚各国互相影响、互惠互利。

D 丝绸之路沿线的各国风情。

E "丝绸之路"的由来。

F 通过丝绸之路，欧亚国家的物质和精神文明也影响了中国。

D 根据短文找出四个正确的句子

☐ 1. 丝绸之路全长超过7000公里。

☐ 2. 丝绸之路是一条从中国通往欧亚大陆的贸易交通线。

☐ 3. 丝绸之路以中国的新疆为终点。

☐ 4. 在丝绸之路开通之前，中国已经有大蒜、大葱等。

☐ 5. 除了佛教以外，其他宗教也通过丝路传入了中国。

☐ 6. 佛教是中国土生土长的宗教。

☐ 7. 通过丝绸之路，中国从欧亚其他国家那里学到了很多东西。

E 用短文中的名词填空

1. 公共_____（第2行）

2. 海上_____（第4行）

3. 工艺_____（第5行）

4. 文化_____（第8行）

5. 动物_____（第13行）

6. _____（第16行）政策

7. 正面_____（第16行）

8. 精神_____（第20行）

144

"世外桃源" 香格里拉

香格里拉在藏语中意为"心中的日月"。它___①___青藏高原的东南边缘，位于云南省的迪庆，海拔3280米。 [1]

香格里拉被世人誉为"世外桃源"。这里有着广阔的草原、清澈的湖泊、蔚蓝的天空、洁白的雪山、原始的森林，再加上成群的牛羊、神秘的寺院，这一切___②___了一幅美丽迷人的风景画。 [5]

香格里拉还被称为"高山大花园""植物王国"，是一个自然景观的旅游胜地。在香格里拉，有上百种珍稀树种和数百种中药材，是一个难得的植物宝藏。

香格里拉是一个多民族、多宗教、多文化并存的地方。这里___③___着勤劳、好客的藏族、白族、回族、苗族等25个民族。香格里拉的居民信仰不同的宗教，有佛教、儒教、道教、天主教、基督教、伊斯兰教等。在生活习惯、服饰、民居建筑以及传统习俗方面，各族人民仍然保持着本民族的特色。 [10]

如画的自然景色，___④___独特的少数民族文化及风情，使香格里拉成了很多游客的必到之处。如果你___⑤___去香格里拉旅游，以下是几则小贴士： [15]

1. 5至7月、9至10月都是雨季，不适合在香格里拉旅游。冬天气温太低，如果___⑥___下雨，路上会结冰，开车和行走都相当危险。

2. 香格里拉气候比较干燥，紫外线辐射强，要___⑦___防晒霜、太阳帽和太阳镜。如果10月以后去，要带羽绒服、帽子、手套和防滑靴。 [20]

3. 香格里拉地处高原，因此不宜做剧烈运动，以防___⑧___高山反应。

从下面的方框里为短文选择最合适的词语填空

| 发现 | 居住 | 带上 | 地处 | 打算 |
| 组织 | 发生 | 组成 | 遇到 | 加上 |

1. _____   2. _____   3. _____   4. _____

5. _____   6. _____   7. _____   8. _____

B 根据短文选择正确答案

1. "意为"（第1行）的意思是
   _____。
   a) 有意思
   b) 有趣
   c) 意思是

2. "世外桃源"（第3行）的意思
   是 _____。
   a) 果园
   b) 高山上的花园
   c) 不受外界影响，想象中的
     美好世界

3. "必到之处"（第15行）的意思
   是 _____。
   a) 可能不会去的地方
   b) 不可能不去的地方
   c) 一般不会去的地方

4. "高山反应"（第21行）的意思
   是 _____。
   a) 在高山上做运动后的感觉
   b) 在高山上攀岩
   c) 人在高山上会出现头痛、
     心跳加快等症状

C 根据短文回答问题

1. 为什么人们称香格里拉为"植物王国"？

2. 香格里拉有什么样的自然景色？

3. 为什么香格里拉是一个多宗教并存的地方？

1. 香格里拉在海拔3280米的高原上。　　　　　　　　　　　　　　　对　　错

   原因：＿＿＿＿＿＿＿＿＿＿＿＿＿＿＿＿＿＿＿＿＿＿＿　　＿＿　＿＿

2. 香格里拉有各种珍奇的花草，但没有中草药。

   原因：＿＿＿＿＿＿＿＿＿＿＿＿＿＿＿＿＿＿＿＿＿＿＿　　＿＿　＿＿

3. 香格里拉的常住居民都是藏族人。

   原因：＿＿＿＿＿＿＿＿＿＿＿＿＿＿＿＿＿＿＿＿＿＿＿　　＿＿　＿＿

4. 香格里拉的独特之处是自然风景加上少数民族风情。

   原因：＿＿＿＿＿＿＿＿＿＿＿＿＿＿＿＿＿＿＿＿＿＿＿　　＿＿　＿＿

5. 每年都有很多游客去香格里拉旅行。

   原因：＿＿＿＿＿＿＿＿＿＿＿＿＿＿＿＿＿＿＿＿＿＿＿　　＿＿　＿＿

☐ 1. 五六月不适合去香格里拉旅游。

☐ 2. 由于香格里拉在高山上，所以游客不能开车进山。

☐ 3. 香格里拉的冬天很冷，再遇上下雨，游客走路千万要小心。

☐ 4. 每年的十一月是香格里拉的雨季。

☐ 5. 香格里拉全年有6个月是雨季。

☐ 6. 十月份以后，游客上香格里拉需带冬衣。

☐ 7. 在香格里拉的高山上，游客最好不要做剧烈运动。

第四单元
第11课

[1]　尊敬的市长先生：

　　　您好！

　　我叫张进林，就读于本市金山国际学校。我今天写信想表达我对我市青少年娱乐活动的一些意见和建议。

[5]　　目前，本市的网民数目近两百万，其中青少年占了相当一部分。最近，青年协会作了一次问卷调查，调查的对象是本市2000个12至20岁的初、高中生。结果发现，45%的青少年首选娱乐活动是网络活动。根据调查结果，一些专家指出，由于政府和社会为青少年提供的娱乐活动种类很

[10]　有限，所以青少年选择上网来消磨他们的课余时间。

　　网络的确已经成为我们生活中的一部分。但由于网络缺乏监管，网上不少色情、暴力等不健康的内容影响了青少年的身心健康，有时还可能造成严重的后果。有些青少年过分依赖网络，上网成瘾。结果，他们的视力、学习成

[15]　绩以及跟人沟通的能力都下降了。

　　对于青少年来说，娱乐生活和社交活动都很重要。具有知识性、挑战性的娱乐活动可以

[20]　扩大青少年的知识面，提高修养，并培养社交技巧。所以，

[25]　我认为市政

府应为本市青少年多提供健康的、有意义的娱乐活动。这样，青少年的业余生活才会丰富多彩。

青少年是社会的未来，政府有责任为他们提供健康、有益的成长环境，把他们培养成有用的人，使其今后为社会服务，为国家作[30]贡献。我希望市长先生能重视这个问题。

此致

敬礼！

张进林

2010年5月4日

生词

1. 就读 jiù dú attend school
2. 表达 biǎo dá express
3. 数目 shù mù number
*4. 协（協）xié joint 协会 xié huì association
5. 问卷 wèn juàn questionnaire
6. 首选 shǒu xuǎn first choice
7. 据（據）jù according to 根据 gēn jù according to
8. 政府 zhèng fǔ government
9. 种类 zhǒng lèi category
10. 限 xiàn limits 有限 yǒu xiàn limited
11. 消 xiāo idle away (the time)
12. 磨 mó waste (time) 消磨 xiāo mó idle away
13. 的确 dí què indeed
14. 乏 fá lack 缺乏 quē fá lack

15. 监（監）jiān supervise 监管 jiān guǎn supervise and control
16. 色情 sè qíng pornographic
17. 暴力 bào lì violent
18. 身心 shēn xīn body and mind
19. 造成 zào chéng cause
20. 后果 hòu guǒ consequence
21. 过分 guò fèn excessive
22. 对于 duì yú with regard to
23. 社交 shè jiāo social contact
24. 具有 jù yǒu have; be provided with
25. 修养 xiū yǎng self-cultivation
26. 业余 yè yú spare time
27. 未 wèi not yet 未来 wèi lái future
28. 益 yì beneficial 有益 yǒu yì beneficial

149

消化课文

1. 根据课文回答问题

1) 本文的作者是谁？他为什么给市长写信？

2) 最近青年协会作了什么调查？调查的对象是谁？

3) 青年协会调查的结果怎么样？为什么会有这样的结果？

4) 网络上的哪些内容会影响青少年的身心健康？

5) 什么样的娱乐和社交活动对青少年有好处？

6) 作者建议市政府为本市青少年提供什么样的活动？

2. 根据实际情况回答问题

1) 在你居住的地方，在哪些公共场所市民可以免费上网？

2) 在你居住的地方，青少年首选的娱乐活动是什么？你认为为什么网络活动在青少年的心目中很重要？

3) 在你居住的地方，政府为青少年提供了哪些娱乐、文化活动？请列出三项。你经常参加哪些活动？你居住的地方有哪些适合青少年参加的慈善活动？

4) 在你居住的地方，政府监管网络上不健康的内容吗？是如何监管的？如果不监管，可能会造成什么后果？

5) 你认为娱乐生活和社交技巧对青少年重要吗？你觉得丰富多彩的娱乐生活应该包括什么？

6) 你居住的地方经常邀请有名的歌星、乐队来演出吗？你看过其中的一场演唱会或者音乐会吗？请谈一谈。

7) 你居住的地方经常举办哪些体育比赛？是什么时候举行的？你参加过吗？请谈一谈。你居住的地方邀请过有名的球队来比赛吗？你去看过吗？

8) 如果你的朋友要来你居住的地方旅游，你会带他/她去看什么演出或表演？去参观哪几个博物馆？

1. 完成句子

Ⓐ例子：我就读于本市金山国际学校。（第3行）

Ⓑ例子：本市的网民数目近两百万，其中青少年占了相当一部分。（第5行）

我出生于＿＿＿＿＿＿。

＿＿＿＿＿＿提供了各种娱乐活动，其中＿＿＿＿＿＿＿＿＿＿。

2. 选择其中一个短语造句

Ⓐ例子：青年协会作了一次问卷调查。（第6行）

作准备/作贡献

Ⓑ例子：结果发现，45%的青少年首选娱乐活动是网络活动。（第7行）

三分之一(1/3)/0.56/三成/打八五折

Ⓒ例子：市政府应为本市青少年多提供健康的、有意义的娱乐活动。（第25行）

为……开设课程/安排住宿/组织活动

3. 用带点的词语模仿例子造句

例子：由于政府和社会为青少年提供的娱乐活动种类很有限，所以青少年选择上网来消磨他们的课余时间。（第9行）

设计娱乐活动既要考虑到知识性又要具有挑战性。

4. 用课文中的动词填空

1) ＿＿＿＿意见（第4行）　　4) ＿＿＿＿修养（第22行）

2) ＿＿＿＿经验（第12行）　　5) ＿＿＿＿社交技巧（第23行）

3) ＿＿＿＿知识面（第20行）　6) ＿＿＿＿娱乐活动（第26行）

实际运用

角色扮演

在这个口语练习中有三个角色:市长、康乐文化署专员及学生代表。你们要讨论政府能为本市青少年组织哪些有意义的娱乐、社交活动。讨论的内容应包括:

- 政府可能提供的娱乐活动
- 资金、人手等问题
- 活动对青少年的影响

例子:

学生:首先感谢市长先生在百忙之中抽出时间来参加这个会议。我写信的目的不是表达不满,而是希望市政府能为青少年组织更多的娱乐和社交活动,使青少年不要整天上网。

市长:我同意你信中的一些看法。市政府已经组织了一些大型的、有益的活动,但种类的确有限。我认为政府、社会、学校、家庭都有责任为青少年提供具有知识性、娱乐性、挑战性的活动,使青少年远离不健康的网站。

专员:如果要开展娱乐、社交等活动,资金和人手是一个问题。今年经济情况不太乐观,康乐文化署没有多余的资金可以安排。但人手方面,我可以安排。

学生:我们学生会成员可以做志愿者,帮助你们一起

组织。我们有些成员很有创意，他们一定很乐意出一把力。

专员：我们署里有几个同事，以前参与组织过大型的活动，比如春节晚会、亚运会等。我可以跟他们商量一下，看看我们能够为本市青少年组织哪些活动，以丰富他们的业余生活。

市长：在资金方面，我想跟商界，比如几个大公司联络一下，看看他们能不能资助。

专员：那倒是个好主意。

学生：我们可以组织歌唱大比拼、网球大奖赛、才艺秀、有奖阅读等活动。希望通过参加这些活动，上网成瘾的青少年人数会减少。

市长：我们组织的活动一定要丰富多彩，这样才能吸引更多的青少年参加。我相信通过我们的共同努力，一定能够达到目标。

参考句子

a) 我认为现在的网站内容缺乏监管，网站上有不少色情、暴力等不健康的内容，影响青少年的身心健康。政府有责任制定法律、法规监管网络。

b) 根据我们的经验，政府很难监管网站上的内容。我们试过了，也很想这样做，但是做不到。

c) 为了扩大学生的知识面，提高他们的修养，我们可以组织一些活动比如专题讨论会、时事辩论会等。

d) 上网的确成了相当一部分学生消磨时间的主要方式。

e) 为了丰富青少年的业余生活，我们可以举办球类比赛、设计比赛、慈善活动、环保活动等。

f) 青少年是社会的未来，我们应该培养他们从小就关心社会、为社会作贡献。我们可以安排他们去老人院或残疾人学校做义工。

153

写作训练

1. 写正式的书信

请你代表学校学生会给本市市长写一封信，表示你支持在本市举办全国运动会。在信里，你要提及：

- 举行大型活动对本市及市民的好处
- 具体的建议
- 能够提供的帮助

参考句子

a) 我今天写信表示支持在本市举办全国运动会，因为我相信在本市举办运动会有很多好处。

b) 运动会不仅能吸引更多的人来本市旅游、消费（xiāo fèi），提高本市的知名度（zhī míng dù），而且还能创造就业（jiù yè）机会。

c) 在准备的过程中，本市需要建旅馆、餐馆及各类设施，还要培训（péi xùn）具备各种技能的人才。

d) 运动会之后，所有的设施都可以给本市市民（shì mín）使用。这样，市民会更加热爱并愿意参与体育活动，以提高身体素质。

e) 我建议政府借这个机会增强市民的环保意识，把本市的绿化做得更好。

f) 我们学校的高年级学生有举办、组织大型活动的经验。我们可以组织学生做志愿者（zhì yuàn zhě）。我们能做的工作有导游、服务员、运动场地工作人员、宣传工作等。

2. 阅读短文并写作文

读了下面的短文后，你对上海青年人的娱乐生活有了更多的了解。请写一篇博客，介绍你所居住地区的青年人的娱乐生活。

新娱乐形式

最近，上海青年会对1000个12至24岁的青年人作了一次调查，[1]
结果发现现在的青年人喜爱的新娱乐形式是网络娱乐、手机娱乐及其他多元化的娱乐活动。这三种娱乐形式已经占到青年人娱乐内容的一半以上。

根据调查，52.8%的青年人主要通过新娱乐形式来减压。在这 [5]
1000名受访者中，26.3%的青年人认为自己承受的压力很大。一个高三学生说，他从今年3月就开始为高考复习了。他每天晚上自习回来后觉得压力特别大，就会上网玩儿一会儿网络游戏。他觉得这样可以调节紧张的心理，减轻学习压力。

在调查中，有近六成的青年人认为新娱乐形式积极、正面的 [10]
影响大于消极、负面的影响，特别是那些多元化的娱乐活动，比如健身运动、交际活动等满足了青年人的娱乐需求，对放松、减压有很好的效果。

在采访中，有些高中生认为，新娱乐形式特别是网络娱乐和动漫会对青年人产生负面的影响。经常通过网络娱乐的青年人容 [15]
易上瘾，这样会影响正常的学习和生活。而且，有些网络游戏和动漫的内容中有不良成分，比如暴力、色情等。

这次调查的负责人指出，社会各界应该加强协作，大力推广健康、向上的新娱乐形式，使娱乐更好地为青年人服务。家长首先要转变对娱乐形式的负面看法。学校也应该教育青年人提高自 [20]
我管理的能力。商界在为青年人提供娱乐产品的时候，不要只为了经济利益，应该根据青年人的特点开发产品，组织并鼓励他们积极参与有益的娱乐活动。

阅读与理解

香港青少年为什么吸毒

[1]　　最近几年，香港的中学生吸毒人数有上升的趋势。众所周知(zhòng suǒ zhōu zhī)，吸毒对青少年的身体健康及生活、学习都有很大的影响。那么青少年为什么会吸毒呢？根据调查分析(fēn xī)，青少年吸毒的原因主要有以下几个：

[5]　　首先，由于无知、好奇(hào qí)而去吸毒的青少年约占70%。在青少年时期，大部分学生人生观(rén shēng guān)还不成熟，思想比较幼稚(yòu zhì)，辨别是非的能力不强。他们对任何事情都充满了好奇心，还有强烈(qiáng liè)的探索欲望(tàn suǒ yù wàng)。有些人开始只想尝试(cháng shì)一下，结果就上瘾了。

　　第二，青少年时期是一段"危险期(wēi xiǎn qī)"。由于他们在生理和心理上

[10]都不成熟，如果碰到不愉快的事，或者感情出了问题，或者遇到了挫(cuò)折(zhé)，他们往往会寻找刺激(xún zhǎo cì jī)来填补(tián bǔ)精神上的空虚(kōng xū)，以寻求安慰(xún qiú ān wèi)。大约有40%的青少年是在以上这些情况下开始吸毒的。

　　第三，有问题的、不温暖(wēn nuǎn)或不稳定(wěn dìng)的家庭往往容易使青少年走上吸毒的道路。在一所戒毒(jiè dú)中心，超过1/3的学生来自破碎(pò suì)的家庭。

[15]　　第四，由于现在的经济条件好了，家长往往宠爱孩子，无条件地满足孩子的物质要求。但当家长稍(shāo)有不能满足孩子的地方，孩子便容易走上吸毒的道路。因家庭溺爱(nì ài)而吸毒的青少年大约占了10%。

　　第五，也有相当一部分青少年受到同伴(tóng bàn)的影响，在他们的鼓动(gǔ dòng)下走上了吸毒的道路。

[20]　　因此，要解决青少年吸毒的问题，社会、家庭、学校一定要共同合作，帮助青少年在困难时期渡过难关(dù guò nán guān)。青少年也应自重、自爱、关注自己的健康，对自己的未来负责。

A 判断正误，并说明原因

1. 这几年，香港的中学生中吸毒的人数越来越多。　　　　对　错

　　原因：＿＿＿＿＿＿＿＿＿＿＿＿＿＿＿＿＿＿＿＿＿＿　＿＿　＿＿

2. 有大约七成的青少年是因为无知、好奇_{hào qí}而开始吸毒的。

　　原因：＿＿＿＿＿＿＿＿＿＿＿＿＿＿＿＿＿＿＿＿＿＿　＿＿　＿＿

3. 在戒毒中心_{jiè dú}里，有不到30%的学生来自破碎_{pò suì}的家庭。

　　原因：＿＿＿＿＿＿＿＿＿＿＿＿＿＿＿＿＿＿＿＿＿＿　＿＿　＿＿

4. 如果家长过分宠爱孩子，孩子也可能会走上吸毒的道路。

　　原因：＿＿＿＿＿＿＿＿＿＿＿＿＿＿＿＿＿＿＿＿＿＿　＿＿　＿＿

5. 只要家庭对孩子多管教，青少年的吸毒问题就能解决。

　　原因：＿＿＿＿＿＿＿＿＿＿＿＿＿＿＿＿＿＿＿＿＿＿　＿＿　＿＿

B 根据短文选择正确答案

1. 吸毒对青少年的＿＿＿＿有很大影响。

　　a) 饮食、健康及生活

　　b) 健康、生活及学习

　　c) 生活、学习及娱乐

2. 青少年时期人生观还不＿＿＿＿，思想比较＿＿＿。

　　a) 成熟；幼稚_{yòu zhì}

　　b) 幼稚；浮躁_{fú zào}

　　c) 强；弱

3. 大约有＿＿＿＿的青少年由于精神空虚_{kōng xū}而吸毒。

　　a) 七成

　　b) 四成

　　c) 一成

4. 解决青少年吸毒问题，需要＿＿＿＿共同合作。

　　a) 社会、国家和政府

　　b) 社会、学校和家庭

　　c) 家庭、邻居和社区

157

C 从短文中选出最合适的动词填空

1. 本市的外籍人口 _____（第5行）全市人口的10%。
   ^(wài jí)

2. 你应该_____（第8行）多做一些运动。

3. 我在学习汉语的过程中_____（第10行）了很多困难。

4. 这位新同学_____（第14行）上海一所本地中学。

5. 父母们总是想办法_____（第16行）子女的需求。

6. 要_____（第20行）青少年逃学的问题需要跟家长合作。
   ^(táo xué)

7. 今年我_____（第22行）组织游学中国的活动。

D 根据短文选择正确答案

1. "众所周知"（第1行）的意思是 _____。
   ^(zhòng suǒ zhōu zhī)

   a) 大家都知道

   b) 观众都知道

   c) 公众场所

2. "无知"（第5行）的意思是 _____。

   a) 无所事事

   b) 没人知道

   c) 没有知识

3. "不温暖"（第13行）的意思是_____。
   ^(wēnnuǎn)

   a) 缺少爱

   b) 没有暖气
      ^(nuǎn qì)

   c) 没有空调

4. "破碎"（第14行）的意思是_____。
   ^(pò suì)

   a) 父母离异
      ^(lí yì)

   b) 没有兄弟姐妹

   c) 没有母亲

5. "无条件地满足"（第15行）的意思是_____。

   a) 要什么给什么

   b) 要的东西得不到

   c) 要学什么就学什么

6. "相当一部分"（第18行）意思是_____。

   a) 一点儿

   b) 挺多

   c) 没几个

凤凰卫视中文台

凤凰卫视有限公司1996年成立____①____香港。凤凰卫视旗下主要有五个频道及两大媒体。五个频道分别为：中文台、资讯台、欧洲台、美洲台、电影台；两大媒体____②____为：《凤凰周刊》、凤凰新媒体。凤凰卫视的目标是全力为全世界华人提供高质量的华语电视节目。其节目具有时代感和感染力，深受广大观众的喜爱和全球华人的支持。自成立以来，凤凰卫视____③____成为电视传媒潮流的领导者。

凤凰卫视中文台于1996年开播。它是全球性华语卫星电视台，也是香港唯一一家24小时用普通话向中国大陆、香港、澳门和台湾省以及亚太、欧美、拉美等地播出的电视台。凤凰卫视中文台立足香港，以沟通大陆、港澳和台湾，服务全世界华人为目标，将中国悠久的历史、博大精深的文化传播给所有华人，____④____帮助华人认识错综复杂、多姿多彩的当今世界。

凤凰卫视中文台节目包罗万象，分评论类、历史人文类、资讯类、访谈类、娱乐时尚类。凤凰卫视中文台的节目与众不同，以新鲜的题材、多样的形式、清新的风格、新奇的内容展示在观众面前，十分符合观众的生活方式和口味。凤凰卫视中文台自开播____⑤____，推出了一系列有影响力的大型特别节目，____⑥____《飞越黄河》、《97香港回归世纪报道》等。

凤凰卫视中文台的节目主持人来自大陆、香港、台湾以及海外。他们有自己的独特风格，而且工作认真投入，深受观众喜爱。

[1]

[5]

第一段

第二段

[10]

第三段

[15]

第四段

[20]

159

以来　及　于　并　比如　分别　和　已经

1. _____　　2. _____　　3. _____

4. _____　　5. _____　　6. _____

B 根据短文选择正确答案

1. 凤凰卫视旗下有_____。
   <small>fènghuáng wèi shì qí xià</small>

   a) 电视台和媒体
   <small>méi tǐ</small>

   b) 报纸和广播站
   <small>guǎng bō</small>

   c) 电视台和报刊
   <small>bào kān</small>

2. 凤凰卫视中文台的观众

   _____。

   a) 全世界都有

   b) 只在大陆

   c) 在港、澳、台

3. 凤凰卫视中文台的节目

   _____播出。
   <small>bō</small>

   a) 白天

   b) 昼夜
   <small>zhòu yè</small>

   c) 夜晚

4. 凤凰卫视中文台的节目

   _____。

   a) 种类不多　　b) 多种多样

   c) 内容单一

5. 相比其他电视台，凤凰卫

   视中文台的节目_____。

   a) 独特、有新意
   <small>dú tè</small>

   b) 没什么特别

   c) 不怎么太好

6. 凤凰卫视中文台的主持人
   <small>zhǔ chí</small>

   来自 _____。

   a) 港、澳、台

   b) 大陆

   c) 中国及国外

C 从短文中找反义词

1. 反对→(　　　　)(第5行)
2. 短暂→(　　　　)(第11行)
   <small>duǎn zàn</small>
3. 简单→(　　　　)(第12行)
4. 普通→(　　　　)(第17行)

160

D 从右边的段落大意中找出最合适的

1. 第一段　□

2. 第二段　□

3. 第三段　□

4. 第四段　□

A 凤凰卫视的过去与将来。

B 凤凰卫视中文台的性质及作用。

C 凤凰卫视的节目主持人。

D 凤凰卫视中文台节目主持人的特色。

E 凤凰卫视中文台的现在与将来。

F 凤凰卫视中文台的节目种类、风格。

G 凤凰卫视的成立、目标及现状。

E 判断正误，并说明原因

1. 凤凰卫视电视节目用的语言是普通话。

　对　错

　原因：_____ ___ ___

2. 凤凰卫视中文台是香港第二家普通话电视台。

　原因：_____ ___ ___

3. 凤凰卫视中文台的服务对象是全世界的华人。

　原因：_____ ___ ___

4. 凤凰卫视中文台的节目多种多样，适合观众的口味。

　原因：_____ ___ ___

5. 观众们都非常喜欢凤凰卫视中文台的节目。

　原因：_____ ___ ___

6. 凤凰卫视中文台的主持人都是大陆人。

　原因：_____ ___ ___

161

快餐文化

第四单元
第12课

[1]　　现代人生活节奏快了，根本就没有时间、精力和耐心像以前一样生活了。快餐文化也因此诞生了。

　　快餐文化的特点是"快"。

　　现代人花在吃饭上的时间少了。他们工作、学习繁[5]忙，没有时间做饭，也没有时间慢慢地品尝、享受美味食品。因此，简便的快餐食品很受欢迎。

　　在物质生活方面，网上购物已经成为现代生活的一部分。现在越来越多的人选择这种购物方式。有些物品质量并不好，但因为现在的东西更新换代太快了，所以有人认[10]为物品不需要坚固、耐用。

　　在精神生活方面，现代人的休闲方式也体现出一个"快"字。很多人喜欢看卡通读物来消磨时间。这些快餐读本内容简单、图片丰富、文字很少。还有很多人喜欢看免费薄小的报纸。虽然这种报纸版面小，但为读者[15]提供国内外新闻，拿在手上读起来很方便。通俗小说也很受广大群众的喜爱，因为现代人不想动脑筋来欣赏长篇文学作品。

[20]　　现在的交通和通讯也比以前快多了。人们乘坐飞机在数小时内就能从一个地方抵达另[25]一个地方。现在很少

有人写书信了，因为人们只要拨打一个电话、发一条短信就可以跟远方的亲戚、朋友联络。

总之，快餐文化已经改变了我们的生活方式。如果你关注一下周围的人和事，就不难发现还有很多快餐文化现象。

生词

1. 奏 zòu play (music)　节奏 jié zòu rhythm; pace
2. 诞生 dànshēng be born
3. 特点 tè diǎn characteristic
4. 美味 měi wèi delicious
5. 简便 jiǎn biàn handy
6. 物质 wù zhì substance
7. 更新换代 gēng xīn huàn dài upgrade
8. 固 gù solid; firm　坚固 jiān gù sturdy
9. 耐用 nài yòng durable
10. 休闲 xiū xián leisure
11. 体现 tǐ xiàn embody; reflect
12. 卡通 kǎ tōng animated cartoon
13. 读物 dú wù reading material
14. 读本 dú běn reader
15. 图片 tú piàn picture
16. 文字 wén zì script; writing
17. 版 bǎn page (of a newspaper)　版面 bǎnmiàn layout
18. 读者 dú zhě reader
19. 国内 guó nèi domestic　国外 guó wài overseas

20. 新闻 xīn wén news
21. 通俗 tōng sú popular
22. 广大 guǎng dà vast; numerous
23. 群 qún crowd; group　群众 qún zhòng the masses
24. 喜爱 xǐ ài like; love
25. 筋 jīn veins　脑筋 nǎo jīn brains; mind　动脑筋 dòngnǎo jīn use one's head
26. 欣 xīn happy; joyful　欣赏 xīn shǎng appreciate; admire
27. 长篇 chángpiān lengthy; long
28. 作品 zuò pǐn works (of literature or art)
29. 抵 dǐ reach　抵达 dǐ dá arrive
30. 书信 shū xìn letter
31. 拨（撥）bō move with hand　拨打 bō dǎ dial
32. 短信 duǎn xìn text message
33. 远方 yuǎnfāng distant place
34. 改变 gǎi biàn change
35. 关注 guān zhù pay close attention (to)

163

消化课文

1. 根据课文回答问题

1) 快餐文化是怎样诞生的？

2) 简便的快餐食品为什么受欢迎？

3) 哪些快餐读物很受欢迎？为什么？请举两个例子。

4) 除了去商店购物以外，如今人们喜欢怎样购物？

5) 现代的交通给人们带来哪些方便？

6) 现在有些物品的质量跟以前的有什么不同？为什么？

2. 根据实际情况回答问题

1) 作者对于快餐文化的看法，你同意吗？为什么？

2) 在你周围，你还能列出一两样快餐文化的现象吗？你觉得这些快餐文化的现象给你带来哪些好处？

3) 你周围喜欢读书的人多吗？他们一般看什么书？看卡通读物的人多还是看小说的人多？你平时有没有阅读的习惯？你一般喜欢看什么样的书？

4) 你居住的地方有免费报纸吗？有哪几种？你看免费报纸吗？如果你看，你最关心哪方面的内容？

5) 你喜欢在网上购物吗？你在网上买过什么东西？你认为网上购物有哪些好处和坏处？

6) 如果你去长途旅游，一般搭乘什么交通工具？你喜欢坐火车旅游吗？坐火车旅游有什么好处和坏处？

7) 在你的成长过程中，你写过信吗？你给谁写过信？你现在还写信吗？你平时怎么与亲戚、朋友联系？

8) 你觉得现在的哪些物品质量比较好？哪些物品不坚固、不耐用？你经常需要购买哪些物品？你一般去哪儿买东西？为什么去那里买？

1. 用带点的词语模仿例子造句

Ⓐ 例子：现代人生活节奏快了，**根本就没有时间**像以前一样生活了。(第1行)

我一天忙到晚，**简直没有时间**看电视。

我现在什么事都在网上做，**甚至**在网上看电影、看杂志、购物等。

Ⓑ 例子：现代人根本就没有时间**像**以前**一样**生活了。(第1行)

现在的交通很方便，**跟**以前**不同**了。

我们学校的课程**跟**10年前的**差不多**。

Ⓒ 例子：**如果**你关注一下周围的人和事，**就不难**发现还有很多快餐文化现象。(第28行)

我们**就要**（快要）期末考试了。

我**连**看电视的时间**都**没有。

只要肯花工夫，你**就**可以把汉语学好。

2. 完成句子

例子：在物质生活方面，网上购物已经成为现代生活的一部分。(第7行)

在学业方面，＿＿＿＿

＿＿＿＿＿＿＿＿＿＿。

3. 从课文中找反义词或近义词

A 反义词

1) 空闲→(　　　)(第4行)　　3) 国外→(　　　)(第15行)

2) 复杂→(　　　)(第13行)　　4) 高雅→(　　　)(第15行)

gāo yǎ

B 近义词

1) 大众→(　　　)(第16行)　　3) 到达→(　　　)(第24行)

2) 搭乘→(　　　)(第22行)　　4) 联系→(　　　)(第27行)

165

口语训练

小组讨论

快餐文化是21世纪的一个普遍现象。你们讨论的题目是：快餐文化对现代人的生活、学习和工作的影响。讨论的内容应包括：

- 还有哪些快餐文化现象？
- 快餐文化给现代人的生活、学习和工作带来了哪些正面和负面的影响？
- 快餐文化现象是好事还是坏事？

例子：

学生1：快餐文化的特点是"快"。如果我们注意一下，我们周围有很多快餐文化现象。因为现代人工作、学习很忙，他们根本就没有时间做饭，所以简便的半成食品很受消费者（xiāo fèi zhě）的欢迎。

学生2：我们家经常买半成品的比萨饼，到家里只要在烤箱里烤几分钟就可以吃了。

学生3：在读书方面，我现在没有时间，也不想动脑筋来欣赏长篇文学作品，只看通俗小说或者卡通读物。今年流行这个作者的作品，明年有可能会出现另一个作者的书。总的来说，现在的事情变化很快。我认为这是好事，因为任何（rèn hé）人都有机会去创造。

学生1：　我不同意你刚才说的。我觉
得这样很浪费人才。比如
说，流行歌曲的寿命很短，
因为过一段时间又有人作出
新的歌曲。

学生2：　我认为快餐文化给我们的生
活带来了不少负面影响。比
如说，现在有些物品质量不
太好，不坚固，也不耐用。
现在的产品更新换代快，这
样商家就有生意做了。我半
年前买了一双球鞋，现在已
经破了，得买新的了。

学生3：　还有，我发现现在大版面的
报纸比以前少多了，而是流
行版面小、免费的报纸。这
种报纸图片多，文字又少又
简单。很多人在上班途中就
能浏览国内外新闻。因此，
这种报纸很受广大读者欢
迎。

学生1：　时代变了，我们的想法也要
变，做事的方法也要变。快
餐文化不管是好事还是坏
事，人们只能接受它，因为
这种现象在我们生活中无处
不在。

参考句子

a) 由于现代通讯非常发达，现
在写信的人不多了。一个电
邮几秒钟就可以发到对方
的邮箱里。由于电邮太方
便，我们每天要看几十个电
邮，但大部分广告电邮可能
跟你没有关系，这浪费了我
们的时间和精力。

b) 现在在大街上你到处都可
以看到用手机打电话的人。
现代人没有耐心，他们想到
一件事情，就拿出手机打个
电话，发个短信。

c) 现在交通十分发达，坐飞
机几个小时就能抵达目的
地，所以现在坐飞机的人
比以前多很多。

d) 现在一次性使用的东西非常
多，纸餐碟、塑料勺、木
筷、纸杯、塑料手套等等，
用起来方便、卫生，也不
贵。

e) 现在很多人休闲时喜欢翻翻
漫画书，因为书里文字少、
图片多，看起来省时，又能
放松一下。

167

写作训练

1. 写投诉信 (tóu sù)

假如你最近买了一样东西，但是质量不好，根本就没法用。你去商店让营业员退货 (tuì huò)，但是营业员不但不退，而且服务态度很差。你写一封信向商店经理投诉这件事。在信里，你要提及：

- 在何时、何地买的物品
- 该物品的质量问题
- 退货的全过程，包括营业员的态度
- 建议解决的办法
- 自己的联络方式

参考句子

a) 我今天写信的目的是想向您反映 (fǎn yìng) 一下有关我从贵店买 iPod 的事。

b) 我上个月8号在贵店买了一个 iPod。可是回到家一试，没有一点儿声音 (shēng yīn)。

c) 第二天，我拿着 iPod 到店里去换。没想到，营业员不但不给我换，而且说是我把 iPod 弄坏 (nòng) 了。对此我非常生气。

d) 我找另一位营业员换，他却说他不管，因为我不是从他手上买的 iPod。我找到了第三位营业员，他说店里卖出的货品不退不换。可是，我的发票 (fā piào) 上写着：七天之内，可以退换货品。

e) 现在商店之间竞争激烈，大家都十分重视服务质量。如果服务不好，就没有顾客来店里买东西。

f) 对此事我向您投诉，希望您能尽快给我答复，帮我解决这个问题。

2. 阅读短文并写回应式作文

读过下面的短文后，对于该不该制止网络语言，你有自己的看法。写一篇博客，谈谈你个人用网络语言的经历及你对网络语言的看法。

网络语言该不该制止

　　网络语言简称"网语"，是21世纪互联网的一个产物。为了便于输入，网民们结合了中文、英文和汉语拼音的特点，发明了一些固定的缩略语，同时也运用一些符号、数字，甚至错别字和生动的图片。 [1]

　　有些比较流行的网语是根据谐音来的，比如："喜欢"谐音成"稀饭"；"气死我了"写成"7456"。有的网语根据拼音或英文的缩写，比如"LG"是"老公"的缩写，"CU"是"See you"的意思；有的是来自联想，例如"灌水"（add water）意思是"向论坛中发帖子"；还有的是新造的合音混合词："不要"成了"表"，"这样子"成了"酱紫"等。除了用文字、数字和字母以外，网语还用符号甚至图片来表达一些特定的意思：如"^^"表示笑，"(^@^)"表示幸运小猪。 [5]

[10]

　　对于网语的广泛使用，社会上不同人士持有不同的态度。有些人认为要规范网语；有些人对网语表示担忧，认为政府应出面制止人们使用；还有些人认为网语是一种字符的狂欢，使用起来方便、快捷。一些文字专家担心，青少年不但在网上使用这些不伦不类的语言，写作文、做功课时，甚至是在考试时，也会不自觉地用到网语，这样会形成习惯，最终影响他们的语文水平。 [15]

　　在互联网时代，虽然网络语言不规范，但是网语却自然地成为一种沟通方式，尤其被年轻人所接受。其实，对于网语现象，不必过分担心。因为在社会不断发展的过程中，符合时代和发展的词语才会被人接受。当然，年轻人也应切记：网语只适合在网上使用，千万不要在其他场合特别是语文学习中使用。 [20]

调节生活节奏

[1]　　现代人的生活节奏非常快，几乎使人疯狂。人们的工作与生活好像上了快车道，许多人感到力不从心。看看周围的人，大家都在为自己的生活、学习、工作忙个不停。虽然大家忙碌的事情可能不一样，但一样的是：脚步越来越快，性子越来越急，吃饭时嘴巴张得越来越

[5]　大，汽车也越开越快。看上去好像大家都适应了快节奏的生活，可是如果让你停下来问问自己："我真的适应这样的生活吗？"大多数人的答案可能是否定的。

　　因此，我们需要时常停下手中的事情，调节一下自己的生活节奏，要不然就会在繁忙的生活中迷失自己，迷失方向。大家可以试一

[10]　试以下几种方法：

　　第一，要管理好自己的时间，分清楚什么是主要的，什么是次要的。

　　第二，要注意锻炼身体。有了健康的身体才能应对压力。我们不能每天都面对着学习、工作、烦恼，而运动是减压的好方法之一。

　　第三，尝试将压力或者心里的事情说出来，比方说写日记、写博

[15]　客。把压力释放出来比闷在心里好。

　　第四，经常跟朋友交流，尤其是跟乐观的朋友交流。

　　第五，要保持一颗感恩、年轻、向上的心，这样一个人才能快乐。

　　第六，给自己放假。一个人不能总是过度劳累，否则身体会吃不消的。尝试周末睡个懒觉，或者抽时间跟家人、朋友外出旅游，换换

[20]　环境，换换心情。

　　今天就开始尝试以上这些方法吧。如果你时常调节自己的生活节奏，你会发现原来生活可以过得更美好。

A 根据短文找出四个正确的句子

□ 1. 现代人的生活节奏太快，结果有一部分人得了精神病。

□ 2. 大部分人每天忙个不停，很少停下来想一想忙什么。

□ 3. 如果一个人车开得太快，他很有可能会迷失方向。

□ 4. 给自己放假是调节生活节奏的好办法。

□ 5. 写日记、博客(bó kè)也是一种减压的方法。

□ 6. 每天睡懒觉可以使生活节奏慢下来。

□ 7. 如果一个人知道感恩(gǎn ēn)，他就会快乐。

B 从短文中选出最合适的动词填空

1. 实际上有很多人都不一定_____（第5行）忙碌(máng lù)不停的现代生活。

2. 有时候，每个人都有必要_____（第8行）一下自己的生活节奏。

3. 如果一个人能把时间_____（第11行）好，他就已经成功了一半。

4. 压力大的人至少每周要_____（第13行）三次，每次半个小时以上。

5. _____（第13行）各种压力，现代人要学会减压。

6. 如果你经常跟乐观的朋友_____（第16行），你也会变成一个快乐的人。

7. 你应该_____（第21行）停下脚步，放下手头的工作，走出自己的小天地。

8. 如果你有一颗年轻、向上的心(kē)，会_____（第22行）生活可以更美好。

C 从短文中找反义词

1. 肯定→(　　)(第7行)

2. 清闲→(　　)(第9行)

3. 主要→(　　)(第11行)

4. 愉快→(　　)(第13行)

5. 悲观→(　　)(第16行)

6. 伤心→(　　)(第17行)

D 给下列词语配上最合适的解释

1. 力不从心 (第2行) ☐
2. 忙个不停 (第3行) ☐
3. 要不然 (第9行) ☐
4. 乐观 (第16行) ☐
5. 感恩 gǎn ēn (第17行) ☐
6. 睡个懒觉 lǎn jiào (第19行) ☐

A 不然的话。

B 早上起得晚。

C 大方、可靠。

D 每天都很忙，一年忙到头。

E 心里想做，但是能力不够。

F 对别人提供的帮助表示感谢。

G 想尽办法想把事情做好。

H 精神愉快，对事情的发展充满信心。 chōngmǎn

E 根据短文回答问题

1. 怎样才能把自己的时间管理好？

2. 有哪些减压的方法？（列出两项）

3. 如果一个人整天忙个不停，结果会怎么样？

F 根据实际情况回答问题

1. 你觉得你的生活、学习、工作节奏快吗？请举一两个例子。

2. 如果你有压力，用什么方法来减压？你的方法有效吗？
   如果效果不大，你打算如何改进？

3. 你认为现代人是否需要换一种方式来生活？为什么？

香港的茶餐厅

　　茶餐厅集快餐与饭馆于一身，是香港最平民化、饮食最地道（dì dao）的场所。在香港，茶餐厅遍布（biàn bù）各区，营业时间不定，通常为早上6时至凌晨（líng chén）1时，铜锣湾（tóng luó wān）、湾仔（wān zǎi）、旺角（wàng jiǎo）等繁华（fán huá）地区的茶餐厅更可能通宵（tōng xiāo）营业。 [1] 第一段

　　茶餐厅的特点是简单快捷（kuài jié）、选择多、价钱实惠（shí huì）。茶餐厅讲究效率，一般都不收小费，顾客用完餐后自己到收银处（shōu yín chù）付费，而且不需要等（děng）候。在茶餐厅里吃饭，从点菜到结账（jié zhàng）都讲求速度（sù dù），非常适合香港人。茶餐厅一般供应各种常餐（cháng cān）、快餐、午餐、特餐（tè cān）等，更有不少香港独有的饮食。茶餐厅供应的各类套餐（tào cān），既营养丰富又物美价廉（wù měi jià lián）。在茶餐厅里吃一顿常餐或快餐只需二三十块港币，而且包含饮料或免费茶水。 第二段 [5]

　　茶餐厅供应的食品和饮料多种多样，有中式的、西式的，当然也有港式的。在茶餐厅里，人们可以吃到各式多士（duō shì）（烤面包）、三明治、蛋挞（dàn tǎ），意粉、各式车仔面（chē zǎi miàn）（一种面条）、扬州炒饭（yáng zhōu）、星洲炒饭、牛肉炒河粉等。部分茶餐厅还供应其他面食，如云吞（yún tūn）（馄饨（hún tun））面、鱼蛋面等。基本上每个茶餐厅都供应烧味，比如叉烧（chā shāo）、烧鹅（shāo é）等。每个茶餐厅必备的港式饮品当然是"港式奶茶"，也叫"丝袜（sī wà）奶茶"。港式奶茶源于（yuán yú）殖民（zhí mín）时期英国人的喝茶方式，即将奶和糖加入红茶。港式奶茶分为冷饮和热饮两种。 [10] 第三段

[15]

　　每逢午饭时段，建筑工人、货车司机、售货员、办公室职员（zhí yuán）等都会光顾（guāng gù）茶餐厅。不同阶层（jiē céng）、行业的顾客在茶餐厅内一边吃饭，一边大声谈论、阅读马经等，成为茶餐厅的一大特色。 第四段

[20]

　　要体验地道的香港生活，非得去一趟茶餐厅不可。 第五段

1. "茶餐厅集快餐与饭馆于一身"（第1行）的意思是 _____。

   a) 在茶餐厅里，顾客吃不到快餐

   b) 茶餐厅是快餐和饭馆的结合体

   c) 茶餐厅不是饭店

2. "茶餐厅是香港最平民化、饮食最地道^{dì dào}的场所"（第1行）的意思是 _____。

   a) 茶餐厅是香港人聚集的场所

   b) 茶餐厅是香港居民的食堂

   c) 在茶餐厅，你能体会到香港普通老百姓的生活及真正港式饮食

3. "每逢午饭时段，办公室职员都会光顾^{zhí yuán   guāng gù}茶餐厅"（第18行）的意思是 _____。

   a) 午饭时间，办公室职员会去茶餐厅用餐

   b) 午饭时间，办公室职员会打电话去茶餐厅叫外卖

   c) 午饭时间，公司老板会去茶餐厅吃午饭

4. "要体验地道的香港生活，非得去一趟茶餐厅不可。"（第21行）的意思是 _____。

   a) 在香港，你一定不能去茶餐厅吃饭

   b) 一定要去茶餐厅亲身体验真正的香港人的生活

   c) 去茶餐厅吃饭不能体验香港人的平民生活

1. _____（第4行）饭菜质量

2. _____（第6行）快节奏的生活需要

3. _____（第7行）各式茶点

4. _____（第20行）长篇小说

5. _____（第20行）旅游景点

6. _____（第21行）本地人的生活

1. 在香港，你到处都可以看到茶餐厅。 　　　　　　　　　　　　对　错

    原因：_____ ___ ___

2. 茶餐厅通常每天营业时间长达12个小时。

    原因：_____ ___ ___

3. 茶餐厅里供应的饭菜既健康，价格又合理。

    原因：_____ ___ ___

4. 在茶餐厅里，吃一顿很平常的午餐不到20块港币。

    原因：_____ ___ ___

5. 在茶餐厅吃饭，一餐的花费包括饮料、茶水。

    原因：_____ ___ ___

6. 在茶餐厅里，你能吃到各种风味的饭菜。

    原因：_____ ___ ___

D　从右边的段落大意中找出最合适的

1. 第一段　□　│　A 茶餐厅里的独特一景。

2. 第二段　□　│　B 茶餐厅的特色：上菜快，品种多，价钱适中。

3. 第三段　□　│　C 茶餐厅是香港生活的缩影。

4. 第四段　□　│　D 具有香港特色茶餐厅的普及程度。

5. 第五段　□　│　E 茶餐厅里供应的饭菜都很健康。

　　　　　　　　│　F 茶餐厅供应多样化的食品。

　　　　　　　　│　G 茶餐厅用自助餐的方式运营。

单元复习

< 生词

第10课

杭州	位于	沿海	浙江省	省会	政治	古都	西湖
山水	闻名	人间	赞美	灵隐寺	六和塔	闷热	
寒冷	特产	名菜	东坡肉	龙井虾仁	丝绸	游船	
宾馆	搭乘	专线	长途	公交	途中	保管	行李
物品	乱	旅游局					

第11课

就读	表达	数目	协会	问卷	首选	根据	政府
种类	有限	消磨	的确	缺乏	监管	色情	暴力
身心	造成	后果	过分	对于	社交	具有	修养
业余	未来	有益					

第12课

节奏	诞生	特点	美味	简便	物质	更新换代
坚固	耐用	休闲	体现	卡通	读物	读本 图片
文字	版面	读者	国内	国外	新闻	通俗 广大
群众	喜爱	动脑筋	欣赏	长篇	作品	抵达
书信	拨打	短信	远方	改变	关注	

杭州位于中国东南沿海　政治、经济、文化中心　自然风景优美

以美丽的山水而闻名　气候温和　四季分明　平均气温在16度左右

旅游的最好季节　冬天相当寒冷　满足游客的需要　传统的工艺品

不同风格、设备齐全的宾馆　搭乘飞机/火车/汽车

保管好行李及物品　注意交通安全/饮食卫生/保护环境

表达意见和建议　作调查　根据调查结果　选择上网来消磨时间

由于……，所以……　活动种类有限　成为生活中的一部分

缺乏监管　影响身心健康　过分依赖网络　能力下降　对于青少年来说

扩大知识面　提高修养　培养社交技巧　丰富多彩

提供健康的、有意义的娱乐活动　为社会服务，为国家作贡献

像……一样　品尝、享受美味食品　简便的食品很受欢迎

在物质/精神生活方面　受广大群众的喜爱　欣赏长篇文学作品

网上购物成为现代生活的一部分　为读者提供国内外新闻

休闲方式体现出一个"快"字　从一个地方抵达另一个地方

改变生活方式　关注周围发生的事　快餐文化现象

第五单元
第13课

[1]   社会的发展给教育带来了新挑战。

     由于现在的学生有很多自由，而且早熟，他们往往自作主张，说话、做事不考虑后果。

     在学校里，有些学生违反校规。他们在课堂上随便
[5] 讲话、说笑，有的学生趁老师不注意发短信、玩儿电脑游戏；有的学生随便迟到、早退，甚至逃课；还有个别的学生偷东西、打架、欺负弱小的同学，甚至还有学生抽烟、吸毒。

     学校该怎样面对新的挑战呢？第一，学校不只是教
[10] 授基础知识和技能的场所，学生也不只是来学校获取知识、应付各种考试的。学校不但要在教学上吸引学生，激发学生的学习动机，培养学生的学习能力，使其养成良好的学习习惯，而且要把他们培养成为有责任感的公民。第二，学校应该培养学生独立思考、辨别是非的能
[15] 力。第三，学校要为学生提供各种健康、有益、有挑战性的课余活动。通过这些活动，学生可以发挥各自的才能，培养各种能力。第四，学校应该制定严格的校规。对于学生中的不良行为，学
[20] 校应及时处理。学校应严格管教那些不遵守校规的学生，给他们适当的处
[25] 罚，比如课后留校、停

课等。学校还应开除那些极少数严重违反校规的学生。

教育好学生不容易。学校、家庭、社会要共同努力，关心青少年的成长，使他们长大后成为有用的人，能为社会作
[30] 贡献。

生 词

1. 面临 miàn lín be faced with
2. 早熟 zǎo shú early-maturing
3. 往往 wǎngwǎng often
4. 主张 zhǔ zhāng view
   自作主张 zì zuò zhǔ zhāng act on one's own
5. 做事 zuò shì act; handle affairs
6. 违（違）wéi violate　违反 wéi fǎn violate
7. 规（規）guī rule; regulation
   校规 xiào guī school regulations
8. 随便 suí biàn do as one pleases
9. 讲话 jiǎng huà speak; talk
10. 趁 chèn while; take advantage of
11. 迟（遲）chí late　迟到 chí dào be late
12. 早退 zǎo tuì leave early
13. 逃 táo escape　逃课 táo kè play truant
14. 个别 gè bié individual
*15. 教授 jiāo shòu teach; instruct
16. 获取 huò qǔ obtain

17. 激发 jī fā stimulate
18. 动机 dòng jī motive
19. 公民 gōngmín citizen
20. 独立 dú lì independent; on one's own
21. 思考 sī kǎo think deeply
22. 发挥 fā huī bring into play
23. 各自 gè zì each
24. 才能 cái néng ability; talent
25. 制定 zhì dìng draw up
26. 严格 yán gé rigid; strict
27. 管教 guǎn jiào subject someone to discipline
28. 遵 zūn abide by; obey　遵守 zūn shǒu comply with
29. 适当 shì dàng appropriate
30. 罚（罰）fá punish　处罚 chǔ fá punish
31. 课后留校 kè hòu liú xiào detention after school
32. 停课 tíng kè suspend classes
33. 开除 kāi chú expel

179

消化课文

1. 根据课文回答问题

1) 现在的学生有哪些特点？

2) 在课堂上，学生有哪些违反校规的现象？

3) 学校的首要任务是什么？

4) 丰富多彩的课余活动可以培养学生的哪些能力？

5) 学校应该怎样管教违反校规的学生？

6) 教育好青年学生是谁的责任？

2. 根据实际情况回答问题

1) 你们学校是一所什么样的学校？你们学校的校规严格吗？请举两个例子。

2) 在你们学校，学生上课时有哪些违反校规的行为？如果被老师发现了，老师会怎样处罚他们？

3) 在你的同学当中，迟到、早退、逃课的现象严重吗？你们学校有没有偷东西、打架、欺负弱小的同学的现象？如果你看到这些现象，会怎么做？学校有哪些规定？

4) 你们学校有人抽烟、吸毒吗？如果抽烟、吸毒者被发现，他们会被开除吗？会受到什么处罚？如果你看到有人抽烟或者吸毒，你会管吗？会怎么管？

5) 如果你们学校的学生违反了校规，最严重的处罚是什么？

6) 你们学校注重培养学生的哪些能力？通过哪些活动来培养？

7) 你们学校的课余活动丰富吗？你今年参加了哪些课余活动？你有什么收获？

8) 在你的成长过程中，你觉得谁对你的影响最大？在哪些方面对你有影响？

1. 完成句子

Ⓐ例子：社会的发展给教育带来了新挑战。

(第1行)

总之，我认为学校应该严格管教违反校规的学生。

Ⓑ例子：有的学生趁老师不注意发短信，有的随便迟到、早退，甚至逃课。(第5行)

Ⓒ例子：第一，学校不只是教授基础知识的场所。第二，学校应该培养学生辨别是非的能力。第三，学校要为学生提供各种有益的活动。第四，学校应该制定严格的校规。(第9~18行)

社会的不断进步给_____带来了_____。

总之，对于那些逃课的学生，_____。

有的活动_____，有的_____，甚至_____。

我们应该怎样做一个好学生呢？第一，_____。第二，_____。第三，_____。第四，_____。

2. 选择其中一个词语造句

例子：由于现在的学生有很多自由，他们往往自作主张。(第2行)

经常/平时/通常/一般/从来不/总是

3. 用带点的词语模仿例子造句

Ⓐ例子：通过这些活动，学生可以发挥各自的才能。(第16行)

Ⓑ例子：对于学生中的不良行为，学校应及时处理。(第18行)

4. 用课文中的动词填空

1) _____校规(第4行)　　　4) _____是非(第14行)

2) _____知识(第9行)　　　5) _____机会(第15行)

3) _____学习动机(第12行)　　6) _____才能(第16行)

181

实际运用

角色扮演

在这个口语练习中有三个角色：学生会主席、副主席和学生代表。在学校里，你们看到一些违反校规的现象。你们的讨论要提及：

• 最近学校里有哪些违反校规的现象？

• 为什么会出现这些现象？

• 这些违反校规的现象给学校带来了哪些挑战？

• 你们给学校提出哪些建议？

例子：

主席：我们今天开会的主要目的是针对最近学校里一些违反校规的现象，讨论一下看能不能给学校提一些建议。

副主席：我也注意到了。有的同学在课堂上不尊重老师，随便讲话。老师提醒了他们好多次，他们还是不听。

学生：我认为这不是学生的错，因为有的老师讲课没有吸引力，学生有时候也听不懂，所以他们才会随便说话。

副主席：我今天上的历史课就很闷，因为老师满堂 mǎn táng 灌 guàn，不给学生参与的机会。我认为在课堂上，老师应该激发学生的学习动机，培养学生的独立思考能力，鼓励学生提问。如果学生对上课的内容感兴趣了，就不会在下面随便说话了。

主席：不管什么原因，学生在学校就是不应该违反校

182

规。犯错的学生就应该受到适当的处罚。我认为学校的校规不够严格，所以现在有越来越多的学生对校规不加理会。

副主席：在我们班里，有个别同学经常迟到、早退，有时候甚至逃课。班主任好像只罚他课后留校。我觉得处罚太轻了。如果有人逃课，学校就应该通知家长，让学生停课一天。

　主席：学校校规好几年没有修改（xiū gǎi）了，有的处罚确实太轻了。

副主席：是啊！学校应该制定严格的校规，比如有人打架、偷东西，就应该严厉（yán lì）处罚，甚至开除他们。

　学生：可是校规是学校制定的，我们有发言权吗？

副主席：我们可以向校长、家长教师协会提建议，看看有哪些校规需要修改。

　主席：我会把今天开会的纪要（jì yào）打印出来，然后大家再看看。我也会去找校长谈一谈，看看我们能为学校做些什么。

参考句子

a) 有些同学好奇心强、胆子大，想挑战校规，做不该做的事。受到处罚时，他们又很后悔（hòu huǐ）。

b) 有些同学喜欢开玩笑，有时候玩笑开过头了，让一些同学受不了。

c) 有些家长忙着工作、赚钱，把管教子女的责任完全推给学校。

d) 有些同学不交或迟交作业、抄别人的作业，学校也不管。

e) 现在的年轻人往往做事自作主张，不考虑后果。

f) 有的同学在校园内抽烟，学校好像也没有人管。他们在低年级的同学面前树立了很不好的形象。学校应重罚（zhòng fá）这些学生。

g) 青少年辨别是非的能力不强，所以学校应该制定严格的校规，让学生知道什么事可以做，什么事不可以做。

h) 对于违反校规的同学，学校也要给他们改正（gǎi zhèng）的机会，这也是青少年成长的一个过程。

写作训练

1. 写建议信

写一封信给你们的校长，对学校今年的教学及管理提出你的看法和改进的建议。在信里，你要提及：

- 学校哪些方面的工作做得不够好？
- 校规应该作哪些调整？
- 你有哪些建议？

参考句子

a) 今年各科老师课后都拼命留作业。他们根本就不理解我们要学六门课。每天为了完成作业，我们连睡觉的时间都没有了。

b) 在课上，有的学生根本听不懂老师在讲什么，回家后还要自学或者请补习老师。

c) 有的老师教书不认真，不负责任，收了学生的作业也不及时改。

d) 学校应该给高中生一些自由，允许他们谈恋爱。

e) 学校应该允许高中生穿便(biàn)服(fú)上学，让他们为上大学作好准备。

f) 学校对迟到、早退、逃课的学生有时候睁(zhēng)一只眼闭(bì)一只眼，处罚也不严。

g) 学校的环保工作做得不够好，很多学生不节约用水、用电，垃圾也没有分(fēn)类(lèi)回收。

h) 学校应该设立(shè lì)奖学金，奖励那些全面发展或有特长的学生。

2. 阅读短文并写回应式作文

你的各科老师在教学中也时常运用多媒体教学手段。参考以下短文，写一篇博客，说一说哪些课适合用多媒体来辅助教学，哪些课适合用传统教学方法。

多媒体教学与传统教学

现在多媒体教学越来越普遍。跟传统教学相比，多媒体教学的 [1]
确有很多优势：第一，多媒体集图、文、声、像的功能为一体，可
从多角度调动学生的情绪、注意力和兴趣；第二，多媒体的交互
性使学生能更多地参与，学习起来会更主动；第三，多媒体软件除
了能形象、生动地演示教学内容以外，还可重复播放、使用，有 [5]
利于解决教学中的难点，课下还可以帮助学生复习；第四，多媒体
可实现个性化教学，能针对不同水平和接受能力的学生；第五，多
媒体信息量大，能节约空间和时间，提高教学效率。

虽然多媒体教学在现代教育中确实起着很大的作用，但我们
也应该注意到，多媒体教学手段不能完全取代传统的教学方法。无 [10]
论是用电脑、投影仪，还是录像机、电视机，都要用到"电"。如
果遇到停电或机器故障，而且事先也没有作好两手准备，那么教师
就会束手无策，从而影响教学效果。跟教师相比，多媒体在教学中
仍然处于辅助的地位，不能代替教师的全部工作。教学过程的各个
环节仍要由教师来组织、展开。传统教学中，教师的个人魅力、 [15]
文化修养、与学生的情感交流等也是多媒体教学无法取代的。

因此，理想的教学应该是：教师在备课时设计并选择最合适的
教学媒体，教学时再配合传统的教学手段。在课堂上，教师还要把
握好多媒体的使用时机，正确处理多媒体和普通教具、语言表达之
间的关系，这样才能获得最佳的教学效果。 [20]

185

阅读与理解

阅读一

[1]   各位观众，大家好！我是主持人黄兴，这位是钱大伟先生。钱先生曾任某大学校长，从事<ruby>高等<rt>gāo děng</rt></ruby>教育事业30余年。今天钱先生将对中国的高等教育 ① 他的看法。

黄：美籍华裔科学家高<ruby>锟<rt>kūn</rt></ruby> ② 了2009年<ruby>诺贝尔<rt>nuò bèi ěr</rt></ruby>物理学奖。您怎么看？

[5] 钱：我听到这个消息也为之感到<ruby>自豪<rt>zì háo</rt></ruby>。自从诺贝尔奖 ③ 以来，已有多位华人科学家获得了该奖。

黄：那您觉得未来在中国的本土会有诺贝尔奖得主吗？

钱：我相信，在不久的将来会有的。中国的科学家不是没有能力，而是目前他们还没有把能力发挥到一定的高度。

[10] 黄：您认为目前中国大学里的<ruby>科研<rt>kē yán</rt></ruby>水平怎么样？

钱：目前，中国有些大学里的科研水平还不高，基础也比较差。但是，近些年也有些科研成果已经达到了国际先进水平，有的已经占有了国际领先地位。

黄：那么，您觉得我国的大学怎样才能 ④ 出<ruby>顶尖<rt>dǐng jiān</rt></ruby>的科学家呢？

[15] 钱：我认为可以在以下几个方面努力。第一，国家要为大学和科研单位 ⑤ 充足的<ruby>经费<rt>jīng fèi</rt></ruby>。第二，研究机构要有<ruby>宽松<rt>kuān sōng</rt></ruby>的研究环境和浓厚的学术气氛。第三，科学家要思想开放、建立自信心。第四，从小培养学生勇于<ruby>创新<rt>chuàng xīn</rt></ruby>、 ⑥ 挑战。

黄：您刚才说到从小培养的问题，您认为我们的中、小学教育应该怎样 ⑦ 中国高等教育的发展？

[20] 钱：中国目前的教育<ruby>制度<rt>zhì dù</rt></ruby>还不太理想，但是近年来很多学校都在进行不同<ruby>程度<rt>chéng dù</rt></ruby>的教育改革。我相信我们一定能找到一种教育制度，既 ⑧ 基础教育，又注重创新，为学生提供发挥他们才能的空间，最终培养出世界一流的科学家。

......

接受　　获得　　培养　　接待　　配合

发表　　合作　　提供　　重视　　设立

1. _____　　2. _____　　3. _____　　4. _____

5. _____　　6. _____　　7. _____　　8. _____

B 根据短文选择正确答案

1. 钱大伟先生_____ 。

　a) 从事高等教育三十多年

　b) 曾经参与中小学教育改革

　c) 现在是某大学校长

2. 钱先生_____ 有信心。

　a) 对高等教育改革效果

　b) 对中小学教育改革

　c) 对高锟获得诺贝尔奖

3. _____获得诺贝尔奖。

　a) 已经有好几位华人科学家

　b) 高锟在华人中是第一个

　c) 未来会有很多中国科学家

4. 钱先生相信_____中国本土会有诺贝尔奖得主。

　a) 在近几年

　b) 不用等太久　　c) 在21世纪

5. 中国大学里_____。

　a) 科研水平普遍比较低

　b) 有些科研成果水平很高

　c) 大学生基础比较差

6. 中国目前的教育制度_____。

　a) 非常完美

　b) 不太理想

　c) 相当好

C 用短文中的名词填空

1. 高等 _____（第2行）

2. 科研 _____（第9行）

3. 研究 _____（第12行）

4. 顶尖的_____（第14行）

5. 办学_____（第16行）

6. 欢快的_____（第17行）

7. 理想的_____（第21行）

8. 发挥创意的_____（第24行）

为短文配题目

☐ 1. 诺贝尔奖奖项

☐ 2. 探讨中国教育的发展方向

☐ 3. 中国的科研水平

☐ 4. 中国的中小学教育如何配合高等教育

E 根据短文找出四个正确的句子

☐ 1. 中国目前的研究机构里的学术气氛相当浓厚。

☐ 2. 科学家们的思想要更开放，这样才会有创新。

☐ 3. 经过几十年的努力，中国的中小学教育制度已经很理想了。

☐ 4. 世界一流的科学家是要从小培养的。

☐ 5. 中小学教育要重视培养学生的创造能力。

☐ 6. 一流的科学家一定有扎实的基础知识。

☐ 7. 中国的科研水平已经达到了国际顶级水平。

F 根据短文回答问题

1. 这篇短文是用什么文体写的？

2. 为什么主持人和钱先生都对高锟感兴趣？

3. 钱先生对理想的中小学教育制度有何期望？

4. 钱先生为什么对中国培养一流的科学家有信心？

188

男女生分开教学好不好

在世界上，大部分中、小学实行男女同校，但是也有一些国家和地区男校和女校分开。一些教育界人士认为，由于男女体质特征的不同，学生的心理和行为也会不同，把男生和女生放在同一个班级，用同一种教学方法对双方都有不利之处。

男女分开上课能顾及男女生的身心发展、学习方式以及兴趣的不同。有研究指出，低年级男生的听觉比较差。如果教师不提高嗓门，男生有时候会听不清老师讲课，因此会对老师讲的课失去兴趣。不少男生还会被误认为有多动症。还有，男生的阅读能力发展得比女生晚。如果在同一个班级里逼男生像女生一样读写，大部分男生达不到老师的要求。在初中阶段，男女生的发育、体能及对运动项目的兴趣有差异。如果男生跟女生一起上体育课，教学的效果就不能保证。

男女分开教学可以使学生的注意力更集中，课上递纸条、使眼色、写情书的现象就不会发生了，这样也能避免出现中学生早恋或单相思的现象。一些老师深有体会地说，男女生分开上课，一些学生不会因为有异性存在而感到难为情，有助于学生积极参与课堂活动。

但是，也有专家担心男女生分开教学不利于学生的心理健康。如果学生长期不接触异性，他们长大后不懂得如何跟异性相处。现在的学生学习很忙，课后的时间不多，很少有机会在学校外面接触到同龄的异性。还有一个问题，男女分校的学生考试成绩是否更好，这还有待我们的考证。

1. 第一段　□
2. 第二段　□
3. 第三段　□
4. 第四段　□

A 世界上的中小学有男女同校和男女分校两种教学模式。
mó shì

B 男女生在学习方法上的差异。

C 男女生分开上课的理由。

D 男女生分开教学的利与弊。

E 男女生分开教学存在的问题及成效有待考证。
cún zài　　　　chéngxiào yǒu dài kǎo zhèng

F 男女生分开教学的优势。

B　判断正误，并说明原因

1. 在各个国家，几乎没有男女生分校教学的情况。　　　　　　　对　　错

　　原因：＿＿＿＿＿＿＿＿＿＿＿＿＿＿＿＿＿＿＿＿＿　　—　　—

2. 虽然男女生的体质特征不同，但他们的心理和行为都相似。

　　原因：＿＿＿＿＿＿＿＿＿＿＿＿＿＿＿＿＿＿＿＿＿　　—　　—

3. 男女生一起上课，适合女生的教学方法男生不一定能接受。

　　原因：＿＿＿＿＿＿＿＿＿＿＿＿＿＿＿＿＿＿＿＿＿　　—　　—

4. 女生的阅读能力比男生发展得早。

　　原因：＿＿＿＿＿＿＿＿＿＿＿＿＿＿＿＿＿＿＿＿＿　　—　　—

5. 男女生在一起上课，他们的注意力更集中。

　　原因：＿＿＿＿＿＿＿＿＿＿＿＿＿＿＿＿＿＿＿＿＿　　—　　—

6. 专家担心男女生分开教学对他们的心理健康不利。

　　原因：＿＿＿＿＿＿＿＿＿＿＿＿＿＿＿＿＿＿＿＿＿　　—　　—

C 给下列词语配上最合适的解释

1. 顾及 (gù jí) (第5行) □ ┃ A 大声说话。
2. 提高嗓门 (sǎngmén) (第6行) □ ┃ B 用眼神说话。
3. 递纸条 (第12行) □ ┃ C 暗暗地 (àn àn) 对某一个人有好感。
4. 使眼色 (第12行) □ ┃ D 遇到困难。
5. 单相思 (dān xiāng sī) (第14行) □ ┃ E 不好意思。
6. 难为情 (nán wéi qíng) (第15行) □ ┃ F 把想说的写在纸条上，然后传给对方。
┃ G 考虑到。
┃ H 回收废纸。

D 根据短文回答问题

1. 为什么低年级男生有时候听不清老师课上讲的内容？

2. 男女生分开上课有哪些明显的好处？请举两个例子。

3. 为什么男女生一起上体育课教学效果会不理想？

4. 如果男女分开教学，在跟异性接触方面会有哪些弊端 (bì duān)？

E 根据实际情况回答问题

1. 你就读的学校是男女同校吗？你怎么看待男女生在一起上课？

2. 在你们班上，总的来说，女生的成绩比男生的好，还是不如男生的？

3. 如果可以选择，你会选择男女同校吗？为什么？

生活方式与现代疾病

第五单元
第14课

[1] 张：观众朋友们好！我叫张军。今天，我们有幸请来了我市现代疾病专家王医生，为我们讲一讲"生活方式与现代疾病"这一热门话题。王医生，现代人的生活方式有哪些特点？

[5] 王：简单地说，现代人的生活很忙碌，精神压力大，饮食不健康，也不均衡，又没有时间运动。有些人还吸烟、喝酒，这些不良嗜好都对健康不利。

张：那么，现代疾病又有哪些呢？

王：主要有心脏病、高血压、糖尿病、癌症等。过去，一般[10] 老年人才得这些疾病，但是，近年来越来越多的年轻人也容易得这些病。因此，现代疾病一定要提早预防。

张：怎样才能预防这些疾病呢？

王：如果仔细分析一下，我们不难看出，绝大多数的现代疾病都跟吃有关。因此，我要劝告大家多吃粗粮，多[15] 吃蔬菜、水果，还要尽量少吃肉，少吃垃圾食品。一日三餐营养要均衡，还要定时、定量进食。另外，现代人要少吃盐，少吃高糖、油腻的食品，少喝饮料。事实上，控制好饮食是预防现代疾病的最佳措施。

张：看来，我们是可以采取措施预防现代疾病的。除了注[20] 意饮食以外，还要注意什么呢？

[25] 王：要长期坚持运动，每周至少运动三次。除了运动以外，生活要
有规律，每天要保证充足的睡眠。还有，要放松，保持良好的
心情，不要过度紧张、劳累。过度紧张和疲劳对健康很有害。
总的来说，身体健康完全靠平时的注意和努力。

张：谢谢王医生！

[30] 王：不用谢。

生词

1. 有幸 yǒu xìng be fortunate
2. 热门 rè mén popular
3. 话题 huà tí subject of a talk
4. 碌（碌） lù busy　忙碌 máng lù busy
5. 嗜 shì have a liking for　嗜好 shì hào hobby; addiction
6. 那么 nà me then; in that case
7. 心脏病 xīn zàngbìng heart disease
8. 尿 niào urine　糖尿病 tángniàobìng diabetes
9. 癌 ái cancer　癌症 ái zhèng cancer
10. 提早 tí zǎo be earlier than planned and expected
11. 防 fáng guard against　预防 yù fáng prevent
12. 仔细 zǐ xì careful
13. 析 xī analyze　分析 fēn xī analyze
14. 劝（勸） quàn try to persuade
劝告 quàngào persuade; advise
15. 大家 dà jiā everybody
16. 粮（糧） liáng grain; food
粗粮 cū liáng coarse food grain
17. 定量 dìngliàng fixed quantity

18. 进食 jìn shí take food
19. 另外 lìng wài in addition; besides
20. 事实 shì shí fact
事实上 shì shí shàng actually; as a matter of fact
21. 控 kòng control　控制 kòng zhì control
22. 措 cuò make plans　措施 cuò shī measure
23. 采取 cǎi qǔ adopt; take
24. 长期 cháng qī long-term
25. 坚持 jiān chí persist on
26. 至少 zhì shǎo at least
27. 规律 guī lǜ regular pattern
28. 保证 bǎozhèng assure; guarantee
29. 充足 chōng zú sufficient
30. 保持 bǎo chí keep; maintain
31. 过度 guò dù excessive
32. 劳（勞） láo fatigue　劳累 láo lèi tired; overworked
33. 疲 pí tired　疲劳 pí láo tired
34. 总的来说 zǒng de lái shuō generally speaking
35. 完全 wánquán completely

193

口语热身

消化课文

1. 根据课文回答问题

1) 王医生是哪方面的专家？她今天要讲什么话题？

2) 现代人的哪些生活方式不利于健康？

3) 人们常说的现代疾病有哪些？

4) 哪些现代疾病是可以预防的？

5) 大多数现代疾病跟什么有关？在饮食方面，现代人应该怎样做才能预防这些疾病？

6) 除了饮食以外，现代人还应该如何预防现代疾病？

2. 根据实际情况回答问题

1) 在你居住的地方，人们的生活节奏快吗？精神压力大吗？表现在哪些方面？

2) 你周围的人经常做哪些运动？在你们国家或地区，最受欢迎的运动有哪些？

3) 在你居住的地方，人们可以在公共场所抽烟吗？哪些公共场所不允许抽烟？如果有人犯规会受到什么处罚？

4) 你们国家或地区的人喜欢喝酒吗？他们常喝什么酒？他们酒后会闹事吗？酒后驾驶的现象严重吗？

5) 在你居住的地方，人们常吃高盐、高糖、高脂肪的食物吗？这对他们的身体有什么影响？

6) 你周围的人注意控制饮食吗？他们是怎么做的？

7) 你周围的人生活有规律吗？他们的睡眠是否充足？他们精神紧张的时候是如何来放松的？

8) 为了保证青年人的饮食健康，政府作了哪些努力？效果怎样？

194

1. 选择其中一个短语造句

Ⓐ例子：请王医生为我们讲一讲"生活方式与现代疾病"这一热门话题。（第2行）

介绍一下/谈谈/说一说

Ⓑ例子：绝大多数的现代疾病都跟吃有关。（第13行）

跟……无关/关系很好/同岁

2. 用所给词语造句

Ⓐ例子："生活方式与现代疾病"这一热门话题（第2行）

饮食与健康 话题

Ⓑ例子：现代人饮食不健康，也不均衡，又没有时间运动。（第5行）

工作忙 又

Ⓒ例子：我要劝告大家多吃粗粮。（第14行）

应该 少喝饮料

Ⓓ例子：每周至少运动三次。（第25行）

这本小说 两遍

3. 用带点的词语模仿例子造句

例子：简单地说，现代人的饮食不健康。（第5行）

事实上，控制好饮食是预防现代疾病的最佳措施。（第18行）

看来，我们是可以采取措施预防现代疾病的。（第19行）

总的来说，身体健康完全靠平时的注意和努力。（第28行）

说实话，现代人的精神压力很大。

4. 从课文中找反义词

1) 古代→（　　　）(第2行)　　4) 极少数→（　　　　）(第13行)

2) 冷门→（　　　）(第3行)　　5) 细粮 →（　　　　）(第14行)

3) 粗心→（　　　）(第13行)　　6) 轻松 →（　　　　）(第27行)

195

口语训练

角色扮演

在这个口语练习中有三个角色：营养师、家长和学生。假设这个学生最近在健康上出现了一些问题，比如他/她的瘦身方法不对、得了肥胖症、经常生病等。营养师在饮食、运动与健康方面给他/她提一些建议。你们的对话要提及：

- 他/她最近出现了什么健康问题？
- 他/她的饮食习惯怎样？
- 他/她应该怎样调整饮食？
- 他/她还应该做哪些运动？

例子：

家长：这是我儿子。他最近体重一直增加，精神也不太好，所以我来向您请教。

营养师：请问，你多大了？最近感觉怎么样？

学生：我17岁。最近我总是觉得精神不好，人家都说我胖了，所以我心情也不好。

营养师：那你告诉我，你每天都吃些什么？做些什么？

学生：我最喜欢吃快餐，也喜欢喝可乐，我几乎每天都要吃一顿快餐，至少喝三罐可乐。我爱上网，每天都跟网友玩儿网上游戏或者看电视连续剧。

营养师：看来你的饮食习惯出了问题。你每天都吃高糖、油腻食品，长期这样下去，你会生病的。为了身体健康，你要尽快改变饮食习惯。你每天至少要吃三份水果、

蔬菜，少吃快餐，少喝可乐。

家长：他生活也没有规律，吃饭不定时，玩儿游戏经常忘记吃饭。他还喜欢晚睡晚起。如果作业做不完，他还经常开夜车。

营养师：那你还要改变生活习惯，保证充足的睡眠。你每周至少应该运动三次。你要调整一下饮食习惯和生活方式，下个月再来见我。

学生：好的。我喜欢打篮球，那我以后争取隔(gé)一天打一次篮球。谢谢您！我会按您说的去做。

（一个月后）

营养师：哎呀，我都快认不出你了！你现在感觉怎么样？

学生：我现在感觉非常好！我在一个月里就减(jiǎn)掉(diào)了20磅(bàng)。我非常满意。

家长：真要感谢您！这孩子不听我们的话，但是他听了您的话，现在身体好了，人也开心了。我们都为他高兴。

营养师：太好了！希望你能坚持下去。

参考句子

a) 每天吃蔬菜、水果，少吃肉，尽量不吃红肉，还要多吃谷类食物、玉米、红薯等粗粮。面包最好吃全麦(quánmài)的，还要多吃高纤维(xiānwéi)、低糖食物。

b) 多做户外活动，多晒太阳，不要老是坐在沙发上看电视或在房间里上网。

c) 保持心情愉快。如果有不愉快的事，就跟好朋友或父母说一说。如果心情不好，长期这样下去也会得病的。

d) 有些学生白天、黑夜颠倒(diāndǎo)。他们白天不抓(zhuā)紧(jǐn)时间，晚上开夜车。如果长期过度劳累、紧张，也会得病。

e) 吃饭时要慢，不要吃得太快，这样有助于消化(xiāohuà)，还不容易吃得太多。

f) 吃饭要定时，生活起居(qǐjū)要有规律。

g) 有些学生总是觉得自己胖，但实际上一点儿都不胖。还有些学生乱吃减肥药。有些减肥药对身体有害。

写作训练

1. 写叙述文

请写一篇文章发表在校刊上，跟将要上高中的学生分享你在高中阶段的学习、生活体验及感受，并提出你的建议。在文章里，你要提及：

- 怎样保持学习与课余活动的平衡 (pínghéng)
- 怎样保持饮食均衡
- 怎样做适当的运动保持身体健康

参考句子

a) 选课的时候，你一定要选自己喜欢的课程，这样你才会愿意花时间去学。如果选的课程你不喜欢，就不容易学好。

b) 高中的第一个学期，不要参加太多的活动，因为你很快会发现高中的课程比初中的难很多。如果你参加太多的活动，就没有充足的时间做功课。

c) 压力大的时候，千万不要通过抽烟、喝酒来减压。这样不仅不能减压，而且可能使你上瘾，对身体有害。

d) 要想有好身体，就要有均衡的饮食，远离垃圾食品。

e) 生活起居 (qǐ jū) 要有规律。不管多忙，也要保证充足的睡眠，这样才不容易生病。

f) 不管多忙，每周一定要坚持锻炼。没有健康的身体，什么事也做不了。

g) 要保持好的心情。如果碰到困难，要用积极的态度来面对。

2. 阅读短文并写回应式作文

读了下面的短文后，你对肥胖带来的危害有了更多的认识。在社区网站上写一篇文章，谈谈你所在社区青少年的肥胖问题及预防肥胖的有效方法。

青少年肥胖问题

1997年，世界卫生组织正式宣布：肥胖是一种疾病。医学界称之为"死亡五重奏"（wǔ chóng zòu）的高血压、高血脂、糖尿病、冠心病（guān xīn bìng）和脑血管疾病都跟肥胖有密切的关系。可见，肥胖已经成为威胁（wēi xié）人类健康的"杀手"。进入21世纪，中国的肥胖人口逐渐增多，其中肥胖儿就占大约10%。 [1]

[5]

现在中国青少年的生活、学习习惯使他们容易患（huàn）肥胖症。如今，人们的生活和经济条件好了，青少年过多地进食高脂肪、高热量的食物，这样的饮食习惯容易导致（dǎo zhì）营养过剩（guò shèng）。再有，学生考试压力大，再加上长时间地坐在电脑和电视机前，缺乏锻炼，过剩的营养消耗（xiāo hào）不掉，肥胖就很容易形成。 [10]

肥胖症会给青少年的身心健康带来负面影响。肥胖不但直接影响到他们的正常（zhèng cháng）发育，而且为日后的健康埋下（mái xià）"定时炸弹（dìng shí zhà dàn）"。肥胖儿还承受（chéng shòu）着很大的心理压力。他们不愿意参加体育活动，因为害怕（hài pà）同学嘲笑（cháo xiào）他们笨拙（bèn zhuō）的身体和动作。在学校，他们往往被其他同学起外号，不被同伴（tóng bàn）接受。长期这样下去，他们可能变得性格怪异、脾气暴躁（bào zào）、内向寡言（guǎ yán）。 [15]

要医治青少年肥胖症不是一件简单的事。到目前为止，没有一种方法可以真正医治肥胖症。因此，解决青少年肥胖问题的有效措施是加强预防。预防的关键（guān jiàn）是改变他们的饮食结构和生活方式。家长要限制（xiàn zhì）孩子过多地摄取（shè qǔ）高热量（rè liàng）、高脂肪的食物，选择含适量（shì liàng）蛋白质和高纤维素（xiān wéi sù）的食品。同时，家长要注意培养孩子的运动习惯，增加体育运动时间，以消耗多余（duō yú）的热量。 [20]

阅读与理解

阅读一

第一段 [1]　　全球变暖已经直接影响到地球的 生态平衡。但很少有人知道人类餐桌上的肉食间接地破坏了地球的环境。有人计算出吃一块牛排对地球变暖的影响等于一辆小汽车行驶两英里排放废气所造成的不良结果。

第二段 [5]　　在最近的50多年里，人类对于肉食的需求量越来越大。现在世界上的 牲畜数目已经是1945年的四倍，也就是说，全世界牲畜的数量是人口的三倍。

第三段　　全世界一共有超过60亿人口，再饲养那么大数目的牲畜，地球怎么承受得了？人类的 生存需要粮食和水，饲养那么多的牲畜也在跟 [10] 人类"抢"粮食和水。有人计算过，在牲畜吃进去的食物中，大约800公斤的植物蛋白只能转化成50公斤的牛肉，也就是说90%以上的植物被白白地浪费了。如果人类能够少吃肉，省下来的粮食可以养活很多人。

第四段　　看来，为了解决粮食的问题，为了保护环境、保持身体健康，吃素是最佳的选择。如果人类改为吃素，那么我们可以少饲养牲畜，这 [15] 样就会减少对环境的破坏。营养专家指出，一个人每周的食肉量不宜超过500克，而过度摄入动物蛋白和脂肪会导致富贵病的发生，比如心脏病、高血压等。吃素对心脏有利，可以降低心血管疾病和 中风的发病率。吃素能增强免疫力，所以素食者往往会 长寿。

第五段　　其实，人们对素食的了解不全面。素食者只要能选择多样化的饭菜，一样能从食物中摄取足够的营养。素食中的蛋白质也相当丰富， [20] 各种坚果的蛋白含量可达30%，谷类约含10%，豆类中的蛋白含量更高，近40%，是肉类的两倍。

1. 第一段　☐
2. 第二段　☐
3. 第三段　☐
4. 第四段　☐
5. 第五段　☐

A 人类对肉食的需求量使 牲 畜数目增加。
B 人类餐桌上的肉食间接地破坏地球的环境。
C 肉食者导致现代疾病的发生。
D 饲 养大量的牲畜浪费粮食和水。
E 吃素者同样能从素食中摄取足够的营养。
F 吃素带来很多好处，同时也能解决人类的粮食问题。
G 吃素能解决粮食问题。

B 判断正误，并说明原因

对　　错

1. 全世界牲畜的数目有60多亿。

　原因：＿＿＿＿＿＿＿＿＿＿＿＿＿＿＿＿＿＿＿＿＿＿＿　＿＿　＿＿

2. 牲畜消耗了地球上大量的粮食和水。

　原因：＿＿＿＿＿＿＿＿＿＿＿＿＿＿＿＿＿＿＿＿＿＿＿　＿＿　＿＿

3. 如果人类少养牲畜，那么我们可以养活更多的人。

　原因：＿＿＿＿＿＿＿＿＿＿＿＿＿＿＿＿＿＿＿＿＿＿＿　＿＿　＿＿

4. 素食者容易得心血管疾病。

　原因：＿＿＿＿＿＿＿＿＿＿＿＿＿＿＿＿＿＿＿＿＿＿＿　＿＿　＿＿

5. 长 寿的人一般都是素食者。

　原因：＿＿＿＿＿＿＿＿＿＿＿＿＿＿＿＿＿＿＿＿＿＿＿　＿＿　＿＿

6. 豆类中的蛋白质含量是肉类的两倍。

　原因：＿＿＿＿＿＿＿＿＿＿＿＿＿＿＿＿＿＿＿＿＿＿＿　＿＿　＿＿

1. 全球变暖使地球　　□　│　A 大约有180亿。

2. 在地球上，牲畜的数目　□　│　B 人的身体会健康一些。

3. 如果人类选择吃素，　□　│　C 心脏病和高血压。

4. 肉吃得太多容易得　　□　│　D 失去生态平衡。

5. 只要素食者吃多样化的饭菜，□│ E 其实素食营养很丰富。

6. 人们对素食的了解不够，□　│　F 营养是一定能保证的。

D　为短文配题目

□ 1. 吃素的好处　　　　　□ 3. 食素更健康

□ 2. 吃肉直接破坏地球　　□ 4. 吃素救地球

E　根据短文找出四个正确的句子

□ 1. 人类正面临着粮食短缺。

□ 2. 目前全世界的人口是1950年的四倍。

□ 3. 坚果中的蛋白质含量很丰富，含大约40%。

□ 4. 更多的人吃素会间接减少对地球的破坏。

□ 5. 素食提供充足的营养，所以食素者不会营养不良。

□ 6. 少吃一块牛排就相当于减少小汽车行驶两百米所排放的废气。

□ 7. 多吃肉既不健康又不环保。

F　从短文中找反义词

A 动词：　1. 失衡→(　　　　)(第1行)　　3. 提升→(　　　　)(第17行)

　　　　　2. 节约→(　　　　)(第12行)　　4. 减弱→(　　　　)(第18行)

B 形容词：1. 直接→(　　　　)(第2行)　　3. 不利→(　　　　)(第17行)

　　　　　2. 优良→(　　　　)(第3行)　　4. 片面→(　　　　)(第19行)

全球性的传染病
chuán rǎn

进入21世纪，新的传染病不断在世界各地出现。这些传染病对人类的健康造成了极大的危害，甚至威胁着人类的生存。由于新发的传染病大都是病毒感染，抗生素对它们也无能为力。

在全球不同的国家或地区，差不多每年都有新发传染病爆发。这些传染病往往是从动物身上传到人的身上。由于气候变暖、人类居住集中、交通频繁，使得传染病传播的范围变广，速度加快。这些疾病严重威胁着人类的健康。

近几年流行的传染病，如非典型肺炎（SARS）、禽流感（H5N1）和甲型流感（H1N1）都来自动物。2003年，在整个亚洲地区特别是中国爆发的非典型性肺炎，病毒传播极快，顿时好像全球都在戒严，人类的一切活动几乎都停止了。几个月之内全球累计病例八千多，死亡率为11%左右。1997年，在香港发现的禽流感引起了世界卫生组织的高度关注。其后，此病一直在亚洲地区零星爆发。直到2005年，疫症不断在亚洲、东欧的多个国家扩散。2008年，甲型流感在墨西哥发现，并很快在世界范围内流行。世界卫生组织一度发出最高级警告。据说，青壮年人比较容易传染甲型流感，这引起了世界性的恐慌。

当传染病在一个国家或地区流行时，如果及早采取隔离措施，这意味着各种交流要中断，尤其影响旅游、运输、商业等。这对该国家或地区造成很大的经济损失。但是，如果行动太慢，可能导致传染病扩散。因此，对付全球性的传染病，所有国家和人民都要行动起来，包括及时通报、积极采取措施防止扩散以及加快研制药物和疫苗。

[1] 第一段

第二段
[5]

第三段
[10]

gāo
dù
líng xīng
yì zhèng
kuò sàn
mò xī gē
[15]
shuō
kǒng huāng

第四段
yì wèi zhe
zhōng duàn
yùn shū
sǔn shī
duì fu
[20]
fáng zhǐ
yán zhì
yì miáo

203

A 从右边的段落大意中找出最合适的

1. 第一段 □
2. 第二段 □
3. 第三段 □
4. 第四段 □

A 几种传染病给人们的生命财产造成巨大的损失。

B 传染病造成的经济损失。

C 传染病的传播途径及范围。

D 全球性的传染病威胁着人类的生存，对医学提出了挑战。

E 各个国家要一起行动对付全球性的传染病。

F 传染病爆发时各国需采取的措施。

B 根据短文选择正确答案

1. "无能为力"（第3行）的意思是 _____。

   a) 不起作用　　b) 很有作用　　c) 起很大的作用

2. "零星"（第13行）的意思是 _____。

   a) 大规模　　b) 少量的　　c) 没有

3. "隔离"（第17行）的意思是 _____。

   a) 不让传染病人接触到其他人　　b) 注射抗生素来医治传染病

   c) 把传染病人跟普通病人放在同一个病房里

4. "中断"（第18行）的意思是 _____。

   a) 继续　　b) 延误　　c) 停止

C 根据短文填写下列表格

传染病	何时发现	何地发现	病例	影响范围
非典型肺炎				
禽流感				
甲型流感				

根据短文找出四个正确的句子

☐ 1. 新的传染病严重地威胁着人类的生存。

☐ 2. 由于人类交往频繁，这使传染病很容易 传 播开。
pín fán chuán bō

☐ 3. 甲型流感的死亡率为11%左右。

☐ 4. 抗生素是医治传染病最佳的药。

☐ 5. 差不多每年都有新的传染病在世界上不同地区出现。

☐ 6. 青少年比较容易传染目前流行的传染病。

☐ 7. 如果传染病在一个地区爆发，很难决定何时隔离这个地区。

E 根据短文选择正确答案

1. 进入21世纪，新的传染病

　　＿＿＿＿。

a) 得到了医治

b) 不时在世界各地出现

c) 能被控制

2. 传染病在全球不同的国家或

地区爆发的原因之一是 ＿＿＿＿。

a) 气候变暖

b) 人类不讲卫生

c) 饮水问题

3. 近几年流行的传染病 ＿＿＿＿。

a) 都是人传染给人

b) 都造成了全球恐慌，一切交
kǒnghuāng
　　流中断

c) 都是从动物传到人的身上

4. 1997年在香港出现的禽流感

　　＿＿＿＿。

a) 在几年内病例达到8000多
bìng lì

b) 在几年内扩散到欧亚国家
kuò sàn

c) 只是在亚洲国家扩散

5. 世界卫生组织 ＿＿＿＿。

a) 一直关注着新的传染病

b) 对任何一种新传染病都会发
jǐng gào
出最高警告

c) 有能力控制传染病扩散

6. 对待全球性的传染病， ＿＿＿＿。

a) 第一件要做的事是中止交通

b) 各国要联合起来，一起行动
lián hé

c) 各国要研制出新的抗生素
yán zhì

**第五单元
第15课**

[1]　　学生会决定在"世界地球日"这一天举办一系列环保活动。

目的： 为了保护校园环境，增强同学们的环保意识，使同学们养成保护环境的习惯。

主题： 保护环境，人人有责

[5]　**对象：** 全校师生

活动时间： 2010年4月22日（世界地球日）下午2点~4点

活动主要内容：

1. 环保知识有奖问答（在图书馆，七至八年级的学生参加）

2. 设计环保传单、海报和小册子，选出最优秀的海报张贴
[10]　在每间教室的布告栏上（七至十一年级的学生参加）

3. 组织环保卫士到校园周围植树、种花、捡垃圾（七至十一年级的学生参加）

4. 环保图片展（在大礼堂，图片由市政府提供）

5. 放映环保纪录片（在戏剧室，全校师生观看）

[15]　6. 环保摄影比赛（在体育馆，欢迎各年级同学参加，参赛者需交一张8 x 12英寸的彩色照片。当天将评选出一等奖、二等奖、三等奖各一名，并颁发奖品，还将有纪念品赠送给每
[20]　个参赛者）

7. 礼物互换（在多媒体教室，礼物必须由同学们自己制作）

8. 旧物回收、捐赠（在校
[25]　务处，包括整洁的衣物、图书、影碟、音乐光碟等）

注意事项：

　　a) 活动当天上午将照常上课，下午的课取消。

[30]　　b) 自明日起，同学们可把礼物、旧物带到学校，集中存放在校务处。
　　　　　学校将有专人看管。

　　c) 参加摄影比赛的照片和环保宣传作品可于活动日之前交给美术系主任。

　　d) 活动当天请同学们穿便服。

学生会

2010年4月5日

生词

1. 系列 xì liè series; set　一系列 yí xì liè a series of
2. 增强 zēngqiáng enhance　3. 传单 chuándān leaflet
4. 海报 hǎi bào poster
5. 册（冊）cè volume; copy　小册子 xiǎo cè zi pamphlet
6. 张贴 zhāng tiē put up (a notice)
7. 布告 bù gào notice; bulletin
8. 栏（欄）lán fence; railing　布告栏 bù gào lán notice board
9. 卫士 wèi shì guard
10. 植 zhí plant　植树 zhí shù tree planting
11. 捡（撿）jiǎn pick up; collect
12. 映 yìng reflect　放映 fàngyìng show; project
13. 纪录片 jì lù piàn documentary
14. 英寸 yīngcùn inch　15. 彩色 cǎi sè colour
16. 评选 píngxuǎn choose through public appraisal
17. 一等 yī děng first-class; top-grade
18. 颁（頒）bān distribute　颁发 bān fā issue

19. 奖品 jiǎng pǐn prize; award
20. 赠（贈）zèng give as a present
　　赠送 zèngsòng give as a present
21. 参赛 cān sài take part in the match
　　参赛者 cān sài zhě player; participant
22. 互换 hù huàn exchange
23. 媒 méi intermediary　媒体 méi tǐ media
　　多媒体 duō méi tǐ multimedia
*24. 由 yóu by (someone)　25. 捐赠 juānzèng donate
26. 校务 xiào wù administrative affairs of a school
27. 整洁 zhěng jié clean and tidy
28. 照常 zhàocháng as usual　29. 取消 qǔ xiāo cancel
30. 存 cún store; keep　存放 cún fàng leave with
31. 专人 zhuān rén a person specially assigned for a task
32. 看管 kān guǎn look after; attend to
33. 之前 zhī qián before　34. 便服 biàn fú informal dress

口语热身

1. 根据课文回答问题

1) 通知中的环保活动将在哪一天举行？那天是什么日子？

2) 七年级的同学当天可以参加哪些活动？请列出三个。

3) "环保卫士"是几年级的同学？他们当天要做些什么？

4) 谁可以观看环保纪录片？纪录片会在哪儿放映？

5) 参加环保摄影比赛的学生要交什么？有哪些奖项？

6) 环保活动当天学校的课程有什么特别的安排？

2. 根据实际情况回答问题

1) 在"地球日"这一天，你们学校会安排什么环保活动？明年的"地球日"，你会建议学校安排什么环保活动？

2) 你周围的同学环保意识强吗？表现在哪些方面？列举两个例子。

3) 你们学校举办过环保知识有奖问答吗？如果没有，你是否想建议学校举办这种比赛？为什么？

4) 你们学校经常组织全校师生参与环保活动吗？请讲一讲最近组织过的一次活动。

5) 你们学校的布告栏里经常张贴宣传环保的海报吗？宣传环保的传单、海报、小册子等一般是谁设计的？你参与过设计吗？学校的布告栏里还应该张贴什么？

6) 你们学校会组织学生植树、种花、捡垃圾吗？你参加过哪些活动？请讲一讲你参与过的一次活动。

7) 你有没有从未打开过的礼物？你一般是怎样处理这些礼物的？你去年过生日收到了什么礼物？

8) 你一般会怎样处理旧衣物和不用的图书、影碟、音乐光碟等物品？你会把它们捐出去义卖吗？

1. 选择其中一个短语造句

Ⓐ 例子：全校师生（第5行）

全市居民/全国人民

Ⓑ 例子：自明日起，同学们可把礼物、旧物带到学校。（第30行）

自从20世纪80年代改革开放以来

从2006年开始

2. 用所给词语造句

例子：礼物必须由同学们自己制作。（第22行）

剧本 由……编写

捐赠物 由……保管

3. 模仿例子缩写词语

Ⓐ 例子：参赛者需交一张彩色照片。（第16行）

（=需要）

Ⓑ 例子：照片可于活动日之前交给美术系主任。

（=可以）　　　　　　　（第32行）

奖品可以放在校务处。

4. 用带点的词语模仿例子造句

例子：当天将评选出一等奖。（第16行）

这个周末全校师生要去海滩捡垃圾。

《地球之日》会在学校礼堂放映。

5. 用课文中的动词填空

1) _____沙滩环境（第2行）　　5) _____活动（第11行）

2) _____环保意识（第2行）　　6) _____电影（第14行）

3) _____传单（第9行）　　7) _____礼物（第21行）

4) _____海报（第9行）　　8) _____旧衣物（第24行）

口语训练

小组讨论

今年的"世界地球日"快到了。作为青年学生，你们可以为环保做些什么？在讨论中，你们要提及在学校或本社区：

- 发现了哪些不环保的现象？
- 可组织哪些活动？
- 希望达到什么目的？

例子：

学生1：我发现我们学校的餐厅很浪费。餐厅为学生提供一次性餐具，每天都会浪费很多塑料、纸和木头。我觉得学校应该鼓励学生自备餐具。

学生2：我同意你的建议。还有，学校的布告栏经常是空的，我们应该在上面张贴一些宣传环保的图片、海报，时刻（shí kè）提醒同学们要注意环保。

学生3：对。我们还应该组织同学们去海滩（hǎi tān）捡垃圾，同时也教育大家不要随手扔垃圾。

学生1：我们可以在下次全校集会（jí huì）上放映一部环保纪录片，教育同学们环保要从每个人做起，从现在做起。

学生2：我们可以举办自然风景摄影比赛，让大

210

家认识到大自然的美丽风景要靠每个人来保护，并鼓励学生更积极地参与保护大自然的活动。

学生3：我们可以建议学校，今年的"世界地球日"允许我们穿便服上学，衣服的颜色要求是蓝色和绿色。募捐来的钱可以为学校购置（gòu zhì）垃圾回收箱。

学生1：我们可以组织环保卫士在校园外的空地上植树、种花。这个花园也可为教学服务，比如说上生物课时，同学们可以在那里上实地课（shí dì）。

学生2：学生会可以安排学生每天轮流打扫（lún liú dǎ sǎo）教室。这样做，学生既培养了劳动（láo dòng）观念，又学会了主动保护环境。

学生3：保护环境是每个人的责任。我们应该经常宣传环保的重要性，增强全民的环保意识。如果每个人每天都坚持注意环保，我相信我们的生活环境会更好。

参考句子

a) 定期组织学生捐出不用的物品、不穿的衣物，然后把它们捐给贫困（pín kùn）地区的儿童。这样，我们不仅能减少浪费，还能帮助别人。

b) 我们要减少搭乘飞机旅游的次数，因为飞机排出（pái chū）的废气（fèi qì）污染空气。相对而言，我们可以选乘火车或汽车，这样既经济又环保。

c) 政府应该发展公共交通，并修建（xiū jiàn）自行车道，鼓励大家多骑自行车。政府还应向买汽车的人多征税（zhēng shuì），提高油价，使更多的人选择公共交通。

d) 礼物包装（bāo zhuāng）纸、盒子，酒瓶、饼干盒、饮料罐（guàn）、购物袋，飞机上的餐具等，用了一次就扔了，实在（shí zài）太不环保了。

e) 普通人家里浪费的现象也很严重：有人开着水龙头刷牙（shuǐ lóng tou shuā yá），房间里没有人也开着灯，晚上开着空调盖被子（gài bèi zi）睡觉。

f) 饭店浪费食物的现象非常严重，每天成吨（dūn）的剩饭、剩菜被扔掉。

211

写作训练

1. 写日记

在"世界地球日"那一天，写一写你的行动及感想。在日记里，你要提及：

- 你做了什么？
- 你有什么感想和遗憾？
- 你今后想做些什么？

参考句子

a) 我去了一个垃圾处理厂作调查，发现扔掉的垃圾数目惊（jīng）人（rén），有很多东西可以再用或回收，但都被扔掉了。

b) 在"世界地球日"这一天，我们学校参加了本市"熄（xī）灯（dēng）一小时"的活动。

c) 我们全家经常讨论怎样在家里节约水、电，回收废物，不买或少买不需要的东西。

d) 本市的回收工作做得不够，浪费的现象还十分严重，让我看了心疼。"地球日"这一天，我跟几个环保组织联系并提出了一些加强回收的建议，但是他们的反应不是很积极。我觉得很失望（shī wàng）。

e) 明年的"地球日"那一天，我会建议学校请"地球之友"人士来校会上发言，宣传环保的重要性。每个班也要定一个环保计划，争取在本学年内落实（luò shí）。

f) 从明年开始，我争取联络住在同一小区的同学，每天早上拼车（pīn chē）上学。

2. 阅读短文并写回应式作文

你对生物塑料有所了解，但是考虑到生物塑料的成本及用料问题，你还是觉得在生活中应该尽量少用塑料制品。为校刊写一篇文章，建议同学们在学校、家里少用塑料制品。

生物塑料

人类提炼(tí liàn)石油做成塑料制品已经有几十年的历史了。这些塑料制品给人类带来了很多方便，但是也带来了难以想象的麻烦，因为塑料废物(fèi wù)很难自然分解(fēn jiě)，燃烧(rán shāo)后又释放(shì fàng)出有毒气体，所以给生态环境造成了污染。 [1]

经过科学家们多年的努力，人类终于找到了"绿色塑料"——生物塑料。生物塑料是以淀粉(diàn fěn)，比如玉米、土豆、小麦等天然(tiān rán)物质为基础，在微生物(wēi shēng wù)的作用下生成的塑料。 [5]

生物塑料用途很广。由于这种塑料不仅坚硬(jiān yìng)、重量(zhòng liàng)轻，可以做成汽车门、船外壳(ké)等用品，而且耐高温、卫生安全有保证，所以可用于餐饮、玩具、医疗(yī liáo)用具、电子产品、食品包装(bāo zhuāng)等。生物塑料对肌肤(jī fū)的适应性也非常好。当生物塑料植入体内一段时间，它会自行(zì xíng)分解成二氧化碳(èr yǎng huà tàn)和水。 [10]

生物塑料发展前景美好。有了生物塑料，人类对石油的消耗(xiāo hào)就会减少。生物塑料不含有毒物质，不会对人类的健康和生态环境造成破坏(pò huài)。全球生物塑料的市场也发展得很快。科学家们预计(yù jì)对生物塑料的需求每年将以10%的速度(sù dù)增长。到2010年，全世界使用的塑料20%将会是生物塑料。 [15]

但是，目前生产生物塑料面临着很大的挑战。生产生物塑料的成本比传统塑料要高出两三倍。由于生产生物塑料需用大量的玉米、小麦(mài)、土豆等农作物，这会引起世界粮食价格上涨。因此，有些科学家正在试用(shì yòng)废木料、野草等代替农作物。而且，生产生物塑料的过程中也会产生二氧化碳，这是个需要解决的问题。 [20]

213

阅读与理解

阅读一

全球变暖

第一段 [1]

　　进入20世纪80年代以来，由于全球变暖，产生"温室效应"，冰川 消融，海平面上升了，这 ① 了自然生态系统的平衡，更威胁到人类的食物供应和居住环境。

第二段

[5]

　　科学家预测，如果人类不立即 ② 行动减少温室气体排放，那么到21世纪末，地球表面的温度将会 ③ 4℃。到那时，地球上的大部分陆地将会变成沙漠，一些土地会被海水淹没，大多数动物将从地球上消失。如果这样，世界上大约只有10亿人能幸存下来，并且要移居到加拿大、西伯利亚、南极洲等冰雪融化的地带。由于农田变成了沙漠、生物大量灭绝，人类的吃饭问题将 ④ 最令人头痛的问题：淡水

[10]

将会变得奇缺，土豆将成为人类的主食。

第三段

　　但是也有一些科学家比较乐观。他们 ⑤ 即使地球上许多地方都变成了沙漠，剩下的可居住区和"生命绿洲"仍然可以维持目前60多亿人口的生存。科学家评估，人类将根据地球资源情况来 重 新 安 置 人口，如今冰天雪地的南极洲将变成 ⑥ 人类居住的"绿洲"。

第四段 [15]

　　为了应对全球变暖，一些科学家提出了一个大胆的设想：围绕地球建立一个人工太空环，遮蔽阳光， ⑦ 地球温度。但是，另外一些科学家认为，这种人工太空环肯定会有副作用，而且这一计划的预算将高得惊人。

第五段

　　2009年12月7日~18日在哥本哈根召开的联合国世界气候大会，有

[20]

192个国家的领导人参加，是最多的国家及国家领导人 ⑧ 的一次国际会议。这次会议被称作"拯救人类的最后一次机会"。大会呼吁各个国家马上采取措施减少二氧化碳的排放，阻止全球暖化。

从下面的方框里为短文选择最合适的词语填空

| 认为 | 影响 | 成为 | 采取 | 参加 |
| 节约 | 上升 | 调节 | 适合 | 预防 |

1. _____ 　　2. _____ 　　3. _____ 　　4. _____

5. _____ 　　6. _____ 　　7. _____ 　　8. _____

B 从右边的段落大意中找出最合适的

1. 第一段 　☐

2. 第二段 　☐

3. 第三段 　☐

4. 第四段 　☐

5. 第五段 　☐

A 悲观(bēi guān)的科学家警告(jǐng gào)人们气候变暖会带来巨大危害(wēi hài)。

B 各国应该马上采取行动，阻止(zǔ zhǐ)全球变暖。

C 全球变暖影响到人类的生存。

D 另一些科学家乐观地面对全球变暖造成的影响。

E 2009年哥本哈根(gē běn hā gēn)世界气候大会的重要性。

F 一些科学家提出大胆(dà dǎn)的设想调节地球的温度(shè xiǎng tiáo jié)。

G 全球变暖并不是那么可怕。

C 根据短文选择正确答案

1. "移居(yí jū)"(第7行)的意思是_____。

　a) 搬到其他地方去住

　b) 流亡到其他地方

　c) 去其他地方开发新天地

2. "最令人头痛的问题"(第9行)的意思是_____。

　a) 很容易解决的问题

　b) 很难解决的问题

　c) 不可能解决的问题

3. "乐观"(第11行)的意思是_____。

　a) 从客观上来看问题

　b) 事情没那么坏，还有希望

　c) 从主观上来看问题

4. "副作用"(第17行)的意思是_____。

　a) 正面的作用

　b) 积极的作用

　c) 除主要作用以外的不好的作用

□ 1. 全球变暖是从20世纪80年代开始的。
□ 2. 如果地球表面的温度上升4度，人类将无法在地球上生存。
□ 3. 全球变暖的结果是人类不得不搬到南极、北极等地去住。
□ 4. 人类应该一齐行动，采取有效的措施，阻止全球暖化。
□ 5. 如果地球温度继续上升，全球气候会变得越来越冷。
□ 6. 全球变暖会影响到自然生态系统的平衡。
□ 7. 如果南极洲的冰雪融化，地球会变成一个大海洋。

1. 由于全球变暖，＿＿＿＿。
   a) 沙漠会变成绿洲
   b) 世界人口会剧增
   c) 冰雪会融化，因此海平面会上升

2. 如果人类不马上减少温室气体排放，到21世纪末＿＿＿＿。
   a) 地球表面温度将会上升4度
   b) 海水将会把沙漠淹没
   c) 所有生物将灭绝

3. 如果农田变成沙漠，生物大量灭绝，＿＿＿＿。
   a) 人类不用吃饭也能活
   b) 人类就会缺粮缺水
   c) 人类就连土豆都种不出来

4. 一些乐观的科学家认为＿＿＿＿。
   a) 人工太空环能把太阳遮住
   b) 人工太空环不会起太大的作用
   c) 单单一个南极洲能让现在的60亿人口住下

5. 一些悲观的科学家认为＿＿＿＿。
   a) 人工太空环能遮住太阳
   b) 人工太空环虽然便宜但有副作用
   c) 如果气候继续恶化，到最后世界上只剩下10亿人口

6. 各国应该马上采取行动，＿＿＿＿。
   a) 希望每年召开一次世界气候大会
   b) 减少二氧化碳的排放
   c) 立即集资建造人工太空环

世界地球日

为了 ___①___ 环境污染问题，1970年4月22日，全美国10000所中小学、2000所高等院校和2000个社区及团体共计2000多万人走上街头，要求政府采取措施控制大气和水污染。美国民间组织提议把4月22日定为"地球日"。 [1]

自从1970年"地球日" ___②___ 后，在全世界范围内得到了各国的响(xiǎng)应(yìng)。环保工作在一定程(chéng)度(dù)上受到了各国的关注，也 ___③___ 了一些进展。1973年，联合国(lián hé guó)成立了联合国环境规划署(guī huà shǔ)，许多国家也都 ___④___ 了环境保护管理机构和科研(kē yán)机构。1989年第44届联合国大会上，环境污染和生态保护成了讨论的热点，最后通过了关于环境保护的决议(jué yì)和宣言(xuān yán)。 [5]

20世纪90年代，"地球日"成了世界上很多国家的特殊日子。1990年4月22日，"地球日"活动的组织者 ___⑤___ 联合国召开高级环境会议，目的是为了阻止(zǔ zhǐ)全球环境恶化(è huà)。1990年的"地球日"这一天，全世界有100多个国家 ___⑥___ 了各种各样的环境保护宣传活动，参加的人达数亿。 [10]

进入21世纪，人类 ___⑦___ 地球的行动受到了全世界的关注。2009年4月22日，第63届联合国大会 ___⑧___ 将今后每年的4月22日定为"世界地球日"。2009年"世界地球日"的主题是"绿色一代"。它呼吁(hū yù)人类积极开发环保能源(néngyuán)，要求个人消费习惯符合(fú hé)环保要求，___⑨___ 一个"无碳(tàn)"的"绿色经济"。 [15]

人类只有一个地球，尊重地球就是尊重生命，拯救(zhěng jiù)地球就是拯救人类的未来。所有热爱地球的人们都应该马上行动起来，把每一天都 ___⑩___ "世界地球日"。 [20]

217

从下面的方框里为短文选择最合适的词语填空

| 诞生 | 当做 | 解决 | 克服 | 建议 | 成立 |
| 创造 | 决定 | 成为 | 举行 | 取得 | 保护 |

1. _____ 2. _____ 3. _____ 4. _____ 5. _____

6. _____ 7. _____ 8. _____ 9. _____ 10. _____

B 判断正误，并说明原因

1. 把4月22日定为"地球日"最初是由美国的民间组织提出　　　　　对　　错
   来的。

   原因：_____　　　——　　——

2. "世界地球日"诞生于1970年4月22日。

   原因：_____　　　——　　——

3. 1990年4月22日这一天，全世界有100多个国家的人民参加
   了保护环境的活动。

   原因：_____　　　——　　——

4. 进入21世纪后，全球越来越多的人关心、保护地球环境。

   原因：_____　　　——　　——

5. "绿色经济"是2009年"世界地球日"的主题。

   原因：_____　　　——　　——

6. 只有保护地球，人类才会有未来。

   原因：_____　　　——　　——

218

C 根据短文选择最适当的解释

1. "环保工作在一定 程 度上受到了各国的关注"(第6行)这句话是指各
   国对环保工作_____。

   a) 多多少少重视起来了　　b) 一点儿都不重视

   c) 非常重视

2. "讨论的热点"(第9行)的意思是_____。

   a) 演讲题目　　　b) 研究的课题　　　c) 热门话题

3. "全球环境恶化"(第12行)的意思是_____。

   a) 全球气温越来越冷　　b) 全球环境越来越差

   c) 全球空气越来越差

4. "一个'无碳'的'绿色经济'"(第17行)是指在这种经济模式中，
   _____。

   a) 碳排放量为零，非常环保　　b) 想尽办法把沙漠变成"绿洲"

   c) 用植树的方法来改善地球环境

D 根据短文找出四个正确的句子

☐ 1. 1973年，世界上很多国家都成立了环境保护和科研机构。

☐ 2. 自从"地球日"在美国诞生后，保护环境受到了各国的重视。

☐ 3. 第63届联合国大会宣布，从2009年开始，每年的4月22日为"世界
   地球日"。

☐ 4. 到2009年为止，人类的个人消费习惯不符合环保的要求。

☐ 5. 2009年的"世界地球日"那一天，在全世界的每个角落都有各种
   保护地球的活动。

☐ 6. 在全球范围内解决环境污染问题和保护环境的工作没有取得什么
   成果。

☐ 7. 20世纪的经济发展在很多方面都符合"绿色经济"的标准。

单元复习

< 生词

第13课

面临　早熟　往往　自作主张　做事　违反　校规
随便　讲话　趁　迟到　早退　逃课　个别　*教授
获取　激发　动机　公民　独立　思考　发挥　各自
才能　制定　严格　管教　遵守　适当　处罚　停课
课后留校　开除

第14课

有幸　热门　话题　忙碌　嗜好　那么　心脏病
糖尿病　癌症　提早　预防　仔细　分析　劝告
大家　粗粮　定量　进食　另外　事实上　控制
措施　采取　长期　坚持　至少　规律　保证
充足　保持　过度　劳累　疲劳　总的来说　完全

第15课

一系列　增强　传单　海报　小册子　张贴　布告栏
卫士　植树　捡　放映　纪录片　英寸　彩色　评选
一等　颁发　奖品　赠送　参赛者　互换　多媒体　*由
捐赠　校务　整洁　照常　取消　存放　专人　看管
之前　便服

带来新挑战　做事不考虑后果　违反/遵守校规　欺负弱小的同学
第一，……；第二，……　教授/获取知识和技能　激发学习动机
培养学习能力　养成良好的学习习惯　成为有责任感的公民
独立思考、辨别是非的能力　发挥才能　适当的处罚　对于不良行为
提供有挑战性的课余活动　关心青少年的成长

生活方式　热门话题　简单地说　生活忙碌，精神压力大
饮食不健康　不良嗜好　对健康不利　提早预防　仔细分析一下
绝大多数的现代疾病都跟吃有关　多吃粗粮　一日三餐营养要均衡
控制饮食是最佳措施　采取措施　生活要有规律　保证充足的睡眠
保持良好的心情　过度紧张和疲劳对健康有害

举办一系列环保活动　为了保护校园环境　增强环保意识　养成习惯
人人有责　有奖问答　设计传单　选出优秀海报　组织环保卫士植树
环保图片展　放映纪录片　欢迎各年级同学参加　评选出一等奖
有纪念品赠送给每个参赛者　旧物回收　照常上课　专人看管
把……存放在校务处　参加摄影比赛　环保宣传作品

词汇表

A

ái	癌 cancer	14
áizhèng	癌症 cancer	14
àn	案 case	7
àosīkǎ	奥斯卡 Oscar	5

B

bānjí	班级 class	2
bānzhǎng	班长 class monitor	1
bān	颁 distribute	15
bānfā	颁发 issue	15
bǎn	版 page (of a newspaper)	12
bǎnmiàn	版面 layout	12
bǎoguì	宝贵 valuable	3
bǎochí	保持 keep; maintain	14
bǎoguǎn	保管 take care of	10
bǎozhèng	保证 assure; guarantee	14
bàodào	报道 report	9
bào	*抱 hold	2
bàoyuàn	抱怨 complain	2
bàolì	暴力 violent	11
bèi	背 back of the body	5
bèijǐng	背景 background	3
bèi	倍 times	1
bèifen	辈分 position in the family hierarchy; generation	6
bǐjìběn diànnǎo	笔记本电脑 laptop	8
biānyuǎn	边远 remote	8
biànfú	便服 informal dress	15
biànlì	便利 convenient	8
biàn	辨 differentiate; distinguish	7
biànbié	辨别 differentiate; distinguish	7
biàn	辩 debate	7
biànlùn	辩论 debate	7
biǎodá	表达 express	11
bīn	宾 guest	10
bīnguǎn	宾馆 guesthouse	10
bìng	并 in addition	5
bō	拨 move with hand	12
bōdǎ	拨打 dial	12
bùzhǐ	不止 more than	3
bùgào	布告 notice; bulletin	15
bùgàolán	布告栏 notice board	15
bù	*部 *a measure word used for books or films*	5

C

cáinéng	才能 ability; talent	13
cǎiqǔ	采取 adopt; take	14
cǎisè	彩色 colour	15
cānsài	参赛 take part in the match	15
cānsàizhě	参赛者 player; participant	15
cáng	藏 hide	5
cè	册 volume; copy	15
cè	策 plan; strategy	4
céng	曾 once	5
céngjīng	曾经 once	5
chāyì	差异 difference	6
chǎn	产 produce	8
chǎnpǐn	产品 product	8
chǎnshēng	产生 produce	8

chángpiān	长篇 lengthy; long	12	
chángqī	长期 long-term	14	
chángtú	长途 long-distance	10	
chèn	趁 while; take advantage of	13	
chēng	称 call	6	
chēnghu	称呼 call; form of address	6	
chéngyǐn	成瘾 become addicted	7	
chéngzhǎng	成长 grow up	7	
chéng	诚 honest; sincere	2	
chéngshí	诚实 honest	2	
chí	迟 late	13	
chídào	迟到 be late	13	
chōngzú	充足 sufficient	14	
chóu	绸 silk	10	
chūshēn	出身 family background	1	
chǔfá	处罚 punish	13	
chǔ	础 plinth	3	
chuándān	传单 leaflet	15	
chuàngzào	创造 create	5	
cìshù	次数 frequency	2	
cūliáng	粗粮 coarse food grain	14	
cún	存 store; keep	15	
cúnfàng	存放 leave with	15	
cuò	措 make plans	14	
cuòshī	措施 measure	14	

D

dāchéng	搭乘 travel by	10
dāpèi	搭配 mix in proportions	9
dá'àn	答案 answer	7
dáfù	答复 reply	3
dàduō	大多 mostly	4

dàjiā	大家 everybody	14
dàlián	大连 Dalian (a city in northern China)	6
dàshì	大事 major issue	8
dàyú	大于 more than	7
dàitì	代替 replace	9
dānqīn	单亲 single parent	4
dānshēn	单身 single; unmarried	4
dǎn	胆 courage	1
dǎn dà	胆大 bold	1
dànshēng	诞生 be born	12
dézhī	得知 get to know	3
díquè	的确 indeed	11
dǐ	抵 reach	12
dǐdá	抵达 arrive	12
dìwèi	地位 position	7
dìngyuè	订阅 subscribe to (a news-paper, a periodical, etc.)	1
dìngliàng	定量 fixed quantity	14
dìngqī	定期 regularly	2
dōngfāng	东方 the East	5
dōngpō	东坡 a famous poet in Song Dynasty	10
dōngpōròu	东坡肉 a kind of pork dish named after a famous poet	10
dòngjī	动机 motive	13
dòng nǎojīn	动脑筋 use one's head	12
dòngxiàng	动向 trend	1
dúlì	独立 independent; on one's own	13
dúshēng zǐnǚ	独生子女 only child	4
dútè	独特 unique	5
dúběn	读本 reader	12

guǎnjiào	管教 subject someone to discipline	13
guāngdié	光碟 disc	8
guǎngdà	广大 vast; numerous	12
guǎngzhōu	广州 Guangzhou (provincial capital of Guangdong Province)	3
guī	规 rule; regulation	13
guīlù	规律 regular pattern	14
guì	*贵 your (respectfully)	1
guìzú	贵族 noble	4
guónèi	国内 domestic	12
guówài	国外 overseas	12
guòdù	过度 excessive	14
guòfèn	过分 excessive	11

H

hǎibào	海报 poster	15
hài	害 harm	9
hánlěng	寒冷 cold	10
hàn	憾 regret	9
hángzhōu	杭州 Hangzhou (provincial capital of Zhejiang Province)	10
hǎoláiwù	好莱坞 Hollywood	5
hǎopíng	好评 favourable comments	5
hǎoshì	好事 good deed	8
hàokè	好客 hospitable	6
héchàngtuán	合唱团 choir	3
hòuguǒ	后果 consequence	11
hū	呼 call	6
hú	湖 lake	10
hùhuàn	互换 exchange	15

huárén	华人 Chinese; foreign citizens of Chinese origin or descent	5
huàjù	话剧 stage play	2
huàtí	话题 subject of a talk	14
huàishì	坏事 bad thing	8
huǎng	谎 lie	7
huī	挥 wave	3
hūn	荤 meat or fish	9
hūnyīn	婚姻 marriage	6
huòdé	获得 gain; win	5
huòqǔ	获取 obtain	13

J

jīchǔ	基础 foundation	3
jīfā	激发 stimulate	13
jíshí	及时 timely	2
jíjiāng	即将 soon	3
jí	疾 disease	9
jíbìng	疾病 disease	9
jí	籍 place of origin	5
jìlù	纪录 record	5
jìlùpiàn	纪录片 documentary	15
jiābèi	加倍 double	1
jiā	佳 good; fine	1
jiādiàn	家电 household electrical appliances	8
jiājiāhùhù	家家户户 every family	8
jiàgé	价格 price	9
jià	*架 put up	5
jiàqī	假期 vacation; holiday	1
jiān	坚 firm	1
jiānchí	坚持 persist on	14

225

láo	劳 fatigue	14	
láolèi	劳累 tired; overworked	14	
lǎonián	老年 old age	4	
lǎoniánrén	老年人 old people; senior citizen	4	
lǐyí	礼仪 courtesy	6	
liáng	梁 beam; bridge	5	
liáng	粮 grain; food	14	
liè	*列 row; line	8	
lièchē	列车 train	8	
lín	临 be faced with	1	
línchuáng	临床 clinical	1	
líng	灵 quick; smart	3	
línghuó	灵活 quick; flexible	3	
língyǐn sì	灵隐寺 Lingyinsi Temple (in Hangzhou)	10	
lìng	*令 make; cause	6	
lìngwài	另外 in addition; besides	14	
liúlì	流利 fluent	3	
liùhé tǎ	六和塔 a famous pagoda in Hangzhou	10	
lóngjǐng	龙井 Dragon Well tea (a kind of green tea)	10	
lóngjǐng xiārén	龙井虾仁 shelled shrimps cooked with Dragon Well tea leaves	10	
lù	碌 busy	14	
lǚyóujú	旅游局 bureau of tourism	10	
lǜ	率 rate	4	
luàn	乱 mess up; random	10	

M

màizuò	卖座 draw large audiences	5	
mánglù	忙碌 busy	14	

méi	媒 intermediary	15	
méitǐ	媒体 media	15	
měi shí měi kè	每时每刻 all the time	7	
měidé	美德 virtue	4	
měihuà	美化 beautify	2	
měiwèi	美味 delicious	12	
mēnrè	闷热 hot and stuffy	10	
miànlín	面临 be faced with	13	
miànshì	面试 interview	1	
míngcài	名菜 famous dish	10	
míngxiǎn	明显 obvious	6	
mó	磨 waste (time)	11	
mò	陌 road	3	
mòshēng	陌生 unfamiliar	3	
mǔqin	母亲 mother	1	
mùdìdì	目的地 destination	8	
mù	募 raise; collect	3	
mùjuān	募捐 make or take up a collection	3	

N

nàme	那么 then; in that case	14	
nàiyòng	耐用 durable	12	
nánxìng	男性 male	6	
nǎojīn	脑筋 brains; mind	12	
nénggàn	能干 capable; competent	2	
nénggòu	能够 can; be able to	9	
nì	腻 greasy	2	
niándài	年代 decade of a century	4	
niánqīng	年轻 young	4	
niánqīngrén	年轻人 young people	4	
niào	尿 urine	14	

227

nóng	浓 thick	5	
nónghòu	浓厚 (of interest) great	5	
nǚxìng	女性 female	6	

P

pāishè	拍摄 take a picture or shoot	5	
pàn	盼 hope	1	
pànwàng	盼望 long for	1	
pí	疲 tired	14	
píláo	疲劳 tired	14	
piān	偏 partial	9	
piānshí	偏食 (have a) partiality for a particular kind of food	9	
piàn	骗 deceive	7	
pǐnzhǒng	品种 variety	2	
pìn	聘 employ; hire	3	
píng	*评 comment	5	
píngwěi	评委 judge	7	
píngxuǎn	评选 choose through public appraisal	15	
pǔbiàn	普遍 general; common	6	
pǔjí	普及 popular	8	

Q

qī	妻 wife	4	
qīzi	妻子 wife	5	
qī	欺 deceive	7	
qīfu	欺负 bully	7	
qíguài	奇怪 unexpected; strange	9	
qiáoliáng	桥梁 bridge	5	
qīnqiè	亲切 warm; close	6	
qín	勤 diligent	1	
qínfèn	勤奋 diligent	1	

qīngshàonián	青少年 youth	7	
qīngqiǎo	轻巧 light and ingenious	8	
qǔxiāo	取消 cancel	15	
quàn	劝 try to persuade	14	
quàngào	劝告 persuade; advise	14	
quēfá	缺乏 lack	11	
què	确 surely	2	
quèshí	确实 really; indeed	8	
quèxìn	确信 be sure	2	
qún	群 crowd; group	12	
qúnzhòng	群众 the masses	12	

R

rèmén	热门 popular	14	
rèqíng	热情 enthusiasm; enthusiastic	1	
rénjì	人际 interpersonal	6	
rénjiān	人间 world; earth	10	
rénxuǎn	人选 candidate	1	
rén	仁 kernel	10	
róng	荣 honour	2	
róngxìng	荣幸 be honoured	2	
rújīn	如今 nowadays	7	
ruǎn	软 soft	8	
ruǎnjiàn	软件 software	8	

S

sèqíng	色情 pornographic	11	
shānshuǐ	山水 scenery with hills and streams	10	
shànyú	善于 be good at	2	
shàn	擅 be good at	3	
shàncháng	擅长 be good at	3	

shāngtǎo	商讨 discuss	2
shàngdàng	上当 be deceived	7
shàngshēng	上升 rise	4
shàngtiáo	上调 raise	9
shàng	尚 prevailing custom	8
shèjiāo	社交 social contact	11
shēnxīn	身心 body and mind	11
shēnzhèn	深圳 Shenzhen (a city in Guangdong province)	3
shèngrèn	胜任 competent; qualified	3
shěng	*省 province	10
shěnghuì	省会 provincial capital	10
shěngshì	省事 save trouble	8
shíshàng	时尚 fashion	8
shíxiàn	实现 realize; achieve	2
shíxíng	实行 implement	4
shǐyòng	使用 use	8
shìjì	世纪 century	4
shìshí	事实 fact	14
shìshí shàng	事实上 actually; as a matter of fact	14
shìwù	事物 thing	7
shìfēi	是非 right and wrong	7
shìdàng	适当 appropriate	13
shì	嗜 have a liking for	14
shìhào	嗜好 hobby; addiction	14
shōurù	收入 income	6
shǒuxuǎn	首选 first choice	11
shòupiàn	受骗 be deceived	7
shūxìn	书信 letter	12
shū	殊 different	3
shù	述 narrate	5

shùmǎ	数码 digital	8
shùmǎ xiàngjī	数码相机 digital camera	8
shùmù	数目 number	11
shuōhuǎng	说谎 tell a lie	7
shuò	硕 big; large	5
shuòshì	硕士 master	5
sīchóu	丝绸 silk	10
sīshēnghuó	私生活 private life	6
sīkǎo	思考 think deeply	13
sì	寺 temple; mosque; monastery	10
sùzhì	素质 quality	9
sù	速 fast; speed	8
suíbiàn	随便 do as one pleases	13
suízhe	随着 along with; following	4
sūnnǚ	孙女 granddaughter (son's daughter)	4
sūnzi	孙子 grandson (son's son)	4
suō	缩 shrink	8
suōduǎn	缩短 shorten	8

T

tā	踏 settle down	1
tāshi	踏实 steady and sure	1
tǎ	塔 pagoda	10
táiwān	台湾 Taiwan (a province of China)	5
tán	*坛 (sports or literary) circle; field	5
tángniàobìng	糖尿病 diabetes	14
táo	逃 escape	13
táokè	逃课 play truant	13
tèchǎn	特产 special local product	10

229

231

zhěngtiān	整天 all day	7
zhèngfāng	正方 (of debaters) those holding affirmative or positive views	7
zhèngquè	正确 correct	7
zhèngzhí	正直 morally upright	3
zhèngshū	证书 certificate	1
zhèngcè	政策 policy	4
zhèngfǔ	政府 government	11
zhèngzhì	政治 politics	10
zhèng	症 symptom	9
zhīqián	之前 before	15
zhīmíng	知名 renowned	5
zhí hū qí míng	直呼其名 directly call one's name	6
zhíjiē	直接 directly	9
zhí	植 plant	15
zhíshù	植树 tree planting	15
zhǐchū	指出 point out	9
zhǐhuī	指挥 conduct	3
zhìshǎo	至少 at least	14
zhìdìng	制定 draw up	13
zhì	治 rule; govern	10
zhōnglǎonián	中老年 middle and old age	6
zhōngnián	中年 middle age	6
zhǒnglèi	种类 category	11
zhòng	众 crowd	5

zhǔzhāng	主张 view	13
zhuānjiā	专家 expert; specialist	1
zhuānrén	专人 a person specially assigned for a task	15
zhuānxiàn	专线 special line	10
zhuǎndá	转达 pass on	2
zhuàn	赚 make a profit	5
zhuànqián	赚钱 make money	5
zhuàng	状 state; shape	2
zhuàngkuàng	状况 condition	2
zhuī	追 pursue	1
zhuīqiú	追求 pursue	1
zǐxì	仔细 careful	14
zìdòng	自动 automatic	8
zì zuò zhǔzhāng	自作主张 act on one's own	13
zǒngde lái shuō	总的来说 generally speaking	14
zòu	奏 play (music)	12
zǔjí	祖籍 ancestral home	5
zuìjiā	最佳 best	1
zūnzhòng	尊重 respect	6
zūn	遵 abide by; obey	13
zūnshǒu	遵守 comply with	13
zuòpǐn	作品 works (of literature or art)	12
zuòshì	做事 act; handle affairs	13

附录：中国地图

政区版

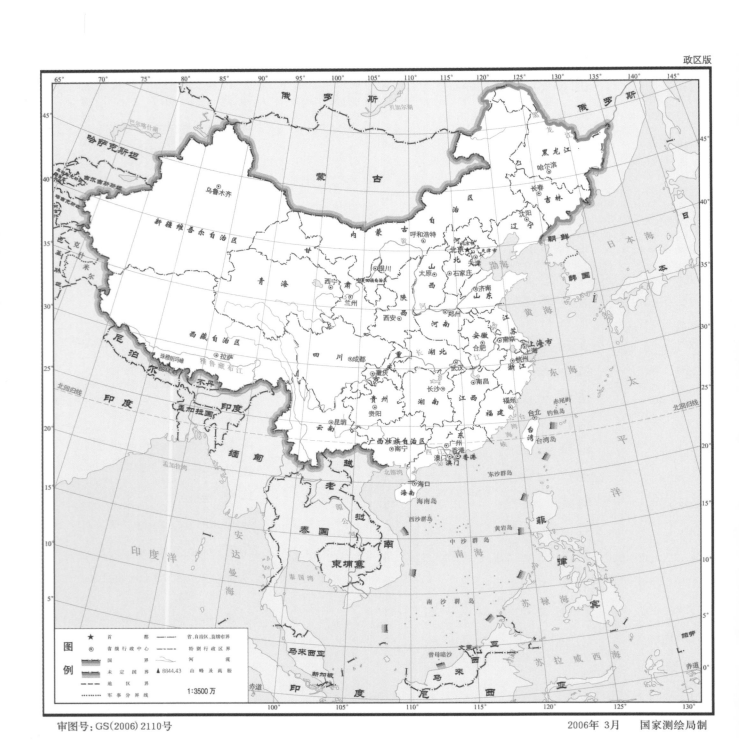

图例
★ 首 都
⊙ 省级行政中心
国 界
未 定 国 界
地 区 界
军事分界线
省、自治区、直辖市界
特别行政区界
河 流
▲ 8844.43 山峰及高程
1：3500万

审图号：GS(2006) 2110号

2006年 3月　国家测绘局制

234